DATE DU

HISTORY IN THE U.S.S.R.
Selected Readings

HISTORY IN THE U.S.S.R.

Selected Readings

Compiled and edited by
MARIN PUNDEFF

Published for

The Hoover Institution on War, Revolution and Peace

Stanford University, Stanford, California

by

CHANDLER PUBLISHING COMPANY

124 Spear Street
San Francisco, California 94105

PREFACE

THIS WORK, which has grown out of teaching and is primarily intended for teaching purposes, is conceived as an introduction to a field—the history of historical scholarship in the Soviet Union—through pertinent documents and writings. The materials presented are formulations of basic Marxist-Leninist doctrine, views of political leaders and influential historians, and official decrees and directives governing the writing and teaching of history. The subject has a nearly fifty-year-long history and has evolved certain distinctive features, yet it is still a virgin field in the Soviet Union. There are no comprehensive surveys or documentary collections, and the limited studies of individual aspects and phases are few. Being the history of "the most political of the sciences," the field has been extremely difficult and dangerous for Soviet scholars to approach. The direct and massive intervention of Stalin in historiography made it impossible during his era to operate with anything but the facts and interpretations he imposed. Only since 1956 has it been made possible for Soviet historians to consider other facts and to attempt a more rational assessment of the history of the post-1917 period and of their own discipline within it. Old dangers and continuing difficulties and limitations which affect their work are therefore reflected in the materials reproduced and cited here.

In contrast, the evolution of historical scholarship in Russia since 1917 has received much attention in the West. Russian émigré historians, as well as German, French, English, and American students, have produced a large body of facts and analysis which, although scattered in many places and languages and still not properly integrated in a synthesizing work, provides a way for understanding what happened to the historical craft in Russia after 1917. This body of facts and analysis is indicated in the references here and in the Suggestions for Further Reading.

Although the monistic and chiliastic history produced in the Soviet Union and the other Communist countries is hardly a better way to the truth than the empirical history which it challenges, the West has important reasons to be interested. First, the native and foreign history currently written for and taught to the captive audience of more than a billion people in the Communist countries from the Elbe to the Amur is being propagated on a scale not known before; the political leaders in control are convinced that the writing and teaching of history is a powerful tool for shaping minds, conditioning people, and attaining political objectives. Knowledge of the nature and content of this new history is not only desirable but imperative.

Second, the early makers of Marxist doctrine left behind the injunction that victorious Communists must write the entire history of mankind *de novo*. Historians in the Communist countries, especially the Soviet Union, are increasingly employed to fulfill this task and refute the past and current writings of non-Marxist historians. Marxist histories of the United States, the origins of the English Parliament, and the revolutions of 1848–49—to cite a few examples—have been produced to challenge and displace existing non-Marxist versions. A great deal of this work is polemical in nature and an elaboration of charges of "bourgeois falsification of history," but with the rising volume of research and publication in these countries, a body of historical writing is coming into existence which challenges in many aspects the non-Marxist history of mankind. With the resources of totalitarian states at their disposal, the managers of this activity, like the managers of the Soviet participation in the Olympic Games, are bent on producing a winning team and overwhelming the opponent. The International Congresses of Historical Sciences, at Stockholm in 1960, and at Vienna in 1965, were arenas to which Soviet historians, seconded by historians from other Communist countries, came to achieve victory over their "bourgeois enemies." The rising confrontation is producing what may be termed the "problem of two histories," which at present is most acute in the field of Russian history. Seceding, whether from conviction or compulsion, after 1917 from Western historiographic traditions, methods, and rules of evidence, historians in the Soviet Union have produced a version of Russia's past, Tsarist and Soviet, which stands in sharp contrast to that pieced together by scholars in Germany, France, Italy, England, and the United States and constantly attacked by Soviet historians as "bourgeois falsification." The problem for the student of Russian past as to what to take and what to discard from these two histories is a very real one. Knowledge of the philosophical assumptions and political imperatives governing the work of Marxist historians is thus indispensable if their work is to be rejected, accepted, or sifted for grains of truth.

Third, the study of the evolution of history in the Soviet Union sheds a great deal of light on the workings of the Marxist societies, since in totalitarian states the writing and teaching of history interlocks tightly with politics, economics, education, and social controls. The writing and teaching of history is an excellent clue to the climate and nature of any society; it is *a fortiori* so to the climate and workings of totalitarian society.

Fourth, evolution means change, and the writing and teaching of history in the Communist countries has been changing. In some countries the area of absolute dogma has been considerably whittled away and further probing, made possible by greater doctrinal flexibility, is going on. Adherence to dogma among Communist historians is, moreover, frequently a matter of personal status; in law-ridden Marxist historiography a human law seems to be operating according to which the younger the historian in age and career, the more doctrinaire he is, or, conversely, the better established the historian, the less dogmatic he is likely to be. Our view of the theoretical assumptions, methods, and practical performance of Communist historians is in danger of becoming frozen, obsolete, and unrealistic if their work is not continuously examined.

The evolution of history as a field of writing and teaching in the Soviet Union since 1917 has had more than its share of the difficulties and jolts which accompany all life processes. It has swung from one extreme to another and, passing through three major phases, has been unremittingly bossed by politics. The first phase (1917–32) saw the emergence of the school of M. N. Pokrovsky, which reduced history to sociological abstractions and an auxiliary of the new "science of society" (*obshchestvovedenie*), and justified the view that he who controls the present controls the past with Pokrovsky's formula that history is "politics retrojected into the past" (*politika oprokinutaia v proshloe*). The second phase (1932–53) saw the destruction of the Pokrovsky school and the restoration of history as a separate and central educational subject, but, remaining highly susceptible to the demands of current politics, history became a favorite tool of Stalin in pursuing his objectives and as a result was turned into a desiccated and stultified exercise in leader glorification. The third phase (1953—) opened with the death of Stalin, which, as in other areas of Soviet intellectual performance, had a revivifying effect on history. While marked by continuing subjection to politics, Soviet history in the current phase of its evolution is showing some reduction of doctrinal rigidity, certain trends toward purer craftsmanship and sophistication, and great diversification and expansion of publication outlets.

What has survived since 1917 without any diminution of its binding force is the central Leninist principle of *partiinost,* that is, unconditional and enthusiastic submission to the interests and demands of the Communist Party. Any scholarship, including historical scholarship, must serve current politics as managed by the party: if it is not party-oriented and party-dominated, scholarship is a menace. In this outlook, all truth is class truth and, since parties speak for classes, all truth is party truth; only subordination to the interests and requirements of the party (*partiinost*) guarantees that the truth will be reached. Historical data are of two types: "facts" (*fakty*) which help to corroborate the law-governed patterns (*zakonomernosti*) that all Marxist history must reveal and illustrate, and "factlings" (*faktiki*) which, although they have indeed occurred, are to be ignored as useless, or obnoxious, in the effort to prove that human history is governed by objective laws, similar to those in natural history, which human beings cannot change or escape. To see no such laws in human affairs and to take both facts and factlings into account, as "bourgeois" historical scholars do, is to reduce history to being a mere "factography" (*faktografiia*). In the frank Communist view, the facts of the past are a plastic material to be molded as current politics require. Hence the changeability of the facts and assessments of Marxist history, which astounds and upsets non-Marxist historians, is a normal and necessary occurrence. Since history, past and future, is for the party to shape, and since the party's mind as to what is true, good, or expedient changes, factual content and personality evaluations undergo frequent and radical alterations. The treatment of Beria as a history subject and Stalin's version of the history of the party, the so-called *Short Course,* to take only two examples, present striking illustrations of such tailoring of the historical fabric to fit and dress up current politics. While Beria was the powerful head of the secret police, his role in history rated three columns and a full-page portrait in "Large Soviet Encyclopedia" (Vol. 5, published in 1950). After he lost out in the power struggle and was executed in 1953, the authorities sent new pages to owners of the encyclopedia with instructions to destroy the Beria article and portrait and insert in their place the new pages, which contained no reference to him whatever. Similarly, while Stalin was the all-powerful dictator, his version of the history of the party was the sole text used and was propagandized as the "model of scientific investigation of history." Since his death the *Short Course* has been discarded and no mention of it is ever made except to illustrate with it how Stalin distorted history.

In bringing the materials in this book together, it has been my conviction that they should speak for themselves and that an intermediary is largely unneeded. My annotations are thus kept to the minimum suggested by classroom experience. In some cases titles have been somewhat modified for brevity and clarity.

This work has benefited from much assistance and encouragement. In particular, I wish to express my appreciation to the Hoover Institution on War, Revolution, and Peace for the financial support which made possible the publication of this volume; to Professor Rodger Swearingen, University of Southern California, and Drs. Delmar T. Oviatt and Joseph B. Ford, San Fernando Valley State College, for continuing support and encouragement; and to Professor Merle Fainsod, Harvard University, for the suggestions in his review of the original mimeographed version of the work in the *American Historical Review.*

MARIN PUNDEFF

CONTENTS

GLOSSARY AND ABBREVIATIONS

RUSSIAN	MEANING IN ENGLISH
FON	Faculty (department) of Social Sciences
Narkompros	People's Commissar (also, Commissariat) of Education
NKVD (later MVD, now KGB)	Ministry of Internal Affairs (police, security)
Partiinost	Party-mindedness, allegiance and submission to the party
RANION	Russian Association of Scientific and Research Institutes in the Social Sciences
R.S.F.S.R.	Russian Soviet Federated Socialist Republic
Sovnarkom, SNK	Council of People's Commissars (since 1946, Council of Ministers)
VKP (B)	All-Union Communist Party (Bolsheviks), the name of the party from 1925 to 1952
Zakonomernost	Law, law-governed pattern, conformity with laws (German, *Gesetzmässigkeit*)

ENGLISH	
CPSU	Communist Party of the Soviet Union, the name of the party since 1952
CC	Central Committee (of the CPSU)

PART ONE

Basic Marxist-Leninist Doctrine

CHAPTER I

KARL MARX AND FRIEDRICH ENGELS

MARXISM—the brain-child of two German intellectuals, Karl Marx (1818–1883) and Friedrich Engels (1820–1895)—is an attempt at constructing a complete philosophical system on traditions and products given to German philosophy by Kant, Herder, and Hegel. In the view of Marxists and non-Marxists alike, the foundation stone of this system, or *Weltanschauung,* a way of seeing and understanding the world around us and in us, is a theory of man's past as it extends into the present and the future. To be a Marxist, say Marxists, is to look at everything historically, to see the process of change in the depth of time, and to locate the tracks (*Gesetzmässigkeiten,* or laws, in the idiom of these German thinkers) of the past which project into the present and the future and determine the course of man's social evolution. As Engels, the lifelong friend and collaborator, put it at Marx's funeral, "Just as Darwin discovered the law of development of organic nature, so Marx discovered the law of development of human history." Marxism is, to use one of its own labels, "historical materialism."

Marxism is thus pre-eminently a theory of history. Marx and Engels, however, left no single statement of their theory of history; its elements are scattered throughout their writings, joint and separate.[1] The earliest beginnings of a theory are found in pieces they wrote in 1844 and 1845. These and other elements appeared next in their joint work *The German Ideology* (completed in 1846), in which they rebelled with vigor and venom against Hegelian idealism then prevalent in Germany. Since it was not published *in toto* until 1932, it is of interest in the history of Marxist ideas rather than for its contemporary effect. Its American editor, R. Pascal, describes it as the "first and most comprehensive statement of historical materialism." The excerpts that follow are from Pascal's edition, K. Marx and F. Engels, *The German Ideology* (New York, 1960), pp. 6–30.[2]

---

[1] The most complete recent guide to their writings is Maximilien Rubel, *Bibliographie des œuvres de Karl Marx, avec en appendice un répertoire des œuvres de Friedrich Engles* (Paris: Rivière, 1956; supplement, 1960). The complex field of "Marxology" is reflected in L. Levin, *Bibliografiia bibilografii proizvedenii K. Marksa, F. Engel'sa, V. I. Lenina* [Bibliography of Bibliographies of the Works of K. Marx, F. Engels, and V. I. Lenin] (Moscow, 1961); in it see especially No. 759, N. V. Starikov, "Engel's ob istorii (bibliografiia)" [Engels on History—Bibliography].

[2] In the recent Soviet collection of readings on Marxist-Leninist philosophy for use in courses on dialectical and historical materialism, *Khrestomatiia po marksistsko-leninskoi filosofii* [Reader on Marxist-Leninist Philosophy] (3 vols.; Moscow, 1961–62), the excerpts from *The German Ideology* follow the *Communist Manifesto,* which opens the first volume, in obvious deference to the manifesto's influence.

1. The German Ideology *

The premises from which we begin are not arbitrary ones, not dogmas, but real premises from which abstraction can only be made in the imagination. They are the real individuals, their activity and the material conditions under which they live, both those which they find already existing and those produced by their activity. These premises can thus be verified in a purely empirical way.

The first premise of all human history is, of course, the existence of living human individuals. Thus the first fact to be established is the physical organization of these individuals and their consequent relation to the rest of nature. Of course, we cannot here go either into the actual physical nature of man, or into the natural conditions in which man finds himself—geological, orohydrographical, climatic, and so on. The writing of history must always set out from these natural bases and their modification in the course of history through the action of man.

Men can be distinguished from animals by consciousness, by religion or anything else you like. They themselves begin to distinguish themselves from animals as soon as they begin to *produce* their means of subsistence, a step which is conditioned by their physical organization. By producing their means of subsistence men are indirectly producing their actual material life.

The way in which men produce their means of subsistence depends first of all on the nature of the actual means they find in existence and have to reproduce. This mode of production must not be considered simply as being the reproduction of the physical existence of the individuals. Rather it is a definite form of activity of these individuals, a definite form of expressing their life, a definite *mode of life* on their part. As individuals express their life, so they are. What they are, therefore, coincides with their production, both with *what* they produce and with *how* they produce. The nature of individuals thus depends on the material conditions determining their production.

This production only makes its appearance with the increase of population. In its turn this presupposes the intercourse of individuals with one another. The form of this intercourse is again determined by production.

The various stages of development in the division of labor are just so many different forms of ownership, i.e., the existing stage in the division of labor determines also the relations of individuals to one another with reference to the material, instrument, and product of labor.

---

* Reprinted by permission of International Publishers Co. Inc. Copyright © 1947. K. Marx and F. Engels, *The German Ideology.*

The first form of ownership is tribal ownership. It corresponds to the undeveloped stage of production, at which a people lives by hunting and fishing, by the rearing of beasts or, in the highest stage, agriculture. In the latter case it presupposes a great mass of uncultivated stretches of land. The division of labor is at this stage still very elementary and is confined to a further extension of the natural division of labor imposed by the family. The social structure is therefore limited to an extension of the family; patriarchal family chieftains; below them the members of the tribe; finally slaves. The slavery latent in the family only develops gradually with the increase of population, the growth of wants, and, with the extension of external relations, of war or of trade.

The second form is the ancient communal and state ownership which proceeds especially from the union of several tribes into a city by agreement or by conquest, and which is still accompanied by slavery. Beside communal ownership we already find movable, and later also immovable, private property developing, but as an abnormal form subordinate to communal ownership. It is only as a community that the citizens hold power over their laboring slaves, and on this account alone, therefore, they are bound to the form of communal ownership. It is the communal private property which compels the active citizens to remain in this natural form of association over against their slaves. For this reason the whole structure of society based on this communal ownership, and with it the power of the people, decays in the same measure as immovable private property evolves. The division of labor is already more developed. We already find the antagonism of town and country; later the antagonism between those states which represent town interests and those which represent country, and inside the towns themselves the antagonism between industry and maritime commerce. The class relation between citizens and slaves is now completely developed.

This whole interpretation of history appears to be contradicted by the fact of conquest. Up till now violence, war, pillage, rape and slaughter, etc., have been accepted as the driving force of history. Here we must limit ourselves to the chief points and take therefore only a striking example— the destruction of an old civilization by a barbarous people and the resulting formation of an entirely new organization of society. (Rome and the barbarians; feudalism and Gaul; the Byzantine Empire and the Turks.) With the conquering barbarian people war itself is still, as hinted above, a regular form of intercourse, which is the more eagerly exploited as the population increases, involving the necessity of new means of production to supersede the traditional and, for it, the only possible, crude mode of production. In Italy it was, however, otherwise. The concentration of landed property (caused not only by buying up and indebtedness but also by inheritance, since, loose living being rife and marriage rare, the old families died out and their possessions fell into the hands of a few) and its conversion into grazing land (caused not only by economic forces still operative today but by the importation of plundered and tribute corn and the resultant lack of demand for Italian corn) brought about the almost total disappearance of the free population. The very slaves died out again and again, and had constantly to be replaced by new ones. Slavery remained the basis of the whole productive system. The plebeians, midway between freemen and slaves, never succeeded in becoming more than a proletarian rabble. Rome, indeed, never became more than a city; its connection with the provinces was almost exclusively political and could therefore easily be broken again by political events.

With the development of private property, we find here for the first time the same conditions which we shall find again, only on a more extensive scale, with modern private property. On the one hand the concentration of private property, which began very early in Rome (as the Licinian agrarian law proves), and proceeded very rapidly from the time of the civil wars and especially under the Emperors; on the other hand, coupled with this, the transformation of the plebeian small peasantry into a proletariat, which, however, owing to its intermediate position between propertied citizens and slaves, never achieved an independent development.

The third form of ownership is feudal or estate-property. If antiquity started out from the town and its little territory, the Middle Ages started out from the country. This different starting-point was determined by the sparseness of the population at that time, which was scattered over a large area and which received no large increase from the conquerors. In contrast to Greece and Rome, feudal development therefore extends over a much wider field, prepared by the Roman conquests and the spread of agriculture at first associated with it. The last centuries of the declining Roman Empire and its conquest by the barbarians destroyed a number of productive forces; agriculture had declined, industry had decayed for want of a market, trade had died out or been violently suspended, the rural and urban populaion had decreased. From these conditions and the mode of organization of the conquest determined by them, feudal property developed under the influence of the Germanic military constitution. Like tribal and communal ownership, it is based again on a community; but the directly producing class standing over against it is not, as in the case of the ancient community, the slaves, but the enserfed small peasantry. As soon as feudalism is fully developed, there also arises antagonism to the towns. The hierarchical system of land ownership, and the armed bodies of retainers associated with it, gave the nobility power over the serfs. This feudal organization was, just as much as the ancient communal ownership, an association against a subjected producing class; but the form of association and the relation to the direct producers were different because of the different conditions of production.

This feudal organization of land ownership had its counterpart in the towns in the shape of corporative property, the feudal organization of trades. Here property consisted chiefly in the labor of each individual person. The necessity for association against the organized robber-nobility, the need for communal covered markets in an age when the industrialist was at the same time a merchant, the growing competition of the escaped serfs swarming into the rising towns, the feudal structure of the whole country: these combined to bring about the guilds. Further, the gradually accumulated capital of individual craftsmen and their stable numbers, as against the growing population, evolved the relation of journeyman and apprentice, which brought into being in the towns a hierarchy similar to that in the country.

The grouping of larger territories into feudal kingdoms was a necessity for the landed nobility as for the towns. The organization of the ruling class, the nobility, had, therefore, everywhere a monarch at its head.

The fact is, therefore, that definite individuals who are productively active in a definite way enter into these definite social and political relations. Empirical observation must in each separate instance bring out empirically, and without any mystification and speculation, the connection of the social and political structure with production. The social structure and the state are continually evolving out of the life-process of definite individuals, but of individuals, not as they may appear in their own or other people's imagination, but as they really are; i.e., as they are effective, produce materially, and are active under definite material limits, presuppositions, and conditions independent of their will.

The production of ideas, of conceptions, of consciousness, is at first directly interwoven with the material activity and the material intercourse of men, the language of real life. Conceiving, thinking, the mental intercourse of men, appear at this stage as the direct efflux of their material behavior. The same applies to mental production as expressed in the language of the politics, laws, morality, religion, metaphysics of a people. Men are the producers of their conceptions, ideas, etc.—real, active men, as they are conditioned by a definite development of their productive forces and of the intercourse corresponding to these, up to its furthest forms. Consciousness can never be anything else than conscious existence, and the existence of men is their actual life-process. If in all ideology men and their circumstances appear upside down as in a *camera obscura,* this phenomenon arises just as much from their historical life-process as the inversion of objects on the retina does from their physical life-process.

In direct contrast to German philosophy which descends from heaven to earth, here we ascend from earth to heaven. That is to say, we do not set out from what men say, imagine, conceive, nor from men as narrated, thought of, imagined, conceived, in order to arrive at men in the flesh. We set out from real, active men, and on the basis of their real life-process we demonstrate the development of the ideological reflexes and echoes of this life-process. The phantoms formed in the human brain are also, necessarily, sublimates of their material life-process, which is empirically verifiable and bound to material premises. Morality, religion, metaphysics, all the rest of ideology and their corresponding forms of consciousness, thus no longer retain the semblance of independence. They have no history, no development; but men, developing their material production and their material intercourse, alter, along with this their real existence, their thinking and the products of their thinking. Life is not determined by consciousness, but consciousness by life. In the first method of approach the starting-point is consciousness taken as the living individual; in the second it is the real living individuals themselves, as they are in actual life, and consciousness is considered solely as *their* consciousness.

This method of approach is not devoid of premises. It starts out from the real premises and does not abandon them for a moment. Its premises are men, not in any fantastic isolation or abstract definition, but in their actual, empirically perceptible process of development under definite conditions. As soon as this active life-process is described, history ceases to be a collection of dead facts as it is with the empiricists (themselves still abstract), or an imagined activity of imagined subjects, as with the idealists.

Where speculation ends—in real life—there real, positive science begins: the representation of the practical activity, of the practical process of development of men. Empty talk about consciousness ceases, and real knowledge has to take its place. When reality is depicted, philosophy as an independent branch of activity loses its medium of existence. At the best its place can only be taken by a summing up of the most general results, abstractions which arise from the observation of the historical development of men. Viewed apart from real history, these abstractions have in themselves no value whatsoever. They can only serve to facilitate the arrangement of historical material, to indicate the sequence of its separate strata. But they by no means afford a recipe or schema, as does philosophy, for neatly trimming the epochs of history. On the contrary our difficulties begin only when we set about the observation and the arrangement—the real depiction—of our historical material, whether of a past epoch or of the present. The removal of these difficulties is governed by premises which it is quite impossible to state here, but which only the study of the actual life-process and the activity of the individuals of each epoch will make evident.

We shall select here some of these abstractions, which we use to refute the ideologists, and shall illustrate them by historical examples.

a) History

Since we are dealing with the Germans, who do not postulate anything, we must begin by stating the first premise of all human existence, and therefore of all history, the premise, namely, that men must be in a position to live in order to be able to "make history." But life involves before everything else eating and drinking, a habitation, clothing, and many other things. The first historical act is thus the production of the means to satisfy these needs, the production of material life itself. And indeed this is a historical act, a fundamental condition of all history, which today, as thousands of years ago, must daily and hourly be fulfilled merely in order to sustain human life. The first necessity therefore in any theory of history is to observe this fundamental fact in all its significance and all its implications and to accord it its due importance. This, as is notorious, the Germans have never done, and they have never therefore had an earthly basis for history and consequently never a historian. The French and the English, even if they have conceived the relation of this fact with so-called history only in an extremely one-sided fashion, particularly as long as they remained in the toils of political ideology, have nevertheless made the first attempts to give the writing of history a materialistic basis by being the first to write histories of civil society, of commerce and industry.

The second fundamental point is that as soon as a need is satisfied, (which implies the action of satisfying, and the acquisition of an instrument), new needs are made; and this production of new needs is the first historical act. Here we recognize immediately the spiritual ancestry of the great historical wisdom of the Germans who, when they run out of positive material and when they can serve up neither theological nor political nor literary rubbish, do not write history at all, but invent the "prehistoric era." They do not, however, enlighten us as to how we proceed from this nonsensical "prehistory" to history proper; although, on the other hand, in their historical speculation they seize upon this "prehistory" with especial eagerness because they imagine themselves safe there from interference on the part of "crude facts," and, at the same time, because there they can give full rein to their speculative impulse and set up and knock down hypotheses by the thousand.

The third circumstance which, from the very first, enters into historical development, is that men, who daily remake their own life, begin to make other men, to propagate their kind: the relation between man and wife, parents and children, the *family*.

The production of life, both of one's own in labor and of fresh life in procreation, now appears as a double relationship; on the one hand as a natural, on the other as a social relationship. By social we understand the cooperation of several individuals, no matter under what conditions, in what manner and to what end. It follows from this that a certain mode of production, or industrial stage, is always combined with a certain mode of cooperation, or social stage, and this mode of cooperation is itself a "productive force." Further, that the multitude of productive forces accessible to men determines the nature of society, hence that the "history of humanity" must always be studied and treated in relation to the history of industry and exchange. But it is also clear how in Germany it is impossible to write this sort of history, because the Germans lack not only the necessary power of comprehension and the material but also the "evidence of their senses," for across the Rhine you cannot have any experience of these things, since history has stopped happening. Thus it is quite obvious from the start that there exists a materialistic connection of men with one another, which is determined by their needs and their mode of production, and which is as old as men themselves. This connection is ever taking on new forms, and thus presents a "history" independently of the existence of any political or religious nonsense which would hold men together on its own.

Only now, after having considered four moments, four aspects of the fundamental historical relationships, do we find that man also possesses "consciousness"; but, even so, not inherent, not "pure" consciousness. From the start the "spirit" is afflicted with the curse of being "burdened" with matter, which here makes its appearance in the form of agitated layers of air, sounds—in short, of language. Language is as old as consciousness, language is practical consciousness, as it exists for other men, and for that reason is really beginning to exist for me personally as well; for language, like consciousness, only arises from the need, the necessity, of intercourse with other men. Where there exists a relationship, it exists for me: the animal has no "relations" with anything, cannot have any. For the animal, its relation to others does not exist as a relation. Consciousness is therefore from the very beginning a social product, and remains so as long as men exist at all. Consciousness is at first, of course, merely consciousness concerning the immediate sensuous environment and consciousness of the limited connection with other persons and things outside the individual who is growing self-conscious. At the same time it is consciousness of nature, which first appears to men as a completely alien, all-powerful, and unassailable force, with which men's relations are purely animal and by which they are overawed like beasts; it is thus a purely animal consciousness of nature (natural religion).

b) *Concerning the production of consciousness*

In history up to the present it is certainly an empirical fact that separate individuals have, with the broadening of their activity into world-historical activity, become more and more enslaved under a power alien to them (a pressure which they have conceived of as a dirty trick on the part of the so-called universal spirit,) a power which has become more and more enormous and, in the last instance, turns out to be the *world market*. But it is just as empirically established that, by the overthrow of the existing state of society by the communist revolution (of which more below) and the abolition of private property which is identical with it, this power, which so baffles the German theoreticians, will be dissolved; and that then the liberation of each single individual will be accomplished in the measure in which history becomes transformed into world-history. From the above it is clear that the real intellectual wealth of the individual depends entirely on the wealth of his real connections. Only then will the separate individuals be liberated from the various national and local barriers, be brought into practical connection with the material and intellectual production of the whole world and be put in a position to acquire the capacity to enjoy this all-sided production of the whole earth (the creations of man). Universal dependence, this natural form of the world-historical cooperation of individuals, will be transformed by this communist revolution into the control and conscious mastery of these powers, which, born of the action of men on one another, have till now overawed and governed men as powers completely alien to them. Now this view can be expressed again in speculative-idealistic, i.e., fantastic, terms as "spontaneous generation of the species" ("society as the subject"), and thereby the series of interrelated individuals can be conceived as a single individual, which accomplishes the mystery of generating itself. It is clear here that individuals certainly make one another, physically and mentally, but do not make themselves either in the non-sense of St. Bruno, nor in the sense of the "unique," of the "made" man.

Our conception of history depends on our ability to expound the real process of production, starting out from the simple material production of life, and to comprehend the form of intercourse connected with this and created by this (i.e., civil society in its various stages), as the basis of all history; further, to show it in its action as State; and so, from this starting-point, to explain the whole mass of different theoretical products and forms of consciousness, religion, philosophy, ethics, etc., etc., and trace their origins and growth, by which means, of course, the whole thing can be shown in its totality (and therefore, too, the reciprocal action of these various sides on one another). It has not, like the idealistic view of history, in every period to look for a category, but remains constantly on the real ground of history; it does not explain practice from the idea but explains the formation of ideas from material practice; and accordingly it comes to the conclusion that all forms and products of consciousness cannot be dissolved by mental criticism, by resolution into "self-consciousness" or transformation into "apparitions," "specters," "fancies," etc., but only by the practical overthrow of the actual social relations which gave rise to this idealistic humbug; that not criticism but revolution is the driving force of history, also of religion, of philosophy and all other types of theory. It shows that history does not end by being resolved into "self-consciousness" as "spirit of the spirit," but that in it at each stage there is found a material result: a sum of productive forces, a historically created relation of individuals to nature and to one another, which is handed down to each generation from its predecessor; a mass of productive forces, different forms of capital, and conditions, which, indeed, is modified by the new generaton on the one hand, but also on the other prescribes for it its conditions of life and gives it a definite development, a special character. It shows that circumstances make men just as much as men make circumstances.

This sum of productive forces, forms of capital and social forms of intercourse, which every individual and generation finds in existence as something given, is the real basis of what the philosophers have conceived as "substance" and "essence of man," and what they have deified and attacked: a real basis which is not in the least disturbed, in its effect and influence on the development of men, by the fact that these philosophers revolt against it as "self-consciousness" and "the unique." These conditions of life, which different generations find in existence, decide also whether or not the periodically recurring revolutionary convulsion will be strong enough to overthrow the basis of all existing forms. And if these material elements of a complete revolution are not present (namely, on the one hand the existence of productive forces, on the other the formation of a revolutionary mass, which revolts not only against separate conditions of society up till then, but against the very "production of life" till then, the "total activity" on which it was based), then, as far as practical development is concerned, it is absolutely immaterial whether the "idea" of this revolution has been expressed a hundred times already, as the history of communism proves.

In the whole conception of history up to the present this real basis of history has either been totally neglected or else considered as a minor matter quite irrelevant to the course of history. History must therefore always be written according to an extraneous standard; the real production of life seems to be beyond history, while the truly historical appears to be separated from ordinary life, something extra-superterrestrial. With this the relation of man to nature is excluded from history and hence the antithesis of nature and history is created. The exponents of this conception of history have consequently only been able to see in history the political actions of princes and states, religious and all sorts of theoretical struggles, and in particular in each historical epoch have had to share the *illusion of that epoch*. For instance, if an epoch imagines itself to be actuated by purely "political" or "religious" motives, although "religion" and "politics" are only forms of its true motives, the historian accepts this opinion. The "idea," the "conception" of these conditioned men about their real practice, is transformed into the sole determining, active force, which controls and determines their practice. When the crude form in which the division of labor appears with the Indians and Egyptians calls forth the caste system in their state and religion, the historian believes that the caste system is the power which has produced this crude social form. While the French and the English at least hold by the political illusion, which is moderately close to reality, the Germans move in the realm of the "pure spirit" and make religious illusion the driving force of history.

The joint work of Marx and Engels that had the greatest ideological and political impact was the "Manifesto of the Communist Party," commonly known as the *Communist Manifesto,* which they wrote in 1847 as the program of the so-called Communist League they had joined earlier. The manifesto was published in their native German in February 1848. Years later, Lenin described it as the work in which "the new *Weltanschauung* . . . as the most comprehensive and profound doctrine of evolution and theory of the class struggle and of the world-historical revolutionary role of the proletariat . . . is defined with the clarity and brilliance of genius." The excerpts reflecting the authors' view of history are from the 1888 English translation edited by Engels and reprinted in Karl Marx and Friedrich Engels, *Selected Works* (2 vols.; Moscow, 1958; "prepared by the Institute of Marxism-Leninism under the Central Committee" of the CPSU), I, 33–65.

2. The Communist Manifesto

The history of all hitherto existing society [3] is the history of class struggles.

---

[3] That is, all *written* history. In 1847, the prehistory of society, the social organization existing previous to recorded history, was all but unknown. Since then, Haxthausen discovered common ownership of land in Russia, Maurer proved it to be the social foundation from which all Teutonic races started in history, and by-and-by village

Freeman and slave, patrician and plebeian, lord and serf, guild-master [4] and journeyman, in a word, oppressor and oppressed, stood in constant opposition to one another, carried on an uninterrupted, now hidden, now open fight, a fight that each time ended, either in a revolutionary reconstitution of society at large, or in the common ruin of the contending classes.

In the earlier epochs of history, we find almost everywhere a complicated arrangement of society into various orders, a manifold gradation of social rank. In ancient Rome we have patricians, knights, plebeians, slaves; in the Middle Ages, feudal lords, vassals, guild masters, journeymen, apprentices, serfs; in almost all of these classes, again, subordinate gradations.

The modern bourgeois society that has sprouted from the ruins of feudal society has not done away with class antagonisms. It has but established new classes, new conditions of oppression, new forms of struggle in place of the old ones.

Our epoch, the epoch of the bourgeoisie, possesses, however, this distinctive feature: it has simplified the class antagonisms. Society as a whole is more and more splitting up into two great hostile camps, into two great classes directly facing each other: Bourgeoisie and Proletariat.

From the serfs of the Middle Ages sprang the chartered burghers of the earliest towns. From these burgesses the first elements of the bourgeoisie were developed.

The discovery of America, the rounding of the Cape, opened up fresh ground for the rising bourgeoisie. The East Indian and Chinese markets, the colonization of America, trade with the colonies, the increase in the means of exchange and in commodities generally, gave to commerce, to navigation, to industry, an impulse never before known, and thereby, to the revolutionary element in the tottering feudal society, a rapid development.

The feudal system of industry, under which industrial production was monopolized by closed guilds, now no longer sufficed for the growing wants of the new markets. The manufacturing system took its place. The guild masters were pushed on one side by the manufacturing middle class; division of labor between the different corporate guilds vanished in the face of division of labor in each single workshop.

---

communities were found to be, or to have been, the primitive form of society everywhere from India to Ireland. The inner organization of this primitive Communistic society was laid bare, in its typical form, by Morgan's crowning discovery of the true nature of the *gens* and its relation to the *tribe*. With the dissolution of these primeval communities society begins to be differentiated into separate and finally antagonistic classes. I have attempted to retrace this process of dissolution in *Der Ursprung der Familie, des Privateigenthums und des Staats* [The Origin of the Family, Private Property, and the State] 2d ed.; Stuttgart, 1886). [Note by Engels to the English edition of 1888.]

[4] Guild master, that is, a full member of a guild, a master within, not a head of a guild. [*Ibid.*]

Meantime the markets kept ever growing, the demand ever rising. Even manufacture no longer sufficed. Thereupon, steam and machinery revolutionized industrial production. The place of manufacture was taken by the giant, Modern Industry, the place of the industrial middle class, by industrial millionaires, the leaders of whole industrial armies, the modern bourgeois.

Modern industry has established the world market, for which the discovery of America paved the way. This market has given an immense development to commerce, to navigation, to communication by land. This development has, in its turn, reacted on the extension of industry; and in proportion as industry, commerce, navigation, railways extended, in the same proportion the bourgeoisie developed, increased its capital, and pushed into the background every class handed down from the Middle Ages.

We see, therefore, how the modern bourgeoisie is itself the product of a long course of development, of a series of revolutions in the modes of production and of exchange.

Each step in the development of the bourgeoisie was accompanied by a corresponding political advance of that class. An oppressed class under the sway of the feudal nobility, an armed and self-governing association in the medieval commune;[5] here independent urban republic (as in Italy and Germany), there taxable "third estate" of the monarchy (as in France), afterwards, in the period of manufacture proper, serving either the semifeudal or the absolute monarchy as a counterpoise against the nobility, and, in fact, cornerstone of the great monarchies in general, the bourgeoisie has at last, since the establishment of Modern Industry and of the world market, conquered for itself, in the modern representative State, exclusive political sway. The executive of the modern State is but a committee for managing the common affairs of the whole bourgeoisie. The bourgeoisie, historically, has played a most revolutionary part.

The bourgeoisie, wherever it has got the upper hand, has put an end to all feudal, patriarchal, idyllic relations. It has pitilessly torn asunder the motley feudal ties that bound man to his "natural superiors," and has left remaining no other nexus between man and man than naked self-interest, than callous "cash payment." It has drowned the most heavenly ecstasies of religious fervor, of chivalrous enthusiasm, of philistine sentimentalism, in

---

[5] "Commune" was the name taken, in France, by the nascent towns even before they had conquered from their feudal lords and masters local self-government and political rights as the "Third Estate." Generally speaking, for the economical development of the bourgeoisie, England is here taken as the typical country; for its political development, France. [*Ibid.*]

This was the name given their urban communities by the townsmen of Italy and France, after they had purchased or wrested their initial rights of self-government from their feudal lords. [Note by Engels to the German edition of 1890.]

the icy water of egotistical calculation. It has resolved personal worth into exchange value, and in place of the numberless indefeasible chartered freedoms, has set up that single, unconscionable freedom—Free Trade. In one word, for exploitation veiled by religious and political illusions it has substituted naked, shameless, direct, brutal exploitation.

The bourgeoisie, during its rule of scarce one hundred years, has created more massive and more colossal productive forces than have all preceding generations together. Subjection of Nature's forces to man, machinery, application of chemistry to industry and agriculture, steam navigation, railways, electric telegraphs, clearing of whole continents for cultivation, canalization of rivers, whole populations conjured out of the ground—what earlier century had even a presentiment that such productive forces slumbered in the lap of social labor?

We see then: the means of production and of exchange, on whose foundation the bourgeoisie built itself up, were generated in feudal society. At a certain stage in the development of these means of production and of exchange, the conditions under which feudal society produced and exchanged, the feudal organization of agriculture and manufacturing industry, in one word, the feudal relations of property, became no longer compatible with the already developed productive forces; they became so many fetters. They had to be burst asunder; they were burst asunder.

Into their place stepped free competition, accompanied by a social and political constitution adapted to it, and by the economical and political sway of the bourgeois class.

A similar movement is going on before our own eyes. Modern bourgeois society with its relations of production, of exchange and of property, a society that has conjured up such gigantic means of production and of exchange, is like the sorcerer who is no longer able to control the powers of the nether world whom he has called up by his spells. For many a decade past the history of industry and commerce is but the history of the revolt of modern productive forces against modern conditions of production, against the property relations that are the conditions for the existence of the bourgeoisie and of its rule. It is enough to mention the commercial crises that by their periodical return put on its trial, each time more threateningly, the existence of the entire bourgeois society. In these crises a great part not only of the existing products, but also of the previously created productive forces, are periodically destroyed. In these crises there breaks out an epidemic that, in all earlier epochs, would have seemed an absurdity—the epidemic of overproduction. Society suddenly finds itself put back into a state of momentary barbarism; it appears as if a famine, a universal war of devastation, had cut off the supply of every means of subsistence; industry and commerce seem to be destroyed; and why? Because there is too much civilization, too much means of subsistence, too much industry, too much commerce. The productive forces at the disposal of society no longer tend to further the development of the conditions of bourgeois property; on the contrary, they have become too powerful for these conditions, by which they are fettered, and so soon as they overcome these fetters, they bring disorder into the whole of bourgeois society, endanger the existence of bourgeois property. The conditions of bourgeois society are too narrow to comprise the wealth created by them. And how does the bourgeoisie get over these crises? On the one hand by enforced destruction of a mass of productive forces; on the other, by the conquest of new markets and by the more thorough exploitation of the old ones. That is to say, by paving the way for more extensive and more destructive crises, and by diminishing the means whereby crises are prevented.

The weapons with which the bourgeoisie felled feudalism to the ground are now turned against the bourgeoisie itself.

But not only has the bourgeoisie forged the weapons that bring death to itself; it has also called into existence the men who are to wield those weapons—the modern working class—the proletarians.

The proletariat goes through various stages of development. With its birth begins its struggle with the bourgeoisie. At first the contest is carried on by individual laborers, then by the workpeople of a factory, then by the operatives of one trade, in one locality, against the individual bourgeois who directly exploits them.

Hitherto, every form of society has been based, as we have already seen, on the antagonism of oppressing and oppressed classes. But in order to oppress a class, certain conditions must be assured to it under which it can, at least, continue its slavish existence. The serf, in the period of serfdom, raised himself to membership in the commune, just as the petty bourgeois, under the yoke of feudal absolutism, managed to develop into a bourgeois. The modern laborer, on the contrary, instead of rising with the progress of industry, sinks deeper and deeper below the conditions of existence of his own class. He becomes a pauper, and pauperism develops more rapidly than population and wealth. And here it becomes evident that the bourgeoisie is unfit any longer to be the ruling class in society, and to impose its conditions of existence upon society as an overriding law. It is unfit to rule because it is incompetent to assure an existence to its slave within his slavery, because it cannot help letting him sink into such a state, that it has to feed him, instead of being fed by him. Society can no longer live under this bourgeoisie; in other words, its existence is no longer compatible with society.

The essential condition for the existence, and for the sway of the bourgeois class, is the formation and augmentation of capital; the condition for capital is wage labor. Wage labor rests exclusively on competition between the laborers. The advance of industry, whose involuntary promoter is the bourgeoisie, replaces the isolation of the laborers, due to competition, by their revolutionary combination, due to association. The development of Modern Industry, therefore, cuts from under its feet the very foundation on which the bourgeoisie produces and appropriates products. What the bourgeoisie, therefore, produces, above all, is its own gravediggers. Its fall and the victory of the proletariat are equally inevitable.

The fullest and most coherent—and at the same time very succinct— formulation of Marx's theory of history came eleven years after the *Communist Manifesto,* in the Preface to his *A Contribution to the Critique of Political Economy,* published in Berlin in 1859. To impassioned present-day followers, Marx produced there "in a flash of genius" the essence of historical materialism; to a more detached student such as Professor Sidney Hook, "this is Marx's own classic statement of how he reached historical materialism and his summary of the position." The passages below are from the English translation in Marx and Engels, *Selected Works,* I, 361–365.

3. Preface to *A Contribution to the Critique of Political Economy*

I was taking up law, which discipline, however, I only pursued as a subordinate subject along with philosophy and history. In the year 1842–43, as editor of the *Rheinische Zeitung,* I experienced for the first time the embarrassment of having to take part in discussions on so-called material interests. The proceedings of the Rhenish Landtag on thefts of wood and parceling of landed property, the official polemic which Herr von Schaper, then *Oberpräsident* of the Rhine Province, opened against the *Rheinische Zeitung* on the conditions of the Moselle peasantry, and, finally, debates on free trade and protective tariffs provided the first occasions for occupying myself with economic questions. On the other hand, at that time when the good will "to go further" greatly outweighed knowledge of the subject, a philosophically weakly tinged echo of French socialism and communism made itself audible in the *Rheinische Zeitung.* I declared myself against this amateurism, but frankly confessed at the same time in a controversy with the *Allgemeine Augsburger Zeitung* that my previous studies did not permit me even to venture any judgment on the content of the French tendencies. Instead, I eagerly seized on the illusion of the managers of the *Rheinische Zeitung,* who thought that by a weaker attitude on the part of the paper they could secure a remission of the death sentence passed upon it, to withdraw from the public stage into the study.

The first work which I undertook for a solution of the doubts which assailed me was a critical review of the Hegelian philosophy of right, a work the introduction to which appeared in 1844 in the *Deutsch-Französische Jahrbücher,* published in Paris. My investigation led to the result that legal relations as well as forms of state are to be grasped neither from themselves nor from the so-called general development of the human mind, but rather have their roots in the material conditions of life, the sum total of which Hegel, following the example of the Englishmen and Frenchmen of the eighteenth century, combines under the name of "civil society," [and] that, however, the anatomy of civil society is to be sought in political economy. The investigation of the latter, which I began in Paris, I continued in Brussels, whither I had emigrated in consequence of an expulsion order of M. Guizot. The general result at which I arrived and which, once won, served as a guiding thread for my studies, can be briefly formulated as follows: In the social production of their life, men enter into definite relations that are indispensable and independent of their will, relations of production which correspond to a definite stage of development of their material productive forces. The sum total of these relations of production constitutes the economic structure of society, the real foundation, on which rises a legal and political superstructure and to which correspond definite forms of social consciousness. The mode of production of material life conditions the social, political, and intellectual life-process in general. It is not the consciousness of men that determines their being, but, on the contrary, their social being that determines their consciousness. At a certain stage of their development, the material productive forces of society come in conflict with the existing relations of production, or—what is but a legal expression for the same thing—with the property relations within which they have been at work hitherto. From forms of development of the productive forces these relations turn into their fetters. Then begins an epoch of social revolution. With the change of the economic foundation the entire immense superstructure is more or less rapidly transformed. In considering such transformations a distinction should always be made between the material transformation of the economic conditions of production, which can be determined with the precision of natural science, and the legal, political, religious, aesthetic, or philosophic—in short, ideological—forms in which men become conscious of this conflict and fight it out. Just as our opinion of an individual is not based on what he thinks of himself, so

can we not judge of such a period of transformation by its own consciousness; on the contrary, this consciousness must be explained rather
from the contradictions of material life, from the existing conflict between
the social productive forces and the relations of production. No social order
ever perishes before all the productive forces for which there is room in it
have developed; and new, higher relations of production never appear
before the material conditions of their existence have matured in the womb
of the old society itself. Therefore mankind always sets itself only such
tasks as it can solve, since, looking at the matter more closely, it will always
be found that the task itself arises only when the material conditions for its
solution already exist or are at least in the process of formation. In broad
outlines Asiatic, ancient, feudal, and modern bourgeois modes of production can be designated as progressive epochs in the economic formation of
society. The bourgeois relations of production are the last antagonistic form
of the social process of production—antagonistic not in the sense of individual antagonism, but of one arising from the social conditions of life of
the individuals; at the same time the productive forces developing in the
womb of bourgeois society create the material conditions for the solution of
that antagonism. This social formation brings, therefore, the prehistory of
human society to a close.

Engels reviewed *A Contribution to the Critique of Political Economy* in
the issues of the London German-language periodical *Das Volk* for August
6 and 20, 1859.[6] He described Marx as "the only one who could undertake
the work of extracting from the Hegelian logic the kernel which comprises
Hegel's real discoveries in this sphere, and to reconstruct the dialectical
method, divested of its idealistic trappings, in the simple shape in which it
becomes the only true form of development of thought." Hegel, Engels
said, had a tremendous historical sense and was the first who attempted to
show a development and an inner coherence in history. The majesty of his
basic idea was still overpowering, and his epoch-making conception of
history was the direct theoretical premise for the new materialist outlook,
but his idealist philosophy had to be turned right side up and his dialectical
method applied to the new materialism coming from the natural sciences.
Marx, Engels was convinced, had fulfilled this task.

The Marxist theory of history evident in the preceding extracts can be
paraphrased as follows: Matter has come into existence first and hence
determines everything else. Man is motivated to act by his material needs.

---

[6] Since Engels did not sign the review, his authorship has been averred on the basis of
literary analysis and indirect evidence. See *Sozialistische Monatshefte,* 1900, pp. 38–46,
where the review is reproduced in full; English translation in Marx and Engels,
Selected Works, I, 366–376.

In seeking to satisfy them, he uses productive forces and enters into production relations. The process of man's existence so determined by his material wants and the resulting economics is not smooth; in fact, it is an unremitting struggle, like the Darwinian struggle in nature, in which men of underpriviledged economic classes fight men of the economic class that holds the advantages in society. History is best understood, therefore, as coming from and showing the effects of a continuous class struggle. The struggle follows Hegel's dialectical pattern: economic evolution brings into existence a class hostile to the class in power and, like thesis and antithesis, the two fight until a synthesis, through violence in most cases, is reached. The dialectical pattern is repeated until the proletariat overpowers the bourgeoisie and establishes a classless society of communism in which the struggle of man against man will end. Being part of nature, the entire social process is governed by laws independent of man's will or wishes. A determined result and not a determining force, man is set on an inevitable course. The only thing he can do is to recognize what is historically inevitable and accept and facilitate its advent.

This then is Marx's bequest of a theory of history or, more properly, this is the theory of history subsequent Marxists have chosen to regard as Marx's bequest. The point is not sophistry. Like the classical oracle, Marx has also said, with customery forcefulness and conviction, that man makes history: "*History* does *nothing,* possesses *no* enormous wealth, fights *no* battles. It is not history but rather *man,* the real, living man, who does everything, possesses everything, fights for everything. 'History' is not some person apart who uses man as means of reaching *her* purposes. History itself is *nothing but* the activity of man pursuing his purposes." [7] It is also evident that both Marx and Engels were concerned over the ways in which their ideas were understood and applied. In letters he wrote seven years after Marx's death, Engels pointed out that "while the material mode of existence is the *primum agens* this does not preclude the ideological spheres from reacting upon it in their turn, though with a secondary effect." The materialist conception of history, he said, has a lot of dangerous friends "to whom it serves as an excuse for *not* studying history. Just as Marx used to say about the French 'Marxists' of the late seventies: 'All I know is that I am not a Marxist.'" This conception, he stressed, held that: "the *ultimately* determining element in history is the production and reproduction of real life. More than this neither Marx nor I have ever asserted. Hence if somebody twists this into saying that the economic element is the *only* determining one, he transforms that proposition into a meaningless, abstract, senseless phrase. . . . Marx and I are ourselves partly to blame for the fact that the younger people sometimes lay more stress on the economic side than is due to it. We had to emphasis the main principle *vis-à-vis* our adversaries, who denied it, and we had not always the time, the

---

[7] *Werke,* II (Berlin, 1962), 98.

place, or the opportunity to allow the other elements involved in the interaction to come into their rights." [8]

Both in its original form and as developed by Lenin, Marxism is "shot through with dualism" [9] and can be used to support both economic determinism and voluntarism as the need of the interpreter happens to dictate. It is not surprising, therefore, that to many the philosophical legacy Marx and Engels left behind is ambiguous.[10]

---

[8] *Selected Works,* II, 486–490.

[9] Robert V. Daniels, "Fate and Will in the Marxist Philosophy," *Journal of the History of Ideas,* XXI, No. 4 (October–December 1960), 538–552.

[10] The literature on the Marxist conception of history is vast. For a critique that has had wide acceptance see Karl Federn, *The Materialist Conception of History* (London, 1939). Other titles are listed in the suggestions for further reading at the end of this book.

CHAPTER II

GEORGI V. PLEKHANOV

ALTHOUGH Marx's homeland, Germany, developed the largest Marxist movement, it was in Russia that the most vigorous offshoots of Marxist thought burgeoned. Introduced in that country after 1872 with translations of *Capital* and the *Communist Manifesto,* Marxism became a polarizing factor: in increasing numbers Russian intellectuals took positions for or against it.[1] Of those who embraced it in this early period, Georgi V. Plekhanov (1856–1918) was the most influential. A scion of petty nobility, Plekhanov went abroad in exile after disillusionment as a Narodnik ("friend of the people," member of the Populist movement in the 1870's) and in the West found a new faith in Marxism. At Geneva he translated the *Communist Manifesto* in 1882 and organized in the following year the first Russian Marxist group, immediately becoming recognized as the mastermind of early Russian Marxism.[2]

In 1895—in reply to polemical articles against Marxism by the Narodnik leader N. K. Mikhailovsky in the journal *Russkoe bogatstvo* ("Russian Treasure")[3]—Plekhanov produced a major treatise entitled *The Development of the Monist View of History.* Characterized by Lenin as a work on which "a whole generation of Russian Marxists was educated," Plekhanov's polemical defense of the Marxist philosophic system is replete with formulations which are part and parcel of the Marxist heritage a student of the doctrine is expected to absorb. Despite his tactical differ-

---

[1] A few Russians had read Marxist works in the original before 1872, but it was the translation of *Capital* that stimulated the dissemination of Marxist ideas in Russia; it is noteworthy that the Russian translation of *Capital* was the first in another language and that it sold in some three thousand copies. On the penetration of Marxism in Russia see Iu. Z. Polevoi, *Zarozhdenie marksizma v Rossii,* [The Origin of Marxism in Russia (Moscow, 1959), and John Plamenatz, *German Marxism and Russian Communism* (London, 1954). The application of Marxism to the study of Russian history before 1917 is discussed in *Ocherki istorii istoricheskoi nauki v SSSR,* [Survey of the History of Historical Science in the U.S.S.R.] (Moscow, 1960), II, 219–291; *Istoriografiia istorii SSSR; s drevneishikh vremen do Velikoi Oktiabr'skoi sotsialisticheskoi revoliutsii* [Historiography of the History of the U.S.S.R., from Earliest Times to the Great October Socialist Revolution] (Moscow, 1961), pp. 330–480; A. L. Shapiro, *Russkaia istoriografiia v period imperializma* [Russian Historiography in the Age of Imperialism] (Leningrad, 1962), pp. 151–234; and V. I. Astakhov, *Kurs lektsii po russkoi istoriografii; chast vtoraia (epokha promyshlennogo kapitalizma)* [Lectures on Russian Historiography, Second Part, The Age of Industrial Capitalism] (Kharkov, 1962), pp. 228–269.

[2] For his biography see Samuel H. Baron, *Plekhanov—The Father of Russian Marxism* (Stanford, Calif., 1963).

[3] For these polemics see James H. Billington, *Mikhailovsky and Russian Populism* (Oxford, 1958).

ences with Plekhanov after 1903, Lenin wrote in 1921 : "I think it proper to observe for the benefit of young members of the Party that one cannot become an *intelligent,* a real Communist unless one has studied—I say advisedly, studied—everything Plekhanov has written on philosophy, for it is the best in world Marxist literature." The "Large Soviet Encyclopedia" describes *The Development of the Monist View of History* as "Plekhanov's most significant philosophical work, written from the positions of revolutionary Marxism." At the centennial of his birth in 1956 the Central Committee of the CPSU honored him as "the first outstanding propagandist of Marxist ideas in Russia and fighter for a scientific materialist world outlook." [4]

Mikhailovsky had written that in contrast to Darwin, who had produced "a few generalizing ideas, most intimately interconnected, which crown a whole Mont Blanc of factual material," Marx had produced disconnected assertions without any foundation of evidence. Plekhanov retorted that Marx did not have to "accumulate mountains of factual material—which had been collected by his predecessors—but to take advantage of this material, among other matter, and begin the study of the real history of mankind from the new point of view." The passages below are from *The Development of the Monist View of History* (Moscow, 1956) as issued in English translation in Plekhanov's centennial year.

4. *The Development of the Monist View of History*

Materialism is the direct opposite of idealism. Idealism strives to explain all the phenomena of Nature, all the qualities of matter, by these or those qualities of the spirit. Materialism acts in the exactly opposite way. It tries to explain psychic phenomena by these or those qualities of matter, by this or that organization of the human or, in more general terms, of the animal body. All those philosophers in the eyes of whom the prime factor is matter belong to the camp of the materialists; and all those who consider such a factor to be the spirit are idealists.

That is all that can be said about materialism in general, about "materialism in the general philosophical sense" : as time built up on its fundamental principle the most varied superstructures, which gave the materialism of one epoch quite a different aspect from the materialism of another.

Materialism and idealism exhaust the most important tendencies of philosophical thought. True, by their side there have almost always existed dualist systems of one kind or another, which recognize spirit and matter as

---

[4] For a sympathetic view of Plekhanov's contribution see Jean Dautry, "Plekhanov et la theorie de l'histoire," *La Pensée,* No. 77 (January–February 1958), pp. 89–95. For a recent restatement of Marxist monism see Howard Selsam, *What Is Philosophy? A Marxist Introduction* (New York, 1962), pp. 37–72.

separate and independent substances. Dualism was never able to reply satisfactorily to the inevitable question: how could these two separate substances, which have nothing in common between them, influence each other? Therefore the most consistent and most profound thinkers were always inclined to monism, i.e., to explaining phenomena with the help of some one main principle (*monos* in Greek means "one"). Every consistent idealist is a monist to the same extent as every consistent materialist. In this respect there is no difference, for example, between Berkeley and Holbach. One was a consistent idealist, the other a no less consistent materialist, but both were equally monistic; both one and the other equally well understood the worthlessness of the dualist outlook on the world, which up to this day is still, perhaps, the most widespread.

In the first half of our century philosophy was dominated by idealistic monism. In its second half there triumphed in science—with which meanwhile philosophy had been completely fused—materialistic monism, although far from always consistent and frank monism.

The bankruptcy of the idealist point of view in explaining the phenomena of nature and of social development was bound to force, and really did force, thinking people (i.e., not eclectics, not dualists) to return to the materialist view of the world. But the new materialism could no longer be a simple repetition of the teachings of the French materialists of the end of the eighteenth century. Materialism rose again enriched by all these acquisitions of idealism. The most important of these acquisitions was the dialectical method, the examination of phenomena in their development, in their origin and destruction. The genius who represented this new direction of thought was Karl Marx.

That the principal cause of the social historical process is the development of the productive forces, we say word for word with Marx: so that here there is no contradiction. Consequently, if it does exist anywhere, it can only be in the question of the relationship between the economy of society and its psychology. Let us see whether it exists.

The reader will be good enough to remember how private property arises. The development of the productive forces places men in such relations of production that the personal appropriation of certain objects proves to be more convenient for the process of production. In keeping with this the legal conceptions of primitive man change. The psychology of society adapts itself to its economy. On the given economic foundation there rises up fatally the ideological superstructure appropriate to it. But on the other hand each new step in the development of the productive forces places men, in their daily life, in new mutual relations which do not correspond to the relations of production now becoming outdated. These new and unprecedented situations reflect themselves in the psychology of men, and very strongly change it. In what direction? Some members of society defend the old order: these are the people of stagnation. Others—to whom the old order is not advantageous—stand for progress; their psychology changes in the direction of those relations of production which in time will replace the old economic relations, now becoming outdated. The adaptation of psychology to economy, as you see, continues, but slow psychological evolution precedes economic revolution.

That the very foundations of the theory of economic materialism remain unconnected among themselves is sheer untruth. One need only read the preface to the *Critique of Political Economy,* to see how intimately and harmoniously they are interconnected. That these propositions have not been tested is also untrue: they have been tested with the help of an analysis of social phenomena, both in *The Eighteenth Brumaire* and in *Capital,* and moreover not at all "particularly" in the chapter on primitive accumulation, as Mr. Mikhailovsky thinks, but absolutely in all the chapters, from the first to the last. If nevertheless this theory has not once been set forth in connection with "a whole Mont Blanc" of factual material, which in Mr. Mikhailovsky's opinion distinguishes it to its disadvantage from Darwin's theory, there's again a misunderstanding here. With the help of the factual material making up, for example, *The Origin of Species,* it is chiefly the mutability of species that is demonstrated; when Darwin touches on the history of a few separate species, he does it only in passing, and only hypothetically; history might have gone this way or other, but one thing was certain—that there had been a history, and that species had varied. Now we shall ask Mr. Mikhailovsky: was it necessary for Marx to prove that mankind doesn't stand still, that social forms change, that the views of men replace one another—in a word, was it necessary to prove the variability of this kind of phenomena? Of course it was not, although in order to prove it, it would have been easy to pile up a dozen "Mont Blancs of factual material." What did Marx have to do? The preceding history of social science and philosophy had piled up a "whole Mont Blanc" of contradictions, which urgently demanded solution. Marx did precisely solve them with the help of a theory which, like Darwin's theory, consists of a "few generalizing ideas, most intimately connected among themselves." When these ideas appeared, it turned out that, with their help, all the contradictions which threw previous thinkers into confusion could be resolved. Marx required, not to accumulate mountains of factual material— which had been collected by his predecessors—but to take advantage of this material, among other matter, and to begin the study of the real history of mankind from the new point of view.

According to the new theory, the historical progress of humanity is determined by the development of the productive forces, leading to changes in economic relations. Therefore any historical research has to begin with studying the condition of the productive forces and the economic relations of the given country. But naturally research must not stop at this point: it has to show how the dry skeleton of economy is covered with the living flesh of social and political forms, and then—and this is the most interesting and most fascinating side of the problem—of human ideas, feelings, aspirations and ideals. The investigator receives into his hands, one may say, dead matter, but an organism full of life has to emerge from his hands.

The development of the social environment is subjected to its own laws. This means that its characteristics depend just as little on the will and consciousness of men as the characteristics of the geographical environment. The productive action of man on nature gives rise to a new form of dependence of man, a new variety of his slavery: economic necessity. And the greater grows man's authority over nature, the more his productive forces develop, the more stable becomes this new slavery: with the development of the productive forces the mutual relations of men in the social process of production become more complex; the course of that process completely slips from under their control, the producer proves to be the slave of his own creation (as an example, the capitalist anarchy of production).

But just as the nature surrounding man itself gave him the first opportunity to develop his productive forces and, consequently, gradually to emancipate himself from nature's yoke—so the relations of production, social relations, by the very logic of their development bring man to realization of the causes of his enslavement by economic necessity. This provides the opportunity for a new and final triumph of consciousness over necessity, of reason over blind law.

Having realized that the cause of his enslavement by his own creation lies in the anarchy of production, the producer ("social man") organizes that production and thereby subjects it to his will. Then terminates the kingdom of necessity, and there begins the reign of freedom, which itself proves to be necessity. The prologue of human history has been played out, history begins.[5]

---

[5] After all that has been said it will be clear, we hope, what is the relation between the teaching of Marx and the teaching of Darwin. Darwin succeeded in solving the problem of how there originate vegetable and animal species in the struggle for existence. Marx succeeded in solving the problem of how there arise different types of social organization in the struggle of men for their existence. Logically, the investigation of Marx begins precisely where the investigation of Darwin ends. Animals and vegetables are under the influence of their physical environment. The physical environment acts on social man through those social relations which arise on the basis of productive forces, which at first develop more or less quickly according to the characteristics of the physical environment. Darwin explains the origin of the species not by an allegedly innate tendency to develop in the animal organism, as Lamarck did, but by the adaptation of the organism to the conditions existing outside it; not by the nature of the organism but by the influence of external nature. Marx explains the

Philosophical monomania—that is, seeking, and claiming to have found, one single master key to the universe—is, of course, not characteristic of Marxism alone. It has repeatedly arisen in history as man has sought simple, easy-to-grasp explanations of the world. If the nineteenth century inclined toward them, the twentieth views them with skepticism, particularly since in practice philosophical monism has led to political monism and ideological orthodoxy and, beyond, to totalitarian monopoly of power and thought.

Another statement of the Marxist view of history was produced by Plekhanov in 1897 in response to the appearance of the French edition of Antonio Labriola's *Essays on the Materialistic Conception of History.* Entitled "The Materialist Conception of History," it is a combative piece adding nothing of significance to the previous statements of the doctrine. It can be read in George Plekhanov, *Essays in Historical Materialism* (New York, 1940).

One of the perplexing difficulties in the writing of history is the problem of assessing the impact of individual human beings, particularly major idea-makers and decision-makers, upon events. The problem, of course, confronts the Marxists as well. In an essay published in 1898 on the role of the individual in history Plekhanov attempted to deal with the problem theoretically and produced what is regarded as the classical Marxist position on it. Plekhanov's answers, however, are far from clear or final, as subsequent readings show; for example, in Stalin's time and under his pressure, the role of the late dictator was vastly exaggerated by Soviet historians, while since his death their assessments of his role have been drastically altered. The excerpts below are from George Plekhanov, *The Role of the Individual in History* (New York, 1940), *passim.*[6]

5. The Role of the Individual in History[*]

III

Again, being conscious of the absolute inevitability of a given phenomenon can only increase the energy of a man who sympathizes with it and who regards himself as one of the forces which called it into being. If such a

---

historical development of man not by the nature of man, but by the characteristics of those social relations between men which arise when social man is acting on external nature. The spirit of their research is absolutely the same in both thinkers. That is why one can say that Marxism is Darwinism in its application to social science (we know that chronologically this is not so, but that is unimportant). [Footnote by Plekhanov.]

[6] For critiques of Plekhanov's views and the general Marxist position on the role of the individual in history see Sidney Hook, *The Hero in History* (Boston, 1957), pp. 75–101, and Leo Yaresh, "The Role of the Individual in History," in *Rewriting Russian History,* ed. Cyril E. Black (2d rev. ed.; New York, 1962), pp. 77–106.

[*] Reprinted by permission of International Publishers Co. Inc. Copyright © 1940. *Essays in Historical Materialism.*

man, conscious of the inevitability of this phenomenon, folded his arms and did nothing, he would show that he was ignorant of arithmetic. Indeed, let us suppose that phenomenon A must necessarily take place under a given sum of circumstances. You have proved to me that a part of this sum of circumstances already exists and that the other part will exist in a given time, T. Being convinced of this, I, the man who sympathizes with phenomenon A, exclaim: "Good!" and then go to sleep until the happy day when the event you have foretold takes place. What will be the result? The following. In your calculations, the sum of circumstances, necessary to bring about phenomenon A, included *my activities,* equal, let us say, to *a.* As, however, I am immersed in deep slumber, the sum of circumstances favorable for the given phenomenon at time T will be, not S, but $S - a$, which changes the situation. Perhaps my place will be taken by another man, who was also on the point of inaction, but was saved by the sight of my apathy, which to him appeared to be pernicious. In that case, force a will be replaced by force b, and if a equals b $(a = b)$, the sum of circumstances favorable for A will remain equal to S, and phenomenon A will take place, after all, at time T.

But if my force cannot be regarded as being equal to zero, if I am a skillful and capable worker, and nobody has replaced me, then we will not have the full sum S, and phenomenon A will take place later than we assumed, or not as fully as we expected, or it may not take place at all. This is as clear as daylight; and if I do not understand it, if I think that S remains S even after I am replaced, it is only because I am unable to count. But am I the only one who is unable to count? You, who prophesied that the sum S would certainly be available at time T, did not foresee that I would go to sleep immediately after my conversation with you; you were convinced that I would remain a good worker to the end; the force was less reliable than you thought. Hence, you, too, counted badly. But let us suppose that you had made no mistake, that you had made allowance for everything. In that case, your calculations will assume the following form: you say that at time T the sum S will be available. This sum of circumstances will include my replacement as a *negative magnitude;* and it will also include, as a *positive magnitude,* the stimulating effect on strongminded men of the conviction that their strivings and ideals are the subjective expression of objective necessity. In that case, the sum S will indeed be available at the time you appointed, and phenomenon A will take place. I think this is clear. But if this is clear, why was I confused by the idea that phenomenon A was inevitable? Why did it seem to me that it condemned me to inaction? Why, in discussing it, did I forget the simplest rules of arithmetic? Probably because, owing to the circumstances of my upbringing, I already had a very strong leaning towards inaction and my conversation with you served as the drop which filled the cup of this laudable inclination to overflowing. That is all. *Only in this sense—as the cause that revealed my moral flabbiness and uselessness—did the consciousness of necessity figure here.* It cannot possibly be regarded as the cause of this flabbiness: the causes of it are the circumstances of my upbringing. And so . . . and so.—arithmetic is very respectable and useful science, the rules of which should not be forgotten even by—I would say, particularly by— philosophers.

But what effect will the consciousness of the necessity of a given phenomenon have upon a strong man who does not sympathize with it and *resists* its taking place? Here the situation is somewhat different. It is very possible that it will cause the vigor of his resistance to *relax*. But when do the opponents of a given phenomenon become convinced that it is inevitable? When the circumstances favorable to it are very numerous and very strong. The fact that its opponents realize that the phenomenon is inevitable, and the relaxation of their energy are merely manifestations of the force of circumstances favorable to it. These manifestations, in their turn, are a part of the favorable circumstances.

But the vigor of resistance will not be relaxed among all the opponents; among some of them the consciousness that the phenomenon is inevitable will cause it to grow and become transformed into the vigor of *despair*. History in general, and the history of Russia in particular, provides not a few instructive examples of this sort of vigor. We hope the reader will be able to recall these without our assistance.

In essence, however, the subjectivists have never been able to solve, or even to present properly, the problem of the role of the individual in history. As against the influence of the *laws* of social-historical progress, they advanced the "activities of critically thinking individuals," and thus created, as it were, a new species of the factors theory; critically thinking individuals were *one factor* of this progress; its own laws were the *other* factor. This resulted in an extreme incongruity. . . . While some subjectivists, striving to ascribe the widest possible role to the "individual" in history, refused to recognize the historical progress of mankind as a process expressing laws, some of their later opponents, striving to bring out more sharply the coherent character of this progress, were evidently prepared to forget that *men make history, and therefore, the activities of individuals cannot help being important in history*. They have declared the individual to be a *quantité négligeable*. In theory, this extreme is as impermissible as the one reached by the more ardent subjectivists. It is as unsound to sacrifice the *thesis* to the *antithesis* as to forget the *antithesis* for the sake of the *thesis*. The correct point of view will be found only when we succeed in uniting the points of truth contained in them into a *synthesis*.

IV

This problem has been interesting us for a long time, and we have long wanted to invite our readers to join us in tackling it. We were restrained, however, by certain fears: we thought that perhaps our readers had already solved it for themselves and that our proposal would be belated. These fears have now been dispelled. The German historians have dispelled them for us. We are quite serious in saying this. The fact of the matter is that lately a rather heated controversy has been going on among the German historians over great men in history. Some have been inclined to regard the political activities of these men as the main and almost the *only* spring of historical development, while others have been asserting that such a view is one-sided and that the science of history must have in view, not only the activities of great men, and not only political history, but historical life as a whole (*das Ganze des geschichtlichen Lebens*). One of the representatives of the latter trend is Karl Lamprecht, author of *The History of the German People*. Lamprecht's opponents accused him of being a *"collectivist"* and a materialist; he was even placed on a par with—*horribile dictu*—the "Social-Democratic atheists," as he expressed it in winding up the debate. When we became acquainted with his views we found that the accusations hurled against this poor savant were utterly groundless. At the same time we were convinced that the present-day German historians were incapable of solving the problem of the role of the individual in history. We then decided that we had a right to assume that the problem was still unsolved even for a number of Russian readers, and that something could still be said about it that would not be altogether lacking in theoretical and practical interest.

Lamprecht gathered a whole collection (*eine artige Sammlung,* as he expresses it) of the views of prominent statesman on their own activities in the historical milieu in which they pursued them; in his polemics, however, he confined himself for the time being to references to some of the speeches and opinions of *Bismarck*. He quoted the following words, uttered by the Iron Chancellor in the North German Reichstag on April 16, 1869:

> Gentlemen, we can neither ignore the history of the past nor create the future. I would like to warn you against the mistake that causes people to advance the hands of their clocks, thinking that thereby they are hastening the passage of time. My influence on the events I took advantage of is usually exaggerated; but it would never occur to anyone to demand that *I should make history*. I could not do that even in conjunction with you, although together, we could resist the whole world. We cannot make history: we must wait while it is being made.

We will not make fruit ripen more quickly by subjecting it to the heat of a lamp; and if we pluck the fruit before it is ripe we will only prevent its growth and spoil it.

Referring to the evidence of Joly, Lamprecht also quotes the opinions which Bismarck expressed more than once during the Franco-Prussian war. Again, the idea that runs through these opinions is that "we cannot make great historical events, but must adapt ourselves to the natural course of things and limit ourselves to securing what is already ripe." Lamprecht regards this as the profound and whole truth. In his opinion, a modern historian cannot think otherwise, provided he is able to peer into the depths of events and not restrict his field of vision to too short an interval of time. Could Bismarck have caused Germany to revert to natural economy? He would have been unable to do this even when he was at the height of his power. General historical circumstances are stronger than the strongest individuals. For a great man, the general character of his epoch is *"empirically* given necessity."

This is how Lamprecht reasons, calling his view a *universal* one. It is not difficult to see the weak side of this "universal" view. The above-quoted opinions of Bismarck are very interesting as a psychological document. One may not sympathize with the activities of the late German Chancellor, but one cannot say that they were insignificant, that Bismarck was distinguished for "quietism." It was about him that Lassalle said: "The servants of reaction are no orators; but God grant that progress has servants like them." And yet this man, who at times displayed truly iron energy, considered himself absolutely impotent in face of the natural course of things, evidently regarding himself as a simple instrument of historical development; this proves once again that one can see phenomena in the light of necessity and at the same time be a very energetic statesman. But it is only in this respect that Bismarck's opinions are interesting; they cannot be regarded as a solution of the problem of the role of the individual in history. According to Bismarck, events occur of themselves, and we can secure what they prepare for us. But every act of "securing" is also an historical event; what is the difference between such events and those that occur of themselves? Actually, nearly every historical event is simultaneously an act of "securing" by somebody of the already ripened fruit of preceding development and a link in the chain of events which are preparing the fruits of the future. How can acts of "securing" be opposed to the natural course of things? Evidently, Bismarck wanted to say that individuals and groups of individuals operating in history never were and never will be all-powerful. This, of course, is beyond all doubt. Nevertheless, we would like to know what their power, far from omnipotence, of course, depends on; under what circumstances it grows and under what circumstances it diminishes. Neither Bismarck nor the learned advocate of the "universal" conception of history who quotes him answers these questions.

V

We do not share Pirenne's pleasant expectations. The future cannot belong to vague and indefinite views, and such, precisely, are the views of Monod and particularly of Lamprecht.

After the stupendous events of the end of the eighteenth century it was absolutely impossible to think any longer that history was made by more or less prominent and more or less noble and enlightened individuals who, at their own discretion, imbued the unenlightened but obedient masses with certain sentiments and ideas. Moreover, this philosophy of history offended the plebeian pride of the bourgeois theoreticians. They were prompted by the same feelings that revealed themselves in the eighteenth century in the rise of bourgeois drama.

The new school did not demand that the historian should be impassive. Augustin Thierry even said quite openly that political passion, by sharpening the mind of the investigator, may serve as a powerful means of discovering the truth. It is sufficient to make oneself only slightly familiar with the historical works of Guizot, Thierry or Mignet to see that they strongly sympathized with the bourgeoisie in its struggle against the lords temporal and spiritual, as well as with its efforts to suppress the demands of the rising proletariat. What is incontrovertible is the following: the new school of history arose in the twenties of the nineteenth century, at a time when the bourgeoisie had already vanquished the aristocracy, although the latter was still striving to restore some of its old privileges. The proud consciousness of the victory of their class was reflected in all the arguments of the historians of the new school. Lastly, the new school may have appeared to be fatalistic because, striving firmly to adopt this point of view, it paid little attention to the great individuals in history.[7] Those who had been brought up on the historical ideas of the eighteenth century found it difficult to accept this. Objections to the views of the new historians poured in from all sides, and then the controversy flared up which, as we have seen, has not ended to this day.

In January, 1826, Sainte-Beuve, in a review, in the *Globe,* of the fifth

---

[7] In a review of the third edition of Mignet's *History of the French Revolution,* Sainte-Beuve characterized that historian's attitude towards great men as follows: "In face of the vast and profound popular emotions which he had to describe, and of the impotence and nullity to which the sublimest genius and the saintliest virtue are reduced when the masses arise, he was seized with pity for men as individuals, could see in them, taken in isolation, only their weakness, and would not allow them to be capable of effective action, except through union with the multitude." [Note in source.]

and sixth volumes of Mignet's *History of the French Revolution,* wrote as follows:

> At any given moment a man may, by a sudden decision of his will, introduce into the course of events a new, unexpected and changeable force, which may alter that course, but which cannot be measured itself owing to its changeability.

It must not be thought that Sainte-Beuve assumed that "sudden decisions" of humans will occur without cause. No, that would have been too naïve. He merely asserted that the mental and moral qualities of a man who is playing a more or less important role in public life, his talent, knowledge, resoluteness or irresoluteness, courage or cowardice, etc., cannot help having a marked influence on the course and outcome of events; and yet these qualities cannot be explained solely by the general laws of development of a nation; they are always, and to a considerable degree, acquired as a result of the action of what may be called the accidents of private life.

French historians say that there was no need at all for France to wage war on the European continent, and that she should have concentrated all her efforts on the sea in order to resist England's encroachments on her colonies. The fact that she acted differently was again due to the inevitable Madame Pomadour, who wanted to please "her dear friend," Maria Theresa. As a result of the Seven Years' War, France lost her best colonies, which undoubtedly greatly influenced the development of her economic relations. In this case feminine vanity appears in the role of the influential "factor" of economic development.

Do we need any other examples? We will quote one more, perhaps the most astonishing one. During the aforesaid Seven Years' War, in August, 1761, the Austrian troops, having united with the Russian troops in Silesia, surrounded Frederick near Striegau. Frederick's position was desperate, but the Allies were tardy in attacking, and General Buturlin, after facing the enemy for twenty days, withdrew his troops from Silesia, leaving only a part of his forces as reinforcements for the Austrian General Laudon. Laudon captured Schweidnitz, near which Frederick was encamped, but this victory was of little importance. Suppose, however, Buturlin had been a man of firmer character? Suppose the Allies had attacked Frederick before he had time to entrench himself? They might have routed him, and he would have been compelled to yield to all the victors' demands. And this occurred barely a few months before a new accidental circumstance, the death of Empress Elizabeth, immediately changed the situation greatly in Frederick's favor. We would like to ask: What would have happened had Buturlin been a man of more resolute character, or had a man like Suvorov been in his place?

In examining the views of the "fatalist" historians, Sainte-Beuve gave expression to another opinion which is also worthy of attention. In the aforementioned review of Mignet's *History of the French Revolution,* he argued that the course and outcome of the French Revolution were determined not only by the general causes which had given rise to the Revolution, and not only by the passions which in its turn the Revolution had roused, but also by numerous minor phenomena, which had escaped the attention of the investigator, and which were not even a part of social phenomena, properly so called. He wrote:

> While these passions (roused by social phenomena) were operating, the physical and physiological forces of nature were not inactive: stones continued to obey the law of gravity; the blood did not cease to circulate in the veins. Would not the course of events have changed had Mirabeau, say, not died of fever, had Robespierre been killed by the accidental fall of a brick or by a stroke of apoplexy, or if Bonaparte had been struck down by a bullet? And will you dare to assert that the outcome would have been the same? Given a sufficient number of accidents, similar to those I have assumed, the outcome might have been the very opposite of what, in your opinion, was inevitable. I have a right to assume the possibility of such accidents because they are precluded neither by the general causes of the Revolution nor by the passions roused by these general causes.

Then he goes on to quote the well-known observation that history would have taken an entirely different course had Cleopatra's nose been somewhat shorter; and, in conclusion, admitting that very much more could be said in defense of Mignet's view, he again shows where this author goes wrong. Mignet ascribes solely to the action of general causes those results which many other, minor, dark and elusive causes had helped to bring about; his stern logic, as it were, refuses to recognize the existence of anything that seems to him to be lacking in order and law.

VI

Are Sainte-Beuve's objections sound? I think they contain a certain amount of truth. But what amount? To determine this we will first examine the idea that a man can "by the sudden decision of his will" introduce a new force into the course of events which is capable of changing their course considerably. We have quoted a number of examples, which, we think, very well explain this. Let us ponder over these examples.

Everybody knows that, during the reign of Louis XV, military affairs went steadily from bad to worse in France. As Henri Martin has observed, during the Seven Years' War, the French army, which always had numerous prostitutes, tradesmen, and servants in its train, and which had three times as many pack horses as saddle horses, had more resemblance to the hordes of Darius and Xerxes than to the armies of Turenne and Gustavus Adolphus. Archenholtz says in his history of this war that the French officers, when appointed for guard duty, often deserted their posts to go dancing somewhere in the vicinity, and obeyed the orders of their superiors only when they thought fit. This deplorable state of military affairs was due to the deterioration of the aristocracy, which nevertheless continued to occupy all the high posts in the army, and to the general dislocation of the "old order," which was rapidly drifting to its doom. These *general* causes alone would have been quite sufficient to make the outcome of the Seven Years' War unfavorable to France. But undoubtedly the incompetence of generals like Soubise greatly increased the chances of failure for the French army which these general causes already provided. Soubise retained his post, thanks to Madame Pompadour; and so we must count the proud Marquise as one of the "factors" significantly reinforcing the unfavorable influence of these general causes on the position of French affairs.

The Marquise de Pompadour was strong not by her own strength, but by the power of the king who was subject to her will. Can we say that the character of Louis XV was exactly what it was inevitably bound to be, in view of the general course of development of social relations in France? No, given the same course of development a king might have appeared in his place with a different attitude towards women. Sainte-Beuve would say that the action of obscure and intangible physiological causes was sufficient to account for this. And he would be right. But, if that is so, the conclusion emerges, that these obscure physiological causes, by affecting the progress and results of the Seven Years' War, also in consequence affected the subsequent development of France, which would have proceeded differently if the Seven Years' War had not deprived her of a great part of her colonies. Does not this conclusion, we then ask, contradict the conception of a social development conforming to laws?

No, not in the least. The effect of personal peculiarities in the instances we have discussed is undeniable; but no less undeniable is the fact that it could occur only *in the given social conditions.*

It follows, then, that by virtue of particular traits of their character, individuals can influence the fate of society. Sometimes this influence is very considerable; but the possibility of exercising this influence, and its extent, are determined by the form of organization of society, by the relation of forces within it. The character of an individual is a "factor" in social development only where, when, and to the extent that social relations permit it to be such.

We may be told that the extent of personal influence may also be determined by the talents of the individual. We agree. But the individual can display his talents only when he occupies the position in society necessary for this. Why was the fate of France in the hands of a man who totally lacked the ability and desire to serve society? Because such was the form of organization of that society. It is the form of organization that in any given period determines the role and, consequently, the social significance that may fall to the lot of talented or incompetent individuals.

But if the role of individuals is determined by the form of organization of society, how can their social influence, which is determined by the role they play, contradict the conception of social development as a process expressing laws? It does not contradict it; on the contrary, it serves as one of its most vivid illustrations.

But here we must observe the following. The possibility—determined by the form of organization of society—that individuals may exercise social influence opens the door to the influence of so-called *accident* upon the historical destiny of nations. Louis XV's lasciviousness was an inevitable consequence of the state of his physical constitution, but in relation to the general course of France's development the state of his constitution was *accidental*. Nevertheless, as we have said, it did influence the fate of France and served as one of the causes which determined this fate. The death of Mirabeau, of course, was due to pathological processes which obeyed definite laws. The inevitability of these processes, however, did not arise out of the general course of France's development, but out of certain particular features of the celebrated orator's constitution, and out of the physical conditions under which he had contracted his disease. In relation to the general course of France's development these features and conditions were *accidental*. And yet, Mirabeau's death influenced the further course of the Revolution and served as one of the causes which determined it.

Still more astonishing was the effect of accidental causes in the above-mentioned example of Frederick II, who succeeded in extricating himself from an extremely difficult situation only because of Buturlin's irresolution. Even in relation to the general course of Russia's development Buturlin's appointment may have been accidental, in the sense that we have defined that term, and, of course, it had no relation whatever to the general course of Prussia's development. Yet it is not improbable that Buturlin's irresolution saved Frederick from a desperate situation. Had Suvorov been in Buturlin's place, the history of Prussia might have taken a different course. It follows, then, that sometimes the fate of nations depends on accidents, which may be called *accidents of the second degree*. *"In allem Endlichen ist ein Element des Zufälligen,"* said Hegel. (In everything finite there are accidental elements.) In science we deal only with the "finite"; hence we can say that all the processes studied by science contain some accidental elements. Does not this preclude the scientific cognition of phenomena? No. *Accident is something relative.* It appears only at the point of intersection of *inevitable* processes. Hence, here, too, accidents do not in the least hinder the scientific investigation of phenomena.

We know now that individuals often exercise considerable influence upon the fate of society, but this influence is determined by the internal structure of that society and by its relation to other societies. But this is not all that has to be said about the role of the individual in history. We must approach this question from still another side.

Sainte-Beuve thought that had there been a sufficient number of petty and dark causes of the kind that he had mentioned, the outcome of the French Revolution would have been the *opposite* of what we know it to have been. This is a great mistake. No matter how intricately the petty, psychological and physiological causes may have been interwoven, they would not under any circumstances have eliminated the great social needs that gave rise to the French Revolution; and as long as these needs remained unsatisfied the revolutionary movement in France would have continued. To make the outcome of this movement the opposite of what it was, the needs that gave rise to it would have had to be the opposite of what they were; and this, of course, no combination of petty causes would ever be able to bring about.

The causes of the French Revolution lay in the character of *social relations;* and the petty causes assumed by Sainte-Beuve could lie only in the *personal qualities of individuals.* The final cause of social relationships lies in the state of the productive forces. This depends on the qualities of individuals only in the sense, perhaps, that these individuals possess more or less talent for making technical improvements, discoveries and inventions. Sainte-Beuve did not have these qualities in mind. No other qualities, however, enable individuals directly to influence the state of productive forces, and, hence, the social relations which they determine, i.e., *economic relations.* No matter what the qualities of the given individual may be, they cannot eliminate the given economic relations if the latter conform to the given state of productive forces. But the personal qualities of individuals make them more or less fit to satisfy those social needs which arise out of the given economic relations, or to counteract such satisfaction. The urgent social need of France at the end of the eighteenth century was the substitution for the obsolete political institutions of new institutions that would conform more to her economic system. The most prominent and useful public men of that time were those who were more capable than others of helping to satisfy this most urgent need. We will assume that Mirabeau, Robespierre and Napoleon were men of that type. What would have happened had premature death not removed Mirabeau from the political stage? The constitutional monarchist party would have retained its considerable power for a longer period; its resistance to the republicans would, therefore, have been more energetic. But that is all. No Mirabeau could, at that time, have averted the triumph of the republicans. Mirabeau's power rested entirely on the sympathy and confidence of the people; but the people wanted a republic, as the Court irritated them by its obstinate defense of the old order. As soon as the people had become convinced that Mirabeau did not sympathize with their republican strivings they would have ceased to sympathize with him; and then the great orator would have lost nearly all influence, and in all probability would have fallen a victim to the very movement that he would vainly have tried to check. Approximately the same thing may be said about Robespierre. Let us assume that he was an absolutely indispensable force in his party; but even so, he was not the only force. If the accidental fall of a brick had killed him, say, in January, 1793, his place would, of course, have been taken by somebody else, and although this person might have been inferior to him in every respect, nevertheless, events would have taken *the same course* as they did when Robespierre was alive. For example, even under these circumstances the Gironde would probably not have escaped defeat; but it is possible that Robespierre's party would have lost power somewhat earlier and we would now be speaking, not of the Thermidor reaction, but of the Floréal, Prairial or Messidor reaction. Perhaps some will say that with his inexorable Terror, Robespierre did not delay but hastened the downfall of his party. We will not stop to examine this supposition here; we will accept it as if it were quite sound. In that case, we must assume that Robespierre's party would have fallen not in Thermidor, but in Fructidor, Vendémiaire or Brumaire. In short, it may have fallen sooner or perhaps later, but it certainly would have fallen, because the section of the people which supported Robespierre's party was totally unprepared to hold power for a prolonged period. At all events, results "opposite" to those which arose from Robespierre's energetic action are out of the question.

Nor could they have arisen even if Bonaparte had been struck down by a bullet, let us say, at the Battle of Arcole. What he did in the Italian and other campaigns other generals would have done. Probably they would not have displayed the same talent as he did, and would not have achieved such brilliant victories; nevertheless the French Republic would have emerged victorious from the wars it waged at that time, because its soldiers were incomparably the best in Europe. Owing to the specific qualities of their minds and characters, influential individuals can change the *individual features of events and some of their particular consequences,* but they cannot change their general *trend,* which is determined by other forces.

VII

It has long been observed that great talents appear everywhere, whenever the social conditions favorable to their development exist. This means that every man of talent who *actually appears,* every man of talent who becomes a *social force,* is the product of *social relations.* Since this is the case, it is clear why talented people can, as we have said, change only individual features of events, but not their general trend; *they are themselves the product of this trend; were it not for that trend they would never have crossed the threshold that divides the potential from the real.*

VIII

Thus, the personal qualities of leading people determine the individual features of historical events; and the accidental element, in the sense that we have indicated, always plays some role in the course of these events, the trend of which is determined, in the last analysis, by so-called general causes, i.e., actually by the development of productive forces and the mutual relations between men in the social-economic process of production. Casual phenomena and the personal qualities of celebrated people are ever so much more noticeable than deep-lying general causes. The eighteenth century pondered but little over these general causes, and claimed that history was explained by the conscious actions and "passions" of historical personages. The philosophers of that century asserted that history might have taken an entirely different course as a result of the most insignificant causes; for example, if some "atom" had started playing pranks in some ruler's head (an idea expressed more than once in *Système de la Nature*).

The adherents of the new trend in the science of history began to argue that history could not have taken any other course than the one it has taken, notwithstanding all "atoms." Striving to emphasize the effect of general causes as much as possible, they ignored the personal qualities of historical personages. According to their argument, historical events would not have been affected in the least by the substitution of some persons for others, more or less capable.[8] But if we make such an assumption then we must admit that the *personal element is of no significance whatever in history,* and that everything can be reduced to the operation of general causes, to the general laws of historical progress. This would be going to an extreme which leaves no room for the particle of truth contained in the opposite opinion. It is precisely for this reason that the opposite opinion retained

---

[8] According to their argument, i.e., when they began to discuss the tendency of historical events to conform to laws. When, however, some of them simply described these phenomena, they sometimes ascribed even exaggerated significance to the personal element. What interests us now, however, are not their descriptions, but their arguments. [Note in source.]

some right to existence. The collision between these two opinions assumed the form of an antinomy, the first part of which was general laws, and the second part was the activities of individuals. From the point of view of the second part of the antinomy, history was simply a chain of accidents; from the point of view of the first part it seemed that even the individual features of historical events were determined by the operation of general causes. But if the individual features of events are determined by the influence of general causes and do not depend upon the personal qualities of historical personages, it follows that these features are *determined by general causes* and cannot be changed, no matter how much these personages may change. Thus, the theory assumes a *fatalistic character*.

As the French Revolution had shown that historical events are not determined by the *conscious* actions of men alone, Mignet and Guizot, and the other historians of the same trend, put in the forefront the effect of *passions,* which often rebelled against all control of the mind. But if passions are the final and most general cause of historical events, then why is Sainte-Beuve wrong in asserting that the outcome of the French Revolution might have been the opposite of what we know it was if there had been individuals capable of imbuing the French people with passions opposite to those which had excited them? Mignet would have said: Because other passions could not have excited the French people at that time owing to the very qualities of human nature. In a certain sense this would have been true. But this truth would have had a strongly fatalistic tinge, for it would have been on a par with the thesis that the history of mankind, in all its details, is predetermined by the *general* qualities of human nature. Fatalism would have appeared here as the result of the disappearance of the *individual in the general*. Incidentally, it is always the result of such a disappearance. It is said: "If all social phenomena are inevitable, then our activities cannot have any significance." This is a correct idea wrongly formulated. We ought to say: if everything occurs as a result of the *general,* then the *individual,* including my efforts, is of no significance. *This* deduction is correct; but it is incorrectly employed. It is meaningless when applied to the modern materialist conception of history, in which there is room also for the *individual*. But it was justified when applied to the views of the French historians in the period of the Restoration.

At the present time, human nature can no longer be regarded as the final and most general cause of historical progress: if it is constant, then it cannot explain the extremely changeable course of history; if it is changeable, then obviously its changes are themselves determined by historical progress. At the present time we must regard the development of productive forces as the final and most general cause of the historical progress of mankind, and it is these productive forces that **determine the consecutive** changes in the social relations of men. Parallel with this *general* cause there are *particular* causes, i.e., the *historical situation* in which the development of the productive forces of a given nation proceeds and which, in the last analysis, is itself created by the development of these forces among other nations, i.e., the same general cause.

Finally, the influence of the particular causes is supplemented by the operation of *individual* causes, i.e., the personal qualities of public men and other "accidents," thanks to which events finally assume their *individual features.* Individual causes cannot bring about fundamental changes in the operation of *general and particular causes* which, moreover, determine the trend and limits of the influence of individual causes. Nevertheless, there is no doubt that history would have had different features had the individual causes which had influenced it been replaced by other causes of the same order.

But let us return to our subject. A great man is great not because his personal qualities give individual features to great historical events, but because he possesses qualities which make him most capable of serving the great social needs of his time, needs which arose as a result of general and particular causes. Carlyle, in his well-known book on heroes and hero-worship, calls great men *beginners.* This is a very apt description. A great man is precisely a beginner because he sees *further* than others, and desires things *more strongly* than others. He solves the scientific problems brought up by the preceding process of intellectual development of society; he points to the new social needs created by the preceding development of social relationships, he takes the initiative in satisfying these needs. He is a hero. But he is not a hero in the sense that he can stop, or change, the natural course of things, but in the sense that his activities are the conscious and free expression of this inevitable and unconscious course. Herein lies all his significance; herein lies his whole power. But his significance is colossal, and the power is terrible.

Bismarck said that we cannot make history and must wait while it is being made. But who makes history? It is made by the *social man,* who is its *sole "factor."* The social man creates his own, social, relationships. But if in a given period he creates given relationships and not others, there must be some cause for it, of course; it is determined by the state of his productive forces. No great man can foist on society relations which *no longer* conform to the state of these forces, or which *do not yet* conform to them. In this sense, indeed, he cannot make history, and in this sense he would advance the hands of his clock in vain; he would not hasten the passage of time, nor turn it back. Here Lamprecht is quite right: even at the height of his power Bismarck could not cause Germany to revert to natural economy.

Social relationships have their inherent logic: as long as people live in given mutual relationships they will feel, think and act in a given way, and no other. Attempts on the part of public men to combat this logic would also be fruitless; the natural course of things (this logic of social relationships) would reduce all his effort to nought. But if I know in what direction social relations are changing owing to given changes in the social-economic process of production, I also know in what direction social mentality is changing: consequently, I am able to influence it. Influencing social mentality means influencing historical events. Hence, in a certain sense, I *can make history,* and there is no need for me to wait while "it is being made."

Monod believes that really important events and individuals in history are important only as signs and symbols of the development of institutions and economic conditions. This is a correct although very inexactly expressed idea; but precisely because this idea is correct it is wrong to oppose the activities of great men to "the *slow progress*" of the conditions and institutions mentioned. The more or less slow changes in "economic conditions" periodically confront society with the necessity of more or less rapidly changing its institutions. This change never takes place "by itself"; it always needs the intervention of *men,* who are thus confronted with great social problems. And it is those men who do more than others to facilitate the solution of these problems who are called great men. But *solving a problem* does not mean being only a "symbol" and a "sign" of the fact that it has been solved.

We think that Monod opposed the one to the other mainly because he was carried away by the pleasant catchword, "slow." Many modern evolutionists are very fond of this catchword. *Psychologically,* this passion is comprehensible: it *inevitably* arises in the respectable milieu of moderation and punctiliousness. . . . But *logically* it does not bear examination, as Hegel proved.

And it is not only for "beginners," not only for "great" men that a broad field of activity is open. It is open for all those who have eyes to see, ears to hear and hearts to love their neighbors. The concept *great* is a relative concept. In the ethical sense every man is great who, to use the Biblical phrase, "lays down his life for his friend."

Deservedly called the "father of Russian Marxism," Plekhanov was probably the best philosophical mind in the international Marxist movement after Marx. Like Marx, he also attempted to be active in proletarian politics and in the strife-torn affairs of the Russian exiles. At the Second Congress of the Russian Social Democratic Workers' (Marxist) Party held at London in 1903 (the first congress, at which the party was organized, was held at Minsk in 1898), he drafted with Lenin's help the party program but proved inferior to the younger man's dynamism, political and organizational skills, and ruthlessness.[9] After 1903, the two men parted company, Lenin heading for the leadership of the Bolshevik wing of the party and ultimate triumph in 1917 and Plekhanov sliding toward the Menshevik wing, decline, and death in 1918.

---

[9] The 1903 program remained in effect until 1919, when a new party program drafted by Lenin superseded it. It was "the first in the world among the programs of the workers' parties in which the idea of the role of the dictatorship of the proletariat was formulated." *Istoriia Kommunisticheskoi partii Sovetskogo Soiuza* [History of the Communist Party of the Soviet Union] (Moscow, 1959), p. 59. For an English translation of the program see Thomas P. Whitney, *The Communist Blueprint for the Future* (New York, 1962), pp. 66–73.

CHAPTER III

VLADIMIR ILYICH LENIN

THE SECOND of the great Russian makers of Marxist doctrine, Lenin (1870–1924, born Vladimir Ilyich Ulianov in the family of a provincial school inspector), amplified voluminously on Marx's ideas and their implications for Russia.[1] While in exile in Siberia, he produced a work of economic history, *The Development of Capitalism in Russia* (1899), with which he became the first Russian—although not a historian—to apply the Marxist conception and method to the writing of Russian history on a large scale. Although Plekhanov chided him for being philosophically shallow, he also penned much on doctrinal as well as practical matters. His most extensive theoretical work is *Materialism and Empirio-Criticism,* written in 1908 when he was in exile in western Europe. It is a rambling elaboration on essentials of Marxism which were then under attack by Russian anti-Marxists, and is characterized by a sharp polemical edge. More succinct and detached in tone are two pieces, "The Three Sources and Three Component Parts of Marxism" and "The Materialist Conception of History," which he wrote in 1913 and 1914 while still in exile. More clearly and pithily than anything else he wrote, they state his understanding of and identification with Marx's theory of history. The two pieces are reproduced from the English translation in V. I. Lenin, *The Three Sources and Three Component Parts of Marxism* (Moscow, n.d.). Other relevant ideas are scattered in his *Imperialism—the Highest Stage of Capitalism* and *State and Revolution,* written in 1916 and 1917, respectively.[2]

6. "The Three Sources and Three Component Parts of Marxism"

Throughout the civilized world the teachings of Marx evoke the utmost hostility and hatred of all bourgeois science (both official and liberal), which regards Marxism as a kind of "pernicious sect." And no other attitude is to be expected, for there can be no "impartial" social science in a society based on class struggle. In one way or another, *all* official and liberal science *defends* wage slavery, whereas Marxism has declared relentless war

---

[1] The latest guide to Lenin's works is *Khronologicheskii ukazatel' proizvedenii V. I. Lenina* [Chronological Guide to the Works of V. I. Lenin] (3 vols.; Moscow, 1959–63).

[2] For a Soviet assessment of Lenin's pre-1917 contributions to historical theory see *Istoriografiia istorii SSSR* (see chap. ii, n. 1), pp. 358–408.

on wage slavery. To expect science to be impartial in a wage-slave society is as silly and naïve as to expect impartiality from manufacturers on the question whether workers' wages should be increased by decreasing the profits of capital.

But this is not all. The history of philosophy and the history of social science show with perfect clarity that there is nothing resembling "sectarianism" in Marxism, in the sense of its being a hidebound, petrified doctrine, a doctrine which arose *away from* the highroad of development of world civilization. On the contrary, the genius of Marx consists precisely in the fact that he furnished answers to questions the foremost minds of mankind had already raised. His teachings arose as the direct and immediate *continuation* of the teachings of the greatest representatives of philosophy, political economy, and socialism.

The Marxian doctrine is omnipotent because it is true. It is complete and harmonious, and provides men with an integral world conception which is irreconcilable with any form of superstition, reaction, or defense of bourgeois oppression. It is the legitimate successor to the best that was created by mankind in the nineteenth century in the shape of German philosophy, English political economy, and French socialism.

On these three sources of Marxism and on its three component parts, we shall briefly dwell.

I

The philosophy of Marxism is *materialism*. Throughout the modern history of Europe, and especially at the end of the eighteenth century in France, which was the scene of a decisive battle against every kind of medieval rubbish, against feudalism in institutions and ideas, materialism has proved to be the only philosophy that is consistent, true to all the teachings of natural science and hostile to superstition, cant, and so forth. The enemies of democracy therefore exerted all their efforts to "refute," undermine, and defame materialism, and advocated various forms of philosophical idealism, which always, in one way or another, amounts to an advocacy or support of religion.

Marx and Engels defended philosophical materialism in the most determined manner and repeatedly explained the profound erroneousness of every deviation from this basis. Their views are most clearly and fully expounded in the works of Engels, *Ludwig Feuerbach* and *Anti-Dühring,* which, like the *Communist Manifesto,* are handbooks of every class-conscious worker.

But Marx did not stop at the materialism of the eighteenth century: he advanced philosophy. He enriched it with the acquisitions of German classical philosophy, especially of the Hegelian system which in its turn led to the materialism of Feuerbach. The chief of these acquisitions is *dialectics,* i.e., the doctrine of development in its fullest and deepest form, free of one-sidedness, the doctrine of the relativity of human knowledge, which provides us with a reflection of eternally developing matter. The latest discoveries of natural science—radium, electrons, the transmutation of elements—have remarkably confirmed Marx's dialectical materialism, despite the teachings of the bourgeois philosophers with their "new" reversions to old and rotten idealism.

Deepening and developing philosophical materialism, Marx completed it, extended its knowledge of nature to the knowledge of *human society.* Marx's *historical materialism* was the greatest achievement of scientific thought. The chaos and arbitrariness that had previously reigned in the views on history and politics gave way to a strikingly integral and harmonious scientific theory, which shows how, in consequence of the growth of productive forces, out of one system of social life another and higher system develops—how capitalism, for instance, grows out of feudalism.

Just as man's knowledge reflects nature (i.e., developing matter) which exists independently of him, so man's *social knowledge* (i.e., his various views and doctrines—philosophical, religious, political, and so forth) reflects the *economic system* of society. Political institutions are a superstructure on the economic foundation. We see, for example, that the various political forms of the modern European states serve to fortify the rule of the bourgeoisie over the proletariat.

Marx's philosophy is finished philosophical materialism, which has provided mankind, and especially the working class, with powerful instruments of knowledge.

II

Having recognized that the economic system is the foundation on which the political superstructure is erected, Marx devoted most attention to the study of this economic system. Marx's principal work, *Capital,* is devoted to a study of the economic system of modern, i.e., capitalist, society.

Classical political economy, before Marx, evolved in England, the most developed of the capitalist countries. Adam Smith and David Ricardo, by their investigations of the economic system, laid the foundations of the *labor theory of value.* Marx continued their work. He rigidly proved and consistently developed this theory. He showed that the value of every commodity is determined by the quantity of socially necessary labor time spent on its production.

Where the bourgeois economists saw a relation between things (the exchange of one commodity for another) Marx revealed a *relation between men.* The exchange of commodities expresses the tie between individual producers through the market. *Money* signifies that this tie is becoming closer and closer, inseparably binding the entire economic life of the individual producers into one whole. *Capital* signifies a further development of this tie: man's labor power becomes a commodity. The wage worker sells his labor power to the owner of the land, factories, and instruments of labor. The worker spends one part of the day covering the cost of maintaining himself and his family (wages), while the other part of the day the worker toils without remuneration, creating *surplus value* for the capitalist, the source of profit, the source of the wealth of the capitalist class.

The doctrine of surplus value is the cornerstone of Marx's economic theory.

Capital, created by the labor of the worker, presses on the worker by ruining the small masters and creating an army of umemployed. In industry, the victory of large-scale production is at once apparent, but we observe the same phenomenon in agriculture as well; the superiority of large-scale capitalist agriculture increases, the employment of machinery grows, peasant economy falls into the noose of money-capital, it declines and sinks into ruin under the burden of its backward technique. In agriculture, the decline of small-scale production assumes different forms, but the decline itself is an indisputable fact.

By destroying small-scale production, capital leads to an increase in productivity of labor and to the creation of a monopoly position for the associations of big capitalists. Production itself becomes more and more social—hundreds of thousands and millions of workers become bound together in a systematic economic organism—but the product of the collective labor is appropriated by a handful of capitalists. The anarchy of production grows, as do crises, the furious chase after markets, and the insecurity of existence of the mass of the population.

While increasing the dependence of the workers on capital, the capitalist system creates the great power of combined labor.

Marx traced the development of capitalism from the first germs of commodity economy, from simple exchange, to its highest forms, to large-scale production.

And the experience of all capitalist countries, old and new, is clearly demonstrating the truth of this Marxian doctrine to increasing numbers of workers every year.

Capitalism has triumphed all over the world, but this triumph is only the prelude to the triumph of labor over capital.

III

When feudalism was overthrown, and *"free"* capitalist society appeared on God's earth, it at once became apparent that this freedom meant a new system of oppression and exploitation of the toilers. Various socialist doctrines immediately began to arise as a reflection of and protest against this oppression. But early socialism was *utopian* socialism. It criticized capitalist society, it condemned and damned it, it dreamed of its destruction, it indulged in fancies of a better order and endeavored to convince the rich of the immorality of exploitation.

But utopian socialism could not point the real way out. It could not explain the essence of wage slavery under capitalism, nor discover the laws of the latter's development, nor point to the *social force* which is capable of becoming the creator of a new society.

Meanwhile, the stormy revolutions which everywhere in Europe, and especially in France, accompanied the fall of feudalism, of serfdom, more and more clearly revealed the *struggle of classes* as the basis and the driving force of all development.

Not a single victory of political freedom over the feudal class was won except against desperate resistance. Not a single capitalist country evolved on a more or less free and democratic basis except by a life and death struggle between the various classes of capitalist society.

The genius of Marx consists in the fact that he was able before anybody else to draw from this and consistently apply the deduction that world history teaches. This deduction is the doctrine of the *class struggle*.

People always were and always will be the stupid victims of deceit and self-deceit in politics until they learn to discover the *interests* of some class or other behind all moral, religious, political, and social phrases, declarations, and promises. The advocates of reforms and improvements will always be fooled by the defenders of the old order until they realize that every old institution, however barbarous and rotten it may appear to be, is maintained by the forces of some ruling classes. And there is *only one* way of smashing the resistance of these classes, and that is to find, in the very society which surrounds us, and to enlighten and organize for the struggle, the forces which can—and, owing to their position, *must*—constitute the power capable of sweeping away the old and creating the new.

Marx's philosophical materialism alone has shown the proletariat the way out of the spiritual slavery in which all oppressed classes have hitherto languished. Marx's economic theory alone has explained the true position of the proletariat in the general system of capitalism.

Independent organizations of the proletariat are multiplying all over the world, from America to Japan and from Sweden to South Africa. The proletariat is becoming enlightened and educated by waging its class struggle; it is ridding itself of the prejudices of bourgeois society; it is rallying its ranks ever more closely and is learning to gauge the measure of its successes; it is steeling its forces and is growing irresistibly.

7. "The Materialist Conception of History"

Having realized the inconsistency, incompleteness, and one-sidedness of the old materialism, Marx became convinced of the necessity of "bringing the science of society . . . into harmony with the materialist foundation, and of reconstructing it thereupon." Since materialism in general explains consciousness as the outcome of being, and not conversely, materialism as applied to the social life of mankind has to explain *social* consciousness as the outcome of *social* being. "Technology," writes Marx (*Capital,* Vol. I), "discloses man's mode of dealing with nature, the process of production by which he sustains his life, and thereby also lays bare the mode of formation of his social relations, and of the mental conceptions that flow from them." In the preface to his *Contribution to the Critique of Political Economy,* Marx gives an integral formulation of the fundamental principles of materialism as extended to human society and its history, in the following words:

"In the social production of their life, men enter into definite relations that are indispensable and independent of their will, relations of production which correspond to a definite stage of development of their material productive forces.

"The sum-total of these relations of production constitutes the economic structure of society, the real foundation, on which rises a legal and political superstructure and to which correspond definite forms of social consciousness. The mode of production of material life conditions the social, political, and intellectual life-process in general. It is not the consciousness of men that determines their being, but, on the contrary, their social being that determines their consciousness. At a certain stage of their development, the material productive forces of society come in conflict with the existing relations of production, or—what is but a legal expression for the same thing—with the property relations within which they have been at work hitherto. From forms of development of the productive forces these relations turn into their fetters. Then begins an epoch of social revolution. With the change of the economic foundation the entire immense superstructure is more or less rapidly transformed. In considering such transformations a distinction should always be made between the material transformation of the economic conditions of production, which can be determined with the precision of natural science, and the legal, political, religious, esthetic, or philosophic—in short, ideological forms in which men become conscious of this conflict and fight it out.

"Just as our opinion of an individual is not based on what he thinks of himself, so can we not judge of such a period of transformation by its own consciousness; on the contrary, this consciousness must be explained rather from the contradictions of material life, from the existing conflict between the social productive forces and the relations of production. . . . In broad outlines Asiatic, ancient, feudal, and modern bourgeois modes of production can be designated as progressive epochs in the economic formation of society." (Cf. Marx's brief formulation in a letter to Engels dated July 7, 1866: "Our theory that the organization of labor is determined by the means of production.")

The discovery of the materialist conception of history, or rather, the consistent continuation and extension of materialism into the domain of social phenomena, removed two chief defects of earlier historical theories. In the first place, they at best examined only the ideological motives of the historical activity of human beings, without investigating what produced these motives, without grasping the objective laws governing the development of the system of social relations, and without discerning the roots of these relations in the degree of development of material production; in the second place, the earlier theories did not cover the activities of the *masses* of the population, whereas historical materialism made it possible for the first time to study with the accuracy of the natural sciences the social conditions of the life of the masses and the changes in these conditions. Pre-Marxian "sociology" and historiography *at best* provided an accumulation of raw facts, collected sporadically, and a depiction of certain sides of the historical process. By examining the whole *complex* of opposing tendencies, by reducing them to precisely definable conditions of life and production of the various *classes* of society, by discarding subjectivism and arbitrariness in the choice of various "leading" ideas or in their interpretation, and by disclosing that all ideas and all the various tendencies, without exception, have their *roots* in the condition of the material forces of production, Marxism pointed the way to an all-embracing and comprehensive study of the process of rise, development, and decline of social-economic formations. People make their own history. But what determines the motives of people, of the mass of people, that is; what gives rise to the clash of conflicting ideas and strivings; what is the sum-total of all these clashes of the whole mass of human societies; what are the objective conditions of production of material life that form the basis of all historical activity of man; what is the law of development of these conditions—to all this Marx drew attention and pointed out the way to a scientific study of history as a uniform and law-governed process in all its immense variety and contradictoriness.

That in any given society the strivings of some of its members conflict with the strivings of others, that social life is full of contradictions, that history discloses a struggle between nations and societies as well as within nations and societies, and, in addition, an alternation of periods of revolution and reaction, peace and war, stagnation and rapid progress or decline— [these] are facts that are generally known. Marxism provided the clue which enables us to discover the laws governing this seeming labyrinth and chaos, namely, the theory of the class struggle. Only a study of the whole complex of strivings of all the members of a given society or group of societies can lead to a scientific definition of the result of these strivings. And the source of the conflicting strivings lies in the difference in the position and mode of life of the *classes* into which each society is divided. "The history of all hitherto existing society is the history of class struggles," wrote Marx in the *Communist Manifesto* (except the history of the primitive community—Engels added subsequently). "Freeman and slave, patrician and plebeian, lord and serf, guildmaster and journeyman, in a word, oppressor and oppressed, stood in constant opposition to one another, carried on an uninterrupted, now hidden, now open fight, a fight that each time ended either in a revolutionary reconstitution of society at large or in the common ruin of the contending classes. . . . The modern bourgeois society that has sprouted from the ruins of feudal society has not done away with class antagonisms. It has but established new classes, new conditions of oppression, new forms of struggle, in place of the old ones. Our epoch, the epoch of the bourgeoisie, possesses, however, this distinctive feature: it has simplified the class antagonisms. Society as a whole is more and more splitting up into two great hostile camps, into two great classes directly facing each other: Bourgeoisie and Proletariat." Ever since the Great French Revolution, European history has very clearly revealed in a number of countries this real undersurface of events, the struggle of classes. And the Restoration period in France already produced a number of historians (Thierry, Guizot, Mignet, Thiers) who, generalizing from events, were forced to recognize that the class struggle was the key to all French history. And the modern era—the era of the complete victory of the bourgeoisie, representative institutions, wide (if not universal) suffrage, a cheap, popular daily press, etc., the era of powerful and ever-expanding unions of workers and unions of employers, etc.—has revealed even more manifestly (though sometimes in a very one-sided, "peaceful," "constitutional" form) that the class struggle is the mainspring of events. The following passage from Marx's *Communist Manifesto* will show us what Marx required of social science in respect to an objective analysis of the position of each class in modern society in connection with an analysis of the conditions of development of each class: "Of all the classes that stand face to face with the bourgeoisie today, the proletariat alone is a really revolutionary class. The other classes decay and finally disappear in the face of modern industry; the proletariat is its special and essential product. The lower middle class, the small manufacturer, the shopkeeper, the artisan, the peasant, all these fight against the bourgeoisie, to save from extinction their existence as fractions of the middle class. They are therefore not revolutionary, but conservative. Nay more, they are reactionary, for they try to roll back the wheel of history. If by chance they are revolutionary, they are so only in view of their impending transfer into the proletariat, they thus defend not their present, but their future interests, they desert their own standpoint to place themselves at that of the proletariat." In a number of historical works (see *Bibliography*),[3] Marx has given us brilliant and profound examples of materialist historiography, of an analysis of the position of *each* individual class, and sometimes of various groups or strata within a class, showing plainly why and how "every class struggle is a political struggle." The above-quoted passage is an illustration of what a complex network of social relations and *transitional* stages between one class and another, from the past to the future, Marx analyzes in order to determine the resultant of historical development.

---

[3] That is, Lenin's bibliography on Marxism appended to the essay. For a recent Soviet restatement of Lenin's views on history see A. M. Pavliuchenko, *V. I. Lenin ob ob'ektivnom kharaktere zakonomernostei obshchestvennogo razvitiia* [V. I. Lenin on the Objective Laws of Social Development] (Minsk, 1960).

PART TWO

Application in the Soviet Union

CHAPTER IV

UNDER LENIN, 1917–1924

ONE OF THE INJUNCTIONS of Marxism to those who espouse it is to seek and achieve "unity of theory and practice." The November revolution in 1917, which brought Lenin and the Bolsheviks to power, opened the way to translating the Marxist-Leninist theories into realities in Russia. The Commissariat of Public Education, headed by Anatolii V. Lunacharskii, with the historian Mikhail N. Pokrovskii as his deputy after May 1918, took charge of education, including the writing and teaching of history, to bring it into line with the theories of Marxism-Leninism and the requirements of the revolutionary regime.

The theory postulated that the old bourgeois society must be dismantled and its institutions and practices demolished before the construction of the new socialist society would begin. In education, this meant throwing out existing curriculums, textbooks, pedagogical practices, and the mass of the teaching staff on all levels. In June 1918, Lenin pointed out to a conference of Soviet teachers: ". . . the main body of the intelligentsia of old Russia is a frank enemy of the Soviet regime, and there is no doubt that it will not be easy to overcome the difficulties which this fact creates." [1]

Lenin also liked to say that the new society was being born from the formula of "Soviet government plus electrification" and that "technology decides everything." In education, this translated into stress on involving the pupils in "activity" situations and training them primarily in technological skills.[2] Soviet education echoed Lenin's ideas: "The old school . . . led the pupils away into hoary antiquity far from democracy, communism, and revolution, nearer to princes, kings, pharaohs, Homers, Titus Livius, and pyramids. The new school must do the opposite; it must shake off the dust of the ages; it must with the students draw nearer to the present time to live actuality, because this actuality, the whole vital life surrounding the students, is living history, much closer and much more important than dead history." [3] As symbols and tools of the old order, textbooks, examinations, homework, and rules of discipline were, in the words of a directive of 1918,

---

[1] *Lenin o narodnom obrazovanii; statii i rechi* [Lenin on Public Education: Articles and Speeches] (Moscow, 1957), p. 247.

[2] For an outline of Lenin's ideas on the so-called polytechnical education see, *ibid.*, pp. 365–366.

[3] Quoted in M. A. Zinoviev, *Soviet Methods of Teaching History* (Ann Arbor, Mich., 1952), p. 49; see also *A. V. Lunacharskii o narodnom obrazovanii* [A. V. Lunacharskii on Public Education] (Moscow, 1958), and L. P. Bushchik, *Ocherk razvitiia shkol'nogo istoricheskogo obrazovaniia v SSSR* [Survey of the Development of History Education in the Soviet Schools] (Moscow, 1961), pp. 87–200. Of interest is Bushchik's account of the influence of John Dewey in this phase.

"banished from the schools." The general objectives and tone of education were defined in the new party program drafted by Lenin and adopted by the Eighth Congress in March 1919. Its section on education given below is translated from the Russian text appended to Volume XVI of Lenin's *Sobranie Sochinenii* ("Collected Works") (Moscow, n.d.).

8. Program of the All-Russian Communist Party (Bolsheviks)

12. In the field of public education, the All-Russian Communist Party sets it as its objective to complete the work begun by the October Revolution of 1917 of transforming the school from a tool of the class domination of the bourgeoisie into a tool for the abolition of class divisions of society and into a tool for the communist regeneration of society.

In the period of the dictatorship of the proletariat, that is, in the period of creating the conditions to make possible the full realization of communism, the school must not only be a vehicle of the principles of communism, but also the vehicle of the ideological, organizational, and educational influences of the proletariat upon the semiproletarian and nonproletarian segments of the masses so as to bring up a generation capable of establishing full communism. The immediate task in this direction at the present time is the further development of the following principles of educational work already established by the Soviet regime:

1. Introduction of free and compulsory general and polytechnical education, suited in its theory and practice for all major branches of production, for all children of both sexes up to the age of seventeen years.

2. Establishment of a network of preschool institutions such as nurseries, kindergartens, clubs, and the like, to improve the social development of women and emancipate them.

3. Full implementation, through instruction in the native language and through coeducation, of the principles of the unified labor school which is unconditionally secular, that is, free from any religious influence whatever, and which cultivates a close tie between instruction and socially useful labor and prepares fully integrated members of the communist society.

4. Supply of all pupils with food, clothing, shoes, and educational materials at state expense.

5. Preparation of new cadres of education workers imbued with the ideas of communism.

6. Attraction of the working people into active participation in the work of education (development of "councils of public education," mobilization of all literate people, and so on).

7. State aid of all types to self-education and self-development of work-

ers and peasants (creation of a network of institutions for education outside the schools, such as libraries, schools for adults, people's homes and universities, courses of lectures, motion-picture theaters, studios, and the like).

8. Widespread development, for persons past the age of seventeen, of professional education related to general polytechnical knowledge.

9. Easy access to the institutions of higher education for all who wish to educate themselves and above all for the working people; attraction of all who are able to do so to teach in the institutions of higher education; elimination of any and all artificial barriers standing between the fresh scientific forces and the teaching opportunities; financial support of the students in order to provide actual opportunity for proletarians and peasants to avail themselves of higher education.

10. Opening and making accessible to the working people all treasures of art created through exploitation of their labor and until now at the exclusive disposal of the exploiters.

11. Unfolding the widest possible propaganda of communist ideas and utilization of the machinery and means of the state for this purpose.

Under the impact of the new outlook and educational philosophy, history was dropped from the curriculum of the schools and its place was assigned to courses first in "political literacy" (*politgramota*) and then in "social science" (*obshchestvovedenie*). In higher education, this policy and the acute lack of Marxist or Marxist-inclined historians led to a similar treatment of history. The history departments of the universities were combined with law and other disciplines to form new "faculties of social sciences" (*fakul'tety obshchestvennykh nauk,* or FON), which the authorities used as agencies for control of the universities and strongholds on the "ideological front." History instruction practically ceased, and the training of a select number of party members to become Marxist historians was entrusted to the so-called Institute of Red Professors, established in 1921 in Moscow and Petrograd, and to other party institutions. The "bourgeois" historians who survived the revolutionary holocaust and did not emigrate were isolated, circumscribed, harassed. Embattled as they were, they held some ground, and for a decade the "historical front," to use another of the official terms of the time, was in a sort of trench warfare, with each side sniping at the other and the "commanding heights" controlled by the party elements.[4] In these circumstances, academic competence dropped to appall-

---

[4] The most detailed, in many ways autobiographical, account of these developments is Konstantin F. Shteppa, *Russian Historians and the Soviet State* (New Brunswick, N.J., 1962). See also A. Presniakov, "Historical Research in Russia during the Revolutionary Crisis," *American Historical Review,* XXVIII, No. 2 (January 1923), 248–257; *Iz istorii Moskovskogo universiteta, 1917–1941* [From the History of Moscow University, 1917–1941] ed. E. N. Gorodetskii *et al.* (Moscow, 1955); and K. T. Galkin, *Vysshe obrazovanie i podgotovka nauchnykh kadrov v SSSR* [Higher Education and the Training of Scientific Personnel in the U.S.S.R.] (Moscow, 1958).

ing levels.[5] By 1928, however, the Institute of Red Professors had produced some fifty Marxist historians, and the regime was ready with these and other cadres to begin the complete conquest of the field of historical scholarship. The central role in all these developments was played by the historian M. N. Pokrovsky (1868–1932). Trained in the school of the great masters V. O. Kliuchevsky and P. G. Vinogradov, he had turned to Marxism and joined Lenin's supporters in the revolutionary year of 1905. Despite its bias, his five-volume *Russkaia istoriia s drevneishikh vremen* ("Russian History from Earliest Times"), first published while he was in exile in western Europe, had established him as a substantial scholar.[6] Burdened with other concerns after taking over, Lenin confined himself to demanding *partiinost* (devotion and service to the party) from all scholarship, including that of history, and gave his full confidence to Pokrovsky as the *spets* (specialist) and hardened fighter for the revolution on the ideological front. As a result, Pokrovsky came to hold all important positions in the field of history and act as its boss on behalf of Lenin and the party. In addition to his job of Deputy People's Commissar of Public Education, he was head of the Socialist Academy of the Social Sciences (established in 1918 and later renamed the Communist Academy), director of the Institute of Red Professors, editor of the vast collection of documents from the Tsarist archives *Krasnyi Arkhiv* ("Red Archive") (106 vols., 1922–41), president of the Society of Marxist Historians, which he set up in 1925, and editor of its journal *Istorik-Marksist* ("Marxist Historian," 1926–41) which became the official organ of the party in the field of history. Ranging far and wide, and backed by the enormous influence of his official posts and Lenin's endorsement, Pokrovsky gained a sizable following of young Marxist historians and devotees and launched what came to be called the "Pokrovsky school" of studying and presenting history.[7] The main characteristics of this school that dominated the 1920's were a broad sociological approach and phraseology, molding the past to suit the requirements of current politics (in accordance with the master's dictum that history was "politics retrojected into the past"), emphasis on impersonal forces and

[5] The leader of a seminar in Contemporary England was asked when the English Parliament was established; he did not know, and he promised to find out. "This is not the way, comrades," Pokrovsky lamented; "one must have the answer ready." M. N. Pokrovsky, *Istoricheskaia nauka i bor'ba klassov* [Historical Science and the Class Struggle] (Moscow, 1933), II, 409.

[6] Abbreviated versions of Pokrovsky's works appeared in translation in the 1930's: *History of Russia from the Earliest Times to the Rise of Commercial Capitalism* (New York, 1931) and *Brief History of Russia* (2 vols.; New York, 1933).

[7] At the celebration of his sixtieth birthday, in 1928, Pokrovsky was praised for having "around himself an entire school of disciples—young Marxist historians who work under his direction in the Communist Academy, the institutions of higher education of the U.S.S.R., the Institute of Red Professors, Russian Association of Scientific and Research Institutes in the Social Sciences, the Society of Marxist Historians, and other scientific institutions which are largely the creation of Mikhail Nikolaevich [Pokrovsky]." *Istorik-Marksist,* No. 9, 1928, p. 83.

"contemporaneity," and deprecation of the Russian national past and its heroes.[8]

In 1920, Pokrovsky produced a brief Marxist rendition of Russian history to the end of the nineteenth century, *Russkaia istoriia v samom szhatom ocherke* ("Russian History in Briefest Outline"), intended for general use in education and propaganda. It won high praise from Lenin, who also suggested some improvements. Excerpts from Pokrovsky's introduction, translated from the third edition of the work (Moscow, 1923), and the full text of Lenin's letter to Pokrovsky, follow.

9. Introduction to M. Pokrovsky, Russian History in Briefest Outline

GENERAL CONCEPTS CONCERNING HISTORY

Why do we need to know the past? Why should we be concerned with what happened ten, a hundred, a thousand, ten thousand years ago? Is it not better to know what follows, what is now occurring, what is around us, on what our life depends?

We study the past precisely in order to understand what is now happening. On earth everything evolves, that is, changes. Hundreds of millions of years ago the earth was an enormous red-hot globe surrounded by vapors, and no life existed nor could exist on it. Tens of millions of years ago life originated on earth. Several millions of years ago there grew on earth a luxuriant vegetation, enormous forests, and multitudes of various animals, aquatic as well as terrestrial. However, this entire universe was not like the one that exists now; all that now exists evolved through a long series of uninterrupted changes from that very universe itself. The plants and animals of today are the descendants of the plants and animals which existed on earth millions of years ago.

---

[8] For characterizations of Pokrovsky's career, ideas, and impact see Thomas R. Hall, "Mikhail Nikolayevich Pokrovsky (1868–1932)," in *Some Historians of Modern Europe*, ed. Bernadotte E. Schmitt (Chicago, 1942), pp. 349–366; Anatole G. Mazour, *Modern Russian Historiography* (Princeton, N.J., 1958), pp. 186–196; Shteppa, *op. cit.*, pp. 3–120; and C. E. Black, "History and Politics in the Soviet Union," in *Rewriting Russian History* (see chap. ii, n. 6), pp. 3–33. The complete bibliography of Pokrovsky's works is in *Istorik-Marksist*, No. 1–2, 1932, pp. 216–248. Mazour's work is bitingly analyzed by the leading Soviet historian and expert in historiography, M. V. Nechkina, in Nechkina *et al.* (eds.), *Protiv burzhuaznoi fal'sifikatsii istorii sovetskogo obshchestva* [Against the Bourgeois Falsification of the History of Soviet Society] (Moscow, 1960), pp. 14–38. For other Soviet views on Pokrovsky reflecting the current party line see *Istoriografiia istorii SSSR* (see chap. ii, n. 1), pp. 469–480, and Shapiro, *op. cit.* (see chap. ii n. 1), pp. 189–208.

How did all this happen? Not accidentally, but in accordance with definite laws. However, if we observe life such as it is now, we will not notice these laws, that is, the regularities of such changes. When people did not study the distant past of the earth and did not unearth the discoverable remains of animals and plants that had existed millions of years ago, scientists believed that the world of today was always the same as at present and that it was created in one stroke. Only a hundred years ago people laughed at the few scholars who dared to assert the opposite. These scholars, however, stated what now seems self-evident, namely, that life on earth evolved gradually in the course of an enormous number of years.

If the study of the earth's past, of the past of animal and plant life, the study of geology and paleontology, demolished the legend that the universe was created at one stroke and does not change, history and archeology demolish the other legend that human society has always been and, therefore, shall always be such as it is. Man changes and shall change, like everything else. Social ways come into existence, other social ways fall apart, in their place rise new ways, and so on. We cannot foresee or envisage the end of these changes, but if we observe them in the course of tens and hundreds of years we shall understand their regularity and learn the laws of such changes. And if we would not be able to conceive graphically what would happen to human society in, let us say, several thousands of years, we could know how and in what ways mankind would change in the course of these thousands of years. He who foresees the future controls that future because, by foreseeing the future, we can prepare for it, take the steps we can to avoid future misfortunes and take the best possible advantage of the benefits which that future will bring us. To know is to foresee, and to foresee is to be, or be able to be, in control. Thus, knowledge of the past gives us control over the future.

This is why it is necessary to know the past.

However, the fact that we can notice the regularity of changes occurring in human society only by observing these changes in the course of a major span of time does not mean that we must necessarily begin our study with the most distant past. We can go the opposite way as well. Indeed, it is easier to notice the regularity of changes occurring in human society if we proceed from the present into the distant past.

Thus, observing what is occurring now or what occurred comparatively recently, we notice the regularity of historical changes, namely, that history is moved by people of definite occupations and changes according to the class which makes history, that is, produces given social changes. We see that when the bulk of the population consisted of peasants history evolved in a way different from the present when the movement is headed by the workers.

At the bottom of all changes lies thus the change in economy, economic change.

What compels man to be economically active? This is self-evident to everyone and needs no great amount of thinking. It suffices to look at what was produced in the past by peasants and what is now produced in factories and shops to understand that. Peasant economy produces grain, meat, wool, flax—in a word, raw materials—which we need to feed and clothe ourselves. From raw materials the factories make meat, canned goods, clothing, shoes—in short, transform the raw materials in such shape as we can more conveniently use them. In the last analysis all this serves to maintain human life. Man thus is economically active in order to be able to exist. This, I repeat, needs no explanation and proof; every child understands it by himself. However, if at the bottom of all historical changes lie economic changes, this means that man is compelled to work by his need, his so-called material needs, his endeavor to protect himself from hunger and cold.

Thus, at the bottom of all man's activity and of all history lie the material needs. Hence the explanation of history which we shall provide is called historical materialism. This understanding of history was contributed first by the social class which first understood the solidarity of common interests of all workers and which leads the present revolution. The materialist conception of history is a proletarian conception of history.

10. Lenin's Letter to Pokrovsky, December 5, 1920

COMRADE POKROVSKY,

I congratulate you very heartily on your success. I like your new book "Brief History of Russia" immensely. The construction and the narrative are original. It reads with tremendous interest. It should, in my opinion, be translated into the European languages.

I will permit myself one slight remark. To make it a textbook (and this it must become), it must be supplemented with a chronological index. This is roughly, what I am suggesting: 1st column, chronology; 2d column, bourgeois view (briefly); 3d column, your view, Marxian, indicating the pages in your book.

The students must know both your book and the index so that there should be no skimming, so that they should retain the facts, and so that they should learn to compare the old science and the new. What do you say to such an addition?

With Communist greetings,

Yours,

LENIN

According to Lenin's wishes, the work became the textbook for the subject. In 1933 it was translated into English. As if to attest its validity, the translation also carried Lenin's letter. After Pokrovsky and his school were condemned in the 1930's for being too schematic and impersonal in presenting the past, Soviet writers made constant use of the second passage of the letter to substantiate the new line—that Lenin had implicitly disapproved of Pokrovsky's approach as superficial and had demanded the writing and teaching of Marxist history filled with facts, people, and dates. Whatever interpretation may be made of Lenin's words, the fact is that Pokrovsky remained the boss of Soviet historiography until his death in 1932. Although in 1931 Stalin began to press a new approach, Pokrovsky continued to be honored until the mid-1930's: for several years after his death the University of Moscow remained named after him (it is now named after M. V. Lomonosov, the eighteenth-century Russian scientist), and the posthumous eighth edition of his *Russian History from Earliest Times* in 1933 carried a note from the publisher (The State Socio-Economic Publishing Office) praising the works of Pokrovsky as being of "exceptionally great [importance] in the development of Marxist-Leninist historiography" and describing his *History* as "still the most complete Marxist presentation of the history of Russia."

As the pace-setter of Soviet historiography, in 1923 Pokrovsky delivered an address before a joint session of the Socialist Academy and the Institute of Red Professors, commemorating the fortieth anniversary of Marx's death. Speaking on the subject of Marx as a historian, he produced a noteworthy statement of what was to him the identity of Marxism and historism. The excerpts translated below are from the text of his address in *Vestnik Sotsialisticheskoi Akademii* ("Bulletin of the Socialist Academy"), IV (1923), 372–384.

11. M. N. Pokrovsky, "Marx as a Historian"

Marx is one of the greatest representatives of the historical method in world literature. Marx is historical to the core. Marxism is historism.

We must be historians because we are Marxists; Bolsheviks, as the speaker before me proved, are indeed Marxists! By its very nature, materialism is primarily a historical outlook. Speaking of essence, idealism has not cognized history, an objective idealism has not cognized the history of man. For it all history, in essence, has been sacred history. Whatever form of objective idealism you may take—the Book of Genesis, Augustine, or Bossuet—you will not see people on the stage acting as free historical agents. You will see an endless chess game of the Lord with the Devil in which men serve as pawns and nothing more. From this angle of vision an immense amount of historical material has been collected. You will find there a divine reason which makes a move with a knight—launches the incursion of Jenghiz Khan into Europe—then makes a move with a pawn—puts on the scene the Swiss—and so on, but in the last analysis you will not see there human history. Subjective idealism, as represented by Kant, liquidated objective idealism and was also unhistorical for a different reason. Since the world is only as we conceive it and nothing more, the world naturally cannot have a history outside the individual. Human history from this point of view is the history of concepts. That is why the history of "ideas" is the favorite topic of this period.

Recognizing on one hand the objective existence of the world and on the other the fact that it was created by nobody, thus removing from the outset all props from under the world, materialism confronted the purely historical question: how has all this come about? This is a pure historical question since all historical questions when cast in a universal form definitely ring in the same way: how has all this happened?

The materialists of the eighteenth century added here the idea of determinism—predetermination of all human actions—an idea succinctly expressed by Laplace in a conversation with Napoleon when Laplace told him: "Give me the elements of the universe in the moment of its creation and I will foretell its fate to its end." In this manner, regardless of the fact that the materialists of the eighteenth century were poor historians, inasmuch as they were materialists they were opening the way for the historical understanding of the world. In the given instance Hegel, the greatest philosopher-historian of the eighteenth century, essentially only translated into the language of German idealist philosophy the wisdom he acquired from the French materialists of the eighteenth century. This is why the wrapping of philosophical idealism is so thin in Hegel and why his idealistic outlook proved so easy to exploit for a completely opposite outlook—the materialist one—as indeed Marxism exploited it.

It is absolutely natural that the founder of dialectical materialism should have been, above all, in a profound manner permeated by historism and should have been a historian in his entire understanding of the world. I will take the liberty of substantiating this with two quotations from Marx separated by an interval of thirty-two years. Here is what Marx wrote to Annenkov in 1845:

It is superfluous to add that men are not free in their choice of productive forces which are the basis of all their history, because every productive force is an acquired force, a product of previous activity. In this manner, the productive forces are the result of the practical energy of men, but this very energy is determined by the conditions in which men find themselves: the productive forces acquired earlier and the social system existing earlier and created not by themselves but by previous generations. Thanks to this simple fact that each succeeding generation finds productive forces acquired by previous generations and these productive forces serve it as raw material in the new production, thanks to this fact there arises a connection in human history and a history of mankind is formed which grows as such in proportion to the growth of the productive forces of men and, consequently, of their social relations. (K. Marx and F. Engels, *Letters,* translation and notes by V. V. Adoratsky, p. 7.)

There can be no clearer statement of the idea—by no means understood by all of us, whether Marxists in quotation marks or without quotation marks—that we cannot bring about a radical historical change *ex nihilo.* This was stated in 1845; in 1877, in his famous letter to the editor of *Otechestvennye Zapiski* ("Notes on the Fatherland"), somewhat changing the form, Marx developed the same thought:

It is now asked, what application to Russia could my critic deduce from my brief historical work? Only the following: if Russia endeavors to become a capitalist nation—and in recent years she has made no insignificant effort in that direction—she will not succeed in attaining this goal unless she converts from the outset a good portion of her peasants into proletarians; then, finding herself one day in the sphere of the capitalist system, she will inevitably fall under the operation of its inexorable laws like all other sinful nations. That is all. To my critic, however, this is too little. He definitely requires turning my work on the genesis of capitalism into a historical-philosophical theory of the general course of economic development and into a theory to which all nations (whatever the historical conditions in which they may be) must submit fatally so as to arrive in the end at such an economic system as would guarantee them the greatest growth of the productive forces of social labor and the most complete development of each individual. But I beg his pardon. This would mean simultaneously doing me a great honor and attributing to me an erroneous opinion of which I am not guilty.

Let us give an example. In various places in *Capital* I make reference to the fate of the plebeians in ancient Rome. At first they were free peasants working for themselves their own plots of land. In the course of Roman history they were gradually rendered propertyless while the same process which tore them from the means of production and subsistence entailed the formation of large-scale landowner-ship as well as of large monetary capital accumulations. Then, one wonderful day, there appeared on one hand free men deprived of everything except the ability to work, and on the other—in order to exploit labor—owners of all appropriated wealth. What happened then? The Roman proletarians became not hired labor but a loitering mob on a much lower moral level than even the poor whites of the southern states of the U.S.A., while what took shape and prospered was not a capitalist but slave-owning method of production (Cf. note 211, p. 688 of the Russian edition of *Capital*). Thus, events, strikingly analogous but occurring in different historical environments, lead to entirely different results. Studying each of these evolutions separately and then comparing them, it would be easy to find the key to understanding these phenomena; however, one must never approach their understanding by using everywhere the same master key of some historical-philosophical theory, the greatest merit of which is in being supra-historical. (Marx and Engels, *Letters*, pp. 239–240.)

Thus, thirty-two years later Marx stressed absolutely clearly that an economic scheme may yield a key for the understanding of actual social relations only if we place such a scheme on a historical basis and begin its application with the question, how did the conditions originate which are to be liquidated at this time? Then we shall obtain the truly useful method of their liquidation. This individuality of social relations Marx emphasizes everywhere, and particularly often in *Capital*, which serves at present as object for surgical exercises to comrades, especially to comrades who like to pose economic problems in strictly abstract form. In every page of it Marx is indeed the same historian as everywhere else.

Here is what Marx wrote in his letter to Kugelmann in 1871, at the blooming of his talent and midway in his writing activity:

To make world history would, of course, be very convenient if the struggle were waged in circumstances of unerringly favorable opportunities. On the other hand, history would have a very mystical character if "chance" played no part. Contingencies form, of course, a component part of the general course of development, being balanced by other contingencies. However, acceleration and retardation depend to a great extent on such "contingencies," among which is such "chance" as the character of the individuals who head at first the movement. (*Letters*, p. 226.)

Here matters come, as you see, almost to the "nose of Cleopatra" to which Plekhanov, standing absolutely faithfully on Marx's ground, indeed came in his work *The Role of the Individual in History*. There it is admitted that Cleopatra's nose may have a certain relative influence, rather minor to be sure. But, of course, "Cleopatra's nose" cannot influence the course of events as a whole; in the whole the influence of "contingencies" is lost, as Marx himself states. As for individual events, their individuality is expressed precisely in that they show the stamp of a given individual. Therefore, in explaining different events one must not fail to invest such individuality with all its characteristics, that is, with the characteristics of the men who create these events. This is all Marx wants to say, and it certainly is elementary truth but one which we, practitioners as well as theoreticians, absolutely tend to forget when we pose the question of the role of the individual in history. Can the individual change the course of history? An individual, even if he were a genius, could not create conditions for an immediate transition to socialism in a country where small-scale producton predominated. Of course not; no individual could do that. But if we take an individual event—October 25, 1917, old style—here personalities, e.g., the personality of Comrade Trotsky, played a major role. Take, furthermore, the entire history of Bolshevism. This, of course, is a world phenomenon called forth by exceptionally general causes transcending our country and our generation; but try to understand the individual moments of the history of Russian Bolshevism from its inception to the latest phase without drawing in the mighty individuality of its leader, and you will fail.

Thus, Marx in his historism comes to the end, to the recognition of a certain influence of the individual moment in history. Marx was always historical, even when he wrote entire pages filled with mathematical formulae. . . .

There are many non-Marxist historians in the world; in my profound conviction, however, Marxists cannot be non-historians. A man who cannot use the historical method is not a Marxist even if he knew by heart all three volumes as well as the fourth volume of *Capital*. He will be, might be, a creature in the Marxist image by his appearance inasmuch as he would assimilate Marxist phraseology and terminology, but a Marxist he will not be. I have, therefore, read this brief and perhaps altogether incomplete report for this solemn session in order to remind our young comrades that they will turn themselves into Marxists only when they take the road shown by Marx, that is, when they constantly remember that every social analysis begins with a historical analysis.

CHAPTER V

THE FIRST INTERREGNUM, 1924–1927

EVEN BEFORE LENIN died in January 1924, a race for the succession began to take shape as it became obvious with his first stroke in May 1922 that his life was ebbing. The leading candidate for his place was Lev Davidovich Bronstein, more generally known as Trotsky (1879–1940), who had been Lenin's right-hand man in the revolution and the ensuing civil war and was marked by an intellect second only to Lenin's in acuity and grasp of Marxist theory. He had, however, a shrewd rival in Iosif Vissarionovich Dzhugashvili, also better known by his revolutionary cryptonym Stalin (1879–1953), who had made himself very useful to Lenin as a party stalwart from the backwoods of Georgia, specialist in problems of the minorities, and doer of jobs no one else would care to take. Enjoying Lenin's confidence, Stalin acquired the jobs of Commissar of Nationalities, Commissar of the Workers' and Peasants' Inspectorate, and Secretary-General of the Central Committee of the Communist Party. Lenin came to realize, however, a year before he died, that the power he had allowed Stalin to amass was luring him to grab for more. In two messages to the Central Committee of December 25, 1922, and January 4, 1923, known as his "Testament," Lenin warned that Stalin had "concentrated an enormous power in his hands" and urged his removal from the post of Secretary-General. Lenin died before the Central Committee took up the matter, and when it did, the issue was sidetracked.

With his eyes on Lenin's place, Stalin quickly moved to create an image of himself as the dead leader's closest and most faithful disciple and hence the man best suited to carry on his work. Trotsky being conveniently away from Moscow (he was at a Black Sea resort because of illness), Stalin took charge of the funeral and delivered his celebrated oration and oath of fidelity to Lenin's ideas and objectives. Later in 1924 he gave a series of lectures at the Sverdlov University explaining the foundations of Leninism. In both cases the effort to identify himself with Lenin is clearly evident. The texts reproduced below are from J. Stalin, *Works*, VI, 47–53, 71–74, 91–93 (Moscow, 1953).[1]

12. Stalin's Oration "On the Death of Lenin"

Comrades, we Communists are people of a special mold. We are made of a special stuff. We are those who form the army of the great prole-

---

[1] For a guide to Stalin's works see Jack F. Matlock, *An Index to the Collected Works of J. V. Stalin* (Washington, 1955).

tarian strategist, the army of Comrade Lenin. There is nothing higher than the honor of belonging to this army. There is nothing higher than the title of member of the party whose founder and leader was Comrade Lenin. It is not given to everyone to be a member of such a party. It is not given to everyone to withstand the stresses and storms that accompany membership in such a party. It is the sons of the working class, the sons of want and struggle, the sons of incredible privation and heroic effort, who before all should be members of such a party. That is why the Party of the Leninists, the Party of the Communists, is also called the Party of the Working Class.

DEPARTING FROM US, COMRADE LENIN ENJOINED US TO HOLD HIGH AND GUARD THE PURITY OF THE GREAT TITLE OF MEMBER OF THE PARTY. WE VOW TO YOU, COMRADE LENIN, THAT WE SHALL FULFILL YOUR BEHEST WITH HONOR!

For twenty-five years Comrade Lenin tended our Party and made it into the strongest and most highly steeled workers' party in the world. The blows of tsarism and its henchmen, the fury of the bourgeoisie and the landlords, the armed attacks of Kolchak and Denikin, the armed intervention of Britain and France, the lies and slanders of the hundred-mouthed bourgeois press—all these scorpions constantly chastised our Party for a quarter of a century. But our Party stood firm as a rock, repelling the countless blows of its enemies and leading the working class forward, to victory. In fierce battles our Party forged the unity and solidarity of its ranks. And by unity and solidarity it achieved victory over the enemies of the working class.

DEPARTING FROM US, COMRADE LENIN ENJOINED US TO GUARD THE UNITY OF OUR PARTY AS THE APPLE OF OUR EYE. WE VOW TO YOU, COMRADE LENIN, THAT THIS BEHEST, TOO, WE SHALL FULFILL WITH HONOR!

Burdensome and intolerable has been the lot of the working class. Painful and grievous have been the sufferings of the laboring people. Slaves and slave-holders, serfs and serf-owners, peasants and landlords, workers and capitalists, oppressed and oppressors—so the world has been built from time immemorial, and so it remains to this day in the vast majority of countries. Scores and indeed hundreds of times in the course of the centuries the laboring people have striven to throw off the oppressors from their backs and to become the masters of their own destiny. But each time, defeated and disgraced, they have been forced to retreat, harboring in their breasts resentment and humiliation, anger and despair, and lifting up their eyes to an inscrutable heaven where they hoped to find deliverance. The chains of slavery remained intact, or the old chains were replaced by new ones, equally burdensome and degrading. Ours is the only country where the oppressed and downtrodden laboring masses have succeeded in throwing off the rule of the landlords and capitalists and replacing it by the rule of the workers and peasants. You know, comrades, and the whole world now admits it, that this gigantic struggle was led by Comrade Lenin and his Party. The greatness of Lenin lies above all in this, that by creating the Republic of Soviets he gave a practical demonstration to the oppressed masses of the whole world that hope of deliverance is not lost, that the rule of the landlords and capitalists is short-lived, that the kingdom of labor *can* be created by the efforts of the laboring people themselves, and that the kingdom of labor must be created not in heaven, but on *earth*. He thus fired the hearts of the workers and peasants of the whole world with the hope of liberation. That explains why Lenin's name has become the name most beloved of the laboring and exploited masses.

DEPARTING FROM US, COMRADE LENIN ENJOINED US TO GUARD AND STRENGTHEN THE DICTATORSHIP OF THE PROLETARIAT. WE VOW TO YOU, COMRADE LENIN, THAT WE SHALL SPARE NO EFFORT TO FULFILL THIS BEHEST, TOO, WITH HONOR!

The dictatorship of the proletariat was established in our country on the basis of an alliance between the workers and peasants. This is the first and fundamental basis of the Republic of Soviets. The workers and peasants could not have vanquished the capitalists and landlords without such an alliance. The workers could not have defeated the capitalists without the support of the peasants. The peasants could not have defeated the landlords without the leadership of the workers. This is borne out by the whole history of the civil war in our country. But the struggle to consolidate the Republic of Soviets is by no means at an end—it has only taken on a new form. Before, the alliance of the workers and peasants took the form of a military alliance, because it was directed against Kolchak and Denikin. Now, the alliance of the workers and peasants must assume the form of economic co-operation between town and country, between workers and peasants, because it is directed against the merchant and the kulak, and its aim is the mutual supply by peasants and workers of all they require. You know that nobody worked for this more persistently than Comrade Lenin.

DEPARTING FROM US, COMRADE LENIN ENJOINED US TO STRENGTHEN WITH ALL OUR MIGHT THE ALLIANCE OF THE WORKERS AND PEASANTS. WE VOW TO YOU, COMRADE LENIN, THAT THIS BEHEST, TOO, WE SHALL FULFILL WITH HONOR!

The second basis of the Republic of Soviets is the union of the working people of the different nationalities of our country. Russians and Ukrainians, Bashkirs and Byelorussians, Georgians and Azerbaijanians, Armenians and Daghestanians, Tatars and Kirghiz, Uzbeks and Turkmenians, are all equally interested in strengthening the dictatorship of the proletariat. Not only does the dictatorship of the proletariat deliver these peoples from fetters and oppression, but these peoples on their part deliver our Republic of Soviets from the intrigues and assaults of the enemies of the working class by their supreme devotion to the Republic of Soviets and their readiness to make sacrifices for it. That is why Comrade Lenin untiringly urged upon us the necessity of the voluntary union of the peoples of our country, the necessity of their fraternal co-operation within the framework of the Union of Republics.

DEPARTING FROM US, COMRADE LENIN ENJOINED US TO STRENGTHEN AND EXTEND THE UNION OF REPUBLICS. WE VOW TO YOU, COMRADE LENIN, THAT THIS BEHEST, TOO, WE SHALL FULFILL WITH HONOR!

The third basis of the dictatorship of the proletariat is our Red Army and our Red Navy. More than once did Lenin impress upon us that the respite we had won from the capitalist states might prove a short one. More than once did Lenin point out to us that the strengthening of the Red Army and the improvement of its condition is one of the most important tasks of our Party. The events connected with Curzon's ultimatum and the crisis in Germany once more confirmed that, as always, Lenin was right. Let us vow then, comrades, that we shall spare no effort to strengthen our Red Army and our Red Navy.

Like a huge rock, our country stands out amid an ocean of bourgeois states. Wave after wave dashes against it, threatening to submerge it and wash it away. But the rock stands unshakable. Wherein lies its strength? Not only in the fact that our country rests on an alliance of the workers and peasants, that it embodies a union of free nationalities, that it is protected by the mighty arm of the Red Army and the Red Navy. The strength, the firmness, the solidity of our country is due to the profound sympathy and unfailing support it finds in the hearts of the workers and peasants of the whole world. The workers and peasants of the whole world want to preserve the Republic of Soviets as an arrow shot by the sure hand of Comrade Lenin into the camp of the enemy, as the pillar of their hopes of deliverance from oppression and exploitation, as a reliable beacon pointing the path to their emancipation. They want to preserve it, and they will not allow the landlords and capitalists to destroy it. Therein lies our strength. Therein lies the strength of the working people of all countries. And therein lies the weakness of the bourgeoisie all over the world.

Lenin never regarded the Republic of Soviets as an end in itself. He always looked on it as an essential link for strengthening the revolutionary movement in the countries of the West and the East, an essential link for facilitating the victory of the working people of the whole world over capitalism. Lenin knew that this was the only right conception, both from the international standpoint and from the standpoint of preserving the Republic of Soviets itself. Lenin knew that this alone could fire the hearts of the working people of the whole world with determination to fight the decisive battles for their emancipation. That is why, on the very morrow of the establishment of the dictatorship of the proletariat, he, the greatest of the geniuses who have led the proletariat, laid the foundation of the workers' International. That is why he never tired of extending and strengthening the union of the working people of the whole world—the Communist International.

You have seen during the past few days the pilgrimage of scores and hundreds of thousands of working people to Comrade Lenin's bier. Before long you will see the pilgrimage of representatives of millions of working people to Comrade Lenin's tomb. You need not doubt that the representatives of millions will be followed by representatives of scores and hundreds of millions from all parts of the earth, who will come to testify that Lenin was the leader not only of the Russian proletariat, not only of the European workers, not only of the colonial East, but of all the working people of the globe.

DEPARTING FROM US, COMRADE LENIN ENJOINED US TO REMAIN FAITHFUL TO THE PRINCIPLES OF THE COMMUNIST INTERNATIONAL. WE VOW TO YOU, COMRADE LENIN, THAT WE SHALL NOT SPARE OUR LIVES TO STRENGTHEN AND EXTEND THE UNION OF THE WORKING PEOPLE OF THE WHOLE WORLD— THE COMMUNIST INTERNATIONAL!

13. *J. Stalin,* The Foundations of Leninism

The foundations of Leninism is a big subject. To exhaust it a whole volume would be required. Indeed, a number of volumes would be required. Naturally, therefore, my lectures cannot be an exhaustive exposition of Leninism; at best they can only offer a concise synopsis of the foundations of Leninism. Nevertheless, I consider it useful to give this synopsis, in order to lay down some basic points of departure necessary for the successful study of Leninism.

Expounding the foundations of Leninism still does not mean expounding the basis of Lenin's world outlook. Lenin's world outlook and the foundations of Leninism are not identical in scope. Lenin was a Marxist, and Marxism is, of course, the basis of his world outlook. But from this it does not at all follow that an exposition of Leninism ought to begin with an exposition of the foundations of Marxism. To expound Leninism means to expound the distinctive and new in the works of Lenin that Lenin contributed to the general treasury of Marxism and that is naturally connected with his name. Only in this sense will I speak in my lectures of the foundations of Leninism.

And so, what is Leninism?

Some say that Leninism is the application of Marxism to the conditions that are peculiar to the situation in Russia. This definition contains a particle of truth, but not the whole truth by any means. Lenin, indeed, applied Marxism to Russian conditions, and applied it in a masterly way. But if Leninism were only the application of Marxism to the conditions that are peculiar to Russia it would be a purely national and only a national, a purely Russian and only a Russian, phenomenon. We know, however, that Leninism is not merely a Russian, but an international phenomenon rooted in the whole of international development. That is why I think this definition suffers from one-sidedness.

Others say that Leninism is the revival of the revolutionary elements of Marxism of the forties of the nineteenth century, as distinct from the Marxism of subsequent years, when, it is alleged, it became moderate, nonrevolutionary. If we disregard this foolish and vulgar division of the teachings of Marx into two parts, revolutionary and moderate, we must admit that even this totally inadequate and unsatisfactory definition contains a particle of truth. This particle of truth is that Lenin did indeed restore the revolutionary content of Marxism, which had been suppressed by the opportunists of the Second International. Still, that is but a particle of the truth. The whole truth about Leninism is that Leninism not only restored Marxism, but also took a step forward, developing Marxism further under the new conditions of capitalism and of the class struggle of the proletariat.

What, then, in the last analysis, is Leninism?

Leninism is Marxism of the era of imperialism and the proletarian revolution. To be more exact, Leninism is the theory and tactics of the proletarian revolution in general, the theory and tactics of the dictatorship of the proletariat in particular. Marx and Engels pursued their activities in the pre-revolutionary period (we have the proletarian revolution in mind), when developed imperialism did not yet exist, in the period of the proletarians' preparation for revolution, in the period when the proletarian revolution was not yet an immediate practical inevitability. But Lenin, the disciple of Marx and Engels, pursued his activities in the period of developed imperialism, in the period of the unfolding proletarian revolution, when the proletarian revolution had already triumphed in one country, had smashed bourgeois democracy and had ushered in the era of proletarian democracy, the era of the Soviets.

That is why Leninism is the further development of Marxism.

It is usual to point to the exceptionally militant and exceptionally revolutionary character of Leninism. This is quite correct. But this specific feature of Leninism is due to two causes: first, to the fact that Leninism emerged from the proletarian revolution, the imprint of which it cannot but bear; second, to the fact that it grew and became strong in clashes with the opportunism of the Second International, the fight against which was and remains an essential preliminary condition for a successful fight against capitalism. It must not be forgotten that between Marx and Engels, on the one hand, and Lenin, on the other, there lies a whole period of undivided domination of the opportunism of the Second International, and the ruthless struggle against this opportunism could not but constitute one of the most important tasks of Leninism.

III. THEORY

From this theme I take three questions:

(1) The importance of theory for the proletarian movement
(2) Criticism of the "theory" of spontaneity
(3) The theory of the proletarian revolution

1. *The importance of theory.* Some think that Leninism is the precedence of practice over theory in the sense that its main point is the translation of the Marxist theses into deeds, their "execution"; as for theory, it is alleged that Leninism is rather unconcerned about it. We know that Plekhanov time and again chaffed Lenin about his "unconcern" for theory, and particularly for philosophy. We also know that theory is not held in great favor by many present-day Leninist practical workers, particularly in view of the immense amount of practical work imposed upon them by the situation. I must declare that this more than odd opinion about Lenin and Leninism is quite wrong and bears no relation whatever to the truth; that the attempt of practical workers to brush theory aside runs counter to the whole spirit of Leninism and is fraught with serious dangers to the work.

Theory is the experience of the working-class movement in all countries taken in its general aspect. Of course, theory becomes purposeless if it is not connected with revolutionary practice, just as practice gropes in the dark if its path is not illumined by revolutionary theory. But theory can become a tremendous force in the working-class movement if it is built up in indissoluble connection with revolutionary practice; for theory, and theory alone, can give the movement confidence, the power of orientation, and an understanding of the inner relation of surrounding events; for it, and it alone, can help practice to realize not only how and in which direction classes are moving at the present time, but also how and in which direction they will move in the near future.

[Discussion of the second and third questions is omitted.]

While Stalin was busy identifying himself with Lenin and reaching victory in the rivalry with Trotsky, the field of history continued to be Pokrovsky's bailiwick. In March 1925 Pokrovsky organized the historians of Marxist persuasion and some old-regime scholars, who were attempting to make an ideological transition to Marxism or at least to fit in with the new circumstances, into a Society of Marxist Historians as an arm of the Communist Academy (the branch in Leningrad, where the Marxists felt like "an inconspicuous island in a bourgeois-historical ocean," was not set up until 1929). The aims and procedures of the society were stated in its statutes "approved by the NKVD" and in an address Pokrovsky delivered on June 1, 1925, at the inauguration of the society. The statutes are here translated, with minor omissions, from the text in *Istorik-Marksist,* No. 1, 1926, pp. 320–322, and Pokrovsky's address, with omissions, from the same, pp. 3–10.

14. Statutes of the Society of Marxist Historians

I. PURPOSES OF THE SOCIETY

1. The Society of Marxist Historians at the Communist Academy shall have as purposes:

(*a*) the unification of all Marxists engaged in scientific work in the field of history;

(*b*) the scientific development of problems of history and Marxist methodology of history;

(*c*) the struggle with the distortion of history by bourgeois scholarship;

(*d*) the critical illumination of current historical literature from the Marxist point of view;

(*e*) the assistance of members of the Society in obtaining scientific literature, access to archives, research travel grants, and the like;

(*f*) the propagation and popularization of the Marxist method and familiarization of the broad masses with the Marxist achievements in the field of history.

2. To attain its purposes the Society shall (*a*) hear and discuss reports in general meetings by members of the Society; (*b*) organize public lectures and debates; (*c*) publish periodicals, collections, bulletins, and the like; (*d*) acquire, sell, and lease any type of property needed for the purposes of the Society and consummate contracts and transactions in accordance with the tasks of the Society.

II. Membership of the Society

3. The Society of Marxist Historians consists of (*a*) regular members and (*b*) corresponding members.

4. As regular members of the Society qualify Marxists who are engaged in scientific historical work and have published, and Marxists in charge of independent courses in history subjects at the institutions of higher education. The first regular members are the constituting members of the Society.

5. As corresponding members qualify persons who, although not meeting the requirements of Article 4, render assistance to the Society through personal participation in the development of scientific problems and through communication of materials to the Society in the form of correspondence, notes, and the like.

6. Election to regular membership in the Society is made at the proposal of the Council in general meeting, with open voting, and by a simple majority of votes cast.

7. Enrollment to corresponding membership is made in the same manner, the entrants having to submit recommendations from regular members of the Society.

III. Rights and Duties of Members of the Society

8. The regular members of the Society have the right to vote in all meetings of the Society.

9. Each regular member of the Society pays membership dues in the amount of one ruble upon admission and three rubles annually.

10. Expulsion from membership in the Society is effected by the general meeting at the proposal of at least ten members of the Society.

11. The corresponding members have advisory votes in the meetings of the Society; membership dues for corresponding members are in the same amount as those for regular members. Expulsion of corresponding members is effected on the same grounds that apply to regular members.

12. Corresponding members can be made regular members of the Society by application to the Council of the Society, whose opinion thereon is referred for final action by the general meeting.

13. The membership lists of the Society are submitted each year to the Presidium of the Communist Academy and the NKVD in two copies.

IV. Management of the Affairs of the Society

14. The affairs of the Society are directed by the Council of the Society, numbering fifteen members and five candidate members elected for one year by the general meeting. On its part the Council elects from its members a Presidium of five members (chairman, deputy chairman, scien-

tific secretary, and two members) and an Editorial Committee of five members.

15. The results of the election of Council of the Society and all subsequent changes therein are submitted for approval by the Presidium of the Communist Academy, whereupon they are communicated to the NKVD.

16. The Council is convened by the chairman as needed.

17. For review of the affairs of the Society a Review Committee consisting of five members and three candidate members is elected by the general meeting of the members of the Society for a one-year term.

18. For resolution of current problems and all affairs of the Society, as well as for hearing scientific reports, the Council calls general meetings of the members of the Society.

19. General meetings are called not less than once a month.

20. A meeting called for resolution of organizational problems is regarded as having a quorum if one-third of the members at hand in Moscow are present.

21. If a scheduled general meeting cannot take place owing to the absence of a quorum, another general meeting is called which will act with any number of members present.

22. The notice for a general meeting is posted by the Council of the Society. Questions suggested by members of the Society for the agenda of the general meeting are discussed in advance by the Council of the Society.

NOTE: Agenda suggestions must be submitted to the Council in writing.

23. Questions in general meetings are resolved by simple majority and open vote. Questions pertaining to amendments of the statutes, expulsion of members, and termination of the affairs of the Society are resolved by a two-thirds' majority of the members present.

24. For organization of research activity, the Council may set up appropriate sections within the Society. The regulations pertaining to the sections shall be worked out by the Council and approved by the general meeting of the Society.

25. The Council of the Society makes a report on the annual activity of the Society, submits it to the Presidium of the Communist Academy, and publishes it for general information. In case the Society publishes no report on its annual activity for three months, the Society shall be considered as having terminated its existence.

26. The area of the activity of the Society is the R.S.F.S.R. With the permission of the Council of the Society, branches thereof can be opened in major cities. The manner of organizing the activity of the branches shall be determined in a special directive worked out by the Council.

27. The seat of the Council of the Society is in Moscow, the Communist Academy.

V. Funds of the Society

28. The funds of the Society are derived from membership dues, income from publications and public lectures, and other sources.

VI. Method of Dissolving the Society

29. The Society may be dissolved:
(a) by decision of the appropriate organs of the government;
(b) by decision of two-thirds of the votes in a general meeting of the members.

30. In case the Society is dissolved, its entire property shall be transferred to the Communist Academy in Moscow by a Liquidating Committee elected therefor by the general meeting of the members of the Society.

15. M. Pokrovsky, "The Tasks of the Society of Marxist Historians"

The need has been felt for a long time to unite the scholarly efforts of the already numerous contingents of Communist comrades who are teaching history in our institutions of higher education as well as the ever increasing number of bourgeois historians who are close to us and who "accept" Marxism. During the years of study, this need is met by the history seminars of the Institute of Red Professors, but as soon as instruction ends, the scholarly ties are severed; yesterday's participants in collective work become solitary individuals, that is, they deteriorate in a rather evident and obvious way. The bourgeois historians moving close to us are completely deprived of an opportunity to become associated with any kind of collective work.

The idea of organizing a society comprising the Marxist historians arose in Leningrad, almost simultaneously as in Moscow, among the Communist historians assigned to work there. But there were too few of them; they were an inconspicuous island in a bourgeois-historical ocean; the local centers felt the danger that the waves of this ocean might overrun the island, and the "dangerous experiment" was not carried through. Now here, in Moscow, we are grounded in an incomparably larger circle of Party youth; here, there is also an "older generation," and we have every prospect, at least every formal prospect, of success.

It does not follow at all from this that our task is a very easy one and that our road is smooth and even. The historical materialism of our day is something much more subtle and complex than the historical materialism of 1917, not to mention 1897.

The dialectic of history does not recognize anything as final; and it required no more than a strong wind to begin to strip the external ornaments from the new edifice, the edifice of "revolutionary Marxism." Our first revolution, as I have felt compelled to say more than once, was the great teacher of Russian historians. After the revolution, many people who had no connection with historical materialism, even those who had quarreled with it fiercely in the nineties, became Marxists. This "post-1905 Marxism" did not prove particularly stable (a case in point is Professor R. Iu. Vipper). But, as compared with the nineties, it resulted in a colossal dissemination of ideas about history which were more or less close to genuine Marxism. The department of police had good reason to become concerned at the end of this period and to start talking about "legal Social-Democratic propaganda" and even about legal Bolshevik propaganda when the writings of Lenin and several other Bolsheviks appeared in Russia. In a word, at the beginning of the second decade of the twentieth century the quantitative dissemination of historical materialism was a fact which no one could deny, not even the Kadets,[2] who, in the face of the enormous popularity enjoyed by historical materialism, were forced to switch from their earlier tactics of ridicule and derision to tactics of silence which they carried to such lengths that several Marxist historical works were not even listed in the bibliographical surveys of *Vestnik Evropy* ("Messenger of Europe") and *Russkaia Mysl'* ("Russian Thought"). It took a noisy trial, which developed around one of these works, and which was brought on by the above-mentioned anxiety of the department of police, to win this honor for it.

However, if quantity was unquestionably on our side, the same cannot be said of quality.

The data which the Free Economic Society collected from its correspondents on the agrarian movement of 1905–6 gave a patently distorted picture. What was needed was the publication of the reports of the gendarmerie—the gendarmes were practical men and did not occupy themselves with tendentious journalism in their secret correspondence—in order to see the true picture of the Russian rural revolution and to convince ourselves that it was far more conscious and far more political, and not nearly so far removed from the workers' revolution, as we had thought. To correct this sin of the old Russian historiography is the foremost task of the coming generation of Marxist historians. Our worker and our peasant must finally have a book in their hands which would depict the past not as the work of landowners and officials but as their own work, the work of peasants and workers.

---

[2] Or Constitutional Democrats (abbreviation made up of the first syllables of the Russian words), a political party of liberals and constitutionalists.

It is more difficult to straighten out another historical kink, since it was a professional deformity which was very useful to us at a certain stage of the development of our craft. I am talking about *economic materialism*. In order to provide a basis for explaining political changes by economic ones, in order to drive out once and for all the saccharine legend of "subjective sociology," which divided all historical figures into good and bad, sympathetic and antipathetic, in order to pave the way for even an elementary scientific understanding of history, we had to collect an enormous amount of economic and, more particularly, historical statistical material. We were proud of it; it made our argument extraordinarily graphic and mathematically incontrovertible, and even now those who pass from an idealist to a materialist understanding of history inevitably go through this door. Historical statistics in themselves are necessary and vital, but to substitute them for history is altogether wrong. One must never forget the words of Marx and Engels—both repeatedly insisted on this point—that, although history is made in a definite economic setting, on a definite economic base, without an understanding of which history itself would remain incomprehensible to us, history nevertheless is made by living human beings who may be directly motivated by other than economic considerations. The analysis of these motives, even of those that are completely individual (Marx deliberately stresses this) does not in the least lead us off the ground of the historical materialist method, and does not convert us into "psychologists."

This defect of ours—these remnants of "economic materialism"—became evident with complete clarity after the imperialist war and the October Revolution. No numerical analysis, no columns of figures in explanation of these events, will take us beyond an understanding of the sociological base on which the events took place. And we must understand the events themselves, and understand them in the Marxist way, that is, in the historical materialistic and dialectic way. It is possible that in the nineties it might have seemed a revelation of genius to explain the beginnings of the 1914 war by fluctuations in the price of wheat (as was done in a work published only seven years ago by an author close to me), but now that we know in the most minute detail about such things as the Russo-French military and the Anglo-Russian naval conventions, now that we know with complete accuracy the complicated machinations behind the assassination of Francis Ferdinand, we realize that wheat prices are irrelevant. The politics of the imperialist war were based on the imperialist economic system without which, to put it simply, there would have been no such politics; but, once it was born out of the womb of finance capitalism, this governmental policy, like every newborn infant which separates from the maternal organism, began to live its own life, and one should not view the entire future life of the child from the standpoint of the fetal period of its existence.

It may be feared that the correction of this anomaly will suffer above all from the "law of inertia"; Engels first noted the substantial practical conveniences of the economic-materialistic explanation of history, but he warned against overenthusiasm for these conveniences. I must buttress my remarks, therefore, with some major authority, and I think that it will not be hard for me to find one. Who was it who approached our October Revolution from the point of view of economic materialism? Above all, of course, our good Mensheviks. According to "the level of the development of productive forces," Russia in 1917 was a country totally unsuited for the initiation of the socialist revolution; here statistics were decisively against us—the figures refused with finality "to go along." Just take a look at the productivity of labor at that time in Russia and abroad, at the ratio between small and large economic enterprises, and so on. Therefore, the Mensheviks opined, in Russia an attempt to overthrow the power of the bourgeoisie was doomed in advance to failure. The bourgeoisie would return immediately (the period of time was originally set at three weeks, as is known), and nothing but the discrediting of socialism would come of the whole thing. Not three weeks have passed, but a little more, nearly six years, and Lenin wrote about these soothsayers: "They all call themselves Marxists, but they understand Marxism in an impossibly pedantic way. The decisive thing in Marxism, namely its revolutionary dialectic, has completely escaped them." And he finished his article with these words: "Needless to say, a textbook written in Kautsky's way was a very useful thing in its time. But it is time to reject the idea that this textbook foresaw all the forms of development that subsequent periods of world history would assume. It is high time to declare that people who think so are simply fools."

This is harshly said but it is said in Lenin's way—right straight in the eye. And since society, undoubtedly, will go the way Lenin indicated—or there would have been no purpose in coming into existence at all—so, undoubtedly, it will have to outgrow, among other things, the "economic materialism" of the nineties which is still firmly set in many of us. The harsh Leninist formula will impel us to go more quickly along this road, and this will help us become not only Marxist historians but Leninist historians. Permit me to conclude my opening remarks with this wish.

CHAPTER VI

UNDER STALIN, 1927–1953

By the end of 1927 Stalin reached a clear-cut victory over Trotsky, who was expelled from the party in November of that year, exiled to Alma-Ata in Soviet Central Asia, and in 1929 deported to Turkey. Among the temporary allies Stalin made in the struggle with Trotsky was the party's leading theoretician, Nikolai I. Bukharin (1888–1938), who produced in the interregnum and later significant formulations of Marxist understanding of history and was eventually liquidated by Stalin in 1938.[1]

In these events Pokrovsky himself played a role very useful to Stalin's immediate purposes. He and Trotsky had locked horns as early as 1922, when he criticized Trotsky's version of the 1905 revolution and Trotsky charged him with "dogmatic mechanization" and "pseudo-Marxism, which confines itself to historical mechanisms, formal analogies, converting historical epochs into a logical succession of inflexible social categories (feudalism, capitalism, socialism, autocracy, bourgeois republic, dictatorship of the proletariat)."[2] Their polemics, largely centered on Trotsky's versions of the 1905 and 1917 revolutions, continued in the ensuing years when Pokrovsky echoed Stalin's views on building "socialism in one country" and condemned Trotsky for his advocacy of the "permanent revolution." Pokrovsky's attacks on Trotsky unquestionably helped the purpose Stalin pursued and may account for the fact that Stalin appeared at Pokrovsky's funeral as one of the pallbearers.

In 1928, the year of his sixtieth birthday, Pokrovsky was widely feted, and the homage paid to him in the pages of *Istorik-Marksist* and elsewhere makes amusing reading in the light of his denunciation a few years later. That year also marked, in economics, the transition from reconstruction and the New Economic Policy to the Five-Year plans and collectivization and, in history, the end of the "coexistence" of the first decade and the beginning of a new phase on the "historical front." Still very vigorous, Pokrovsky headed a broad offensive launched by the regime to liquidate the surviving "bourgeois" scholars. In a wave of purges, arrests, trials, and exiles that kept the entire field of scholarship in turmoil until 1932, more than a hundred and twenty historians (among them many eminent scholars, such as S. F. Platonov, E. V. Tarle, Iu. V. Got'e, and S. V. Rozhdestvensky) were arrested, investigated, and sent into exile from which many

---

[1] See Sidney Heitman, "Between Lenin and Stalin: Nikolai Bukharin," in *Revisionism: Essays on the History of Marxist Ideas*, ed. Leopold Labedz (New York, 1962), pp. 77–90, and his bibliography of Bukharin's works cited there.

[2] Leon Trotsky, *The History of the Russian Revolution* (Ann Arbor, Mich., 1957), I, 463–470.

never returned.[3] The purge brought Pokrovsky to the peak of his power and influence. For the needs of the war that was being waged against the "class enemy" and for the "militant education of the masses," he initiated in 1931 the publication of a new journal, *Bor'ba Klassov* ("Class Struggle," 1931–36), which was to be focused on the study of the postwar period. In a noteworthy address in 1931 Pokrovsky surveyed the results of the warfare, the achievements of the Society of Marxist Historians, and the tasks in the period ahead. The excerpts below are translated from the text of the address as published in *Istorik-Marksist*, No. 21, 1931, pp. 3–7.

16. M. Pokrovsky, "The Tasks of Marxist Historical Science in the Reconstruction Period"

The Society of Marxist Historians began functioning in 1925, toward the end and at the very height of the reconstruction period. One of the fundamental problems of this period was the utilization of bourgeois specialists. We were compelled to build communism with the hands of noncommunists, and resolving the issue whether or not these hands were clean and capable was one of the conditions for the success of this construction work. Hence the first task the Society had to undertake in the matter of tying theory with practice was the ideological scrutiny of the specialists, the history specialists we inherited from bourgeois Russia. At the very moment the reconstruction period came to an end, these specialists produced a whole series of works, which amounted to declarations (Petrushevsky, Tarle, Bakhrushin, and others).[4] These declarations made it possible to establish

---

[3] Konstantin F. Shteppa, *Russian Historians and the Soviet State*, p. 49. In a staged trial, Platonov, Tarle, and others were charged with plotting to restore the monarchy with the help of the Vatican. For another eyewitness account and casualty list see V. V. Chernavin, "The Treatment of Scholars in the USSR," *Slavonic and East European Review*, XI, No. 33 (April 1933), 710–714.

[4] The case of Tarle (1875–1955) is of particular interest. He had begun his career before 1917 as a historian of the French revolutionary and Napoleonic period and, like others, had sought to adapt himself to the new situation; he had even been admitted into the Society of Marxist Historians. Pokrovsky, however, regarded him as a "pseudo-Marxist," and in the purge of 1931 he became the object of particularly vicious torment and was banished to the east. After Pokrovsky was discredited and the renewed German *Drang nach Osten* began to be felt, Tarle reappeared in the late 1930's as his history of the Russian national effort against the French in 1812 became useful in preparing the Russian nation to face the Germans. He further adapted his work to the requirements of the situation and eventually came to be honored by the regime as one of the acceptable bourgeois historians. His entire historical writings have recently been republished (1957–61) in twelve volumes. For the vicissitudes of Tarle's career see Ann K. Erickson, "E. V. Tarle: The Career of a Historian under the Soviet Regime," *American Slavic and East European Review*, XIX, No. 2 (April 1960), pp. 202–216, and Edgar Hösch, "Der historiographische Umbruch in Russland: Tarle als

what kind of people they were in their world view and how suitable they were for us comrades in the building of communism. In the Society a number of reports were read about the work of these bourgeois specialists, and the reports made it clear that it was quite impossible to build communism with their hands.

Here the Society fulfilled its elementary Party duty, and, I repeat, acted completely in the spirit of the directive on tying theory with practice, because at that time both the scientific research work and, to a significant degree, the teaching in our universities, were in the hands of the specialists who underwent critical examination in our Society. The taking of a large part of the research work from their hands—that is, liquidation of the RANION history institute and the opening of a history institute in the Communist Academy—was one of the consequences of this examination. Unfortunately, we did not succeed then in reaching the higher citadel of the old historiography, the second department of the All-Union Academy of Sciences, and these dyed-in-the-wool reactionary historians were removed from their posts in a quite different connection and much later. We succeeded only in averting the spread of this harmful growth in the body of Soviet historiography by blocking the establishment of a new historical institute within the walls of the Academy of Sciences.

This first fulfillment by the Society of Marxist Historians of its immediate Party duty evoked manifest disapproval by several circles which at that time still seemed to be completely on the Party's side (now some of the representatives of these circles are formally outside the Party, whereas others have been formally condemned by the Party and have been kept only on the condition that they reform). The unmasking of the bourgeois historians in the way in which it was done in our discussions and in the pages of *Istorik-Marksist* appeared to these circles as "revolutionary infantilism," and one of the pioneers in unmasking the anticommunist ideology of our old professors, Comrade Fridliand, was immediately punished for it by a supremely insolent review in a publication edited at that time by Slepkov. . . .

Thus, first of all in connection with the unmasking of Petrushevsky, Tarle, and Co., the Society of Marxist Historians had to come to grips for the first time with its principal enemy in the period ahead—the deviationists. Since then we have had to concern ourselves very little with native bourgeois historians, because the major ones among them have already been

---

Beispiel," *Saeculum*, XI (1960), No. 3, 199–219. An example of what the regime unleashed on the "class enemy on the historical front" is G. Zaidel and M. Tsvibak, *Klassovyi vrag na istoricheskom fronte; Tarle i Platonov i ikh shkoly* [The Class Enemy on the Historical Front; Tarle and Platonov and Their Schools] (Moscow, 1931).

unmasked by us, and the others were taken care of by the appropriate institutions, and the frank confessions they have made relieved us of any obligation to unmask them.

Thus, in the new phase we were obliged to unmask not bourgeois specialists (except for the Western ones—here our unmasking work was much delayed; for example, our critique of Dopsch's theory was completed only this year), but their friends and followers among the Party deviationists—both right and "left." This was an immeasurably more difficult and more vital struggle than the preceding one. At a time when the bourgeois historians, as honest reactionaries, were formulating their views more or less clearly, the opportunists, from among the Party deviationists with individual exceptions, did everything to avoid this, justifying Lenin's famous description of opportunism: "When we speak of the struggle with opportunism, we must never forget the characteristic traits of all contemporary opportunism in any and all fields; its vagueness, its diffuseness, and its elusiveness. The opportunist, by his very nature, avoids a definite and irrevocable statement of the question, looks for compromise, wriggles like a snake between mutually exclusive points of view, trying to 'agree' with each, reducing his disagreements to corrections, doubts, mild-natured and innocent desires, etc., etc."

Our contemporary opportunists are especially fond of hiding behind Lenin, concocting each time out of quotations from Lenin the kind of dish that no Menshevik would refuse. The words are genuinely Leninist, but not a drop of Leninist content is left in them because the words are torn out of context and because other words of Lenin which would explain the quotations in a quite different sense are carefully hidden from the reader. On inexperienced people, particularly on inexperienced young people, this hailstorm of quotations undoubtedly makes some impression. It must be remembered that Bernstein's famous book—the gospel of opportunism—is also sprinkled with quotations from Marx and Engels, although its primary aim was to prove revolutionary Marxism wrong.

Self-criticism is another camouflage of the opportunists. When an opportunist is caught saying anti-Party things, falsifying Lenin and actually fighting against Leninism, a violent shriek goes up at once about the suppression of self-criticism.

There can be no Leninist study of any subject whatever without the link between theory and practice, that there exists no apolitical science that can be detached from the current class struggle; these are self-evident matters, but what is the link between theory and practice on the historical front?

Here there are two conceptions of this question, one of which is undoubtedly a narrow-minded approach to the question, that is, completely unLeninist; only the second is correct. The first formula of linking theory and practice proposed to us maintains that historians must take an active part in putting our archives in order and using them. This is absolutely right as far as it goes. Historians must undertake this work. But it would be extremely shortsighted to understand in this way the link between theory and practice in the field of history. It would mean an unbelievable humiliation for that science which Marx and Engels were prepared to consider the "only" science and about which they were prepared to say that "nearly all ideology results either in a distorted understanding of this history (the history of human beings), or in rendering it completely abstract. Ideology itself is only one aspect of this history."

It is the essence of history, as has been said repeatedly, that it is the *most political* of all sciences, and the link between theory and practice in it is in the fact that history must interpret directly and tirelessly the current class struggle for the masses, must uncover the roots, sometimes deeply concealed, of class contradictions; in a word, it must reveal and subject to a merciless Marxist-Leninist analysis all those political conflicts which are going on before our eyes—which is impossible without a historical approach to these conflicts. I have already had occasion to point out that the roots of the right and of the "left" deviations, grown long before us, are not to be found only in the first years of the New Economic Policy, when some comrades managed to recall, of all the things Lenin had formulated about the NEP, only that "the New Economic Policy signifies a transition to the restoration of capitalism to a considerable degree," and did not remember that in the same speech Lenin said that "the dictatorship of the proletariat is the most furious and bitter struggle, in which the proletariat must fight against the whole world," and that the NEP is simply another solution to the same problem that arose in the very earliest years.

This Leninist course was entirely forgotten by certain comrades ten years ago, and when the means of reaching socialism changed sharply, these comrades remained in old positions, positions which were condemned by Lenin ten years ago. However, as I had occasion to remark elsewhere, these are not the deepest roots of present-day opportunist tendencies. Not speaking of the general source of all opportunism, the petty-bourgeois outlook— the "sociological" root, so to speak, of opportunism—it is not difficult to trace its concrete historical roots, if not for centuries, at least for decades. At this point we come upon a very curious fact. We encounter the present tangle of right and left deviations in the seventies in the tangle of the Narodniks, who maintained unanimously that the Russian government at that time was a supra-class organization and that the peasant was the hero and creator of all Russian history. This deification of the individual peasant of that time appears now as a special historical form of the struggle against collectivization and against the liquidation of the kulaks as a class, and it is marvelously in logical accord with Trotsky's thesis that capitalism was "implanted" in our country by a supra-class organization, that is, by the autocracy, and that it was "implanted" on an extremely primitive economic base. This is why only "people with peculiarly constructed minds" can talk about socialism in Russia.

All of these things are closely interrelated and they can be brought to light only by *historical* analysis. In this historical analysis of the contemporary political situation, without which the political situation cannot be understood, there is to be found the specific form for the union of theory and practice which is peculiar to history.

All historical works of Marx and Engels and all of Lenin's historical works and analyses were devoted to this purpose and answered this need. Not one of our great teachers was concerned with history for history's sake. To open parentheses, the study of history for history's sake—it can now be taken as established—was always undertaken by puny and untalented historians, or by clever people who wished to hide their own political faces behind a pile of quotations, and with the help of this pile to promote views which, in fact, corresponded to the political interests of one or another class. In particular, bourgeois democracy, with its system of stultifying the masses, has worked out the formula of "objective" history, a formula which, unfortunately, still to this day clouds the vision of many of our comrades. It is not that they fail to acknowledge theoretically that service in the proletariat's political struggle against the bourgeois world both inside and outside the U.S.S.R. constitutes their primary task; they understand this, theoretically, that is, bookishly, cut off from reality, but this theoretical understanding by itself is not worth a broken penny because it is in itself a stigma, the mark of Cain, standing for the rupture of theory and practice. Only he who fights in history for the interests of the proletariat, who chooses accordingly his subjects, his opponent, and his appropriate weapon for the fight with the opponent, is a genuine Leninist historian.

We must brace ourselves now on this front, and the sooner the better. Perhaps, the historians of the U.S.S.R. may need to exert themselves less here, although it must be said that the writing of the history of the peoples of the U.S.S.R. is still a matter of the future, and there is a whole vast area which we have only begun to develop—the area of the nationality question and of everything that is connected with it; the fight against imperial chauvinism, as the major danger, and against local nationalisms, as a secondary danger, the repulse of which is no less urgent, has only been touched by us. So the historians of the U.S.S.R., too, have nothing particular to boast about.

However, the situation on the front of Western history most urgently requires reinforcement. The leaders on this front should have noticed that the linking of theory and practice in their area began spontaneously, in spite of them, among the rank and file; actually, students of Western history in the Institute of Red Professors are all connected with sections of the

Comintern and work there, and it was appropriate that one of the leaders of the Comintern was invited to open a discussion on Western history. But where are the actual leaders in Western history? They are sitting somewhere in the thick woods of the French Revolution or in the history of the most ancient period of German social-democracy, or in some other quite remote places, which, both by their remoteness and by the manner in which they are being investigated, represent an unquestionable break between theory and practice. Here chronology is not the matter at issue. Engels studied the history of primitive societies and was very much interested in the history of ancient Egypt: he needed both in order to formulate the conception of historical materialism, which was a perfectly proper concern in the days when Marxism was being founded. Now the question of social formations, that is, the question of feudalism, of natural economy, even of tribal customs as it relates to the study of the peoples of the U.S.S.R., is the most urgent question, even though all these things are now dealt with in the first pages of our history textbooks. The question is not one of chronology, but of approach, of whether we study history as such, falling into the traps of crafty bourgeois researchers, who actually are pursuing definite class aims, or whether we take history as a weapon in the class struggle, as a means of exposing each and every "ideology" of our bourgeois enemies as well as of the opportunists who are closer to us and who sometimes conceal themselves under Party slogans. It is in the struggle with bourgeois historiography and with opportunism, and in the merciless unmasking of both, that the fundamental union of theory and practice on the historical front takes place. To this is added, of course, a whole host of specific tasks having to do with the history of the class struggle which is currently under way in various countries, and with the task of serving those organizations, the Comintern in the first instance, which cannot get along without historians on both the Western and Eastern fronts. Unless we resolve these many concrete questions, which we do not need to enumerate here, our historical work can easily degenerate into polemics that are quite superficial and require no historical knowledge, and one fine day we may hear the question: since the Party press handles this kind of thing magnificently, why do we have historians at all?

We must never forget this. History is the concrete investigation of concrete social questions. In this investigation we must beat our enemy, and we must so define this research that it corresponds to our purposes. The most important thing here is to unite the historical work we are carrying on with the proletariat's struggle against wage slavery. Where this union is not achieved, there is no genuine Leninist history.

By 1932, for all his apparent power, Pokrovsky was beginning to lose his grip on the field of history. The lodgment of Stalin in Lenin's place and the industrialization program he launched after 1928 created new circumstances and new demands. Stalin had little of the internationalist outlook of Lenin and Trotsky, and his formula of building "socialism in one country" and making Russia the powerful home base of the revolution intrinsically favored a more traditional type of history which, while retaining the language of historical materialism, was to give recognition to national forces and make Russians proud of their past virtues and current achievements. The industrialization program, moreover, required well-schooled young generations to man the jobs of remaking Russia. Under Stalin the regime began to revive the traditional view that, whatever the field, competence came from solid grounding in the experience of past generations. "Cadres" (that is, qualified personnel), Stalin liked to say, "decide everything."

Thus, by the beginning of the 1930's, "a contradiction of particular intensity had arisen between the demands of practice in socialist construction and the existing system of education."[5] A new approach had to be taken to eliminate the "activity" school, with its laxity in learning and discipline, and press a carefully organized and administered process of "mastery of knowledge." The first step along this road was the Central Committee's decree of July 25, 1930, introducing universal compulsory education through the fourth grade. The second step was the Committee's decree of September 5, 1931, "On the Elementary and Secondary School," calling for intensive struggle against the "theory of the 'withering away' of the school" and the debasement of the function of the teacher, and for development of "individuals who are well educated and who have proper mastery of the basic branches of knowledge."[6] In general, this new approach meant greater historism, that is, historical background approach, in the presentation of all subjects and firmer texture of facts, personalities, and dates in the historical account itself.

At the very time, therefore, when through the purge Pokrovsky was achieving complete control of historical scholarship, the sands were shifting under his feet under the pressures of higher policy. Moreover, the writing and teaching of history began to reflect the keen interest of Stalin in altering the presentation of the recent Soviet past so as to expunge Trotsky's role in it, brand him as the archvillain, and depict himself as Lenin's closest associate and most faithful disciple. Unlike Lenin, who had no rivals in leading the Bolshevik regime and needed no hagiography, Stalin was a rather obscure functionary who had clawed his way to the top and after victory needed a retouched public image of himself. Gradually, a pressure was generated to doctor the history of the party and the regime and create the version Stalin required. However, not all historians responded to the new line, and in the general turmoil, which he skillfully managed from

---

[5] *Osnovy kommunisticheskogo vospitaniia* [Foundations of Communist Education] (Moscow, 1960), pp. 158–159.

[6] Texts of the decrees in *Sbornik rukovodiashchikh materialov o shkole* [Collection of Guiding Materials concerning the Schools] (Moscow, 1952), pp. 33–52.

above, Stalin proceeded to shoot at his own special targets among the real and alleged supporters of Trotsky and "falsifiers" of recent party history. With liquidations hitting right and left, Stalin wrote a sharp letter to the editors of *Proletarskaia revoliutsiia* ("Proletarian Revolution," 1921–41, a party review devoted to questions of party history) which was later hailed by Stalinist historians as marking a new stage in the writing and teaching of history in the Soviet Union. The excerpts from the letter below are from the English translation in Stalin, *Works,* XIII, 86–104 (Moscow, 1955).

17. Stalin's Letter to Proletarskaia revoliutsiia, November 1931

DEAR COMRADES,

I emphatically protest against the publication in the magazine *Proletarskaia revoliutsiia* (No. 6, 1930) of Slutsky's anti-Party and semi-Trotskyist article, "The Bolsheviks on German Social-Democracy in the Period of Its Pre-War Crisis," as an article for discussion.[7]

Slutsky asserts that Lenin (the Bolsheviks) underestimated the danger of *Centrism* in German Social-Democracy and in prewar Social-Democracy in general; that is, he underestimated the danger of camouflaged opportunism, the danger of conciliation toward opportunism. In other words, according to Slutsky, Lenin (the Bolsheviks) did not wage an irreconcilable struggle against opportunism, for, in essence, underestimation of Centrism is tantamount to refraining from a thoroughgoing struggle against opportunism. It follows, therefore, that in the period before the war Lenin was not yet a real Bolshevik; that it was only in the period of the imperialist war, or even at the close of the war, that Lenin became a real Bolshevik.

Such is the tale Slutsky tells in his article. And you, instead of branding this new-found "historian" as a slanderer and falsifier, enter into discussion with him, provide him with a forum. I cannot refrain from protesting against the publication of Slutsky's article in your magazine as an article for discussion, for the question of Lenin's *Bolshevism,* the question

---

[7] It is of interest that A. Slutsky happened to live in the Red Presnia district of Moscow where N. S. Khrushchev had recently been appointed First Party Secretary by Stalin. On December 15, 1931, the district passed, undoubtedly at the initiative of Khrushchev, a special resolution condemning Slutsky for "deliberate utilization of Party literature for propaganda of Trotskyism, the spearhead of the counterrevolutionary bourgeoisie," and expelling him from the party. In January 1932 the party stalwarts of the district were commended for having dealt "a decisive rebuff to the attempts of the Trotskyite contrabandists to falsify the history of our Party. They threw out from their ranks the Trotskynite Slutsky who had disguised himself." See Lazar Pistrak, *The Grand Tactician: Khrushchev's Rise to Power* (New York, 1961), pp. 78–79.

whether Lenin *did* or *did not wage* an irreconcilable struggle, based on principle, against Centrism as a certain form of opportunism, the question whether Lenin *was* or *was not* a real Bolshevik, cannot be made into a subject of discussion.

In your statement entitled "From the Editorial Board," sent to the Central Committee on October 20, you admit that the editorial board made a mistake in publishing Slutsky's article as a discussion article. That is all to the good, of course, despite the fact that the statement of the editorial board is very belated. But in your statement you commit a fresh mistake by declaring that "the editorial board considers it to be politically extremely urgent and necessary that the entire complex of problems pertaining to the relations between the Bolsheviks and the prewar Second International be further analyzed in the pages of *Proletarskaia revoliutsiia.*" That means that you intend once again to draw people into a discussion on questions which are axioms of Bolshevism. It means that you are again thinking of converting the subject of Lenin's Bolshevism from an axiom into a problem requiring "further analysis." Why? On what grounds?

Everyone knows that Leninism was born, grew up, and became strong in relentless struggle against opportunism of every brand, including Centrism in the West (Kautsky) and Centrism in our country (Trotsky, etc.). This cannot be denied even by the downright enemies of Bolshevism. It is an axiom. But you are dragging us back by trying to turn an axiom into a problem requiring "further analysis." Why? On what grounds? Perhaps through ignorance of the history of Bolshevism? Perhaps for the sake of a rotten liberalism, so that the Slutskys and other disciples of Trotsky may not be able to say that they are being gagged? A rather strange sort of liberalism, this, exercised at the expense of the vital interests of Bolshevism. . . .

What, exactly, is there in Slutsky's article that the editorial board regards as worthy of discussion?

Slutsky asserts that Lenin (the Bolsheviks) did not pursue a line directed toward a rupture, toward a split with the opportunists in German Social-Democracy, with the opportunists in the Second International of the prewar period. You want to open a discussion on this Trotskyist thesis of Slutsky's. But what is there to discuss? Is it not obvious that Slutsky is simply slandering Lenin, slandering the Bolsheviks? Slander must be branded as such and not made the subject of discussion.

As you see, the editorial board made a mistake in permitting a discussion with a falsifier of the history of our Party.

What could have impelled the editorial board to take this wrong road?

I think that they were impelled to take that road by rotten liberalism, which has spread to some extent among a section of the Bolsheviks. Some

Bolsheviks think that Trotskyism is a faction of communism—one which makes mistakes, it is true, which does many foolish things, is sometimes even anti-Soviet, but which, nevertheless, is a faction of communism. Hence a certain liberalism in the attitude toward the Trotskyists and Trotskyist-minded people. It scarcely needs proof that such a view of Trotskyism is deeply mistaken and harmful. As a matter of fact, Trotskyism has long since ceased to be a faction of communism. As a matter of fact, Trotskyism is the advanced detachment of the counterrevolutionary bourgeoisie, which is fighting against communism, against the Soviet regime, against the building of socialism in the U.S.S.R.

Who gave the counterrevolutionary bourgeoisie an ideological weapon against Bolshevism in the shape of the thesis that building socialism in our country is impossible, that the degeneration of the Bolsheviks is inevitable, etc.? Trotskyism gave it that weapon. It is no accident that in their efforts to prove the inevitability of the struggle against the Soviet regime all the anti-Soviet groups in the U.S.S.R. have been referring to the well-known Trotskyist thesis that building socialism in our country is impossible, that the degeneration of the Soviet regime is inevitable, that a return to capitalism is probable.

Who gave the counterrevolutionary bourgeoisie in the U.S.S.R. a tactical weapon in the shape of attempts at open actions against the Soviet regime? The Trotskyists, who tried to organize anti-Soviet demonstrations in Moscow and Leningrad on November 7, 1927, gave it that weapon. It is a fact that the anti-Soviet actions of the Trotskyists raised the spirits of the bourgeoisie and let loose the wrecking activities of the bourgeois experts.

Who gave the counterrevolutionary bourgeoisie an organizational weapon in the form of attempts at setting up underground anti-Soviet organizations? The Trotskyists, who organized their own anti-Bolshevik illegal group, gave it that weapon. It is a fact that the underground anti-Soviet work of the Trotskyists helped the anti-Soviet groups in the U.S.S.R. to assume an organized form.

Trotskyism is the advanced detachment of the counterrevolutionary bourgeoisie.

That is why liberalism in the attitude toward Trotskyism, even though the latter is shattered and camouflaged, is blockheadedness bordering on crime, on treason to the working class.

That is why the attempts of certain "writers" and "historians" to smuggle disguised Trotskyist rubbish into our literature must meet with a determined rebuff from Bolsheviks.

That is why we cannot permit a literary discussion with the Trotskyist smugglers.

It seems to me that "historians" and "writers" of the Trotskyist smuggler category are for the present trying to carry out their smuggling work along two lines.

Firstly, they are trying to prove that in the period before the war Lenin underestimated the danger of Centrism, thereby leaving the inexperienced reader to surmise that, in consequence, Lenin was not yet a real revolutionary at that time; that he became one only after the war, after he had "re-equipped" himself with Trotsky's assistance. Slutsky may be regarded as a typical representative of this type of smuggler.

We have seen above that Slutsky and Co. are not worth making much fuss about.

Secondly, they are trying to prove that in the period prior to the war Lenin did not realize the necessity of the growing over of the bourgeois-democratic revolution into a socialist revolution, thereby leaving the inexperienced reader to surmise that, in consequence, Lenin at that time was not yet a real Bolshevik; that he realized the necessity of this growing over only after the war, after he had "re-equipped" himself with Trotsky's assistance. Volosevich, author of *A Course in the History of the CPSU (B)*, may be regarded as a typical representative of this type of smuggler.

True, as far back as 1905 Lenin wrote that *"from the democratic revolution we shall at once, and just to the extent of our strength, the strength of the class-conscious and organized proletariat, begin to pass to the socialist revolution,"* that *"we stand for uninterrupted revolution,"* that *"we shall not stop halfway."* True, a very large number of facts and documents of a similar nature could be found in the works of Lenin. But what do the Voloseviches care about the facts of Lenin's life and work? The Voloseviches write in order, by decking themselves out in Bolshevik colors, to smuggle in their anti-Leninist contraband, to utter lies about the Bolsheviks and to falsify the history of the Bolshevik Party.

As you see, the Voloseviches are worthy of the Slutskys. Such are the "highways and byways" of the Trotskyist smugglers.

You yourselves should realize that it is not the business of the editorial board of *Proletarskaia revoliutsiia* to facilitate the smuggling activities of such "historians" by providing them with a forum for discussion.

The task of the editorial board is, in my opinion, to raise the questions concerning the history of Bolshevism to the proper level, to put the study of the history of our Party on scientific, Bolshevik lines, and to concentrate attention against the Trotskyist and all other falsifiers of the history of our Party, systematically tearing off their masks.

That is all the more necessary since even some of our historians—I am speaking of historians without quotation marks, of *Bolshevik* historians of our Party—are not free from mistakes which bring grist to the mill of the Slutskys and Voloseviches. In this respect, even Comrade Yaroslavsky is

not, unfortunately, an exception; his books on the history of the CPSU
(B), despite all their merits, contain a number of errors in matters of
principle and history.

With communist greetings,

J. STALIN

Thereafter, while Stalin was alive, it became a consistent practice in
party history writings to carry violent attacks on Trotsky as, in Stalin's
favorite characterization, Judas Iscariot, and to deny him any significant
role in the events of the 1917–27 decade, of which he was undeniably a
major maker. Thus arose the Stalinist system of historical falsification
which Trotsky sought to combat from abroad with numerous exposés and
historical writings. However, while the world was able to compare the two
Bolshevik versions and draw its own conclusions, the people of Russia had
to wait until 1956 for the historical truth that the regime administers to
become more truthful.

In 1932 the tightening of the educational process was carried further by
a Central Committee decree of August 25, which called for firm academic
plans, curriculums, textbooks, and classroom procedures. The stabilization
of the curriculum was accompanied by demands for doing away with the
"nihilism" of the "Down with the Textbook" slogan of the 1920's and the
tentativeness of the existing teaching tools.[8] On February 12, 1933, the
Central Committee issued a decree calling for "stable textbooks in all
subjects to liquidate the existing 'method' of endless 'redrafting' of textbooks." The excerpts from the decrees below are translated from the texts
in *Sbornik rukovodiashchikh materialov o shkole* (see n. 6, above), pp.
59–70.

18. Decree of August 25, 1932, on Curricula and Administration of the Elementary and Secondary Schools

The Central Committee of the VKP (B) finds that the elementary and
secondary schools in the R.S.F.S.R. in the past year have registered notable
progress with the introduction of universal compulsory education and
transition toward a systematic mastery of knowledge on the basis of
definite academic plans, curriculums, and schedules. However, there is still
no complete elimination of the fundamental shortcoming of the schools,
namely, the fact that "the training in the schools does not provide a
sufficient amount of general-education knowledge and handles unsatisfacto-

---

[8] F. F. Korolev, *Sovetskaia shkola v period sotsialisticheskoi industrializatsii* [The
Soviet School in the Period of Socialist Industrialization] (Moscow, 1959), p. 84.

rily the task of training for the technical schools and the higher institutions in general individuals who are well educated and who have proper mastery of the basic sciences (physics, chemistry, mathematics, native language, geography, etc.)." (Decree, CC of the VKP (B), September 5, 1931.)

The CC of the VKP (B) decrees:

1. With reference to the curriculums, the basic shortcomings [include, among others,] an insufficiently historical approach to the curriculums in social studies evident in the fact that they provide an extremely weak idea of the historical past of peoples and countries, the evolution of human society, etc. An essential shortcoming is the fact that there are still no developed curriculums in history.

Accordingly, the CC proposes: (1) that the People's Commissar of Education of the R.S.F.S.R. reorganize by January 1, 1933, the curriculums of the elementary and secondary schools so as to assure an actual, lasting, and systematic mastery of the foundations of sciences, knowledge of the facts, and habits of correct speech, writing, mathematical exercises, etc.; (2) that in reorganizing the curriculums he be guided by the following: . . . (d) significant strengthening of the elements of historism in the social studies curriculums . . . and illustrating the basic subdivisions and topics of these subjects with factual material and historical digressions and comparisons; (g) recognition as absolutely necessary that the secondary schools assure each student of proficiency in one foreign language.

2. With reference to organization of the school work so as to strengthen the learning process, the CC of the VKP (B) proposes that the People's Commissars of Education of the Union Republics . . . organize the learning process in the schools on the following basis: (a) the basic unit in the organization of learning in the elementary and secondary schools must be the lesson involving a given group of pupils and proceeding on a strictly delineated schedule with a firm enrollment of pupils; (b) the teacher must systematically in proper sequence present the subject taught by him and train the pupils in work with the textbook . . .

19. Decree of February 12, 1933, on Textbooks

1. The policy of the R.S.F.S.R. People's Commissariat of Education and Ogiz[9] in the preparation of textbooks is recognized as wrong.

2. The following are condemned and rescinded as contravening the decisions of the CC of the VKP (B):

(a) The circular letter of August 1918 of the Unified Schools Section of the R.S.F.S.R. People's Commissariat of Education, stating that "textbooks must altogether be banished from the school."

---

[9] The State Publishing Office.

(b) The decree of March 28, 1930, of the Board of the People's Commissariat of Education, recognizing it as "impossible to adhere at the present time to the principle of textbook stabilization."

(c) The resolution of May 16, 1930, of the All-Russian Conference on Schoolbooks . . . which states: "The textbook must in no case be stable . . . The Conference firmly rejects the principle of textbook stabilization."

(d) The decision of the presidium of the CC of Education Workers' Union of March 3, 1930, terming the decision to standardize the textbooks for [use during] three-year periods as "wrong and politically harmful."

3. Publication of so-called "workbooks" and "watered-down textbooks" which supplant the actual textbooks and do not provide systematic knowledge in the subjects studied at school is to cease at once.

The People's Commissariat of Education and Ogiz are to assure the publication of stable textbooks, intended to be used over many years, in the native language, mathematics, geography, physics, chemistry, natural science, etc., scheduling their publication not later than July 15, 1933, so as to introduce them with the opening of the school year on September 1, 1933.

4. The rule is established that each textbook must be approved by the Board of the People's Commissariat of Education upon prior and thorough examination and that no changes may be made in the textbook without a special decision of the Board of the People's Commissariat of Education.

5. The existing method of publishing textbooks independently in each province, area, and autonomous republic of the R.S.F.S.R. is ended. In each subject there must be a single obligatory textbook approved by the People's Commissariat of the R.S.F.S.R. and published by Uchpedgiz.[10]

Upon Pokrovsky's death in 1932, his historiographic empire began to fall apart or to be actively broken up. The Institute of Red Professors, RANION, the Communist Academy, and the Society of Marxist Historians all were gradually dismantled and the functions providing leadership in the field of history and supervising it were vested in the Institute of History of the Academy of Sciences of the U.S.S.R.[11] Created in 1936 from remnants of Pokrovsky's organizations after the Academy was moved from Leningrad to Moscow to complete its bolshevization, the Institute of

---

[10] The publishing office for educational materials.

[11] The Society of Marxist Historians was dissolved in 1934. Later, one of its prominent young members and a product of the Pokrovsky school, Anna M. Pankratova, spoke of "the sorry times of the sterile 'sociological' discussions in the Society of Marxist Historians." *Pravda*, September 8, 1939.

History received a virtual monopoly of historical research and publication which it exercised well into the postwar period.[12]

It has been said that it was Pokrovsky's good fortune to die before the steps were taken to destroy his work, influence, and considerable independence as a scholar. It has also been said that, from the perspective of subsequent developments in Soviet history writing, his school was the only genuine attempt to create a Marxist historiography. At any rate, what now arose was the Stalinist totalitarianism which pressed the elimination of whatever intellectual independence still survived in the party, the enforcement of rigorous theoretical dogmatism, and the regimentation of all areas of life to serve the purposes of Stalin's regime. Prominent among these purposes were the preparation of the Russian people through patriotic education and propaganda to face the German threat, and the restoration of traditional history to serve this education and make possible the creation of a "great leader" myth. The drastic step in the field of history was the joint decree of the Central Committee of the VKP (B) and the Council of People's Commissars of May 16, 1934, which, without explicitly mentioning Pokrovsky, condemned the "abstract sociological schemes" of his school and inaugurated the return to more conventional history of people, facts, and dates. The decree also set up several teams to write new textbooks to replace the products of Pokrovsky's era and reopened the history departments in the universities for a more traditional approach to the training of historians. The decree, given in full below, is translated from the text in *Istorik-Marksist,* No. 37 (1934), pp. 83–84.

20. Decree of May 16, 1934, on the Teaching of History in the Schools

The Council of People's Commissars of the U.S.S.R. and the CC of VKP (B) find that the teaching of history in the schools of the U.S.S.R. is unsatisfactorily handled. Textbooks and instruction have an abstract, schematic nature. Instead of teaching civic history in a lively and engaging way, with statement of the most important events and facts in their chronological sequence and with characterizations of historical personalities, the students are given abstract definitions of socioeconomic formations, thus replacing the well-connected exposition of civic history with abstract sociological schemes.

The decisive condition for enduring mastery of a history course by students is the observance of historical and chronological sequence in the

---

[12] For the organization and functions of the Institute see Alexander Vucinich, *The Soviet Academy of Sciences* (Stanford, Calif., 1956), pp. 26–27, which also discusses a number of other Academy units dealing with history.

statement of historical events, with strict implantation in the students' memory of the important historical events, historical personalities, and chronological dates. Only such a history course can ensure the comprehensibility, clarity, and concreteness of the history material that the students need; correct analysis and correct generalization of historical events leading the student to Marxist understanding of history are possible only on this basis.

In accordance with this, the Council of People's Commissars of the U.S.S.R. and the Central Committee of the VKP (B) decree:

1. Preparation by June 1935 of the following new history textbooks: (a) history of the ancient world, (b) history of the Middle Ages, (c) modern history, (d) history of the U.S.S.R., (e) modern history of dependent and colonial countries.

2. Approval of the following list of members of groups entrusted with compiling the new historical textbooks: history of the ancient world—Prof. S. I. Kovalev (principal), academician N. M. Nikolsky, A. S. Svanidze, and Prof. A. V. Minulin; history of the Middle Ages —Prof. E. A. Kosminsky (principal), Prof. A. I. Gukovsky, O. V. Trachtenberg, and A. I. Malyshev; modern history—academician N. M. Lukin (principal), Prof. C. S. Fridliand, Prof. V. M. Dalin, Prof. G. S. Zaidel, and Docent A. V. Efimov; history of the U.S.S.R. —Prof. N. N. Vanag (principal), Prof. B. D. Grekov, Prof. A. M. Pankratova, and Prof. S. A. Piontkovsky; modern history of dependent and colonial countries—K. B. Radek (principal), K. Z. Gabidulin, Prof. N. I. Konrad, A. S. Mukhadzhi, M. S. Godes, M. D. Kokin, L. I. Madyar, P. A. Mif, and F. A. Rothstein.

3. In order to train qualified specialists in history, the reopening as of September 1, 1934, of departments of history in the Moscow and Leningrad universities, with the contingent of students to be admitted in the autumn set at 150 for each department, and to fix the course of training at five years.

Chairman of the Council of People's Commissars of the U.S.S.R.,
V. MOLOTOV
Secretary of the Central Committee of the VKP (B) J. STALIN

Beginning in 1934, history was reinstated in the curriculum of the ten-grade secondary schools. A joint party-government decree of June 9 of that year reintroduced elementary history of the U.S.S.R. with brief data from general history in the third (80 hours) and fourth (40 hours) grades; history of the ancient Orient and Greece in the fifth (80 hours) and Rome in the sixth (40 hours) and medieval history to the eleventh century in the sixth (40 hours) and to the eighteenth century in the seventh grade (80 hours).[13] Another decree, of September 3, 1935, cracked down on a "major portion of the education workers" for "not having outgrown yet the stupid anti-Leninist theory of the 'withering-away of the school,'" prescribed in detail the lengths of school time, and reinstated the prerevolutionary system of grading.

The preparation of the new textbooks ordered by the decree of May 16, 1934, did not proceed satisfactorily. Acting as an evaluation committee, on August 8, 1934, Stalin and two of his closest associates, Sergei M. Kirov (1886–1934) and Andrei A. Zhdanov (1896–1948), rendered a report which found the speedily prepared outline for the textbook on the history of the U.S.S.R. full of misconceptions and errors; another report by them, dated August 9, 1934, found the outline of the modern history textbook somewhat better, but still rather replete with confusion.[14] Excerpts from the official announcement in *Pravda* on January 27, 1936, making public the two reports, follow, translated from the text in *Sbornik rukovodiashchikh materialov o shkole,* pp. 82–89.

21. "On the Front of Historical Science," Pravda, January 27, 1936

Attributing a great importance to the proper organization of the teaching of civic history in the schools of the U.S.S.R., the Council of People's Commissars of the U.S.S.R. and the CC of the VKP (B) on May 16, 1934, adopted and published the well-known decree concerning "The Teaching of Civic History in the Schools of the U.S.S.R." [They] decreed the creation of five teams for the preparation of new textbooks and approved the personnel of these teams.

On August 14, 1934, the CC of the VKP (B) and the Council of People's Commissars approved the observations submitted by Comrades Stalin, Kirov, and Zhdanov concerning the outlines of the new textbooks on history of the U.S.S.R. and modern history.

---

[13] Subsequent regulations required students in the last three grades (eighth, ninth, and tenth) to be exposed to a systematic course of U.S.S.R. history from earliest time to the present, including local republic history (255 hours), and a course of modern history since the French Revolution (164 hours). For a comparison of this program and the history curriculum of the eleven-grade secondary school, in operation from 1958 to 1964, see Marin Pundeff, "History in Soviet Education since 1958," *Harvard Educational Review,* XXXII No. 1 (Winter 1962), 66–80. The history curriculum of the present ten-grade school is in Seymour N. Rosen, *Significant Aspects of Soviet Education,* U.S. Office of Education Bulletin No. 15 (Washington, 1965), pp. 20–23.

[14] A particularly difficult problem has been the matter of fitting Russian history into the periodization required by the five socioeconomic formations postulated by Marx in Reading No. 3 (primitive-communal, slaveowning, feudal, capitalist, and socialist). For a discussion of the matter see Leo Yaresh, "The Problem of Periodization," in Black, *op. cit.* (see chap. ii, n. 6), pp. 34–77.

In these observations both outlines were subjected to detailed analysis and rigorous criticism, and it was established that the outline for the history of the U.S.S.R. was particularly unsatisfactory, abounding in a large number of unscientific and, from the point of view of Marxism, illiterate definitions and being afflicted by extreme shoddiness which is especially inadmissible in a "textbook in which each word and each definition must be weighed." Major as well as minor shortcomings also afflicted the outline for the modern history textbook.

The observations of Comrades Stalin, Kirov, and Zhdanov showed in a thorough way the direction in which the outlines and the textbooks under preparation were to be revised. Nevertheless, the Sovnarkom of the U.S.S.R. and the CC of the VKP (B) are compelled to state that the history textbooks now submitted to the Sovnarkom and the CC for consideration are in a large part unsatisfactory and continue to be afflicted by the same shortcomings indicated above. Especially unsatisfactory are the textbook in the history of the U.S.S.R., submitted by the team of Professor Vanag, and the textbooks in the elementary course in the history of the U.S.S.R. for the elementary schools, submitted by the teams of Mints and Lozinsky. The fact that the authors of the cited textbooks continue to insist on historical definitions and conditions which have repeatedly been exposed as wrong by the party, and which are patently worthless and grounded in the well-known errors of Pokrovsky, cannot be viewed by the Sovnarkom and the CC but as evidence that anti-Marxist, anti-Leninist, essentially liquidationist, and anti-scientific conceptions of historical science have taken root among some of our historians and especially the historians of the U.S.S.R. The Sovnarkom and the CC of the VKP (B) emphasize that these injurious tendencies and attempts to liquidate history as a science are related above all to the propagation of the erroneous historical views typical of the so-called "historical school of Pokrovsky" among some of our historians. The Sovnarkom and the CC point out that the task of overcoming these injurious views is the necessary precondition for the preparation of textbooks in history as well as for the development of Marxist-Leninist historical science and the rise of history training in the U.S.S.R., which have a most important meaning for the cause of our country and party and for the education of the next generation.

In accordance with this the Sovnarkom of the U.S.S.R. and the CC of the VKP (B) have decreed the creation of a commission of the Sovnarkom and the CC for review, basic improvement, and, if needed, rewriting of the history textbooks already written. This commission has been given the right to set up teams for reviewing the individual textbooks as well as to announce a competition for the preparation of textbooks to replace those which might be found by the commission to need a radical rewriting. The Sovnarkom and the CC have also decreed the publication in the press of the observations of Comrades Stalin, Kirov, and Zhdanov and of other materials concerning this matter.

OBSERVATIONS CONCERNING THE OUTLINE OF THE TEXTBOOK IN THE HISTORY OF THE U.S.S.R.

The team of Vanag has not fulfilled the assignment and has even failed to understand the assignment. It has put together an outline of *Russian history* and not a *history* of the U.S.S.R., that is, a history of Russia but without the history of the peoples which went into the makeup of the U.S.S.R. . . .

The outline does not stress the annexationist and colonialist role of the Russian tsarism together with the Russian bourgeoisie and landowners ("Tsarism is the Prisonhouse of Peoples").

The outline does not stress the counterrevolutionary role of the Russian tsarism in foreign policy from the time of Catherine II to the 1850's and beyond ("Tsarism as an International Gendarme").

The outline reduces to one category feudalism and the prefeudal period when the peasants were still not bound to the soil, and also the autocratic system of government and the feudal system when Russia was dismembered into many independent pseudo-states.

The outline reduces to one category the concepts of reaction and counterrevolution, revolution "generally," bourgeois revolution, and bourgeois-democratic revolution.

The outline does not give the conditions and sources of the national liberation movement of the peoples of Russia subjugated by tsarism, and thus the October Revolution as a revolution freeing these peoples from national suppression remains unexplained as to motives, as also does the creation of the U.S.S.R.

The outline abounds in banal and trite definitions of all sorts concerning "police terror of Nicholas I," "Razinshchina" and "Pugachevshchina," "advance of the landlords' counterrevolution of the 1870's," "first advances of the industrial revolution," "first advances of tsarism and bourgeoisie in the struggle with the 1905–7 revolution," and so forth. The authors of the outline blindly copy the trite and absolutely unscientific definitions of bourgeois historians of all kinds, forgetting that they must teach our youth Marxist, scientifically grounded definitions.

The outline does not reflect the role and influence of the West European bourgeois-revolutionary and socialist movements in the formation of the bourgeois-revolutionary movement and the proletarian-socialist movement in Russia. The authors of the outline obviously have forgotten that the

Russian revolutionaries regarded themselves as disciples and followers of the noted leaders of bourgeois-revolutionary and Marxist thought in the West.

The outline does not take into account the roots of the first imperialist war and the role of tsarism in that war as a rearguard of the West European imperialist states; likewise no account is taken of the dependence of Russian tsarism as well as Russian capitalism upon West European capital, and as a result the significance of the October Revolution as the liberation of Russia from her semicolonial status remains unexplained as to motives.

The outline does not take into account the existence, before the World War, of a general European political crisis which expressed itself above all in the decline of bourgeois democracy and parliamentarianism, and as a result the significance of the Soviets in world history as bodies of proletarian democracy and agencies of the freeing of workers and peasants from capitalism remains unexplained as to motives.

The outline does not take into account the struggle of currents within the ruling Communist Party of the U.S.S.R. and the fight against Trotskyism as a manifestation of petty-bourgeois counterrevolution.

And so on and so forth.

It must be said in general that the outline has been put together in an extremely shoddy manner and is rather illiterate from the point of view of Marxism.

We regard as necessary the radical rewriting of the outline in the spirit of the positions stated above, the fact being taken into account that the assignment is to produce a *textbook* in which each word and each definition must be weighed, rather than to produce irresponsible journalistic writings in which one may babble about anything and in any way and disregard the sense of responsibility.

We need a textbook in the history of the U.S.S.R. in which, first, the history of Great Russia is not separated from the history of the other peoples of the U.S.S.R. and, second, the history of the peoples of the U.S.S.R. is not separated from general European and, indeed, world history.

I. Stalin
August 8, 1934   A. Zhdanov
S. Kirov

Observations Concerning the Outline of the Textbook in
Modern History

Owing to the fact that modern history is particularly rich in content and packed with events, and in view of the fact that, if one takes the period up to the October Revolution, the most important event in the history of bourgeois countries is the victory of the French Revolution and the consolidation of capitalism in Europe and America, we think that it would be best if the textbook in modern history opens with a chapter on the French Revolution. For connection with the preceding events it might contain a limited introduction with a brief exposition of the basic developments of the Dutch and English revolutions and leave the detailed exposition of the developments of the Dutch and English revolutions for the end of the textbook in medieval history.

As the principal shortcoming of the outline we regard the fact that it does not emphasize with sufficient sharpness the profound difference and contrast between the French (bourgeois) revolution and the October (socialist) revolution in Russia. The main axis of the textbook must be exactly this idea of the contrast between the bourgeois and socialist revolutions. To show that the French (and any foreign) bourgeois revolution, having freed the people of the chains of feudalism and absolutism, imposed on it new chains, the chains of capitalism and bourgeois democracy, whereas the socialist revolution in Russia destroyed any and all chains and freed the people of all forms of exploitation—this should be the red thread of the textbook in modern history.

Therefore, it should not be allowed that the French Revolution is simply called "great"; it should be called and treated as *bourgeois* revolution.

Similarly, our socialist revolution in Russia should not be called simply the October Revolution; it should be called and treated as a *socialist* and *soviet* revolution.

In accordance with this the outline of the textbook in modern history should be rewritten by choosing corresponding definitions and terms.

We regard the division of modern history in the outline into two parts as being inadequately explained as to reasons and fortuitous, produced by some unknown criterion. We would consider it better to divide modern history into three parts:

First part: from the French bourgeois revolution to the Franco-Prussian War and the Paris Commune (excluding the latter). This will be the period of the victory and consolidation of capitalism in the leading countries.

Second part: from the Franco-Prussian War and the Paris Commune to the victory of the October Revolution in Russia and the end of the imperialist war (inclusive of the latter). This will be the period of the beginning of the decline of capitalism, the first blow at capitalism by the Paris Commune, the transformation of the old "free" capitalism into imperialism, and the destruction of capitalism in the U.S.S.R. by the forces of the October Revolution, opening a new era in the history of mankind.

Third part: from the end of 1918 (end of the war) to the end of 1934.

This will be, on the one hand, the period of the postwar imperialism in the capitalist countries, economic and political crisis in these countries, and fascism and intensification of the struggle for colonies and spheres of influence, and, on the other hand, the period of civil war and intervention in the U.S.S.R., the first Five-Year Plan and the start of the second Five-Year Plan in the U.S.S.R., victorious building of socialism in our country, uprooting of the last survivals of capitalism, victory and rise of socialist industry in the U.S.S.R., victory of socialism in the countryside, and victory of the kolkhozes and sovkhozes on the other. We consider it a major error that the authors of the outline cut off history in 1923. This error must be corrected by bringing the history to the end of 1934. In accordance with this, it is necessary to make a reconstruction and reallocation of the material in the parts and chapters.

It would be well to free the outline of old, trite expressions such as "old regime," "new regime," etc. It would be better to replace them with "precapitalist regime" or, better yet, "absolutist-feudal regime"; instead of "new regime," use "regime of capitalism and bourgeois democracy." By such a change the so-called "new regime," that is, capitalist regime, will be seen as an *old* regime as compared with the Soviet regime in the U.S.S.R., which represents a higher type of organization of human society.

It would be well also to free the outline of the excessive abundance of "ages." "Age of the Consulate," "Age of Napoleon," "Age of the Directory"—are there not too many ages?

It appears to us wrong that the colonial question has received a disproportionately small space in the outline. While people like George Sand, Spengler, Kipling, etc., have been given ample attention, the colonial question and its status in a country like, let us say, China have received little attention.

It would also be well to replace the term "unification of Germany and Italy" with the term "reconsolidation of Germany and Italy as independent states." Otherwise the impression could be created that one refers not to the struggle for reconsolidation of such previously dismembered states as Germany and Italy, but to the unification of these states in one state.

In general, the outline in modern history in our opinion has been put together in a better way than the outline in the history of the U.S.S.R., but there is nevertheless plenty of confusion in it.

I. Stalin

August 9, 1934   S. Kirov

A. Zhdanov

The preparation of the new textbooks continued to proceed unsatisfactorily. The commission set up to judge the manuscripts announced in

1937 that it was unable to award the first prize, that the second prize went to a manuscript edited by Professor A. V. Shestakov, which was to be issued as the textbook for U.S.S.R. history in the third and fourth grades, and that encouragement prizes were awarded to the historians I. I. Mints, M. V. Nechkina, A. M. Pankratova, and three others. Among the shortcomings of the manuscripts submitted, the jury cited the tendency to regard the annexation of the Ukraine (1654) and Georgia (1801) by Russia as an absolute evil whereas it should more properly be seen as a relative and lesser evil compared with the alternative facing the Ukrainians and Georgians of being absorbed by Poland and Turkey, respectively.[15] All the required textbooks were eventually produced. Taken together, they became, with their emphases, selection of facts, and interpretations, an "essential historiographic document on the new stage" in the writing and teaching of history in the Soviet Union.[16]

The assassination of Kirov in December 1934 gave Stalin the opportunity (for which he was apparently waiting) [17] to begin a purge unprecedented in its design, savagery, and size. By 1938, when the purge reached its peak, the victims were millions from all walks of Soviet life: old-guard Bolsheviks, party functionaries, military leaders, bureaucrats, intellectuals, scholars, working people, purgers, and purgers of purgers. Party stalwarts like Bukharin, Rykov, Zinoviev, Kamenev, Radek, and Tomsky were classed as Trotskyists and "enemies of the people," and some were put through staged trials and shot.[18] Trotsky's response from abroad to these developments was to point out that the alleged Trotskyists had been Stalin's staunch allies in the Stalin-Trotsky struggle and to publish profuse evidence on the "Stalin school of falsification." The piece below is Trotsky's Foreword to the American edition of his *The Stalin School of Falsification* (New York, 1937).[19]

---

[15] *Pravda*, August 22, 1937. This is the origin of the "lesser evil" formula. In 1951 the idea was revived by M. V. Nechkina, who asked for an exchange of views on it. See *Voprosy istorii* [Problems of History], No. 4, 1951, pp. 44–48. At the Nineteenth Congress, in 1952, however, speakers rebuked *Voprosy istorii* for reopening the matter, and the delegate from Azerbaijan, M. D. Bagirov, complained that this had made the struggle with "bourgeois nationalism" in the minority areas more difficult. The new formula pressed by the party is that the annexations have been an "absolute good" for the peoples annexed. *Voprosy istorii*, No. 9, 1952, p. 11; see also Konstantin F. Shteppa, "The 'Lesser Evil' Formula," in Black, *op. cit.*, pp. 107–120, and Lowell R. Tillett, "Shamil and Muridism in Recent Soviet Historiography," *American Slavic and East European Review*, XX, No. 2 (April 1961), pp. 253–269.

[16] M. Nechkina, Iu. Poliakov, and L. Cherepnin. "Nekotorye voprosy istorii sovetskoi istoricheskoi nauki" [Certain Questions in the History of Soviet Historical Science], *Kommunist*, No. 9, 1961, pp. 58–70.

[17] See reading No. 32, Khrushchev's speech of 1956 on Stalin's crimes.

[18] For these developments, see Leonard Schapiro, *The Communist Party of the Soviet Union* (New York, 1960), pp. 399–434.

[19] For a bibliography of Trotsky's works see his three-volume biography by Isaac Deutscher, *The Prophet Armed, The Prophet Unarmed,* and *The Prophet Outcast* (New York and London, 1954–63). A comprehensive reconstruction of Trotsky's part in Bolshevik history, the biography extends to 1940, when Trotsky was murdered in

22. Foreword to L. Trotsky, The Stalin School of Falsification *

The Moscow trials, which so shocked the world, signify the death agony of Stalinism. A political regime constrained to use such methods is doomed. Depending upon external and internal circumstances, this agony may endure for a longer or shorter period of time. But no power in the world can any longer save Stalin and his system. The Soviet regime will either rid itself of the bureaucratic shell or be sucked into the abyss.

This volume does not deal with the Moscow trials, to which my new book, *The Crimes of Stalin,* is wholly devoted. The Moscow juridical amalgams did not, however, fall from the sky, but were the inexorable products of the past, first of all, that is, of the "Stalin school of falsification." The present volume will, I believe, prove of assistance to everyone who seeks to understand the ideological and political genesis of the Moscow trials. Without possessing the knowledge of its genesis, it is in general impossible to understand anything in this world, including a frame-up.

To enter now into a theoretical controversy with the Stalinists would be a complete anachronism. These people—and I have in mind of course the leaders and not the duped and befuddled followers—have completely and decisively broken with Marxism and are veering convulsively from one empirical formula to another, accommodating themselves to the needs of the Soviet ruling caste. But it remains an incontestable historical fact that the preparation of the bloody judicial frame-ups had its inception in the "minor" historical distortions and "innocent" falsification of citations. The bureaucracy found it indispensably necessary to adapt Bolshevism to its own needs. This could not be done otherwise than by corroding the soul of Bolshevism. To the revolutionary essence of Bolshevism the bureaucracy gave the name of "Trotskyism." Thus it created the spindle on which to wind in the future its falsifications in all the spheres of theory and practice.

In the political sphere, the initiative in this work—it is impermissible to slur over this in silence—was assumed by the deceased Zinoviev, the herald of the struggle against Trotskyism from 1923 to 1925. But already at the end of 1925, Zinoviev became frightened by the consequences of his own

Mexico in order to silence him. For a characterization of Trotsky as a historian see Bertram D. Wolfe, "Trotsky as Historian," *Slavic Review,* XX, No. 3 (October 1961), 495–502. See also Robert H. McNeal, "Trotsky's Interpretation of Stalin," *Canadian Slavonic Papers,* V (1961), 87–97.

* Reprinted by permission of Merit Publishers from L. Trotsky, *The Stalin School of Falsification.* New York: Pioneer Publishers, 1937.

initiative and came over to the ranks of the Opposition. What happened thereafter is only too well known. In the *economic* sphere, the theoretical weapons against Trotskyism were forged by Bukharin: "the underestimation of the peasantry," "super-industrialization," etc. The fate of Bukharin is no less well known: the official champion of pure Leninism was soon proclaimed a "bourgeois liberal," was later pardoned, and is now in jail awaiting trial.

The most prominent place in the struggle against "Trotskyism" was accorded to *historical questions*. These involved both the history of the development of Russia as a whole, as well as the history of the Bolshevik party and the October Revolution in particular. The deceased M. N. Pokrovsky must unquestionably be acknowledged as the most authoritative Soviet historian. For a number of years, he waged, with a vehemence peculiar to him, a struggle against my general views on the history of Russia and especially my conception of the October Revolution. Everything written by the other "communist" critics on this theme was merely a parroting of the ideas of Pokrovsky. While taking due cognizance of the erudition, conscientiousness, and talent of the deceased scholar, it is impermissible not to state that Pokrovsky failed to master the method of Marxism, and instead of providing an analysis of the continued interaction of all the elements in the historical process, he provided for each occasion mechanistic constructions *ad hoc,* without bothering about their dialectic interconnection. A few years ago such an appraisal sounded like blasphemy. Pokrovsky was the supreme authority of Soviet science. The reign of his school was absolute. His textbooks or the textbooks of his disciples circulated in millions of copies. Shortly before his death, he was idolized as the lawgiver in the domain of scientific thought. But already in 1935, steps were taken suddenly and all the more drastically to review his heritage. In the course of a few months, Pokrovsky was completely cashiered, crushed, and discredited. He probably escaped the prisoner's dock only by his timely demise. It would naturally be absurd to expect that Pokrovsky's school has been liquidated in the interests of Marxism. No, Pokrovsky is accused of lacking patriotism, of irreverence toward Russia's past, of lacking national pride!

In what did Stalin's own theoretical work express itself? In nothing. All he did was to exploit his fellow-traveler theorists, in the interests of the new ruling caste. He will enter into the annals of the history of "thought" only as the organizer of the greatest school of falsification. But for this very reason Stalin, more truly and completely than anybody else, expresses the ideological physiognomy of the new ruling stratum. Each theoretical formula of anti-Trotskyism (whether it involved Zinoviev, Bukharin, or Pokrovsky) became at the very next stage an intolerable burden to the new masters of the situation. Official "theory" is today transformed into a blank sheet of paper on which the unfortunate theoreticians reverently trace the contours of the Stalinist boot. Retreating with seven-league strides from its Bolshevik past, the bureaucracy at first devoured at each successive stage its own theoreticians. Nowadays that is no longer adequate. The bureaucracy cannot be reconciled with anything but the destruction of the entire old generation of Bolsheviks. Such is the consummation of the Soviet Thermidor!

*   *   *

This volume contains no little material for the political characterization of the four most prominent men in the last two Moscow trials: Zinoviev-Kamenev, on the one hand; Radek-Piatakov, on the other. The previous aberrations in politics and theory of both these couples act to facilitate in the extreme the understanding of their conduct in court, just as, on the other hand, the judicial trials cast a livid light on the preceding zigzags of these unfortunate victims of the GPU.

Zinoviev and Kamenev were the initiators of the struggle against me in 1923. Piatakov and Radek—the former by three-quarters, the latter by half —stood in the camp of the Opposition. In 1926, Zinoviev and Kamenev joined the Opposition; at the same time, Radek and Piatakov became stauncher in their oppositional credo. In November 1927, Zinoviev and Kamenev turned to the path of capitulation. They were followed first by Piatakov, and then by Radek.

The specter of Trotskyism was first pushed forward by the "triumvirate" (Zinoviev, Kamenev, and Stalin) in 1924. In 1926, Zinoviev, at a meeting of the Opposition center, told how the "triumvirate" had decided to revive artificially the old, prerevolutionary, long-forgotten differences between Lenin and myself in order, by using the specter of Trotskyism as a cover, to wage a struggle against Trotsky. This story of Zinoviev is corroborated by the letters of Radek (December 25, 1927) and Piatakov (January 2, 1928) which the reader will find in this volume. Both these letters were written in the days when Zinoviev and Kamenev, to justify their capitulation, were once again pushing forward the specter of Trotskyism which they themselves had already exposed, while Radek and Piatakov were still seeking to maintain their old positions. But in the course of the very next year, Piatakov and after him Radek, too, found themselves compelled to resort to the official legend of Trotskyism, so as to prepare and justify their own capitulation. In these instances of ideological demoralization was reflected the growing social pressure of the bureaucracy.

The old accusations ("permanent revolution," "underestimation of the peasantry," etc.) proved altogether inadequate for the purpose of crushing the Opposition and, later, of rooting it out physically. There ensued an epoch of criminal amalgams, at first petty and partial, and later ever more monstrous. The series of recantations of Zinoviev-Kamenev, growing in geometric progression, brought them in August 1936 to the prisoner's dock, charged with the assassination of Kirov, i.e., a crime with which they certainly had less connection than Stalin himself. In the days of the trial of Zinoviev and Kamenev, Radek and Piatakov rushed into print with exceptionally revolting articles in which, pretending a belief in the indictment, they demanded death for the accused. But soon thereafter, both of them found themselves in the prisoner's dock and were compelled to make confessions infinitely surpassing in monstrosity the fictitious crimes of Zinoviev-Kamenev. Conclusion? To play tricks with history is impermissible, especially in an epoch of great shocks and convulsions.

*   *   *

But how can one believe—naïve people will say—that Stalin was capable of such a frightful frame-up, that he was able to find for this frame-up a staff of executives, including the accused themselves, and did not, at the same time, meet with any resistance either on the part of his closest associates or in the judicial apparatus? Only those can be astonished by it who were asleep during the preceding evolution of the U.S.S.R. The process of handpicking and training the apparatus in the spirit of the Stalin school of falsification has already endured for fourteen years. Even though in fragmentary form, this book contains numerous authentic documents which serve to characterize the different stages of the subjugation of the party, the corruption of the apparatus, and the poisoning of the conscience of the ruling stratum, in the name of a "monolithism" that is false through and through. The innumerable theoretical forgeries and historical frame-ups, referred to in these pages, represent in essence nothing but a series of designs and sketches for those hellish frescoes with which Stalin has shocked the conscience of the entire world. Control Commissions, as far back as 1924, got used to demanding false confessions from former Oppositionists. Emulating Zinoviev, Kamenev, Radek, and Piatakov, many thousands of capitulators got used to issuing false statements. The papers carried articles dealing with these statements, which neither the authors nor the informed readers believed in for an instant. In each new edition of Lenin's *Collected Works,* the notes were subjected to a drastic revision : the minuses were replaced by pluses, the pluses by minuses. In encyclopedias and other reference books, the biographies were made over anew every year or so and events were delineated in a new manner—for the sake of exalting some while demoting others. Thousands of writers, historians, and economists in the U.S.S.R. write by command what they do not believe. Professors in universities and schoolteachers are compelled to change written textbooks in a hurry in order to accommodate themselves to the successive stage of the official lie. The spirit of the Inquisition thoroughly impregnating the atmosphere of the country feeds, as we have already said, from profound social sources. To justify their privileges the ruling caste perverts the theory which has as its aim the elimination of all privileges. The lie serves, therefore, as the fundamental ideological cement of the bureaucracy. The more irreconcilable becomes the contradiction between the bureaucracy and the people, all the ruder becomes the lie, all the more brazenly is it converted into criminal falsification and judicial frame-up. Whoever has not understood this inner dialectic of the Stalinist regime will likewise fail to understand the Moscow trials.

The death agony of Stalinism signifies the death agony of the Comintern. This international organization is now the main internal obstacle in the path of the emancipation of the working class. The selection of people without honor and without conscience has reached the same appalling proportions in the Comintern as in the state apparatus of the U.S.S.R. The "leaders" by special appointment change their "convictions" upon instructions by telegraph. They organize campaigns of vilification against Zinoviev who used to be their infallible authority, against Bukharin whom they used to acclaim as their leader, against Radek whom only yesterday they reverently cited in the struggle against Trotskyism. The functionaries of the Comintern represent in all relations—theoretical, political, and moral—a type which is the polar opposite of the revolutionist. They hang on to Stalin, who in turn needs them for the maintenance of his tyranny in the U.S.S.R. The Moscow trials reveal to the very bottom the inner rottenness of the Comintern. After an initial period of bewilderment and vacillation, its swift disintegration is inevitable. It may take place much sooner than the collapse of the Stalinist system in the Soviet Union. The Second International has contrived in a number of countries to establish intimate connections with the Comintern in the period of its complete degeneration. The collapse of the Comintern must inevitably deal a cruel blow to the social democracy. But this does not mean that the world proletariat will be left without leadership. At the cost of terrible defeats and sacrifices, the main responsibility for which falls upon the Soviet bureaucracy, the proletarian vanguard will find its historic road. Ever more confidently will it rally its ranks under the banner of the Fourth International, which is already rising today on the shoulders of its predecessors.

Once again, as after the elimination of Trotsky, Stalin's triumph necessitated the rewriting of the history books of the land in order to eliminate the purged "enemies of the people" from public memory and tell the confused people what the past really was. The first step in this new "Operation Palimpsest" was the publication of a new version of the history of the party authenticated by Stalin and the new Central Committee he put together while the purge was decimating the old one. The concise *History of the Communist Party of the Soviet Union (Bolsheviks)—Short Course,* issued in October 1938, was officially billed as "edited by a commission of the Central Committee" and "authorized by the CC of the CPSU (B), 1938," and was intended as the handbook of official truth in party and regime history as well as of official interpretation of Marxism-Leninism. For this reason Stalin personally wrote the theoretical section of Chapter IV on "Dialectical and Historical Materialism." [20]

The *Short Course,* as the new party history came to be universally known, was immediately propagandized as the product of Stalin's genius and the "greatest repository of Marxism-Leninism." Eventually issued in more than forty million copies and in many languages, it was the tool with which Stalin's version of the recent past and notions of doctrinal orthodoxy were enforced while he was alive.[21] A unique document on Stalin's rule, it should be read in its entirety. The excerpts below are from the English edition published in Moscow in 1951.

---

[20] While Stalin's authorship of the theoretical section is beyond dispute, the authorship of the rest of the *Short Course* has been a matter of conjecture and controversy. Stalin's official "Short Biography" published in 1939 stated that the *Short Course* was compiled by the commission "working under Stalin's guidance and with his active assistance." Writing in 1942, Pankratova indicated that the specialist in party history, E. M. Iaroslavsky, "was one of the basic authors and one of the editors of the *Short Course* . . . written under the direction of Comrade Stalin" (see Reading No. 27). The second "corrected and expanded" edition of the "Short Biography" issued in 1947, however, stated that the *Short Course* was "written by Comrade Stalin and approved by a commission of the CC of the VKP (B)." Judging from the gnomic style of the *Short Course,* which is the same as the style of the theoretical section and which was characteristic of everything Stalin personally wrote, it would appear that Stalin's mind fashioned the whole work and that Iaroslavsky was only his amanuensis. However, in his exposé of Stalin's crimes in 1956, Khrushchev charged that Stalin claimed as his own "the work created by a group." See *Joseph Stalin: A Short Biography* (New York, 1941), p. 85; *Joseph Stalin: A Political Biography* (New York, 1949), p. 87; and Gustav Wetter, *Dialectical Materialism* (London, 1958), p. 180, note 1.

[21] The *Short Course* was reissued as late as 1955, but fell into disuse after Khrushchev's destalinization campaign in 1956. It was superseded in 1959 by a new official version edited by B. N. Ponomarev and entitled *Istoriia Kommunisticheskoi Partii Sovetskogo Soiuza* (also available in an English edition, *History of the Communist Party of the Soviet Union*). For an appraisal see L. Schapiro's review in *Problems of Communism,* IX, No. 1 (January–February 1960) pp. 58–61, and Panas Fedenko, *Khrushchev's New History of the Soviet Communist Party* (Munich, 1963). The confusion of the interim period between the two versions of the party history is reflected in *Materialy vsesoiuznogo soveshchaniia zaveduiushchikh kafedrami obshchestvennykh nauk* [Materials of the All-Union Conference of Holders of Chairs in the Social Sciences] (Moscow, 1958).

23. Chapter IV, Section 2, "Dialectical and Historical Materialism," History of the Communist Party of the Soviet Union (Bolsheviks)—Short Course

Dialectical materialism is the world outlook of the Marxist-Leninist party. It is called dialectical materialism because its approach to the phenomena of nature, its method of studying and apprehending them, is *dialectical,* while its interpretation of the phenomena of nature, its conception of these phenomena, its theory, is *materialistic.*

Historical materialism is the extension of the principles of dialectical materialism to the study of social life, an application of the principles of dialectical materialism to the phenomena of the life of society, to the study of society and of its history.

When describing their dialectical method, Marx and Engels usually refer to Hegel as the philosopher who formulated the main features of dialectics. This, however, does not mean that the dialectics of Marx and Engels is identical with the dialectics of Hegel. As a matter of fact, Marx and Engels took from the Hegelian dialectics only its "rational kernel," casting aside its Hegelian idealistic shell, and developed dialectics further so as to lend it a modern scientific form.

> "My dialectic method," says Marx, "is not only different from the Hegelian, but is its direct opposite. To Hegel . . . the process of thinking, which, under the name of 'the Idea' he even transforms into an independent subject, is the demiurgos (creator) of the real world, and the real world is only the external, phenomenal, form of 'the Idea.' With me, on the contrary, the ideal is nothing else than the material world reflected by the human mind, and translated into forms of thought." (*Capital,* Vol. 1, p. xxx, George Allen & Unwin Ltd., 1938.)

When describing their materialism, Marx and Engels usually refer to Feuerbach as the philosopher who restored materialism to its rights. This, however, does not mean that the materialism of Marx and Engels is identical with Feuerbach's materialism. As a matter of fact, Marx and Engels took from Feuerbach's materialism its "inner kernel," developed it into a scientific-philosophical theory of materialism and cast aside its idealistic and religious-ethical encumbrances. We know that Feuerbach, although he was fundamentally a materialist, objected to the name materialism. Engels more than once declared that "in spite of the [materialist] foundation," Feuerbach "remained . . . bound by the traditional idealist fetters," and that "the real idealism of Feuerbach becomes evident as soon as we come to his philosophy of religion and ethics." (Karl Marx, *Selected Works*, Eng. ed., Moscow, 1946, Vol. 1, pp. 373, 375.)

Dialectics comes from the Greek *dialego*, to discourse, to debate. In ancient times dialectics was the art of arriving at the truth by disclosing the contradictions in the argument of an opponent and overcoming these contradictions. There were philosophers in ancient times who believed that the disclosure of contradictions in thought and the clash of opposite opinions was the best method of arriving at the truth. This dialectical method of thought, later extended to the phenomena of nature, developed into the dialectical method of apprehending nature, which regards the phenomena of nature as being in constant movement and undergoing constant change, and the development of nature as the result of the development of the contradictions in nature, as the result of the interaction of opposed forces in nature.

In its essence, dialectics is the direct opposite of metaphysics.

1) The principal features of the *Marxist dialectical method* are as follows:

a) Contrary to metaphysics, dialectics does not regard nature as an accidental agglomeration of things, of phenomena, unconnected with, isolated from, and independent of, each other, but as a connected and integral whole, in which things, phenomena, are organically connected with, dependent on, and determined by, each other.

The dialectical method therefore holds that no phenomenon in nature can be understood if taken by itself, isolated from surrounding phenomena, inasmuch as any phenomenon in any realm of nature may become meaningless to us if it is not considered in connection with the surrounding conditions, but divorced from them; and that, vice versa, any phenomenon can be understood and explained if considered in its inseparable connection with surrounding phenomena, as one conditioned by surrounding phenomena.

b) Contrary to metaphysics, dialectics holds that nature is not a state of rest and immobility, stagnation and immutability, but a state of continuous movement and change, of continuous renewal and development, where something is always arising and developing, and something always disintegrating and dying away.

The dialectical method therefore requires that phenomena should be considered not only from the standpoint of their interconnection and interdependence, but also from the standpoint of their movement, their change, their development, their coming into being and going out of being.

The dialectical method regards as important primarily not that which at the given moment seems to be durable and yet is already beginning to die away, but that which is arising and developing, even though at the given moment it may appear to be not durable, for the dialectical method considers invincible only that which is arising and developing.

"All nature," says Engels, "from the smallest thing to the biggest, from a grain of sand to the sun, from the Protista to man, is in a constant state of coming into being and going out of being, in a constant flux, in a ceaseless state of movement and change." (F. Engels, *Dialectics of Nature.*)

Therefore, dialectics, Engels says, "takes things and their perceptual images essentially in their interconnection, in their concatenation, in their movement, in their rise and disappearance." (F. Engels, *Anti-Dühring.*)

c) Contrary to metaphysics, dialectics does not regard the process of development as a simple process of growth, where quantitative changes do not lead to qualitative changes, but as a development which passes from insignificant and imperceptible quantitative changes to open, fundamental changes, to qualitative changes; a development in which the qualitative changes occur not gradually, but rapidly and abruptly, taking the form of a leap from one state to another; they occur not accidentally but as the natural result of an accumulation of imperceptible and gradual quantitative changes.

The dialectical method therefore holds that the process of development should be understood not as movement in a circle, not as a simple repetition of what has already occurred, but as an onward and upward movement, as a transition from an old qualitative state to a new qualitative state, as a development from the simple to the complex, from the lower to the higher:

"Nature," says Engels, "is the test of dialectics, and it must be said for modern natural science that it has furnished extremely rich and daily increasing materials for this test, and has thus proved that in the last analysis nature's process is dialectical and not metaphysical, that it does not move in an eternally uniform and constantly repeated circle, but passes through a real history. Here prime mention should be made of Darwin, who dealt a severe blow to the metaphysical conception of nature by proving that the organic world of today, plants and animals, and consequently man too, is all a product of a process of development that has been in progress for millions of years." (*Anti-Dühring.*)

d) Contrary to metaphysics, dialectics holds that internal contradictions are inherent in all things and phenomena of nature, for they all have their negative and positive sides, a past and a future, something dying away and something developing; and that the struggle between these opposites, the struggle between the old and the new, between that which is dying away and that which is being born, between that which is disappearing and that which is developing, constitutes the internal content of the process of development, the internal content of the transformation of quantitative changes into qualitative changes.

The dialectical method therefore holds that the process of development from the lower to the higher takes place not as a harmonious unfolding of phenomena, but as a disclosure of the contradictions inherent in things and phenomena, as a "struggle" of opposite tendencies which operate on the basis of these contradictions.

"In its proper meaning," Lenin says, "dialectics is the study of the contradiction *within the very essence of things.*" (Lenin, *Philosophical Notebooks,* p. 263.)

And further:

"Development is the 'struggle' of opposites." (Lenin, *Collected Works,* Vol. 13, p. 301.)

Such, in brief, are the principal features of the Marxist dialectical method.

It is easy to understand how immensely important is the extension of the principles of the dialectical method to the study of social life and the history of society, and how immensely important is the application of these principles to the history of society and to the practical activities of the party of the proletariat.

If there are no isolated phenomena in the world, if all phenomena are interconnected and interdependent, then it is clear that every social system and every social movement in history must be evaluated not from the standpoint of "eternal justice" or some other preconceived idea, as is not infrequently done by historians, but from the standpoint of the conditions which gave rise to that system or that social movement and with which they are connected.

The slave system would be senseless, stupid, and unnatural under modern conditions. But under the conditions of a disintegrating primitive communal system, the slave system is a quite understandable and natural phenomenon, since it represents an advance on the primitive communal system.

The demand for a bourgeois-democratic republic when tsardom and bourgeois society existed, as, let us say, in Russia in 1905, was a quite understandable, proper, and revolutionary demand, for at that time a bourgeois republic would have meant a step forward. But now, under the conditions of the U.S.S.R., the demand for a bourgeois-democratic republic would be a senseless and counterrevolutionary demand, for a bourgeois republic would be a retrograde step compared with the Soviet republic.

Everything depends on the conditions, time and place.

It is clear that without such a *historical* approach to social phenomena, the existence and development of the science of history is impossible, for only such an approach saves the science of history from becoming a jumble of accidents and an agglomeration of most absurd mistakes.

Further, if the world is in a state of constant movement and development, if the dying away of the old and the upgrowth of the new is a law of development, then it is clear that there can be no "immutable" social systems, no "eternal principles" of private property and exploitation, no "eternal ideas" of the subjugation of the peasant to the landlord, of the worker to the capitalist.

Hence, the capitalist system can be replaced by the Socialist system, just as at one time the feudal system was replaced by the capitalist system.

Hence, we must not base our orientation on the strata of society which are no longer developing, even though they at present constitute the predominant force, but on those strata which are developing and have a future before them, even though they at present do not constitute the predominant force.

In the eighties of the past century, in the period of the struggle between the Marxists and the Narodniks, the proletariat in Russia constituted an insignificant minority of the population, whereas the individual peasants constituted the vast majority of the population. But the proletariat was developing as a class, whereas the peasantry as a class was disintegrating. And just because the proletariat was developing as a class the Marxists based their orientation on the proletariat. And they were not mistaken, for, as we know, the proletariat subsequently grew from an insignificant force into a first-rate historical and political force.

Hence, in order not to err in policy, one must look forward, not backward.

Further, if the passing of slow quantitative changes into rapid and abrupt qualitative changes is a law of development, then it is clear that revolutions made by oppressed classes are a quite natural and inevitable phenomenon.

Hence, the transition from capitalism to Socialism and the liberation of the working class from the yoke of capitalism cannot be effected by slow changes, by reforms, but only by a qualitative change of the capitalist system, by revolution.

Hence, in order not to err in policy, one must be a revolutionary, not a reformist.

Further, if development proceeds by way of the disclosure of internal contradictions, by way of collisions between opposite forces on the basis of these contradictions and so as to overcome these contradictions, then it is clear that the class struggle of the proletariat is a quite natural and inevitable phenomenon.

Hence, we must not cover up the contradictions of the capitalist system, but disclose and unravel them; we must not try to check the class struggle but carry it to its conclusion.

Hence, in order not to err in policy, one must pursue an uncompromising proletarian class policy, not a reformist policy of harmony of the interests of the proletariat and the bourgeoisie, not a compromisers' policy of "the growing of capitalism into Socialism."

Such is the Marxist dialectical method when applied to social life, to the history of society.

2) It is easy to understand how immensely important is the extension of the principles of philosophical materialism to the study of social life, of the history of society, and how immensely important is the application of these principles to the history of society and to the practical activities of the party of the proletariat.

If the connection between the phenomena of nature and their interdependence are laws of the development of nature, it follows, too, that the connection and interdependence of the phenomena of social life are laws of the development of society, and not something accidental.

Hence, social life, the history of society, ceases to be an agglomeration of "accidents," and becomes the history of the development of society according to regular laws, and the study of the history of society becomes a science.

Hence, the practical activity of the party of the proletariat must not be based on the good wishes of "outstanding individuals," not on the dictates of "reason," "universal morals," etc., but on the laws of development of society and on the study of these laws.

Further, if the world is knowable and our knowledge of the laws of development of nature is authentic knowledge, having the validity of objective truth, it follows that social life, the development of society, is also knowable, and that the data of science regarding the laws of development of society are authentic data having the validity of objective truths.

Hence, the science of the history of society, despite all the complexity of the phenomena of social life, can become as precise a science as, let us say, biology, and capable of making use of the laws of development of society for practical purposes.

Hence, the party of the proletariat should not guide itself in its practical activity by casual motives, but by the laws of development of society, and by practical deductions from these laws.

Hence, Socialism is converted from a dream of a better future for humanity into a science.

Hence, the bond between science and practical activity, between theory and practice, their unity, should be the guiding star of the party of the proletariat.

Further, if nature, being, the material world, is primary, and consciousness, thought, is secondary, derivative; if the material world represents objective reality existing independently of the consciousness of men, while consciousness is a reflection of this objective reality, it follows that the material life of society, its being, is also primary, and its spiritual life secondary, derivative, and that the material life of society is an objective reality existing independently of the will of men, while the spiritual life of society is a reflection of this objective reality, a reflection of being.

Hence, the source of formation of the spiritual life of society, the origin of social ideas, social theories, political views, and political institutions, should not be sought for in the ideas, theories, views, and political institutions themselves, but in the conditions of the material life of society, in social being, of which these ideas, theories, views, etc., are the reflection.

Hence, if in different periods of the history of society different social ideas, theories, views, and political institutions are to be observed; if under the slave system we encounter certain social ideas, theories, views, and political institutions, under feudalism others, and under capitalism others still, this is not to be explained by the "nature," the "properties," of the ideas, theories, views, and political institutions themselves but by the different conditions of the material life of society at different periods of social development.

Whatever is the being of a society, whatever are the conditions of material life of a society, such are the ideas, theories, political views, and political institutions of that society.

In this connection, Marx says:

> "It is not the consciousness of men that determines their being, but, on the contrary, their social being that determines their consciousness." (*Selected Works,* Eng. ed., Moscow, 1946, Vol. 1, p. 300.)

Hence, in order not to err in policy, in order not to find itself in the position of idle dreamers, the party of the proletariat must not base its activities on abstract "principles of human reason," but on the concrete conditions of the material life of society, as the determining force of social development; not on the good wishes of "great men," but on the real needs of development of the material life of society.

The fall of the utopians, including the Narodniks, Anarchists, and Socialist-Revolutionaires, was due, among other things, to the fact that they did not recognize the primary role which the conditions of the material life of society play in the development of society, and, sinking to idealism, did not base their practical activities on the needs of the development of the material life of society, but, independently of and in spite of these needs, on "ideal plans" and "all-embracing projects" divorced from the real life of society.

The strength and vitality of Marxism-Leninism lies in the fact that it does base its practical activity on the needs of the development of the material life of society and never divorces itself from the real life of society.

It does not follow from Marx's words, however, that social ideas, theories, political views, and political institutions are of no significance in the life of society, that they do not reciprocally affect social being, the development of the material conditions of the life of society. We have been speaking so far of the *origin* of social ideas, theories, views, and political institutions, of *the way they arise,* of the fact that the spiritual life of society is a reflection of the conditions of its material life. As regards the *significance* of social ideas, theories, views, and political institutions, as regards their *role* in history, historical materialism, far from denying them, stresses the important role and significance of these factors in the life of society, in its history.

There are different kinds of social ideas and theories. There are old ideas and theories which have outlived their day and which serve the interests of the moribund forces of society. Their significance lies in the fact that they hamper the development, the progress, of society. Then there are new and advanced ideas and theories which serve the interests of the advanced forces of society. Their significance lies in the fact that they facilitate the development, the progress, of society; and their significance is the greater, the more accurately they reflect the needs of development of the material life of society.

New social ideas and theories arise only after the development of the material life of society has set new tasks before society. But, once they have arisen, they become a most potent force, which facilitates the carrying out of the new tasks set by the development of the material life of society, a force which facilitates the progress of society. It is precisely here that the tremendous organizing, mobilizing, and transforming value of new ideas, new theories, new political views, and new political institutions manifests itself. New social ideas and theories arise precisely because they are necessary to society, because it is *impossible* to carry out the urgent tasks of development of the material life of society without their organizing, mobilizing, and transforming action. Arising out of the new tasks set by the development of the material life of society, the new social ideas and theories force their way through, become the possession of the masses, mobilize and organize them against the moribund forces of society, and thus facilitate the overthrow of these forces, which hamper the development of the material life of society.

Thus social ideas, theories, and political institutions, having arisen on the basis of the urgent tasks of the development of the material life of society, the development of social being, themselves then react upon social being, upon the material life of society, creating the conditions necessary for completely carrying out the urgent tasks of the material life of society, and for rendering its further development possible.

In this connection, Marx says:

"Theory becomes a material force as soon as it has gripped the masses." (*Zur Kritik der Hegelschen Rechtsphilosophie.*)

Hence, in order to be able to influence the conditions of material life of society and to accelerate their development and their improvement, the party of the proletariat must rely upon such a social theory, such a social idea, as correctly reflects the needs of development of the material life of society, and which is therefore capable of setting into motion broad masses of the people and of mobilizing them and organizing them into a great army of the proletarian party, prepared to smash the reactionary forces and to clear the way for the advanced forces of society.

The fall of the "Economists" and Mensheviks was due among other things to the fact that they did not recognize the mobilizing, organizing, and transforming role of advanced theory, of advanced ideas and, sinking to vulgar materialism, reduced the role of these factors almost to nothing, thus condemning the Party to passivity and inanition.

The strength and vitality of Marxism-Leninism is derived from the fact that it relies upon an advanced theory which correctly reflects the needs of development of the material life of society, that it elevates theory to a proper level, and that it deems it its duty to utilize every ounce of the mobilizing, organizing, and transforming power of this theory.

That is the answer historical materialism gives to the question of the relation between social being and social consciousness, between the conditions of development of material life and the development of the spiritual life of society.

3) *Historical Materialism*

It now remains to elucidate the following question: what, from the viewpoint of historical materialism, is meant by the "conditions of material life of society" which in the final analysis determine the physiognomy of society, its ideas, views, political institutions, etc.?

What, after all, are these "conditions of material life of society," what are their distingishing features?

There can be no doubt that the concept "conditions of material life of society" includes, first of all, nature which surrounds society, geographical environment, which is one of the indispensable and constant conditions of material life of society and which, of course, influences the development of society. What role does geographical environment play in the development of society? Is geographical environment the chief force determining the physiognomy of society, the character of the social system of man, the transition from one system to another?

Historical materialism answers this question in the negative.

Geographical environment is unquestionably one of the constant and indispensable conditions of development of society and, of course, influences the development of society, accelerates or retards its development. But its influence is not the *determining* influence, inasmuch as the changes and development of society proceed at an incomparably faster rate than the changes and development of geographical environment. In the space of three thousand years three different social systems have been successively superseded in Europe: the primitive communal system, the slave system, and the feudal system. In the eastern part of Europe, in the U.S.S.R., even four social systems have been superseded. Yet during this period geographical conditions in Europe have either not changed at all, or have changed so slightly that geography takes no note of them. And that is quite natural. Changes in geographical environment of any importance require millions of years, whereas a few hundred or a couple of thousand years are enough for even very important changes in the system of human society.

It follows from this that geographical environment cannot be the chief cause, the *determining* cause of social development, for that which remains almost unchanged in the course of tens of thousands of years cannot be the chief cause of development of that which undergoes fundamental changes in the course of a few hundred years.

Further, there can be no doubt that the concept "conditions of material life of society" also includes growth of population, density of population of one degree or another, for people are an essential element of the conditions of material life of society, and without a definite minimum number of people there can be no material life of society. Is not growth of population the chief force that determines the character of the social system of man?

Historical materialism answers this question too in the negative.

Of course, growth of population does influence the development of society, does facilitate or retard the development of society, but it cannot be the chief force of development of society, and its influence on the development of society cannot be the *determining* influence because, by itself, growth of population does not furnish the clue to the question why a given social system is replaced precisely by such and such a new system and not by another, why the primitive communal system is succeeded precisely by the slave system, the slave system by the feudal system, and the feudal system by the bourgeois system, and not by some other.

If growth of population were the determining force of social development, then a higher density of population would be bound to give rise to a correspondingly higher type of social system. But we do not find this to be the case. The density of population in China is four times as great as in the U.S.A., yet the U.S.A. stands higher than China in the scale of social development, for in China a semifeudal system still prevails, whereas the U.S.A. has long ago reached the highest stage of development of capitalism. The density of population in Belgium is 19 times as great as in the U.S.A., and 26 times as great as in the U.S.S.R. Yet the U.S.A. stands higher than Belgium in the scale of social development; and as for the U.S.S.R., Belgium lags a whole historical epoch behind this country, for in Belgium the capitalist system prevails, whereas the U.S.S.R. has already done away with capitalism and has set up a Socialist system.

It follows from this that growth of population is not, and cannot be, the chief force of development of society, the force which *determines* the character of the social system, the physiognomy of society.

a) What, then, is the chief force in the complex of conditions of material life of society which determines the physiognomy of society, the character of the social system, the development of society from one system to another?

This force, historical materialism holds, is the *method of procuring the means of life* necessary for human existence, the *mode of production of material values*—food, clothing, footwear, houses, fuel, instruments of production, etc.—which are indispensable for the life and development of society.

In order to live, people must have food, clothing, footwear, shelter, fuel, etc.; in order to have these material values, people must produce them; and in order to produce them, people must have the instruments of production with which food, clothing, footwear, shelter, fuel, etc., are produced; they must be able to produce these instruments and to use them.

The *instruments of production* wherewith material values are produced, the *people* who operate the instruments of production and carry on the production of material values thanks to a certain *production experience* and *labor skill*—all these elements jointly constitute the *productive forces* of society.

But the productive forces are only one aspect of production, only one aspect of the mode of production, an aspect that expresses the relation of men to the objects and forces of nature which they make use of for the production of material values. Another aspect of production, another aspect of the mode of production, is the relation of men to each other in the process of production, men's *relations of production*. Men carry on a struggle against nature and utilize nature for the production of material values not in isolation from each other, not as separate individuals, but in common, in groups, in societies. Production, therefore, is at all times and under all conditions *social* production. In the production of material values men enter into mutual relations of one kind or another within production, into relations of production of one kind or another. These may be relations of cooperation and mutual help between people who are free from exploitation; they may be relations of domination and subordination; and, lastly, they may be transitional from one form of relations of production to another. But whatever the character of the relations of production may be, always and in every system, they constitute just as essential an element of production as the productive forces of society.

Here is a rough picture of the development of productive forces from ancient times to our day. The transition from crude stone tools to the bow and arrow, and the accompanying transition from the life of hunters to the domestication of animals and primitive pasturage; the transition from stone tools to metal tools (the iron axe, the wooden plow fitted with an iron colter, etc.), with a corresponding transition to tillage and agriculture; a further improvement in metal tools for the working up of materials, the introduction of the blacksmith's bellows, the introduction of pottery, with a corresponding development of handicrafts, the separation of handicrafts from agriculture, the development of an independent handicraft industry and, subsequently, of manufacture; the transition from handicraft tools to machines and the transformation of handicraft and manufacture into machine industry; the transition to the machine system and the rise of modern large-scale machine industry—such is a general and far from complete picture of the development of the productive forces of society in the course of man's history. It will be clear that the development and improvement of the instruments of production was effected by men who were related to production, and not independently of men; and, consequently, the change and development of the instruments of production was accompanied by a change and development of men, as the most important element of the productive forces, by a change and development of their productive experience, their labor skill, their ability to handle the instruments of production.

In conformity with the change and development of the productive forces of society in the course of history, men's relations of production, their economic relations also changed and developed.

Five *main* types of relations of production are known to history: primitive communal, slave, feudal, capitalist, and Socialist.

The basis of the relations of production under the primitive communal system is that the means of production are socially owned. This in the main corresponds to the character of the productive forces of that period. Stone tools, and, later, the bow and arrow, precluded the possibility of men individually combating the forces of nature and beasts of prey. In order to gather the fruits of the forest, to catch fish, to build some sort of habitation, men were obliged to work in common if they did not want to die of starvation, or fall victim to beasts of prey or to neighboring societies. Labor in common led to the common ownership of the means of production, as well as of the fruits of production. Here the conception of private ownership of the means of production did not yet exist, except for the personal ownership of certain implements of production which were at the same time means of defense aganst beasts of prey. Here there was no exploitation, no classes.

The basis of the relations of production under the slave system is that the slaveowner owns the means of production; he also owns the worker in production—the slave, whom he can sell, purchase, or kill as though he were an animal. Such relations of production in the main correspond to the state of the productive forces of that period. Instead of stone tools, men now have metal tools at their command; instead of the wretched and primitive husbandry of the hunter, who knew neither pasturage nor tillage, there now appear pasturage, tillage, handicrafts, and a division of labor between these branches of production. There appears the possibility of the exchange of products between individuals and between societies, of the accumulation of wealth in the hands of a few, the actual accumulation of the means of production in the hands of a minority, and the possibility of subjugation of the majority by a minority and the conversion of the majority into slaves. Here we no longer find the common and free labor of all members of society in the production process—here there prevails the forced labor of slaves, who are exploited by the nonlaboring slaveowners. Here, therefore, there is no common ownership of the means of production or of the fruits of production. It is replaced by private ownership. Here the slaveowner appears as the prime and principal property owner in the full sense of the term.

Rich and poor, exploiters and exploited, people with full rights and people with no rights, and a fierce class struggle between them—such is the picture of the slave system.

The basis of the relations of production under the feudal system is that the feudal lord owns the means of production and does not fully own the worker in production—the serf, whom the feudal lord can no longer kill, but whom he can buy and sell. Alongside of feudal ownership there exists individual ownership by the peasant and the handicraftsman of his implements of production and his private enterprise based on his personal labor. Such relations of production in the main correspond to the state of the productive forces of that period. Further improvements in the smelting and working of iron; the spread of the iron plow and the loom; the further development of agriculture, horticulture, viniculture, and dairying; the appearance of manufactories alongside the handicraft workshops—such are the characteristic features of the state of the productive forces.

The new productive forces demand that the laborer shall display some kind of initiative in production and an inclination for work, an interest in work. The feudal lord therefore discards the slave as a laborer who has no interest in work and is entirely without initiative, and prefers to deal with the serf, who has his own husbandry, implements of production, and a certain interest in work essential for the cultivation of the land and for the payment in kind of a part of his harvest to the feudal lord.

Here private ownership is further developed. Exploitation is nearly as severe as it was under slavery—it is only slightly mitigated. A class struggle between exploiters and exploited is the principal feature of the feudal system.

The basis of the relations of production under the capitalist system is that the capitalist owns the means of production, but not the workers in production—the wage laborers, whom the capitalist can neither kill nor sell because they are personally free, but who are deprived of means of production and, in order not to die of hunger, are obliged to sell their labor power to the capitalist and to bear the yoke of exploitation. Alongside capitalist property in the means of production we find, at first on a wide scale, private property of the peasants and handicraftsmen in the means of production, these peasants and handicraftsmen no longer being serfs, and their private property being based on personal labor. In place of the handicraft workshops and manufactories there appear huge mills and factories equipped with machinery. In place of the manorial estates tilled by the primitive implements of production of the peasant, there now appear large capitalist farms run on scientific lines and supplied with agricultural machinery.

The new productive forces require that the workers in production shall be better educated and more intelligent than the downtrodden and ignorant serfs, that they be able to understand machinery and operate it properly. Therefore, the capitalists prefer to deal with wage workers, who are free from the bonds of serfdom and who are educated enough to be able properly to operate machinery.

But having developed productive forces to a tremendous extent, capitalism has become enmeshed in contradictions which it is unable to solve. By producing larger and larger quantities of commodities, and reducing their prices, capitalism intensifies competition, ruins the mass of small and medium private owners, converts them into proletarians and reduces their purchasing power, with the result that it becomes impossible to dispose of the commodities produced. On the other hand, by expanding production and concentrating millions of workers in huge mills and factories, capitalism lends the process of production a social character and thus undermines its own foundation, inasmuch as the social character of the process of production demands the social ownership of the means of production; yet the means of production remain private capitalist property, which is incompatible with the social character of the process of production.

These irreconcilable contradictions between the character of the productive forces and the relations of production make themselves felt in periodical crises of overproduction, when the capitalists, finding no effective demand for their goods owing to the ruin of the mass of the population which they themselves have brought about, are compelled to burn products, destroy manufactured goods, suspend production, and destroy productive forces at a time when millions of people are forced to suffer unemployment and starvation, not because there are not enough goods, but because there is an overproduction of goods.

This means that the capitalist relations of production have ceased to correspond to the state of productive forces of society and have come into irreconcilable contradiction with them.

This means that capitalism is pregnant with revolution, whose mission it is to replace the existing capitalist ownership of the means of production by Socialist ownership.

This means that the main feature of the capitalist system is a most acute class struggle between the exploiters and the exploited.

This, however, does not mean that changes in the relations of production, and the transition from old relations of production to new relations of production, proceed smoothly, without conflicts, without upheavals. On the contrary, such a transition usually takes place by means of the revolutionary overthrow of the old relations of production and the establishment of new relations of production. Up to a certain period the development of the productive forces and the changes in the realm of the relations of production proceed spontaneously, independently of the will of men. But that is so only up to a certain moment, until the new and developing productive forces have reached a proper state of maturity. After the new productive forces have matured, the existing relations of production and their upholders—the ruling classes—become that "insuperable" obstacle which can only be removed by the conscious action of the new classes, by the forcible acts of these classes, by revolution. Here there stands out in bold relief the *tremendous role* of new social ideas, of new political institutions, of a new political power, whose mission it is to abolish by force the old relations of production. Out of the conflict between the new productive forces and the old relations of production, out of the new economic demands of society, there arise new social ideas; the new ideas organize and mobilize the masses; the masses become welded into a new political army, create a new revolutionary power, and make use of it to abolish by force the old system of relations of production, and to firmly establish the new system. The spontaneous process of development yields place to the conscious actions of men, peaceful development to violent upheaval, evolution to revolution.

"The proletariat," says Marx, "during its contest with the bourgeoisie is compelled, by the force of circumstances, to organize itself as a class . . . by means of a revolution, it makes itself the ruling class, and, as such, sweeps away by force the old conditions of production." (*The Communist Manifesto,* in *Selected Works,* Eng. ed., Moscow, 1946, Vol. 1, p. 131.)

And further:

"The proletariat will use its political supremacy to wrest, by degrees, all capital from the bourgeoisie, to centralize all instruments of production in the hands of the state, i.e., of the proletariat organized as the ruling class, and to increase the total of productive forces as rapidly as possible." (*Ibid.,* p. 129.)

"Force is the midwife of every old society pregnant with a new one." (*Capital,* Vol. 1, p. 776.)

Here is the formulation—a formulation of genius—of the essence of historical materialism given by Marx in 1859 in his historic Preface to his famous book, *Critique of Political Economy:*

"In the social production of their life, men enter into definite relations that are indispensable and independent of their will; these relations of production correspond to a definite stage of development of their material forces of production. The sum total of these relations of production constitutes the economic structure of society—the real foundation, on which rises a legal and political superstructure and to which correspond definite forms of social consciousness. The mode of production of material life determines the social, political, and intellectual life process in general. It is not the consciousness of men that determines their being, but, on the contrary, their social being that determines their consciousness. At a certain stage of their development, the material productive forces in society come in conflict with the existing relations of production, or—what is but a legal expression for the same thing—with the property relations within which they have been at work before. From forms of development of the productive forces these relations turn into their fetters. Then begins an epoch of social revolution. With the change of the economic foundation the entire immense superstructure is more or less rapidly transformed. In considering such transformations a distinction should always be made between the material transformation of the economic conditions of production, which can be determined with the precision of natural science, and the legal, political, religious, aesthetic, or philosophic—in short, ideological forms in which men become conscious of this conflict and fight it out. Just as our opinion of an individual is not based on what he thinks of himself, so can we not judge of such a period of transformation by its own consciousness; on the contrary, this consciousness must be explained rather from the contradictions of material life, from the existing conflict between the social productive forces and the relations of production. No social order ever disappears before all the productive forces for which there is room in it have been developed; and new, higher relations of production never appear before the material conditions of their existence have matured in the womb of the old society itself. Therefore, mankind always sets itself only such tasks as it can solve; since, looking at the matter more closely, we will always find that the task itself arises only when the material conditions necessary for its solution already exist or are at least in the process of formation." (*Selected Works,* Eng. ed., Moscow, 1946, Vol. 1, pp. 300–301.)

Such is Marxist materialism as applied to social life, to the history of society.

Such are the principal features of dialectical and historical materialism.

It will be seen from this what a theoretical treasure was safeguarded by Lenin for the Party and protected from the attacks of the revisionists and renegades, and how important was the appearance of Lenin's book, *Materialism and Empirio-Criticism,* for the development of our Party.

After the *Short Course* was published, the Central Committee issued a decree giving the general lines of the party propaganda work which was henceforth to be conducted on the basis of the *Short Course.* The decree's basic purpose was to embed the notion of orthodoxy: that there was only one orthodox line of knowing and reasoning and that this line was given in the *Short Course.* The excerpts below are translated from the text in *Kommunisticheskaia partiia Sovetskogo Soiuza v rezoliutsiiakh i resheniiakh s" ezdov, konferentsii i plenumov TsK, Chast III, 1930–1954* ("The Communist Party of the Soviet Union in Resolutions and Decisions of Congresses, Conferences, and Plenums of the CC, Part III, 1930–1954") (Moscow, 1954), pp. 316–332.

24. Decree of November 14, 1938, on Party Propaganda

The publication of the *Short Course* is a major event in the ideological life of the Bolshevik party.

The *Short Course* is a most important tool in the task of mastering Bolshevism and arming the members of the party with Marxist-Leninist theory, that is, with knowledge of the laws of social development and political struggle, and a tool for raising the political vigilance of party and nonparty Bolsheviks and placing the propaganda of Marxism-Leninism on an appropriately high theoretical level.

In producing the *Short Course* the Central Committee has pursued the following objectives:

1. It has been necessary to give the party a uniform guide to the history of the party, a guide representing the official interpretation, authenticated by the Central Committee, of the basic questions of the history of the VKP (B) and Marxism-Leninism, free from any arbitrary interpretations. With the publication of the *Short Course* approved by the Central Committee, an end is put to arbitrariness and confusion in the writing of the history of the party, which had occurred in a number of previously published textbooks on the history of the party.

2. In producing the *Short Course* the Central Committee has aimed at liquidating the harmful split in the area of propaganda between Marxism and Leninism which has developed in recent years and which has led to teaching Leninism as separate doctrine divorced from Marxism, dialectical and historical materialism, and the history of the party, forgetting that Leninism grew and developed from Marxism, that Marxism is the foundation of Leninism, and that without knowing this foundation Leninism cannot be understood.

3. In contrast to certain old textbooks presenting the history of the VKP (B) primarily around historical personalities and aiming at instructing the cadres in personalities and their biographies, the *Short Course* presents the history of the party by unfolding the basic ideas of Marxism-Leninism and aims at instructing party cadres primarily in the *ideas* of Marxism-Leninism.

In producing the *Short Course* the Central Committee aims at teaching the doctrine of Marxism-Leninism on the basis of historical facts. The Central Committee has realized that such a presentation of Marxist-Leninist theory serves best the interests of the cause inasmuch as it is better, more natural, and more comprehensible to demonstrate the basic ideas of Marxism-Leninism through historical facts, inasmuch as the history of the VKP (B) itself is Marxism-Leninism in action, and inasmuch as the correctness and viability of Marxist-Leninist theory have been verified by practice—in the experience of the class struggle of the proletariat—and the Marxist-Leninist theory itself developed and enriched itself in closest contact with practice and through the theoretical reduction of the experience of the revolutionary struggle of the proletariat.

4. In producing the *Short Course* the Central Committee aims at freeing the Marxist literature from oversimplification and vulgarization in the interpretation of a number of questions of the theory of Marxism-Leninism and the history of the party.

Such vulgarization and oversimplification have found expression, for example, in the views, obviously anti-Marxist and long condemned by the party, concerning the role of the individual in history which have been spread until recently by certain pseudo-theoreticians and propagandists proceeding from a semi-Socialist-Revolutionary position.

The incorrect interpretation of the question of the victory of socialism in our country is a case of similar vulgarization and oversimplification.

The distortions of Marxist-Leninist ideas on the question of the nature of war in the contemporary period, the lack of understanding of the distinction between just and unjust wars, and the incorrect view of Bolsheviks as *sui generis* "pacifists" have had wide currency.

In recent times in historical science the anti-Marxist distortions and vulgarizations have been related to the so-called school of Pokrovsky, which perversely interpreted historical facts and, contrary to historical materialism, explained them in the light of the present, rather than in the light of the conditions in which the historical events occurred, and thus perverted the actual history.

5. In producing the *Short Course* the Central Committee aims to demonstrate effectively the power and significance of Marxist-Leninist theory which scientifically uncovers the laws of the development of society, a theory which teaches the use of these laws in guiding the revolutionary activity of the proletariat, a theory which, like all science, constantly develops and perfects itself and which is not afraid of replacing individual obsolete positions and deductions with new positions and deductions corresponding to new historical conditions.

The Central Committee has proceeded from the belief that without knowing Marxism-Leninism, without mastering Bolshevism, and without overcoming their theoretical lag, our cadres will be lame in both legs since the task of correctly guiding all areas of socialist construction demands the mastery of Marxist-Leninist theory by the practical workers and demands the skill of being guided by theory in solving problems of practical work.

It is wrong to think that the task of mastering the theory is only up to the powers of a small circle of functionaries. The mastery of Marxist-Leninist theory is something everyone can accomplish. More than ever before, under the Soviet regime and the victory of socialism in the U.S.S.R., unlimited opportunities have been created for our leading cadres to master successfully the Marxist-Leninist theory and study the history of the party and the works of Marx, Engels, Lenin, and Stalin. To master the theory of Marxism-Leninism one needs only willingness, persistence, and strength of character in order to reach this goal. If it is possible to master other sciences like physics, chemistry, or biology, there can be no doubt that it is possible to master fully the science of Marxism-Leninism.

6. In producing the *Short Course* the Central Committee aims at helping the cadres which are involved in theoretical and propaganda work to reform themselves, improve the quality of their work, begin to liquidate their theoretical lag, remove the shortcomings and gaps in their ideological training, and lift the propaganda work to the appropriate level.

All these objectives defined by the Central Committee have been reached in the *Short Course*.

To foster the propagation of the new history, the Central Committee also in 1938 established a special history library, the "State Public History Library of the R.S.F.S.R." in Moscow. By 1957 the library held more than a million volumes. It has played a key part in spreading the official history versions and has issued numerous "recommended reading" lists.

The condemnation of the history produced by Pokrovsky's school and the relegation of the pre-1938 versions of the Soviet past to limbo created a vacuum which was filled by a new type of Marxist history, produced by old historians who made the necessary transition to Stalinism and by new workers in the field. Written in the circumstances of probable involvement in a war with Germany, the new history stressed the role of the great leader, the theme of German aggression against the Slavs through the centuries, and the promotion of what was officially called "Soviet patriotism." Heroes of the Russian national past (Alexander Nevsky, Dmitry Donskoy, Kuzma Minin, Alexander Suvorov, Mikhail Kutuzov, and others) were again brought into focus and, along with more controversial figures like Ivan the Terrible and Peter the Great, who had built the power of the state at all cost against internal and external opposition, were systematically extolled, while patriotic pride was given free rein to develop.

The current national hero exalted by this type of history was, of course, Stalin. Officially called *Vozhd* (the exact Russian equivalent of *Führer* and *Duce*), he was placed next to Lenin in the center of everything that had occurred in Russia since 1917. Soviet historians vied with each other and with party propagandists in glorifying him as a universal genius, father of the masses, and leader without peer in the history of mankind.

Among the older generation of historians who made the transition to Stalinism was the historian of medieval Russia, Boris D. Grekov (1882–1953), who now began to rise to prominence. Having dodged the storms of the earlier phases, Grekov wrote solid history as he had been trained to do before 1917 and, with his emphasis on the autochthonous development of the Russian state, became useful for Stalin's purposes. He became director of the Institute of History at the Academy Sciences in 1937 and gradually acquired other important positions in the field of history.[22] A younger historian who also rose at this time and made a career from unabashed sycophancy around Stalin was Anna M. Pankratova (1897–1957,) a 1925 graduate of the Institute of Red Professors specializing in the history of the Russian labor movement and professor at the University of Moscow since the reopening of the history department in 1934. Writing on the first anniversary of the publication of the *Short Course,* she fawned in a way which might be found revolting but which won her Stalin's endorsement as one of the court historiographers or hagiographers. Whether believing what she wrote or being simply pragmatic, Pankratova panegyrized:

"The year of work on the historical front which has passed under the mark of Stalin's *Short Course of the History of VKP (B)* was a year of creativity and joy. The great book has become the handbook of Soviet historians, their solid support in work, and their wise tutor and guide. The rich content of Stalin's remarkable creation, its profound ideas, iron logic, internal unity, organic coalescence of factual material, and theoretical generalizations, as well as the noble simplicity of the style, the conciseness of the embossed formulations, the clarity and readability of the exposition, capture one's attention, engross, and compel one to study and work in the new way, and give stimulus to a *creative* attitude in the work in the field of history.

"The ossification of thought which the deadening formulae and abstract sociological schemes of Pokrovsky's antiscientific methodology had brought on is now completely demolished.

"In stating the bases of dialectical and historical materialism which constitutes the theoretical foundation of the truly scientific communist view of the world, the *Short Course of the History of VKP (B)* has

---

[22] An important post which Grekov held from 1947 to 1951 was that of director of the Academy's Institute of Slavic Studies, which was created to meet the needs of Soviet political and intellectual tutelage over the Slavic countries after the war. For a bibliography of his works see *Kratkie Soobshcheniia Instituta Slavianovedeniia* [Brief Communications of the Institute of Slavic Studies], No. 12, 1954, pp. 86–98.

graphically shown the way to end the inadmissible neglect of the questions of theory. The *Short Course* has given Soviet historians a statement of the basic positions of Marxist-Leninist methodology of history unmatched in its profundity." [23]

One of the loudest voices in the chorus of glorifiers of Stalin belonged to Nikita S. Khrushchev (1894—.) A farm boy from the Kursk area, in the years before the revolution he had drifted to the industrial regions of the Ukraine, where he eked out a living as a miner and locksmith. In 1918 he joined the Bolsheviks in the Ukraine and fought in the Civil War engagements there. Battle-tested, energetic, and verbal, he found his *metier* in party organizational work and soon caught the attention of the party leaders in the Ukraine (Lazar M. Kaganovich and others) for unerringly adhering to Stalin's line in the Stalin-Trotsky conflict. In 1929 he was rewarded by being transferred to Moscow for study at the Industrial Academy and organizational work at the center. Developing under Stalin's eyes as an *apparatchik* (organization man) *par excellence,* he rose swiftly: in 1931 he was made party secretary of the largest Moscow city district; in 1934 he was elected member of the Central Committee and in the next year was given additional responsibility as party secretary of the entire Moscow province; in 1938 he was co-opted an alternate member of the Politbureau, which Stalin was replenishing after the purge; and in 1939 he became a full-fledged member of that highest policy-making body in the Soviet Union. He held this membership during the rest of Stalin's era without interruption. Between 1938 and 1949 he was Stalin's emissary in the Ukraine, returning to Moscow in 1949 for work in the party secretariat, where Stalin's death found him.[24]

One of the basic reasons for Khrushchev's rise was Stalin's need for new loyal men. Another was undoubtedly Khrushchev's readiness to do as the *Vozhd* willed. A sample of his part in the articulation of the new history and the glorification of Stalin is the article he wrote on the occasion of Stalin's sixtieth birthday in 1939, published together with similar articles by V. M. Molotov, K. E. Voroshilov, L. M. Kaganovich, A. I. Mikoian, L. P. Beria, and G. M. Malenkov in the volume *Stalin* (New York, 1940). Khrushchev's theme reflects his party standing as an expert on the Ukrainian and other minority problems. His article is reproduced below with minor omissions.

---

[23] *Pravda,* September 8, 1939. On the tenth anniversary of the *Short Course,* in 1948, the Academy of Sciences held a special commemorative meeting at which Pankratova read a similar panegyric. See *Vestnik Akademii Nauk SSSR* [Bulletin of the Academy of Sciences of the U.S.S.R.], No. 10, 1948, pp. 17–38.

[24] It is, of course, not a coincidence that Khrushchev rose in the years of the purge. For his role in it and for other aspects of his life and career see Pistrak, *op. cit.;* Konrad Kellen, *Khrushchev: A Political Portrait* (New York, 1960); George Paloczi-Horvath, *Khrushchev: The Making of a Dictator* (Boston, 1960); and Roy MacGregor-Hastie, *The Man from Nowhere* (New York, 1961).

25. N. Khrushchev, "Stalin and the Great Commonwealth of Nations"

Today, on the sixtieth anniversary of Comrade Stalin's birth, all eyes will be turned on our great leader of nations, on our dear friend and father.

Working people all over the world will write and speak words of love and gratitude about him.

Their enemies will foam at the mouth with rage when putting pen to paper or speaking on this theme.

The working men of the world see in Comrade Stalin their leader, their liberator from the yoke of capitalism. In Comrade Stalin the people of our country behold their teacher, friend, and father.

The enemies of the people view Comrade Stalin as their most dangerous foe. The imperialists of all countries know full well that every word uttered by Comrade Stalin is backed by a people one hundred and eighty-three million strong, that every idea advanced by Comrade Stalin is endorsed by the great and mighty multinational Soviet people, the hope of the oppressed in every land and a mortal menace to international imperialism.

Stalin is a son of the working people. The whole life of this great man has been dedicated to the revolutionary struggle for the establishment of communist society.

The biography of Comrade Stalin is the heroic epic of the battles and victories of the working people—the workers, peasants, and intellectuals.

The biography of Comrade Stalin is the glorious epic of our Bolshevik Party.

The biography of Comrade Stalin is the epic of the revolutionary struggle of the working class against its oppressors—the landlords and capitalists.

In the struggle for the creation of the great Party of the Bolsheviks Comrade Stalin was ever in the lead, was ever by Lenin's side. He never yielded an inch in the struggle for the purity of the Bolshevik ranks, was ever engaged in uncompromising combat with the opportunists of every shade and color. He fought them as a matter of principle—Mensheviks, Socialist-Revolutionaries, Narodniks, and bourgeois nationalists. From early youth Comrade Stalin devoted himself to the cause of the laboring masses, to the struggle of the people against capitalism, for communism. In this struggle Comrade Stalin has always shown himself uncompromising and indefatigable.

No matter how much the myrmidons of the tsar, his gendarmes and police, might try to keep Comrade Stalin away by force from those fighting in the ranks of the working class, no matter how much they might try to stow him away in jails and places of exile in far-off Siberia, they never succeeded in doing so for long.

Comrade Stalin never relaxed his struggle for a moment. Even while in jail he kept up a relentless fight against the enemies of the working class. From jail he would establish contact with revolutionary workers and lead their struggle. While in exile he maintained close connections with the Party, and, like Lenin, continued to direct the struggle of the Party, the struggle of the working class.

Comrade Stalin always took advantage of the first opportunity to escape from exile to be once more in the midst of the fighters for the workers' cause, once more to lead this struggle, to organize the working people for the storming of the citadels of tsarism and capitalism.

Stalin was the close friend and associate of the great Lenin. Lenin together with Stalin created the great Bolshevik Party, the Party of a new type, the revolutionary Party of the working class. Stalin gave Lenin true support in the struggle to establish the Bolshevik Party, in the struggle for the purity of its ranks.

In Comrade Stalin the working class and all toilers possess the greatest man of the present era, a theoretician, leader, and organizer of the struggle and victory of the working class and of all toilers, against capitalism and for communism.

Comrade Stalin is an outstanding theoretician, an outstanding authority in many fields, including the national question. On the eve of the first Russian revolution he already taught the working class that it could not be victorious over tsarism and capitalism without a correct solution of the national problem. He formulated our Party's fundamental propositions on the national question, and later, in 1913, elaborated them in his brilliant work entitled *Marxism and the National Question*.

This book refuted the treacherous opportunist views of the Second International on the national question.

Lenin and Stalin hammered out a Bolshevik program on the national question. According to the doctrine laid down by Comrade Stalin, the national question is part of the general question of the proletarian revolution. Comrade Stalin teaches that in the epoch of imperialism the national question is inseparably connected with the whole international situation.

Together with Lenin, Stalin explained the Bolshevik principle of the international solidarity of the workers. Together with Lenin, Stalin showed that the proletariat could not be victorious over tsarism and capitalism without prosecuting a correct national policy. This was particularly true of so multinational a country as Russia.

Comrade Stalin made it plain that one of the factors on which the fate of the revolution in Russia depended was the correct solution of the national question. Lenin and Stalin taught that tsarist Russia was a prison of nations spreading the virus of national animosity, a prison in which the landlords and capitalists incited one nationality against another so that they might utilize this national dissension to plunge the laboring masses into still greater bondage and magnify their exploitation.

The Bolshevik Party had the proper approach to the solution of the national question in Russia. Its solution must be credited largely to Comrade Stalin. It was under his leadership that the Bolshevik Party firmly cemented all nationalities, all peoples of what was formerly Russia, and on the basis of mutual trust and confidence, on the basis of the great amity of nations, established the Soviet state, the great Union of Soviet Socialist Republics.

On Lenin's initiative, the realization of this great historic task was entrusted to Comrade Stalin. From 1917 to 1923 Comrade Stalin was People's Commissar of Nationalities. The Declaration of Rights of the Peoples of Russia, that famous historic document, was his. This instrument of paramount importance proclaimed the fraternal trust and confidence, the great amity, that governs the peoples of our land. Stalin took a leading part in the formation of each one of the national republics of our great Soviet Union. He was in direct charge of the struggle for the Soviet Ukrainian Republic. He personally participated in the establishment of the Byelorussian Soviet Socialist Republic. He was the founder of the Soviet Socialist Republics of Transcaucasia and Central Asia. He treated each nationality of our country with the love and affection of a father and helped them build their own free Soviet life. Today we are in a position to state that as a result of the enormous work performed by our Bolshevik Party, as a result of the untiring efforts of our great Stalin, the Soviet Union has been converted into a mighty, invincible socialist state of workers and peasants which effectively exerts its influence on international affairs, so that our enemies are compelled to reckon with it.

Stalin is the symbol of the unbreakable friendship that welds the great Soviet people. All nations of the Soviet Union see in Stalin their friend, their father, their leader.

Stalin is the friend of the people, a title he gained by his simple ways.

Stalin is the father of the people by virtue of the love he bears them. Stalin is the leader of nations for the wisdom with which he guides their struggle.

Comrade Stalin's greatness lies in the fact that he, a true son of the people who has felt the full weight of the hardships that beset the lives of those who struggle in its cause, has always directed his revolutionary energies to the enhancement of the welfare of the toiling population. All our might, all our invincibility, repose in the people. Their creative power is a mighty force, as Stalin never tires of telling us.

The Bolshevik Party is invincible because it is linked with inseparable bonds to the great community of working people. And Stalin's greatness is the greatness of our free Soviet people.

That explains, said Comrade Stalin, why "our government and Party have no interests and concerns apart from those of the people." But before the creative power of the people could manifest itself, before the fountain of popular creative genius could start to gush, the people had to achieve their social and national freedom, there had to be created the Bolshevik Party, a party that could ensure the laboring masses their national and social emancipation.

Lenin and Stalin were the creators and organizers of such a Bolshevik, revolutionary party. Together with Lenin, Stalin built, cleansed, and consolidated this Bolshevik Party. After Lenin's death Comrade Stalin successfully maintained the purity of the Bolshevik Party and of its principles as taught by Lenin. He defended our Party in its desperate fight with the Trotskyites, the Rights, the Mensheviks, Socialist-Revolutionaries, and bourgeois nationalists—with all these enemies of the working people.

Today, when we honor Comrade Stalin's sixtieth birthday, we celebrate the victory of the working class, the victory of our Bolshevik Party, the victory of Leninism.

The working class was victorious because its struggle was led by the Bolshevik Party, and the Bolshevik Party was created by Lenin and Stalin.

The working people were victorious because they established large-scale industry, for which we are indebted to Comrade Stalin, the untiring champion of the socialist industrialization of the country.

The people were victorious because the alliance between the working class and the laboring peasantry was a success. For this, too, we are indebted to Comrade Stalin, who steadily fought for such an alliance.

Socialism was victorious in our country because our peasantry secured the wherewithal to make the change to socialist construction, and for this we are indebted to the collective farm system of which Stalin was the founder.

The defense of our existence as an independent state requires the firm coherence of our entire people. And this coherence we possess. All nations composing our great Soviet Union are firmly knit in solidarity. This solidarity is the product of Comrade Stalin's brilliant theory underlying our national policy on the national question; it is the product of the application of this policy in practice.

The people won the right of the great Soviet Union to existence because they have their valorous Red Army and Navy, and the Army and Navy are the creation of our great Stalin, who increases their might with every day. All nationalities of the Soviet Union proclaim their manifold successes and attribute them to him who inspired them, Comrade Stalin.

The Ukrainian people have particular cause for rejoicing at the celebration of the sixtieth birthday of their leader, friend, and teacher, Comrade Stalin, because during the years of Civil War Stalin exercised the direct leadership of their struggle for liberation from the imperialist forces of intervention, from Petliura, Makhno, and Denikin, because Comrade Stalin daily directs socialist construction in the Ukraine.

The Ukrainian people are profoundly grateful to Comrade Stalin for the deliverance of their fellow Ukrainians who had been enduring the heavy yoke of the Polish gentry and capitalists. The Ukrainian people give thanks to Comrade Stalin for the reunion of the great Ukrainian people in one Ukrainian state.

Today, on the sixtieth anniversary of Comrade Stalin's birth, let us exclaim rejoicingly: "Long life to you, our beloved Stalin, and may you prosper the cause of toiling humanity."

By 1939 the first graduating class from the history departments of the universities was ready to teach in the secondary schools or to do advanced work of specialization. On the basis of regulations issued by the Sovnarkom on March 31, 1939, a uniform program (*aspirantura*) leading to the first advanced degree of *kandidat istoricheskikh nauk* ("candidate of historical sciences") was established in the universities and scientific institutions. The program, capped by a dissertation, is roughly equivalent to that of the American Ph.D. and is ordinarily the prerequisite for bestowal of the next degree of *doktor istoricheskikh nauk* ("doctor of historical sciences"), which is granted, currently without a formal program of studies, after defense of a dissertation or in recognition of major contributions to scholarship.[25] In the universities and teachers' colleges (pedagogical institutes) the history curriculum continued to improve. At the University of Moscow, which serves as the paragon in Soviet higher education, three new chairs were established in 1939 in addition to the five (for ancient history, medieval history, modern and contemporary history, Russian history, and history of colonial and dependent areas) with which the department was reopened in 1934: history of the Southern and Western Slavs, archeology, and ethnography.[26]

25 *Pedagogicheskaia Entsiklopediia* [Pedagogical Encyclopedia] (Moscow, 1964), Vol. I, cols. 132–133, 772–773; Nicholas DeWitt, *Education and Professional Employment in the USSR* (Washington, 1961), pp. 378–409.

26 *Iz istorii Moskovskogo universiteta, 1917–1941* (see chap. iv, n. 4), pp. 259–286, and William K. Medlin, "The Teaching of History in Soviet Schools: A Study in Methods," in *The Politics of Soviet Education,* ed. George Z. F. Bereday and Jaan Pennar (New York, 1960), pp. 100–116.

In the realm of historiographic policy, the denunciations of Pokrovsky reached a climax in 1939–40 when the Academy's History Institute published two volumes of essays criticizing his views and writings. Edited by the institute director, Grekov, who was emerging as the official historian of ancient Russia and the head of the new school of "national Bolshevik historiography," the two volumes were written in the tone of the Zaidel-Tsvibak book against Tarle and Platonov in 1931 (cited in note 4); as Soviet historians now point out, even the title of the second volume, which appeared in 1940, was changed to "Against the Anti-Marxist Conception of M. N. Pokrovsky"—the first volume having appeared under the title "Against the Historical Conception of M. N. Pokrovsky"—so as to leave no doubt that his views and work had been heresy.[27] The opening piece by A. M. Pankratova denounced his school as a "base for wrecking activities by enemies of the people unmasked by the organs of the NKVD, by the Trotskyist-Bukharinist hirelings of fascism, and by wreckers, spies, and terrorists who had skillfully camouflaged themselves with the aid of the harmful and anti-Leninist historical conceptions of M. N. Pokrovsky."

A more restrained but similarly negative evaluation of Pokrovsky was produced in 1941 by N. L. Rubinshtein in his *Russkaia istoriografiia* ("Russian Historiography"), which was the first Marxist attempt to evaluate the writings of Russian history in Russia from early times to the 1930's.[28] While Pokrovsky was alive and in power, Rubinshtein had been

---

[27] M. V. Nechkina, Iu. A. Poliakov, and L. V. Cherepnin, "O proidennom puti," in *Sovetskaia istoricheskaia nauka ot XX k XXII s''ezdu KPSS; istoriia SSSR* [Soviet Historical Science from the Twentieth to the Twenty-second Congress of the CPSU: History of the U.S.S.R.], ed. N. M. Druzhinin and others (Moscow, 1962), p. 15.

[28] There is no full-scale survey in any language of Soviet historiography in regard to policies as well as organization of research and products. Rubinshtein devoted only one-eighth of his 650 pages to the Soviet period, discussing in four individual chapters the work and impact of N. A. Rozhkov, Pokrovsky, Lenin, and Stalin. Earlier article-length surveys are cited in M. V. Nechkina, "O periodizatsii istorii sovetskoi istoricheskoi nauki," *Istoriia SSSR* [History of the U.S.S.R.], No. 1, 1960, pp. 77–91. A Soviet survey of the work of the first twenty-five years in various fields of native as well as foreign history, *Dvadtsat' piat'let istoricheskoi nauki v SSSR* [Twenty-five Years of Historical Science in the U.S.S.R.] (Moscow, 1942; see reading no. 27) provides much information and comment revealing the political line in 1942. The work of 1942–55 is broadly reported in A. L. Sidorov's paper "Osnovnye problemy i nekotorye itogi razvitiia sovetskoi istoricheskoi nauki," read at the Tenth International Congress of Historical Sciences (Rome, 1955) and published in *Desiatyi mezhdunarodnyi kongress istorikov v Rime* [The Tenth International Congress of Historians in Rome] (Moscow, 1956), pp. 5–55. The work of 1956–61 in Russian history is surveyed in great detail in the volume cited in the preceding note; a companion volume for the work in European and American history has also been published, entitled *Sovetskaia istoricheskaia nauka ot XX k XXII s''ezdu KPSS; istoria zapadnoi Evropy i Ameriki* [Soviet Historical Science from the Twentieth to the Twenty-second Congress of the CPSU: History of Western Europe and America] (Moscow, 1963). The six-volume general survey *Ocherki istorii istoricheskoi nauki v SSSR* (Moscow, 1955), which is in the process of being published by the Academy's History Institute, will cover the work of 1917–62 in its last three volumes, but only the first three have appeared so far. A "bibliography of the history of historical science in the U.S.S.R." is in preparation

one of his supporters in the Tarle affair and other matters; writing on the occasion of Pokrovsky's sixtieth anniversary, he had praised him for a "profound and subtle analysis" that had taught young Soviet historians valuable lessons.[29] Rubinshtein's tergiversation in 1941 did not make him secure from attack later on; in the late 1940's he, too, went through the agony of being denounced for having failed to appreciate fully the theoretical importance of Lenin and Stalin to historical scholarship. The excerpts translated below are from his chapter on Pokrovsky in *Russkaia istoriografiia* (Moscow, 1941), pp. 575–599.

26. N. L. Rubinshtein, "Pokrovsky"

The historiographic analysis of the scholarly work of Pokrovsky presents in certain respects a considerable difficulty. The problem is that in the development of Russian historical science Pokrovsky occupies a rather special place. He traveled a long road of evolution: coming out of the historical school of Kliuchevsky and starting with a bourgeois historical conception, Pokrovsky soon entered upon a resolute struggle with bourgeois ideology and took the path of an ideological rapprochement with Marxism. The rapprochement with Marxism determined the ideological direction of his thought, but he never was a true Marxist. The ideological rapprochement became consolidated in practice by a rapprochement of action with revolutionary Marxism in the revolutionary struggle of the Russian proletariat, which took Pokrovsky into the ranks of the Bolshevik party and of the active participants in the October Revolution and the Soviet reconstruction.

During the struggle with the bourgeois historical schools for the creation of a Soviet historical science, his position as a Bolshevik historian placed Pokrovsky at the head of Soviet historical scholarship.

Pokrovsky stood out in Russian historical science not as a radical front-rank representative during the period of the crisis in bourgeois science, but as a leader of Soviet historians creating a Soviet historical science and as an agent in a given phase. Naturally, the requirements upon the historian in these two phases and the criteria for the evaluation of his work were different; what might have been meritorious in the first historical phase turned out to be complete unsuitability in the second.

This, however, is not all. In Soviet Russia Pokrovsky had disciples, the so-called historical school of Pokrovsky. This school developed the errone-

---

(*Voprosy istorii*, No. 1, 1962, pp. 209–214). The most satisfactory Western surveys are the works by Shteppa, Mazour, and Black cited earlier (see, respectively, chap. iv, n. 4 and n. 7, and chap. ii, n. 6).
[29] *Istorik-Marksist*, No. 9, 1928, pp. 58–78.

ous anti-Marxist positions of the historical scheme of Pokrovsky; some did that unconsciously without subjecting the positions to Marxist-Leninist criticism, while others did it as wreckers hiding their anti-Soviet ideological activity behind the master's authority.

Carefully watching the state of Soviet historical science, the party and the government pointed out in the beginning of 1936 that "anti-Marxist, anti-Leninist, essentially liquidationist, and antiscientific conceptions of historical science" had taken root among some of our historians and especially the historians of the U.S.S.R.: "The Sovnarkom and the CC of the VKP (B) emphasize that these injurious tendencies and attempts to liquidate history as a science are related above all to the propagation of the erroneous historical views typical of the so-called 'historical school of Pokrovsky' among some of our historians."

The 1905–7 revolution completed the ideological break of Pokrovsky with bourgeois liberalism and moved him into the ranks of the Bolshevik party and even into the Moscow committee of the party. He recognized then "the theory of class struggle as the motive force of history" but at the same time he remained on the theoretical positions of economic materialism and even published in 1906 a pamphlet under this title.

In 1917 Pokrovsky rejoined the ranks of the Bolshevik party. In the October days he was placed at the head of the Moscow Soviet of Workers' Deputies, and in the spring of 1918 he began his activity as Deputy People's Commissar of Education, head of Soviet historical science, and director of the Communist Academy, of the Institute of Red Professors, and of other history centers.

In his report "Leninism and Russian History" at the conference of Marxist historians in 1929, Pokrovsky defines the essence of Marxism as follows: "Economic materialism, that is, economic interpretation of history, alone or even economic materialism plus class struggle—this still is not Marxism. Only he who recognizes the political deductions from Marxism, who recognizes the dictatorship of the proletariat, is a true Marxist." To this formulation Pokrovsky returns repeatedly. In this definition of Marxism the limit of Pokrovsky's methodological evolution is clearly evident. "Economic materialism *plus* class struggle," a principle of adding (in other cases subtracting) and simple appending to the old—this expresses most directly the mechanical nature of his methodology.

The undialectical nature and mechanicalness of the world outlook of Pokrovsky represent his basic vice and his inability to reconstruct his views.

The class struggle was for Pokrovsky an aspect of politics rather than an objective historical basis. Marx spoke of the class struggle as the operation of the basis for inevitability in history and an actual law of social development in the class society. Pokrovsky spoke of "politics retrojected into the past." His conception of the class struggle did not incorporate the laws of class struggle and was only a subjective interpretation of history.

Instead of a Marxist understanding of the class struggle as the content of the historical process as a whole, the class struggle was segregated as a special system of facts in a special "history of the revolutionary movement." In reality this produced not a purified but a constricted and abstract understanding of the class struggle, detached from the concrete interconnection of events and thus deprived of the internal determinism and law-governed pattern of its own development. The revolutionary struggle itself thus became a series of revolutionary flashes torn from an understanding of the class struggle which pierces the entire content of history.

This determined the relation of Pokrovsky's scheme and his historical method to the facts and the concreteness of historical reality. He does not reveal the law-governed pattern of the class struggle with a tangible and factual content; from the historical reality were gleaned those facts which constitute a direct manifestation of this class struggle.

Along with the tangible facts, the living and concrete individual was also dropped as a component part of the historical process. Here, too, Pokrovsky thought that he was headed toward Marxism whereas in fact he distorted its doctrine. In the recognition of the historical role of the individual Pokrovsky saw only a populist cult of the heroic personality. However, proving that ". . . heroes do not make history but history makes heroes and, therefore, heroes do not make the people but the people make heroes and move history forward," Marxism has also pointed out that "heroes and outstanding personalities can play an important role in the life of society to the extent that they are able to grasp correctly the conditions of social development and to understand how to change them for the better." [30]

In the ensuing years, the issue of Pokrovsky and his influence was pressed out of the focus of attention by the war and the necessity of mobilizing all forces to meet the German onslaught. Historians, like everyone else, bent their efforts in line with the slogan "All for the Front, All for Victory." As history appeared to be repeating itself, they went back to the old themes of the patriotic heroism of the Russian people, the solidarity of all Slavs against the German *Drang nach Osten* and recurrent aggression, and the role of the great figures of the Russian national past in times of similar crisis. Use of historians to expose the "fascist falsification of history" had begun in the late 1930's. In 1939, in line with this purpose, the History Institute sponsored the publication of a collection of pieces by Tarle, E. A. Kosminskii, and others, *Protiv fashistskoi fal'sifikatsii istorii*

---

[30] Here Rubinshtein quotes from p. 16 of the Russian edition of the *Short Course*.

("Against the Fascist Falsification of History") edited by F. I. Notovich. The collection, however, came out embarrassingly close to the signing of the Nazi-Soviet pact and was left unused by Soviet propaganda in the ensuing two years.

When the Germans became enemies once again, the anti-German tone rose to a screaming pitch. Since all Slavic nations were invaded by the Germans, one of the themes to develop and exploit now was that of anti-German common cause with wide roots in the recent and distant past of all Slavs. An All-Slavic Committee was immediately formed in Moscow under the guidance of Soviet and refugee Slavists (Grekov, N. S. Derzhavin, Z. R. Nejedly, and others) to promote this theme in every way possible. The committee began publication of the monthly *Slaviane* ("Slavs"; 1942–58), whose "principal task" was to foster "the unity of the Slavic peoples in the struggle against Hitler's Germany" and to "illumine the glorious pages of the history of the Slavic peoples [and their] contributions to the civilization of mankind." The old themes of Russian Pan-Slavism were thus rewoven with those of Russian nationalism. By training and interests, the surviving old-regime historians fitted well into this new orientation and once again began to play a major role in historical scholarship.

The preoccupations of the war years are best reflected in Pankratova's Introduction to the comprehensive assessment of Soviet historical scholarship in the first quarter of a century of its existence, *Dvadtsat' piat' let istoricheskoi nauki v SSSR* ("Twenty-five Years of Historical Science in the U.S.S.R."), published in 1942 by the History Institute and edited by V. P. Volgin, Tarle, and Pankratova. The volume contains valuable surveys of all fields of history in which Soviet historians had been active: Russian history (all phases) and foreign history (ancient world, Middle Ages, Byzantine history, Slavic studies, Oriental studies, and modern history). Pankratova's Introduction, parts of which are translated below, summed up the evolution of Soviet historiography since 1917 and its tasks in the war.

27. A. M. Pankratova, "Twenty-five Years of Soviet Historical Science"

Soviet historical science makes a recapitulation of its work of a quarter of a century in the days of the Great Patriotic War of the Soviet Union against Hitler's Germany.

In his address to the leadership of the Academy of Sciences of the U.S.S.R., Comrade Stalin placed upon the center of Soviet scholarship the task of "heading the movement of the innovators in the field of science in the raging struggle with the vicious enemy of our people and the other freedom-loving peoples, the German fascism." He expressed conviction that the Soviet scholars "will fulfill with honor their great patriotic duty to the Motherland in the tough times of the Great Patriotic War of the Soviet people against the German invaders."

The scientific workers of all disciplines and in all fields are urgently working toward the realization of the main task—the earliest possible defeat of Hitlerism. Soviet science together with its center, the Academy of Sciences of the U.S.S.R. and all its institutes, has moved forward in the conditions of the great patriotic war as a progressive science clearly comprehending its duty to hasten the historical hour of the doom of the vicious enemy of mankind, fascism.

Historical science in the U.S.S.R. serves now this task also. It contributes to the ideological arming of the Soviet people by explaining the lofty and noble objectives of the great patriotic war as the most just war in history. It unmasks the barbarian ideology of fascism. It demonstrates on the basis of the laws of the class struggle and on the basis of the study of our best historical traditions that "our cause is just and that victory shall be ours." The latter deduction is not an agitator's slogan but the result of a profound knowledge of the laws of history.

II

The classics of Marxism-Leninism have constantly taught the proletariat that revolutionary social theory is a weapon incomparable in its power. Theory allows the proletariat to realize its condition and the objectives of its struggle. Theory helps it find loyal allies. Theory discloses to it the weak and vulnerable points of the enemy. Theory shows whence and how classes came in the past and where they may go in the future.

It is not an accident that all ideologists of the progressive classes of society have sought and seek support in history and that all reactionaries resort to the falsification of history. It is not an accident that the very rise of historical science was connected with the period of the rise of the bourgeoisie as a class. However, even in the most creative period of its existence, the bourgeoisie could not create a stable methodological foundation for history. The bourgeoisie was unable either to assess correctly the past development of mankind or to understand the direction of its future development. It failed to discover, therefore, the possibility of scientific foreseeing.

III

The victory of the October Socialist Revolution provided a new angle of seeing the past and, as Engels foresaw, compelled the writing of all history *de novo*. The Soviet government created an unprecedented material foundation for a powerful surge of Soviet historical science. In the course of the gigantic reorganization of all social relations there arose an interest of the masses in history.

However, in the first period of the development of Soviet historical science, from 1917 to 1924, idealistic or vulgar-materialistic views concerning history still survived in almost all segments of the historical front. In part, leadership in historical science was in the hands of persons remote from Marxism. Scientific and research institutions as well as university chairs in history were headed not infrequently by active anti-Marxists. Old bourgeois historians at times openly came out in their works and lectures against Marxism and spoke out against the dictatorship of the proletariat. In the form of historical studies, they waged as fierce a struggle against the proletarian revolution on the historical front as the armed bourgeois-landlord counterrevolution did on the fronts of the civil war.

In the autumn of 1931, the remarkable letter "On Certain Questions of the History of Bolshevism" by Comrade Stalin to the editors of *Proletarskaia Revoliutsiia* was published. It signalized the serious danger of smuggling in, under the guise of history, of the contraband Trotskyism which gives the world bourgeoisie an ideological weapon in its stuggle against the dictatorship of the proletariat. Comrade Stalin asked historians not only to deny a forum to slanderers and falsifiers of history, but also to wage a merciless struggle against rotten liberalism in questions of theory. He called upon Soviet historians to launch a positive and creative work and, in particular, to place the effort of studying the history of our party on scientific Bolshevik tracks. The letter of Comrade Stalin summoned the historians to intensify revolutionary vigilance on the theoretical front, particularly in relation to the new methods of the class enemy, which strives surreptitiously to penetrate and disorganize the ranks of the builders of socialism.

In the decree of the CC of the VKP (B) and the Sovnarkom of May 16, 1934, the major shortcomings in teaching were also pointed out. Under the guise of history, students had been served abstract definitions of socioeconomic formations while the narration of civic history had been replaced by abstract sociological schemes.

On the basis of the decree of the CC of the VKP (B) and the Sovnarkom of the U.S.S.R. concerning the development of history education, history departments were introduced in the structure of the universities. They were given the task of training new qualified cadres of historians educated in the Marxist way.

A major handicap in the development of historical science was the anti-Marxist and antiscientific views of the "school" of Pokrovsky. By replacing objective historical knowledge and the study of the concrete development of history with abstract schemes and sterile antiscientific sociological conceptions, the "school" of Pokrovsky held back the development of civic history on the basis of Marxist-Leninist methodology. More than that, this "school" brought direct harm to the work of educating the young genera- tions in the spirit of Soviet patriotism. It ignored the study of the heroic traditions of the great Russian people and failed to arm the youth with sentiments of love toward the Motherland and hatred toward its enemies.

In August 1934, Comrades Stalin, Kirov, and Zhdanov made known their "Observations Concerning the Outlines of Textbooks" on the history of the U.S.S.R. and on modern history, commissioned to be produced by teams of several authors. The outlines of textbooks submitted by the authors were subjected in the "Observations" to the most trenchant criti- cism. At the same time the "Observations" gave very important methodo- logical suggestions for all knotty problems of history. These suggestions became a Bolshevik program for the further development of historical science in the U.S.S.R. In their critical observations concerning the outlines of history textbooks, Comrades Stalin, Kirov, and Zhdanov proceeded from the position that the popular masses in the U.S.S.R. should know the scientific and objective civic history of mankind, which would teach them to understand the movement of the classes and would arm them with the knowledge of the laws and perspectives of social development.

A veritable holiday for the entire historical front was the appearance of the *Short Course of the History of the VKP (B)*, written under the direction and with the immediate participation of Comrade Stalin. A great example of truly scientific and profoundly ideological historical work, the *Short Course of the History of the VKP (B)* has had an enormous significance for the entire historical front.

Of inestimable methodological importance to historians of all specialties has been and is the chapter by Comrade Stalin on dialectical and historical materialism. A definition of historical science and its tasks and objectives is given in this chapter with exceptional clarity and profundity.

Since 1936–37, Soviet historical science, based on the achievements of the preceding years, has moved swiftly ahead. This third period in its development is marked by a number of synthesizing works and above all by the production of textbooks in all historical disciplines.

The new Soviet textbooks are not a mere popularization of previously accumulated factual materials but a definite creative result of the accom- plishments of Soviet historical science.

IV

Marxist-Leninist historical science alone has produced a scientifically argumented periodization of world history. At its basis is the doctrine developed by Marx, Engels, Lenin, and Stalin concerning socioeconomic formations, with its most significant idea of the dictatorship of the proletariat.

The development of the periodization of world history by Comrade Stalin is not limited to extending the Marxist-Leninist doctrine of the formations. Comade Stalin has brought out the process of the acceleration of human history.

Stalin's profound analysis of all basic phases of the history of human society and his all-encompassing characterization of the actual progress made in each phase of the life of mankind are a remarkable contribution to the treasury of Marxism-Leninism, the significance of which is enormous not only for historical science but for all other sciences connected with the study of the history of human society. The periodization of the basic phases of the history of human society given by Comrade Stalin constitutes a profound methodological foundation for concrete historical investigations in all fields of historical science.

V

We must dwell in particular on the problems connected with the history of the Bolshevik party and the Comintern. The huge inheritance of Lenin, the development of which increasingly attracts the attention of Soviet historians, and the works of Comrade Stalin are a granitic foundation on which the truly scientific study of the history of the All-Union Communist Party is being conducted. The enormous importance of this effort is evident in the fact that Comrade Stalin personally has devoted a large share of his attention to the matter of putting together the history of the party. Under his immediate direction and closest participation, a *Short Course of the History of the VKP (B)* has been produced. Among the historians working voluminously and fruitfully in the history of the Bolshevik party one should assign the first place to a member of the Academy, E. M. Iaroslavskii. A historian educated broadly and comprehensively, Academician Iaroslavskii devotes his main attention to the history of the three revolutions in the U.S.S.R. and the history of the Bolshevik party. He was one of the basic authors and one of the editors of the *Short Course of the History of the VKP (B)*, written under the direction of Comrade Stalin. His concise but exceptionally valuable studies devoted to the life and work of Lenin and Stalin are books which are educating millions of Soviet citizens.

An enormous contribution to the history of Bolshevism is Comrade Beria's work *On the Question of the History of the Bolshevik Organizations in the Transcaucasian Regions*. This book initiated the documentary study of the life and work of Comrade Stalin with which the history of the Bolshevik organizations in the Transcaucasian regions is closely connected.

VI

What are the tasks at present on the historical front in the U.S.S.R.? The tasks are entirely defined by the demands and exigencies of the Great Patriotic War against Hitlerite barbarian fascism.

The task of increasing the ideological armament of the entire Soviet people—who are waging the greatest and most just patriotic war in history for the preservation of the basic achievements of their national civilization as well as that of mankind in general—is foremost before all Soviet historians and the scholarly centers encompassing them.

Above all, Soviet historians must give a profoundly truthful illumination of the heroic past of the peoples of the Soviet Union. Historians in the U.S.S.R. are writing the history of their Motherland as fervent patriots. They are endeavoring to show clearly and concretely to the contemporary generations the glorious historical traditions of the Russian people, which are traditions of fervent love of the Motherland and intense hatred toward its enemies and of self-sacrifice and steadfastness in the struggle against masters and enslavers.

The images of the great Russian patriots and heroes of the liberation struggle of the peoples of the U.S.S.R. must be enveloped in glory and carefully preserved for future generations in the works of Soviet historians.

In connection with this positive work of major importance Soviet historians have to carry out a critical effort in the re-examination of the negative attitude toward our traditions entrenched in past years and of the underestimation of our glorious past cultivated by the "school" of Pokrovsky.

Armed with the knowledge of the laws of social development, and using the scientific method of Marxism-Leninism, progressive Soviet historical science must fulfill and shall fulfill the progressive social tasks assigned to it.

The dislocations caused by the war, including the evacuation of the Academy's History Institute to Uzbekistan, nearly suspended historical work from 1942 to 1944. In propaganda work, however, the Grekov school of Russian nationalism and Pan-Slavism couched in Marxist terms moved in high gear. Like the school's head, many older historians of "bourgeois" background and training reasserted themselves through their competence and usefulness in propagandizing these familiar themes. Among the older historians, Tarle, whose work on the Napoleonic era ideally suited him for drawing the needed parallels between the "Patriotic War" of 1812 and the "Great Patriotic War" now raging, achieved complete triumph over his tormentors of a decade earlier. As one of the speakers at the "Jubilee

Session" of the Academy of Sciences commemorating the twenty-fifth anniversary of the Revolution, he had the opportunity to point from the highest rostrum in the land to the "intellectual devastation" wrought by Pokrovsky's school, which, he said, "in the fullest sense of the word, abolished Russian history." [31] Grekov himself presented similar views at the session [32] and formulated his historiographic "credo" (as his fellow Slavist V. I. Picheta termed it) in a paper on "Lenin and Historical Science" which he read at the general meeting of the Academy in 1944.[33]

Ending in the greatest victory in Russian history, the war extended Soviet influence into the entire Slavic area and deep into Central Europe and created a situation in which even the most farfetched visions of prerevolutionary Russian nationalism and Pan-Slavism appeared realized. To meet the needs of this situation, in 1945 the Academy produced a comprehensive plan for the tasks of historical scholarship after the war, including its role in the anticipated combat with American and other "bourgeois" historians. Essential portions of the plan are translated below from the text in *Istoricheskii zhurnal* ("Historical Journal"), No. 3, 1945, pp. 60–75.

28. The 1945 Plan for Postwar Historical Work

I

Bourgeois historiography has been unable, even at the point of its highest development, to create durable methodological foundations for historical science. Historians of the first half of the nineteenth century posed the problem of historical laws but did not solve it. Only the founders of scientific socialism, Marx and Engels, by developing and proving the theory of historical materialism, opened "the road to the scientific study of history as process unified and governed by laws in all its immense multiplicity and contradictoriness." [34]

In the past several decades West European and American bourgeois historians have attained a considerable degree of perfection in the technique of historical investigation and have considerably expanded, due to the successes of archeology, the chronological framework of history. However, they have almost completely refused to make an effort to establish the

[31] E. V. Tarle, "O sovetskoi istoriografii," in *Iubileinaia sessiia Akademii Nauk SSSR posviashchennaia 25-letiiu Velikoi Oktiabr'skoi Sotsialisticheskoi Revoliutsii* [Jubilee Session of the Academy of Sciences of the U.S.S.R. Devoted to the Twenty-fifth Anniversary of the Great October Socialist Revolution] (Moscow, 1943), pp. 150–159.

[32] B. D. Grekov, "Razvitie istoricheskikh nauk v SSSR za 25 let," *ibid.*, pp. 140–149.

[33] It can be read in his *Izbrannye trudy* [Selected Works] (Moscow, 1960), III, 369–383.

[34] Lenin, *Sochineniia*, XVIII, 13 [Footnote in source].

general laws of historical evolution. In those instances where such effort was made in the past several decades, it has vividly attested the impotence of bourgeois historical thought, which is unable to lift itself above the most vulgar eclecticism.

In the majority of its representatives, Western historical "science" has more and more frankly relinquished its own past and has eagerly emphasized the impossibility of disclosing the objective laws of the historical process or the inapplicability of the very concept of objective law to it. The theoretical justification for this position has been provided for historians by the representatives of reactionary neo-Kantian philosophy, Rickert, Windelband, and others. Naturally, historians infected by such a philosophy were at best only able to produce a certain systematization of the raw facts collected by them or a description of an isolated series of historical phenomena. Generalizations from facts and disclosure of the inner connections of phenomena took less and less noteworthy place in historical works.

It must be said that the fascist pseudo-science has a weak echo (only among the pro-fascist circles) in the democratic countries. The majority of historians in these countries view the fascist "theories" negatively, even though they do not always express this attitude as sharply as these theories deserve.

Only a relatively small number of Western historians in the democratic countries adhere to materialist positions. These are primarily scholars working in economic history or influenced to one degree or another by Marxism. It is true that they are mainly imbued with the vulgar conceptions of the so-called "economic materialism." Nevertheless, thanks to their materialist positions these historians primarily produce valuable synthesizing works. Due to the growth of interest in the works of Soviet historians and their methodology and to the struggle against the fascist pseudoscience, these historians will grow in number and will draw nearer to true historical materialism in their methodology. Certain signs of this process can already be noticed.

The history of the development of Soviet historical science is a history of the swift dissemination of the Marxist-Leninist materialist understanding of history and its victory over historical idealism and its survivals and over all types of perversions of Marxism-Leninism. By the time of the Great October Socialist Revolution, Russian historical science already had its own materialist tradition. The list of this heritage of the prerevolutionary period should be headed, of course, by the works of Lenin and Stalin. The book *Development of Capitalism in Russia* can be taken as the paragon of the application of the materialist method to the study of economic history of Russia. Stalin's work *Marxism and the National Question,* by its elucidation of the question of the origin of nations and creation of state forms, has given historians formulations which are of immense importance beyond the understanding of the pertinent phenomena in Russian history; its argumentation and deductions are so universally valid that no historian of the West or of the East can do without it.

A major part in the dissemination of the materialist understanding of history was also played in their time by the numerous works of Plekhanov.

During the first years after the Great October Socialist Revolution, idealist or vulgar materialist views of history were still very influential in almost all sectors of the historical front. In the ideological field a struggle went on which reflected the class struggle being waged in the country. In the historical literature of this period one can find works that prove historically the inevitability of the restoration of capitalism, works that provide material for the bourgeois-nationalist groups, and works that propagandize Trotskyist and right-opportunist formulations. The most enduring and extremely harmful for the development of our historical science has been the influence of the anti-Marxist views of the "school" of Pokrovsky, which pushed its unscientific positions under the banner of allegedly most orthodox Marxism. In replacing objective historical knowledge and the study of the concrete development of history with abstract sociological schemes, the "school" of Pokrovsky harassed the Marxist-Leninist study of civic history and inflicted direct damage upon the education of the young generations.

In some sectors of the historical front the traditions of "Pokrovshchina" [35] have continued to be felt until very recent times. The schematicism and failure to understand the dialectics of the historical process, which typified the "school" of Pokrovsky and expressed themselves in Pokrovsky and his disciples in an indiscriminate condemnation of the entire past of the Russian state and all its representatives, are currently manifesting themselves in reverse form, in attempts at indiscriminate and antiscientific praise of the prerevolutionary past of Russia.

II

In drafting the general plan of works in the field of history for the coming years, it is necessary to take into account the general historical setting in which the work will take place. The destruction of fascism will lead (1) to the colossal strengthening of the world-historical role of the U.S.S.R. as the decisive force in the struggle with fascism, and (2) to the clear realization of the moral-political and military superiority of the democratic countries over the fascist countries. Interest is sharply rising

---

[35] The Russian term formed from a name and the ending *"shchina"* means all things connected with the individual—his ideas, habits, deeds, influence, etc.—and usually has a pejorative meaning.

throughout the world in the U.S.S.R., in the history of the Russian people and the other peoples of the Soviet Union, in the history of the evolution of democratic ideas and institutions, in international relations and the history of relations between the countries participating in the anti-fascist coalition in particular, and in the history of wars and military science. More than ever before, people in foreign countries will heed the voice of Soviet scholarship. On the other hand, anti-Marxist tendencies and groupings may again come to life in historical scholarship abroad as a reaction to the growth of the influence of the U.S.S.R. It is known that in the prewar years many problems were tackled in West European and American historical scholarship only because their solution was likely, in the opinion of the respective circles, to strike a blow at the Marxist understanding of history. Furthermore, one must not underestimate the importance of the fascist and pro-fascist tendencies of falsification in historical science. These tendencies may survive in some places even after the destruction of fascism if a persistent struggle is not waged against them, with Soviet scholarship playing as it should the leading role in it. Thus, our historical science faces enormous tasks of extraordinary responsibility. Meanwhile, in a number of fields of investigation, Soviet historical science, even though possessed of methodological superiority, is significantly lagging in the quantity of work, publication of sources, etc. Numerous problems in our science are entirely inadequately handled or not handled at all from the point of view of Marxism-Leninism.

These are the general considerations which have guided the Institute of History and the Division of History and Philosophy in drafting the general plan of works in history.

*   *   *

Problems of U.S.S.R. History. Writing the history of the peoples comprised in the U.S.S.R. constitutes obviously the fundamental task of the Soviet scholarly institutions. Among the various problems of U.S.S.R. history, we consider it necessary to single out as foremost the following categories:

I. Cultural history of the peoples of the U.S.S.R.
II. History of Russian social thought
III. History of Russian science and its influence upon the development of world science
IV. History of cities of the U.S.S.R.
V. History of manufacturing in Russia
VI. History of social classes in the U.S.S.R.
VII. History of the Russian state
VIII. History of the international relations of Russia

IX. History of Russian military art, Russian army, and Russian navy

X. History of the individual peoples of the Soviet Union

XI. History of the Civil War

XII. History of the Soviet state

XIII. History of the industrialization of the U.S.S.R.

XIV. History of the collectivization of agriculture

XV. History of nodal points of the war

XVI. History of the partisan movement

XVII. History of the people's militia

XVIII. History of individual military units

XIX. History of war industry

XX. History of individual republics, areas and districts in the years of the Patriotic War

XXI. History of collectivized peasantry in the Patriotic War

Problems of World History. In studying world history, our scholarly institutions face four basic tasks: (1) illumination of nodal points of the historical process from the point of view of historical materialism and construction thereby of a genuinely scientific history of mankind; (2) refutation of unscientific idealistic conceptions in the field of history and unmasking of the falsifications of fascist "historians"; (3) investigation of those points in the history of foreign countries the understanding of which contributes to the elucidation of the historical evolution of our own country; (4) study of the history of countries close to ours in geographic location or historical destiny, particularly and especially the history of the Slavic peoples. In accordance with this, the Division of History and Philosophy designates the following problems of world history as the fundamental problems for the next few years.

In the field of ancient history:

I. International relations in antiquity—above all, relations among the countries of the East and then relations between countries of the East and West.

II. Slavery and feudalism in the history of countries of the East. On this question there is a sharp difference between the dominant views of the Soviet and foreign historians. While the latter place the beginning of feudal relations in distant antiquity, Soviet historians insist on the late origin of feudalism.

III. The problem of the socioeconomic structure and development of the countries of the Hellenistic East. The development of archeological, papyrological, and numismatic materials and the introduction of new concepts of socioeconomic analysis in studying them have called forth the task of elucidating the socioeconomic structure and development of the countries of the Hellenistic East. At the same time, major novel developments in the foreign literature have brought about the definition and elucidation of many questions of the history of the Hellenistic East in an obviously perverse way ("planned economy" in Ptolemaic Egypt and the like). This demands an increased attention from Soviet Orientalists to the socioeconomic history of the countries of the Hellenistic East, all the more so since several of these countries occupied parts of the southern and southeastern territory of the present-day Soviet Union.

IV. Slaveowning and feudal formations and their interrelation in the concrete history of ancient societies. The questions of the decay of the slaveowning formation, the emergence of the elements of the feudal formation within it, and the nature and concrete forms of the social revolution which cleared the way for the development of feudal relations are questions of enormous scientific significance, so far insufficiently illumined from the Marxist-Leninist point of view.

V. Ideological crisis of the ancient world. The ideological currents that accompanied the process of decay of the ancient slaveowning societies have for a long time attracted the attention of historians. The literature devoted to the rise of Christianity is indeed immense. Nevertheless, there are still quite a few questions requiring study or re-examination. Soviet historical science in this field should continue the work done in its time by the best bourgeois scholarship and re-examine the heritage left by it from the point of view of historical materialism.

VI. Greek Black Sea littoral. The comprehensive study of the ancient and Scythian civilizations and their interrelationship has a great significance not only for the understanding of the history of the ancient world, but for the elucidation of the early history of our country as well.

In the field of medieval history:

I. History of medieval peasantry. Reference is made to the study of the history of the peasantry as the basic mass of the working people in the Middle Ages in the individual countries of Europe in the various stages of the development of feudal society. By working on this problem, the Soviet historians continue the best traditions of Russian medieval studies connected with the names of Vinogradov, Petrushevski, and Savin.

II. Religious and sociopolitical ideologies in the Middle Ages. This problem has for a long time been the domain of idealist historians who have created in this field numerous legends and reactionary distortions.

It is necessary to re-examine again the material on this problem from the dialectical-materialist point of view.

III. Peculiarities of the evolution of medieval Germany. The study of this problem is necessary in order to elucidate the prior conditions of the economic and political development of Germany in the succeeding period leading to the establishment of the most predatory imperialist state in the world. It is also needed for the purpose of unmasking the fascist idealization of the medieval German empire.

IV. History of Byzantine feudalism. This problem includes the topics of "Genesis of Byzantine feudalism and Slavdom," "Byzantine and feudal estate-holding," and "Feudalism and the fall of the Byzantine Empire."

V. International role of Byzantium. The following topics pertain here: "Byzantium and Rus," "Byzantium and the Slavs," "Byzantium and Western Europe," and "Byzantium and the East."

The place occupied by Byzantium in the international relations of medieval Europe and the Orient is absolutely unique. Byzantium represents a sort of nodal point where the interests of Kievan and Muscovite Rus, the countries of western Europe, the countries of the Near East, and the countries of the Mediterranean area crossed each other. This problem has a great significance for the history of Rus and its international relations.

In the field of the history of the East in the Middle Ages:

VI. Russian people and the peoples of the medieval East.
VII. Rise of feudalism in the countries of the medieval East.

In the field of modern history:

I. Agrarian relations on the eve of and during the bourgeois revolutions. Regardless of the fact that there are quite a few studies devoted to this problem in historical science, it must not be considered as sufficiently studied from the point of view of the requirements placed upon our Marxist-Leninist science. As examples of individual topics in this field, the following may be pointed out: "Feudal reaction on the eve of the bourgeois revolution" and "Agrarian relations and revolutionary conditions."

II. Industrial revolution in western Europe and the United States of America. Contemporary bourgeois historical science has made much effort in the last decades to oppose the Marx-Engels conception of the industrial revolution with the conception of the evolutionary development of the capitalist forms of industry. The apologist purpose of these efforts is clear to us. However, huge factual material has been employed in these works. Our task is to oppose the apologist interpretation of the industrial revolution with its truly scientific and dialectical-materialist interpretation. For this it is necessary to carry out much work of collecting, analyzing, and interpreting pertinent historical sources.

III. History of social classes in modern times. Individual problems for investigation in this field are the insufficiently studied history of the working class, peasantry, and petty bourgeoisie. The inadequate study of the history of the petty bourgeoisie from the Marxist-Leninist point of view should be emphasized. The role of the petty bourgeoisie in the class struggle of the eighteenth and nineteenth centuries cannot be regarded as deserving no attention from the historian. This group of problems comprises the topics on the history of the labor movement.

IV. History of social thought in the eighteenth and nineteenth centuries. Here rise as most relevant to the present the problems of the history of progressive social thought, democratic and socialist. However, it is extremely important to study the various manifestations of reactionary thought which constitute the antecedents of fascism. This is also necessary for the purpose of a complete elucidation of the genesis and nature of fascism and for the purpose of the struggle with the pro-fascist tendencies in Western historical science.

V. Genesis and development of imperialism and its specificities in individual countries. The study of this problem presupposes work on the history of imperialism in individual countries. The basic topic here, of course, is "Genesis and development of predatory German imperialism."

VI. National liberation movements in the countries of western Europe. It is necessary to re-examine the material carefully from a new angle of vision. As examples of desirable topics we suggest "The Slavic movement of 1848–49" and "The national liberation movement in Italy."

On these questions bourgeois historiography in general and German historiography in particular have created and embedded quite a few prejudices in the public mind.

VII. History of international relations in the nineteenth and twentieth centuries. The importance of this section for understanding the international relations of the present time is clear to anyone.

VIII. The English revolution of the seventeenth century.

IX. The revolution of 1848–49.

In the field of contemporary history: In contemporary history the central group of problems is undoubtedly constituted by the Second World War and its preparation. The efforts of our historians in the immediate period ahead should be addressed to these problems. The full elucidation of the historical process which led to the Second World War requires a careful and comprehensive study of the social and political history of the principal countries of Europe and America in the age of imperialism and, especially, in the period between the two wars.

An enormous problem in scope and significance is the history of the war itself.

In the field of the history of Slavic peoples: The rise of interest in the life and history of the Slavic peoples resulting from the Great Patriotic War requires the separation of the problems of Slavic studies in a special group. Russian Slavic studies in the past made quite a few contributions, and Russian Slavists resolved many important problems in all fields of Slavic studies. However, our prerevolutionary Slavic studies also had a number of shortcomings of a methodological and political nature. Soviet Slavic studies, despite the existence of individual outstanding investigators and investigations, are undoubtedly lagging behind in meeting the demands placed on them by life. It is urgently necessary to unite all forces in Slavic studies, attract many young workers, and restore and strengthen the ties with Slavists abroad. By using the whole heritage of prerevolutionary Slavic studies, Soviet Slavists have the task of lifting the history of the Slavic peoples to a new high level and illuminating it with the light of Marxist-Leninist historical science.

Among the problems arising here in addition to the problem of "Ethnogenesis of the Slavic peoples," we may mention the following:

I. Problem of the origin and development of state and law among the Slavic peoples.

II. History of the struggle of the Slavic peoples for freedom.

III. The cultural unity of the Slavic peoples. The investigation of this problem on the basis of a study of artifacts, language, folklore, etc., constitutes the immediate task of Slavic studies in our countries as well as abroad.

IV. Russian-Slavic relations. This problem requires the efforts of historians of various specialties. It is necessary to study the political, economic, and cultural ties of Russia with the Western and Southern Slavs in the various stages of historical development, with special attention to modern times (nineteenth century).

In the field of modern and contemporary history of the peoples of the East. The basic groups of problems in this field are:

I. "Relations between the countries of the West and the countries of the East in the nineteenth and twentieth centuries."

II. "Colonial policy of states toward the countries of the East."
III. "National movements in the countries of the East."
IV. "History of agrarian relations in the countries of the East."
V. "History of social thought in the countries of the East."

In the first group of problems, Soviet historians should regard the following as foremost: "Russia and her eastern neighbors." The second group consists of the following basic problems: "Forms and methods of colonial subjugation"; "Struggle of states for colonies"; and "Policy toward colonies in the Second World War." It is also extremely important to begin work on the study of ideology in the Eastern countries of Japan, China, and India. The study of sociopolitical and philosophic ideas is the necessary condition for the correct understanding of the slogans and programs of the groupings struggling within these countries.

The series of problems of contemporary history of the countries of the East involves the cycle of:

VI. Pacific Ocean problems, the study of which is the task of the special Pacific Ocean Institute. Central place among these problems is held and shall be held in the next several years by (1) general political problems of the war in the Pacific; (2) questions of colonial policy of Pacific countries; and (3) study of proposals for postwar changes in the political and economic status of the Pacific.

The plan should include the following topics relative to the above field:

1. "History of the war in the Pacific." Here are envisaged monographs on questions of diplomatic and military history of the war in the Pacific as well as works characterizing conditions in the individual Pacific countries during the Second World War. First of all, the following monographs are projected: "Japanese-American relations on the eve of the war in the Pacific," "India and the war in the Pacific," and "The colonial system and the war in the Pacific."

2. "Postwar political status of the Pacific." Here are envisaged monographs devoted to analysis of numerous proposals and plans for the postwar organization of the Pacific as well as concrete studies characterizing the postwar changes and conditions in the individual Pacific countries such as Japan and her colonies, China (including Manchuria and Inner Mongolia), French Indochina, Thailand, Burma, British Malaya, the Philippines, Dutch East India, Oceania, Australia, New Zealand, Alaska, the western states of the U.S.A., Canada, Mexico and other Latin American countries of the Pacific basin, and, separately, India (which, even though not a Pacific country, is politically drawn into the orbit of the "Pacific problem").

3. "The Soviet Union and the Pacific countries." Monographs are proposed to disclose the great and honorable role of the U.S.S.R. as a force actively working for the establishment of justice and lasting peace in the Pacific. Concretely, works are projected to show the growth of the ideological-political influence of the Soviet Union upon certain social strata in the various Pacific countries, the responses to the Leninist-Stalinist national policy in dependent and colonial countries of the Pacific basin, the gigantic growth of the international prestige of the Soviet state resulting from the heroic and victorious struggle of the Soviet people against Hitlerite Germany. In the first place, a work on "The influence of the Great Patriotic War of the Soviet Union upon the liberation struggle in China" is projected.

Setting for themselves broad research tasks, historians are not turning away from major synthesizing works which sum up the monographic work completed. These synthesizing works are needed for the broad masses of readers as well as for the historians themselves as an antidote to the extremes of narrow specialization; when correctly formulated, they are not only not in the way of research but are a condition fostering its growth. Several such synthesizing works on historical subjects are planned in our institutes. These are, above all, a multivolume "History of the U.S.S.R. from earliest times," a multivolume "History of Russian culture," and, finally, "World History." All these publications have in major part been prepared and must be pushed forward and completed. The need is felt to produce a multivolume "History of international relations and diplomacy" and a historical encyclopedia. It is absolutely necessary to prepare a series of volumes of the synthesizing type for the thirtieth anniversary of the October Socialist Revolution.

No less important for the development of historical science is the publication of historical sources. In this respect we have fallen behind in recent years; the volume of publication of sources has sharply decreased. Meanwhile, many sources published earlier have become bibliographic rarities. It is necessary to begin the systematic serial publication of various types of sources of the history of the peoples of the U.S.S.R., such as public documents, chronicles, memoirs, etc. The sources of the history of each people should be published in uniform pattern and in strict observance of the basic principles of scholarly publication of sources. Many foreign countries are ahead of us in this respect. In almost all countries of Europe, the sources of their history are systematically published. We possess the scientific manpower for the execution of this task. The methods of publication are developed to a degree of excellence. In order to place the study of history on strictly scientific foundations, it is necessary to begin at once the organization of the work involved in the systematic publication of documents.

In this connection, it is of particularly great importance to resume the publication of the multivolume series "International relations in the age of imperialism" and to prepare and publish the diplomatic documents pertaining to the 1918–1941 period.

At the same time, it is necessary for us to undertake seriously work in historiography. Precise knowledge of the history of our science is one of the tools of the struggle for a correct approach to its development and against the various errors and distortions. Regrettably, in this field, too, we have done very little in recent years; research in historiography is done in craftsmanlike fashion and on a scale which does not satisfy at all. The Division is in favor of creating a special commission on historiography.

Finally, we must strengthen and in some cases actually renovate the work in the auxiliary historical disciplines. Without numismatics, paleography, historical geography, etc., there can be no work in a number of most important historical problems. In the meantime, however, the number of scholars having mastery of the material of these disciplines in our country has not risen but has catastrophically dropped. We must achieve here a decisive reversal and guarantee the proper development of the still weak nuclei in the auxiliary historical disciplines organized in the Institute of History and the Institute of History of Material Culture.

All this enormous program cannot, of course, be realized by the Institute of History of the Academy of Sciences alone, no matter how much we increase its staff. It presupposes the co-operation of many scientific institutions and, first of all, of the scientific institutions of the academies of the union republics and branches of the U.S.S.R. Academy of Sciences as well as the chairs at the institutions of higher education. Thus, the history of the culture of the Georgian people, the history of the Georgian people, and the history of the Georgian peasantry should be studied by the Institute of History of the Georgian Academy of Sciences, and so on.

For a successful solution of the major tasks facing us on the historical front, it is necessary to carry out in the next several years the following organizational plans:

I. Create a special Archeographic Commission of union-wide scope to regulate the work on preparation of historical sources for publication in the entire country.

II. Ensure to historians access to documents held in the archives and aids facilitating the speediest investigation of documents (publication of lists of archival holdings, descriptions, guides, etc.).

III. Strengthen in every way the international ties of historians.

IV. Strengthen the ties of the Institute of History with other institutes and chairs working in the field of history and in the areas of adjacent and related disciplines (Institute of Philosophy, Institute of Economics, Institute of Ethnography, etc.) for co-ordination of effort directed toward the solution of common tasks. Establish around the Institute a wide circle of historians connected with it through their work.

V. Establish (along with improving the *Istoricheskii zhurnal*) a number of periodicals on questions of history to publish research papers, critical reviews, and bibliographic information.

The postwar years to the death of Stalin (1945–53) witnessed in history as in the general area of ideology and education the stiffening of the characteristic features of Stalin's regime: theoretical dogmatism, intellectual orthodoxy, Soviet patriotism (with periodic attacks on Western culture and the "rootless cosmopolitanism" of the Jews), and totalitarian coercion. In the early part of this period, management of Soviet intellectual life seemed to be assigned to A. A. Zhdanov (head of the "Propaganda and Agitation" department of the Central Committee since 1938), who in 1946 delivered a scathing attack against the "grovelers" before "decadent bourgeois culture," which, he said, was "in a state of miasma and corruption." [35] Zhdanov's regime came to end with his death in 1948, but "Zhdanovshchina" did not. The atmosphere and themes remained the same in the ensuing years when Georgi M. Malenkov (1902–) began to move to the fore as Stalin's closest associate and manager of ideological affairs.

In accordance with the 1945 plan, historical work was pushed in almost all of the designated directions. The leading history journal, *Istoricheskii zhurnal*, was reorganized and retitled *Voprosy istorii* ("Problems of History"; 1945–) and allowed to grow to its present annual size, which is twice that of its American counterpart, *the American Historical Review*. Slavic and Byzantine studies, in which Russian prerevolutionary scholarship had performed well, were now recalled from the limbo where early Marxist zeal and Pokrovsky's influence had committed them. Because of their close identification with Slavophilism, Pan-Slavism, and Tsarist interests, Slavic studies had been viewed by the Marxists before the revolution with intense hostility which became policy for most of the two decades after 1917. By the late 1930's, however, the Stalinist change in historiographic policy and the necessity of preparing for a confrontation with Germany brought about renewed recognition of the importance of Slavic studies to Russian interests. In 1939 a section for Slavic studies was set up in the Institute of History, and in 1942 a "Slavic Commission" was established under the Presidium of the Academy of Sciences to stimulate and co-ordinate work in all aspects of Slavic studies.[36] In January 1947

---

[35] It is illustrative of Zhdanov's importance at the time that the University of Leningrad was (and remains) named after him.

[36] For the plan of its work see *220 let Akademii Nauk SSSR* [Two Hundred and Twenty Years of the Academy of Sciences of the U.S.S.R.] (Moscow, 1945), p. 272.

these were amalgamated as the Institute of Slavic Studies of the Academy of Sciences to serve as the central Soviet agency for the execution, promotion, and co-ordination of studies in Bulgarian, Czechoslovak, Polish, and Yugoslav history.[37] In 1948, teams of scholars associated with the new institute were commissioned to produce general country histories for Bulgaria, Czechoslovakia, Poland, and Yugoslavia intended for use in the Soviet Union and abroad as summations and guideposts of the growing Marxist historiography in this field.[38] Byzantine studies—rejected after 1917 because the two bulwarks of the order that had been overthrown, Tsarist autocracy and the Orthodox Church, had grown out of Byzantine traditions—received similar impetus with the establishment of a section in the Institute of History in 1944 and the resumption of the publication of the well-known prerevolutionary periodical *Vizantiiskii vremennik* ("Byzantine Journal") in 1947.[39]

Another field—that of Oriental studies—in which prerevolutionary Russian scholarship had preformed well, fared considerably better in the interwar period. The Soviet government's interest in actual and potential revolutionary conditions in Asia reflected itself in toleration and some encouragement of old-regime Orientalists and, with the establishment of an Institute of Oriental Studies in the Academy in 1930, in active promotion of work in this field.[40] An area in which the work envisaged by the 1945 plan

---

[37] V. Picheta, "Institut slavianovedeniia Akademii nauk SSSR i ego zadachi" [The Institute of Slavic Studies of the Academy of Sciences of the U.S.S.R. and Its Tasks], *Voprosy istorii*, No. 5, 1947, pp. 165–167.

[38] Eventually, histories of Bulgaria (2 vols.; 1954–55), Czechoslovakia (3 vols.; 1956–60), Poland (3 vols.; 1954–58), and Yugoslavia (2 vols.; 1963) were produced. For the products of the Institute and Soviet scholars in the general field of Slavic studies see the two-volume bibliography compiled by I. A. Kaloeva for 1918–60 and 1961–62, *Sovetskoe slavianovedenie; literatura o zarubezhnykh slavianskikh stranakh na russkom iazykye*, [Soviet Slavic Studies: Literature on the Slavic Countries Abroad in the Russian Language] (Moscow, 1963). See also Marin Pundeff, "Sowjetische Forschungsarbeiten zur neuzeitlichen Balkan-Geschichte," *Saeculum*, XV, No. 3 (1964), 273–297.

[39] For Soviet work in Byzantine studies see the numerous historiographic and bibliographic articles in *Vizantiiskii vremennik*; Z. V. Udal'tsova, *Osnovnye problemy vizantinovedenii v sovetskoi istoricheskoi nauke* [Basic Problems of Byzantine Studies in Soviet Historical Science] (Moscow, 1955) ; and N. P. Sokolov, *Sorok let sovetskogo vizantinovedeniia* [Forty Years of Soviet Byzantine Studies] (Gorki, 1959).

[40] For a discussion of Soviet Oriental studies in the postwar years see Rodger Swearingen, "Asian Studies in the Soviet Union," *Journal of Asian Studies*, XVII (1958), 515–537. Studies pertaining to China are listed in *Bibliografiia Kitaia*, comp. P. E. Skachkov (Moscow, 1960) ; Japan, in *Bibliografiia Iaponii* (Moscow, 1960) ; India, in *Bibliografiia Indii* (Moscow, 1965) ; Southeast Asia, in *Bibliografiia Iugovostochnoi Azii* (Moscow, 1960) ; Turkey, in *Bibliografiia Turtsii* (Moscow, 1959) ; and Outer Mongolia, in *Mongol'skaia Narodnaia Respublika; bibliografiia knizhnoi i zhurnal'noi literatury na russkom iazyke, 1935–1950* [Mongolian People's Republic: Bibliography of Books and Articles in Russian, 1935–1950] (Moscow, 1953) and its extension *Bibliografiia Mongol'skoi Narodnoi Respubliki; knigi i stat'i na russkom iazyke, 1951–1961* [Bibliography of the Mongolian People's Republic: Books and Articles in Russian, 1951–1961] (Moscow, 1963).

was not allowed to proceed while Stalin was alive was the study of the history of the Second World War and its Soviet phase termed the Great Patriotic War.[41] Barring the professionals from a genuine study of the war, the regime gave the field to the party propagandists to build new Stalinist myths, such as the portrayal of the forced retreat in the face of the German fury in 1941 as a preconceived plan of "active defense" devised by Stalin, the praising of Stalin as the "greatest commander of all ages," and the quashing of all questions concerning the massive Soviet defeats and the chaos, disorganization, and defection at the front and in the rear in the early part of the "Great Patriotic War." The result of this policy was absence of any publication of documents and sources or of serious monographic works; for all practical purposes, Stalin's wartime writings and speeches, last published in 1949, constituted the official history of the war until 1953.[42]

The approach maintained in the postwar years is well conveyed in M. A. Zinov'ev, *Osnovnye voprosy metodiki prepodavaniia istorii* (Moscow, 1948). This manual on methods of teaching history was issued by the Academy of Pedagogical Sciences of the R.S.F.S.R., the principal Soviet agency having jurisdiction over methodological, administrative, and curricular problems in education. It has been translated under the auspices of the American Council of Learned Societies as *Soviet Methods of Teaching History* (Washington, 1952). The opening chapter, on "Tasks and Content of Historical Teaching Methods" (omitting the footnotes), follows.

29. M. A. Zinoviev, Soviet Methods of Teaching History

The importance of historical education in the system of general secondary education is clear to every Soviet pedagogue. The newspaper *Pravda* in its edition of January 27, 1936, wrote concerning the attention given historical education by the Central Committee of the Party, guided by the great Stalin: "It (the Central Committee) sees, as did Marx, Engels, and

---

[41] This designation, which the regime promoted, grew out of the parallel with the war of 1812 against the French, termed the Patriotic War in traditional Russian history.

[42] For a discussion of the handling of history in 1945–53 see Matthew P. Gallagher, *The Soviet History of World War II: Myths, Memories, and Realities* (New York, 1963), pp. 37–127. Later work is listed in G. A. Kumanev, *Velikaia Otechestvennaia Voina Sovetskogo Soiuza, 1941–1945 gg.; bibliografiia sovetskoi istoricheskoi literatury za 1946–1959 gg.* [The Great Patriotic War of the Soviet Union, 1941–1945: Bibliography of the Soviet Historical Literature, 1946–1959] (Moscow, 1960) and *Velikaia Otechestvennaia Voina Sovetskogo Soiuza, 1941–1945 gg.; rekomendatel'nyi ukazatel' literatury* [The Great Patriotic War of the Soviet Union: Bibliography of Recommended Literature] (Moscow, 1965).

Lenin, that history is a powerful weapon in the struggle for socialism. The popular masses of the U.S.S.R. must know the real history of mankind, the history of the enslavement and liberation of the working masses; they must know where we come from and where we are going, because this will increase tenfold the conviction of workers and kolkhoz members in the inevitable victory of socialism and will give them a knowledge of the conditions of this victory. They must get a concrete idea of the sources of power, of the methods of domination by the exploiting classes, an idea of the sources of power and the methods of struggle of the working masses for liberation. They must get, not a dead scheme of arising and decaying social-economic formations, but a concrete picture of a class struggle with the characteristics of their leaders, concrete characteristics of class relations in this struggle, because only in this way will history teach them that which is its objective, as a political science, that is, about the struggle for power and its preservation."

We are obliged to improve and increase our work in the field of the ideological-political education of youth first of all by the decision of the Central Committee of the Party concerning the periodicals *Zvezda* ("The Star") and *Leningrad* and the subsequent decision on questions of ideological-political education.

History is a powerful weapon of communist education and it must wholly serve the cause of the struggle for communism.

"Historism" is a distinctive trait of Marxist-Leninist conceptions of the world. The laws of historical development were discovered for the first time by Marx and Engels, and Lenin and Stalin developed them further and adapted them to the new stage of social development.

Comrade Stalin wrote: "It is clear that the existence and development of the science of history is impossible without such a historical approach to social phenomena because such an approach to the matter prevents the science of history from being converted into a chaos of fortuities and into a series of the most ridiculous errors."

By cultivating and developing in students "historism," that is, a historic attitude with regard to the phenomena of social life, we establish in their consciousness the bases of dialectic thinking. In this respect the task of the school consists of showing the student "the process of the development of mankind in history" and in showing that "nature also has its history in time."

In cultivating in the student a historical attitude in regard to life, we must be guided by the following directions of Lenin, given in his lecture "On the State": "not to forget the basic historical connections, to consider every problem from the point of view of how a given historical phenomenon originated, what were the main stages of its development, and from the point of view of its development see what ultimately became of this phenomenon."

The bourgeois school did not and could not manage the task of cultivating the historical attitude toward life on the part of students because true "historism" is alien to the bourgeois mentality.

If one is to be a consistent historian, he necessarily admits that the bourgeois order is destined to destruction, an admission which cannot be made by a thinker who bases himself on bourgeois premises. That is why such a thinker does not utilize historical categories for the basis of the bourgeois social structure.

In this regard the Soviet school differs radically from the bourgeois. Soviet history teachers have mastered dialectic and historical materialism. As we know, the historical development of mankind proceeds according to the rules of materialistic dialectics; as a result of this, history teachers in Soviet secondary schools are able to demonstrate to their students dialectics in action over thousands of years. It is possible that a student will not hear a word from the teacher about the rules of dialectic development in the form of abstract formulae, for instance, about the transition from quantity to quality, about dialectic jumping, about the unity of opposites, the role of ideas, and so forth but he will gain a practical acquaintance with dialectics while still in school through history lessons. Following the concrete facts of history and drawing conclusions from them, the student will think dialectically and will only later learn that he is thinking according to the laws of materialistic dialectics. In order to attain that important educational aim, the teacher is bound to organize his teaching carefully, thinking over how to reveal dialectics in history to the students. Unfortunately our Soviet method of teaching history in secondary schools to date has never brought up for discussion the question of cultivating on the part of students a historical attitude toward life. And meanwhile it is now comparatively easy to reflect on the basic theses of dialectics applicable to the teaching of history, because in Stalin's work "On Dialectic and Historical Materialism" we have a brilliant and at the same time brief and clear exposition of the laws of dialectic development.

The teaching of Marxism-Leninism about the system of relationships between historical phenomena in the form of the teaching of social and economic structures, through which the peoples of the world have to pass in their historic development, do not contradict the representation of history as a multiform process, proceeding differently in different countries. In this connection, the following thought of Marx acquires a particularly significant meaning: "The same economic basis—the same from the aspect of the primary conditions, thanks to the infinitely varying empiric circumstances, natural conditions, racial relationships, acting outside of historical influ-

ences, etc.—may reveal in its manifestations endless variations and gradations, which can be understood only by an analysis of these given empirical
circumstances."

The task of the method of teaching history is to show how to teach
students in the form of a school course of specific history the basic
principles of Marxist-Leninist historical science.

This task is divided into two parts. It is necessary: (1) to determine
the bases of the science, and (2) to develop the methods of teaching these
bases.

The bases of the science are determined by the program according to
which lessons are conducted in the schools. The history program determines
the tasks and the contents of history courses, their extent and sequence in
the different school grades.

Methods and modes of teaching history are various and are determined:
(1) by the content and character of the historical material which has to be
studied by the students; (2) by the individual qualities of the teacher, his
experience, age, temperament, education, etc.; (3) by the individual composition of the class, the mental development of the students, their age and
sex, general conditions of work in the school and by other circumstances.

All this indicates the diversity of the teaching process. But this diversity
does not prevent the method of teaching history from being a science. Just
as in historical science, the infinite diversity of historic processes in various
countries makes it possible for Soviet scientists to determine historic systems of relationships—so in the method of teaching history the infinite
variety of the pedagogical process in different teachers, in different classes
and at different times of teaching history—makes it possible for us to
determine pedagogical laws. For underlying the fundamentals of teaching
are the psychological processes, which, for all their variety, proceed in
conformity with certain laws.

That is why we can speak also of the systems of relationships of
pedagogical processes in the field of teaching history, determine them, and
study the conditions of their course. It is these pedagogical relationships
that are studied by historical teaching method.

There are two basic methods of research in the field of the method of
teaching history: (1) scientific-pedagogical observation and the study of
teaching methods (study of teaching experience) in school and (2) pedagogical experiments. The task of both of these methods is to determine
pedagogical facts, the study and generalizations of which constitute the task
of teaching method as a science.

In applying methods of scientific observation and experiment, the researcher must strive to determine the authenticity of the pedagogical fact
and consequently to have the pedagogical process at the time of the scien-

tific observation and experiment proceed under natural conditions and remain unaltered in the presence of the investigator-experimentalist. This is necessary inasmuch as the teacher and the students often feel and work differently at the time of investigation in the presence of strangers from what they usually do.

Thus, the determination of pedagogical facts in the field of history teaching by means of observation and experiment, their description, generalization, and the drawing of pedagogical relationships for this on the basis of given materialistic dialectics all form the content of the science of the method of teaching history. We must distinguish the *method* of teaching history from teaching history. Teaching method is theory, and teaching is practice, that is, the application of theory. Marxism-Leninism teaches us that theory adds sureness to practice, gives the force of orientation and the comprehension of internal connections; practice without theory is blind. That is why every teacher of history must study teaching method.

V. I. Lenin said: "It would be incorrect to think that it is enough to adopt communist slogans [and] conclusions of communist science without having absorbed all the facts the consequence of which is communism itself. . . . We have no need of learning by rote but we need to develop and improve the memory of every student through the knowledge of basic facts, because communism would become an inanity, an empty placard, the communist would be but a simple boaster, if all acquired ideas were not assimilated into his consciousness."

Thus, mastery of good teaching can be ensured only by creative application of method in the practice of teaching.

A teacher who has not studied method teaches blindfolded without picturing to himself clearly the end results of his work. He has not yet embraced the process of teaching as a whole, often does not foresee the difficulties and makes mistakes which have been described long ago in method. It is only after many years of work, and not always even then, that teachers rectify their mistakes and become sure of their pedagogical work. But it happens often that bad modes of work which the teacher applied, having no knowledge of method, become habits.

Teaching method gives a description of the process of teaching as a whole, shows difficulties, possible errors, indicates ways of attaining better results in teaching. This makes teachers conscious of their work; they work systematically and it accelerates greatly the process of developing a teacher into a master of pedagogy. A teacher can also become a master of pedagogy after several years of work even without method, but one must bear in mind that individual experience is limited while collective experience, described and scientifically adapted in teaching method, is unlimited and makes it possible for teachers to develop broadly their pedagogical capabilities.

The scientific working-over and description of collective teaching experience excludes the so-called "prescriptionist" methods of history as worthless. It often occurs that a teacher expects from "methods of (teaching) history" detailed indications on separate lessons. "Prescriptions" regulating a determined order of structure and the conducting of a lesson bind the creative capacities of teachers, prevent their pedagogical growth. In reducing the teaching method to an assemblage of methodological elaborations, prescriptions prevent the further growth of method as a science.

In his work a secondary-school teacher of history deals with very complex historical processes and facts, where economic questions are interwoven with political struggle, and cultural factors are closely linked with economic and cultural events. The teachers have to expose and reveal historic processes, where struggling masses are participants, and where prominent historical personalities play a considerable role. In short, teachers deal not with factors of a certain isolated part of history, as economic factors only, or facts of class struggle of military-historical importance, etc., but with facts depicting a historical process in its entirety, in all its complexity. It is true that in courses of history in secondary schools one deals more with economic and cultural factors, but these facts are always interlaced and closely connected with various other facts.

Because of the great complexity of historical material there can be very different forms of its rendering, the utilization of most diverse methodic means. That is why the "methodic prescription" assuming only one form of exposition of historic material and no other establishes the predominance of patterns, kills the live, creative source in teaching, and dries up vital pedagogical work. This explains why one cannot reduce method to a gathering of prescriptions.

Along with "the prescription method" appears so-called "methodic nihilism," which is a complete denial of teaching method. Its clearest description was formulated by Professor Vipper in his article published in the periodical review *Mir Bozhii* in 1893. In his article Professor Vipper considers method as a combination of the technical modes of teaching; he refuses to recognize teaching method as a science and calls it scholasticism. He asserts that it is enough for a student preparing himself to become a teacher to complete the general university course. He wrote: "There is no doubt that the general university course developing the mental outlook of the future teacher, will give him a more substantial base for his future activity, than the investing in him of 'preparations of pedagogical pharmacies.'"

Unfortunately, the negative attitude toward teaching method, the refusal to recognize it as a scientific discipline, is still widespread among some scientific workers and many teachers. Such views can be explained by erroneous representation of the problems and contents of teaching method. Professor Vipper as well as all nihilists of method imagine teaching method as a combination of technical modes of teaching with no connection with the material which is taught; in other words, they picture quite incorrectly the tasks of history teaching methods. But the method of teaching history, as we have seen, has the precise purpose of determining the content of historical knowledge which has to be mastered by the students, and, in the second place, of determining the methods of transmitting this knowledge. That is why it is absurd to repudiate teaching method by misinterpreting its tasks and content and by ascribing to this science content which it does not have.

Developing principles and a system of teaching, the method of teaching history necessarily deals with history as with a single subject of instruction, as a subject possessing certain common aspects in the fifth as well as in the seventh and ninth classes, which does not eliminate, of course, some differences in the teaching of history depending upon the year taught. As a subject of instruction, history possesses some well-known peculiarities, distinguishing it from other subjects (for instance, mathematics, the Russian language, etc.). The task of the method of teaching history is to determine the educational and indoctrinational properties of history as a subject of instruction, to make it clear that history by its content is a bearer of communist indoctrination and that communist indoctrination is not a sort of appendage to the content, introducing some thesis or other differing from the true exposition of historical events. A teacher must understand that history is in itself scientifically, that is, in the light of the Marxist-Leninist outlook and truthful exposition, a perfect weapon for the communist indoctrination of students.

The question of the analysis of historic facts, of their generalization, the development and forming of general historical concepts, and the bringing of students to the understanding of the Marxist conception of history is a very important part of the method of teaching history. Teachers must understand clearly exactly in what the analysis and generalization of historic events consist, what kinds of generalizations are made in school practice, how general concepts develop in students' minds, how and when it is most expedient to perform the work of bringing students to a Marxist understanding of history.

A part of teaching method is devoted to a clarification of the question of the history of the development of methodic thought in the field of teaching history in secondary schools. At present one cannot develop consciously the problems of teaching history without knowing the history of the origin and development of methodic concepts. From this historical outline of the development of method a teacher will learn about the most popular and authoritative manuals and textbooks of the past, about typical peculiarities of preparing and giving lessons, and about the purposes of teaching history. All this broadens the teacher's horizons, enriches his experience, and introduces a still greater consciousness into his work.

The last remaining years of the Stalin era were marked by further moves to intimidate the intellectuals and scholars and to tighten the controls over their thinking and work. In 1948, the head of the State Planning Commission since 1938 and former associate of Zhdanov in the Leningrad purges, N. A. Voznesenskii (1903–1950), published a book on the Soviet economy in the Second World War, *Voennaia ekonomika SSSR v period Otechestvennoi voiny*,[43] in which he propounded the thesis that the socialist economy is determined by the state planning agencies, that the state is the "driving power" in such an economy, and that the state's planning activities constitute its law of development. A lucid and succinct exposition, the book was acclaimed in the party press and won new prestige for its youthful and dynamic author in party circles. Although it was most deferential to Stalin and propounded views which Stalin himself had expressed, the book and its author became the object of Stalin's ire. In several statements culminating in the essay *Economic Problems of Socialism in the U.S.S.R.* (Moscow, 1952), Stalin personally set forth the official line in economics. Voznesenskii's book was declared "anti-Marxist and unscientific" and was confiscated; meanwhile its author disappeared from public life and was shot on Stalin's orders in 1950.[44]

The purposes of intimidating and controlling the historians were served by several prolonged discussions of the question of a Marxist periodization of Russian history and the significance for historiography of the essay *Marxism and Problems of Linguistics* (Moscow, 1950), with which Stalin set forth the official line in the field of linguistics. A vexatious central problem to Soviet historians, the matter of meaningfully periodizing Russian history from the Marxist view of the five successive economic formations had been extensively discussed two decades earlier, but only minor aspects were settled. A consensus seemed reached at that time that Russia had skipped the slaveowning formation and that the feudal formation in Russia extended from the establishment of a state in the ninth century to the liquidation of serfdom in the nineteenth. However, even these formulas were not elevated to the status of dogma, and the whole problem of Marxist periodization continued to harass the work of Soviet historians. In December 1948 the Institute of History of the Academy sponsored a new discussion, initiated with a report by one of its members, Professor S. V.

---

[43] See the American Council of Learned Societies translation, *The Economy of the USSR During World War II* (Washington, 1948).

[44] See Khrushchev's 1956 speech, in reading no. 32, and Druzhinin, *op. cit.*, pp. 514–515. In the years since 1956 steps have been taken to restore Voznesenskii and his work to good standing; a Soviet biography of him has been announced as forthcoming.

Bakhrushin. Bakhrushin proposed a dual principle for establishing the periods in Russian history by using socioeconomic phenomena of the basis as well as political phenomena of the superstructure. The resulting exchanges again produced little that has remained firm, but did serve as occasions for the regime to make its controls felt.[45]

A situation with ludicrous and grotesque elements developed with the appearance of Stalin's pronouncement on linguistics. The theories of N. Ia. Marr (1864–1934) and his school had been regarded as the extension of Marxism into the field of linguistics and were the basis of the work of Soviet archeologists and historians of the early Slavs such as Grekov, N. S. Derzhavin, and others; one of the signs of Marr's supreme authority was the fact that the Academy's Institute of History of Material Culture was named after him. In his pronouncement, Stalin branded Marr's views and school as "anti-Marxist and unscientific" and called for eradication of the "cult of Marr." Linguists, archeologists, historians, and others in the Soviet Union and the satellite countries hastened to make apologies for having been blind to Marr's sins.[46] After Stalin's death his intervention in the field of linguistics has been blamed for "erroneous assertions" concerning the interrelationship between basis and superstructure.[47]

---

[45] For a full discussion of the periodization problem and its status in 1929–34 and 1948–53 see Leo Yaresh, "The Problem of Periodization," in Black, *op. cit.*, pp. 34–77, and Shteppa, *op. cit.*, pp. 242–275.

[46] See, for example, Derzhavin's letter to *Voprosy istorii* (No. 7, 1952, pp. 153–155). For the repercussions in the satellite countries see, *ibid.*, No. 8, 1952, pp. 121–138. The whole episode is discussed in Shteppa, *op. cit.*, pp. 285–318, and Wetter, *op. cit.* (see, above, n. 20), pp. 196–202.

[47] *Istoriia Kommunisticheskoi partii Sovetskogo Soiuza* (2d ed.; Moscow, 1962), pp. 621–624.

CHAPTER VII

THE SECOND INTERREGNUM, 1953–1955

THE SECOND INTERREGNUM was opened by Stalin's death in March 1953 and the establishment of a "collective leadership" to fill the void. Seniority in the collective leadership appeared to be held by Malenkov, who became Prime Minister, Viacheslav M. Molotov (1890—), Foreign Minister, and Lavrentii D. Beria (1899–1953), head of the police, but in the redistribution of power Khrushchev ended up by being the ranking secretary in the party secretariat.

Employing Stalin's strategy of the 1920's, Khrushchev proceeded from the secretariat to build personal alliances and connections through new personnel appointments for an eventual bid for supreme power. In the end of 1953 he helped to remove Beria from his key position and carry out his condemnation and execution, for having been, among other things, an agent of British intelligence since 1919.[1] In retrospect it appears that Khrushchev had achieved victory in his struggle for power with Malenkov by January 1955.[2] Indeed, in February of that year Malenkov stepped down as Prime Minister, being replaced by Khrushchev's nominee for the position, Nikolai A. Bulganin (1895—); Khrushchev's conduct of the reconciliation with Yugoslavia in Belgrade in May 1955 demonstrated that he had prevailed over Molotov, who was dropped from the post of Foreign Minister in the following year.

Beyond some statements in the party press warning against the "cult of personality" without specifying Stalin, the brief period of the second interregnum showed no changes in Soviet historiography. Authoritative material on history was published in Volume 19 of the second edition of the *Bol'shaia Sovetskaia Entsiklopediia* ("The Large Soviet Encyclopedia"), which is one of the most effective vehicles of official information and positions in the Soviet Union. Bearing the *podpisano k pechati* ("signed for printing") date of June 16, 1953, the volume was obviously prepared for the press before or shortly after Stalin died.[3] Its several articles dealing

---

[1] The charge was that he was recruited by British intelligence while he headed the Bolshevik apparatus in his native Georgia and Transcaucasia. His book *On the Question of the History of the Bolshevik Organizations in the Transcaucasian Regions,* detailing events of this period and glorifying Stalin's part in them, was published in 1935 and hailed as an "enormous contribution to the history of Bolshevism." See reading no. 27.

[2] Phillip E. Mosely, "Khrushchev's Party Congress," *Foreign Affairs,* January 1962, p. 187.

[3] For the meaning of this imprimatur in Soviet books and the procedures of Soviet censorship see Boris I. Gorokhoff, *Publishing in the USSR* (Bloomington, Ind., 1959), pp. 80–81, 257.

with history accordingly reflect views dominant in Stalin's time. The articles are translated in substantial part.

30. The Large Soviet Encyclopedia, Volume 19, Articles on Historism, etc.

HISTORISM

Historism is one of the basic principles of the dialectical approach to the study of nature and society, requiring consideration of objects, phenomena, and events in their origin and development as related to the concrete historical conditions which have produced them. In order to approach scientifically the solution of problems of social life, V. I. Lenin teaches that it is most important to "keep in mind the basic historical connection and consider each problem from the point of view of how the given event appears in history, what major stages it has undergone in its evolution, thus seeing what it has become now." (*Works*, 4th ed., Vol. 29, p. 436.) The Marxist dialectical method views all phenomena and events in their internal linkage and the process of their interaction. There are no isolated phenomena in the world; each phenomenon is connected with another. Thus, it is possible to understand a phenomenon or event only through a historical approach to it and through consideration of the concrete historical setting with which this phenomenon or event is connected.

V. I. Lenin teaches that without a historical approach to social phenomena it is impossible for history to exist and develop as a science, inasmuch as only such an approach rescues the historical science from its transformation into a chaos of chance occurrences and a pile of most absurd errors.

The origins of historism are found in the views of the West European Utopian socialists, especially those of Saint-Simon. Hegel attempted to view phenomena historically, that is, in a definite, even though perverted and abstract, connection with history. Hegel's historism, however, was built on a fallacious idealistic foundation and was addressed solely toward the past. Hegel tried to cast Prussia as the apex of social and historical evolution and proclaimed the eternity of monarchy in its constitutional form.

The most profound development of the principle of historism in the entire pre-Marxian literature is in the works of the Russian revolutionary democrats. (V. G. Belinsky, A. I. Herzen, N. G. Chernyshevsky, and N. A. Dobroliubov).

The Marxist-Leninist principle of historism is in radical contrast to the methodology of bourgeois sociology, which is antihistorical and metaphysical in its very basis. Bourgeois sociology of the nineteenth and twentieth centuries proceeds from a direct negation of the principle of historism and rejects the law-governed nature of the development of society (Neo-Kantian school, etc.). The hostile attitude of the ideologists of the bourgeoisie toward the principle of historism is caused by the fact that the objective study of the phenomena of social life in their connection with the conditions which produced them proves incontrovertibly the historically transitory nature of the capitalist society and its inevitable doom. Marxist historism is a tool of correct and objective reflection of reality; it is free from any substitution of abstract, lifeless schemes for concrete study of phenomena and events. Marxist historism rejects any distortion of reality and any tendentious illumination of the facts of the past outside and independently of the concrete historical conditions in which they occurred. Guided by the principle of historism, K. Marx and F. Engels proved the temporary and transitory nature of the capitalist system and the historically inevitable victory of communism.

The Communist Party has always condemned and exposed the deviations from the principle of historism. In the early 1930's the CC of the VKP (B) exposed the antihistorical conception of the so-called "school" of M. N. Pokrovsky, which pervertedly interpreted historical events and illuminated them from the point of view of the present rather than from the point of view of the conditions in which they occurred, and thus distorted actual history.

F. Engels pointed out that after the victory of the socialist revolution the state would wither away. I. V. Stalin, developing Marxism further, has indicated that the formula of F. Engels is correct for certain conditions, that is, for the conditions of the victory of socialism in all countries or in the majority of countries, but that it is not applicable when socialism is victorious in one isolated country while in all other countries capitalism is supreme. In these conditions the country of the victorious revolution must not weaken but in every way strengthen its state. Consequently, both formulas are correct, though not absolutely, each for its own time.

HISTORIOGRAPHY

Historiography is the science studying (a) the history of the accumulation of knowledge concerning the development of human society and the perfection of the methods of historical investigation, (b) the history of the struggle of currents in the field of interpretation of social phenomena reflecting the struggle of classes, (c) the history of the discovery of the laws of historical development, and (d) the history of the victory of Marxist-Leninist historical science over bourgeois pseudo-science.

Historiography was transformed into a science only with the appearance of Marxism. The basis of scientific historiography is Marxism-Leninism. Soviet historiography wages a resolute struggle against the bourgeois and bourgeois-nationalist falsifiers of history. It exerts a major influence on the development of historiography in the countries of people's democracy and on the progressive historiography in the capitalist countries. The reactionary bourgeois historiography, which is in a state of complete decay and decadence, expresses the interests of the imperialist bourgeoisie and has become one of the ideological weapons of the instigators of war.

HISTORICAL MATERIALISM

Historical materialism is the science of the laws of development of human society originated by K. Marx and F. Engels and developed by V. I. Lenin and the disciple and continuator of the work of Lenin, I. V. Stalin. Historical materialism provides the only scientific understanding of history and serves as a method of cognizing social phenomena. Historical materialism is the extension of the positions of dialectical materialism to the phenomena of the life of society, to the study of society, and to the study of the history of society. Historical materialism represents the scientific-historical foundation of Marxism and arms the party of the proletariat with knowledge of the objective laws of the development of society which is necessary for the successful direction of the revolutionary struggle of the proletariat aiming at the annihilation of capitalism and the construction of communism.

Prior to the emergence of Marxism, fallacious philosophical views concerning the development of society, namely, the idealistic understanding of history, held sway. Idealism still typifies bourgeois sociology. The adherents of the idealistic understanding of history see the basis of the development of society not in the conditions of material life, not in social existence, but in the evolution of ideas, views, and historical notions of people. V. I. Lenin points out that historical theories of this type confine themselves to analysis of idea impulses behind the historical activity of people without studying these impulses, without discerning the objective conformity to laws of the development of the system of social relationships, and without seeing the roots of these relationships in the stage of development of material production; such theories do not encompass the actions of the masses of the people, who are the true makers of history.

The essence of historical materialism was formulated in a genius-like manner by K. Marx in the Preface to *Critique of Political Economy*.[4]

As a result of the creation of dialectical and historical materialism by K. Marx and F. Engels, for the first time in history philosophical materialism

---

[4] The article quotes here the statement of the theory reproduced in reading no. 3.

was completed "to the top" and extended to the understanding of society. "As Darwin discovered the law of the evolution of the organic world, so Marx discovered the law of the evolution of human history, that is, the simple fact hidden until now under ideological incrustations that people must first eat, drink, have shelter, and clothe themselves before they can engage in politics, science, art, religion, etc.; that, consequently, the production of immediate material necessities for life and thus each given stage of the economic development of a people or an era make up the basis upon which take shape the governmental institutions, legal notions, art, and even religious ideas of a given people and [are the basis] by which they should be explained rather than vice versa, as it has been done so far." (F. Engels, in K. Marx and F. Engels, *Selected Works,* Vol. 2, 1952, p. 157.)

The discovery of the materialistic understanding of history by K. Marx and F. Engels has made it possible to explain the evolution of society as a natural-history process; that is, as a law-governed process subordinated to objective laws which are independent of human will. Knowledge of these laws and their utilization in practical activity allow the proletariat and its party to solve successfully the problems of the revolutionary reorganization of society.

HISTORY

History (from the Greek *istoria*—narrative, story of something known, investigation) is (1) in general and broad sense, any process of development. In this meaning, the term *history* is applicable without exception to all phenomena in the life of nature and human society. "We know," K. Marx and F. Engels wrote, "only one science, the science of history. Viewing history from two sides, it can be divided into history of nature and history of man. However, these two sides are inseparably linked; since man has existed, the history of nature and the history of man have mutually conditioned each other." (*Works,* Vol. 4, p. 8 n.) (2) Science studying the "evolution of human society as a unitary and, in its vast many-sidedness and contradictory nature, law-governed process." (See V. I. Lenin, *Works,* 4th ed. Vol. 21, p. 41.)

History is one of the most important social sciences. The theoretical and methodological basis of history as a science is historical materialism, which represents the extension of the positions of dialectical materialism to the study of social life. The extension of materialism to the field of social phenomena is one of the greatest contributions of K. Marx and F. Engels, the creators of scientific communism. The emergence of Marxism in the middle of the nineteenth century was a revolution in all science having a world-historical significance. Marxism was the first to discover the objective laws of historical development of society. With the emergence of

Marxism, history for the first time became a genuine science. The process of the development of historical knowledge running through several millennia is, therefore, divided into two basically different periods: a pre-Marxist period when history was still not a science in the true sense of the term, and the period of scientific history which began with the emergence of Marxism.

The beginnings of accumulation of historical knowledge and emergence of historical thinking go back to remote antiquity. An immense part in the accumulation of historical knowledge was played by the appearance of writing. The oldest known historical works are the various monuments of the countries of the ancient Orient: inscriptions on stones (the oldest among these, the ancient Egyptian "Palermo Stone," dates back to the end of the fourth or beginning of the third millennium B.C.); summaries and chronicles of events in Egypt, Sumer, Akkad, Babylonia, Assyria, and Persia; Hittite chronicles and Urartu inscriptions (first millennium B.C.). Compared with the other countries of the ancient Orient, ancient China had the greatest development of historical knowledge, the first historical works appearing in the sixth to the third centuries B.C. The first historical work presenting the history of China from earliest times to the second century B.C. was the book by one of the major thinkers of antiquity, Ssu-ma Ch'ien (145-86 B.C.) entitled *Shih Chi* ("Historical Notes"). Among the historical works of ancient Greece, the oldest are the works of the logographers (sixth and fifth centuries B.C.), Herodotus (fifth century B.C.), who was regarded for many centuries in Europe as the "Father of History," Thucydides, and Xenophon. Polybius attempted to write a world history. Basic aspects of the history of Greece and Rome were presented by Plutarch in the form of biographies of outstanding historical personalities. In ancient Rome historical works appeared in the form of chronicles or annals. Among the historians of ancient Rome the leading ones are Livy, Tacitus, and Ammianus. The oldest Armenian and Georgian historical works belong to the first centuries A.D.

Russian written historical literature appeared in the tenth century. The largest historical work of early Russia was the *Povest' vremennykh Let* ("Chronicle of Bygone Years"), which was imbued with the patriotic idea of struggle for the unity of the Russian lands. The most important products of early Russian historical thinking in the eleventh to the seventeenth century were the numerous chronicles.

For many centuries—in the period of the slaveowning and feudal system and in that of the consolidation of the capitalist system—an immense amount of factual historical material was accumulated and a large quantity of historical works by historians of various countries and peoples appeared. However, typical of all these works—even of those which were written by representatives of social strata progressive for their time—was the idealistic understanding of the process of social development. The entire course of the historical process and the individual events in the life of society were viewed by the authors of these works as a manifestation of "God's will" (or of many gods), "Divine Providence," some sort of "divine world spirit" or absolute "idea," or, at best, as the result of the free creativity of the human mind, that is, as sociopolitical and ethical theories and concepts of individuals. In the works of the ancient and medieval historians and chroniclers which have reached us, the data concerning actual events are mixed with religious-mythological legends, epic sagas, and sometimes inventions by the authors of these works. Ecclesiastical-religious ideology put a very heavy imprint upon the historical works of the middle ages.

Even in the period of the establishment and consolidation of capitalist relationships when bourgeois historiography played a certain progressive role in the struggle with feudal-ecclesiastical conceptions of the history of society, bourgeois historiography stood entirely on idealistic and unscientific grounds. Attacking the theological views concerning social life, the writers of the age of the bourgeois revolutions in the seventeenth and eighteenth centuries proclaimed another idealistic principle of explaining history, that of rationalism (F. Voltaire, J.-J. Rousseau, and others). It is typical that even the bourgeois philosophers and historians who approached materialistically (although metaphysically) the phenomena of nature (F. Bacon and T. Hobbes in England; D. Diderot, P. Holbach, and C. Helvetius in France) remained idealists in the field of history. The major representatives of bourgeois historiography in the West (F. Guizot, A. Thierry, F. Mignet) and gentry-bourgeois historiography in Russia (N. M. Karamzin, T. N. Granovsky, S. M. Solov'iov, V. O. Kliuchevsky, N. I. Kareev, I. V. Luchitsky, M. M. Kovalevsky, and others) were not able to explain scientifically the course of the historical evolution of society. This applies also to the representatives of West European utopian socialism (G. Babeuf, A. Saint-Simon, and C. Fourier).

The doctrine of the founders of Marxism-Leninism, the views of K. Marx, F. Engels, V. I. Lenin, and I. V. Stalin concerning the basic questions of the development of human society, and their discovery of the most important inherent laws of this development have created the scientific basis of the development of history as a science.

Marxism-Leninism teaches that the laws of science reflect objective processes in nature or society. "Marxism understands the laws of science, whether laws of natural science or laws of political economy, as a reflection of objective processes occurring independently of human will. Men can discover these laws, know them, study them, reckon with them in their actions, and use them in the interest of society, but they cannot alter or remove these laws. Nor can they construct or create new laws of science." (I. Stalin, *Economic Problems of Socialism in the U.S.S.R.,* 1952, p. 4.) The laws of the evolution of society are as knowable as are the laws of the evolution of nature and, consequently, have the significance of objective truths.

The laws of the evolution of society, which, like the laws of the evolution of nature, are objective and operating independently of human will, have a number of distinctive characteristics as compared to the latter. Thus, the majority of the laws of economic evolution of society are of limited duration and operate only during a given historical period. In the economic field, the discovery and application of a new law infringing upon the interests of the evanescent forces of society will meet with powerful resistance on their part, and thus a social force is needed that can overcome this resistance. Marxism-Leninism teaches that the mechanical application of the laws of nature, such as biological laws, to the area of social life—as it is done by bourgeois pseudo-scholars and preachers of the so-called "social Darwinism," Malthusianism, and the like—is antiscientific. Marxism-Leninism also teaches that along with laws operating throughout the entire course of human history there are special laws typical only of one or several social formations. For the science of history the investigation of special law-governed patterns of the development of socialist society by the classics of Marxism-Leninism has an immense significance.

The whole diversified history of human society can be scientifically explained only by proceeding from the materialistic principle that the material life of society, that is, its existence, is primary, whereas its spiritual life is secondary and derivative, and that the material life of society is an objective reality existing independently of human will, whereas the spiritual life of society is a reflection of this objective reality and a reflection of existence.

The main force in the system of conditions of material life of society which determines the character of the social system and the development of society from one system into another is the method of producing the material goods needed by society to live and develop. The other conditions of material life of society—geographic setting and growth of population—have an influence upon the development of society by accelerating or retarding it, but they cannot be the main force of the development of society. The basis of the historical process is the evolution of the means of production of material goods, or the development of productive forces and production relationships. The changes in the method of production inevitably cause the alteration of the entire social system. The nature of the method of production in a society determines in essence the nature of the society itself, as well as its ideas, theories, political concepts, and institutions. The changes and development of the methods of production always start with changes and development of the productive forces, and above all with changes and development of tools of production. The productive forces are the most mobile and revolutionary element of production; they are the determining element in the development of production because the changes in the productive and economic relations of men in society are determined by the changes in the state of productive forces. The totality of production of relationships, K. Marx pointed out, "constitutes the economic structure of society, that is, the real basis upon which rises a legal and political superstructure and to which certain forms of social consciousness correspond." (K. Marx, *Critique of Political Economy,* 1951, p. 7.)

In studying from all sides the basis of society, Marxist-Leninist historical science also gives much attention to the explanation of the active role of social ideas, theories, political concepts, and institutions in the history of society. "The superstructure is produced by the basis but this does not mean at all that it merely reflects the basis or that it is passive, neutral, or indifferently reacting to the fate of its basis, the fate of the classes, and the nature of the system. To the contrary, having come into existence, it becomes a powerful active force, actively helps its basis to take final shape and consolidate itself, and takes all steps to help the new system to break and liquidate the old basis and the old classes." (I. Stalin, *Marxism and Problems of Linguistics,* 1952, p. 7.)

The analysis of phenomena in the basis and the superstructure and their interaction makes it possible to evaluate correctly the concrete course of historical events in their mutual interrelation and causal determination.

Emphasizing the decisive role of the popular masses in the evolution of the historical process, Marxism-Leninism teaches that history is made by the people who produce the material goods without which society cannot exist or develop. This determines the true role of the popular masses in history.

". . . The history of the evolution of society is above all a history of the evolution of production, a history of the methods of production succeeding one another in the course of centuries, and a history of the evolution of the productive forces and the production relationships of men.

"This means that history of social development is at the same time a history of the producers of material goods themselves or a history of the working masses who are the fundamental forces of the process of production and who assure the production of material goods necessary for the existence of society.

"This means that the historical science, if it wishes to be a real science, can no longer reduce the history of social development to the actions of kings and military leaders and to the actions of 'conquerors' and 'subjugators' of states; it must, above all, take up the history of the producers of material goods, that is, the history of the working masses and the history of peoples.

"This means that the key for the study of history of society must be sought not in the heads of men or the views and ideas of society, but in the method of production practiced by society in each historical period, that is, in the economics of society.

"This means that the foremost task of historical science is the study and discovery of the laws of production, laws of development of the productive forces and production relationships, and the laws of the economic development of society." (I. Stalin, *Problems of Leninism,* 11th ed., 1952, p. 591.)

Bourgeois historians regard the popular masses as a "mob" which is led by outstanding personalities or "heroes." Basically antagonistic to Marxism-Leninism is the reactionary cult of the individual in history which amounts to an idealistic exaggeration of the role of the individual, attribution of supernatural qualities to it, superstitious worship of it, and dismissal of the role of masses, classes, and parties. Marxist-Leninist science exposed these Populist and Socialist-Revolutionary theories and proved that the real maker of history is the people. Heroes and outstanding personalities may play an important role in the life of society only to the extent to which they correctly understand how to change the conditions of material life of society for the better, to which they correctly express the interests and needs of the forces and classes in the forefront, and to which the masses support them. Heroes do not make history; the people push history forward and make heroes.

The discovery of the objective laws of social development, the establishment of the true role of the popular masses and class struggle in the history of society, and the profound study of the concrete features and laws of the development of capitalism made it possible for K. Marx, F. Engels, V. I. Lenin, and I. V. Stalin to arm the proletariat of the entire world with a clear understanding of its world-historical mission as the only class which is capable of leading and bringing to total victory the revolutionary struggle for the annihilation of capitalism, establishment of the dictatorship of the proletariat, abolition of the exploitation of man by man, and construction of the socialist society. The work of I. V. Stalin, *Economic Problems of Socialism in the U.S.S.R.,* reveals the laws of the future of historical development of Soviet society and the conditions of the gradual transition to communism.

History as a science is closely related to the other social sciences, such as political economy, philosophy, juridical sciences, archeology, ethnography, linguistics, literature, art, etc. At the same time history has its distinctive features. The special nature of history as a science consists in the fact that it analyzes the process of the evolution of society as a whole, the totality of the phenomena of social life, and all its aspects in their interconnection and interdetermination. The study of the historical process as a unitary whole does not preclude individual historians' concentration on certain aspects of this process or study of historical events and phenomena relating either to the economic basis or to the field of the political superstructure, culture, etc.; however, in all cases they must study these events and phenomena against the background of the general historical process while the results of their special investigations must enrich the understanding of certain era or stage in the development of society or of the historical process as a whole. History studies the phenomena of social life in their full concreteness and total diversity, reconstructing on the basis of historical sources the characteristic and specific features of the individual historical events and processes and at the same time showing the general and the main aspect which is contained in these events and processes and revealing the laws typical of certain socioeconomic formations or periods in the evolution of these formations in given concrete conditions of life of the nation or people. The subject of historical science is, therefore, the entire totality of phenomena of the life of society in various ages and various countries. The understanding of history as a world-historical process is impossible without the deepest study, from all sides, of the history of the individual peoples, nations, and nationalities. Thus, the study of the history of peoples in all specific features of their national evolution and the study of economic, political and cultural ties among peoples are for historical science a task of primary importance.

The establishment of the facts and accumulation of factual material have an exceptionally great significance for historical science because facts, that is, concrete historical phenomena and events, provide the historian with a basis for scientific generalizations and the establishment of specific or general laws in the history of peoples. Authenticity of the factual material is one of the indispensable requirements placed upon any historical investigation.

In exposing the falsified selection of facts by bourgeois scholars V. I. Lenin wrote: "In the area of social phenomena there is no method more widely practiced and more bankrupt than the extraction of individual insignificancies [5] and the game of examples. To select examples involves no effort and has no, or purely negative, meaning since what matters is the concrete historical setting of the individual cases. If taken in their entirety and interconnection, facts are not only a 'stubborn' but also an unconditionally conclusive matter. Insignificancies, if taken out of the whole and out of

---

[5] Lenin's word is *faktiki* ("factlings"), connoting disdain.

the interconnection, and if they are desultory and arbitrary, are merely a plaything, if nothing worse." (*Works,* 4th ed., Vol. 23, p. 266.) In order to create a real basis for investigation of social phenomena, "it is necessary to take not individual facts but the entire totality of the facts relating to the question under study without a single exception" (*ibid.*).

Marxist-Leninist science views history of society as a progressive process in which evolution proceeds from the inferior to the superior. Marxism-Leninism provided the first strictly scientific basis for the periodization of world history by establishing five basic types of production relationships and, consequently, five socioeconomic formations in history the nature of which is determined by the dominant method of production: primitive-communal, slaveowning, feudal, capitalist, and, finally, the communist system, whose first stage is socialism. A most important task of historical science is to show the growth of the new social relationships and the struggle of the new with the old, of that which is being born with that which is dying, and of the progressive with the reactionary. Furthermore, the definition of the historical meaning of certain phenomena (e.g., political movements, uprisings, wars, and many others) requires the investigating historian to analyze the essence of the phenomena or events in the light of the general course of the historical process both in the given country and in the entire world. Therefore, each social system and movement in history must be evaluated not from the point of view of "eternal justice" or some such preconceived idea, as is done by bourgeois historians, but from the point of view of the conditions which produced this system and social movement and with which they are connected.

Marxism-Leninism teaches that everything depends on conditions, time, and place, and that the existence and development of scientific knowledge concerning history is impossible without a historical approach to social phenomena inasmuch as only such an approach rescues historical science from conversion into a chaos of chance occurrences and a pile of most absurd errors.

The Marxist historian must show the process of development of society such as it has been and is in reality. The uncritical application to phenomena of past historical eras of criteria with which it is possible and necessary to approach the phenomena of the present was, for example, a characteristic feature of the anti-Marxist so-called "school" of M. N. Pokrovsky. Asking the historians to eradicate decisively the anti-Marxist and vulgarizing conceptions of Pokrovsky's "school," the CC indicated in 1938 that the "school" of Pokrovsky "perversely interpreted historical facts and, contrary to historical materialism, explained them in the light of the present rather than in the light of the conditions in which the historical events occurred and thus perverted the actual history." (*Decisions of the Party*

Concerning Publishing: A Collection, 1941, pp. 173–174). Marxist-Leninist science requires the concrete study of historical phenomena, made on the basis of the methodology of historical materialism. Marxism-Leninism rejects the mechanical application of ready formulas to all the diverse phenomena of the historical evolution of society. K. Marx irately protested against the attempts to depict Marxism as a sort of "universal master key" with which a ready answer can be immediately produced for any questions. The discovery of the objective laws of the evolution of society does not terminate the continued study of history; rather, it creates the most propitious conditions for its investigation. Being an enemy of dogmatism, Marxism-Leninism requires the historian to use a creative approach in investigating social development. Supererudition, Talmudism, and quotation mania have nothing in common with Marxism-Leninism.

In studying the past of human society in unbreakable relation to the contemporary life of peoples, establishing the laws of the evolution of society in the various stages of its existence, and divulging those phenomena and profound forces which will determine the future course of events, historical science provides thereby most valuable material for the scientific prevision of the future historical process and the future fate of peoples. This is one of the basic differences between Marxist-Leninist historical science and bourgeois pseudo-science, which is incapable of disclosing the basic tendencies and laws of the historical development of mankind and unable to foresee the course of historical events.

The bourgeois historians preaching misanthropic racist views divide all peoples into "superior" and "inferior," "civilized" and "uncivilized," and "historical" (possessing history) and "unhistorical" (standing at a low level of development and possessing no history at all). These "scholars" see the beginning of history of mankind in the appearance of the first state entities or the first evidences of writing. Marxist-Leninist historical science decisively rejects any division of peoples into "superior" or "historical" and "inferior" or "unhistorical" and notes as unscientific the separation of a special "prehistoric era." F. Engels indicated that man came into history such as he was when he "first moved out of the animal (in the narrowest sense of the term) kingdom." (F. Engels, *Anti-Dühring,* 1951, p. 167.)

Studying the history of the evolution of society since earliest times, Marxist-Leninist historical science denies the reactionary point of view of many bourgeois historians who assert that the historical science is primarily expected to study the remote past and should not study recent history and contemporary historical events and phenomena since this interferes with preservation of "scientific objectivity" and "impartiality." The historians standing on the positions of Marxism-Leninism proceed from the only correct position, that the historical process of the evolution of society must be studied in its continuity and in the ties of the past with the present right up to the events and phenomena of the contemporary world. The study of the history of Soviet society and the recent history of the countries of the West and the East since the Great October Socialist Revolution is of primary importance. The deepening study of the history of society, of the succession of socioeconomic formations, of the history of class struggle, and of the revolutionary transformations in the field of social and governmental organization has an immediate practical significance since it arms the working class and all progressive humanity with the practical experience of revolutionary struggle, of struggle for peace and genuine democracy, and of struggle for construction of socialist and communist society.

In contrast to bourgeois objectivism, the guiding principle of Marxist-Leninist historical science is the principle of communist party-mindedness. The party-mindedness of the Marxist-Leninist historical science is a manifestation of its scientific objectivity since Marxist-Leninist theory alone discovered the objective laws of social evolution, which are independent of human will and which correspond to the vital interests of the working class and all working people. V. I. Lenin indicated that "on the one hand, the materialist carries through his objectivism more consistently, profoundly, and fully than the objectivist. He does not limit himself to pointing out the necessity of the process, but goes on to explain which socioeconomic formation gives content to this process and which class determines this necessity. . . . On the other hand, materialism incorporates, so to say, party-mindedness by making it necessary in any evaluation of events to maintain candidly and openly the viewpoint of a definite social group." (*Works*, 4th ed., Vol. 1, pp. 380–381.) The objective laws which govern the evolution of society lead with an iron necessity toward the triumph of communism. Workers of the capitalist countries struggling for their emancipation and workers who have removed the mastery of capitalists and landlords and are building a new life are directly interested in the creation of a scientifically objective picture of the historical development of society and in the revelation of the objective laws and tendencies of that development. "Our party," G. M. Malenkov said in the report to the nineteenth congress of the CPSU, "is strong because it is guided in all its activity by Marxist-Leninist theory. Its policy is based on scientific knowledge of the laws of social development." (G. Malenkov, *Report to the Nineteenth Congress of the Party Concerning the Work of the Central Committee of the VKP (B)*, 1952, p. 77.) The study of these laws makes it possible for the working people to master them, to learn how to apply them, to use them in the interest of society, and to assist with all their conscious and purposeful work the earliest triumph of the new over the old. Conversely, the exploiting classes are not interested in the disclosure of the actual and objective laws of social development, fear the coming events, and vainly try to halt the progressive course of historical development and turn back the wheel of history.

In numerous books and articles on questions of "philosophy of history," "methodology of history," "sociology," and so on, bourgeois historians proclaim that the task of "objective" history is merely the establishment of historical facts and their description and the accumulation of factual material, that is, naked factology (*faktologiia*). The establishment and description of facts are used by bourgeois historians for the purpose of frankly falsifying history. F. Engels wrote: "The bourgeoisie turns everything into merchandise, including history. Through the force of its very nature and the force of the conditions of its existence, it is typical for the bourgeoisie to adulterate all merchandise; it has also adulterated history. Indeed, that work sells best in which the falsification of history best suits the interests of the bourgeoisie." (*Marx-Engels Archives,* Vol. 10, 1948, p. 104.)

Bourgeois historians and publicists have made it their principal task to "render void" the materialistic understanding of history and ignore or pervert the laws of social development discovered by Marxist-Leninist science. The crusade of bourgeois sociologists and historians against Marxism-Leninism has shown with greatest clarity the shift of bourgeois historiography to the tracks of the most frantic reaction. A particularly monstrous nature is assumed by the bourgeois distortion of history in the capitalist countries since the Great October Socialist Revolution and the period of the general crisis of capitalism. Falsification of historical events and facts, propaganda of racism, cosmopolitanism, coercion, and aggressive war, fierce hatred of the ideas of communism and the camp of peace and democracy led by the U.S.S.R.—these are the characteristic features of contemporary bourgeois historiography, as also of the entire bourgeois ideology and culture placed in the service of American and British imperialism.

The complete decline of bourgeois "science" in the U.S.A., England, and the other capitalist countries in the period of imperialism and the ever deepening general crisis of the world capitalist system is evident particularly in the fact that the bourgeois historians have increasingly slipped to positions of most reactionary subjective idealism and agnosticism. Contemporary bourgeois historiography, which serves the purposes of imperialist policy and, above all, the policy of the ruling circles of the U.S.A. and England, is typified, on the one hand, by efforts to dress itself up in the toga of "apoliticalness" and "impartiality" and, on the other, by statements unprecedented in their cynical candor concerning the direct subordination of historical science to the purposes of contemporary imperialist policy. Thus, the president of the American Historical Association, C. Read, speaking in 1949 before the historians of the U.S.A., declared that the historian finds in the past what he seeks and selects the facts of the past in direct harmony with the scheme existing in his head and with what appears desirable from the social point of view. A professor at the University of London, G. Renier, stands in his book *History, Its Purpose and Method,* like C. Read, on the positions of pragmatism and subjective idealism and completely denies the existence of any objective laws in the historical process. On this "ground" he tries to "prove" that the result of the study of history cannot be scientific prevision and that in general history cannot be a science that provides a picture of objective reality. The ideologists of the imperialist reaction are afraid to admit the objective subordination to laws of the development of society and the possibility of scientifically foreseeing the historical process because this would mean admission of the inevitability of the doom of capitalism.

While bourgeois historiography has become ever more reactionary and has reached a dead end, Marxist-Leninist historical science has grown and developed in an intransigent struggle with the reactionary bourgeois historiography, including the right-wing socialist historical "science," and has unswervingly proceeded on the road of creative growth and enrichment of historical knowledge.

The historical science was the arena of a fierce ideological struggle. Under the guidance of the Communist Party, the "conceptions" of bourgeois ideologists were shattered, the falsifying findings of Trotskyists and other inimical groupings were smashed, and the complete triumph of Marxism-Leninism in the Soviet historical science was assured. Of the greatest importance in exposing the Trotskyist and all other kinds of falsifiers of history was I. V. Stalin's letter "Concerning Certain Questions of the History of Bolshevism," addressed to the editors of the journal *Proletarskaia revoliutsiia* and published in November 1931. An enormous role in the development of historical science in the U.S.S.R. was played by the destruction of the anti-Marxist and vulgarizing "school" of M. N. Pokrovsky, which was carried out by the Soviet historians under the guidance of the Communist Party. The decrees of the Sovnarkom of the U.S.S.R. and the CC of the VKP (B) "Concerning the Teaching of Civic History in the Schools of the U.S.S.R." of May 16, 1934, and January 26, 1936, the "Observations" of I. V. Stalin, S. M. Kirov, and A. A. Zhdanov concerning the outlines of the textbooks on the history of the U.S.S.R. and modern history, and the ruling of the jury of the government commission conducting the competition for the best history textbook (1937) exposed fully the anti-Marxist nature of Pokrovsky's "school," which had taken a position against the Marxist principle of historism in the evaluation of historical phenomena.[6]

---

[6] For the decree of May 16, 1934, and the "Observations" of Stalin, Kirov, and Zhdanov see readings nos. 20 and 21.

Of major significance for the development of the Soviet historical science was the publication in 1938 of the *History of the All-Union Communist Party (Bolsheviks)*: *Short Course,* which is a model of scientific investigation of history.

Under the guidance of the Communist Party, the Soviet historians have achieved a series of successes in the investigation of the history of the U.S.S.R. and general history. In the works of Soviet historians are studied such problems as the development of feudalism in Russia, the history of the class struggle and revolutionary movement, and the history of the heroic struggle of the peoples of the Soviet Union against foreign enslavers. A significant development was made by historical science in the Union republics, and for the first time the scientific history of a number of peoples of the U.S.S.R. began to be written. The history of the mighty Russian people is studied by Soviet historians in connection with the history of all peoples inhabiting the territory of the U.S.S.R. For the first time, Marxist textbooks of history for the schools of secondary and higher education were prepared.

The Soviet historians have produced major works which have received high praise in the scholarly community. Such are the works of B. D. Grekov in the history of the evolution of feudal relations and the history of the peasantry in Russia; of B. A. Rybakov in the history of crafts in ancient Russia; of P. I. Liashchenko in the history of national economy; of M. N. Tikhomirov in the history of Russian towns; of S. V. Bakhrushin in the history of Siberia and class struggle in the Russian state; of K. V. Basilevich in the history of the Russian centralized state; of I. I. Smirnov in the history of the class struggle of the peasantry; of A. V. Artsikhovsky, S. P. Tolstov, S. V. Kiseliov, P. N. Tret'iakov, and others who have made major discoveries in the field of archeology; of N. M. Druzhinin in the history of the peasantry in the nineteenth century; of M. V. Nechkina in the history of the Russian revolutionary-liberational movement; of A. M. Pankratova and A. L. Sidorov in the history of the labor movement and the history of Russia in the period of imperialism; of V. I. Picheta, A. D. Udal'tsov, and N. S. Derzhavin in the history of Slavic peoples; of P. A. Zhilin in the history of the Patriotic War of 1812; of B. G. Gafurov in the history of Tadzhikistan; of N. Berdzenishvili, I. Dzhavakhishvili, S. Dzhanashia, and G. V. Khachapuridze in the history of Georgia; of Ia. Ia. Zutis and Ia. P. Krastyn in the history of Latvia; of V. I. Avdiev, I. Iu. Krachkovsky, V. V. Struve, V. S. Sergeev, A. V. Mishulin, N. A. Mashkin, E. A. Kosminsky, S. D. Skazkin, N. P. Gratsiansky, S. I. Arkhangel'sky, M. M. Smirin, A. Iu. Iakubovsky, V. P. Volgin, E. V. Tarle, V. P. Potiomkin, A. S. Erusalimsky, V. M. Khvostov, F. V. Potiomkin, and others in the field of general history and a number of other investigations which have amounted to a serious contribution to the development of Soviet historical science.

The proceedings of the Nineteenth Congress of the party were a clear reflection of the enormous concern of the CPSU with the still greater intensification of the ideological work and the fullest development of science, including historical science. Serious shortcomings and errors in the work of Soviet historians were subjected to just criticism at the Nineteenth Congress of the party. The criticism of the party helps the Soviet historical science address all its powers to the liquidation of shortcomings and assures the future growth of Soviet historical science. The Communist Party requires of Soviet historians the decisive overcoming of the anti-Marxist cult of personality in history; struggle with the manifestations of supererudition, dogmatism, and quotation mania; unfolding of wide scientific criticism and contest of opinions; and creation of solid Marxist-Leninist studies in which the great historical role of the working popular masses and the role of the working class and its vanguard, the Communist Party, must be correctly demonstrated.

The work on the problems of historical science in the U.S.S.R. is concentrated in a number of scientific and research institutions and the country's institutions of higher education: Institute of History of the U.S.S.R. Academy of Sciences; Marx-Engels-Lenin-Stalin Institute of the CC of the CPSU; Academy of Social Sciences of the CC of the CPSU; Higher Party School of the CC of the CPSU; Institute of History of Material Culture; Institute of Slavic Studies of the U.S.S.R. Academy of Sciences; appropriate institutes of the republican academies of sciences and branches of the U.S.S.R. Academy of Sciences; universities; teachers' colleges; Historical and Archival Institute; State Historical Museum; and local historical and ethnographic museums and other institutions. The training of historians takes place in the historical and historical-philological faculties of the universities and teachers' colleges; the universities, teachers' colleges, Academy of Social Sciences of the CPSU, Academy of Sciences of the U.S.S.R., republican academies of sciences, and branches of the U.S.S.R. Academy of Sciences have advanced programs (*aspirantura,* and *doktorantura* in a number of scientific institutions) which prepare research historians and instructors in institutions of higher education.

History is a required subject in the secondary and technical schools of the U.S.S.R., the humanistic faculties of the institutions of higher education, the Higher Party School of the CC of the CPSU, the republican and regional party schools, and the universities of Marxism-Leninism.

The Institute of History of the U.S.S.R. Academy of Sciences publishes the monthly review *Voprosy istorii* ("Problems of History"), the occasional volumes of essays *Istoricheskie Zapiski* ("Historical Notes"), and the collections of historical documents *Istoricheskii arkhiv* ("Historical Archives"). A specialized journal is *Vestnik drevnei istorii* ("Journal of Ancient History") ; collective volumes *Srednie veka* ("Middle Ages") and *Vizantiiskii vremennik* ("Byzantine Journal") are also published. A large amount of historical studies and materials is published in the learned publications of the various institutes, academies, universities, and other institutions which conduct scientific and research work in the field of history and historiography.

Fruitfully working upon the paramount problems of world history, the Soviet historical science exerts an enormous influence on the development of progressive historical science in the entire world. The Soviet historians maintain a close relationship with the progressive historians of other countries and render creative assistance to the Marxist historians of the countries of people's democracy in their struggle for the victory of Marxism-Leninism in historical science. In the countries of people's democracy the Marxist-Leninist historical science has attained notable successes. From the very first years of the existence of the people's democratic regimes in these countries, Marxist-Leninist historical science has actively served the cause of fulfilling the tasks of the popular revolution and successfully moving the countries of people's democracy along the road to socialism. The development of historical science in these countries takes place amid an acute struggle of Marxist historians with representatives of bourgeois historiography. Utilizing the experience and accomplishments of Soviet historical science, the Marxist historians of the countries of people's democracy are at work upon the principal problems of the history of their countries and general history.

HISTORY IN THE SCHOOLS

History is one of the basic subjects in the Soviet schools, the purpose of the study of which is mastery of the foundations of historical science by the students. In their decree of May 16, 1934, "Concerning the Teaching of Civic History in the Schools of the U.S.S.R.," the Sovnarkom of the U.S.S.R. and the CC of the VKP (B) found the teaching of this subject to be unsatisfactory and indicated that the history textbooks as well as the teaching itself bore an abstract and schematic nature. This condition in the teaching of civic history in the schools of the U.S.S.R. was a direct result of the anti-Marxist, anti-Leninist, essentially liquidationist and antiscientific views of historical science connected, above all, as the Sovnarkom of the U.S.S.R. and the CC of the VKP (B) pointed out, with the dissemination among certain Soviet historians of the erroneous and harmful conceptions of the so-called historical "school" of Pokrovsky.

In accordance with the decree of the CC of the VKP (B) of June 9,

1934, concerning the "Introduction of an Elementary Course in General History and History of the U.S.S.R. in the Primary and Incomplete Secondary Schools," an elementary course in the history of the U.S.S.R. with brief data of general history is taught in the primary schools (until 1945, in the third and fourth grades; since 1945, in the fourth grade only); history of the ancient world in the fifth and sixth grades (the course ends in the first semester of the sixth grade); history of the Middle Ages in the sixth (second semester) and seventh grades; modern history and history of the U.S.S.R. in the eighth and ninth grades; and history of the U.S.S.R. in the tenth grade.

In contrast to the teaching of history in bourgeois schools which falsify science to suit the capitalists, the teaching of history in the Soviet schools gives the students genuine scientific knowledge, objective history of social relations disclosing the laws of the historical process, history of the means of production, and along with that the history of the working masses, history of peoples, history of the class struggle and revolutionary movement, the world-historical significance of the Great October Socialist revolution, and history of the struggle of the Soviet people for the triumph of communism. The teaching of history in the Soviet schools is imbued with communist party-mindedness and inculcates in the students the feeling of Soviet patriotism, Soviet national pride, intransigence toward the ideology of cosmopolitanism, and devotion to the interests of the Soviet people and state.

"HISTORY OF THE VKP (B) : SHORT COURSE"

History of the VKP (B) : Short Course is the scientific history of the Communist Party of the Soviet Union for the period from its founding by V. I. Lenin to 1937. The book was published under the editorship of a committee of the CC of the party and was approved by the Central Committee.

The *Short Course of the History of the VKP (B)* is the only guide to the history of the CPSU approved by the Central Committee and representing a scientific interpretation of the problems of the history of the party and Marxism-Leninism. The questions concerning the role of the individual in history, the just and unjust wars, the victory of socialism in the U.S.S.R., the role and significance of the socialist state, the Soviet intelligentsia, and other major questions developed in the works of the classics of Marxism-Leninism and in the decisions and documents of the CPSU have found a correct illumination in the history of the Communist Party of the Soviet Union. The fourth chapter of the book incorporates the work of I. V. Stalin entitled "Dialectical and Historical Materialism," which states the theoretical bases of the Communist Party in closest connection with the history and policy of the CPSU and shows, as does the entire book, the unity of theory and practice in the activity of the Communist party.[7] The *Short Course of the History of the VKP (B)* shows the unity, totality, and consistency of the doctrine of K. Marx, F. Engels, V. I. Lenin, and I. V. Stalin, that is, the unity of Marxism-Leninism. In the end of the book is shown the significance of the mastery of Marxist-Leninist theory. To master Marxist-Leninist theory means to know how to enrich this theory with the new experience of the revolutionary movement, enrich it with new formulations and deductions, develop it and move it forward, without being halted by the fact that, proceeding from the essence of the theory, one replaces some of its formulations and deductions which have proved obsolete with new formulations and deductions corresponding to the new historical setting. Marxist-Leninist theory is not dogma; it is a guide for action.

The *Short Course of the History of the VKP (B)* shows how the Communist Party fulfills its directing and guiding function in Soviet society. The teaching concerning the party, as developed by V. I. Lenin, allows the party to organize all practical activity and assure a leading role for itself under any conditions. The party works out the correct policy by basing itself upon the Marxist-Leninist theory which scientifically explains the objective laws of the development of society and by basing itself upon the experience of the masses.

In the decision of November 14, 1938, concerning "The Organization of Party Propaganda in Connection with the Publication of the *Short Course of the History of the VKP (B)*," the CC of the party stressed that with the publication of this book, the cadres of the Communist Party and the Soviet state received a new and powerful ideological weapon and an encyclopedia of basic knowledge in the field of Marxism-Leninism.[8] The *Short Course of the History of the VKP (B)* was made the basis of the propaganda of Marxism-Leninism. This publication became the handbook for tens of millions of communists and nonparty people. It received the widest possible circulation. From October 1938 to October 1, 1952, the *Short Course of the History of the VKP (B)* was published in forty million copies.

Another authoritative statement formulated during the second interregnum concerned historiography as a science. As envisaged in the 1945 plan, work in the history of historical scholarship in Russia, prerevolutionary and Soviet, was fostered by establishing the Commission on History of Historical Science in 1947 and attaching it to the Academy Institute of

---

[7] See reading no. 23.
[8] Reading no. 24.

History. In 1955 the commission produced the first volume of a projected six-volume survey *Ocherki istorii istoricheskoi nauki v SSSR* ("Survey of the History of Historical Science in the U.S.S.R.") which is intended to cover the historical writing of the various peoples in the country in the Tsarist and Soviet periods. Only the first three volumes, covering developments to 1917, have appeared so far. The introduction to the first volume represents an extensive definition of historiography from the Marxist point of view as prevalent in 1954 when the volume was prepared for the press. It is translated below in full.

31. Introduction to Survey of the History of Historical Science in the U.S.S.R., Volume 1

Historiography is the science of studying the history of the accumulation of knowledge concerning the development of human society; the history of the improvement of the methods of historical investigation; the history of the struggle of various currents in the field of interpretation of social phenomena reflecting the struggle of classes; the history of discovery of the laws of historical development; and the history of the victory of Marxist-Leninist historical science over bourgeois pseudo-science.

Historiography has the same theoretical and methodological foundation as all other social sciences, namely historical materialism, which represents the extension of dialectical materialism to the area of social phenomena and, in particular, to the study of the history of society. Having its own subject distinct from the subject of historical science, historiography rests on the same methodological foundations as historical science itself.

In contrast to the idealistic conceptions of bourgeois historians, Marxist-Leninist historical science proceeds from the thesis that the material life of society is primary and its spiritual life is secondary and derivative. The principal force in the system of conditions of the material life of society which determines the character of the social order and the forward movement of society is the method of producing material goods. Marxism-Leninism sees the basis of the historical process in the development of methods of production and the development of the productive forces and production relationships of people; the totality of production relationships "forms the economic structure of society, that is, the real basis upon which rises a legal and political superstructure to which certain social forms of consciousness correspond." (K. Marx, *Critique of Political Economy,* Moscow, 1953, p. 7.)

In contrast to bourgeois historical theories which often reduce the process of historical development to the actions of "great men"—monarchs, military leaders, and other public men—Marxist-Leninist historical science holds that, above all, history is made by people producing material goods, without whom society cannot live and develop. Therefore, the history of society is, above all, the history of the working masses and the history of the people.

Reducing the historical process to the activities of "great men," the bourgeois theories propagandize the cult of personality in history. In contrast to this, Marxist-Leninist historical science, proceeding from the angle of studying the history of the producers of material goods, studies the role of prominent individuals in all areas of social life from fundamentally different standpoints. The bourgeois historians regard the popular masses as passive environment and "crowd" dominated and led by "prominent individuals" and "heroes." In appraising the activities of historical personalities, Marxist-Leninist science proceeds to establish to what social class a personality belongs, the interests of which social groups he reflects, and the extent to which his activity echoes the best and uppermost aspirations of the popular masses and the progressive tendencies of social development or, contrariwise, whether it reflects the reactionary drives of the exploiting classes.

In contrast to bourgeois theories covering up in all possible ways the role of the class struggle in the development of society, Marxist-Leninist historical science regards the class struggle as the most important propulsion force in the development of a society consisting of antagonistic classes. "Dialectic," V. I. Lenin writes, "requires the study of a given social phenomenon from all sides in its development and the reduction of the external and apparent aspects to the basic propelling forces and to the development of productive forces and class struggle." (V. I. Lenin, *Works,* Vol. 21, pp. 193–194.)

This does not mean at all that Marxist-Leninist historical science ignores the active role of social ideas, theories, political views and institutions in the history of society. To the contrary, in contrast to bourgeois idealistic and metaphysical theories, Marxist-Leninist science clarifies the true place and role of the social superstructure in the historical process. In studying the socioeconomic development of society, the history of the working masses, class struggle, and revolutionary and national-liberational movements, and the history of the struggle for socialism and communism, Marxist-Leninist science devotes a great deal of attention to clarifying the active role of the social superstructure in the history of society because the superstructure, "having come into existence, constitutes a major active force, actively helps its basis to take shape and consolidate itself, and takes all measures to help the new order to overcome and liquidate the old basis and the old classes." (J. Stalin, *Marxism and Problems of Linguistics,* Moscow, 1954, p. 7.)

Depicting from all sides the superstructure of society, historical science gives much attention to the development of the culture of nations—sciences, literature, arts, ethical norms, etc.—in the total process of the development of society.

Historical science is closely connected with the other social sciences: philosophy, political economy, juridical sciences, linguistics, study of literature, study of arts, etc. Along with that, its specific distinction is the fact that historical science regards the process of the development of society as a whole and studies not only economic history, history of political institutions, history of international relations, history of culture, etc., but the entire totality of the phenomena of social life from all sides and in their interrelation and interdetermination. The study of the historical process as a unitary whole does not preclude individual historians from concentrating their attention on one or another set of facets of this process or from investigating the historical events and phenomena relating, for example, to the economic basis to the area of the political superstructure, and so on, provided that in all cases they study these events and phenomena against the backdrop of the entire historical process and that the results of their individual investigations enrich the understanding of the historical process as a whole.

In contrast to some bourgeois theories, Marxist-Leninist historical science regards the totality of the history of society as a progressive process consisting of a succession of socioeconomic formations.

Marxism-Leninism first provided a strictly scientific basis for the periodization of world history by defining in the historical process five basic types of production relationships and, accordingly, five socioeconomic formations whose nature is determined by the prevailing method of production: primitive-communal, slaveowning, feudal, capitalist, and, finally, socialist. The most important task of historical science is to demonstrate the laws of development typical of all socioeconomic formations as well as of the individual formations at one or another stage of their development. The task of the historian is to demonstrate the inception and growth of new social relations, the struggle of the new with the old, of that which is being born with that which is dying, of the progressive with the reactionary, and to make evident the ultimate victory of the new over the old. The nature and historical significance of this or that phenomenon and its progressive or reactionary character can be correctly determined only by relating it to the concrete historical conditions of the time. Historism, that is, the study of social phenomena in the concrete totality of the historical conditions, is one of the indispensable requirements of Marxist-Leninist historical science. The historian must show the process of the development of society such as it actually has been. Scientific objectivity is incompatible with modernization, that is, with an arbitrary application to phenomena of past historical epochs of such criteria as may and should be used in studying the phenomena of the present. The modernization of history, as a form of its falsification, is a characteristic feature of bourgeois historical theories which attempt, for example, to find capitalist relations in the epoch of the slaveowning formation.

Marxist-Leninist historical science holds that the understanding of history as a world-historical process is impossible without a most profound and comprehensive study of the history of individual peoples. The study of the history of peoples in all specific aspects of their development and the simultaneous study of the economic, political, and cultural relations between nations are the most important tasks of historical science.

Bourgeois historians preaching misanthropic racist views divide peoples into "superior" and "inferior," "civilized" and "uncivilized," "historical," or possessing a history of their own, and "nonhistorical," or standing at a low level of development and altogether lacking a history of their own. Marxist-Leninist historical science decisively rejects any division of peoples into "superior" or "historical" and "inferior" or "nonhistorical" and regards all peoples as being equally capable of historical development and possessed of a history of their own.[9]

In studying the history of society since ancient times, Marxist-Leninist historical science also rejects the reactionary viewpoint of many bourgeois historians who assert that history is meant to study only the past and predominantly the remote past, and that it is under no obligation to bring its investigation to the present and study contemporary events; the study of the phenomena of the present interferes with the preservation of "scientific objectivity" and "impartiality." Marxist-Leninist historical science holds that the only correct approach is to study the historical process in close relation of the past with the present, from ancient times to the events of our own day. The study of the history of the Soviet society and of the modern history of foreign countries has a primary importance; beyond its theoretical importance, the study of these periods has an immense practical significance in the struggle for constructing the communist society.

The bourgeois historians have long ceased to aid the development of historical science and have turned their "science" into a weapon for the falsification of history. Engels himself wrote: "The bourgeoisie turns everything into merchandise, including, of course, history. By the force of

---

[9] As the reader will detect, this and other passages are almost verbatim reproductions of the formulations in the "Large Soviet Encyclopedia" (reading no. 30). Very characteristic of Stalin's time, this method assured the official formulations of uniform propagation. From an author's point of view, it also protected him against charges of tampering with "the line."

its very nature and the conditions of its life, it is typical of the bourgeoisie to adulterate all merchandise; it has also adulterated history. Indeed, that work is best remunerated in which the falsification of history serves most directly the interests of the bourgeoisie." (*Marx and Engels Archive*, Vol. 10, Moscow, 1948, p. 104.) The falsification takes the shape above all of negation of objective law-governed patterns (*zakonomernosti*) in the historical process. The bourgeois historians and sociologists assert that such law-governed patterns do not exist, that the historical process represents in itself an accumulation of fortuitous facts and that the tasks of historical science consist simply in the establishment and description of these facts. V. I. Lenin stressed that such a "science" is typified by a "despair as to the possibility of scientifically understanding the present, by an abdication from science, by an endeavor to spit on all generalizations, hide from all laws of historical development, and conceal the forest behind trees." (V. I. Lenin, *Works*, Vol. 20, p. 179.)

The negation of historical law-governed patterns and the veneration of the single fact found wide acceptance with the advent of the epoch of imperialism. In the West this found its final expression in the neo-Kantian theory of H. Rickert and W. Windelband, and in Russia in the works of A. S. Lappo-Danilevsky, P. N. Miliukov, and others. Such a stand serves as a camouflage of the direct falsification of history since negation of the law-governed nature of the historical process actually means the replacement of objective historical law-governed patterns with subjective schemes; the bourgeois historians fit the factual material into their reactionary schemes so as to provide a historical justification of the capitalist system. Voluntarism has always been typical of bourgeois historical theories; however, this subjective arbitrariness is particularly characteristic of contemporary reactionary "science" abroad.

Thus, speaking before the historians of the United States in 1949, the president of the American Historical Association, Conyer Read, stated that the historian finds in the past what he seeks and selects the facts of the past in close harmony with the scheme existing in his head and with what appears desirable "from a social point of view." In his book *History, Its Purpose and Method* (1950), the London University professor, G. Renier, like C. Read, completely denies the existence of any objective, law-governed nature of the historical process. On this "basis" he tries to prove that the result of the study of history cannot be scientific forecasting (*predvidenie*) and that history in general cannot be a science providing a picture of objective reality. The ideologists of imperialist reaction and the warmongers are afraid to admit the objective, law-governed nature of the development of society and the possibility of scientific forecasting of the historical process since this would mean admission of the inevitability of the doom of capitalism. The imperialist bourgeoisie of the United States, England and other capitalist countries has turned bourgeois historical "science" into a servant of its reactionary and predatory policy.

Marxist-Leninist historical science wages resolute struggle against the falsification of history. Marxist-Leninist science holds that the establishment of facts and the accumulation of factual material has an exceptionally important significance for historical science inasmuch as facts, that is, concrete historical phenomena and events, serve as the basis for scientific study of history. Authenticity of the factual material is one of the indispensable requirements of any historical investigation. However, the establishment of facts alone does not constitute the final objective of the historical investigation; it represents only its beginning. Facts must serve as means of becoming cognizant of historical law-governed patterns. Such objective, law-governed patterns lead with an iron inexorability to the triumph of communism. The proletariat, its Communist Party, and Marxist-Leninist science are in a direct manner interested in the creation of a scientific and objective picture of the historical development of society and in the uncovering of the objective laws and tendencies of this development.

The strength of Marxism-Leninism is that, by uncovering the law-governed nature of the historical process, it provides the possibility of determining the path of the development of society. In studying the past of human society in uninterrupted relation to the contemporary life of peoples, in establishing the laws of the development of society at the various stages of its existence, and in revealing in their inception those phenomena which will determine the subsequent course of events, Marxist-Leninist historical science provides most valuable material for scientific forecasting of the future historical process and the future destinies of nations.

In contrast to the hypocritical assertion of "impartiality" and "objectivity" of science by the bourgeois scholars, Marxist-Leninist science elevates as governing principle the principle of communist party-mindedness (*partiinost*). The party-mindedness of Marxist-Leninist historical science fully converges with its scientific objectivity since it rests on the objectively existing laws of social development. V. I. Lenin pointed out that "on one hand, a materialist carries through his objectivism more consistently, profoundly, and fully than an objectivist. He does not stop with pointing to the necessity of the process, but explains which socioeconomic formation gives content to this process and which class determines this necessity. On the other hand, materialism incorporates, so to speak, a party-mindedness in that it compels one to base himself frankly and openly on the viewpoint of a given social group in any assessment of events." (V. I. Lenin, *Works*, Vol. 1, pp. 380–381.)

At a time when the bourgeois historical "science" wound up in a dead end, Marxist-Leninist historical science grew and developed in relentless struggle with bourgeois ideology and unswervingly went along the path of creative growth.

Historiography, as history of historical science, rests upon the basic principles of Marxist-Leninist historical science. They serve as the most important criteria with which historiography approaches the general assessment of this or that trend in the history of historical thought and the evaluation of the work of this or that historian. From the standpoint of these basic criteria, historiography divides all history of historical thought into two periods: the pre-Marxist, prescientific period when history, regardless of some individual accomplishments, had not yet become a true science; and the Marxist, scientific period when, in the middle of the nineteenth century, the founders of Marxism, K. Marx and F. Engels, created their scientific theory and formulated the basic propositions in the area of historical science. The emergence of Marxism signified a world-historical revolution in the area of ideology and an epoch qualitatively new and fundamentally different from the preceding period in the development of historical knowledge, which thenceforth turned into a true science.[10]

In the historiography of the Marxist period one should separate the historiography of the epoch of capitalism (first period: from the emergence of Marxism to the 1890's, when Lenin made his appearance; and second period: from the 1890's to the Great October Socialist Revolution) from the historiography of the Soviet period (from the Great October Socialist Revolution to the present).

However, to establish two basic periods in the history of historical knowledge—prescientific and scientific—does not at all mean to ignore the accomplishments of historical thought which were made during the prescientific period. Marxist historical science and Marxist historiography, like Marxism in general, came into being not in a vacuum; they utilized and reworked all positive accomplishments of previous historical thought. The criterion of historism which is binding in historical science is also binding in historiography. The evaluation of this or that trend or of the works of individual historians must be made in direct relation to the contemporary historical conditions and to the accomplishments of prior historical thought. A series of historical theories and individual propositions of the pre-Marxist period represented a definite step forward when compared with the

---

[10] In 1961 this central point was questioned by S. L. Peshtich, *Russkaia istoriografiia XVIII veka* [Russian Historiography of the Eighteenth Century] (Leningrad, 1961). While accepting the division into pre-Marxist and Marxist periods in the development of historical science, Peshtich states that "it is necessary to admit that history became a science even before Marxism" and that the entire pre-Marxist period cannot be viewed as prescientific. This assertion that it was not Marx and Engels who made history into a science runs counter to fundamental theoretical positions maintained in the past.

preceding stage of development and to a certain extent prepared the ground for the deductions of Marxist science.

The historical views of the great Russian revolutionary-democrats of the nineteenth century, V. G. Belinsky, A. I. Herzen, N. G. Chernyshevsky, and N. A. Dobroliubov, constitute the pinnacle of historical science in Russia in the pre-Marxist period. The superiority of the methodology of the Russian revolutionary-democrats over the bourgeois historical theories determined their superiority in the field of historiography as well. The historical views of these revolutionary-democrats are typified by an effort to understand the historical process as a law-governed process, to apply dialectic to cognition of social life, and to uncover the causes of the historical development of society. Their outstanding merit is that they saw in the popular masses the true makers of history, came close to the correct understanding of the role of the class struggle in the development of society, produced an incisive critique of the order based on feudalism and serfdom, and worked for the revolutionary overthrow of that order. Their views on the history of society developed in the direction of materialist understanding of social life. However, owing to the backwardness of socioeconomic relations in feudal Russia, the Russian revolutionary-democrats only moved toward historical materialism and could not fully overcome idealism in the understanding of social development.

Proceeding from the decisive principle of Marxist-Leninist historical science concerning the primacy of material life of society, Marxist-Leninist historiography regards the history of historical science not as a chaotic accumulation of theories and names but as a definite part of the ideological superstructure of this or that society. Marxist-Leninist historiography regards the history of historical science as a part of the history of social thought. The task of historiography is not only to establish this or that historical phenomenon, but to explain it by proceeding from the given historical conditions.

This means that Marxist-Leninist historiography regards the history of historical science as one of the reflections of the class struggle in the area of the social sciences. This is why historiography sees it as one of its principal tasks to uncover the class nature of the struggle of currents in the historical science and to explain why certain problems become basic in this struggle at one or another period and how these problems are resolved by the representatives of this or that current. Proceeding from the fundamental thesis of historical science concerning the progressive character of the struggle of the popular masses for social, political, and national freedom, historiography devotes special attention to currents reflecting the aspirations of the popular masses. If historical science must, above all, be history of the people and their struggle for progress in society, then historiography must represent, above all, a history of the development of progressive historical thought and a history of its leading role in the development of historical science. The task of historiographic science is to single out in any given period the leading progressive trend regardless of whether it is, especially in the initial stage of its development, a particularly noticeable phenomenon or not. In this respect historiography naturally devotes special attention to the history of Marxist-Leninist historical science as a history of true science which has played a determining role in the history of historical thought. Proceeding from the fundamental principle of historical science, that of regarding all phenomena in their interconnection and development, historiography particularly emphasizes the significance of contemporary Soviet Marxist-Leninist historical science. The development of the Soviet historical thought has a major theoretical and practical significance in the struggle for victory of the communist ideology. Soviet historiography approaches its subject not in an objectivist way or from the standpoint of establishing certain historiographic phenomena, but from the standpoint of militant and singularly objective communist party-mindedness.

In contrast to the cosmopolitanism of bourgeois falsifying historiography, Marxist-Leninist historiography proceeds from the fact that historical science develops in the framework of a given country and is national in character. In showing its class character, a given historiographic phenomenon at the same time takes on a national form. Only by studying what class they represent and in what country they occur can one correctly and comprehensively assess a given historiographic trend and a given historian.

One of the most important tasks of historiography is the study of the history of development of methods and techniques of historical investigation and procedures for interpretation of historical sources. Marxist-Leninist historiography stresses the fact that the investigatory technique of a historian is in close relationship to his historical theory and his methodological principles.

With the present volume, the Institute of History of the Academy of Sciences of the Soviet Union begins the publication of *Survey of the History of Historical Science in the U.S.S.R.*, which will embrace the history of historical thought in our country from ancient times to the present. The writing of a history of historical science in our country required the team of authors to show the basic moments in the development of historiography in the U.S.S.R. and to resolve a number of specific problems deriving from the special nature of the development of historical science in the Soviet Union.

Above all, a history of historical science in a multinational state such as the Soviet Union is a history of a science whose creators have been the numerous peoples inhabiting our country. Any work claiming to present historiography in the U.S.S.R. must embrace the historiography of the peoples of the U.S.S.R. All earlier efforts to write a generalizing study of historiography were reduced to a presentation almost exclusively of Russian historiography. The present work makes it its task to present the history of historical science of the peoples of the U.S.S.R. from ancient times to the present. The accomplishment of this task required the close co-operation of the Institute of History of the Academy of Sciences of the U.S.S.R. with the institutes of the academies of sciences of the Union republics.

The authors' team also made it its task to show the true significance of historical science in our country. Previous works on historiography, even some published in the Soviet period, had attempted to depict historical science in Russia as a reflection of West European historical thought and regarded foreign scholars as the first initiators of historical science in Russia. In this manner the independent nature of historical science in our country and the immense contribution which our historians made to historical science in national as well as foreign history were denied. The historiography of the peoples of the U.S.S.R. was thus subjected to direct or indirect disfiguration. In contrast to this, in the present work it is shown that one of the initiators of historical science in our country, M. V. Lomonosov, was a representative of the advanced science of his time. The scientific-historical views of the Russian revolutionary-democrats of the 1840's through the 1860's stood considerably higher than the views of the contemporary bourgeois historiographers. They contained elements of materialist explanation of history. Even bourgeois-liberal historical thought in Russia had achieved a series of undeniable accomplishments as compared with West European and American historiography. S. M. Solov'ev, N. I. Kareev, I. V. Luchitsky, P. L. Vinogradov, and M. M. Kovalevsky in their better moments stood considerably higher than the contemporary bourgeois historical science abroad.

The history of historical science in the U.S.S.R. represents a notable illustration of the fact that the stubborn struggle between the nobility and bourgeois-liberal current, on the one hand, and the revolutionary-democratic and later Marxist current, on the other, ended in the complete victory of Marxist-Leninist historical science. This struggle placed its imprint upon the very history of historical science in our country.

In ancient times popular aspirations and historical traditions were preserved in oral folklore creations and only in part were reflected in written documents. At the end of the eighteenth century, alongside the official nobility current in historical science in Russia there developed a bourgeois-liberal current. The distinctive feature of historical science in Russia at that time was the emergence of a revolutionary-enlightening current, the spokesman of which was A. N. Radishchev. It found its continuation in the historical views of the Decembrists, and in the 1830's and 1840's was supplanted by the revolutionary-democratic current personified by V. S. Belinsky and A. I. Herzen. This current received its highest expression in the historical views of N. G. Chernyshevsky and N. A. Dobroliubov. Before the serfdom reform of 1861, the bourgeois-liberal current, converging on a number of issues with the nobility current and together with it taking a position against the revolutionary-democrats, was still unable to part definitively with democratic ideas. A personification of this entanglement of liberalism and democratism was T. N. Granovsky. After the reform of 1861 Russian liberalism definitively broke with democratism. The reactionary and falsifying character of bourgeois historiography became more and more apparent.

It is with the 1890's and the beginning of the work of V. I. Lenin that the Marxist-Leninist stage in the development of historical science opens. In Russia of that time the opening of this stage was to a certain extent prepared by the work of G. V. Plekhanov, who made a considerable contribution to the propagation of Marxism in our country.

Marxist-Leninist historical science developed in an unceasing fight with Populist, bourgeois-liberal, gentry-monarchical, Menshevik, and various other historical conceptions inimical to Marxism. The decisive shattering of these antiscientific conceptions is one of the incontrovertible proofs of the immense strength of Marxist-Leninist theory, which Marxist-Leninist historical science takes as its guide.

With the victory of the Great October Socialist Revolution there began a new stage in the history of Marxist-Leninist historical science which has received in our country new and limitless opportunities for development.

CHAPTER VIII

UNDER KHRUSHCHEV, 1955–1964

THE SUPREME POWER which Khrushchev was beginning to wield seems to have reached and influenced the work of Soviet historians by the autumn of 1955. At the Tenth International Congress of Historians, in Rome in September 1955, the main report on "Basic Problems and Some Achievements in the Evolution of Soviet Historical Science" still referred to Stalin as the "continuator of Lenin's work." [1] The spokesman delivering it, however, was not Anna Pankratova, as it might have been expected in Stalin's time, but a historian much less identified with Stalin and his historiographic policy, A. L. Sidorov. In fact, the volume of the papers read by Soviet participants in the congress, published by the History Institute in 1956, omitted Pankratova's contribution with a note that the author would publish it elsewhere. [2]

The full extent of Khrushchev's power to make history, past and present, was made plain by his famous "secret" speech of February 25, 1956, before the Twentieth Congress of the CPSU, on the subject of Stalin's crimes and the pernicious "cult of personality." One of the most important documents of the twentieth century, the speech was made before a closed session of select participants in the congress and was never released in full in the Soviet Union. However, a copy of the speech, "obtained from a confidential source," was released by the U.S. Department of State on June 4, 1956. [3]

---

[1] This was the first international congress attended by Soviet historians after the Sixth Congress, in Oslo in 1928, and the Seventh, in Warsaw in 1933. For a view of the Soviet performance see Pieter Geyl, *Encounters in History* (Cleveland, 1961), pp. 341–351.

[2] *Desiatyi mezhdunarodnyi kongress istorikov v Rime* (see chap. vi, n. 28), last (unnumbered) page.

[3] What was published in the Soviet Union was a brief "Decree on the Cult of Personality and Its Consequences" adopted by the congress "unanimously" on February 25, 1956, after "having heard the report of Comrade Khrushchev." A further, much more detailed decree was adopted by the Central Committee on June 3 for the purpose of "overcoming the cult of personality and its consequences." Texts of both decrees are in *Voprosy ideologicheskoi raboty, sbornik vazhneishikh reshenii KPSS (1954–1961 goda)* [Problems of Ideological Work: Collection of the Most Important Decisions of the CPSU, 1954–1961] (Moscow, 1961), pp. 11–12 and 77–95. The authenticity of the speech as released by the Department of State has been confirmed by the fact that it has never been repudiated by Soviet authorities, and foreign communist parties, including the American Communist Party, have accepted it as a basis of their reactions. The Twenty-second Congress of the party, in October 1961, produced further details in what has been termed Khrushchev's "destalinization" campaign. The Department of State text has been published in a number of places. A convenient collection featuring it together with other pertinent materials is *The Anti-Stalin Campaign and International Communism: A Selection of Documents Edited by the Russian Institute, Columbia University* (New York, 1956). For a thoroughgoing analysis of the speech see Bertram D. Wolfe, *Khrushchev and Stalin's Ghost* (New York, 1957). For Khrushchev's earlier views see reading no. 25.

Of enormous importance for the writing and teaching of contemporary history in the U.S.S.R. and elsewhere, the speech is reproduced below in extensive part.

32. N. S. Khrushchev, "On the Cult of Personality and Its Consequences"

Comrades! In the report of the Central Committee of the Party at the XXth Congress, in a number of speeches by delegates to the Congress, as also formerly during the plenary CC/CPSU sessions, quite a lot has been said about the cult of the individual and about its harmful consequences.

After Stalin's death the Central Committee of the Party began to implement a policy of explaining concisely and consistently that it is impermissible and foreign to the spirit of Marxism-Leninism to elevate one person, to transform him into a superman possessing supernatural characteristics akin to those of a god. Such a man supposedly knows everything, sees everything, thinks for everyone, can do anything, is infallible in his behavior.

Such a belief about a man, and specifically about Stalin, was cultivated among us for many years.

The objective of the present report is not a thorough evaluation of Stalin's life and activity. Concerning Stalin's merits, an entirely sufficient number of books, pamphlets, and studies had already been written in his lifetime. The role of Stalin in the preparation and execution of the Socialist Revolution, in the Civil War, and in the fight for the construction of Socialism in our country is universally known. Everyone knows this well. At the present we are concerned with a question which has immense importance for the Party now and for the future—with how the cult of the person of Stalin has been gradually growing, the cult which became at a certain specific stage the source of a whole series of exceedingly serious and grave perversions of Party principles, of Party democracy, of revolutionary legality.

Because of the fact that not all as yet realize fully the practical consequences resulting from the cult of the individual, the great harm caused by the violation of the principle of collective direction of the Party and because of the accumulation of immense and limitless power in the hands of one person—the Central Committee of the Party considers it absolutely necessary to make the material pertaining to this matter available to the XXth Congress of the Communist Party of the Soviet Union.

Allow me first of all to remind you how severely the classics of Marxism-Leninism denounced every manifestation of the cult of the individual. In a letter to the German political worker, Wilhelm Bloss, Marx stated: "From my antipathy to any cult of the individual, I never made public during the existence of the International the numerous addresses from various countries which recognized my merits and which annoyed me. I did not even reply to them, except sometimes to rebuke their authors. Engels and I first joined the secret society of Communists on the condition that everything making for superstitious worship of authority would be deleted from its statute. Lassalle subsequently did quite the opposite."

Sometime later Engels wrote: "Both Marx and I have always been against any public manifestation with regard to individuals, with the exception of cases when it had an important purpose; and we most strongly opposed such manifestation which during our lifetime concerned us personally."

The great modesty of the genius of the revolution, Vladimir Ilyich Lenin, is known. Lenin had always stressed the role of the people as the creator of history, the directing and organizational role of the Party as a living and creative organism, and also the role of the Central Committee.

Marxism does not negate the role of the leaders of the workers' class in directing the revolutionary liberation movement.

While ascribing great importance to the role of the leaders and organizers of the masses, Lenin at the same time mercilessly stigmatized every manifestation of the cult of the individual, inexorably combated the foreign-to-Marxism views about a "hero" and a "crowd," and countered all efforts to oppose a "hero" to the masses and to the people.

Lenin taught that the Party's strength depends on its indissoluble unity with the masses, on the fact that behind the Party follow the people— workers, peasants, and intelligentsia. "Only he will win and retain the power," said Lenin, "who believes in the people, who submerges himself in the fountain of the living creativeness of the people."

Lenin spoke with pride about the Bolshevik Communist Party as the leader and teacher of the people; he called for the presentation of all the most important questions before the opinion of knowledgeable workers, before the opinion of their Party; he said: "We believe in it, we see in it the wisdom, the honor, and the conscience of our epoch."

Lenin resolutely stood against every attempt aimed at belittling or weakening the directing role of the Party in the structure of the Soviet State. He worked out Bolshevik principles of Party direction and norms of Party life, stressing that the guiding principle of Party leadership is its collegiality. Already during the prerevolutionary years Lenin called the Central Committee of the Party a collective of leaders and the guardian and interpreter of Party principles. "During the period between congresses," pointed out

Lenin, "the Central Committee guards and interprets the principles of the Party."

Underlining the role of the Central Committee of the Party and its authority, Vladimir Ilyich pointed out: "Our Central Committee constituted itself as a closely centralized and highly authoritative group . . ."

During Lenin's life the Central Committee of the Party was a real expression of collective leadership of the Party and of the nation. Being a militant Marxist-revolutionist, always unyielding in matters of principle, Lenin never imposed by force his views upon his co-workers. He tried to convince; he patiently explained his opinions to others. Lenin always diligently observed that the norms of Party life were realized, that the Party statute was enforced, that the Party congresses and the plenary sessions of the Central Committee took place at the proper intervals.

In addition to the great accomplishments of V. I. Lenin for the victory of the working class and of the working peasants, for the victory of our Party, and for the application of the ideas of scientific Communism to life, his acute mind expressed itself also in this, that he detected in Stalin in time those negative characteristics which resulted later in grave consequences. Fearing for the future fate of the Party and of the Soviet nation, V. I. Lenin made a completely correct characterization of Stalin, pointing out that it was necessary to consider the question of transferring Stalin from the position of the Secretary General because of the fact that Stalin was excessively rude, that he did not have a proper attitude toward his comrades, that he was capricious and abused his power.

In December 1922 in a letter to the Party Congress Vladimir Ilyich wrote: "After taking over the position of Secretary General Comrade Stalin accumulated in his hands immeasurable power and I am not certain whether he will be always able to use this power with the required care."

This letter—a political document of tremendous importance, known in the Party history as Lenin's "testament"—was distributed among the delegates to the XXth Party Congress. You have read it, and will undoubtedly read it again more than once. You might reflect on Lenin's plain words, in which expression is given to Vladimir Ilyich's anxiety concerning the Party, the people, the State, and the future direction of Party policy.

Vladimir Ilyich said: "Stalin is excessively rude, and this defect, which can be freely tolerated in our midst and in contacts among us Communists, becomes a defect which cannot be tolerated in one holding the position of the Secretary General. Because of this, I propose that the comrades consider the method by which Stalin would be removed from this position and by which another man would be selected for it, a man, who above all, would differ from Stalin in only one quality, namely, greater tolerance, greater loyalty, greater kindness and a more considerate attitude toward the comrades, a less capricious temper, etc."

This document of Lenin's was made known to the delegates at the XIIIth Party Congress, who discussed the question of transferring Stalin from the position of Secretary General. The delegates declared themselves in favor of retaining Stalin in this post, hoping that he would heed the critical remarks of Vladimir Ilyich and would be able to overcome the defects which caused Lenin serious anxiety.

Comrades! I will not comment on these documents. They speak eloquently for themselves. Since Stalin could behave in this manner during Lenin's life, could thus behave toward Nadezhda Konstantinovna Krupskaya, whom the Party knows well and values highly as a loyal friend of Lenin and as an active fighter for the cause of the Party since its creation—we can easily imagine how Stalin treated other people. These negative characteristics of his developed steadily and during the last years acquired an absolutely insufferable character.

As later events have proven, Lenin's anxiety was justified: in the first period after Lenin's death Stalin still paid attention to his (i.e., Lenin's) advice, but later he began to disregard the serious admonitions of Vladimir Ilyich.

When we analyze the practice of Stalin in regard to the direction of the Party and of the country, when we pause to consider everything which Stalin perpetrated, we must be convinced that Lenin's fears were justified. The negative characteristics of Stalin, which, in Lenin's time, were only incipient, transformed themselves during the last years into a grave abuse of power by Stalin, which caused untold harm to our Party.

We have to consider seriously and analyze correctly this matter in order that we may preclude any possibility of a repetition in any form whatever of what took place during the life of Stalin, who absolutely did not tolerate collegiality in leadership and in work, and who practiced brutal violence, not only toward everything which opposed him, but also toward that which seemed to his capricious and despotic character, contrary to his concepts.

Stalin acted not through persuasion, explanation, and patient co-operation with people, but by imposing his concepts and demanding absolute submission to his opinion. Whoever opposed this concept or tried to prove his viewpoint, and the correctness of his position, was doomed to removal from the leading collective and to subsequent moral and physical annihilation. This was especially true during the period following the XVIIth Party Congress when many prominent Party leaders and rank-and-file Party workers, honest and dedicated to the cause of Communism, fell victim to Stalin's despotism.

We must affirm that the Party had fought a serious fight against the Trotskyites, rightists, and bourgeois nationalists, and that it disarmed ideologically all the enemies of Leninism. This ideological fight was carried on successfully, as a result of which the Party became strengthened and tempered. Here Stalin played a positive role.

It was precisely during this period (1935–1937–1938) that the practice of mass repression through the government apparatus was born, first against the enemies of Leninism—Trotskyites, Zinovievites, Bukharinites, long since politically defeated by the Party, and subsequently also against many honest Communists, against those Party cadres who had borne the heavy load of the Civil War and the first and most difficult years of industrialization and collectivization, who actively fought against the Trotskyites and the rightists for the Leninist Party line.

Stalin originated the concept "enemy of the people." This term automatically rendered it unnecessary that the ideological errors of a man or men engaged in a controversy be proven; this term made possible the usage of the most cruel repression, violating all norms of revolutionary legality, against those who were only suspected of hostile intent, against those who had bad reputations. This concept, "enemy of the people," actually eliminated the possibility of any kind of ideological fight or the making of one's views known on this or that issue, even those of a practical character. In the main, and in actuality, the only proof of guilt used, against all norms of current legal science, was the "confession" of the accused himself; and, as subsequent probing proved, "confessions" were acquired through physical pressures against the accused.

This led to glaring violations of revolutionary legality, and to the fact that many entirely innocent persons, who in the past had defended the Party line, became victims.

We must assert that in regard to those persons who in their time had opposed the Party line, there were often no sufficiently serious reasons for their physical annihilation. The formula, "enemy of the people," was specifically introduced for the purpose of physically annihilating such individuals.

Lenin's wisdom in dealing with people was evident in his work with cadres.

An entirely different relationship with people characterized Stalin. Lenin's traits—patient work with people; stubborn and painstaking education of them; the ability to induce people to follow him without using compulsion, but rather through the ideological influence on them of the whole collective—were entirely foreign to Stalin. He (Stalin) discarded the Leninist method of convincing and educating; he abandoned the method of ideological struggle for that of administrative violence, mass repressions, and terror. He acted on an increasingly larger scale and more stubbornly through punitive organs, at the same time often violating all existing norms of morality and of Soviet laws.

Arbitrary behavior by one person encouraged and permitted arbitrariness in others. Mass arrests and deportations of many thousands of people, execution without trial and without normal investigation, created conditions of insecurity, fear, and even desperation.

Lenin used severe methods only in the most necessary cases, when the exploiting classes were still in existence and were vigorously opposing the revolution, when the struggle for survival was decidedly assuming the sharpest forms, even including a civil war.

Stalin, on the other hand, used extreme methods and mass repressions at a time when the revolution was already victorious, when the Soviet state was strengthened, when the exploiting classes were already liquidated and Socialist relations were rooted solidly in all phases of national economy, when our Party was politically consolidated and had strengthened itself both numerically and ideologically. It is clear that here Stalin showed in a whole series of cases his intolerance, his brutality, and his abuse of power. Instead of proving his political correctness and mobilizing the masses, he often chose the path of repression and physical annihilation, not only against actual enemies, but also against individuals who had not committed any crimes against the Party and the Soviet government. Here we see no wisdom but only a demonstration of the brutal force which had once so alarmed V. I. Lenin.

Lately, especially after the unmasking of the Beria gang, the Central Committee has looked into a series of matters fabricated by this gang. This revealed a very ugly picture of brutal willfulness connected with the incorrect behavior of Stalin. As facts prove, Stalin, using his unlimited power, allowed himself many abuses, acting in the name of the Central Committee, not asking for the opinion of the Committee members nor even of the members of the Central Committee's Political Bureau; often he did not inform them about his personal decisions concerning very important Party and government matters.

Considering the question of the cult of an individual we must first of all show everyone what harm this caused to the interests of our Party.

Vladimir Ilyich Lenin had always stressed the Party's role and significance in the direction of the socialist government of workers and peasants; he saw in this the chief precondition for a successful building of socialism in our country. Pointing to the great responsibility of the Bolshevik Party, as a ruling party in the Soviet state, Lenin called for the most meticulous observance of all norms of Party life; he called for the realization of the principles of collegiality in the direction of the Party and the state.

Collegiality of leadership flows from the very nature of our Party, a party built on the principles of democratic centralism. "This means," said Lenin, "that all Party matters are accomplished by all Party members—directly or through representatives—who without any exceptions are subject to the same rules; in addition, all administrative members, all directing collegia, all holders of Party positions are elective, they must account for their activities and are recallable."

It is known that Lenin himself offered an example of the most careful observance of these principles. There was no matter so important that Lenin himself decided it without asking for advice and approval of the majority of the Central Committee members or of the members of the Central Committee's Political Bureau.

In the most difficult period for our Party and our country, Lenin considered it necessary regularly to convoke congresses, Party conferences, and plenary sessions of the Central Committee at which all the most important questions were discussed and where resolutions, carefully worked out by the collective of leaders, were approved.

So it was during Lenin's life.

Were our Party's holy Leninist principles observed after the death of Vladimir Ilyich?

Whereas during the first few years after Lenin's death Party Congresses and Central Committee plenums took place more or less regularly, later, when Stalin began increasingly to abuse his power, these principles were brutally violated. This was especially evident during the last fifteen years of his life. Was it a normal situation when over thirteen years elapsed between the XVIIIth and XIXth Party Congresses, years during which our Party and our country had experienced so many important events? These events demanded categorically that the Party should have passed resolutions pertaining to the country's defense during the Patriotic War and to peacetime construction after the war. Even after the end of the war a Congress was not convened for over seven years.

Central Committee plenums were hardly ever called. It should be sufficient to mention that during all the years of the Patriotic War not a single Central Committee plenum took place. It is true that there was an attempt to call a Central Committee plenum in October 1941, when Central Committee members from the whole country were called to Moscow. They waited two days for the opening of the plenum, but in vain. Stalin did not even want to meet and to talk to the Central Committee members. This fact shows how demoralized Stalin was in the first months of the war and how haughtily and disdainfully he treated the Central Committee members.

In practice Stalin ignored the norms of Party life and trampled on the Leninist principle of collective Party leadership.

Stalin's willfulness vis-à-vis the Party and its Central Committee became fully evident after the XVIIth Party Congress which took place in 1934.

Having at its disposal numerous data showing brutal willfulness toward Party cadres, the Central Committee has created a Party Commission under the control of the Central Committee Presidium; it was charged with investigating what made possible the mass repressions against the majority of the Central Committee members and candidates elected at the XVIIth Congress of the All-Union Communist Party (Bolsheviks).

The Commission has become acquainted with a large quantity of materials in the NKVD archives and with other documents and has established many facts pertaining to the fabrication of cases against Communists, to false accusations, to glaring abuses of socialist legality—which resulted in the death of innocent people. It became apparent that many Party, Soviet, and economic activists who were branded in 1937–38 as "enemies" were actually never enemies, spies, wreckers, etc., but were always honest Communists; they were only so stigmatized, and often, no longer able to bear barbaric tortures, they charged themselves (at the order of the investigative judges—falsifiers) with all kinds of grave and unlikely crimes. The Commission has presented to the Central Committee Presidium lengthy and documented materials pertaining to mass repressions against the delegates to the XVIIth Party Congress and against members of the Central Committee elected at that Congress. These materials have been studied by the Presidium of the Central Committee.

It was determined that of the 139 members and candidates of the Party's Central Committee who were elected at the XVIIth Congress, 98 persons, i.e., 70 per cent, were arrested and shot (mostly in 1937–38). (*Indignation in the hall.*)

What was the composition of the delegates to the XVIIth Congress? It is known that 80 per cent of the voting participants of the XVIIth Congress joined the Party during the years of conspiracy before the Revolution and during the Civil War; this means before 1921. By social origin the basic mass of the delegates to the Congress were workers (60 per cent of the voting members).

For this reason, it was inconceivable that a Congress so composed would have elected a Central Committee, a majority of which would prove to be enemies of the Party. The only reason why 70 per cent of the Central Committee members and candidates elected at the XVIIth Congress were branded as enemies of the Party and of the people was that honest Communists were slandered, accusations against them were fabricated, and revolutionary legality was gravely undermined.

The same fate met not only the Central Committee members but also the majority of the delegates to the XVIIth Party Congress. Of 1,966 delegates with either voting or advisory rights, 1,108 persons were arrested on charges of antirevolutionary crimes, i.e., decidedly more than a majority. This very fact shows how absurd, wild, and contrary to common sense were the charges of counterrevolutionary crimes made out, as we now see, against a majority of participants at the XVIIth Party Congress. (*Indignation in the hall.*)

This was the result of the abuse of power by Stalin, who began to use mass terror against the Party cadres.

What is the reason that mass repressions against activists increased more and more after the XVIIth Party Congress? It was because at that time Stalin had so elevated himself above the Party and above the nation that he ceased to consider either the Central Committee or the Party. While he still reckoned with the opinion of the collective before the XVIIth Congress, after the complete political liquidation of the Trotskyites, Zinovievites, and Bukharinites, when as a result of that fight and socialist victories the Party achieved unity, Stalin ceased to an ever greater degree to consider the members of the Party's Central Committee and even the members of the Political Bureau. Stalin thought that now he could decide all things alone and all he needed were statisticians; he treated all others in such a way that they could only listen to and praise him.

After the criminal murder of S. M. Kirov, mass repressions and brutal acts of violation of socialist legality began. On the evening of December 1, 1934, on Stalin's initiative (without the approval of the Political Bureau—which was passed two days later, casually) the secretary of the Presidium of the Central Executive Committee, Yenukidze, signed the following directive:

> I. Investigative agencies are directed to speed up the cases of those accused of the preparation or execution of acts of terror.
>
> II. Judicial organs are directed not to hold up the execution of death sentences pertaining to crimes of this category in order to consider the possibility of pardon, because the Presidium of the Central Executive Committee [of the] U.S.S.R. does not consider as possible the receiving of petitions of this sort.
>
> III. The organs of the Commissariat of Internal Affairs (NKVD) are directed to execute death sentences against criminals of the above-mentioned category immediately after the passage of sentences.

This directive became the basis for mass acts of abuse against socialist legality. During many of the fabricated court cases the accused were charged with "the preparation" of terroristic acts; this deprived them of any possibility that their cases might be re-examined, even when they stated before the court that their "confessions" were secured by force, and when, in a convincing manner, they disproved the accusations against them.

It must be asserted that to this day the circumstances surrounding Kirov's murder hide many things which are inexplicable and mysterious and demand a most careful examination. There are reasons for the suspicion that the killer of Kirov, Nikolayev, was assisted by someone from among the people whose duty it was to protect the person of Kirov. A month and half before the killing, Nikolayev was arrested on the grounds of suspicious behavior, but he was released and not even searched. It is an unusually suspicious circumstance that when the Chekist assigned to protect Kirov was being brought for an interrogation on December 2, 1934, he was killed in a car "accident" in which no other occupants of the car were harmed. After the murder of Kirov, top functionaries of the Leningrad NKVD were given very light sentences, but in 1937 they were shot. We can assume that they were shot in order to cover the traces of the organizers of Kirov's killing. (*Movement in the hall.*)

Mass repressions grew tremendously from the end of 1936 after a telegram from Stalin and Zhdanov, dated from Sochi on September 25, 1936, was addressed to Kaganovich, Molotov, and other members of the Political Bureau. The content of the telegram was as follows:

"We deem it absolutely necessary and urgent that Comrade Yezhov be nominated to the post of People's Commissar for Internal Affairs. Yagoda has definitely proved himself to be incapable of unmasking the Trotskyite-Zinovievite bloc. The OGPU is four years behind in this matter. This is noted by all Party workers and by the majority of the representatives of the NKVD." Strictly speaking, we should stress that Stalin did not meet with and therefore could not know the opinion of party workers.

This Stalinist formulation that the "NKVD is four years behind" in applying mass repression and that there is a necessity for "catching up" with the neglected work directly pushed the NKVD workers on the path of mass arrests and executions.

The mass repressions at this time were made under the slogan of a fight against the Trotskyites. Did the Trotskyites at this time actually constitute such a danger to our Party and to the Soviet state? We should recall that in 1927 on the eve of the XVth Party Congress only some 4,000 votes were cast for the Trotskyite-Zinovievite opposition, while there were 724,000 for the Party line. During the ten years which passed between the XVth Party Congress and the February-March Central Committee Plenum, Trotskyism was completely disarmed; many former Trotskyites had changed their former views and worked in the various sectors building socialism. It is clear that in the situation of socialist victory there was no basis for mass terror in the country.

The majority of the Central Committee members and candidates elected at the XVIIth Congress and arrested in 1937–38 were expelled from the Party illegally through the brutal abuse of the Party Statute, because the question of their expulsion was never studied at the Central Committee Plenum.

Now when the cases of some of these so-called "spies" and "saboteurs" were examined it was found that all their cases were fabricated. Confessions of guilt of many arrested and charged with enemy activity were gained with the help of cruel and inhuman tortures.

At the same time Stalin, as we have been informed by members of the Political Bureau of that time, did not show them the statements of many accused political activists when they retracted their confessions before the military tribunal and asked for an objective examination of their cases. There were many such declarations, and Stalin doubtlessly knew of them.

The Central Committee considers it absolutely necessary to inform the Congress of many such fabricated "cases" against the members of the Party's Central Committee elected at the XVIIth Party Congress.

Many thousands of honest and innocent Communists have died as a result of this monstrous falsification of such "cases," as a result of the fact that all kinds of slanderous "confessions" were accepted, and as a result of the practice of forcing accusations against oneself and others. In the same manner were fabricated the "cases" against eminent Party and state workers—Kossior, Chubar, Postyshev, Kosarev, and others.

In those years repressions on a mass scale were applied which were based on nothing tangible and which resulted in heavy cadre losses to the Party.

The vicious practice was condoned of having the NKVD prepare lists of persons whose cases were under the jurisdiction of the Military Collegium and whose sentences were prepared in advance. Yezhov would send these lists to Stalin personally for his approval of the proposed punishment. In 1937–38, 383 such lists containing the names of many thousands of Party, Soviet, Komsomol, Army, and economic workers were sent to Stalin. He approved these lists.

A large part of these cases are being reviewed now and a great part of them are being voided because they were baseless and falsified. Suffice it to say that from 1954 to the present time the Military Collegium of the Supreme Court has rehabilitated 7,679 persons, many of whom were rehabilitated posthumously.

Mass arrests of Party, Soviet, economic, and military workers caused tremendous harm to our country and to the cause of socialist advancement.

Mass repressions had a negative influence on the moral-political condition of the Party, created a situation of uncertainty, contributed to the spreading of unhealthy suspicion, and sowed distrust among Communists. All sorts of slanderers and careerists were active.

Facts prove that many abuses were made on Stalin's orders without reckoning with any norms of Party and Soviet legality. Stalin was a very distrustful man, sickly suspicious; we knew this from our work with him. He could look at a man and say: "Why are your eyes so shifty today," or "Why are you turning so much today and avoiding looking me directly in the eyes?" The sickly suspicion created in him a general distrust even toward eminent Party workers whom he had known for years. Everywhere and in everything he saw "enemies," "two-facers," and "spies."

Possessing unlimited power he indulged in great willfulness and choked a person morally and physically. A situation was created where one could not express one's own will.

When Stalin said that one or another should be arrested, it was necessary to accept on faith that he was an "enemy of the people." Meanwhile, Beria's gang, which ran the organs of state security, outdid itself in proving the guilt of the arrested and the truth of materials which it falsified. And what proofs were offered? The confessions of the arrested—and the investigative judges accepted these "confessions." And how is it possible that a person confesses to crimes which he has not committed? Only in one way— because of application of physical methods of pressuring him, tortures, bringing him to a state of unconsciousness, deprivation of his judgment, taking away of his human dignity. In this manner were "confessions" acquired.

When the wave of mass arrests began to recede in 1939, and the leaders of territorial Party organizations began to accuse the NKVD workers of using methods of physical pressure on the arrested, Stalin dispatched a coded telegram on January 20, 1939, to the committee secretaries of oblasts and krais, to the Central Committees of republic Communist Parties, to the People's Commissars of Internal Affairs and to the heads of NKVD organizations. This telegram stated:

> The Central Committee of the All-Union Communist Party (Bolsheviks) explains that the application of methods of physical pressure in NKVD practice is permissible from 1937 on in accordance with permission of the Central Committee of the All-Union Communist Party (Bolsheviks). . . . It is known that all bourgeois intelligence services use methods of physical influence against the representatives of the socialist proletariat and that they use them in their most scandalous form. The question arises as to why the socialist intelligence service should be more humanitarian against the mad agents of the bourgeoisie, against the deadly enemies of the working class and the kolkhoz workers. The Central Committee of the All-Union Communist Party (Bolsheviks) considers that physical pressure should still be used

obligatorily, as an exception applicable to known and obstinate enemies of the people, as a method both justifiable and appropriate.

Thus, Stalin had sanctioned in the name of the Central Committee of the All-Union Communist Party (Bolsheviks) the most brutal violation of socialist legality, torture and oppression, which led as we have seen to the slandering and self-accusation of innocent people.

The power accumulated in the hands of one person, Stalin, led to serious consequences during the Great Patriotic War.

When we look at many of our novels, films, and historical "scientific studies," the role of Stalin in the Patriotic War appears to be entirely improbable. Stalin had foreseen everything. The Soviet Army, on the basis of a strategic plan prepared by Stalin long before, used the tactics of so-called "active defense," i.e., tactics which, as we know, allowed the Germans to come up to Moscow and Stalingrad. Using such tactics the Soviet Army, supposedly thanks only to Stalin's genius, turned to the offensive and subdued the enemy. The epic victory gained through the armed might of the Land of the Soviets, through our heroic people, is ascribed in this type of novel, film, and "scientific study" as being completely due to the strategic genius of Stalin.

We have to analyze this matter carefully because it has a tremendous significance not only from the historical, but especially from the political, educational, and practical point of view.

What are the facts of this matter?

Before the war our press and all our political-educational work was characterized by its bragging tone: when an enemy violates the holy Soviet soil, then for every blow of the enemy we will answer with three blows and we will battle the enemy on his soil and we will win without much harm to ourselves. But these positive statements were not based in all areas on concrete facts, which would actually guarantee the immunity of our borders.

During the war and after the war Stalin put forward the thesis that the tragedy which our nation experienced in the first part of the war was the result of the "unexpected" attack of the Germans against the Soviet Union. But, Comrades, this is completely untrue. As soon as Hitler came to power in Germany he assigned to himself the task of liquidating Communism. The Fascists were saying this openly; they did not hide their plans. In order to attain this aggressive end all sorts of pacts and blocs were created, such as the famous Berlin-Rome-Tokyo axis. Many facts from the prewar period clearly showed that Hitler was going all-out to begin a war against the Soviet state and that he had concentrated large armed units, together with armored units, near the Soviet borders.

Documents which have now been published show that by April 3, 1941, Churchill, through his ambassador to the U.S.S.R., Cripps, personally warned Stalin that the Germans had begun regrouping their armed units with the intent of attacking the Soviet Union. It is self-evident that Churchill did not do this at all because of his friendly feeling toward the Soviet nation. He had in this his own imperialistic goals—to bring Germany and the U.S.S.R. into a bloody war and thereby to strengthen the position of the British Empire. Just the same, Churchill affirmed in his writings that he sought to "warn Stalin and call his attention to the danger which threatened him." Churchill stressed this repeatedly in his dispatches of April 18 and in the following days. However, Stalin took no heed of these warnings. What is more, Stalin ordered that no credence be given to information of this sort, in order not to provoke the initiation of military operations.

We must assert that information of this sort concerning the threat of German armed invasion of Soviet territory was coming in also from our own military and diplomatic sources; however, because the leadership was conditioned against such information, such data was dispatched with fear and assessed with reservation.

Despite these particularly grave warnings, the necessary steps were not taken to prepare the country properly for defense and to prevent it from being caught unawares.

And what were the results of this carefree attitude, this disregard of clear facts? The result was that already in the first hours and days the enemy had destroyed in our border regions a large part of our air force, artillery, and other military equipment; he annihilated large numbers of our military cadres and disorganized our military leadership; consequently we could not prevent the enemy from marching deep into the country.

Very grievous consequences, especially in reference to the beginning of the war, followed Stalin's annihilation of many military commanders and political workers during 1937–41 because of his suspiciousness and through slanderous accusations. During these years repressions were instituted against certain parts of military cadres, beginning literally at the company and battalion commander level and extending to the higher military centers; during this time the cadre of leaders who had gained military experience in Spain and in the Far East was almost completely liquidated.

Stalin was very much interested in the assessment of Comrade Zhukov as a military leader. He asked me often for my opinion of Zhukov. I told him then, "I have known Zhukov for a long time; he is a good general and a good military leader."

After the war Stalin began to tell all kinds of nonsense about Zhukov, among others the following, "You praised Zhukov, but he does not deserve it. It is said that before each operation at the front Zhukov used to behave as follows: he used to take a handful of earth, smell it, and say, 'We can begin the attack,' or the opposite, 'The planned operation cannot be carried out.' " I stated at that time, "Comrade Stalin, I do not know who invented this, but it is not true."

It is possible that Stalin himself invented these things for the purpose of minimizing the role and military talents of Marshal Zhukov.

In this connection Stalin very energetically popularized himself as a great leader; in various ways he tried to inculcate in the people the version that all victories gained by the Soviet nation during the Great Patriotic War were due to the courage, daring, and genius of Stalin and of no one else.

Comrades, let us reach for some other facts. The Soviet Union is justly considered as a model of a multinational state because we have in practice assured the equality and friendship of all nations which live in our great Fatherland.

All the more monstrous are the acts whose initiator was Stalin and which are rude violations of the basic Leninist principles of the nationality policy of the Soviet state. We refer to the mass deportations from their native places of whole nations, together with all Communists and Komsomols without any exception; this deportation action was not dictated by any military considerations.

The willfulness of Stalin showed itself not only in decisions concerning the internal life of the country but also in the international relations of the Soviet Union.

The July Plenum of the Central Committee studied in detail the reasons for the development of conflict with Yugoslavia. It was a shameful role which Stalin played here. The "Yugoslav affair" contained no problems which could not have been solved through Party discussions among comrades. There was no significant basis for the development of this "affair"; it was completely possible to have prevented the rupture of relations with that country. This does not mean, however, that the Yugoslav leaders did not make mistakes or did not have shortcomings. But these mistakes and shortcomings were magnified in a monstrous manner by Stalin, which resulted in a break of relations with a friendly country.

I recall the first days when the conflict between the Soviet Union and Yugoslavia began artificially to be blown up. Once, when I came from Kiev to Moscow, I was invited to visit Stalin who, pointing to the copy of a letter lately sent to Tito, asked me, "Have you read this?" Not waiting for my reply, he answered, "I will shake my little finger—and there will be no more Tito. He will fall."

We have dearly paid for this "shaking of the little finger." This statement reflected Stalin's mania for greatness, but he acted just that way: "I will shake my little finger—and there will be no Kossior"; "I will shake my little finger once more and Postyshev and Chubar will be no more"; "I will shake my little finger again—and Voznesenskii, Kuznetsov, and many others will disappear."

But this did not happen to Tito. No matter how much or how little Stalin shook, not only his little finger but everything else that he could shake, Tito did not fall. Why? The reason was that, in this case of disagreement with the Yugoslav comrades, Tito had behind him a state and a people who had gone through a severe school of fighting for liberty and independence, a people which gave support to its leaders.

You see to what Stalin's mania for greatness led. He had completely lost consciousness of reality; he demonstrated his suspicion and haughtiness not only in relation to individuals in the U.S.S.R., but in relation to whole parties and nations.

We have carefully examined the case of Yugoslavia and have found a proper solution which is approved by the peoples of the Soviet Union and of Yugoslavia as well as by the working masses of all the People's Democracies and by all progressive humanity. The liquidation of the abnormal relationship with Yugoslavia was done in the interest of the whole camp of socialism, in the interest of strengthening peace in the whole world.

Let us also recall the "affair of the Doctor-Plotters." (*Animation in the hall.*) Actually there was no "affair" outside of the declaration of the woman doctor Timashuk, who was probably influenced or ordered by someone (after all, she was an unofficial collaborator of the organs of state security) to write Stalin a letter in which she declared that doctors were applying supposedly improper methods of medical treatment.

Such a letter was sufficient for Stalin to reach an immediate conclusion that there were doctor-plotters in the Soviet Union. He issued orders to arrest a group of eminent Soviet medical specialists. He personally issued advice on the conduct of the investigation and the method of interrogation of the arrested persons. He said that the academician Vinogradov should be put in chains, another one should be beaten. Present at this Congress as a delegate is the former Minister of State Security, Comrade Ignatiev. Stalin told him curtly, "If you do not obtain confessions from the doctors, we will shorten you by a head." (*Tumult in the hall.*)

Stalin personally called the investigative judge, gave him instructions, advised him on which investigative methods should be used; these methods were simple—beat, beat, and, once again, beat.

Shortly after the doctors were arrested, we members of the Political Bureau received protocols with the doctors' confessions of guilt. After distributing these protocols, Stalin told us, "You are blind like young kittens; what will happen without me? The country will perish because you do not know how to recognize enemies."

The case was so presented that no one could verify the facts on which the investigation was based. There was no possibility of trying to verify facts by contacting those who had made the confessions of guilt.

We felt, however, that the case of the arrested doctors was questionable. We knew some of these people personally because they had once treated us. When we examined this "case" after Stalin's death, we found it to be fabricated from beginning to end.

This ignominious "case" was set up by Stalin; he did not, however, have the time in which to bring it to an end (as he conceived that end), and for this reason the doctors are still alive.

Comrades! The cult of the individual acquired such monstrous size chiefly because Stalin himself, using all conceivable methods, supported the glorification of his own person. This is supported by numerous facts. One of the most characteristic examples of Stalin's self-glorification and of his lack of even elementary modesty is the edition of his *Short Biography* which was published in 1948.

This book is an expression of the most dissolute flattery, an example of making a man into a godhead, of transforming him into an infallible sage, "the greatest leader," "sublime strategist of all times and nations." Finally no other words could be found with which to lift Stalin up to the heavens.

In the draft text of his book appeared the following sentence: "Stalin is the Lenin of today." This sentence appeared to Stalin to be too weak, so in his own handwriting he changed it to read: "Stalin is the worthy continuer of Lenin's work, or, as it is said in our Party, Stalin is the Lenin of today." You see how well it is said, not by the nation but by Stalin himself.

It is possible to give many such self-praising appraisals written into the draft text of that book in Stalin's hand. Especially generously does he endow himself with praises pertaining to his military genius, to his talent for strategy.

I will cite one more insertion made by Stalin concerning the theme of the Stalinist military genius.

"The advanced Soviet science of war received further development," he writes,

at Comrade Stalin's hands. Comrade Stalin elaborated the theory of the permanently operating factors that decide the issue of wars, of active defense and the laws of counteroffensive and offensive, of the co-operation of all services and arms in modern warfare, of the role of big tank masses and air forces in modern war, and of the artillery as the most formidable of the armed services. At the various stages of the war Stalin's genius found the correct solutions that took account of all the circumstances of the situation. (*Movement in the hall.*)

And further, writes Stalin:

Stalin's military mastership was displayed both in defense and offense. Comrade Stalin's genius enabled him to divine the enemy's plans and defeat them. The battles in which Comrade Stalin directed the Soviet armies are brilliant examples of operational military skill.

In this manner was Stalin praised as a strategist. Who did this? Stalin himself, not in his role as a strategist but in the role of an author-editor, one of the main creators of his self-adulatory biography.

Such, comrades, are the facts. We should rather say shameful facts.

And one additional fact from the same *Short Biography* of Stalin. As is known, *The Short Course of the History of the All-Union Communist Party (Bolsheviks)* was written by a commission of the Party Central Committee.

This book, parenthetically, was also permeated with the cult of the individual and was written by a designated group of authors. This fact was reflected in the following formulation on the proof copy of the *Short Biography* of Stalin:

A commission of the Central Committee, All-Union Communist Party (Bolsheviks), under the direction of Comrade Stalin and with his most active personal participation, has prepared a *Short Course of the History of the All-Union Communist Party (Bolsheviks)*.

But even this phrase did not satisfy Stalin; the following sentence replaced it in the final version of the *Short Biography:*

"In 1938 appeared the book, *History of the All-Union Communist Party (Bolsheviks), Short Course,* written by Comrade Stalin and approved by a commission of the Central Committee, All-Union Communist Party (Bolsheviks)." Can one add anything more? (*Animation in the hall.*)

As you see, a surprising metamorphosis changed the work created by a group into a book written by Stalin. It is not necessary to state how and why this metamorphosis took place.

A pertinent question comes to our mind: if Stalin is the author of this book, why did he need to praise the person of Stalin so much and to transform the whole post-October historical period of our glorious Communist Party solely into an action of "the Stalin genius"?

Did this book properly reflect the efforts of the Party in the socialist transformation of the country, in the construction of socialist society, in the industrialization and collectivization of the country, and also other steps taken by the Party which undeviatingly traveled the path outlined by Lenin? This book speaks principally about Stalin, about his speeches, about his reports. Everything without the smallest exception is tied to his name.

And when Stalin himself asserts that he himself wrote the *Short Course of the History of the All-Union Communist Party (Bolsheviks)*, this calls at least for amazement. Can a Marxist-Leninist thus write about himself, praising his own person to the heavens?

In speaking about the events of the October Revolution and about the Civil War, the impression was created that Stalin always played the main role, as if everywhere and always Stalin had suggested to Lenin what to do and how to do it. However, this is slander of Lenin. (*Prolonged applause.*)

I will probably not sin against the truth when I say that 99 per cent of the persons present here heard and knew very little about Stalin before the year 1924, while Lenin was known to all; he was known to the whole Party, to the whole nation, from the children up to the graybeards. (*Tumultuous, prolonged applause.*)

All this has to be thoroughly revised, so that history, literature, and the fine arts properly reflect V. I. Lenin's role and the great deeds of our Communist Party and of the Soviet people—the creative people. (*Applause.*)

Comrades! The cult of the individual has caused the employment of faulty principles in Party work and in economic activity; it brought about rude violation of internal Party and Soviet democracy, sterile administration, deviations of all sorts, covering up of shortcomings and varnishing of reality. Our nation gave birth to many flatterers and specialists in false optimism and deceit.

We should also not forget that due to the numerous arrests of Party, Soviet, and economic leaders, many workers began to work uncertainly, showed overcautiousness, feared all which was new, feared their own shadows, and began to show less initiative in their work.

Take, for instance, Party and Soviet resolutions. They were prepared in a routine manner often without considering the concrete situation. This went so far that Party workers, even during the smallest sessions, read their speeches. All this produced the danger of formalizing the Party and Soviet work and of bureaucratizing the whole apparatus.

Stalin's reluctance to consider life's realities and the fact that he was not aware of the real state of affairs in the provinces can be illustrated by his direction of agriculture.

All those who interested themselves even a little in the national situation saw the difficult situation in agriculture, but Stalin never even noted it. Did we tell Stalin about this? Yes, we told him, but he did not support us.

Why? Because Stalin never traveled anywhere, did not meet city and kolkhoz workers; he did not know the actual situation in the provinces.

He knew the country and agriculture only from films. And these films had dressed up and beautified the existing situation in agriculture.

Many films so pictured kolkhoz life that the tables were bending from the weight of turkeys and geese. Evidently Stalin thought that it was actually so.

Vladimir Ilyich Lenin looked at life differently; he was always close to the people; he used to receive peasant delegates, and often spoke at factory gatherings; he used to visit villages and talk with the peasants.

Stalin separated himself from the people and never went anywhere. This lasted tens of years. The last time he visited a village was in January 1928 when he visited Siberia in connection with grain deliveries. How then could he have known the situation in the provinces?

In the situation which then prevailed I have talked often with Nikolai Alexandrovich Bulganin; once when we two were traveling in a car, he said, "It has happened sometimes that a man goes to Stalin on his invitation as a friend. And when he sits with Stalin, he does not know where he will be sent next, home or to jail."

One of the oldest members of our Party, Kliment Yefremovich Voroshilov, found himself in an almost impossible situation. For several years he was actually deprived of the right of participation in Political Bureau sessions. Stalin forbade him to attend the Political Bureau sessions and to receive documents. When the Political Bureau was in session and Comrade Voroshilov heard about it, he telephoned each time and asked whether he would be allowed to attend. Sometimes Stalin permitted it, but always showed his dissatisfaction. Because of his extreme suspicion, Stalin toyed also with the absurd and ridiculous suspicion that Voroshilov was an English agent. (*Laughter in the hall.*) It's true—an English agent. A special tapping device was installed in his home to listen to what was said there. (*Indignation in the hall.*)

Let us consider the first Central Committee Plenum after the XIXth Party Congress when Stalin, in his talk at the Plenum, characterized Vyacheslav Mikhailovich Molotov and Anastas Ivanovich Mikoyan and suggested that these old workers of our Party were guilty of some baseless charges. It is not excluded that had Stalin remained at the helm for another several months, Comrades Molotov and Mikoyan would probably have not delivered any speeches at this Congress.

Stalin evidently had plans to finish off the old members of the Political Bureau. He often stated that Political Bureau members should be replaced by new ones.

We should in all seriousness consider the question of the cult of the individual. We cannot let this matter get out of the Party, especially not to the press. It is for this reason that we are considering it here at a closed Congress session. We should know the limits; we should not give ammunition to the enemy; we should not wash our dirty linen before their eyes. I think that the delegates to the Congress will understand and assess properly all these proposals. (*Tumultuous applause.*)

Comrades, we must abolish the cult of the individual decisively, once and for all; we must draw the proper conclusions concerning both ideological-theoretical and practical work.

It is necessary for this purpose:

First, in a Bolshevik manner to condemn and to eradicate the cult of the individual as alien to Marxism-Leninism and not consonant with the principles of Party leadership and the norms of Party life, and to fight inexorably all attempts at bringing back this practice in one form or another.

To return to and actually practice in all our ideological work the most important theses of Marxist-Leninist science about the people as the creator of history and as the creator of all material and spiritual good of humanity, about the decisive role of the Marxist Party in the revolutionary fight for the transformation of society, about the victory of Communism.

In this connection we will be forced to do much work in order to examine critically from the Marxist-Leninist viewpoint and to correct the widely spread erroneous views connected with the cult of the individual in the sphere of history, philosophy, economy and of other sciences, as well as in literature and the fine arts. It is especially necessary that in the immediate future we compile a serious textbook of the history of our Party which will be edited in accordance with scientific Marxist objectivism, a textbook of the history of Soviet society, a book pertaining to the events of the Civil War and the Great Patriotic War.

Perhaps the most succinct and widely used statement on history as a discipline published after Khrushchev's secret speech is the Introduction to *Istoriia SSSR, Tom I, S drevneishikh vremen do 1861 g.* ("History of the U.S.S.R.," Vol. I, "From Earliest Times to 1861") (Moscow, 1956), edited by M. V. Nechkina and others and adopted by the Ministry of Higher Education for use as a textbook in the universities and teachers colleges. The textbook, of which the second volume covering the period from 1861 to 1917 was published in 1959, is the successor to the two-volume textbook first published in 1939 and revised in 1947. The translation below represents the doctrinal portions of the Introduction.

33. Introduction to History of the U.S.S.R., Volume 1

SUBJECT AND AIMS OF THE HISTORY OF THE U.S.S.R.

The history of our Fatherland studies the development of human society on the territory of the U.S.S.R. as a law-governed process (*zakonomernyi protsess.*) The history of the U.S.S.R. endeavors to generalize the facts of the past of our country on the basis of Marxist-Leninist methodology and to know the totality of the phenomena of the past in all its complexity and contradiction as a process governed by objective laws of development. In studying the past of the peoples of the U.S.S.R. it is necessary to explain both the general laws of social development and those particular law-governed developments (*zakonomernosti*) which are characteristic in various epochs and peoples, and those peculiarities which have been evoked by concrete conditions of historical existence.

Knowledge of the laws of social development helps one to orient himself in the present, carry out changes in society, foresee the future. Here lies the close connection between science and practice. The strength of the giants of science—the leaders and organizers of the revolutionary struggle of the proletariat, Marx, Engels, Lenin—and the strength of the Communist Party of the Soviet Union are in the fact that they have always acted with the weapons of knowing the laws of social development in their hands.

Negation of the objective conformity to laws (*zakonomernosti*) of historical development leads to simple registration of historical facts, to subjectivism and voluntarism, that is, to unscientific explanation of the historical process solely by the will and subjective intentions of individuals.

The history of the U.S.S.R. investigates the interconnection and interdetermination of all aspects of the development of the peoples of our Fatherland (economics, social relations, political system, international relations, ideology, etc.). Bourgeois historian-idealists have sought the key to explaining historical phenomena in the ideas and impelling motives behind the actions of individuals and in those objectives which they set for themselves. Marxism-Leninism has proved that man's views, ideas, and theories themselves depend upon the conditions of material life in society. The basis of the historical process is the development of the method of producing material goods, which in itself represents the unity of the productive forces of society (tools of labor, productive experience of individuals, and their habits of work) and of the production relationships (relationships of persons in the process of production).

The production relationships constitute the basis (economic system) of society to which corresponds a definite superstructure (political, legal, religious, philosophical, artistic, and other notions of society as well as political and other institutions). In attributing a determining role in the historical process to the method of producing material goods, Marxist-Leninist historical science also gives proper attention to the study of the role of the superstructure, particularly as forces actively participating in the development of the basis.

The bourgeois historian-idealists exaggerate the role of individual prominent personalities and heroes in the historical process and because of that they devote principal attention to government leaders in power, military men, and so on. Marxism-Leninism proves that the determining role in the historical process is played by the popular masses, the creators of material and cultural values. This, however, does not mean that Marxist-Leninist theory denies the role of the individual in history. Recognizing the importance of the activities of individual men, Marxist-Leninist historical science believes that such activities reflect the interests of definite classes or social groups and that their results depend upon the extent to which they meet the demands of social development.

Prior to the victory of socialism in the history of the U.S.S.R., as in the history of any country, the moving force in the development of a society consisting of antagonistic classes was the class struggle. The existence of classes and class struggle was admitted by the bourgeois historians themselves. In contrast to bourgeois science, Marxism-Leninism established that the existence of classes is connected only with specific historical phases in the development of production, that the struggle of classes leads to the dictatorship of the proletariat, and that the dictatorship of the proletariat constitutes a transition to the abolition of classes and to a classless society. (See K. Marx and F. Engels, *Selected Letters,* Moscow, 1953, p. 63.)

At the foundation of the Marxist understanding of history lies the teaching concerning socioeconomic formations. In the light of this teaching, Marxist-Leninist historical science endeavors to understand the multiplicity of political forms, the variety of local and ethnic peculiarities in social development in the course of millennia, and the complexity of contemporary existence of societies with different levels of development. The classics of Marxism-Leninism have divided the history of mankind into five formations succeeding to one another with law-conforming regularity: (1) primitive-communal, (2) slaveowning, (3) feudal, (4) capitalist, (5) socialist. At the basis of this division of history lies the method of producing material goods which determines the nature of the social system and the political and spiritual life of people in the period of this or that formation. Each formation is governed both by the general laws of historical development and the specific laws characteristic only of a given formation. The history of the U.S.S.R. provides a picture of the development of all formations.

Each formation moves through several law-governed stages in its development: period of origination and establishment; period of decadence during which in the womb of the old system there are born new phenomena disintegrating it and in the end leading to the victory of the new formation. Thus, in studying the history of each formation, an important task of the historian is to uncover the struggle of the old with the new and the struggle of the progressive with the reactionary phenomena.

The history of society as a whole represents a progressive process of succession of socioeconomic formations. In studying the succession of socioeconomic formations in the history of our country, as in the history of any country, it is necessary to take into account the law of the correspondence of productive relationships to the nature and level of productive forces. The progressive development of the formation continues as long as the productive relationships allow room for the growth of the productive forces. When the productive relationships turn from propelling the productive forces into impeding them and barring them from further growth, the death of the formation becomes inevitable.

The Marxist-Leninist historical science is party-minded (*partiina*). The party-mindedness of the Marxist-Leninist historical science converges with true scholarship because the interests of the revolutionary proletariat demand knowledge of the objective conformity to laws of historical development. The party-mindedness of Marxist-Leninist science excludes falsification, embellishment, or, conversely, darkening of history; it presupposes establishment of truth through study of objective laws of historical development which prepare the ground for the revolution and the transition to socialism. The purpose of science is to master these laws and use them in the interests of the proletarian revolution and the building of socialism. Therefore, Marxist-Leninist historical science is a weapon in the struggle for communism. Negation of the principle of party-mindedness of science leads to bourgeois objectivism, that is, to denial of class analysis of historical phenomena and of their evaluation as phenomena typical of a given social system. In trying to prove the eternity of private property, social inequality, class contradictions, racial discrimination, religion, etc., the reactionary bourgeois scholars turn to the history of early formations and arbitrarily attribute to them features of contemporary capitalism.

NEED TO USE THE DATA OF OTHER SCIENCE IN HISTORICAL STUDY

In waging a struggle against all manifestations of bourgeois ideology and methodology in the field of history, the Soviet historical science uses all fine achievements of bourgeois historiography. In the study of the history of the U.S.S.R. it is necessary to utilize the data of various sciences. For the proper reconstruction of the conditions of existence of man in one or another epoch it is necessary to know the geographic environment surrounding him, the influence of which has been in inverse ratio to man's ability to cope with nature. Geology, paleontology, paleobotany, and paleozoology, armed at present with exact methods of investigation, make it possible for the historian to determine the nature of the geographic environment and its changes and to date the duration of distant epochs in the history of mankind.[4]

AIMS AND ORGANIZATION OF THE TEXTBOOK ON HISTORY OF THE U.S.S.R.

In a textbook on the history of the U.S.S.R. the history of the Russian people must be presented in close connection with the histories of the other peoples of our Fatherland. At the same time, the close connection of the history of our country with the histories of foreign countries and peoples must be shown, and the role of the peoples of our country in the world-historical process must be disclosed.

The development of the historical science and the necessity of taking into account its achievements created the need for writing a new textbook on the history of the U.S.S.R. Undertaking this task, the authors' team and the editorial committee based their thinking on the necessity of dividing the material into volumes according to the periodization of the historical process in formations. The first volume of the present textbook is devoted to the primitive-communal and slaveowning system on the territory of the U.S.S.R. and the feudal formation. The material is developed to the abolition of serfdom in 1861. The second volume encompasses the history of the peoples of the U.S.S.R. in the period of capitalism; the third, the history of Soviet society.

The first volume of the textbook is divided in five parts corresponding to the basic period in the history of our country.

The first part is devoted to a description of the primitive-communal and slaveowning system on the territory of the U.S.S.R. Here the problem is posed as to the origins of the Slavs, and the history of the Eastern Slavs to the fourth century, when a process of development of classes began among them, is considered.

In the second part the crisis in the slaveowning system's production relationships is shown, the earliest feudal societies on the territory of the U.S.S.R. (Transcaucasia, Central Asia) are described, and, finally, the problem of the genesis and consolidation of the feudal system of production among the Eastern Slavs (which advanced to feudalism as a result of the

---

[4] Uses of data from anthropology, archeology, ethnography, folklore, and linguistics are also briefly explained.

disintegration of the primitive-communal system, avoiding the slaveowning system of production) and the creation and development of the ancient Russian state (to the beginning of the twelfth century) are examined.

The third part of the textbook is devoted to the period of the flowering of feudalism in Russia. In this part is presented the history of the Russian and other peoples of our Fatherland in the period of feudal decentralization of Russia (beginning of twelfth—end of fifteenth century) and the creation and consolidation of the Russian centralized state (end of fifteenth—beginning of seventeenth century). The presentation ends with a characterization of the first peasant war in Russia, in the beginning of the seventeenth century, and the heroic struggle of the Russian people against the Polish-Swedish interventionists.

The chronological framework of the fourth part embraces the history of the peoples of our country from the 1620's to the middle of the eighteenth century. This period is characterized on the one hand by intensification of feudal oppression, formation of the system of serfdom, and sharp intensification of class contradictions which expressed themselves in a series of antifeudal uprisings, of which the largest was the peasant war led by S. T. Razin. On the other hand, in this period there were born in the womb of the feudal formation new phenomena of a bourgeois nature, and an all-Russian market and industry begin to take shape.

In the last (fifth) part of the textbook the history of the peoples of our country in the second half of the eighteenth century and the first half of the nineteenth century is examined; [this is the period] when the development of the feudal production relationships in Russia was increasingly out of joint with the growing productive forces, and when the process of the decay of the feudal serfdom system advanced and led in the second quarter of the nineteenth century to its crisis.

Taking into consideration the existence at present of synthesizing works and courses on the history of the individual peoples of the U.S.S.R., the authors' team and the editors did not see it to be their task to give a continuous narrative of the factual history of each people in all its length, but endeavored to trace the basic and leading lines and the law-governed developments in the history of the peoples and their interconnection with the destinies of the Russian people.

More attention than in the previous textbooks has been devoted to the problems of economic history and the history of culture. The problem of the formation of the Russian, Ukraninian, and Belorussian ethnic groups and nations has been raised.

The meaning of Khrushchev's "de-Stalinization" speech to Soviet historians was that they faced the ticklish task of revising the history of the decades in which Stalin had a part. While the guidelines for rewriting Stalin's role in the purges, for example, were plain enough, those for treating other areas of the history of the party—to the regime, the most important segment of all history—were at best obscure. Stimulated by the developments at the Twentieth Party Congress and the general "thaw" since 1953, some historians ventured into such taboo areas as the revolutionary role of the Mensheviks before 1917 and the party's vacillating policies at the time. The most prominent of these venturesome historians was the deputy editor-in-chief of *Voprosy istorii*, E. N. Burdzhalov, who gave space to probing articles and wrote one himself. In essence, these articles questioned the "gilding of historical reality" and called for respect for the facts in the history of the prerevolutionary period. At a conference in Leningrad, Burdzhalov even enunciated a theory of the diminishing truthfulness of Soviet historians according to which the historians of the 1920's "wrote more truthfully than the historians of the 1930's, and the latter more truthfully than the historians of the 1950's." [5]

Alarmed by the ferment in the U.S.S.R., the upheavals in Poland and Hungary, and the spreading infection of "revisionism," the Soviet leadership took the matter in hand. On March 9, 1957, the Central Committee issued a special decree which found the editors of *Voprosy istorii*, Pankratova and Burdzhalov, to have made "theoretical and methodological mistakes" leading to departure from the principle of *partiinost*, and ordered changes in personnel and policy. Pankratova, already ill (she died in May 1957), was left in her position with an admonition, but Burdzhalov was fired and several members of the editorial board were replaced.[6] The new board promptly published a statement promising reforms and strict observance of *partiinost* in its work.

The decree below is translated from the text in *Spravochnik partiinogo rabotnika* ("Handbook of the Party Worker") (Moscow, 1957), pp. 381–382. The excerpts from the board's statement are from the English translation in *Current Digest of the Soviet Press*, IX, No. 28 (August 21, 1957), 3–10.

34. Decree of March 9, 1957, on Voprosy istorii

The CC of the CPSU notes that since the Twentieth Congress of the CPSU the journal *Voprosy istorii* has published a number of substantial

---

[5] For this and other details of the Burdzhalov affair see Merle Fainsod, "Soviet Russian Historians, or: the Lesson of Burdzhalov," *Encounter*, March 1962, No. 102, pp. 82–89.

[6] Pankratova was succeeded by a party specialist in the history of the civil war and intervention, S. F. Naida, who gave way in June 1960, to a specialist in the history of international relations and the British Commonwealth, V. G. Trukhanovskii. Trukhanovskii's choice is indicative of the reorientation of the journal toward problems of foreign policy, historiography of non-Soviet subjects, and controversies with foreign, especially American and British, non-Marxist historians.

materials on various problems of historical science. At the same time the journal has permitted the occurrence of theoretical and methodological mistakes which show a tendency toward departure from the Leninist principles of party-mindedness (*partiinost*) in scholarship.

The journal's leading article on "The Twentieth Congress and the Tasks of Research in Party History" (issue No. 3 for 1956), the editorial article "Concerning the Article of Bugaev" (issue No. 7), the article of Comrade Moskalev (issue No. 8), and several others blur the fundamental disagreements between Bolsheviks and Mensheviks on such a basic question as the hegemony of the proletariat in the revolution, embellish the role of the Mensheviks and belittle the guiding role of the Bolsheviks in the 1905–7 revolution, lack the Leninist criticism of the schismatic activities of the Mensheviks and their opportunism in crucial problems of the revolution, and distort the history of the party's struggle to form an alliance of the working class and the peasantry. In its consideration of questions of the party's struggle against the Trotskyists and right-wing opportunists, the journal is silent on the point that in their fight against the party they overstepped the limits of Soviet legality.

In his article "Concerning the Tactics of the Bolsheviks in March and April, 1917" published in the journal's issue No. 4 and in his statements at the readers' conferences, Comrade Burdzhalov attempted, by way of criticism of the cult of the individual, to expand the role of Zinoviev in 1917 and treated the questions of the ideological and political struggle of our party in an objectivist spirit. By dishonestly using historical documents, he tried to prove that until Lenin's return to Russia the party in essence held semi-Menshevik positions and that "unifying" tendencies in respect to the Mensheviks were strong in the party.

In its editorial articles in issues Nos. 1 and 7 for 1956, the journal *Voprosy istorii* in effect oriented the Soviet historians toward a weakening of the struggle with bourgeois ideology in historiography. It is noteworthy that the journal abandoned the criticism of revisionist and nationalist views which have been particularly widespread in the Yugoslav press.

The editor-in-chief of the journal, Comrade Pankratova, and the deputy editor-in-chief, Comrade Burdzhalov, have for a long time rejected all criticism of the journal. In the work of the editorial office the principles of collective leadership have been grossly violated by Comrade Burdzhalov.

The CC of the CPSU decrees:

1. To recognize as erroneous the position of the journal *Voprosy istorii* in a number of articles in which certain fundamental aspects of the history of the CPSU are incorrectly illuminated.

To obligate the editorial board of the journal *Voprosy istorii* to secure a consistent observance of the Leninist principle of party-mindedness in historical science and a decisive struggle against the manifestations of bourgeois ideology and attempts at revision of Marxism-Leninism.

2. To point out to the editor-in-chief of the journal *Voprosy istorii,* Comrade A. M. Pankratova, the serious shortcomings which she has allowed to develop in the direction of the journal.

3. To relieve of his duties the deputy editor-in-chief of the journal *Voprosy istorii,* Comrade E. N. Burdzhalov, because of errors in the direction of the journal.

4. To appoint Comrade N. I. Matiushkin as first deputy editor-in-chief of the journal *Voprosy istorii,* relieving him of his duties as deputy editor-in-chief of the Government Publishing Office for Political Literature (Gospolitizdat). To create in the editorial office of the journal the additional position of deputy editor-in-chief in charge of questions of the history of foreign countries.

5. To order the Department of Science, Institutions of Higher Education, and Schools, the Department of Propaganda and Agitation of the CC of the CPSU, and the Presidium of the Academy of Sciences of the U.S.S.R. to take steps toward the strengthening of the editorial board and personnel of the editorial office of the journal.

35. *Statement of* Voprosy istorii

Historiography is one of the most important sectors of the ideological front. Soviet historians are studying the history of their motherland and other countries, exposing ideas and theories hostile to Marxism-Leninism, and fighting all bourgeois falsifications of social events, particularly the fictions concocted by the apologists of capitalism to slander the U.S.S.R. and the other socialist countries. Soviet historians have made great contributions to the study of the life and struggle of the peoples of the world at various stages of their development, to showing the decisive role of the working masses in history, and to the exposition of man's advance along the road of democracy and socialism.

Along with the historians of the countries of the socialist camp and progressive scholars in capitalist countries, Soviet historians are lined up against reactionary bourgeois historians and are exposing the tendentious nature of their researches. On Soviet historians depends unslackening vigilance against the moves of our ideological opponents, unswerving observance of the Leninist principle of Party allegiance in scholarship.

The Twentieth Party Congress ushered in a new stage in the development of Soviet historiography, as in other fields of knowledge. The Congress outlined majestic prospects for further economic, scientific, and cultural advance; it resolutely condemned dogmatism and Talmudism and set the aim of completely eliminating the harmful consequences of the cult of the individual leader. By doing so, the Twentieth Congress helped to enliven creative work in all spheres of Soviet science and scholarship. Carrying out the Congress decisions, the workers of the ideological front have begun to link their work more closely with concrete economic and cultural tasks.

The work of Soviet historians is being reorganized in the light of the decisions and instructions of the Twentieth Party Congress. They are waging a struggle to free historiography completely of the harmful incrustations of the cult of the individual leader, which caused serious distortions in the judgment of phenomena and events of the past. Our scholars are concentrating on study of the outstanding questions of our own and world history. They are seeking to study more deeply the experience of socialist construction and of the liberation movement of the working masses, to show in everything the full stature of the world-historic role of our people and our party.

The Party and government have created all the conditions necessary for creative work by Soviet scholars. The source materials at the command of researchers have been enriched and enlarged. They now have broader opportunities for work on archive documents of both pre-Soviet and Soviet times. In studying modern problems of our country's history, Soviet researchers can acquaint themselves directly with the work of state institutions, enterprises, and public organizations. Scholars have access to the foreign press and literature published abroad, and they maintain direct contacts with historians of other countries, particularly with their colleagues of the people's democracies.

All this, combined, is facilitating an advance in Soviet historiography. Inspired by the ideas of Marxism-Leninism and imbued with a feeling of Soviet patriotism and proletarian internationalism, our historians are stubbornly and persistently seeking to achieve a truthful treatment of phenomena of the past and present and are arming the working people with scientific knowledge of the historical process.

A responsible role is played by our scholars in studying the work of the Communist Party and Soviet state. They are showing the world-historic significance of the experience of the working people of the U.S.S.R., who have built a socialist society and are advancing toward communism. This experience is the precious heritage of all progressive mankind. It arms the Communist and Workers' Parties and the masses whom they lead in the struggle for democracy and socialism, it lightens their efforts in the liberation movement and in building a new life, and it teaches Bolshevist party allegiance, vigilance toward and intolerance of compromise with class enemies.

The advance in historiography after the Twentieth Party Congress was reflected in some degree in the magazine *Voprosy istorii*. Important problems of both our own and world history were raised in its pages. The magazine published informative and interesting articles on revolutionary populism (*narodnichestvo*), on the history of the Civil War, on problems of periodization, on source materials and research in them, on historiography and other problems. However, in many instances the editors of the magazine did not meet their responsible obligations properly. What is more, in treating certain important problems they committed serious methodological errors and violated the principles of Marxist-Leninist Party allegiance, sometimes slipping into bourgeois objectivism.

The magazine's efforts to examine in a new light certain questions of the history of the Soviet Communist Party and of Soviet society sometimes in actuality came down to incorrect treatment of events of the past, to distortion of questions long settled and providing no cause for doubts. Some officials of the magazine lost the sense of responsibility for the work entrusted to them and did not show the necessary seriousness in judging historical problems, where haste and thoughtlessness are particularly dangerous and where deep and comprehensive analysis of life phenomena in their interrelationship and interdependence is required—and especially a Party, a Leninist approach to facts and events.

The Soviet historian is not a sideline observer, a clerk or a mechanical copyist of materials, a collector of information which may happen to come into his hands by chance. He cannot base his conclusions on unchecked data torn from the context of events and contradicting the actual course of the historical process. In investigating this or that question, our scholars maintain a class point of view, a Marxist-Leninist stand; they identify the social goal of the forces in action in the historical arena, and they stand clearly and unambiguously on the side of progress against reaction, the side of the revolution against counterrevolution, the side of democracy and socialism against imperialism.

At the very dawn of the proletarian movement in our country Lenin pointed out:

"Not a single living person *can fail to take a stand on the side* of one or another class (once he has realized their relationships), can fail to be overjoyed by the success of the given class and to be saddened by its failures, can fail to be indignant at those who are inimical to this class, at those who hinder its development by spreading backward views, etc., etc."

Bourgeois historiography tries to conceal the class nature of its historical studies and resorts to all kinds of disguises to do so, but the proletariat and the masses whom it leads operate quite differently. In contrast to the false pose of objectivity assumed by the bourgeoisie and its scholars, with their declarations of the supraclass nature of history and the other social sciences, the proletariat and its Marxist-Leninist vanguard present Communist Party allegiance in science, firm and consistent championing of their class position, diametrically opposed to bourgeois objectivism.

Marxism-Leninism has irrefutably demonstrated that there is not and cannot be supraclass ideology in a society divided into hostile classes, there is not and cannot be supraclass social science suitable for serving equally the interests of different social groups. Social science always has been and remains party science. Hence it is silly and ridiculous to make any attempts to depart from the criteria of Party allegiance in judging the work of bourgeois scholars or scholars expressing the interests of other exploiting classes.

Attempts to conceal the discarding of Party allegiance under an assumed concern for "objectivity" in analyzing social phenomena also cannot hold water. It is materialism that champions real, genuinely scientific objectivity —materialism, which, as V. I. Lenin taught, incorporates Party allegiance, "making it incumbent in any judgment of events to side directly and openly with the standpoint of a definite social group." It is all the more important to emphasize this because the mistakes committed by *Voprosy istorii* follow primarily the line of bourgeois objectivism.

It is well known that *Voprosy istorii* is descended from and continues the work of such periodicals as *Istorik-Marksist* and *Bor'ba klassov,* which did a great deal to give a Party interpretation of major events in the life and work of the Party and people. One of the outstanding historians of our party, Ye. M. Yaroslavsky, headed the magazine *Istorik-Marksist* for a long time. But, whereas *Voprosy istorii,* like its forerunners, used to maintain a firm stand of Bolshevist party allegiance, the editors have committed a series of important errors of late, errors tending toward departure from the Leninist principles of Party allegiance in scholarship. While raising voices of protest against vulgarization and oversimplification in the work of some scholars, individual staff members themselves sometimes took the path of sensation and of concessions to bourgeois objectivism, concessions incompatible with genuine scholarship.

These staff members misunderstood the tasks set by the Twentieth Party Congress in the sphere of ideological work. Instead of a principled approach to the treatment of historical phenomena and events, instead of a deeper presentation of the work of the Communist Party of the Soviet Union on the basis of careful study of concrete materials and comprehensive analysis of the Party's uncompromising struggle with enemies of

Marxism-Leninism, they began in effect to blunder into a liberal interpretation of the Party policy. With this approach, contradictions which had existed in the Party were played down, and militant Bolshevist refusal to compromise with anti-Party forces and groupings were often ignored, toned down, or presented in distorted fashion.

Some of the staff members interpreted the Twentieth Party Congress directive on the need to ensure peaceful coexistence between the socialist camp and the imperialist camp as a policy of "relaxing" the struggle against ideological opponents of Marxism-Leninism, a policy of peaceful coexistence of socialist and bourgeois ideologies.

*   *   *

What were the basic trends in the errors in *Voprosy istorii?* First, the magazine distorted some questions of the history of the Communist Party of the Soviet Union in both the pre-Soviet and the Soviet periods. Some of the articles wrongly described the history of the Soviet state, particularly in the initial period of Soviet rule. Almost nothing was done to expose revision in its present stage. There were erroneous evaluations of the policy of the chief imperialist states, and, above all, of the U.S.A.; this led to weakening the ideological struggle against the American imperialists' aggressive, antipopular activity. There were mistaken attempts at re-examination of the attitude taken by Soviet historians, as well as historians of other socialist countries, toward the works of reactionary bourgeois scholars.

In dealing with the history of the Communist Party of the Soviet Union the magazine in a number of instances gave an erroneous treatment of the Menshevist and Bolshevist stands at various stages in the Party's development, failed to show properly the fundamental difference in their policies and practical work in the course of the revolutionary movement, and did not describe the extremely sharp conflict of principle which went on between the Leninists and the opportunists; moreover, in some articles in the magazine there were attempts to idealize the role of the Mensheviks, to misrepresent real history and to revise scientifically established views.

The editorial "The Twentieth Party Congress and Problems of Research in Party History," [7] carried in issue No. 3, 1956, also violated the principles of Leninist party allegiance in the treatment of Party history. While the editorial did advance certain scientifically correct and valuable propositions, nevertheless the mistakes made earlier by the magazine were not corrected and were offered to the reader as something advanced in the work of the journal, as the new word in historical scholarship.

The articles "Tactics of the Bolsheviks in March and April, 1917" (No. 8, 1956) [8] and "More on Tactics of the Bolsheviks in March and April,

---

[7] *Current Digest of the Soviet Press,* VIII, No. 19 (June 20, 1956), 6–9.
[8] *Current Digest of the Soviet Press,* VIII, No. 39 (November 7, 1956), 3–5.

1917," by E. N. Burdzhalov, formerly assistant editor-in-chief of the magazine, did the greatest damage to scientific treatment of Party history. In these articles, under the guise of criticizing the I. V. Stalin cult, E. N. Burdzhalov tried to accentuate Zinoviev's role in 1917 and treated major questions of the ideological and political struggle of the Bolshevist party in that period in an objectivist spirit. By unscrupulous use of documents, E. N. Burdzhalov tried to prove that the Party essentially had upheld semi-Menshevist positions before Lenin's return to Russia and that allegedly there had been a strong tendency within its ranks to unite with the Mensheviks.

Specific mistakes in Burdzhalov's articles were considered in detail in the magazines *Partiinaia zhizn* ("Party Life") and *Kommunist*.[9] Hence there is no need to examine the content of his articles in detail.

The author tries sweepingly to besmirch the activity of I. V. Stalin, equating his position with that of Kamenev, Zinoviev, and other representatives of opportunism. But the more Burdzhalov tries to do this, the clearer we see the tendentiousness of his arguments. Although I. V. Stalin did waver greatly on tactical matters before V. I. Lenin's return to Russia, his stand was never identical with that of Kamenev. An attempt to equate Stalin and Kamenev is, in effect, falsification of Party history and attests to Burdzhalov's failure to understand the essence of the Party's struggle to eliminate the consequences of the cult of the individual leader.

Despite the gravity of I. V. Stalin's mistakes, we cannot view his activity solely through the prism of these mistakes. This would be a distortion of actual Party history, in which I. V. Stalin figures as an outstanding Marxist-Leninist who played a major role in exposing and routing the enemies of the Party and in fighting for the triumph of the Party's cause. If the author, who so zealously pays lip service to scientific objectivity, had actually proceeded from this requirement in evaluating the activity of I. V. Stalin, he would not have had to range far and wide searching for mistakes, and only mistakes, or to revise a number of key questions of Party history.

Even more unfounded are attempts to confuse the harm done by the cult of the individual leader with the entire activity of the Party and people at the given stages of the development of the Soviet state, failing to see that the mistakes of the cult of the individual leader and the activity of the Party and the people are not at all one and the same. Although the I. V. Stalin cult did great harm to our country, it would be a flagrant error to identify it with the policy and the practical work of the Party and the people, who accomplished great things even in these conditions. Attempts to

---

[9] *Current Digest of the Soviet Press,* IX, No. 2 (February 20, 1957), 5–6, and No. 17 (June 5, 1957), 3–8.

do so lead objectively to belittling the successes of the Party and the Soviet state.

Workers on the ideological front, including historians, still have much to do to help the party complete its struggle for fully eliminating the consequences of the cult of the individual leader. In this struggle, however, it is necessary resolutely to oppose the revisionist tendencies that are encountered abroad, since these tendencies are dictated by the desire to blacken the role of our party, to belittle and distort it. The struggle against revisionism is all the more important in view of the fact that international imperialist reaction is striving in every way to use for its own selfish aims the works being done by our party to eliminate the consequences of the cult of the individual leader.

"We have recently been accused in the West of being 'Stalinists' and 'followers of Stalin,'" said Comrade N. S. Khrushchev, First Secretary of the Party Central Committee. "In reply to this we have already declared more than once that to our minds the term 'Stalinist,' like Stalin himself, is inseparable from the great title of Communist. When one speaks of the cause of the revolution, defense of the proletariat's class interests in the revolutionary struggle against our class enemies, Stalin courageously and unyieldingly defended the cause of Marxism-Leninism. We criticized Stalin not for having been a bad Communist. We criticized him for certain deviations, negative qualities, for having made serious errors. . . . However, in the most important respect—for Marxist-Leninists the chief and the most important matter is defense of the interests of the working class, of the cause of socialism and the struggle against the enemies of Marxism-Leninism—in this main and most important respect, may God grant, as the saying goes, that every Communist will be able to fight as Stalin fought.

"The opponents of Communism have purposely invented the word 'Stalinist' and they are trying to make it a term of opprobrium. For all of us Marxist-Leninists who have devoted our whole lives to the revolutionary struggle for the interests of the working class and its fighting vanguard, the Leninist party, Stalin's name is inseparable from Marxism-Leninism. For this reason, each of us members of the CPSU wants to be true to the cause of Marxism-Leninism, to the struggle for the interests of the working class, as Stalin was true to this cause."

It is easy to see that direct connection between the editors' mistaken views of Menshevism and their views of opportunism on the world scene. In neither case was the magazine concerned about intensifying vigilance with respect to political tendencies inimical to the working class, and it failed to show the bitter struggle waged by the Bolsheviks and revolutionary Marxists of other countries against the opportunists. The harm of the editors' position is quite evident in the present-day situation, when opportunistic, revisionist elements have become active in some of the fraternal Communist and Workers' Parties and when, therefore, it is particularly necessary to expose their ideology. Despite the fact that the Soviet and foreign press has regularly carried articles sharply criticizing the political and ideological views of present-day revisionism, the editors of *Voprosy istorii* have not reacted to them even once. They have ignored criticism of the revisionism and nationalism that have lately attained currency in the foreign press.

Take, for instance, the recent counterrevolutionary events in Hungary. Both the foreign and the Soviet press animatedly responded to the problems connected with these events, exposing the activity of the enemies of the Hungarian people and their opportunistic accomplices within the ranks of the working class and its party. *Voprosy istorii,* however, avoided treating these problems. It did not publish articles about the Hungarian counterrevolution in 1919, when the Hungarian Soviet Republic was stifled, or materials about the history of the ideological and political preparation of the antipopular uprising in Hungary in October 1956, or about the activity of the counterrevolution and renegades from Marxism-Leninism during the uprising itself. This showed not only lack of the necessary effective work by the magazine but also its inability to react to burning questions of the day properly and from positions of historiography.

The following fact is also quite important. Soviet historiography has made considerable progress in recent years in exposing the aggressive nature of American imperialism and its antipopular activity at various stages of history, that is, during World War I and the Great October Socialist Revolution in Russia, during the preparation [for] and the actual intervention of foreign states against our country, during the revival of German imperialism's armed might and the unleashing of World War II, and in today's situation. However, *Voprosy istorii* kept aloof from the work being done by Soviet historians and other scholars, publishing nothing to support their studies. On the contrary, it carried some articles that conflicted with works on American imperialism by Soviet researchers.

Voprosy istorii also fell short of the mark in treating a number of other cardinal foreign policy problems which are of tremendous importance today in the extremely acute struggle between the camp of imperialism and the camp of socialism.

In recent years *Voprosy istorii* published a considerable number of articles and materials on questions of bourgeois historiography. But in these questions, too, the magazine was not consistent throughout. The editors were right, for example, in objecting to some historians' simplified attitude toward the studies of bourgeois scholars, whereby the results of the latter's work were completely and entirely denied and the factual data collected by them ignored. But, while wisely condemning an oversimplified approach to bourgeois historiography, the editors at the same time actually opposed the principle of party allegiance in evaluating the bourgeois heritage. Some Soviet historians were sharply criticized precisely for having decisively condemned the reactionary nature of the works of various bourgeois scholars.

Readers have objected strongly also to the magazine's position on foreign scholars' influence on the works of historians and other scholars of our country. While persistently opposing the disregard of this influence by some persons and disclosing the harm of national narrowness in treating the development of Soviet social thought, the editors at the same time greatly exaggerated the importance of foreign influences on the development of social ideas in Russia and made these influences a self-sufficient factor, which in some cases was given prominence by the magazine.

This approach had the result of belittling the independence and importance of Soviet scholarship. While correctly raising their voice against "jingoism," the editors failed to consider properly another, still more important fact—the need for constant and systematic treatment of the genuine patriotic traditions of the peoples of Russia and for a profound disclosure of their historic achievements and their enormous contribution to the development of world scholarship. In a number of cases this led to a distortion of historical perspective and to a one-sided and tendentious evaluation of the past and slackened the editors' concern for showing the patriotic deeds of our heroic ancestors. It is quite natural, therefore, that the Soviet academic community sharply criticized the magazine's erroneous line and counterposed to it a truly patriotic and truly internationalist position, one that is alien to national nihilism and to indifference to the achievements of Soviet scholarship and advanced social thought.

There is no justification for the editors' failure to deal in the magazine with the progressive significance of the unification of a number of areas of the Transcaucasus, Central Asia, and the Far East with Russia. This is all the more regrettable in that some historians and men of letters have been guilty of errors in this question.

The above-cited facts show that all has not been well in the work of *Voprosy istorii* in recent years. Despite the fact that the Soviet academic community and the press repeatedly have called attention to shortcomings in the work of the magazine, the editors have not drawn the proper conclusions from the comradely advice and warnings given them.

The editors' position was also not corrected in the U.S.S.R. Academy of Sciences' History Institute, of which the magazine was the organ. The directors of the institute did not utilize every means at their disposal to influence the editors' stand and to demand that the magazine radically improve its work.

The serious shortcomings and mistakes in the magazine's work are largely due to the fact that the role of the editorial board as a collegial directing body was essentially reduced to naught. E. N. Burdzhalov, former assistant editor, frequently violated the principles of collectivity and acted on his own. Thus, his erroneous articles were published despite the disagreement and outright protests of a number of board members. Meetings of the editorial board were not called regularly. Many board members did not show up at meetings or read the materials sent to them.

In view of the grave shortcomings and mistakes in the work of *Voprosy istorii,* the Presidium of the U.S.S.R. Academy of Sciences has taken steps to reinforce the editorial leadership and staff. A new editorial board has been appointed. The magazine has been withdrawn from the jurisdiction of the History Institute and placed under the U.S.S.R. Academy of Sciences' Division of Historical Sciences. Steps have been taken to improve the work of the editorial staff radically and to normalize its relations with academic institutions and the *aktiv* of contributors.

The new editorial board considers it its cardinal duty and most urgent task to eliminate the shortcomings in the work of *Voprosy istorii.* It recognizes the articles about the magazine carried in the press, above all those in *Pravda, Partiinaya zhizn,* and *Kommunist,* to be correct. It highly values the concern about the magazine shown by Soviet scholars during discussion of the magazine at academic institutes and educational institutions. The editorial board will study carefully the comments made and will utilize whatever is valuable to reorganize the work of the magazine.

The magazine faces responsible tasks in dealing with fundamental problems of Soviet and world history. These tasks are determined, above all, by the decisions of the Twentieth Party Congress, by the forthcoming fortieth anniversary of the Great October Socialist Revolution, by the need for a comprehensive disclosure of the world-historic significance of the Soviet Union, its historical path and experience, its tremendous efforts in the struggle for peace and world-wide security of nations. They are linked, further, with the need for greatly improving treatment of major problems of general history, particularly the history of the rise and development of the people's democracies. It is necessary to counterbalance the false flood of reactionary bourgeois historical literature with Marxist-Leninist studies of these problems, to develop a genuine offensive against bourgeois ideology and the views of revisionists.

The editors should focus their attention on questions of Soviet patriotism and proletarian internationalism, on comprehensively showing the historical path of the Soviet people in the struggle for socialism and communism, and on disclosing the great advantages of the socialist system over the capitalist. While devoting the necessary space in the magazine to the pre-Soviet history of the peoples of the U.S.S.R., and particularly their revolutionary and national-liberation movement, the editorial board considers it a major task to publish materials on contemporary problems of Soviet and world history.

The editorial board will pay particular attention to resolutely restoring the principles of Party allegiance in the evaluation of historical phenomena, principles that have been violated in the magazine of late. It will wage an adamant struggle against distortions of the historical process, against relapses into bourgeois ideology in historiography, and for purity of Marxist-Leninist theory.

The editorial staff will oppose any attempts to sacrifice considerations of principle to the special interests of individual scholars, to distract the magazine's attention from the fundamental problems of history, or to supplant a creative discussion of questions with a clash between individual groups of persons guided by personal rather than scholarly considerations.

A basic reorganization of the work of *Voprosy istorii* is also necessary because it has now become the organ of the U.S.S.R. Academy of Sciences' Division of Historical Sciences. Whereas before it was connected, and only formally, with an academic institute, it now has a direct and immediate relationship with the work of all the institutes of the U.S.S.R. Academy of Sciences' Division of Historical Sciences. This will not only expand the academic base of the magazine and offer better opportunity for enlisting contributors, but will influence the choice of subject matter.

The importance of this circumstance becomes greater in view of the establishment of a number of new specialized journals: *Voprosy istorii KPSS* ("Questions of History of the Communist Party of the Soviet Union"), *Istoria SSSR* ("History of the U.S.S.R."), *Novaya i noveishaya istoria* ("Recent and Modern History"), and others. It is necessary to specify more clearly the sphere of activity of each magazine, to eliminate, insofar as possible, duplication in materials published, and for each magazine to find its place in the general task of elucidating Soviet and world history. As the organ of the U.S.S.R. Academy of Sciences' Division of Historical Sciences, *Voprosy istorii* must naturally focus its attention on the most important problems and refrain from dealing with topics that are narrowly specialized.

In the new conditions the magazine must pay considerably more attention to elucidating the history of the development of the Soviet socialist republics and to the work of their academic institutions dealing with history. The geographical distribution of its contributors' *aktiv* must also be changed. Whereas formerly the contributors to the magazine were largely staff members of academic institutions in Moscow, now it is highly desirable and necessary to enlist considerably more writers from other areas, so that the magazine may more fully represent the academic forces of our country as a whole.

The editorial board asks the country's historians to take active part in the magazine and relies on their help and support. Only if it receives this will it be able to accomplish the responsible and urgent tasks that confront it in present-day conditions.

The severity with which the party dealt with Burdzhalov and alleged departures from *partiinost* and the wave of attacks on "revisionism," Yugoslav and other, in the party press created the impression that the regime was turning to a kind of "neo-Stalinism" and that the "thaw" was ending in a new "freeze." [10] In retrospect, it appears that the party action stemmed from the fear caused by the Hungarian revolution and from the resulting struggle between the Khrushchev faction and what he labeled as an "antiparty group" composed of Molotov, Malenkov, Kaganovich, and others. Khrushchev's victory over the group in June 1957,[11] and the containment of the upheaval in eastern Europe may well account for the fact no further measures of "restalinization" ensued. From the point of view of the victors of June 1957, the dismissal of Burdzhalov apparently has been deemed a sufficient measure to tell Soviet historians to write and teach with the interests of the party—as defined by the current leadership—always in mind. The fact that Burdzhalov's career was cut short and for a while he disappeared from view has undoubtedly induced his fellow historians to draw appropriate conclusions for their own careers and work. The aims of the regime in drawing and maintaining the limits of permissible historical discussion have thus been served without other measures of overt repression.

In the years since these developments, Soviet spokesmen have asserted that Soviet historical scholarship is in a new stage of development. The dogmatism and ossification which impeded their work under Stalin have been overcome, they say, and their freedom from the "cult of personality" and their expanded opportunities for historical work are leading them to do more and better work than ever before. While these claims are reminiscent of Pankratova's panegyrics in the 1930's when Stalin broke the dogmatism and ossification of the Pokrovsky school and ushered in a "new stage in Soviet historical scholarship," within the Soviet reality the facts support the assertion. So long as *partiinost* is observed, the bonds around historians

---

[10] For a more detailed analysis of the 1956–59 period see Alexander Dallin, "Recent Soviet Historiography," in *Russia under Khrushchev*, ed. Abraham Brumberg (New York, 1962), pp. 470–488, and Vera Piroschkow, "Sowjetische Geschichtswissenschaft im inneren Widerstreit (1956–1959)," *Saeculum*, XI (1960), No. 1–2, 180–198.

[11] On the crisis of June 1957 see Roger Pethybridge, *A Key to Soviet Politics: The Crisis of the Anti-Party Group* (New York, 1962).

are considerably loosened, dogmatism is officially condemned, publication outlets are ample, and archives are much more accessible. The result has been a notable rise in the volume of historical output.[12] A number of new journals have been started to provide space for specialized work and to allow *Voprosy istorii* to play the role of dominant historical journal: *Istoriia SSSR* ("History of the U.S.S.R."), *Voprosy istorii KPSS* ("Problems of History of the CPSU),[13] *Novaia i noveishaia istoriia* ("Modern and Contemporary History"), *Voenno-istoricheskii zhurnal'* ("Journal of Military History"), and many others. Numerous collective works have also been launched: *Vsemirnaia istoriia* ("World History"), in ten volumes, representing the first large-scale attempt to fit the entire history of mankind into a Marxist-Leninist interpretation;[14] *Istoriia Velikoi Otechestvennoi voiny Sovetskogo Soiuza, 1941–1945* ("History of the Great Patriotic War of the Soviet Union"), in six volumes;[15] *Istoriia SSSR* ("History of the U.S.S.R."), in eleven volumes; *Istoriia kommunisticheskoi partii Sovetskogo Soiuza* ("History of the Communist Party of the Soviet Union"), in six volumes; *Istoriia diplomatii* ("Diplomatic History"), a five-volume second edition of a work first published in 1941–45; *Sovetskaia istoricheskaia entsiklopediia* ("Soviet Historical Encyclopedia"), in twelve volumes; and many others. The opening of the archives has led to the initiation of documentary series on the revolutions of 1905 and 1917, Russian diplomatic history in the nineteenth and twentieth centuries, and other subjects. The stenographic records of earlier party congresses, suppressed in Stalin's time for good political reasons, are again made available.

What was unquestionably novel in the years 1956–64 was the Khrushchev stamp on the facts and interpretation of Soviet history from 1917 to 1953. The condemnation of the "cult of personality" has led to greater emphasis upon the role of the party and the masses it leads (which made easier the magnification of Khrushchev's role in past events) and develop-

---

[12] This is best reflected in the two volumes of *Sovetskaia istoricheskaia nauka ot XX k XXII s"ezdu KPSS* (see chap. vi, n. 2, 7).

[13] The Central Committee decree of January 12, 1957, establishing the journal defines its basic tasks as fostering "scientific work on questions of the history of the party, especially in the postrevolutionary period; rendering assistance to teachers and propagandists in the study and teaching of the history of the party in the institutions of higher education and in the system of party education; reviewing the literature in the field of history of the party; and developing the history of the fraternal communist and workers' parties and of the international labor movement." Text of the decree in *Spravochnik partiinogo rabotnika*, pp. 372–373.

[14] For a detailed analysis of the first seven volumes see Georg Stadtmüller, "Die neue sowjetische Weltgeschichte," *Saeculum*, XI (1960), No. 4, 292–384.

[15] The fertile publishing on the history of the war since 1956 and the revision of Stalin's role in it are discussed in Gallagher, *op. cit.* (chap. vi, n. 42), pp. 128–175. See also A. Hillgruber and H. A. Jacobsen, "Sowjet-Kommunistische Kriegsgeschichtsschreibung 1945–1961," *Wehrwissenschaftliche Rundschau*, XI (1961), No. 10, 546–556; V. Matsulenko and V. Sekistov, "Historiographie soviétique de la deuxième guerre mondiale," *Revue d'histoire de la deuxième guerre mondiale*, XI (1961), 71–88; and the comprehensive bibliography in Vol. VI of *Istoriia Velikoi Otechestvennoi Voiny Sovetskogo Soiuza, 1941–1945*.

ment of a cult of Lenin. The study of party history, as revised and supplemented by ideological indoctrination, has been intensified on all levels of education and propaganda.[16] The first statement of the new version for general use appeared in Volume 50 of the "Large Soviet Encyclopedia," devoted to the U.S.S.R. and bearing the imprimatur date of August 15, 1957.[17] A new textbook on party history to replace Stalin's *Short Course* was published in 1959 under the general editorship of B. N. Ponomarev;[18] in contrast to the *Short Course,* it deals only with history and leaves the theoretical and doctrinal aspects to other publications.[19]

The fundamental educational reforms which Khrushchev introduced with the Central Committee theses "On strengthening the relationship of the school with life and the further development of public education in the country" of November 12, 1958, also entailed significant changes in the structure and content of history education.[20] Intended to implement Lenin's ideas of "polytechnical education" and bring study and work together, the reforms increased general education from seven to eight years and established requirements for practical work from primary school to university training. To sample opinion regarding the proposed changes in the history curriculum of the new eleven-year secondary schools, the Academy of Pedagogical Sciences of the R.S.F.S.R. initiated discussions among history professors and teachers. The results of the discussions were summarized in a statement by the academy in *Pravda* on September 16, 1959, which served as the basis for a decree "On certain Changes in the Teaching of History in the Schools" jointly issued on October 8, 1959, by the Central Committee and the Council of Ministers. Coming a quarter of a century after the 1934 decree, the new decree on history steered a middle

---

[16] A Central Committee decree of June 18, 1956, for example, introduced the requirement of three "social sciences" courses for all students in institutions of higher education: History of the CPSU, 224 hours (120 hours of lectures and 104 hours of seminar work), Political Economy, 300 hours (184 hours of lectures and 116 hours of seminar work), and Dialectical and Historical Materialism, 140 hours (70 hours of lectures and 70 hours of seminar work). The syllabi for the three courses with the officially approved bibliographies are translated in *Administration of Teaching in Social Sciences in the USSR* (Ann Arbor, Mich., 1960).

[17] It is translated in Robert Maxwell (ed.), *Information USSR: An Authoritative Encyclopedia about the Union of Soviet Socialist Republics* (New York, 1962), pp. 105–254.

[18] The *Istoriia kommunisticheskoi partii Sovetskogo Soiuza* was reissued in an expanded edition in 1962. For a detailed analysis of the two editions see Panas Fedenko, *Khrushchev's New History of the Soviet Communist Party* (Munich, 1963).

[19] *Osnovy marksistskoi filosofii* [Fundamentals of Marxist Philosophy] (Moscow, 1959) and *Osnovy Marksizma-Leninizma* [Fundamentals of Marxism-Leninism] (Moscow, 1960). The latter has been published in English and was reissued in a revised edition in 1963. Both contain lengthy sections on the materialist conception of history.

[20] The most comprehensive treatment of the reforms is Nicholas DeWitt, *Education and Professional Employment in the USSR* (Washington, 1961). For their effect on history education at the various levels see also Bushchik, *op. cit.* (chap. iv, n. 3), pp. 390–489; Pundeff, *op. cit.* (chap. vi, n. 13); and Seymour M. Rosen, *Higher Education in the USSR* (Washington, 1963), pp. 1–25.

course between Pokrovsky's sociological schematicism (which the 1934 decree condemned) and Stalin's stress on the great leader, and introduced two "concentric" phases in the history curriculum of the eleven-year schools. The text of the statement of September 16, 1959, below is from the translation in *Current Digest of the Soviet Press* (XI, No. 37, 14–15), October 14, 1959; the decree is translated from the text published in *Uchitel'skaia gazeta* ("Teachers' Gazette"), November 3, 1959.

36. Statement on the Teaching of History in Schools, September 16, 1959

The reorganization of the public education system, the introduction of compulsory eight-year education, and the expansion of secondary education enhance the educational role of the schools and set forth as a major task the improvement of study in the fundamentals of the sciences, including history.

The system for history instruction in U.S.S.R. schools was defined by the May 16, 1934, decree of the U.S.S.R. Council of People's Commissars and the Party Central Committee "On the Teaching of Civil History in U.S.S.R. Schools." In subsequent years, the system underwent minor changes. At present the teaching of history is organized as follows: in the fourth grade, a short course in the history of the U.S.S.R. is given; in the fifth grade and the first half of the sixth grade, ancient history is studied; in the second half of the sixth grade and the seventh grade, medieval history is studied; in grades eight, nine and ten, a systematic course in U.S.S.R. history from ancient times to the present is taught, together with a systematic course in modern history. In 1957 the study of the recent history of foreign countries was introduced in the senior class of the secondary school. Moreover, in each Union republic the history of that particular republic is taught.

Until 1955–56, the U.S.S.R. Constitution was taught in the eighth grade, but in view of the difficulty of this material for eighth-grade students, the subject was shifted to the tenth grade. Beginning with the 1959–60 academic year, the study of the U.S.S.R. Constitution will be introduced in the tenth grade, with instruction in the civil, criminal, labor, and several other branches of Soviet law.

The study of history in the schools is of enormous significance in inculcating the fundamentals of the Marxist-Leninist world view in young people.

The study of history consistently opens up before the pupils a picture of the development of human society in a form accessible to them, and they gradually acquire, by learning specific historical facts, a correct understanding of the phenomena of social life.

The existing system of history instruction in schools has proved itself for the most part. Nevertheless, there are serious shortcomings in the teaching of history.

It cannot be considered normal that graduates of incomplete secondary schools have a meager knowledge of the history of the U.S.S.R. because they have studied it only in the fourth grade of elementary school. This shortcoming must now be eliminated, especially in view of the transition to universal compulsory eight-year education. It must also be pointed out that the school history course is overloaded with secondary materials; many of the existing textbooks have fallen behind the present-day level of learning, are written in a dry language unintelligible to the students, and need radical improvement. The teaching of history in the schools is still not fully utilized for the purposes of indoctrination. It often boils down to the teacher's bland repetition of facts contained in the texts, without sufficient use of visual aids or vivid influences on the students' emotions.

With the aim of improving history instruction in the schools, the Russian Republic Academy of Pedagogy has worked out a draft for perfecting the system of school history education.

As the draft was being prepared, it was made to take into account the many suggestions voiced by history teachers, scholars, and broad circles of the Soviet public during the nationwide discussion of the theses of the Party Central Committee and the U.S.S.R. Council of Ministers concerning schools and during the discussion by the U.S.S.R. and Union-republic Supreme Soviets of the reorganization of the public education system.

The present draft was discussed among teachers, instructors in higher educational institutions, and scholars of the Russian and other Union republics. From this emerged the following system for teaching the history and Constitution of the U.S.S.R. and other Union republics in the schools of the country.

It is suggested that in the fourth grade the teaching of U.S.S.R. history be retained as an independent subject, given in the form of brief episodic accounts from the history of the U.S.S.R., fully suitable for children of that age, which should stimulate the children's interest in the history of their motherland. The fourth-grade textbooks must accordingly be built around vivid stories from native history, arranged chronologically without any pretense of conveying complete historical information. The lessons in the fourth grade should be conducted primarily by the method of explanatory reading.

It is suggested that materials in existing programs and texts in ancient and medieval history be somewhat abbreviated and simplified. Ancient history should be studied only in the fifth grade and medieval history only in the sixth, with 70 hours of each subject given.

The study of ancient and medieval history in the eight-year school is essential for providing the students with a correct understanding of the history of society's development and for raising the young people's general cultural level.

It is suggested that in the seventh and eighth grades an elementary course in U.S.S.R. history, to include the most important facts about the social and state structure of the Soviet Union and about the modern and recent history of foreign countries, be introduced. The proposed class time for history courses in the seventh and eighth grades is about 180 hours, including 110 hours of U.S.S.R. history, 20 hours of information about the social and state structure of the Soviet Union, and 50 hours of facts about the modern and recent history of foreign countries.

The elementary course in U.S.S.R. history, along with essential facts from the modern and recent history of foreign countries in a form accessible to adolescents, will provide graduates of eight-year schools with a certain degree of completeness in historical knowledge and a better understanding of our country's role in world history and of contemporary historical events.

At the second stage of secondary education, a systematic course in modern and recent history (about 160 hours) and a systematic course in U.S.S.R. history (about 170 hours) are recommended for the ninth, tenth, and eleventh grades in all types of secondary schools. In the latter course, the greatest attention should be concentrated on U.S.S.R. history in the nineteenth and twentieth centuries, especially on the Soviet period of our country's history, and the concluding chapter should deal extensively with the Twenty-first Party Congress and its decisions.

Besides this, the study in the eleventh grade of the U.S.S.R. Constitution and the Constitutions of the Union republics, along with basic facts about the civil, labor, collective farm, criminal and various other branches of Soviet law (about 70 hours), is suggested as a separate subject. The study of this subject will leave the graduates of secondary schools better prepared for practical work.

The introduction in schools of the Union republics of courses in the history of the republic concerned is no light achievement. The school reorganization and the improvement of the system for teaching history in the schools will make it possible to improve and expand history instruction, including studies in the history of the Union republics. It is advisable for each Union republic to be allowed to determine the system for teaching its own history.

In the system for teaching history in the schools, the greatest attention is thus given to U.S.S.R. history. Graduates of schools will also have acquired a sufficient knowledge of the history of foreign countries.

History courses in secondary schools must provide students with a scientific understanding of the laws of society's development in a form intelligible to them and must develop in them a conviction about the inevitable victory of communism, while revealing the role of the popular masses as the true makers of history and the historical significance of the individual.

In a history course, special attention should be given to explaining the role of the Communist Party as the directing and guiding force in Soviet society and to a study of the modern stage of communist construction in the U.S.S.R. It is also necessary to show in detail the formation and development of the socialist system, the growth of national liberation movements, and the major events in the modern and recent history of other countries.

History instruction in school is intended to bring up the young people in the spirit of communist ideals, socialist patriotism, proletarian internationalism, and a deep respect for labor, and to facilitate the training of students for an active public life.

The prospective changes in the teaching of history give rise to the necessity for drafting new programs and creating new textbooks in all branches of the school course in history and in the Constitution. The intended completion date for the drafting of new programs in history and the Constitution for all types of general-education schools is January 1, 1960.

To ensure the high scientific and pedagogical level of the new textbooks, it is imperative to create a series of authors' collectives from among the most qualified scientific workers and the most experienced teachers.

It is intended that the following will be prepared through competitions and published by June 1, 1961: a book of stories from U.S.S.R. history for the fourth grade; a textbook on ancient history for the fifth grade; a textbook of medieval history for the sixth grade; a U.S.S.R. history textbook for the seventh and eighth grades; textbooks on modern and recent history of foreign countries for the ninth, tenth, and eleventh grades; and a textbook on the U.S.S.R. Constitution for the eleventh grade. The publication of the U.S.S.R. history textbook for the ninth, tenth, and eleventh grades is intended sometime before June 1, 1962.

Work is proceeding in all the Union republics on the composition of school textbooks in the history and Constitutions of the republics. There is reason to suppose that this work will be finished in a year or eighteen months.

The Russian Republic Academy of Pedagogy hopes that the History

Institutes of the U.S.S.R. Academy of Sciences and the Union-republic Academies of Sciences, instructors at universities and pedagogical institutes, and experienced teachers will take an active part in the composition of new textbooks for the schools. It is also important for the scientific institutions, with the participation of the best teachers, to examine the manuscripts submitted to the Union-republic Ministries of Education by the authors' collectives.

In the course of two or three years, it will be necessary to publish anthologies and readers in history for secondary school students and to increase the publication of popular science and fictional literature on the history and social and state structure of the U.S.S.R. for students of various ages. It is also necessary to expand the output of historical maps and pictures to meet the demand for them in the schools, to increase the publication of other visual aids in the history and Constitution of the U.S.S.R., and to expand the production of educational films.

In the near future, the Russian Republic Academy of Pedagogy will prepare methodological guides for teachers of history in the various grades.

The Russian Republic Academy of Pedagogy hopes that the Party and Soviet public, teachers, scholars, and public education personnel will declare in the press their views on the present draft for improving the teaching of history in the schools.

37. Decree of October 8, 1959, on Changes in the Teaching of History in the Schools

For the purpose of improving the teaching of history and U.S.S.R constitution in the schools, the Central Committee of CPSU and the Council of Ministers of the U.S.S.R. *decree:*

1. The sequence of the study of history in the schools shall be as follows: in the fourth grade, episodic stories from the history of the U.S.S.R., in the fifth grade, elementary course of the history of the ancient world; in the sixth grade, elementary course of the history of the Middle Ages; in the seventh and eighth grades, elementary course in the history of the U.S.S.R., with the most important data concerning the social and governmental organization of the Soviet state as well as with data from the modern and contemporary history of foreign countries; in the ninth to eleventh grades, sys-

tematic course in the history of the U.S.S.R. and systematic course in the modern and contemporary history of foreign countries.

The U.S.S.R. constitution, with data from the civil, criminal, labor, and other branches of Soviet law and the basic provisions of the constitution of the respective union republic, shall be studied in the eleventh grade of the secondary school.

2. The course in history in the secondary school must aid the development in the pupils, in a form accessible to them, of the scientific understanding of the laws of the history of the evolution of society; must form in the pupils the conviction of the inevitability of the doom of capitalism and the victory of communism; and must consistently disclose the role of the popular masses as the true makers of history and creators of material and spiritual values, as well as the significance of the individual in history.

The study of the questions of the current stage of communist construction and the disclosure of the role of the Communist Party as the leading, directing, and guiding force in Soviet society assumes at present a special significance.

The teaching of history and other general education subjects in the schools is called upon to bring the young people up in the spirit of communist devotion to ideas and morality, of intolerance toward bourgeois ideology, in the spirit of socialist patriotism and proletarian internationalism, of profound respect for labor, and to promote the preparation of the pupils for an active public life.

3. The Central Committees of the communist parties and the Councils of Ministers of the Union republics shall be instructed to consider the question of the study of the history of the Union republic in the schools.

4. To supply the schools with new textbooks, the Ministry of Education of the R.S.F.S.R. shall prepare and publish, through competitions, new textbooks in history written graphically and convincingly at a high scientific and methodological level and in a language accessible to the pupils: the book of stories on the history of the U.S.S.R. for the fourth grade, the textbook of history of the ancient world for the fifth grade, the textbook of the Middle Ages for the sixth grade, and the textbook of history of the U.S.S.R. for the seventh and eighth grades by June 1, 1961, and the textbook of modern and contemporary history of foreign countries for the ninth to eleventh grades, the textbook of the U.S.S.R. constitution for the eleventh grade, and the textbook of U.S.S.R. history for the ninth to the eleventh grades by June 1, 1962. It is recommended that the

Ministry of Education of the R.S.F.S.R. publish individual text-books for the most complex courses of history in trial editions.

For the preparation of the textbooks of history and the U.S.S.R. constitution, authors' collectives shall be organized from among scholars and the best schoolteachers, assuring them appropriate conditions for work on the textbooks.

The Institute of History of the U.S.S.R. Academy of Sciences, the Institutes of History of the Academies of Sciences of the Union republics, and the Academy of Pedagogical Sciences of the R.S.F.S.R. shall take active part in the preparation of the textbooks in history as well as in the scholarly examination and discussion of the textbook manuscripts submitted by the various authors' collectives to the ministries of education of the Union republics.

5. The ministries of education of the Union republics shall:

    a) Develop by January 1, 1960, teaching plans in history and the U.S.S.R. constitution for all types of general-education schools.

    b) Publish textbooks of the history of the Union republics by June 1, 1961.

    c) Issue in three to five years collections of readings and books for outside reading in history for the pupils of the secondary schools and increase the publication of scientifically popularized and fictional literature in history and the social and governmental organization of the U.S.S.R. addressed to the various ages of the pupils as well as of methods aids for the teachers. They shall take steps to increase the publication of historical maps, pictures, and other visual aids on history and the U.S.S.R. constitution and to step up the release of instructional films keyed to the history courses in the schools.

6. The Ministry of Education of the R.S.F.S.R. and the Academy of Pedagogical Sciences of the R.S.F.S.R. shall be instructed to work out in two months' time proposals for the improvement of history education in the secondary general-education schools for working and rural youth as well as for preparation of special textbooks in history for schools of this type.

7. The Central Committees of the communist parties and the Councils of Ministers of the Union republics, the local area (*krai*) committees, and the regional committees of the party shall increase their vigilance for quality in the teaching of history and the U.S.S.R. constitution in the schools, shall accord systematically the necessary assistance to the teachers of history in raising their theoretical knowledge, and shall take steps to raise the qualifications of the

teachers. They shall consider and approve practical measures for the training of numbers of history teachers in the institutions of higher education in accordance with the needs of their schools, bearing in mind that in the very near future only persons with higher education in history are to be admitted to teaching history in the eight-year and secondary schools.

The preparation of new history textbooks, necessitated by the restructuring of the curriculum of the new eleven-year school and the changes in facts and interpretation, was initiated by a decree of February 23, 1960, of the Council of Ministers opening a nationwide competition for manuscripts. The terms of the competition stated: "The textbooks must be written in conformity with the contemporary requirements of historical and pedagogical science, in a graphic and persuasive manner, and in language understandable to the students. They must aid the rearing of the youth in the spirit of devotion to communist ideals and morality as well as of intolerance to bourgeois ideology and in the spirit of socialist patriotism and proletarian internationalism as well as of profound respect for labor, and must also promote the preparation of the students for active public life. The textbooks must conform to the draft programs for history prepared by the Academy of Pedagogical Sciences of the R.S.F.S.R." [21] Intended to supersede the textbooks commissioned by Stalin's decree of 1934 and written by Pankratova (her textbook underwent seventeen editions) and others, the new textbooks were originally promised for 1962–63 (grades 4–8) and 1963–64 (grades 9–11), but delays in producing some of them developed.

In the process of renovating history as well as ideology, the Central Committee issued on January 9, 1960, a decree "On the Tasks of Party Propaganda in Present-Day Conditions" to supersede Stalin's decree of 1938 and draw the lines for ideological work. [22] A lengthy document, it discusses all aspects and vehicles, including history, of party propaganda. Its meaning for historians was explained in editorials in *Voprosy istorii* and elsewhere. [23] Later in 1960, *Voprosy istorii* published a comprehensive review of achievements and tasks in the field of history, followed by a statement on the new format of the journal. [24] The essential parts follow.

---

[21] *Voprosy istorii*, No. 4, 1960, pp. 221–222.

[22] See reading No. 24. The text of the 1960 decree is translated in *Current Digest of the Soviet Press*, XII, No. 2 (February 10, 1960), 17–23.

[23] See, for example, "The Party Central Committee Resolution 'On the Tasks of Party Propaganda in Present-Day Conditions' and Historical Science," *Voprosy istorii*, No. 6, 1960, 3–9, translated in *Current Digest of the Soviet Press*, XII, No. 31 (August 31, 1960), 8–10.

[24] *Voprosy istorii*, No. 8, 1960, pp. 3–21, translated in *Current Digest of the Soviet Press*, XII, No. 40 (November 2, 1960), 6–14.

38. Editorial, "Soviet Historical Science at a New Stage of Development"

The study of history has never been mere curiosity, a withdrawal into the past for the sake of the past. Over the course of many centuries mankind has tried to delve into the recent as well as the remote past, eager to discover in history an explanation of the present and to foresee the future, having come to know the past. Historical science—and the path that mankind has traveled over many centuries bears witness to this fact—always serves, above all, the needs of the times. By its nature and by its social function, historical science has always been called upon to serve the most timely requirements of society's ideological life, and the whole history of historical knowledge and the entire course of development of historical science irrefutably testify to this. Historical science has been and remains an arena of sharp ideological struggle; it has been and remains a class, party science.

The experience of history is the criterion of the correctness of any historical theory. The struggle of ideas, trends, and theories constituting the basic content of the process of development of historical science is based on actual contradictions in social development and reflects the struggle among the classes and their parties. Historical science and the present day are indissolubly linked. The present cannot be correctly understood without the data of historical science. Knowledge of the paths of society's development in the past helps to understand the present and to foresee the future. Such is the dialectical tie of history and life.

The experience of history has irrefutably demonstrated that the teaching of Marxism-Leninism gives the only explanation of the laws of the historical process that is true and conforms to objective reality. The victory of the Great October Revolution, the building of socialism in our country, and the rise of the world socialist system graphically and convincingly testify that Marxism quite correctly foresaw the course of history, disclosed its laws, and pointed the way to "a scientific study of history as a single process which in all its many varied aspects and contradictions develops in conformity with natural laws." (V. I. Lenin, *Works,* Vol. 21, p. 41.) Marxism-Leninism placed teaching concerning society on firm scientific foundations and established history as the science of the gradual development of society from ancient times to the present day, a science that views the entire age-old path of mankind as a lawful, natural historical process, the basic content of which is the replacement of social-economic formations, the inevitable downfall of exploiting societies, and the victory of communism.

Herein lies the great effective force of Soviet historical science. "Our views are supported by history itself, by reality at every step," wrote V. I. Lenin. (*Works,* Vol. 10, p. 7.)

The successful development of Soviet historical science is ensured by the concern and leadership of the Communist Party, the policy of which is based on the creative application and development of Marxism-Leninism.

Our ideological opponents contend that the party spirit of Soviet historiography is incompatible with objective scientific research. This reflects the unwillingness of some and the inability of others to take note of the achievements of Marxist historiography. The great force of Marxist-Leninist doctrine is that it places in the researcher's hands the only correct and scientific creative method of objective, comprehensive study of social phenomena and processes. This method requires thorough and precise analysis of facts and events taken in their real interdependence. It is not fragmentary little facts [*faktiki*] and examples, not isolated illustrations, but the sum total of the factual material relating to the question under study that must be the basis of historical research. Marxist historians follow the instructions of the founder of Soviet historical science, V. I. Lenin, who taught: "In the sphere of social phenomena there is no device more widespread and more invalid than that of seizing upon *isolated* little facts [*faktiki*], playing with examples. To select examples in general is no difficult task, but this has no meaning, or a purely negative one, since the whole point lies in the historical concrete situation of individual cases. Facts, if taken *as a whole, in their interrelation,* are not only stubborn but also unquestionably conclusive things. Little facts [*faktiki*], if taken outside their entirety, outside their interrelation, if fragmentary and arbitrary, are merely a toy or something even worse." (*Works,* Vol. 23, p. 266.)

V. I. Lenin stressed that in research work "it is necessary to try to establish a foundation of precise and indisputable facts on which one could rely and with which one could counter any of those general or abstract arguments that are so endlessly abused in some countries in our times. If this is to be a real foundation, it is necessary to take not isolated facts but the *sum total* of facts relating to the question under examination, *without a single* exception; otherwise the suspicion—and a fully legitimate one—arises that the facts have been chosen or selected arbitrarily, that a 'subjective' concoction to justify perhaps a dirty event is being served up instead of the objective relation and interdependence of historical phenomena in their entirety." (*Ibid.,* pp. 266–267.)

Marxism-Leninism, which revealed the objective laws of social development and armed historians with a knowledge of them, for the first time created the possibility of a strictly scientific investigation of factual material.

Soviet historical science is successfully developing precisely because it is guided by the creative method of Marxism-Leninism and consistently observes the principle of historicity, of profound objective analysis of historical reality, combined with a class, party approach to phenomena of social life, always remembering that history is organically linked with the living activity of the masses, the creators of history, that "history is *nothing but* the activity of man pursuing his aims." (K. Marx and F. Engels, *Works,* 2d ed., Vol. 2, p. 102.) Adherence to the Communist stand cannot fail to coincide with the highest scientific objectivity, for Marxism-Leninism is the only true theory of social development, a fact confirmed by the practice of history. Eternally living, developing Marxist-Leninist teaching underlies the successes of Soviet historical science.

The superiority of Marxist-Leninist methodology to bourgeois theories of social development does not mean that a nihilistic attitude should be adopted toward all bourgeois historiography. The contribution that bourgeois historiography has in its time made to the development of scholarship we assess at its true worth and in a number of questions still avail ourselves of the works of notable historians of the past. Soviet historians give thoughtful consideration to everything positive which was achieved by their predecessors and which is now being produced not only by progressive foreign scholars but by honest researchers who do not subscribe to Marxist-Leninist views.

V. I. Lenin observed that Marxist science had captured the minds of the millions-strong masses because it rested on the firm foundation of human knowledge. Marx, after studying the laws of development of human society, "grasped the inevitability of a capitalist development leading to communism and, most important, proved this purely on the basis of the most precise, the most detailed, the most profound study of that capitalist society and by having fully assimilated all that earlier science had given. Everything created by human society he critically reworked, not leaving a single point untouched." (V. I. Lenin, *Works,* Vol. 31, pp. 261–262.)

The twentieth century has been a time of deepening crisis for bourgeois historiography. The aggravation of all the contradictions of capitalism in the period of imperialism, and particularly in the period of the general crisis of capitalism, has resulted in sharp lines being drawn in the ranks of the bourgeois intellectuals and among historians in particular. Reactionary bourgeois scholars are trying to use historical science to defend the exploiter system, to justify all the abominations of imperialism. Our attitude to the works of these historians may be characterized by the words of V. I. Lenin. Terming the bourgeois professors of political economy and philosophy "the learned minions" of the class of capitalists and theologians, Vladimir Ilyich noted: "The task of Marxists in both instances is to succeed in assimilating and adapting the discoveries made by these 'minions' (you won't take a step, for instance, in studying new economic developments without availing yourself of the works of these minions), and to be able to divest them of their reactionary slant, to be able to carry on *their own* line and contend against the *entire line* of the forces and classes hostile to us." (*Ibid.*, Vol. 14, p. 328.)

Soviet historians know that the peaceful coexistence of states with different social-economic systems does not mean the slackening of the ideological struggle, on the front of historical science in particular. In this struggle they are upholding the methodological principles of Soviet historical science and its accomplishments, vigorously propagandizing historical materialism, convincingly disclosing the theoretical untenability of bourgeois historiography and the politically reactionary nature of its various trends, exposing the falsifiers of history and rebuffing the revisionists.

Among the bourgeois historians there are scholars who see the contradictory nature of the bourgeois system, condemn certain of its aspects, and are seeking to gain insight into the course of the historical process. The erroneous methodological premises of these researchers keep them from producing genuinely scientific works of history. But they have been responsible for a number of useful works on concrete history, valuable for their underlying study of sources and their systematization of factual material. Soviet scholars readily and sincerely support the utmost expansion of international ties not only with Marxist historians but with honest bourgeois historians as well. They do so because such ties serve the cause of strengthening peace and disseminating the achievements of Soviet historiography and enable foreign scholars to see the strides made by our historical science and to become convinced of the correctness of Marxist-Leninist methodology. It is essential for Marxist historians, in turn, to be familiar with contemporary bourgeois historical science, with its achievements in the field of research on concrete questions and its schools, techniques, and trends. Soviet historians agree with pure and open hearts to the development of international contacts; consistently defending their fundamental positions, they are striving for honest and vigorous co-operation in all that is necessary for the development of historical science and for the discharge of its responsibilities to the present and to the peoples fighting for peace and a better future for mankind.

Five years ago Soviet historians took part in the work of the Tenth International Congress of Historical Sciences in Rome, at which our scholars read a number of papers and delivered a number of reports that evoked great interest in the international scholarly community.

Now the next, the Eleventh International Congress of Historical Sciences is gathering in Stockholm; our historical science will be fittingly represented at this congress. The historians of the U.S.S.R. go to Stockholm amid a new advance in Soviet historical science. Foreign scholars will once again be able to see that in the land of victorious socialism the most favorable conditions have been created for the development of historical science.

*   *   *

Since the Twentieth and Twenty-first Party Congresses, a new stage has begun in the development of Soviet historical science. Big and responsible tasks confront historians in the light of the Party Central Committee's decree of January 9, 1960, "On the Tasks of Party Propaganda in Present-Day Conditions." Now that the Soviet Union has entered the period of the comprehensive building of communism, the social sciences have an enormously enhanced role to play in the communist education of the working people. Historians are called upon to make their contribution to the great cause of building a communist society.

Marxist-Leninist doctrine has received creative development in the decisions of the Communist Party of the Soviet Union and of the fraternal communist and workers' parties; these decisions provide a comprehensive analysis of the present stage in the development of society. This has enriched and armed our historical science ideologically. Elimination of the consequences of the cult of the individual helped to spur the creative activity of the historians and to vitalize work in all fields of historical science.

At the same time, some people have construed rectification of the errors engendered by the cult of the individual as the revision of fundamental theses and conclusions worked out in Soviet historical science in the preceding period. Individual historians made theoretical and methodological mistakes that showed a tendency to deviate from the Leninist principles of party orientation in scholarship. Tendencies of this sort, manifested in particular in the journal *Voprosy istorii,* met with a unanimous rebuff from the Soviet scholarly community, which vigorously criticized the mistakes and distortions committed. In reinforcing the militant principles of party spirit in Soviet historical science and in combating all sorts of manifestations of revisionism, historians were greatly aided by the Party Central Committee's March 9, 1957, decree "On the Magazine *Voprosy Istorii,*" which stressed the need for consistent adherence to the Leninist principle of party spirit in historical science.

In the time that has elapsed since this decree was adopted, Soviet historians have achieved many successes in the struggle against bourgeois ideology and revisionism. Many articles and special collections have been published in which bourgeois falsification of history and revisionism in historiography have been exposed. It should, however, be said that the historians' efforts along these lines must be stepped up even further. Not always have we been conducting a genuine offensive against bourgeois ideology along the entire front of historical science; we have at times been underestimating the necessity of combating ideological opponents in the fields of the history of the most recent period as well as of more remote times. The struggle against bourgeois historiography—and all the more so an offensive—cannot reduce merely to polemics and the exposure of works by reactionary historians. It is important, above all, to produce substantial scholarly studies that embrace the entire historical process, in particular the history of Soviet society and the most recent history of foreign countries.

The struggle against bourgeois ideology has been and continues to be the foremost task of our historians. It helps the best representatives of bourgeois historical science to understand the fallacy of its methodological principles and political tendencies and to draw closer to the genuinely scientific methodology of Marxism-Leninism. This places a special responsibility on Soviet historians and demands that they wage the struggle against bourgeois ideology systematically, topic by topic, and convincingly in all areas of historical science.

A thorough study of the theory of Marxism-Leninism is the cardinal factor ensuring the successful development of Soviet scholarship. A major event in our country's ideological life is the launching of the publication of the second edition of the *Works* of K. Marx and F. Engels and of the fifth edition of V. I. Lenin's collected works, the *Complete Works*. Soviet historians are doing considerable work on a study of the writings of the founders of Marxism-Leninism. But in this area a great deal still remains to be done. We do not yet have generalizing works devoted to the importance of the Leninist heritage for historical science, although the number of articles that to one degree or another consider separate aspects of this subject is considerable. A particularly large number of such articles were published on the occasion of the ninetieth anniversary of Vladimir Ilyich's birth.

The publication of party documents and of the works of N. S. Khrushchev and other leaders of the Communist Party of the Soviet Union and the international Communist and workers' movement has great importance for historians.

The most important field of research for Soviet historians is the history of the Communist Party of the Soviet Union. Historians working on party history comprise one of the leading detachments of Soviet historical science. Research on party-history problems has assumed great scope in recent years. A major advance in this field has been the new generalizing work entitled "History of the Communist Party of the Soviet Union," which deals with the heroic history of the party, for the first time analyzes in detail the past twenty years in the history of the Party, years filled with events of the greatest moment, and corrects a number of mistakes that appeared in literature on party history written in previous years.

Research on the activities of Vladimir Ilyich Lenin, founder of the Communist Party and the Soviet state, study of the enormously rich Leninist heritage, has assumed vast scope. The ninetieth anniversary of V. I. Lenin's birth was marked by the appearance of a large number of books and articles. Among them the new edition of the "Biography of V. I. Lenin" is of great importance.

A characteristic feature of the new stage in the development of Soviet historical science is the broadening of the range of problems dealt with in scholarly studies and the creation of generalizing works that encompass the whole process of the development of human society or particular periods.

The wide scope of research work in all directions and the creative co-operation of scholars in various specialties were what paved the way for the publication of such an important generalizing work as the multivolumed "World History."

This work, the result of the creative effort of a large group of historians, sums up the results of the more than forty years of development of Soviet historical science. The Soviet "World History" for the first time examines the entire process of world history in the light of a single and unified conception based on the Marxist teaching concerning social-economic formations. On the basis of the vast and varied material on the history of various countries and peoples the "World History" shows the unity of the process of world history and the validity of those general laws of the development of human society discovered by K. Marx, F. Engels, and V. I. Lenin. A major principle of Soviet historiography—the principle of the historical equality of all peoples of the world—is consistently sustained in the "World History." This work shows the utter untenability of any sort of racist, Europo-centrist, pan-Islamist, chauvinist or nationalist theory. The profound feeling of respect for all peoples, for their history and for their contribution to the treasure-house of world culture, a feeling that is characteristic of socialism, guides the Soviet scholars working on the "World History"—a history of peoples, not of kings and generals.

A generalization of the results of studies done by specialists is contained in recently published textbooks and study aids on the history of the U.S.S.R. and on world history. A special volume of the "Large Soviet Encyclopedia" (second edition) entitled "Union of Soviet Socialist Republics," which contains a systematic outline of the history of the U.S.S.R. from earliest times to the present day and an outline of the history of our historical science, has been published in an enormous edition in the U.S.S.R. and translated into many foreign languages.

Now that significant new strides have been made in Marxist-Leninist research on various stages of domestic history, scholars are beginning the writing of a multivolume generalizing work entitled "History of the U.S.S.R." A fundamental "History of Russian Art" is coming out and work is under way on a "History of Russian Culture." A universal reference work on world history—the twelve-volume "Soviet Historical Encyclopedia"—is being prepared in the country for the first time.

Characteristic of the development of Soviet historical science in our day is the decisive shift of historians to the study of processes directly related to the present, to life, and to the practice of communist construction. The attention of researchers is being drawn more and more to the history of Soviet society and, in the field of foreign history, to the recent period.

A number of difficulties are involved in the study of the present. Figuratively speaking, the researchers here have to tread "virgin soil" and to pose and resolve entirely new problems in scholarship. They do not have such a rich arsenal of research already done as do historians working on problems of the past. Frequently the very collection of material on a particular problem is of great value, laying the groundwork for deeper research in the future.

Soviet historical science has made a step forward in this direction in the past few years. Only a few years ago, scholarly output on the history of Soviet society consisted primarily of magazine articles; monographs were quite a rarity. Of course, the scope and level of research on the history of Soviet society are not yet up to the demands of the times or the growing requirements of the Soviet reader. We have few fundamental research works on the history of Soviet society. Scholars should be bolder in tackling contemporary problems. But one cannot at the same time fail to note that more and more scholarly works (to say nothing of popular literature of a scholarly nature for a mass readership) devoted to questions of the history of the building of socialism and communism have been appearing. This is coming to be the principal trend of historical research in the U.S.S.R.

Soviet historians have been devoting a great deal of attention to comprehensive study of the greatest event of world history—the Great October Socialist Revolution. More than 600 books came out in our country on the occasion of the fortieth anniversary of the October Revolution; in addition, a vast number of articles and other works were published. A fundamental work entitled "The History of the Great October Socialist Revolution" will be written by a collective group of scholars. Many studies and documentary publications on the history of the revolution of 1905–7—the "dress rehearsal" for the Great October Revolution—were prepared on the occasion of its fiftieth anniversary.

Soviet researchers have been concentrating on a study of the history of the masses—the true creators of history. The guiding role of the Communist Party, the history of the working class and collective farm peasantry, the history of the alliance between the working class and the peasantry—these are the major subjects being treated by our scholarship.

The Soviet people's heroic exploit in the Great Patriotic War of 1941–45 is being studied thoroughly and comprehensively by historians. Monographs and memoirs are being published. Note should be taken of the importance of the work now under way on a multivolume "History of the Great Patriotic War, 1941–1945" (the first volume has already been published). This work is called upon to disclose comprehensively and thoroughly the sublime epopee of the struggle of the Soviet people, led by the Communist Party, for their freedom and independence and for the liberation of the peoples of other countries from fascism.

Research is also under way in the field of postwar history: materials are being assembled and the first attempts are being made to generalize them in monographs, pamphlets, dissertations, and articles. It must be stressed, however, that life and the practice of building communism call upon historians for more vigorous treatment of the history of Soviet society in the postwar period.

Progress in studying the history of Soviet society has made it possible to produce a generalizing book entitled "History of the U.S.S.R.: Epoch of Socialism." This work is a major accomplishment of our historiography. The scholars' task now is to bring out a multivolume history of Soviet society.

Significant strides have been made by historians of the Union republics. Bourgeois historiography, as is known, reflecting the chauvinistic and nationalistic aspirations of the exploiter classes, proceeds from the profoundly reactionary principle of dividing peoples into "historical" and "nonhistorical." Under a victorious socialist system the peoples of the U.S.S.R. have fully manifested the wealth of their creative powers. In close contact with the scholars of Moscow, Leningrad, and other scientific centers of the country, the historians of the Union and autonomous republics are working on major problems of the history of all the Soviet peoples. They have produced many monographs and generalizing works on the history of the peoples of the U.S.S.R. from the most ancient times to the present day.

Soviet historians are paying considerable attention to combating reactionary bourgeois historiography and working out the history of historical science. Collections of articles directed against the falsification of history have appeared. The first volume of "Outlines of the History of Historical Science in the U.S.S.R." has been published and Volumes II and III have been prepared. A work is being written on the history of historical science in the years of the Soviet regime (1917–60).

The study of methodological problems, which has been intensified of late, necessitates that work in this direction be further stepped up. The important task of the historians consists in thorough elaboration of the theory of the historical process and of methods of historical research. For this, business-like co-operation should be arranged with scholars in other social science: philosophers, economists, legal scholars, and literature specialists.

Research on the history of the people's democracies and the recent history of the capitalist countries is proceeding on a wide front. Not only monographs have been produced but also generalizing works: two volumes of a "History of Bulgaria," three volumes of a "History of Czechoslovakia," and three volumes of a "History of Poland," prepared by the U.S.S.R. Academy of Sciences' Slavic Studies Institute.

Our scholars' works on world history describe the processes involved in the general crisis of capitalism, elucidate the history of the international communist and workers' movement, expose the lie of the bourgeoisie's apologists concerning the present state of the capitalist countries and disclose the world-historic role of the Great October Socialist Revolution.

Soviet historical science, forcefully exposing the piratical nature of the imperialist warmongers, serves the noble cause of preserving peace through the world. A truthful treatment of the history of the Soviet state's foreign policy and of international relations in the age of imperialism is called upon to play a big role in this. The second (five-volume) edition of the "History of Diplomacy" is now being published.

Soviet historians are doing successful research in various fields of world history, its ancient, medieval, and modern periods. Problems of ancient history are being studied thoroughly (the works of Academicians A. I. Tiumenev, V. V. Struve, and others). Soviet medievalists are working fruitfully, solving complex problems of the social-economic and political history of the European Middle Ages (works of Academician S. D. Skazkin and others). Work has begun on a three-volume "History of Byzantium." The study of the history of the peoples of Asia and Africa is expanding. A collective work entitled "Outlines of the Modern History of Japan" has been produced. Work is proceeding on a "Modern History of India." The newly established Africa Institute is developing its scientific activity. Groups of scholars have recently finished the second and third volumes of "Modern History."

History is a concrete science based on accurately established factual material. It is therefore of great importance for the development of this science that its facilities for the study of source materials be developed. The documentary resources of Soviet historiography have noticeably expanded in recent years, primarily as a result of the introduction into scholarly circulation of a large number of documents on the most recent period. On the basis of a government decision adopted in 1956, researchers have been given broad access to documents on the history of Soviet society. This has been a key factor in the new successes of our historians in their study of the history of Soviet society and international relations of the recent period.

Publication of archive documents has expanded. On the occasion of the fortieth anniversary of the Great October Socialist Revolution alone more than 100 collections of documents containing 22,000 new items were published. A multivolume series of documents entitled "The Great October Socialist Revolution" and an Academy edition of "Decrees of the Soviet Regime" are being published. A series of documentary collections on the history of the 1905–7 revolution has also appeared. A number of multivolume publications of great importance for illuminating the history of foreign policy and international relations are being put out. These include "Documents of U.S.S.R. Foreign Policy" and "The Foreign Policy of Russia in the 19th and Beginning of the 20th Centuries: Documents of the Russian Ministry of Foreign Affairs." Documentary materials on the history of the Second World War have been published that are of exceptional importance for exposing bourgeois falsifiers of history. These are: "Correspondence between the Chairman of the U.S.S.R. Council of Ministers and the Presidents of the U.S.A. and Prime Ministers of Great Britain during the Great Patriotic War of 1941–1945" and "Franco-Soviet Relations during the Great Patriotic War of 1941–1945."

Many documents on the histories of the peoples of the U.S.S.R. in the periods of feudalism and capitalism are being published. Note should be taken of the fruitful work of the U.S.S.R. Academy of Sciences' Archeographic Commission, under the direction of Academician M. N. Tikhomirov, on the publication of the "Complete Collection of Russian Chronicles." Publication of the "Records of the Social-Economic History of Northeast Rus" is continuing. Historians and literary scholars have jointly published a number of monuments of the social-political thought and literature of medieval Russia. Several new publications are devoted to major popular movements—the peasant wars of the seventeenth and eighteenth centuries and the peasant movement in the nineteenth century. Many documents are being published in the Union and autonomous republics, where archeographic work is assuming ever greater scope. Much attention has recently been paid to the publication of documents on the history of Russia's relations with the countries of the East.

Creative co-operation in the publication of documents is developing between Soviet and foreign historians. The state archives of the U.S.S.R. and the people's democracies have published three volumes of documents entitled "From the History of International Proletarian Solidarity." These collections are a contribution to the struggle against revisionism and for the purity of Marxism-Leninism and the proletarian solidarity and international amity of peoples. Historians of the U.S.S.R., Czechoslovakia, Bulgaria and Poland are preparing documentary publications on Soviet-Czechoslovak and Soviet-Polish friendly relations and on the liberation of Bulgaria from the Turkish yoke.

The expansion of source materials is a vivid index of the development of Soviet scholarship in the past few years.

The Party and government are showing constant concern about expanding publishing facilities for historical science. The number of historical journals in the country has grown. From 1957 through 1959 the following were published: *Voprosy istorii KPSS; Istoria SSSR; Novaya i noveishaya istoria; Voyenno-istorichesky zhurnal* ("Journal of Military History") ; *Ukrainsky istorichesky zhurnal* ("Ukrainian Historical Journal") ; *Istorichesky arkhiv* ("Historical Archive") ; *Sovremenny vostok* ("The East Today") ; and *Sovetskaya arkheologia* ("Soviet Archeology"). *Istoricheskiye zapiski* ("Historical Notes") of the Academy of Sciences' History Institute is appearing. The journal *Istoricheskiye nauki* ("Historical Sciences") is being published in the system of the higher schools (in the series *Nauchniye doklady vysshei shkoly* ["Scientific Reports of Higher Schools"]). Collections devoted to specific epochs or problems are appearing regularly: *Sredniye veka* ("Middle Ages"), *Vizantiisky vremennik* ("Byzantine Chronicle"), *Problemy istochnikovedenia* ("Problems of the Study of Source Materials"), *Voprosy istorii religii i ateizma* ("Problems of the History of Religion and Atheism"), *Materialy po istorii SSSR* (Materials on U.S.S.R. History"), *Materialy po istorii zemledelia i selskovo khozyaistva v SSSR* ("Materials on the History of Farming and Agriculture in the U.S.S.R."), *Yezhegodnik muzeya istorii religii i ateizma* ("Annual of the Museum of the History of Religion and Atheism"), *Arkheografichesky yezhegodnik* ("Archeographic Annual"), and *Skandinavsky sbornik* ("Scandinavian Collection"). Numerous *Trudy* ("Works") and *Ucheniye zapiski* ("Scholarly Notes") of the country's scientific and higher educational institutions are being published.

A growing number of books on history are being published. In addition to the publication of new research works, the works of the greatest Soviet historians (S. V. Bakhrushin, B. D. Grekov, E. V. Tarle, and others) as well as the best works of the prerevolutionary historians (an eight-volume edition of the collected works of V. O. Klyuchevsky; S. M. Soloviov's multivolumed "History of Russia from Ancient Times," V. P. Tatishchev's "Russian History," etc.) are being reissued.

The organizational forms of scientific work have changed and broadened. A number of new scientific institutions have sprung up (such as the Africa Institute and the Institute of World Economics and International Relations) ; some changes have been made in the organization of the work of established scientific institutions. Scientific councils on specific problems have been set up to co-ordinate the research being done by the historians of various institutions throughout the country: councils on the history of socialist and communist construction in the U.S.S.R. (chairman M. P. Kim), on the history of the peoples' national-liberation struggle against colonialism and the history of the development of the Eastern countries that have taken the path of independence (chairman B. G. Gafurov), on the history of the Great October Socialist Revolution (chairman I. I. Mints), on the study of the historical prerequisites of the Great October Socialist Revolution (chairman A. L. Sidorov) and on the origin of capitalism (chairman S. D. Skazkin). Creative groups for the study of major problems of domestic history as well as the history of individual countries of the East are functioning in the History Institute of the U.S.S.R. Academy of Sciences: groups for the study of the history of the peasantry and of agriculture in the U.S.S.R. (V. P. Danilov in charge), for research on the revolutionary situation in Russia in the 1850's and 1860's (M. V. Nechkina in charge), for the study of the history of socialist ideas (B. F. Porshnev in charge), and for the study of the history of France (V. P. Volgin in charge), Spain and Britain (I. M. Maisky in charge of both groups), Italy (S. D. Skazkin in charge), and Germany (A. S. Yerusalimsky in charge). Committees on the history of historical science (M. V. Nechkina in charge) and on the history of the agriculture and peasantry of Russia (N. M. Druzhinin in charge) are also fruitfully at work in the History Institute.

The work of the scientific councils, committees, and creative groups makes possible more precise co-ordination of the research being done by a broad circle of historians in the fields of domestic and foreign history. A remarkable feature of these new forms in the guidance of research work and its co-ordination is the fact that the scientific councils and groups for specific countries and problems are not administrative but public creative organizations. This is evidence that in the period of the comprehensive building of communism public forms play an ever growing role in the administration of various spheres of social and cultural development.

The establishment of scientific councils and groups for specific problems and countries helps to expand creative scientific discussions, which are being conducted at scientific conferences, sessions, and meetings, as well as in the press. The broad discussion of various problems and the lively exchange of views are yielding good scientific results.

Another feature of the development of Soviet historical science at the present stage is the increasing proportion of collective works. This form of scientific work creates big possibilities for effective research. It facilitates thorough treatment of all aspects of a problem and permits maximum utilization of the energies and knowledge of each specialist for the solution of specific problems. The creation of collective works by no means obviates the necessity of expanding individual work on monographs.

New contingents of historians are being carefully trained in our country and, together with the prominent scholars of the older generation, are successfully engaged in solving complex research tasks. Many measures have been put into effect in the past few years to improve the training of young specialists and raise the quality of dissertations. Stricter requirements have been set for admission to graduate studies, which are attracting the most able youth, as a rule with scientific and teaching experience. Even before being defended, dissertations must now be published, although only in part. Standards have been raised for dissertations being defended and special stress is being laid on their scientific timeliness.

The recent decision of the Party Central Committee and Soviet government putting in order the system for defending dissertations is very important for reinforcing scientific personnel; it grants the Higher Certification Commission the right, upon the representation of the academic councils of higher educational institutions and research institutes, to divest of academic degrees persons upon whom an academic title has been conferred mistakenly as well as persons who are not actively engaged in creative work in science. Scientific activity is now under the careful control of the public; this helps strengthen the close tie of science with life and with the practice of building communism. All this contributes to the reinforcement of our science and to the growth of scientific cadres.

With every year interest in a knowledge of history is growing in our country and the dissemination of this knowledge is assuming increasingly broader scope.

The growing interest of broad strata of the working people in the study of history is indicated by such facts as the yearly influx of young people into the departments of history and historical philology at higher educational institutions. In connection with the recent reorganization of the system of higher education in the U.S.S.R. there has been a particular increase in the influx into the higher educational institutions' evening and correspondence divisions of young persons desirous of devoting themselves to the study of history.

History is one of the most important subjects in secondary school. The decree of the Party Central Committee and U.S.S.R. Council of Ministers "On Certain Changes in the Teaching of History in the Schools" (October 8, 1959) states: "The secondary-school history course should help develop in the pupils, in a form comprehensible to them, a scientific understanding of the laws of development of society, implant in them the conviction that the doom of capitalism and victory of communism are inevitable, and consistently disclose the role of the masses as the true makers of history and creators of material and spiritual values, as well as the importance of the individual in history." [25]

Soviet working people are also acquiring knowledge of history in the extensive party education network, in the universities of culture and lecture bureaus, and through self-education.

It is the duty of scholars to participate vigorously in disseminating historical knowledge and in popularizing it. A task of special importance is to produce good textbooks for higher and secondary schools. In this respect much has been done in the past few years. New higher-school textbooks have been written on all three periods of the history of the U.S.S.R. New textbooks on the history of the Middle Ages, on modern history, and on the history of the countries of the East have been published. Next in line is the creation of textbooks for secondary schools. An open competition has been announced toward this end. The schools are waiting for good, substantial textbooks.

The needs of the Soviet school do not stop here, however. Very important is the publication of general and specialized lecture courses for higher educational institutions (this is particularly necessary in view of the development of the system of evening and correspondence education). The secondary schools need a variety of anthologies, readers for the pupils, and texts for the teachers. Finally, popular literature of a scientific nature on various problems of history is needed for a broad readership.

All this places honorable tasks on Soviet historians, whose duty is to bring knowledge to the masses and forward the great work of their communist education and the development of socialist culture.

An important feature of the development of Soviet historical science at the present stage is the considerable expansion of international contacts. Our historians' collaboration with scholars of the other socialist countries has become especially close. Soviet scholars have shared actively in the preparation of a number of generalizing works by the historians of these countries. Joint sessions of archeologists of the U.S.S.R., Bulgaria, Poland, the German Democratic Republic, Rumania, and Mongolia have been held. Polish, Czechoslovak, and Bulgarian scholars participated in the conferences on Old Russian literature held in Leningrad. Soviet scholars took part in the work of the Third Congress of Historians of Czechoslovakia. A discussion of the nature of the November revolution in Germany was held jointly with the historians of the German Democratic Republic.

Many useful meetings have taken place in the past years between Soviet

---

[25] *Uchitelskaya gazeta,* November 3, 1959. The decree is translated in reading no. 37.

scholars and the historians of capitalist countries. The historians of the Soviet Union maintain contact with more than 150 foreign scientific institutions. An Anglo-Soviet colloquium and a Franco-Soviet conference of historians proceeded well. Soviet specialists have taken part in international congresses and conventions of Byzantine specialists, orientalists, archivists, numismatists, and sinologists, in the work of international committees on the history of parliamentary and representative institutions and on the history of social movements and structures, and in a seminar on cultural ties between West and East and an international congress on "classical" philology and history. Soviet researchers have worked in the archives of France and Sweden, and Swedish historians in the archives of the U.S.S.R. Many scholars from capitalist countries have taken part in the work of a number of conferences and sessions and in other scientific undertakings in the U.S.S.R. (the Congress of Slavists, etc.) and have delivered lectures in Soviet research institutes and higher educational institutions. The mutual exchange of graduate and undergraduate students for training in research and educational institutions has been developing between the U.S.S.R. and foreign countries.

*   *   *

The tireless concern of the Communist Party and Soviet government have ensured new successes for historical science. These are expressed, above all, in the rise in the level of theoretical scholarship and increase in the amount of scientific output, in the expansion of work on source materials and of the range of problems dealt with in historical research, in the improved organization of scientific work, in the further strengthening and growth of the contingents of scholars, in the establishment of new scientific institutions, and in the expansion of publishing facilities.

At the same time one cannot overlook the shortcomings that exist in the work of the research institutes and the work of the historians. The Party Central Committee's decree "On the Tasks of Party Propaganda in Present-Day Conditions" states: "Many economists, philosophers, historians, and other scholarly personnel have not overcome elements of *dogmatism,* do not have a bold and creative approach to life and to the experience of the masses' struggle, are poorly elaborating timely theoretical and practical questions, and are often held in the toils of outdated and fruitless problems." [26]

The Communist Party calls upon historians to direct all their energies and creative powers into the working out of problems advanced by the process of building a communist society. Toward this end scholars must make vigorous use of the entire arsenal of resources. It is their duty to

---

[26] "On the Tasks of Party Propaganda in Present-Day Conditions," Decree of the Party Central Committee, State Political Publishing House, 1960, p. 10.

show the great truth of history, to draw deeper generalizations from mankind's experience, to disclose convincingly and on the basis of concrete historical material the laws of social development and the heroic traditions of our people and the toiling masses of other countries, and to propagandize the ideas of Soviet patriotism and proletarian internationalism.

Scientific institutions should participate actively in the communist education of the working people and in studying the processes and developments taking place in the U.S.S.R., in the socialist system as a whole, and in the capitalist countries.

A central task of historians of the U.S.S.R. is to combat bourgeois ideology and expose bourgeois reformist and revisionist historiography. Soviet researchers must rebuff hostile ideology in all areas of historical science—above all, those concerned with the history of Soviet society and with recent history. Needless to say, this does not mean lessening the attention paid to current problems or to earlier periods of history. The reactionary forces of the capitalist world, which are falsifying history, must not be permitted to gain control over the study of remote epochs.

The tasks can be accomplished correctly and promptly only on the basis of a clear-cut, well-thought-out system of planning of research work. Research institutes should engage in more purposeful planning of scholarly work, so that primary stress is laid on topical subject matter and on the solution of major problems in the shortest possible time and with a concentration of all creative forces. Planning must be so adjusted as to ensure proper placement of people, establishment of creative groups for the writing of collective research works, skillful combination of work on monographs with the production of works of a generalizing nature, and intelligent use of the powers of experienced scholars and talented young people.

Efficiency in the publication of scholarly works is of decisive importance, for only then can scholarly data become the possession of the masses. Prompt publication of books and articles on timely subjects will ensure active participation by historians in the communist education of the working people and in the struggle with bourgeois ideology.

The task, therefore, is for historians to strive for a further improvement in the quality of research, and the institutes, publishing houses, and journals for comprehensive treatment of the major problems of history and increased publication of scholarly output, for the extensive popularization of historical information, for higher demands on writers, and for the careful selection of manuscripts for publication.

Only if the creative efforts of workers in all the social sciences are well co-ordinated can the production of fundamental generalizing works on urgent topics be ensured. At present work is still not co-ordinated well either among historians, economists, and philosophers on a nationwide scale or among historians, archeologists, ethnographers, and specialists in other allied sciences. Co-ordination is an important function of officials not only of the U.S.S.R. Academy of Sciences but of the U.S.S.R. Ministry of Higher and Specialized Secondary Education.

The scientific councils on specific problems should play a big role in eliminating duplication of research topics and in the struggle for topicality and high standards of scholarly output. Generalizations must be drawn from their experience and their activity critically analyzed. They are called upon to contribute seriously to the co-ordination of scientific work, to make recommendations on specific scientific questions, and to promote the creative exchange of opinions and the collective solution of problems under discussion. Experience has shown that some councils have been holding scientific sessions without proper organization and without the texts of papers and reports prepared in advance. As a result, no active discussion ensues. In such cases the scientific sessions lose a precious feature—the creative exchange of opinions.

Soviet historical science appears before the whole world as an advanced science that is disclosing the objective content of the historical process. Its distinguishing feature is a lofty humanism, for it serves the noble ends of peace and progress. Studying the events of both the recent and the remote past, Soviet historical science is at the same time indissolubly linked by its whole content to the present day; it looks, too, toward the future and serves the cause of communism.

Our scholarship reveals the great force of the people—the makers of history—and the importance of constructive labor in all spheres of material and spiritual production. It rouses in people the noble feelings of love of country, respect for labor, and abhorrence of any exploitation of man by man. Through an analysis of the concrete material of history, Soviet scholars are showing that all roads in our age lead to communism and that capitalism is doomed. Soviet historical science inculcates in the peoples of the U.S.S.R. a feeling of optimism and confidence in their powers, discloses the broad historical perspective of the present day, and makes possible a profound and comprehensive understanding of the present in the light of the entire experience of history and the objective laws of the historical process.

The truthful works of Soviet historians, in particular works on the most recent period, are evoking a most hostile reaction in the camp of imperialism. This means the blows have been hitting the mark.

Now that our country has embarked upon the period of the comprehensive building of communism and the decisive stage of the peaceful competition between socialism and capitalism has been launched, the importance of historical science and its responsibility not only to contemporaries but to future generations have grown as never before. The victory of socialism in the peaceful competition with capitalism is historically determined and inevitable. The aggressive forces of world imperialism are intent on disrupting peaceful competition and unleashing a new world war. The sole possible outcome of a third world war is the complete destruction of the capitalist system. But the peoples of all countries want peace, not war. The mighty camp of socialism, which is the reliable bulwark of peace, is firmly resolved to prevent the outbreak of a new war. The correlation of forces that has now formed is such that war can be ruled out of the life of human society. But if peace is to be safeguarded, resolute and vigorous action is needed. One of the most important tasks facing the historians is to expose the essence of the aggressive policy of imperialism.

Soviet historians, in co-operation with the progressive scholars of all lands, are waging an indefatigable struggle against reaction. The importance of international contacts among historians is especially growing in our time, when the imperialist circles are taking the path of overt acts of provocation and trying to block the victory of the ideas of peaceful competition among countries with different social-economic systems. The Soviet Union is not succumbing to these provocations but is working steadfastly and vigorously for a relaxation of international tension and implementation of a program of general and total disarmament. Nikita Sergeyevich Khrushchev, the great champion of peace, has by his vigorous activity won the ardent gratitude and broadest support of all the world's peoples. He has been tirelessly exposing the machinations of the imperialist warmongers and with singular firmness upholding the dignity of the U.S.S.R. and all the socialist countries. As do all the Soviet people, the historians fully approve and support the firm peaceful policy of the Communist Party and Soviet government.

Wholehearted devotion to its people and to its Communist Party, defense of the interests of ordinary people all over the world, propaganda of the ideas of the equality and friendship of all peoples on earth, and determination in exposing the reactionary ideology of imperialism—these are the principal qualities characterizing Soviet historical science. It sees its functions in serving a better future for all mankind. Communism—the most just society on earth—will be this future. The selfless labor of Soviet historians is directed toward this noble end.

ON THE CHARACTER AND STRUCTURE OF THE JOURNAL
"VOPROSY ISTORII"

The U.S.S.R. Academy of Sciences' History Division recently approved the character and structure of the journal *Voprosy istorii.*

In working out the character and clarifying the structure of the journal, the History Division proceeded from the position that *Voprosy istorii* should be the central general-history journal for Soviet historians.

By its nature the journal is a scholarly publication that elucidates the working out, on the basis of Marxist-Leninist doctrine, of the foremost problems in the work of all institutions engaged in research in the field of history. The principle of integrated treatment of problems of historical science should find broad reflection in *Voprosy istorii*. Toward this end, the journal's work plan must consider the main trends in the work of the institutes and scientific councils that are part of the History Division.

The journal must at the same time take into account the interests and requirements of the broad community of historians; it must rely upon the participation of historians working in the system of the U.S.S.R. Academy of Sciences and in Academy institutes of the Union and autonomous republics, and upon the scientific community of all the country's research and educational institutions.

Voprosy istorii should be a journal of broad specialization that touches on the subjects of greatest importance in various fields of historical science. Moreover, in accordance with the Party Central Committee's decree "On the Tasks of Party Propaganda in Present-Day Conditions," the journal must devote its main attention to a treatment of basic problems in the history of the Communist Party of the Soviet Union and of Soviet society, of the world socialist system, of the world Communist, workers', and general democratic movement, of the present stage in the general crisis of capitalism, of the disintegration of the colonial system of imperialism and of the development of the national-liberation struggle of the peoples of Asia, Africa, and Latin America and to the struggle against bourgeois ideology in its various manifestations; it is also called upon to deal systematically with major problems in the history of the modern period, the Middle Ages, and the ancient world, in archeology and ethnography, in the history of the arts, and in auxiliary historical disciplines.

The materials published in the journal should be creative scholarly works, including surveys based on solid documentation with thorough scientific arguments and theoretical deductions and generalizations that make an unmistakable forward step in the study of the question under investigation and disclose the general and specific laws of the development of history. Only on this basis can *Voprosy istorii* fulfill the tasks stemming from the Party Central Committee's decision of January 9, 1960, and become the party's reliable assistant in the matter of party propaganda and the communist education of the working people.

The journal should strive to publish primarily theoretical articles, articles concerned with major problems, and historiographical articles. Special attention should be given to the preparation and publication of articles dealing with questions of the theory of the historical process. At the same time the journal should find space for articles on specific questions of the historical process. These articles can also deal with problems touched upon to one degree or another in other history journals. The publication of materials with similar subject matter in different journals will prevent the establishment of a monopoly by one or another publication in specific fields of historical science, a monopoly harmful for science. At the same time, however, it is essential that one journal not duplicate another. Toward this end, closer contacts should be arranged between editorial boards in order to ensure co-ordination of their work plans.

Voprosy istorii is called upon for systematic publication of discussion materials on major problems of historical science.

The journal's editorials should outline a concrete work program that directs the efforts of historians toward solution of the most pressing tasks of historical science.

The journal should inform its readers regularly and in detail of the state of all departments of historical science in the U.S.S.R. and of the state of historical science abroad. To this end, it should carry articles dealing with the accomplishments and shortcomings of Soviet historiography and the state of historical science in the U.S.S.R. and the other countries of the socialist camp, and articles analyzing the struggle of the various schools and trends in bourgeois historiography and criticizing its philosophical foundations and the latest bourgeois and revisionist conceptions. It should also publish critical surveys of Soviet and foreign journals, thematic reviews of new books and articles, critiques of individual publications that are of serious interest, and notices about new books and articles.

The journal should also offer detailed information on the work of the bureau of the U.S.S.R. Academy of Sciences' History Division and its institutes and on the research work and scientific life of the country's higher educational establishments and other scientific institutions.

The journal should print materials on the creative life of eminent historians of the U.S.S.R. and other countries of the socialist camp, as well as of progressive historians of the capitalist countries.

Voprosy istorii will succeed in becoming the leading central history journal if it substantially raises the theoretical level of the articles and scientific criticism published in the magazine. While mercilessly exposing the invalidity and reactionary nature of bourgeois and revisionist conceptions, the journal should also serve as a model of principled, comradely, well-reasoned, patient, and conscientious criticism of individual mistakes of Soviet and progressive foreign scholars.

In keeping with the journal's new character, the History Division has made several changes in its structure. *Voprosy istorii* is to consist of four sections: "Articles," "Historical Science in the U.S.S.R.," "Historical Science Abroad," and "Letters and Notes."

The "Articles" constitute the journal's main section, and half of each issue will be allotted to them. Articles on theoretical problems, historiography, the study of source materials and specific historical questions for all periods of history, as well as on archeology, the history of the arts and ethnography, will be published in this section. Articles on key problems may as a rule run to two author's signatures [about 12,000 words]; in individual cases they may be longer. Articles on specific questions should not exceed one and a half author's signatures.

The section "Historical Science in the U.S.S.R." will feature materials on the work of the U.S.S.R. Academy of Sciences' History Division and of the scientific councils, reviews of the most important works of Soviet historians, notes on books, and surveys of Soviet history journals. It is intended that this section will regularly carry a list of the scholarly and popular-scholarly books by Soviet authors that have come out in the month preceding the date of which the issue of *Voprosy istorii* is sent to press, as well as a list of articles published over the same month in the history journals, collections, and scholarly notes of research institutes and higher educational institutions of the U.S.S.R. It is contemplated that this section will also carry information on the publication abroad of works by Soviet historians.

The editors of *Voprosy istorii* are desirous that every reader be able to find in this section information on the books and articles published by Soviet historians, archeologists, and ethnographers in the areas of historical knowledge that interest him. Far more space will be allotted than before to the publication of information on the work of institutes of the History Division, scientific councils, and groups, on scientific conferences and sessions of historians, and on the research work of the history faculties and departments of the Soviet Union's higher educational institutions.

The section "Historical Science Abroad" will inform the reader about the development of historical science in the people's democracies and the work of historians in the capitalist countries through the publication of reviews of the major works by foreign authors, surveys of foreign history journals, and notes on books. A list of articles carried in the history journals of the people's democracies will be regularly published, as well as information on reviews in foreign publications of works by Soviet scholars. Each issue will contain a critical digest of 15 to 20 articles of particular interest to the Soviet historian published in various foreign history journals. This section will also carry information on the work of foreign institutions doing research in the history field and on scholarly congresses and sessions held abroad.

In the section "Letters and Notes" our readers will be able to share their research findings in the fields of history, archeology, and ethnography; to voice their ideas on specific materials published in our journal or on the work of the magazine as a whole, in cases where this can and should be done within the framework of a short article; to take exception, when necessary, to what the author of an article or review has said; and to propose specific measures aimed at improving research in the field of history, the teaching of history, and the dissemination of historical knowledge among the broad masses.

In each issue the editors will publish brief items on the authors whose articles appear in the journal.

Inasmuch as *Voprosy istorii* circulates not only in the U.S.S.R. but abroad as well, the journal will publish résumés of its articles in English. This should make it easier for foreign readers to examine the contents of our journal.

The new character and structure of *Voprosy istorii* take effect beginning with issue No. 8. Discussion of these changes by historians in Moscow and several other of the country's scientific centers has shown that they meet with the approval of our community of historians. The wishes and critical comments that the journal hopes to hear from staff members of research institutes working in the fields of history, archeology, ethnography, and the history of the arts and from instructors in the history faculties and departments of higher educational institutions; and also—and this is extremely important—the broader and more active participation of these scholars in the journal, as authors, will help the editorial board and staff of *Voprosy istorii* to carry on the work of improving the journal.

Illustrative of Khrushchev's emphasis of the role of the masses in the making of history is the first chapter of a new party textbook *Istoriia SSSR* ("History of the U.S.S.R."), prepared by the Higher Party School of the Central Committee and published in 1960. A one-volume presentation of the entire span of Russian history, including the Soviet period, the textbook is intended for use in the party schools. Its Chapter I (omitting the footnotes) is translated below.

39. Chapter I of History of the U.S.S.R.

SUBJECT, METHOD, AND OBJECTIVES OF THE COURSE: FOUNDATIONS OF MARXIST-LENINIST THEORY AND METHODOLOGY OF HISTORY

Subject and Method of History as a Science

The history of the U.S.S.R. is a science studying the process of the origination and development of human society on the territory of our country. The theoretical foundation of Marxist historical science is historical materialism. K. Marx and F. Engels incontrovertibly proved that at the base of the progressive movement of mankind lies the evolution of the means of production, which are determined in each historical period by the nature of the productive forces and the production relationships which correspond to them. History is an objective process whose course is determined in conformity with laws by the succession of socioeconomic formations.

The evolution of the historical process is determined by laws operating beyond the will and wish of men. "Contemporary materialism," Engels pointed out, "sees in history a process of the evolution of mankind, and its task, therefore, is to discover the laws of the movement of this process."

V. I. Lenin developed and rendered concrete the Marxist conception of the subject of history as a science. History, he pointed out in his article "Karl Marx," is a science studying the evolution of society as a "unitary process conforming to laws in all its immense multiplicity and contradictoriness." V. I. Lenin stressed that only Marxism had overcome the limited view of the bourgeois sociologists, who at best dwelled upon "ideas as motives of the historical activity of men, failing to capture the objective law-governed nature of the evolution of the system of social relationships."

These theoretical positions determine the subject of the history of the U.S.S.R. as a science studying the evolution of society on the territory of our multinational country.

Previous historical theories, V. I. Lenin said, "did not embrace . . . the activities of the *masses* of the people," that is, the activity of the popular masses which Marxism-Leninism sees as the decisive force of history and creators of all material and spiritual values.

The concept of the "people" is invested by Marxism-Leninism with a content fundamentally different from that given it by bourgeois and petty-bourgeois sociology, which regards the people as a "supra-class" and "supra-national" category. By the term "people" Marxism-Leninism means first of all the working masses. V. I. Lenin always resolutely fought against concealment of "the failure to understand the class antagonisms within the people" through disquisitions about the people. The class struggle is the motive force of history which, as V. I. Lenin emphasizes, determines "the evolution of society."

The growth of the role of the popular masses in history is an objective law of social evolution. "Together with the growth of the stability of a historical action," K. Marx and F. Engels wrote, "the size of the masses whose product it is will also grow."

The role of the popular masses has especially grown with the appearance of the working class in the arena of history. The class struggle has risen to a new level as it has come to be waged by the proletariat in economic, political, and ideological forms.

The true and total flourishing of the creative role of popular masses comes with the liquidation of the exploiting classes and the factors causing exploitation of man by man. As socialism achieves victory, it brings along the annihilation of the profound contradiction, typical of all antagonistic formations, between the decisive role which belongs to the working masses and their suppressed status in the exploitative societies.

In his report to the Twenty-first Congress of the CPSU, N. S. Khrushchev noted that "if the power falls into the hands of the working class and the socialist system is established, the people are afforded an opportunity to develop the economy of their country at a pace immeasurably faster than under capitalism."

Decisively rejecting the idealistic pseudo-theory of "heroes and mob," Marxism-Leninism discloses the objective laws of the historical activity of the masses. In so doing, Marxism-Leninism attributes a major importance to the subjective factors in the historical process. These factors include the activity of classes and of parties and party leaders, the degree of organization and consciousness of the masses, the activity of states, the role of science in history, etc.

Marxism-Leninism has created the only scientific conception of the role of the individual in history. It considers this role in an organic unity with the interests of classes and parties giving rise to the historical personality.

The study of the subjective factors in all the multiplicity of their concrete manifestations constitutes an important task of Marxist historical science.

Marxism-Leninism has armed historical science not only with a scientific theory but with a truly scientific method of investigation, the method of scientific analysis.

The profound statement of the basic propositions of Marxist methodology is to be found in V. I. Lenin's work "Statistics and Sociology." V. I. Lenin stressed there the fundamental proposition of the Marxist method of scientific investigation, that is, the necessity of "taking not individual facts but the entire totality of the facts relevant to the question under consideration without a single exception . . ."

Of greatest importance in the methodology of history are the laws and categories of materialistic dialectics. "Dialectical logic," V. I. Lenin noted, "requires that the subject is taken in its evolution. . . ." Quantitative changes, Marxism teaches, lead to qualitative changes by leaps, upsets, and revolutions. The internal contradictions which are inherent in the historical phenomena determine the upward development of society from inferior forms to superior.

At a time when the favorite way of bourgeois historians is to seek historical analogies, parallels, or, conversely, historical "contrasts," Marxist methodology demands a strict, concretely historical approach to the evaluation of any phenomena of the past. Thus, as V. I. Lenin repeatedly stressed, only the study of the past from all sides and the analysis and synthesis of all totalities of facts can lead the historians to correct and truly scientific deductions.

At the present time, particularly, bourgeois historiography is dominated by a negation of the possibility of knowing the phenomena of the past and, consequently, a negation of history itself as a science. The negation of the law-governed nature of history is intended to disarm ideologically the masses, prove the "indestructibility" of the capitalist system, and "disprove" the Marxist doctrine of the inescapable revolutionary doom of capitalism.

The entire practice of Marxist historical science proves the possibility of knowing the historical process. The materialistic conception of history, V. I. Lenin said, makes it possible to derive scientific deductions "with the precision of natural history," that is, makes it possible to investigate the past with the precision of objective truth. The criterion of truth, as V. I. Lenin pointed out, is "the practice of all of humanity."

The scientific generalization of the historical experience always makes it possible to see more clearly the tasks and perspectives of the future. For this reason historical science occupies an important place in the revolutionary and remaking practice of the Communist Party and the Soviet state.

A most important principle of Marxist historical science is its party-mindedness. The party-mindedness of historical science is the expression of its class character. Since the great remaking role of the working class led by the Communist Party is determined by the law-governed course of the historical process, the entire previous history of society is in essence an objective preparation for the historical mission of the proletariat. The proletariat is the only class whose basic interests are connected with the truly scientific understanding of history in all the stages of its evolution. The class interests of the proletariat do not need any falsification, modernization, embellishment, or debasement of history. The party-mindedness of Marxist historical science is the supreme expression of scientific objectivity.

Thus, only the Communist Party speaks openly of the party-mindedness of its world outlook. "Materialism," V. I. Lenin wrote, "embodies party-mindedness in itself, so to speak, by demanding that the viewpoint of a definite social group be taken openly and frankly in any assessment of events."

The policy of the Communist Party constitutes the vital foundation of the Soviet social and governmental system. It expresses the fundamental interests of the people. In Soviet conditions, party-mindedness is inseparably tied with people-mindedness. "He who wishes to be with the people," N. S. Khrushchev says, "will always be with the party. He who stands stably on the positions of the party will always be with the people."

In contrast to Marxism, bourgeois ideologists and contemporary revisionists do everything to gloss over and veil the party-mindedness of scholarship. The expression of the party-mindedness of bourgeois historiography is its objectivism and hypocritical disquisitions about "pure," "non-party," and "supra-class" scholarship.

The Communist Party not only speaks openly about the party-mindedness of its world outlook, but also wages incessantly a struggle for it. The militant party-mindedness of Marxist historical science is manifested in its profound study of the life of the working masses and of the great creative role of the people, and in the truly scientific nature of its historical studies and its struggle against bourgeois conceptions and for the purity of Marxist-Leninist theory in historical science.

Study of the History of the Age of Socialism: A Most Important Task of Historical Science

A most important stage in the development of Soviet historical science was [marked by] the Twentieth Congress of the CPSU.

The Congress summoned the Soviet scholars to put a decisive end to dogmatism and pseudo-erudition and to launch a daring and creative development of the current problems of communist construction. In the light of the decisions of the Congress, a most important task of Soviet historians is the deepened and comprehensive study of the history of the Soviet socialist society.

The party has created for Soviet historians all necessary conditions for the successful realization of these tasks. New archival collections have become accessible. Historical literature has been enriched by a considerable number of memoirs, a prominent place among which is occupied by reminiscences about V. I. Lenin. New historical journals, on the history of the U.S.S.R. and on problems of the history of the CPSU, have been started. In the Ukraine, a journal on the history of that region has commenced publication. The work of writing the history of factories and plants has been resumed.

A new testimony of the incessant solicitude of the party for the development of historical science is the decision of the CC of the CPSU concerning the preparation of a scholarly work, the "History of the Great Patriotic

War." The direction of this work is entrusted to a commission headed by Academician P. N. Pospelov.

In guiding the work of Soviet historians toward a daring and creative development of the most important scientific problems, the party also resolutely struggles for party-mindedness in scholarship and for purity of its theory. On March 9, 1956,[27] the CC of the CPSU adopted a decree concerning errors in the journal *Voprosy istorii*. In certain articles published in that journal, the tactics of the party in the period from February to October 1917 were discussed in a profoundly erroneous way. Attempts were made to gloss over the opportunistic tactics of the Mensheviks and the Socialist Revolutionaries in the years of the first Russian revolution. In the discussion articles of the journal it was "proved" that the program of the Bolsheviks did not envisage the nationalization of the land and that after the victory of the October Revolution a process of the peaceful growing of capitalism into socialism took place in our country. The journal subjected to revision such a fundamental proposition of Leninism as the alliance of the working class and the peasantry.

A substantial result of the work of Soviet scholars in implementing the directives of the Twentieth Congress is the publication of synthesizing works such as the "History of the Communist Party of the Soviet Union," prepared by a team of historians (headed by the corresponding member of the U.S.S.R. Academy of Sciences, B. N. Ponomarev), the "History of the U.S.S.R.: Age of Socialism," and the "World History," and a considerable number of studies which appeared in connection with the fortieth anniversary of the Revolution.

The Twenty-first Congress of the CPSU opened wide horizons before Soviet historical science. As it was stressed at the Congress, a most important task of workers in the social sciences in present-day conditions is the study and generalization of the experience of communist construction in our country.

The formal study of history, as the CC of the CPSU and the U.S.S.R. Council of Ministers decree "On Certain Changes in the Teaching of History in the Schools," adopted on October 8, 1959, states, must "aid in developing in the pupils, in a form accessible to them, a scientific understanding of the laws of the history of the evolution of society, form in the pupils the conviction of the inevitability of the doom of capitalism and the victory of communism, and consistently disclose the role of the popular masses as the true makers of history and creators of material and spiritual values, as well as the significance of the individual in history." The great significance of the study of problems of the contemporary stage of commu-

---

[27] A typographical error in the original; the decree was adopted on March 9, 1957.

nist construction and the disclosure of the role of the Communist Party as the leading, directing, and guiding force in Soviet society is stressed in the decree of the CC of the CPSU "On the Tasks of Party Propaganda in Present-Day Conditions."

The study of history is intended to aid in the inculcation of communist devotion to ideas, intolerance toward bourgeois ideology, socialist patriotism, and proletarian internationalism.

Khrushchev's emphasis on the popular masses as the real makers of history did not seem to be merely a return to Leninist orthodoxy. It was related rather to his denunciation of Stalin's policies and practices which began at the Twentieth Congress of the Party and moved into a second phase at the Twenty-second Congress, in 1961.[28] Why did Khrushchev choose to dissociate himself from his erstwhile patron and his ways? Why did he stress the role of the masses as the makers of past, current, and future history? The answers are complex, but Khrushchev's central point seems to have been that the rapport between the communist leadership and the popular masses must be rebuilt and reinforced. He seems to have been convinced that Stalin's rule of terror, liquidations, and self-glorification had resulted in a dangeros alienation of the masses from the regime, manifest during the Second World War in widespread sedition and disloyalty. Having been Stalin's emissary in the area of the greatest sedition, the Ukraine, Khrushchev knew at first hand the result of Stalin's methods and appears to have been determined to make certain that, if another supreme crisis should arise, the popular masses of the Soviet Union would make history for the regime rather than for the enemy.

Stimulated by the denunciation of Stalin and the rehabilitation of many of his victims at the Twentieth Congress of the party, Soviet historians began to seek a more rational assessment of the history of their discipline since 1917. The various problems involved—including the troublesome matters of periodizing the career of Soviet historical scholarship and defining Pokrovsky's role in it—required discussion if the last three volumes of the ambitious history of historical scholarship in Russia, *Ocherki istorii istoricheskoi nauki v SSSR,* devoted to the postrevolutionary period, were to be meaningfully completed. In 1958 the Commission on History of Historical Scholarship in the Academy of Sciences, which is publishing this work, initiated a general discussion on the "periodization of the history of Soviet historical science." Inevitably, the discussion became enmeshed with the problems of assessing the role of Pokrovsky from 1917 to 1932.

Being a good Leninist and a victim of Stalin's intervention in historiography, Pokrovsky seemed destined for a reconsideration after 1956. Cau-

---

[28] For Khrushchev's reports to the congress see the official Soviet translations in *Documents of the 22nd Congress of the CPSU* (2 vols.; New York, 1961). The new party program adopted by the congress is in Jan F. Triska (ed.), *Soviet Communism: Programs and Rules* (San Francisco, 1962).

tious comments that a review was needed began to appear in the ensuing years, but it was not until the Twenty-second Congress, in 1961 that the reassessment was officially launched. Speaking before the congress, the head of the CPSU's Department of Agitation and Propaganda, L. F. Il'ichev, depicted Pokrovsky as an old Bolshevik who had been done wrong by Stalin, and recalled Lenin's appreciation of his work.[29] The result was a spate of articles by party propagandists and historians seeking to "restore Pokrovsky to his rightful place in Soviet historical science." [30] As the dialogue continues, the essence of the reassessment of Pokrovsky and the results of the discussion concerning the periodization of Soviet historical scholarship have been reviewed by the chairman of the Academy commission (now Scientific Council) M. V. Nechkina. Her summation published in *Istoriia SSSR* (No. 2, 1962, pp. 57–78) is translated below in substantial part.

40. M. V. Nechkina, "Summing up the Discussion concerning the Periodization of the History of Soviet Historical Science"

The discussion concerning the periodization of the history of Soviet historical science, the preliminary results of which we are assessing in the atmosphere of the creative upsurge evoked by the decisions of the Twenty-second Congress of the CPSU and by the adoption of the new program of the party, has been exceptionally meaningful and fruitful. This new and almost untouched field of science arouses great interest among historians. This is evident in both the liveliness of the consideration of the historiographic reports and the breadth of the questions taken up by the articles in this journal.

The discussion which has been carried out has not aimed at solving all controversial questions and reaching final decisions. The study of historiography is still in the beginning stage. We are, in effect, planning a housing development rather than moving families into a building already erected. To stimulate investigation, formulate a number of new problems, determine the existing forces, define the immediate tasks, and elucidate the controversial points was a significant objective of the discussion. It is not at all necessary—especially at the beginning of any work—to have a "unified" opinion on all questions; creative work is unthinkable without individual search and hypotheses of all kinds.

---

[29] Translation in *Current Digest of the Soviet Press*, XIV, No. 2 (February 7, 1962), 21–23.

[30] For the more significant articles see *Kommunist*, No. 4, 1962; *Istoriia SSSR*, No. 3, 1962; and *Voprosy istorii*, No. 3, 1962.

The opening of the discussion in the press was preceded by a great deal of collective work of preparation on the part of historians. On two occasions (in 1958 and 1959) reports dealing with the general subject of the periodization of the history of Soviet historical science were discussed in the History Institute of the Academy of Sciences, while special meetings devoted to historiography heard reports on individual periods in the development of Soviet historical science. The reports evoked a lively debate in which took part not only representatives of the old generation whose life ran through all the periods and stages of Soviet science, but also young historians who are studying the road traveled on the basis of a rich documentary heritage and testimonies of the older comrades. In the beginning of 1960 the discussion was carried into the pages of the journal *Istoriia SSSR*. From the materials received, the journal published twelve articles and one extensive communication concerning the collective consideration of the problems by historians in Leningrad. In all, more than fifty historians took part in the discussions in the press and in the History Institute.

All these facts allow us to say that the question is ripe and evokes great interest. Knowledge of the road traveled by a science is necessary for the growth of that science, for the successful discharge of the tasks it faces, and for the systematic and unrelenting struggle with foreign falsifiers. Knowledge of the history of science is also necessary for the development of Soviet culture and for its flowering. The interest in the history of our science speaks in itself of the growth, development, and richness of results achieved; it means recognizing and regarding this as a rising and moving process. Is it premature to begin the work on this little-studied process with the questions of periodization? Is it not better to begin by carefully collecting factual material, taking stock and bringing to light individual smaller aspects, and then taking up the questions of periodization? In my opinion, the answer in this case can certainly be: no, it is not premature. The history of Soviet historical science has its special features; its factual material is generally well known to historians and merged with their biographies. If history is made by people, historical science is made by historians or, more precisely, by people creating historical works. They are aware of a sea of facts concerning the history of their own field where their work has been their life. They have collected an enormous amount of material which, for investigations of other "virgin" areas, would have to be extracted from the recesses of archives. In this case, the material has evolved through their personal life-experiences. This is why it is proper to begin by considering the periodization of the historiographic process. This will immediately bring to light much material, introduce order in it, and facilitate and to a certain extent accelerate the subsequent research in historiography even if the later work introduces corrections in the preliminarily delineated stages. It is already possible to draw the basic outlines of the process.

The discussion was characterized by a diversity of topics. It included both articles which on the whole took up the question of the periodization of Soviet historical science (F. E. Los, E. A. Lutskii, M. E. Naidenov, N. N. Stepanov, A. L. Shapiro, S. O. Shmidt, and others) and papers devoted to individual stages of periodization (G. D. Alekseeva, V. F. Inkin, and A. G. Chernykh—and we should add here S. M. Dubrovskii, S. A. Shelud'ko, and others who delivered reports at the historiographic meetings of the History Institute but have not yet published them).[31] There were also problem studies devoted to the historiography of individual questions: historiography of the Great October Socialist Revolution (E. N. Gorodetskii), the question of training of cadres of Soviet historians in 1921–29 (L. V. Ivanova), and Soviet historiography of Russian imperialism (K. N. Tarnovskii). Besides the basic subject of the periodization of this history of Soviet historical science, the participants in the discussion dealt in passing with numerous other historiographic problems of cardinal significance, such as the question of the function of historical science in Soviet society and its role in the building of communism, the content of historiography as a subject, the problem of the bourgeois heritage in Soviet historical science and the general relation of the latter to the preceding historical development, and the question of the place and role of historiography itself in the body of historical knowledge. One of the most important questions is the question of the world significance of Soviet historical science and its influence in other countries upon the development of progressive ideology of liberation and upon the development of culture. This question was dealt with meaningfully and on the basis of much factual material in an article by R. Sh. Tagirov (Kazan).

The question of the history of historical science among the various peoples of our Fatherland has a special importance. The historiography of the individual peoples merges into the concept of history of Soviet historical science and constitutes an inseparable part of it. The historiographic roads traveled by the individual peoples in their scientific progress are far from identical. They are distinguished by great individuality, which includes individual chronological limits and stages of internal development. The question of this individuality was clearly formulated by F. E. Los in the case of Ukrainian historiography. However, it was still quite inade-

---

[31] Alekseeva, Inkin, and Chernykh addressed in their articles to the initial period of Soviet historiography in the first years of the Soviet regime; the reports of Dubrovskii and Shelud'ko were devoted to the development of Soviet historical science in the decade of 1924–34.

quately aired in the discussion. A negative aspect of the discussion was the small number of participants representing historical work in our republics.

A special and very essential question transcending the framework of periodization—the complex question of M. N. Pokrovsky and his place and role in the development of Soviet historical science—has emerged. Having at first evoked quite significant differences of opinion, this question was then marked by an obvious convergence of views. The following basic positions are hardly controversial. It is clear to all that there is no question of a "return" to Pokrovsky. We have moved far ahead now. No one seeks to suppress the question of Pokrovsky's errors; the knowledge and correction of these errors have been and are an achievement of Soviet historical science. However, Pokrovsky must be restored to the significant place in the history of the development of Marxist historical science which belongs to him. It is necessary to analyze carefully not only the errors but the many positive sides of the products of his work. It is necessary to study him in his development and to know his evolution as a scholar. It is necessary to end the general denigration of the work of this prominent Soviet Marxist scholar which was practiced by the majority of historians in the era of the cult of Stalin's personality. The question of Pokrovsky was treated in those years as the sum total of his errors and nothing else; the positive sides of his work were entirely ignored and the evaluation of Pokrovsky turned into an unqualified black spot. This was basically wrong. Not only the scholarly but the public significance of the work of this great political functionary was unjustifiably defamed. The situation must be corrected. The execution of this major historiographic task is, of course, a matter for serious documentary study in the field of history or historical science and cannot be regarded as settled by a presentation of general formulas. To begin such work of study is a task of the historians of historical science that cannot be postponed.

A topic given special attention in the discussion was the question of the crisis of bourgeois historical science. The crisis had its beginning, as is known, in the pre-Soviet period, but without an analysis of this phenomenon the problem of the failure of bourgeois historical science in the U.S.S.R. cannot be properly posed.

Another special subject—the peculiarity of the historiographic development of individal problems—emerged in the controversies concerning the periodization of the history of Soviet historical science. Because of certain inherent peculiarities, the periodization of their historiography can depart somewhat from the general chronological delimitations. Thus, for the historiography of imperialism as a special scientific problem, Tarnovskii persuasively demonstrated that the chronological limits of its internal development fall on much earlier dates; this especially topical question matured, and evolved faster than others in the circumstances of the acute ideological-political struggle; the internal watershed in its evolution is 1926–28, according to Tarnovskii.

In the discussions in Leningrad, Iu. S. Tokarev raised with justification the question of the special significance of the historiography of the CPSU and the need for studying it.

Let us now move to the subject which was the special concern of the discussion, the periodization of the history of Soviet historical science. The following questions held a central place in the controversy:

> What should be the principle or criterion for the periodization of the history of Soviet historical science?
>
> What are the major fundamental periods through which Soviet historical science has passed?
>
> What more limited internal stages in the development of our science are identifiable within the major periods?

Many participants in the discussion talked about the criterion or principle of periodization which had been proposed. Let me note that "criterion of periodization" and "principle of periodization" are the same thing, namely, the reason for dividing the process of development into individual consecutive phases. Some participants in the discussion have in vain separated one from the other. Furthermore, contradicting his own criticism, one author even cited the specific list of the main aspects of the historiographic process. I had indicated not a "multitude" of these but only four: (1) general conception of the historical process, (2) research problems derived from it, (3) methods of research and new methodological issues, and (4) utilization of new sources.

Since the discussion, this list may be supplemented by a fifth aspect—the new organizational forms of science (collective works, products of scholarly symposia, etc.). The common premises of all these "aspects" are, evidently, the social processes which take place in the country and, of course, the class struggle in the historical segment of time when it exists. This must be emphasized with all clarity. Indeed, what is involved is the study of phenomena of the superstructure growing out of a given social basis, as was pointed out above.

However, can one settle in this case for the formula that the class struggle is the basic and sole criterion of periodization? We are moving from a class society to a classless one, and even at the stage of the victory and consolidation of socialism we lack reasons for operating with the criterion of the appearance of new class enemies confronting historical science within our country. The historical limitation of a criterion which periodizes historical science abstractly and constantly "according to the class struggle" has been well demonstrated by N. V. Efremenkov. It is necessary, of course, to take into account the class struggle in foreign historical science and our struggle with foreign falsifiers. Despite all their importance, however, these phenomena cannot serve as basic criteria in the periodization of Soviet historical science itself.

The basic historiographic facts are the works of historians. They alone create the substance of the evolving science. Through them we in historiography study the acute and tense ideological struggle in the field of science.

In the discussion, another criterion of periodization, appearing to the critics as much more precise, was suggested in opposition to the one proposed.

"Obviously," writes Naidenov, "some principle is needed to show the limits between the various stages in the development of historical science. It is not necessary to collect a multitude of facts characterizing the various aspects of this process. Possibly, it is enough to take only those facts which most graphically characterize the content of the new phenomena rising in the course of the evolution of science. The time of the rise of these phenomena—or, more precisely, the time when these new phenomena begin to play a decisive role in the development of science by concentrating, as in a focus, all of the essential aspects of this process—is the chronological limit which separates the earlier development from the later. Such is the significance, undoubtedly, of the facts of the appearance of new ideological enemies of Soviet historiography."

We cannot agee with the proposed criterion at all. First of all, is this not too much honor to the enemies of Soviet historiography? The appearance of hostile conceptions cannot be the criterion of the development of Soviet science, by the very nature of the matter. Such a criterion leaves in the shadow the phenomena of the development of science as such and its positive conquests. Thinking about the proposed criterion, it is impossible to avoid the question: What is the future of poor historical science? Will it not come to a halt in its development if its ideological enemies—this "powerful force" entailing succession of periods in its growth—disappear?

Such a criterion, as might be expected, turns out to be inapplicable in dividing the internal stages of the second major period of Soviet historiography, which Naidenov agrees to begin with 1934. We ask, then, who was the "new ideological enemy" here? Was it not Pokrovsky? And why so? As Naidenov correctly thinks, however, Pokrovsky "was not hostile to Leninism." What happened to the basic criterion? And why does Pokrovsky appear only at this point? He appeared much earlier. And the main thing is, as we see, that he cannot be treated as an "enemy" of Soviet historiography. All the more so since the critic himself rightly finds his activity progressive and even Marxist.

Let us move further along the periods. The period of the war (1941–45), identified by Naidenov, is set apart, as he himself indicates, not on the basis of the rise of a new ideological enemy of Soviet historiography (fascism, as is known, appeared earlier than 1941), but on the basis of two other features: the nature of the new problems and the considerable expansion of work in the history of the U.S.S.R. and in general history during those years. The years 1946–56 are, again, set apart, not on the basis of the proposed principle, and the rise of new ideological enemies of Soviet historiography is correctly left out of consideration. The proposed general criterion is also left to rest in peace in relation to the subsequent periods. It is difficult to imagine that the critic "did not notice" that he failed to apply his own principle in at least five internal stages in the development of the history of historical science which he identified. What can better demonstrate the bankruptcy of the proposed criterion? Lutskii, Shapiro, and Efremenkov justifiably disputed the proposed criterion and showed that Naidenov himself could not apply it to the factual material of the most recent major periods of the victory of socialism and the advanced construction of communism. The criterion of periodization "according to the class struggle" is inapplicable in the history of the classless society.

It is absolutely evident that the Leninist period in the history of historical science begins with the publication of Lenin's first works in the first half of the 1890's. These works disclosed the most important historical conception of the rise of the new capitalist formation in Russia and the succession of feudalism by capitalism. Without a moment's hesitation, Naidenov disputes the position that Soviet historical science after the Great October Revolution received an already immense Leninist contribution and began its work by leaning on it. He finds that "in reality there was nothing of the kind." Professional historians who stood on Marxist positions were few, and Marxist historians "were not able to begin their work by relying on the Leninist contribution" since they did not know it. The result is a rather dark picture: Lenin was a solitary figure in historical science, and historians began to know his works only years after he died. However, Lenin did write and publish his works for the masses. Regardless of the underground form of publication, his word did reach the masses and did affect them. Why should historians be excluded from this circle? It turns out that the beginning of the Leninist period in the history of historical science came to an abrupt end in 1917. If Naidenov is to be believed, a dark period set in, during which Pokrovsky's conception prevailed and displaced Lenin's conception. Most categorically put, historians adopted not Lenin's conception but Pokrovsky's conception, and thus the Marxist development of historians, according to Naidenov, stood on a rather low level; even the Society of Marxist Historians, whatever qualifications may be made, turned out to be nothing more than "an organization of the school of Pokrovsky." How can this proposition be reconciled with the correct view of the same author that the acute ideological struggle within the party induced cohesion and consolidation of the Marxist forces on the historical front which "found expression in the creation of the All-Russian Society of Marxist Historians"? The cohesion and consolidation of forces did not take place on a Leninist foundation? In my opinion, it is wrong to place the consolidation of Marxist historians solely in the decade of 1924–34. What about the establishment of the Socialist Academy (1918), the Marx-Engels Institute (1920), the Commission for the Study of the History of the Party (1920), the Institute of Red Professors (1921), and even RANION (1923)—did these developments play no part in the consolidation of the Marxist historians? It turns out that only in the second half of the 1930's, many years after Lenin's death, Soviet historians finally became aware of the Leninist heritage and took up Leninist positions. In my opinion, this conception cannot be accepted. It lacks the idea of the uninterrupted development of Marxist-Leninist historical science, the idea of its progressive movement, and the understanding of Lenin's true role in it.

No one denies the complexity and peculiarity of the situation in the first stages of the development of historical science, which comprise roughly one and a half decades after the revolution. The dominance of Pokrovsky's conceptions at that time does not eliminate the question of the development of the Leninist period of the history of historical science which began before the revolution. First of all, Pokrovsky did not alone constitute historical science. Many historians lived and worked without being members of the "school of Pokrovsky" or submitting to the influence of its errors. To reduce the entire Marxist historical science to Pokrovsky would be a peculiar "cult of the personality" of Pokrovsky. However, this is not all. Lenin's conception penetrated into the scholarly consciousness of Pokrovsky himself and of his disciples. Secondly, Pokrovsky's own conception comprised not only errors; he held views which reflected Lenin's generalizations. The illustrations can be multiplied, but what has been said suffices to show that in the years when Pokrovsky held numerous leading posts and made his errors, the Leninist period in the development of historical science continued and expressed itself in numerous facts, partly despite Pokrovsky's influence and partly thanks to him.

The greatest controversies were provoked by the question of setting apart an initial stage in the development of Soviet historical science.[32]

---

[32] I must note that in my first report on periodization (1958) in the History Institute, this stage was not identified and I spoke generally of a first period in the development of historical science from 1917 to the middle of the 1930's (more exactly to 1934–36). However, many historians of Soviet society speaking in the debates convinced me of the appropriateness of identifying an initial take-off stage. [Note in source.]

Several historians (the Academician I. I. Mints, A. P. Kuchkin, and I. B. Berkhin) spoke against establishing such a stage and regarded the first years in the development of historical science after 1917 as a mere continuation of the Leninist period which had started earlier. The establishment of this stage is required by the very fact that Marxist historical science emerged from the revolutionary underground into the sphere of governmental existence, of the university lectern, and of the general publication media and became able to set up the necessary historical organizations and institutions.

Considering all this, it seems that the historians favoring the establishment of the first stage, rather than those opposing it, are right. What remains is only the controversy as to its terminal date.

The suggested limit of the stage—1923—encountered a number of objections. While Lutskii extends the "first years" only up to the 1920's and thus narrows this stage, the majority of those who objected favored its extension; Los, Tarnovskii, and Efremenkov suggest that this stage extended to 1924–25 and coincided with the period of the reconstruction of the national economy in the U.S.S.R.

Although I attach no decisive importance to a difference of one or two years, I think that more arguments were produced in favor of the first suggested date (1923) as the end of the first stage.

Several voices were raised in favor of dividing the years 1924–1934 (or 1936) into two stages. Tarnovskii's proposal to regard the period of 1924–29 as "the beginning of the consolidation of the Leninist conception" should not be accepted; we should remain on the position of the uninterrupted development of the Leninist period in historiography, whose beginning is unanimously placed in the middle of the 1890's.

A characterization of 1928 as a dividing line was also pressed in Naidenov's article, in accordance with his criterion, on the basis of the appearance of right capitulationists and bourgeois nationalists of the type of Iavorskii in the Ukraine and the struggle with them. It should be noted that the struggle with the right capitulationists and bourgeois nationalists began before 1928 and that the proposed criterion is in conflict with the factual material. It is also difficult to regard this year as the "beginning" of the criticism of Pokrovsky's errors on the part of his disciples. The selection of 1928 as a dividing line is not sufficiently persuasive, and there is hardly a reason for dividing internally into two stages the great dynamic decade of 1924–34, saturated with phenomena of significant growth of Marxist thought and acute struggle with the ideological enemies of Marxism-Leninism and marked by the possibility that arose among the historians themselves of overcoming Pokrovsky's errors.

The majority of the participants in the discussion agreed to begin the second major period in the development of Soviet historical science with the decrees of the party and the government in 1934–36 which had a cardinal importance for the development of Soviet historical science. This position rightly causes no controversies. However, a number of historians deem it necessary to expand this dividing strip by including 1937, while others include 1938.

It is true that the basic documentary materials of the watershed stage are comprised in a wider chronological frame than the one first indicated. Let us recall for the readers, especially the younger ones, the sequence of the publication of these historic decrees which played an enormous role in the development of Soviet historical science.

On May 16, 1934, the Sovnarkom and the CC of the VKP (B) issued a decree on the teaching of civic history in the schools of the U.S.S.R. which spoke of the unsatisfactory approach to the teaching of history in the schools and its abstract, schematic nature. Pokrovsky was not yet mentioned here, although the characterization of some of the errors objectively pertained to him and was in somewhat different form repeated in two other documents published much later and directly referring to him. Less than three months after the decree of May 16, 1934, the well-known "Observations Concerning the Outline of the Textbook in the History of the U.S.S.R." were written over the signatures of I. Stalin, A. Zhdanov, and S. Kirov (August 8, 1934), followed by "Observations Concerning the Outline of the Textbook in Modern History" (August 9, 1934) signed by the same authors (in another order of last names). These observations were not published at the time and became known only through copies and word of mouth to a very narrow circle of historians. The decision to publish them was taken by the Sovnarkom and the CC of the VKP (B) one and a half years after they were written (January 26, 1936). On the day following their confirmation (January 27), *Pravda* published an official communication entitled "In the Council of People's Commissars of the U.S.S.R. and the CC of the VKP (B)." It recalled with extensive quotations the decree of May 16, 1934, cited other decrees concerning the teaching of history and history textbooks, and for the first time mentioned Pokrovsky.

On August 22, 1937, *Pravda* published the decision of the jury of the government commission concerning the competition for the best textbook for the third and fourth grades of the secondary schools in U.S.S.R. history, signed "Jury of the Competition." Nothing was said directly in relation to Pokrovsky. The text (composed by a member of the jury, Ia. A. Iakovlev, assisted by V. Bystrianskii, and edited by Stalin) [33] contained

---

[33] In particular, the well-known text concerning the annexation of Georgia to Russia, first published together with the formula of the "lesser evil," was personally added by I. V. Stalin. [Footnote in source.]

important critical observations concerning the textbooks for the primary schools presented in the competition by numerous authors (in all, more than seventy manuscripts were received).

Thus, until 1938 no special decrees of the Sovnarkom and the CC of the VKP (B) devoted to Pokrovsky's errors or mentioning his name were published. The campaign against Pokrovsky was launched on a wide scale in 1937 and 1938 on the basis of the communication entitled "In the Council of People's Commissars of the U.S.S.R. and the CC of the VKP (B)." The name of Pokrovsky and the mention of his errors and of the errors of his "school" first occur in the decree of the CC of the VKP (B) of November 14, 1938, devoted to propagandizing the just published *Short Course of the History of the VKP (B.)* Thus, the expression "the 1934–1936 decrees of the CC of the VKP (B) concerning the errors of Pokrovsky" current among historians should not be regarded as accurate. No decrees of the CC of the VKP (B) concerning Pokrovsky himself were published in those years. What was published was the official communication of 1936 whose meaning spread in practice in a spate of directives concerning the teaching of history and the state of historical science issued in the years indicated.

In this context, of interest is the proposal of N. N. Stepanov to set apart 1934–37 as a special transitional stage. For us the understanding of the meaning of these years is important: great creative work was started, Lenin was assimilated more widely and deeply, and historical science began to rise to another level. However, there developed errors connected with the cult of Stalin's personality. The destruction of many historians in the years of the cult of Stalin's personality wrought irreparable damage upon Soviet historical science. It should be marked as a failure of the discussion that the question of the influence of the cult of Stalin's personality upon historical science was inadequately treated.

The special characteristics indicated also affected the brief stage of the prewar years from the end of 1937 to the beginning of the war in 1941. With all these serious features, it was impossible to unfold one's work in these tense three years which were in effect absorbed in historiography by the work on the textbooks. Monographs were conceived and begun but were hardly ever finished; huge collective works of generalizing nature, often in many volumes, were planned but as a rule remained unrealized—they were dashed to the ground by the insuperable difficulties in the illumination of the Soviet period arising from the cult of Stalin's personality.

Unity of many features ties together in one unified whole the span of almost twenty years (1934–53 if one counts from the first decrees in 1934, or 1937–56 if one takes as a starting date the general historical periodization and as a terminal date the Twentieth Congress of the CPSU). Efremenkov, speaking at the end of the discussion, was right in noting that the separation of 1941–45 and 1946–56 into individual stages does not evoke objections by historians.

Historians of historical science rightly and unanimously date the beginning of the new contemporary period from 1956. Historical science in our time is a participant in the advanced construction of communism. Soviet science is a faithful helper of the party. Its tasks are great and honorable. To demonstrate and study the activity the people as the makers of history, to help the formation of the world outlook of the builders of communist society through the study of the law-governed nature of the historical evolution unalterably proceeding through the changing antagonistic formations to the liquidation of class society and to communism, to raise and maintain on a high level the study of the Soviet period in our history, to study the role of the party as the leader of the laboring masses in the great construction of the classless society, and to show the place and significance of the socialist camp in the world and in the struggle for peace and for the vital interests of the working humanity—these are the foremost tasks of historians.[34]

In the three years following the Twenty-second Congress, Soviet historians labored to translate the theory and decisions adopted by the congress into practice. The new party program adopted by the congress is a blueprint for moving the Russian segment of human society into the final stage of evolution forecast by Marx, the stage of communism, in which a new consciousness and material plenty would produce the classless society of Marx's millennium and obviate the dictatorship of the proletariat, and the true history of man would begin. In the process of moving from socialism into communism, Soviet historians are told, Soviet society faces "three interrelated tasks: the creation of the material and technical base of communism, the formation of communist social relations, and the upbringing of the new man." Historians, as all scientists, have the highest duty to "give the party and the people maximum assistance in successfully solving these great tasks." [35]

Along with these internal tasks, a no less important external task, Soviet historians are told, is the "struggle against the bourgeois falsification of

[34] This most recent stage in the development of Soviet historical science is more fully elucidated in the article of M. V. Nechkina, Iu. A. Poliakov, and L. V. Cherepnin, "Some Questions of the History of Soviet Historiography," *Kommunist*, No. 9, 1961, pp. 58–70 [translated in *Current Digest of the Soviet Press*, XIII, No. 30 (August 23, 1961), 12–18] [Note in source].

[35] See B. N. Ponomarev's report before the national conference on measures to improve the training of historians, *Voprosy istorii*, No. 1, 1963, pp. 3–35, and the *Pravda* summary translated in *Current Digest of the Soviet Press*, XIV, No. 51 (January 16, 1963), 36–37. The full account of the conference (held on December 18–21, 1962) with the recommendations adopted is in *Voprosy istorii*, No. 2, 1963, pp. 3–75.

history." As Engels enjoined, all history written by the bourgeoisie must be rewritten because the bourgeoisie adulterates history, as it adulterates merchandise, in order to make profit and serve its interests. The entire history of mankind must be written *de novo*, Soviet historians are told, in order to show that the past has merely been a prologue to communism and to disclose the pattern of mankind's advance toward communism. The struggle against the bourgeois falsifiers is to be waged in all realms of thought and all areas of investigation, from philosophy of history to the history of Zanzibar.[36] The mobilization for this coming battle of the histories has been massive: new institutes for the history of the peoples of Asia, Africa, and Latin America have been established in the Academy of Sciences, amply staffed and provided with publication outlets, and are required to carry the struggle into these areas where Western historians have traditionally led.[37] Monographic and generalizing works are being produced in significant numbers in these fields, as well as in West European and American history, and in all cases the effort is made to translate the most important of these products into the respective languages and induce their wide dissemination. International meetings such as the Eleventh International Congress of Historians in Stockholm in 1960 and the Twelfth Congress in Vienna in 1965 have been attended with the same purposes in mind.[38] Thus, whatever they may do and wherever they may be, Soviet historians are under the compulsion of their own convictions or of the political power to contribute to the maintenance of the image of the U.S.S.R. as the champion of true humanism and to the production of weapons for the *kto kogo* ("who will bury whom") struggle which Lenin defined in 1921 and which Khrushchev updated in 1962.

[36] *Ibid.*, No. 1, 1962, pp. 3–13; *Istoriia SSSR*, No. 1, 1962, pp. 200–208. For other recent directives see *Current Digest of the Soviet Press* and the quarterly *Soviet Studies in History*.

[37] The recent four-volume survey *Historical Writing on the Peoples of Asia* (London, 1961–62) regrettably fails to show the nature and extent of Soviet work in this field. The essays included are brief and uninformed.

As an illustration of Soviet area studies, much of the Soviet work in Latin American history is comprehensively described and listed in Leo A. Okinshevich and Cecilia J. Gorokhoff, *Latin America in Soviet Writings, 1945–1958* (Washington, 1959), Juan A. Ortega y Medina, *Historiografía Soviética Iberoamericanista (1945–1960)* (Mexico City, 1961), and S. S. Mikhailov, "Izuchenie Latinskoi Ameriki v Sovetskom soiuze" [The Study of Latin America in the Soviet Union], *Voprosy istorii*, No. 4, 1962, pp. 98–106.

[38] For the Soviet participation in the Stockholm congress see *XI⁶ Congrès International des Sciences Historiques: Rapports* (6 vols.; Uppsala, 1960) and Panas Fedenko, "Soviet Views on the 1960 World Historical Congress," *Studies on the Soviet Union*, I (1961), No. 1, 115–124.

BIBLIOGRAPHY

1. In Russian

A. V. Lunacharskii o narodnom obrazovanii [A. V. Lunacharskii on Public Education]. Moscow, 1958.

Astakhov, V. I. *Kurs lektsii po russkoi istoriografii. Chast' vtoraia (Epokha promyshlennogo kapitalizma)* [Lectures on Russian Historiography. Second Part. Age of Industrial Capitalism]. Kharkov, 1962.

Bibliografiia Iaponii [Bibliography of Japan]. Moscow, 1960.

Bibliografiia Indii [Bibliography of India]. Moscow, 1965.

Bibliografiia Iugovostochnoi Azii [Bibliography of Southeast Asia]. Moscow, 1960.

Bibliografiia Kitaia [Bibliography of China]. Moscow, 1960.

Bibliografiia Mongol'skoi Narodnoi Respubliki, Knigi i stat'i na russkom iazyke (1951–1961) [Bibliography of the Mongolian People's Republic: Books and Articles in the Russian Language, 1951–1961]. Moscow, 1963.

Bol'shaia Sovetskaia Entsiklopediia [The Large Soviet Encyclopedia], Vol. 19. Moscow, 1953.

Bushchik, L. P. *Ocherk razvitiia shkol'nogo istoricheskogo obrazovaniia v SSSR* [Survey of the Development of History Education in the Soviet Schools]. Moscow, 1961.

Desiatyi mezhdunarodnyi kongress istorikov v Rime, sentiabr' 1955 g., doklady sovetskoi delegatsii [The Tenth International Congress of Historians in Rome, September, 1955: Reports of the Soviet Delegation]. Moscow, 1956.

Dvadtsat piat let istoricheskoi nauki v SSSR [Twenty-five Years of Historical Science in the U.S.S.R.]. Moscow, 1942.

220 let Akademii Nauk SSSR [220 Years of the Academy of Sciences of the U.S.S.R.]. Moscow, 1945.

Galkin, K. T. *Vysshee obrazovanie i podgotovka nauchnykh kadrov v SSSR* [Higher Education and the Training of Scientific Personnel in the U.S.S.R.]. Moscow, 1958.

Grekov, B. D. *Izbrannye trudy* [Selected Works]. Vol. III, Moscow, 1960.

Istoriia Velikoi Otechestvennoi voiny Sovetskogo Soiuza, 1941–1945 [History of the Great Patriotic War of the Soviet Union, 1941–1945]. 6 vols. Moscow, 1960–65.

Istoriia Kommunisticheskoi partii Sovetskogo Soiuza [History of the Communist Party of the Soviet Union]. Moscow, 1959.

Istoriia Kommunisticheskoi Partii Sovetskogo Soiuza [History of the Communist Party of the Soviet Union]. 2d enlarged ed., 1962.

Istoriia SSSR, Tom I, S drevneishikh vremen do 1861 g. [History of the U.S.S.R., Vol. I, From Earliest Times to 1861]. Moscow, 1956.

Istoriia SSSR [History of the U.S.S.R.]. Moscow, 1960.

Istoriografiia istorii SSSR. S drevneishikh vremen do Velikoi Oktiabr'skoi sotsialisticheskoi revoliutsii [Historiography of the History of the U.S.S.R.: From Earliest Times to the Great October Socialist Revolution]. Moscow, 1961.

Iubileinaia sessiia Akademii Nauk SSSR posviaschchennaia 25-letiiu Velikoi Oktiabr'skoi Sotsialisticheskoi Revoliutsii [Jubilee Session of the Academy of Sciences of the U.S.S.R. Devoted to the 25th Anniversary of the Great October Socialist Revolution]. Moscow, 1943.

Iz Istorii Moskovskogo universiteta (1917–1941) [From the History of Moscow University]. Moscow, 1955.

Kaloeva, I. A. *Sovetskoe slavianovedenie. Literatura o zarubezhnykh slavianskikh stranakh na russkom iazyke* [Soviet Slavic Studies: Literature on the Slavic Countries Abroad in the Russian Language]. 2 vols. (for 1918–1960 and 1961–1962). Moscow, 1963.

Khrestomatiia po marksistsko-leninskoi filosofii [Reader on Marxist-Leninist Philosophy]. 3 vols. Moscow, 1961–62.

Khronologicheskii ukazatel' proizvedenii V. I. Lenina [Chronological Index to the Works of V. I. Lenin]. 3 vols. Moscow, 1959–63.

Kommunisticheskaia partiia sovetskogo soiuza v rezoliutsiiakh i resheniiakh suezdov, konferentsii i plenumov TsK, Chast III, 1930–1954 [The Communist Party of the Soviet Union in Resolutions and Decisions of Congresses, Conferences, and Plenums of the CC, Part III, 1930–1954]. Moscow, 1954.

Korolev, F. F. *Sovetskaia shkola v period sotsialisticheskoi industrializatsii* [The Soviet School in the Period of Socialist Industrialization]. Moscow, 1959.

Kumanev, G. A. *Velikaia Otechestvennaia voina Sovetskogo Soiuza (1941–1945 gg.). Bibliografiia sovetskoi istoricheskoi literatury za 1946–1959 gg.* [The Great Patriotic War of the Soviet Union, 1941–1945: Bibliography of the Soviet Historical Literature, 1946–1959]. Moscow, 1960.

Lenin o narodnom obrazovanii: statii i rechi [Lenin on Public Education: Articles and Speeches]. Moscow, 1957.

Lenin, V. I. *Sobranie Sochinenii* [Collected Works]. Vol. XVI. Moscow, n.d.

Levin, L. *Bibliografiia bibliografii proizvedenii K. Marksa, F. Engel'sa, V. I. Lenina* [Bibliography of Bibliographies of the Works of K. Marx, F. Engels, and V. I. Lenin]. Moscow, 1961.

Materialy vsesoiuznogo soveshchaniia zaveduiushchikh kafedrami obshchestvennykh nauk [Materials of the All-Union Conference of Holders of Chairs in the Social Sciences]. Moscow, 1958.

Mongol'skaia Narodnaia Respublika: Bibliografiia knizhnoi i zhurnal'noi literatury na russkom iazyke. 1935–1950 [Mongolian People's Republic: Bibliography of books and articles in the Russian language, 1935–1950]. Moscow, 1953.

Ocherki istorii istoricheskoi nauki v SSSR [Survey of the History of

Historical Science in the U.S.S.R.]. Moscow, 1955— 3 vols. to date.
Osnovy kommunisticheskogo vospitaniia [Foundations of Communist Education]. Moscow, 1960.
Osnovy marksistskoi filosofii [Fundamentals of Marxist Philosophy]. Moscow, 1959.
Osnovy Marksizma-Leninizma [Fundamentals of Marxism-Leninism]. Moscow, 1960.
Pavliuchenko, A. M. *V. I. Lenin ob ob'ektivnom kharaktere zakonomernostei obschchestvennogo razvitiia* [V. I. Lenin on the Objective Nature of the Laws of Social Development]. Minsk, 1960.
Pedagogicheskaia Entsiklopediia [Pedagogical Encyclopedia]. Vol. I. Moscow, 1964.
Peshtich, S. L. *Russkaia istoriografiia XVIII veka. Chast' I* [Russian Historiography of the 18th Century, Part I]. Leningrad, 1961.
Pokrovsky, M. N. *Istoricheskaia nauka i bor'ba klassov* [Historical Science and the Class Struggle]. 2 vols. Moscow, 1933.
Polevoi, Iu. Z. *Zarozhdenie marksizma v Rossii* [The Origin of Marxism in Russia]. Moscow, 1959.
Protiv burzhuaznoi fal'sifikatsii istorii sovetskogo obshchestva [Against the Bourgeois Falsification of the History of Soviet Society]. Moscow, 1960.
Rubinshtein, N. L. *Russkaia istoriografiia* [Russian Historiography]. Moscow, 1941.
Sbornik rukovodiashchikh materialov o shkole [Collection of Guiding Materials concerning the Schools]. Moscow, 1952.
Shapiro, A. L. *Russkaia istoriografiia v period imperializma* [Russian Historiography in the Age of Imperialism]. Leningrad, 1962.
Sokolov, N. P. *Sorok let sovetskogo vizantinovedeniia* [Forty Years of Soviet Byzantine Studies]. Gorky, 1959.
Sovetskaia istoricheskaia nauka ot XX k XXII s'ezdu KPSS. Istoriia SSSR [Soviet Historical Science from the 20th to the 22nd Congress of the CPSU: History of the U.S.S.R.]. Moscow, 1962.
Sovetskaia istoricheskaia nauka ot XX k XXII s'ezdu KPSS. Istoriia zapadnoi Evropy i Ameriki [Soviet Historical Science from the 20th to the 22nd Congress of the CPSU: History of Western Europe and America]. Moscow, 1963.
Spravochnik partiinogo rabotnika [Handbook of the Party Worker]. Moscow, 1957.
Udal'tsova, Z. V. *Osnovnye problemy vizantinovedenii v sovetskoi istoricheskoi nauke* [Basic Problems of Byzantine Studies in Soviet Historical Science]. Moscow, 1955.
Velikaia Otechestvennaia voina Sovetskogo Soiuza (1941–1945 gg.). Rekomendatel'nyi ukazatel' literatury [The Great Patriotic War of the Soviet Union, 1941–1945: Bibliography of Recommended Literature]. Moscow, 1965.
Voprosy ideologicheskoi raboty, sbornik vazhneishikh reshenii KPSS (1954–1961 goda) [Problems of Ideological Work: Collection of the

Most Important Decisions of the CPSU, 1954–1961]. Moscow, 1961.
Zaidel, G., and Tsvibak, M. *Klassovyi vrag na istoricheskom fronte: Tarle i Platonov i ikh shkoly* [The Class Enemy on the Historical Front: Tarle and Platonov and Their Schools]. Moscow, 1931.

*   *   *

Istoricheskii zhurnal [Historical Journal], No. 3, 1945.
Istorik-Marksist [Marxist Historian], No. 1, 1926; No. 9, 1928; No. 1–2, 1932.
Kratkie soobshcheniia Instituta Slavianovedeniia [Brief Communications of the Institute of Slavic Studies], Vol. 12, 1954.
Mikhailov, S. S. "Izuchenie Latinskoi Ameriki v Sovetskom Soiuze" [The Study of Latin America in the Soviet Union], *Voprosy Istorii,* No. 4, 1962.
Nechkina, M. V. "O periodizatsii istorii sovetskoi istoricheskoi nauki" [Concerning the Periodization of the History of Soviet Historical Science], *Istoriia SSSR* [History of the U.S.S.R.], No. 1, 1960.
Nechkina, M., Poliakov, Iu., and Cherepnin, L. "Nekotorye voprosy istorii sovetskoi istoricheskoi nauki" [Certain Problems of the History of Soviet Historical Science], *Kommunist* [Communist], No. 9, 1961.
Picheta, V. "Institut slavianovedeniia Akademii nauk SSSR i ego zadachi" [The Institute of Slavic Studies of the Academy of Sciences of the U.S.S.R. and Its Tasks], *Voprosy Istorii* [Problems of History], No. 5, 1947.
Proletarskaia revoliutsiia [Proletarian Revolution], November 1931.
Uchitel'skaia gazeta [Teachers' Gazette], November 3, 1959.
Vestnik Akademii Nauk SSSR [Bulletin of the Academy of Sciences of the U.S.S.R.], No. 10, 1948.
Vestnik Sotsialisticheskoi Akademii [Bulletin of the Socialist Academy], Vol. IV, 1923.
Voprosy istorii [Problems of History], No. 4, 1951; No. 9, 1952.

2. In Western languages

Administration of Teaching in Social Sciences in the USSR. Ann Arbor, Mich., 1960.
The Anti-Stalin Campaign and International Communism: A Selection of Documents Edited by the Russian Institute, Columbia University. New York, 1956.
Baron, Samuel H. *Plekhanov—The Father of Russian Marxism.* Stanford, Calif., 1963.
Billington, James H. *Mikhailovsky and Russian Populism.* Oxford, 1958.
Black, C. E. (ed.). *Rewriting Russian History.* 2d. rev. ed. New York, 1962.

Deutscher, Isaac. *The Prophet Armed, The Prophet Unarmed,* and *The Prophet Outcast.* 3 vols. London and New York, 1954–63.

DeWitt, Nicholas. *Education and Professional Employment in the USSR.* Washington, 1961.

Documents of the 22nd Congress of the CPSU. 2 vols. New York, 1961.

XI-e Congrès International des Sciences Historiques: Rapports. 6 vols. Uppsala, 1960.

Fedenko, Panas. *Khrushchev's New History of the Soviet Communist Party.* Munich, 1963.

Federn, Karl. *The Materialist Conception of History.* London, 1939.

Gallagher, Matthew P. *The Soviet History of World War II: Myths, Memories and Realities.* New York, 1963.

Gorokhoff, Boris I. *Publishing in the USSR.* Bloomington, Ind., 1959.

Historical Writing on the Peoples of Asia. 4 vols. London and New York, 1961–62.

Hook, Sidney. *The Hero in History.* Boston, 1957.

Joseph Stalin: A Political Biography. New York, 1949.

Joseph Stalin: A Short Biography. New York, 1941.

Kellen, Konrad. *Khrushchev: A Political Portrait.* New York, 1960.

Lenin, V. I. *The Three Sources and Three Component Parts of Marxism.* Moscow, n.d.

MacGregor-Hastie, Roy. *The Man from Nowhere.* New York, 1961.

Matlock, Jack F. *An Index to the Collected Works of J. V. Stalin.* Washington, 1955.

Marx, Karl, and Engels, Friedrich. *The German Ideology,* ed. R. Pascal. New York, 1960.

——, ——. *Selected Works.* 2 vols. Moscow, 1952.

Maxwell, Robert (ed.). *Information USSR: An Authoritative Encyclopedia about the Union of Soviet Socialist Republics.* New York, 1962.

Mazour, Anatole. G. *Modern Russian Historiography.* Princeton, N.J., 1958.

Okinshevich, Leo A. *Latin America in Soviet Writings: A Bibliography* [1917–1964]. 2 vols. Baltimore, 1966.

Ortega y Medina, Juan A. *Historiografía Sovietica Iberoamericanista (1945–1960).* Mexico City, 1961.

Paloczi-Horvath, George. *Khrushchev: The Making of a Dictator.* Boston, 1960.

Pethybridge, Roger. *A Key to Soviet Politics: The Crisis of the Anti-Party Group.* New York, 1962.

Pistrak, Lazar. *The Grand Tactician: Khrushchev's Rise to Power.* New York, 1961.

Plamenatz, John. *German Marxism and Russian Communism.* London, 1954.

Plekhanov, Georgi. *The Development of the Monist View of History.* Moscow, 1956.

——. *Essays in Historical Materialism.* New York, 1940.

Pokrovsky, M. N. *Brief History of Russia.* 2 vols. New York, 1933.
————. *History of Russia from the Earliest Times to the Rise of Commercial Capitalism.* New York, 1931.
Rosen, Seymour M. *Higher Education in the USSR.* Washington, 1963.
————. *Significant Aspects of Soviet Education.* U.S. Office of Education Bulletin 1965, No. 15. Washington, 1965.
Rubel, Maximilien. *Bibliographie des œuvres de Karl Marx: avec en appendice un répertoire des œuvres de Friedrich Engels.* Paris: Rivière, 1956; supplement, 1960.
Schapiro, Leonard. *The Communist Party of the Soviet Union.* New York, 1960.
Selsam, Howard. *What Is Philosophy? A Marxist Introduction.* New York, 1962.
Shteppa, Konstantin F. *Russian Historians and the Soviet State.* New Brunswick, N.J., 1962.
Stalin, J. *Works,* Vol. VI. Moscow, 1953.
Triska, Jan F. (ed.). *Soviet Communism: Programs and Rules.* San Francisco, 1962.
Trotsky, Leon. *The History of The Russian Revolution.* Ann Arbor, Mich., 1957.
Voznesensky, N. A. *The Economy of the USSR during World War II.* Washington, 1948.
Vucinich, Alexander. *The Soviet Academy of Sciences.* Stanford, Calif., 1956.
Wetter, Gustav. *Dialectical Materialism.* London, 1958.
Whitney, Thomas P. *The Communist Blueprint for the Future.* New York, 1962.
Wolfe, Bertram D. *Khrushchev and Stalin's Ghost.* New York, 1957.
Zinoviev, M. A. *Soviet Methods of Teaching History.* Ann Arbor, Mich., 1952.

*   *   *

Current Digest of the Soviet Press, IX, No. 28 (August 21, 1957); XI, No. 37 (October 14, 1959); XII, No. 40 (November 2, 1960).
Dallin, Alexander. "Recent Soviet Historiography," in *Russia under Khrushchev,* ed. Abraham Brumberg (New York, 1962).
Daniels, Robert V. "Fate and Will in the Marxian Philosophy of History," *Journal of the History of Ideas,* XXI, No. 4 (October–December 1960).
Dautry, Jean. "Plekhanov et la theorie de l'histoire," *La Pensée,* No. 77 (January–February 1958).
Erickson, Ann K. "E. V. Tarle: The Career of a Historian under the Soviet Regime," *American Slavic and East European Review,* XIX, No. 2 (April 1960).
Fainsod, Merle. "Soviet Historians, or The Lesson of Burdzhalov," *Encounter,* No. 102 (March 1962).

Fedenko, Panas. "Soviet Views on the 1960 World Historical Congress," *Studies on the Soviet Union,* I, No. 1 (1961).

Hall, Thomas R. "Mikhail Nikolayevich Pokrovsky (1868–1932)," in *Some Historians of Modern Europe,* ed. Bernadotte E. Schmitt (Chicago, 1942).

Heitman, Sidney. "Between Lenin and Stalin: Nikolai Bukharin," in *Revisionism: Essays on the History of Marxist Ideas,* ed. Leopold Labedz (New York, 1962).

Hillgruber, A., and Jacobsen, H. A. "Sowjet-Kommunistische Kriegsgeschichtsschreibung 1945–1961," *Wehrwissenschaftliche Rundschau,* XI, No. 10 (1961).

Hösch, Edgar. "Der historiographische Umbruch in Russland: Tarle als Beispiel," *Saeculum,* XI, No. 3 (1960).

McNeal, Robert H. "Trotsky's Interpretation of Stalin," *Canadian Slavonic Papers,* Vol. V (1961).

Matsulenko, V. and Sekistov, V. "Historiographie soviétique de la deuxième guerre mondiale," *Revue d'histoire de la deuxième guerre mondiale,* Vol. XI (1961).

Medlin, William K. "The Teaching of History in Soviet Schools: A Study in Methods," in *The Politics of Soviet Education,* ed. George Z. F. Bereday and Jaan Pennar (New York, 1960).

Mosely, Philip E. "Khrushchev's Party Congress," *Foreign Affairs,* January 1962.

Piroschkow, Vera. "Sowjetische Geschichtswissenschaft im inneren Widerstreit (1956–1959)," *Saeculum,* XI, No. 1–2 (1960).

Presniakov, A. "Historical Research in Russia during the Revolutionary Crisis," *American Historical Review,* XXVIII, No. 2 (January 1923).

Pundeff, Marin. "History in Soviet Education since 1958," *Harvard Educational Review,* XXXII, No. 1 (Winter 1962).

———. "Sowjetische Forschungsarbeiten zur neuzeitlichen Balkan-Geschichte," *Saeculum,* XV, No. 3 (1964).

Stadtmüller, Georg. "Die neue sowjetische Weltgeschichte," *Saeculum,* XI, No. 4 (1960).

Swearingen, Rodger, "Asian Studies in the Soviet Union," *Journal of Asian Studies,* XVII, No. 3 (May 1958).

Tillett, Lowell R. "Shamil and Muridism in Recent Soviet Historiography," *American Slavic and East European Review,* XX, No. 2 (April 1961).

Wolfe, Bertram D. "Trotsky as Historian," *Slavic Review,* XX, No. 3 (October 1961).

SUGGESTIONS FOR FURTHER READING

There is no comprehensive Western, or for that matter Soviet, bibliography of the history of historical scholarship in the U.S.S.R. The reader is reminded that the basic works cited in the text contain useful bibliographies. In addition, the searching student should examine *Istoriia istoricheskoi nauki v SSSR; dooktiabr' skii period. Bibliografiia,* edited by M. V. Nechkina and others (Moscow, 1965), which lists writings to 1963 on the subject before 1917 and is due to be supplemented by a bibliography for developments in the 1917–66 period; Vol. II of *Guide to Russian Reference Books,* by Karol Maichel (Stanford, Calif., 1964); and *Basic Russian Publications* and *Russia and the Soviet Union,* both edited by Paul L. Horecky (Chicago, 1962, 1965).

1. In Western languages

Acton, H. B. *The Illusion of the Epoch: Marxism-Leninism as a Philosophical Creed.* Boston, 1957.

Achminow, Herman. "Mythos und Wahrheit in der Geschichtslehre von Marx," *Saeculum,* XI, No. 3 (1960), 266–294.

"All-Union Conference of Historians," *Current Digest of the Soviet Press,* XIV, No. 51, January 16, 1963.

Anweiler, Oskar, and Meyer, Klaus. *Die sowjetische Bildungspolitik seit 1917: Dokumente und Texte.* Heidelberg, 1961.

Avrich, Paul H. "The 'Short Course' and Soviet Historiography," *Political Science Quarterly,* December 1960, 539–553.

Bober, M. M. *Karl Marx's Interpretation of History.* Cambridge, Mass., 1948.

Böss, Otto. "Die Geschichte der sowjetischen Historiographie; zur Diskussion ihrer Periodisierung (1960–1962)," *Jahrbücher für Geschichte Osteuropas,* XI, No. 4 (December 1963), 561–592.

Carew Hunt, R. N. *The Theory and Practice of Communism.* London, 1957.

Chard, Chester S. "Soviet Scholarship on the Pre-History of Asiatic Russia," *Slavic Review,* XXII, No. 3 (September 1963), 538–546.

Crankshaw, Edward. *Khrushchev: A Career.* New York, 1966.

Donnert, E. "Pokrovskijs Stellung in der sowjetischen Geschichtswissenschaft," *Jahrbuch für Geschichte der UdSSR und der volksdemokratischen Länder Europas,* VII (1963), 35–60.

Glezerman, G. *The Laws of Social Development.* Moscow, 1960.

Gregor, A. James. *A Survey of Marxism: Problems in Philosophy and the Theory of History.* New York, 1965.

Grzybowski, K. "History in the Remaking," *Problems of Communism,* XI, No. 2 (March-April 1962), 63–67.

Guins, George. "Soviet Historians and the Peasant Reform of 1861," *Studies on the Soviet Union,* II, No. 3 (1962), 107–112.

"Historians Discuss Their Tasks after the Congress," *Current Digest of the Soviet Press*, XIV, No. 10, April 4, 1962.

Hösch, Edgar. *Evgenij Viktorovic Tarle (1875–1955) und seine Stellung in der sowjetischen Geschichtswissenschaft*. Wiesbaden, 1964.

Horak, Stephan M. "Ukrainian Historiography, 1953–1963," *Slavic Review*, June 1965, pp. 258–272.

Huttenbach, Henry R. "The Education of a History Major at Moscow State University," *AHA Newsletter*, June 1966, pp. 31–37.

Jablonowski, Horst. "Die Geschichte Asiens in der Sovethistoriographie nach dem Zweiten Weltkrieg," *Saeculum*, X, No. 2–3 (1957), 298–311.

Jackson, George D. "Western Studies of International Socialism as Seen by a Soviet Historian," *Slavic Review*, September 1963, pp. 530–537.

Jacobs, Wilbur R., and Masson, Edmund E. "History and Propaganda: Soviet Image of the American Past," *Mid-America*, XLVI, No. 2, April 1964.

Keep, John (ed.). *Contemporary History in the Soviet Mirror*. New York, 1963.

"Keeping Tabs on Western Historians of Russia," *Current Digest of the Soviet Press*, XIV, No. 19, June 6, 1962.

Kennan, George F. "Soviet Historiography and America's Role in the Intervention," *American Historical Review*, LXV, No. 2 (January 1960), 302–322.

Kon, I. S. *Die Geschichtsphilosophie des 20. Jahrhunderts*. 2 vols. Berlin, 1964.

McNeal, R. H. "Khrushchev and Clio," *International Journal*, XV, No. 1 (Winter 1959), 49–58.

Marko, Kurt. "Die Sowjetrussische Historiographie der Gegenwart und ihr Verhältnis zu Europa," *Moderne Welt*, V, No. 2 (1964), 209–216.

———. *Sowjethistoriker zwischen Ideologie und Wissenschaft*. Cologne, 1964.

Mehnert, Klaus. *Stalin versus Marx: The Stalinist Historical Doctrine*. New York, 1952.

Ostrovitjanov, K. V. *Social Sciences in the U.S.S.R.* The Hague, 1965.

"Outline of a Planned 11-Volume History of USSR," *Current Digest of the Soviet Press*, XIII, No. 12, April 19, 1961.

Philipp, Werner. "Wandlungen der Sowjethistoriographie," in *Marxismus-Leninismus: Geschichte und Gestalt* (Berlin, 1962), pp. 69–88.

Plekhanov, Georges, *Introduction à l'histoire sociale de la Russie*. Paris, 1926.

Pokrovsky, M. N. *Page d'histoire; la methode du matérialisme historique appliquée à quelques problèmes historiques concrets*. Paris, 1929.

"Pravda Outlines Tasks of Multivolume Party History," *Current Digest of the Soviet Press*, XIV, No. 25, July 18, 1962.

Riha, Thomas. "Soviet Historians Today," *Russian Review*, July 1964, pp. 259–264.

Rogger, Hans. "Politics, Ideology, and History in the USSR: The Search

for Coexistence," *Soviet Studies,* XVI, No. 3 (January 1965), 253–275.
Stökl, G. "Der historische Materialismus und die Geschichtswissenschaft in der Sowjetunion," *Österreichische Osthefte,* I, No. 2 (1959).
Straube, F., "Der Aufschwung der sowjetischen Geschichtswissenschaft nach dem XX. Parteitag der KPdSU," *Jahrbuch für Geschichte der UdSSR und der volksdemokratischen Länder Europas,* VIII (1964), 361–373.
Thornton, Thomas Perry (ed.). *The Third World in Soviet Perspective: Studies by Soviet Writers on the Developing Areas.* Princeton, N.J., 1964.
Tillett, Lowell R. "Soviet Second Thoughts on Tsarist Colonialism," *Foreign Affairs,* January 1964, pp. 309–319.
Vucinich, A. "Soviet Theory of Social Development in the Early Middle Ages," *Speculum,* XXVI (1951), 243–254.
Wolfe, Bertram D. "Operation Rewrite: The Agony of Soviet Historians," *Foreign Affairs,* October 1952.
Yakobson, Sergius "Conflict and Change in Soviet Historical Scholarship," *Bucknell Review,* December, 1965.

2. In Russian

Asmus, V. F. *Marks i burzhuaznyi istorizm.* Moscow, 1933.
Astakhov, V. I. *Kurs lektsii po russkoi istoriografii. Chast'pervaia (do serediny XIX veka).* Kharkov, 1959.
———. *Kurs lektsii po russkoi istoriografii (do kontsa XIX v.).* Kharkov, 1965.
Beskrovnyi, L. G. *Ocherki voennoi istoriografii Rossii.* Moscow, 1962.
Bibliografiia Afganistana. Moscow, 1965.
Bibliografiia Afriki. Moscow, 1964.
Cherniak, E. B. *Burzhuaznaia istoriografiia rabochego dvizheniia.* Moscow, 1960.
———. *Istoriografiia protiv istorii (Kritika reaktsionnoi istoriografii epokhi krusheniia kapitalizma.* Moscow, 1962.
Dement'ev, I. P. *Amerikanskaia istoriografiia grazhdanskoi voiny v SShA (1861–1865).* Moscow, 1963.
Diligenskii, G. G. "Marksistsko-leninskaia teoriia i konkretnoistoricheskoe issledovanie," *Voprosy istorii,* No. 3, 1963, pp. 88–100.
Gavrilichev, V. A. *Velikaia Frantsuzkaia burzhuaznaia revoliutsiia kontsa XVIII veka v sovetskoi istoriografii (1917–1960 gg.).* Kazan, 1961.
Grushin, B. A. *Ocherki logiki istoricheskogo issledovaniia.* Moscow, 1961. Review essay by Marin Pundeff, *History and Theory,* IV, No. 1 (1964), pp. 72–78.
Illarionov, V. T. *Vvedenie v istoriografiiu drevneishei istorii.* Gorki, 1960.
Il'ichev, L. F. *Obshchestvennye nauki i kommunizm.* Moscow, 1963.
Istoriia i sotsiologiia. Moscow, 1964.
Kon, I. S. *Filosofskii idealizm i krizis burzhuaznoi istoricheskoi mysli.*

Moscow, 1959. Review by Marin Pundeff, *American Historical Review,* October 1961, pp. 175–176. See above, in Western languages section, for revised German edition.

Kosminskii, E. A. *Istoriografiia srednikh vekov.* Moscow, 1963.

Kritika burzhuaznykh kontseptsii istorii Rossii perioda feodalizma. Moscow, 1962.

Kritika noveishei burzhuaznoi istoriografii. Moscow, 1961.

Krivoguz, I. M., *et al.* "Osnovnye napravleniia sovetskoi istoriografii novogo vremeni," *Voprosy istorii,* No. 6, 1965, pp. 87–104.

Kunina, A. E. "Metodologicheskie poiski v amerikanskoi burzhuaznoi istoriografii (po stranitsam amerikanskikh zhurnalov)," *Novaia i noveishaia istoriia,* No. 2, 1964, pp. 132–137.

Lavrovskii, V. M. "K voprosu o predmete i metode istorii kak nauki," *Voprosy istorii,* No. 4, 1966, pp. 72–77.

Metodologicheskie i istoriograficheskie voprosy istoricheskoi nauki. Tomsk, 1964.

Musaelian, Zh. S. *Bibliografiia po kurdovedeniiu.* Moscow, 1963.

Naidenov, M. E. "O leninskom etape v istoricheskoi nauke," *Voprosy istorii,* No. 2, 1966, pp. 21–37.

Nechkina, M. V. (ed.). *Istoriia i Istoriki: Istoriografiia istorii SSSR.* Moscow, 1965.

Nekotorye problemy istorii sovetskogo obshchestva (istoriografiia). Moscow, 1964.

"O metodologicheskikh voprosakh istoricheskoi nauki," *Voprosy istorii,* No. 3, 1964, pp. 3–68.

Peshtich, S. L. *Russkaia istoriografiia XVIII veka. Chast' II.* Leningrad, 1965.

Poliakov, Iu. A. "Kommunisticheskoe vospitanie i istoriia," *Voprosy istorii,* No. 7, 1963, pp. 3–18.

Pripisnov, V. I. "O sootnoshenii istoricheskogo materializma i istoricheskoi nauki," *Voprosy filosofii,* No. 1, 1961, pp. 103–113.

Protiv fal'sifikatsii istorii. Moscow, 1959.

Protiv fal'sifikatsii istorii KPSS. Moscow, 1964.

Protiv fal'sifikatorov istorii Vtoroi mirovoi voiny. Moscow, 1959.

Protiv fal'sifikatsii istorii Vtoroi mirovoi voiny. Moscow, 1964.

Rol' narodnykh mass i lichnosti v istorii. Moscow, 1957.

Sherbatov, G. *Arabistika v SSSR.* Moscow, 1959.

Sherman, I. L. *Sovetskaia istoriografiia grazhdanskoi voiny v SSSR (1920–1931).* Kharkov, 1964.

Sherstobitov, V. P., and Vinnik, D. F. "Razvitie istoricheskoi nauki v Sovetskoi Kirgizii (1917–1964 gg.)," *Voprosy istorii,* No. 2, 1965, pp. 3–26.

Shusharin, V. P. *Sovremennaia burzhuaznaia istoriografiia drevnei Rusi.* Moscow, 1964. Review by Jesse D. Clarkson, *American Historical Review,* April 1965, pp. 842–843.

Shvedova, O. I. *Istoriki SSSR. Ukazatel' pechatnykh spiskov ikh trudov.* Moscow, 1941.

Sidorov, A. L. "Nekotorye razmyshleniia o trude i opyte istorika," *Istoriia SSSR,* No. 3, 1964, pp. 118–138.

Smirnov, N. A. *Ocherki istorii izucheniia Islama v SSSR.* Moscow, 1954, analyzed in Ann K. S. Lambton, *Islam and Russia* (London, 1956).

Sokolov, O. D. "V. I. Lenin i formirovanie bol'shevistskikh vzgliadov M. N. Pokrovskogo," *Voprosy istorii,* No. 8, 1963, pp. 30–41.

Stroitel'stvo kommunizma i obshchestvennye nauki. Moscow, 1962.

Tarnovskii, K. N. *Sovetskaia istoriografiia rossiiskogo imperializma.* Moscow, 1964.

Tursunbaev, A. B. *Protiv burzhuaznoi fal'sifikatsii istorii Kazakhstana.* Alma Ata, 1963.

Ustinov, V. A. *Primenenie vychislitel'nykh mashin v istoricheskoi nauke.* Moscow, 1964.

Vainshtein, O. L. "Stanovlenie sovetskoi istoricheskoi nauki (20-e gody)," *Voprosy istorii,* No. 7, 1966, pp. 32–47.

———. *Zapadnoevropeiskaia srednevekovaia istoriografiia.* Moscow, 1964.

"V. I. Lenin o partiinosti v istoricheskoi nauke," *Voprosy istorii,* No. 4, 1958, pp. 3–22.

Vinogradov, K. B. *Burzhuaznaia istoriografiia pervoi mirovoi voiny.* Moscow, 1962.

Zhukov, E. M. (ed.). *Vsesoiuznoe soveshchanie o merakh uluchsheniia podgotovki nauchno-pedagogicheskikh kadrov po istoricheskim naukam, 18–21 dekabria 1962 g.* Moscow, 1964.

"Zhurnal i istoricheskaia nauka," *Voprosy istorii,* No. 1, 1966, pp. 3–14.

INDEX OF NAMES

Monetary Policy in the United States

CONSULTING EDITOR

Richard Thorn
University of Pittsburgh

Monetary Policy

in the

United States

T H O M A S   M A Y E R

University of California at Davis

RANDOM HOUSE

New York

To Dorothy

Preface

There are several ways in which one can approach monetary policy. One is to emphasize history, to discuss the origin and evolution of our present central bank and the actions it has taken in various years. The other is to focus on an evaluation of monetary policy by discussing the advantages and disadvantages of monetary policy as a stabilization tool. Within a short book one cannot do both adequately and I have chosen the latter alternative. This has the advantage of dealing with currently relevant issues rather than with the issues of the past. It does, however, have one disadvantage—the problems discussed in this book are still unsettled. I have tried to present both sides of the numerous debates, with the result that the reader may find himself in the position of the businessman who wanted to hire a one-armed economist since he was tired of hearing the man's predecessor say, "On the one hand . . . but on the other hand." However, this cannot be helped. Monetary policy is a field in which economists have achieved very considerable insight but little agreement. To pretend that there is agreement by presenting primarily one point of view would be less than candid. Similarly, to avoid controversial problems by ignoring them and discussing, instead, "factual" material such as changes in the Federal Reserve Act, would give the reader little perspective on current problems. Having to choose among the three risks of being bewildering, less than candid, or irrelevant, I chose the first of these. I am dealing with unsettled issues because the unsettled issues are, unfortunately, the significant ones.

In writing this book I have tried to keep in mind that monetary policy is not an independent subject, but is part of general economics. I have, therefore, tried to pay some attention to the underlying microeconomic basis of statements about monetary policy, and also to introduce the results of recent econometric studies. I have summarized the findings of these studies in the text and given the details, as well as explanations of statistical techniques, in footnotes. In addition, I have liberally cited sources in footnotes rather than placing them only into a "further reading" section in the hope of tempting the reader to go to these sources. A textbook should be a summary of, and a guide to, the original literature—not a complete substitute for it.

As far as background is concerned, I am assuming that the reader has some familiarity with monetary institutions, for example, that he knows something about the structure of the Federal Reserve System and the factors increasing or decreasing bank reserves, and that he has had a limited exposure to monetary theory.

In conclusion, I would like to express my gratitude for helpful comments to Thomas Cargill, John Culbertson, Milton Friedman, David Laidler, Charles Schotta, Harlan Smith, W. P. Strassmann, Richard Thorn, and Clark Warburton, none of whom are, of course, responsible for any remaining errors. I am also indebted for typing a difficult manuscript to Mrs. Edna Pitts, Dennis Fanucchi, and Mrs. Dolores Byrne. Last, but not least, I would like to express my gratitude to the editors, Mr. Theodore Caris and Miss Susan Sperling.

Davis, California   *Thomas Mayer*
October, 1967

Contents

Monetary Policy in the United States

The Goals
of Monetary Policy

Monetary policy has several major goals. They are full employment, price stability, economic growth, and balance of payments equilibrium. Table 1.1 shows the extent to which we have met the goals in recent years. There is widespread agreement about the desirability of these goals, but they are only vaguely defined in the general consensus and stand partly in a competitive relationship to each other. So let us look at them in greater detail.

Full employment is, of course, entirely consistent with some frictional unemployment, that is, an unemployment rate of 3 or 4 percent as measured by our statistical series. Whether the target should be a 3 percent rate, a 4 percent rate, or a 5 percent rate is a matter of dispute, with conservatives generally advocating a higher rate than liberals. To some extent, what is considered an acceptable level of unemployment seems to depend upon the actual unemployment rates of the recent past; for example, in 1934 a 5 percent unemployment rate would probably have been considered full employment.

Price stability, also, is not a straightforward idea. To be realistic, price stability must be interpreted as consistent with some quite minor price changes, but should this be one quarter of 1 percent per year, or can it be as high as 1 or even, perhaps, 2 percent? This problem is complicated by the fact that the Consumer Price Index appears to have an upward bias. New commodities are included in the index only after they have come into fairly common use so that the index does not catch the price decline which usually occurs as a commodity evolves from a specialty into a generally used one. Moreover, the index does not give

TABLE 1.1 Selected Economic Indicators 1947–1966

Year	Real GNP in 1958 Prices (Billions of dollars)	Unemployment Rate	Labor Force Time Lost Through Unemployment and Part-Time Employment[a]	Consumer Price Index (1957–1959 = 100)	Wholesale Price Index (1957–1959 = 100)	GNP Price Index (1958 = 100)	Surplus or Deficit in the Balance of Payments[b] (Billions of dollars)	U.S. Gold Stock Plus Foreign Currency Holdings[c] (Billions of dollars)
1948	323.7	3.8%	—	83.8	87.9	79.6	.8	24.4
1949	324.1	5.9	—	83.0	83.5	79.1	.1	24.6
1950	355.3	5.3	—	83.8	86.8	80.2	-3.5	22.8
1951	383.4	3.3	—	90.5	96.7	85.6	-.8	22.9
1952	395.1	3.1	—	92.5	94.0	87.5	-1.2	23.3
1953	412.8	2.9	—	93.2	92.7	88.3	-2.2	22.1
1954	407.0	5.6	—	93.6	92.9	89.6	-1.5	21.8
1955	438.0	4.4	—	93.3	93.2	90.9	-1.2	21.8
1956	446.1	4.2	5.1%[d]	94.7	96.2	94.0	-1.0	22.1
1957	452.5	4.3	5.3	98.0	99.0	97.5	.6	22.9
1958	447.3	6.8	8.1	100.7	100.4	100.0	-3.4	20.6
1959	475.9	5.5	6.6	101.5	100.6	101.6	-3.9	19.5
1960	487.7	5.6	6.7	103.1	100.7	103.3	-3.9	17.8
1961	497.2	6.7	8.0	104.2	100.3	104.6	-2.4	17.1
1962	529.8	5.6	6.7	105.4	100.6	105.8	-2.2	16.2
1963	551.0	5.7	6.4	106.7	100.3	107.2	-2.7	15.9
1964	580.0	5.2	5.8	108.1	100.5	108.9	-2.8	15.8
1965	614.4	4.6	5.0	109.9	102.5	110.9	-1.3	14.6
1966	647.7[p]	3.9	4.2	113.1	105.8[p]	114.2[p]	-1.2[e]	14.6[p]

a Beginning 1963 this series is not strictly comparable with preceding data.   b Liquidity basis.

c Convertible foreign currencies held by United States monetary authorities only.   d Data not available prior to 1956.

e Average for first three quarters at seasonally adjusted rates.   p denotes preliminary.

SOURCE: *1967 Economic Report of the President* (Washington, D.C.: Executive Office of the President, 1967), pp. 214, 216, 239, 262, 264, 307, and 312.

sufficient weight to quality improvements. An obvious example is medical services. Suppose that a physician's fee rises from $5 to $10 per visit, but that diseases which formally required three visits to cure can now be cured in one visit. Has the price of medical services gone up or down? The Consumer Price Index treats such a situation as a price increase. In view of this bias in the index, should one define price stability as an annual increase by 1 or 2 percent in the Consumer Price Index rather than as a constant Consumer Price Index?

Another problem is whether the price level should be measured by the Consumer Price Index, by the Wholesale Price Index, or by the GNP deflator.[1] This question can have quite important policy implications. Thus, in the period from 1960 to 1964, the Consumer Price Index rose by 4.8 percent, while the Wholesale Price Index was virtually stable. In these years, should the Federal Reserve have been worrying about inflation or rejoicing in price stability?

Economic growth involves the problem of deciding what rate of growth is sustainable. Federal Reserve officials have suggested that the growth rate may, at certain times, be increased in the *short run* by inflationary policies, but that such growth would not be sustainable in the *long run* and that monetary policy should aim at sustainable growth. But the concept of sustainable growth is imprecise and, therefore, a difficult one on which to base monetary policy.

Finally, the concept of balance-of-payments equilibrium is, also, not clear cut. To start with, different methods of measuring the balance of payments yield different results and, in addition, it is not at all clear whether balance-of-payments *equilibrium* is

[1] There has been much controversy in the past whether one should use, as a guide to monetary policy, the Wholesale Price Index or the Consumer Price Index. (The GNP deflator is a recent innovation.) The Consumer Price Index has the advantage of tying in better with our ultimate welfare interests than does the Wholesale Index. But, on the other hand, the Consumer Price Index is sluggish and signals price changes much more slowly than does the Wholesale Price Index and, in addition, the quality change problem is more severe for the Consumer Price Index than it is for the Wholesale Price Index. For a detailed discussion, see Lloyd Mints, *Monetary Policy for a Competitive Society* (New York: McGraw-Hill, 1950), Chapter 7.

consistent with a small *deficit* in the balance of payments. The dollar is used as a reserve currency by many countries and, since the demand for international reserves grows with time, some deficit in the United States balance of payments may be consistent with balance-of-payments equilibrium. Clearly, the size of such an "equilibrium deficit," and even its very existence, is a matter of judgment.

These four goals—full employment, price stability, economic growth, and balance-of-payments equilibrium—are not the only goals that monetary policy has pursued. During World War I, the overriding goal of monetary policy was to facilitate the sale of government securities, while during World War II and until 1951, the dominant goal of monetary policy was to maintain stable prices for government securities. Another goal is the maintenance of the private enterprise system, to the extent that the Federal Reserve has tried to limit the extent to which monetary policy interferes with the free-market mechanism. Moreover, a major aim of Federal Reserve policy has been to ensure the soundness of the banking system by limiting the occurrence of money market conditions that would tempt banks to make unsound loans. While this aim can, in principle, be treated as merely a *means* to the goals discussed above, the Federal Reserve has given it so much emphasis that, at least at times, it has almost appeared to be an independent goal. Thus in 1929 the Federal Reserve was so eager to limit speculation that it disavowed any concern with "the larger public consequences" of its action to limit speculation.[2]

While most people agree on the desirability of the Federal Reserve's current goals, there is some dissent. A small minority of observers feel that periodic depressions (and, hence, unemployment) are a "good thing" because in a depression, weak and inefficient firms are weeded out and labor is kept docile.

Similarly, price stability is not accepted as desirable by everyone. Some economists, again a fairly small minority, ad-

---

[2] See Clark Warburton, "Monetary Disturbances and Business Fluctuations in Two Centuries of American History," Leland Yeager (ed.), *In Search of a Monetary Constitution* (Cambridge, Mass.: Harvard University Press, 1962), p. 86.

vocate that prices should not remain stable, but that they should fall as productivity increases. In discussing this issue, which was debated extensively in the 1920's, economists have often stressed the impact of price changes on the income distribution. If prices are kept stable and the fruits of rising productivity are distributed by rising factor payments, then, it is said, "rentiers" and other fixed-income groups, do not share the benefits of rising productivity. On the other hand, if output prices decline and factor prices remain stable as productivity rises, then all segments of the economy can share in the gain. But this reasoning is not valid. If the public correctly anticipates the behavior of the price level, the remuneration of "fixed" income groups will then, *in the long run* (to which any discussion of goals necessarily relates) be adjusted to take account of changes in the price level. For example, if prices are falling at the rate of 2 percent per year, and if, in the absence of this price decline, the equilibrium rate of interest is 5 percent, it will become 3 percent. Similarly, if prices are known to be rising, certain salaries which are now fixed would include a built-in escalation factor. Adopting a policy of letting prices decline secularly would, however, provide a substantial once-and-for-all gain for long-term creditors and a loss to long-term debtors; the converse applies to a policy of inflation.

By and large, however, economists are opposed to secularly falling prices for fear that such a policy will make it difficult to maintain full employment. For example, if it is known that prices are falling at the rate of 2 percent per year, the real rate of interest then has a "floor" at 2 percent or more since it is impossible to get the money rate of interest below zero. Consequently, it may not be possible to force the rate of interest down far enough to achieve full employment. Moreover, given the extent of price inflexibility in our economy, a policy that attempts to distribute the gains in productivity by allowing prices to fall rather than by encouraging money incomes to rise faces serious difficulties.[3]

The converse policy goal of generally rising prices has, *in and*

[3] Note, however, that complete unanimity among economists about the effect of falling prices on employment does not exist. Thus, according to Professor Milton Friedman, the experience of the 1870's, when rapid eco-

of itself, few supporters. While a number of economists advocate a moderate degree of secular inflation they generally do so because they think that pursuing such a policy would make it easier to maintain full employment, *not* because they like inflation per se.

The next goal, rapid economic growth, is one that seems, at first glance, to be clearly desirable. But while almost nobody would object to rapid growth if it could be obtained without cost, some economists think that the cost (for example, the need to raise the saving-income ratio) is too high.[4]

Finally, there is the goal of balance-of-payments equilibrium. One dispute in this area centers on the question of whether monetary policy should be used to maintain balance-of-payments equilibrium at all, or whether, instead, a system of flexible (or freely fluctuating) exchange rates should be adopted. In such a system, the price of foreign currencies fluctuates so that it maintains the balance of payments in equilibrium by varying the prices of currencies. Another possible way of handling a potential balance-of-payments disequilibrium is to impose exchange control, that is, to limit foreign payments by government regulations. Until the late 1950's the balance of payments generally did not play an important role in American monetary policy; it is only since then that the Federal Reserve has had to worry about a threat to the United States gold stock. Most other countries have not been that fortunate, and in many countries balance-of-payments considerations play a major role in determining monetary policy.

But even if one accepts the Federal Reserve's current goals in

---

nomic growth occurred in spite of falling prices, shows that the economy can adjust to any price trend as long as it is stable enough to be predictable.

Back in the 1920's, a major argument for secularly falling prices was that allowing the price level to remain stable required a secular increase in the quantity of money. In some business cycle theories which were prominent in the 1920's, it was held that an increase in the quantity of money would initiate a business cycle. These cycle theories are now out of favor.

[4] On this issue, see James Tobin, "Economic Growth as an Objective of Government Policy," *American Economic Association Papers and Proceedings,* Vol. 54 (May, 1964), pp. 1–20. (See also the "Comments" on this paper by Harry Johnson and Herbert Stein, *Ibid.,* pp. 21–27.)

broad general terms, there remain serious problems when one gets down to specifics. One of these is the multiplicity of goals. There is a serious question as to whether these goals are compatible. The general feeling of the Federal Reserve is that they *are* compatible, and, indeed, that they are interrelated. In this view, price stability (or perhaps a slowly declining price level) is necessary to maintain full employment and sustainable economic growth. While inflation might help to raise employment and the growth rate in the short run, an inflationary boom leads to maladjustments that make the subsequent recession much more severe. Conversely, sharply falling prices are bad for employment, so that price stability (or, perhaps, gently falling prices) and full employment are a single package rather than competing goals. Similarly, price stability and balance-of-payments equilibrium are compatible because this equilibrium can only be achieved if the domestic price level is kept under control with the result that we do not price ourselves out of foreign markets. As Chairman Martin of the Board of Governors put it:

> There is a tendency to speak of international versus domestic goals. This seems to me to be only the latest version of a series of problems formulated in terms of unrealistic alternatives. Over the years we have seen counterposed, full employment or price stability, social objectives or financial objectives, and stagnation or inflation. . . . The underlying fallacy of this approach is that it assumes that we can concentrate on one major goal without considering collateral, and perhaps deleterious side effects on other objectives. But we cannot. If we were to neglect international financial equilibrium, or price stability, or financial soundness in our understanding zeal to promote faster domestic growth, full employment, or socially desirable programs, we would be confronted with general failure. . . .[5]

Similarly, in 1958 in a joint reply to a question posed by the Senate Finance Committee, the twelve Federal Reserve Bank presidents said:

[5] Quoted in David Eastburn, *The Federal Reserve on Record* (Philadelphia: Federal Reserve Bank of Philadelphia, n.d.), pp. 24–25. (The passage comes from Chairman Martin's testimony before the Joint Economic Committee in 1963.)

In principle, stable prices, business stability at high levels of production and employment and economic growth are mutually consistent. In practice, inconsistencies may at times develop. Excessive expansion or contraction in major sectors of the economy tends to be accompanied by inflationary or deflationary tendencies; too much emphasis on one objective may impair ability to achieve others.

Rising prices usually lead to waste, inefficiency, misdirected use of resources, and, eventually, to a boom which ends in a depression. . . . A considerable degree of price stability (or perhaps even gradually declining prices), therefore, would appear to be an essential, although not a sufficient, condition for achieving business stability and steady economic growth.

Reasonably full employment is also consistent with achieving sustained economic long-term growth. Unemployment and idle facilities represent a waste of economic resources. On the other hand, attempts to maintain full employment at a maximum level without regard to price stability may inhibit economic growth. . . . Attempts directed primarily towards maintaining employment at a maximum level also create an economic climate which is not conducive to the most efficient use of economic resources. When demand is pressing against capacity, the emphasis is on getting more output. Costs and prices are secondary considerations.[6]

Thus, the Federal Reserve sees little conflict between its goals. The feeling that various policy goals are compatible is one that is common and natural among government officials. A belief that goals are *not* compatible would require an official to choose among them and to support policies that would hinder the achievement of one or more of our national goals. Obviously, the people who have to make the hard decisions, unlike those who merely write books about them, tend to play down the conflict among goals. This should not be interpreted to deny that there is *some* complementarity among the various goals—for example, a wild speculative boom probably *does* make the ensuing recession worse by causing excessive investment and other maladjustments. But, although there is some degree of complementarity, there is also some potential for conflict among them.

[6] *Ibid.*, pp. 18–19.

Full employment and price-level stability may conflict in several ways. For example, if we have "cost-push" inflation, that is, inflation initiated by sellers of either labor or products pushing up their prices, it may be necessary to create so much unemployment and excess capacity so that sellers cease to demand higher prices in order to curb such an inflation. There is a great deal of literature about the relation between wage changes and unemployment (the so-called "Phillips Curve") which suggests that it would take substantial unemployment to insure that wages rose no faster than productivity.[7]

Another, and perhaps more relevant, way in which full employment and price-level stability may be incompatible is the following. Stabilization policies take some time to become effective and since our forecasting ability is still fairly limited, a policy of insuring that aggregate demand will be sufficient for full employment will sometimes result in aggregate demand being excessive, and, hence, inflationary. (Conversely, a policy of managing aggregate demand so that it is never great enough to be inflationary is likely to lead, at times, to a deficiency of aggregate demand.) A very firm commitment to full employment will, therefore, tend to be inflationary. Hence, it *may* be inflation rather than price stability that is compatible with full employment. Even in the long run it is quite doubtful that moderate inflation is bad for employment. In the postwar period we have had a moderate secular inflation, at least as measured by our price indexes, and it has not resulted in maladjustments leading to a severe depression.

Similarly, so far at least, there is little evidence that price stability is necessary for rapid economic growth. Looking at growth rates and price trends in various countries in the postwar period one sees little correlation between the two.[8] While this is

[7] See Lawrence Klein and Ronald Bodkin, "Empirical Aspects of the Trade-Offs among Three Goals: High Level Employment, Price Stability, and Economic Growth," in Commission on Money and Credit, *Inflation, Growth and Employment* (Englewood Cliffs, N.J.: Prentice-Hall, 1964), pp. 389–401, and the literature cited therein.

[8] See Klein and Bodkin, *op. cit.*, p. 407. For a detailed list of ways in which inflation helps or hinders economic growth, see U.S. Joint Economic Committee, *Review of the Report of the Commission on Money and Credit,*

not firm evidence that moderate inflation does not hurt the growth rate, it is at least suggestive.

Price stability and balance-of-payments equilibrium, too, are not necessarily related. Granted that inflation tends to worsen the balance of payments, it is not at all clear that price *stability* is consistent with balance-of-payments equilibrium. If foreign prices are rising, balance-of-payments equilibrium may require rising prices in the United States to prevent a recurrence of a dollar shortage. On the other hand, if world demand shifts away from United States products and assets, or if the United States develops a greater taste for imports or for foreign assets, balance-of-payments equilibrium will then require a *decline* in the United States price level. Given changes in world trade patterns and in foreign prices, it would be a coincidence if balance-of-payments considerations would call for a stable price level.[9]

The other two goals, full employment and rapid growth, may also be inconsistent with balance-of-payments equilibrium since both full employment and rapid growth are likely to lead to an increase in imports. To be sure, rapid growth *may* also spur exports and, in addition, may make domestic investment so profitable that an improvement in the capital account offsets, or more than offsets, the deterioration of the current account. But there is no assurance that this would actually happen.

Given this possible clash of goals, what should the Federal Reserve do? It would not have enough tools to aim at all of its goals, simultaneously, even if these goals were not mutually conflicting. But as long as the Federal Reserve is officially committed to multiple goals, it must claim that any action taken to achieve any one goal does not conflict with the achievement of another goal. This puts the Federal Reserve under very great pressure to be vague and obscure in its statements and thinking at times. This problem could be solved by requiring monetary policy to

---

Hearings (Washington, D.C.: 79th Congress, First Session, August 14–18, 1961), pp. 374–487.

[9] This assumes stable exchange rates and no changes in trade barriers. The balance-of-payments problem is discussed in detail in Delbert Snider, *International Monetary Relations* (New York: Random House, 1966).

concentrate on one goal only. The goal usually suggested is price-level stability. This was proposed in a Congressional bill that led to important Congressional hearings in the mid-1920's and has been proposed, on-and-off, though without success, since then.[10] Concentrating on this single goal can be defended in several ways. It can be said that the various goals are, at least to some extent, interrelated so that, while stabilizing the price level would not necessarily guarantee full employment and balance-of-payments equilibrium, it would go a long way toward meeting these goals, too.[11] Since monetary policy is not capable of completely achieving all the above goals it should, in the opinion of some, be confined to the more feasible task of meeting one of them directly. For the other goals, the favorable by-products of meeting the one chosen goal should be relied on. A second approach is the claim that monetary policy is not the only stabilization tool but is supplemented by fiscal policy. If monetary policy is directed toward maintaining price stability, fiscal policy can be left to deal with the employment problem.[12] Another

---

[10] See, for instance, Henry Simons, "Rules versus Authorities in Monetary Policy," reprinted in American Economic Association, *Readings in Monetary Theory* (Homewood, Ill.: Richard D. Irwin, 1951), pp. 337–368, and Jacob Viner, "Problems of Monetary Control," in *Essays in International Finance, No. 45* (Princeton, N.J.: International Finance Section, Princeton University, 1964), p. 35.

[11] For example, if businessmen have the assurance of price stability, they are less likely to cut back investment during a recession than if they expect prices to fall. Opinions vary on the extent to which price stability would help to prevent fluctuations in output. Economists who accept a monetary theory of the cycle or one stressing maladjustments tend to give more weight to price stability as a curative factor than those economists who accept a more Keynesian explanation such as the multiplier-accelerator mechanism.

[12] But note two problems here. First, this division of labor still leaves two goals—economic growth and balance-of-payments equilibrium—untended. (It is *not* correct to say that flexible exchange rates, unaided by monetary policy, could take care of the balance-of-payments problem—see Robert Mundell, "Problems of Monetary and Exchange Rate Management in Canada," *National Banking Review*, Vol. 2, No. 1 [September, 1964], pp. 77–86.) Second, since output and the price level are connected (which is, after all, what a stable aggregate supply curve implies), an attempt to handle them separately would fail if full employment and price stability are incompatible.

possibility is to use fiscal policy to achieve the domestic goals and confine monetary policy to dealing with the balance-of-payments problem. Since monetary policy has a *comparative* advantage over fiscal policy in dealing with a balance-of-payments disequilibrium, such a division of labor has much to recommend it.[13] But because of the difficulties in using fiscal policy successfully for domestic stabilization, monetary policy (whether rightly or wrongly) is used for this task, too.

Confining monetary policy to a single goal provides a yardstick for evaluating the performance of the money managers. As long as monetary policy does *not* have a single goal, anyone attempting to evaluate the record of monetary policy faces an exasperating task, as exemplified by the following comment of Senator Proxmire to Chairman Martin at a Congressional hearing:

> I have the greatest respect for your ability, and I think that you are an outstanding and competent person, and everybody agrees with that, but the fact is, that when you try to come down and discuss this in meaningful specific terms, it is like nailing a custard pie to the wall. . . . And frankly, Mr. Martin, without specific

---

[13] Note that this is a comparative, and not necessarily an absolute, advantage. The reason monetary policy has this comparative advantage is that it affects the balance of payments in two ways. Like fiscal policy it affects the current account by changing the level of income and, hence, imports and exports. In addition, by changing interest rates, monetary policy has some effect on the capital account of the balance of payments. (To be sure, fiscal policy also has some indirect effects on interest rates since these are influenced by the level of income. Clearly, however, monetary policy has more control over interest rates than does fiscal policy.) In fact, it can be shown that the opposite policy of using fiscal policy to cure a balance-of-payments disequilibrium and monetary policy to achieve the domestic goals leads to instability. See Robert Mundell, "The Appropriate Use of Monetary and Fiscal Policy for Internal and External Stability," *Staff Papers,* Vol. 9 (March, 1962), pp. 70–77. But there are also disadvantages in using monetary policy as the balance-of-payments adjustment mechanism. If capital flows are determined by balance-of-payments considerations they are diverted from their fundamental task of shifting capital from capital surplus to capital deficit regions. Moreover, using interest rates to adjust the balance of payments may tend to raise interest rates on a world scale. See Richard Ablin, "Fiscal-Monetary Mix: A Haven for the Fixed Exchange Rate?," *National Banking Review,* Vol. 4 (December, 1966), pp. 199–204.

goals, criteria, guidelines, it is impossible to exercise any Congressional oversight over you, and I think you know it.[14]

The Federal Reserve has not accepted the view that it should confine itself to the pursuit of a single goal. Instead, it has stressed the interrelatedness of goals and, hence, the need to look at the behavior of the whole economy rather than at any single index in isolation. Moreover, the Federal Reserve believes that since many factors not under its control influence the price level or any other criterion, it cannot pledge itself to keep the price index or any other index stable.[15] This attitude is illustrated in the exchange between Chairman Martin and Senator Douglas reprinted as an Appendix to this chapter.

Given the fact that the Federal Reserve aims at several goals at the same time, can one say that it gives more emphasis to one goal than to another? This important question deserves as straightforward an answer as is possible. Unfortunately, several difficulties make it impossible. First, to state that the Federal Reserve prefers, say, price stability to full employment, is meaningless unless one first specifies the quantities involved. For example, in all probability, the Federal Reserve prefers a 1 percent price increase per year to continuous unemployment of 10 percent, and, at the same time, prefers a 3 percent unemployment rate with stable prices to a situation in which unemployment is only 2 percent but prices are rising at an annual rate of 20 percent. To state whether the Federal Reserve prefers one goal to another one must specify the "trade-off" between the two.[16] Note, moreover, that this trade-off is not constant but changes as the levels of the variables change. A rise in unemployment by one percent-

---

[14] Cited in John Culbertson, *Full Employment or Stagnation?* (New York: McGraw-Hill, 1964), pp. 154–155.

[15] As mentioned above, there is also a technical problem of deciding which price index to stabilize; is the Consumer Price Index to be interpreted as "the" price index, or is it the Wholesale Price Index or the GNP deflator? There is enough divergence among these indexes to make this a serious problem.

[16] This is simply a manifestation of the fact that you generally cannot tell if someone prefers commodity A to commodity B unless you know the quantities of A and B being offered.

age point gives rise to less concern if it means a rise from 2 percent to 3 percent than if it means a rise from 5 percent to 6 percent. The problem is further complicated by the fact that Federal Reserve officials never state explicitly what they consider the proper trade-off to be.

It is, therefore, *not* possible to give a straightforward answer to the question posed above. However, it is possible to give a roundabout answer, by comparing the Federal Reserve's trade-off with that of, say, the Council of Economic Advisers in recent years.[17] It appears that the Federal Reserve attaches *relatively* more importance to price stability and relatively less importance to full employment than does the Council of Economic Advisers. Similarly, the Federal Reserve seems to be more concerned with balance-of-payments equilibrium and less concerned with economic growth than is the Council of Economic Advisers.[18] Note, however, two qualifications to these statements. First, they are not based on any hard and fast evidence, but are merely the general impressions of some economists. Second, these statements do not, by any means, imply that the Federal Reserve is not interested in full employment and economic growth, or that the Council of Economic Advisers does not value price stability and balance-of-payments equilibrium—it is merely a matter of degree. Various interest groups have their spokesmen in the government—the farmers have the Department of Agriculture, business has the Department of Commerce, and labor the Department of Labor; to some extent the Federal Reserve seems to look upon itself as the only spokesman for creditors and other fixed-income groups who would be hurt by inflation.

[17] Another possibility, though one fraught with statistical problems, is to take an indicator of monetary policy, and to make it a function of the unemployment rate, rate of price increase, etc. One can then determine, statistically, the role that each of these variables plays in determining Federal Reserve policy. For the most recent attempts to do this see John Wood, "A Model of Federal Reserve Behavior," George Horwich (ed.), *Monetary Process and Policies: A Symposium* (Homewood, Ill.: Richard D. Irwin, 1967), pp. 135–166, and Thomas Havrilesky, "A Test of Monetary Policy Action," *Journal of Political Economy*, Vol. 77 (June, 1967), pp. 299–304.

[18] This statement refers to the average attitude of recent Councils and, hence, reflects the results of recent elections. Future election results may change the picture.

This choice of relative priorities, perhaps more than any other area of Federal Reserve policy, provoked a great deal of criticism. Consider, for example, the following recent episode. In the period 1958–1962, unemployment rates were high (varying from 6.8 percent in 1958 to 5.5 percent in 1959) and the rate of economic growth was disappointing.[19] The cumulative gap between potential and actual output during this period was $170 billion (in 1962 prices) so that, even if some allowance is made for the fact that a full employment policy could not achieve full potential output, the failure to adopt expansionary policies cost the nation $25 billion per year in this period.[20] But since the Consumer Price Index was rising in this period from 100.7 in 1958 to 105.4 in 1962 and the balance of payments was in deficit, the Federal Reserve adopted a tight money policy in spite of high unemployment. While the money supply had been allowed to grow at an annual rate of just over 2 percent from 1948 to 1958, it grew at an average rate of only ½ of 1 percent from mid-1959 to mid-1962. Monetary policy has therefore been blamed for initiating the 1960 recession as well as for the very slow recovery that followed.[21] Similarly, the Federal Reserve has been blamed for other recessions, the 1937 downturn, for example.

So much for the general goals of monetary policy. Obviously, one cannot jump from these general goals to specific directives for actions in day-to-day operations. For example, if the Federal Open Market Committee were to tell its account manager at the New York Federal Reserve Bank to conduct operations so as to maintain price stability and full employment, the account manager would have to translate these general goals into specific ones for such daily operations such as raising excess reserves to, say,

[19] See Table 1.1.

[20] Culbertson, *op. cit.*, p. 22.

[21] *Ibid.*, pp. 123–128. Professor Culbertson attributes the Federal Reserve's tight money policy not only to a deemphasis on full employment relative to price stability, but also to its emphasis on credit conditions—a point discussed in Chapter 7 below. The best defense of the restrictive policy is that velocity was rising in these years, hence only a small increase in the money stock was "needed." But the critics of the Federal Reserve respond by saying that velocity was rising because the restrictive monetary policy had raised interest rates. This increase in interest rates subsequently reduced investment.

$500 million. (Such discretion is, of course, not given to the account manager.) The goals discussed in this chapter are high level goals which are used to deduce lower level goals, and it is these lower level goals which are the immediate guides to action. They are discussed in Chapter 3; before coming to them we must look at the tools of monetary policy.

Preview

At this point it might be useful to provide a brief outline of what is to come. Chapter 2 discusses the tools of monetary policy, the ways in which the Federal Reserve changes bank reserves. The following chapter, which deals mainly with the effect of changes in bank reserves on the money stock and on interest rates, also discusses the money market goals and criteria used by the Federal Reserve. Chapter 4 carries the story forward by looking at the effects which changes in interest rates and the money stock, in turn, have on expenditures. The following chapter describes the resource allocation effects of monetary policy. Chapter 6 raises the question of whether monetary policy is fast enough in its effects to be a useful stabilization tool, and the final chapter pulls this material together by comparing alternative monetary policies.

FURTHER READING

Eastburn, David. *The Federal Reserve on Record*. Philadelphia: Federal Reserve Bank of Philadelphia, n.d., pp. 15–27.

Goldenweiser, Emanuel. *Monetary Management*. New York: McGraw-Hill, 1949, Chapter 4.

Gordon, Robert. *Business Fluctuations*. New York: Harper & Row, 1961, Chapter 18.

Harriss, C. L. *Money and Banking*. Boston: Allyn and Bacon, 1965, Chapter 21.

Hart, Albert, and P. Kenen. *Money, Debt and Economic Activity*. Englewood Cliffs, N.J.: Prentice-Hall, 1961, Chapters 9 and 20. (The first of these chapters gives a summary of the historical record of prices and employment.)

Klein, Lawrence, and R. G. Bodkin. "Empirical Aspects of the Trade-

Offs among Three Goals: High Level Employment, Price Stability and Economic Growth," in Commission on Money and Credit. *Inflation, Growth and Employment.* Englewood Cliffs, N.J.: Prentice-Hall, 1964, pp. 367–428.

Mundell, Robert, "The Appropriate Use of Monetary and Fiscal Policy for Internal and External Stability," International Monetary Fund, *Staff Papers,* Vol. 9 (March, 1962), pp. 70–77.

Rothwell, J. C. "Aiming at a Moving Target," *Federal Reserve Bank of Philadelphia Business Review* (April, 1964), pp. 3–19. (This article summarizes changes in the Federal Reserve's view of its goals.)

Scitovsky, Tibor and Ann. "Inflation versus Unemployment: An Examination of their Effects," in Commission on Money and Credit. *Inflation, Growth and Employment.* Englewood Cliffs, N.J.: Prentice-Hall, 1964, pp. 429–470.

Trescott, Paul. *Money, Banking, and Economic Welfare.* New York: McGraw-Hill, 1965, Chapter 18.

Viner, Jacob. "Problems of Monetary Control," in *Essays in International Finance, No. 45.* Princeton, N.J.: International Finance Section, Princeton University Press, 1964.

APPENDIX TO CHAPTER 1

The Federal Reserve's Criteria

The following discussion about fiscal policy among Chairman Martin of the Board of Governors, Senator Paul Douglas of Illinois, and Mr. Young, Associate Director of the Federal Reserve's Division of Research and Statistics, illustrates the Federal Reserve's belief that action must be based on many criteria rather than on a single one:[1]

[1] The occasion was a hearing of the Joint Economic Committee in 1958; it is quoted in David Eastburn, *The Federal Reserve on Record, op. cit.,* pp. 22–24.

MR. MARTIN. I would not use any one index. I would—

SENATOR DOUGLAS. What group, what family of indexes would you use?

MR. MARTIN. Well, I think we would have to cover the whole waterfront on that.

SENATOR DOUGLAS. Let's get to some of the docks on the waterfront. Production?

MR. MARTIN. Production index.

SENATOR DOUGLAS. Employment?

MR. MARTIN. Employment.

SENATOR DOUGLAS. Unemployment?

MR. MARTIN. Unemployment.

SENATOR DOUGLAS. What else?

MR. MARTIN. Mr. Young, what would you—

MR. YOUNG. I think you would go across the board—on new orders—

SENATOR DOUGLAS. What?

MR. YOUNG. You would go across the board on new orders and inventories—

SENATOR DOUGLAS. If you go across the board, what would you look at?

MR. MARTIN. New orders, inventories—

MR. YOUNG. What is happening in the securities markets?

SENATOR DOUGLAS. What is happening to production? It was 145 in August.

MR. MARTIN. January, 133.

SENATOR DOUGLAS. A fall of twelve points. What is that?

MR. YOUNG. Around 8 percent.

MR. MARTIN. Seven to 8 percent.

SENATOR DOUGLAS. If it should go down below 10 percent would you regard that as significant?

MR. YOUNG. I think you would want to look at the movement against typical patterns in the past also.

SENATOR DOUGLAS. You say in past recessions the fall in production has not exceeded 10 percent?

MR. YOUNG. For a moderate recession it is something like 10 percent.

SENATOR DOUGLAS. All right. Now, then, suppose it exceeds 10 percent. What I am trying to get at is that you are the doctor, one of the doctors, sitting by the bedside of the patient . . .

Now, you feel his pulse. You find out what his temperature is.

An M.D. has certain standards. If the temperature rises to, say, 103, something is wrong. He does not worry very much at 99¾.

Do you have anything in the back of your mind as to where you might have a critical point? Would you say a fall of 10 percent in production should begin to—

MR. MARTIN. I would not want to be pinned to a level. I think that you have got to—

SENATOR DOUGLAS. Suppose you had a fall of 15 percent. Would you worry?

MR. MARTIN. The further the fall—

SENATOR DOUGLAS. You do not think fiscal policy should come in if production fell 15 percent?

MR. MARTIN. I would not—just could not answer that on a specific basis.

SENATOR DOUGLAS. Suppose it fell 20 percent?

MR. MARTIN. I am not—

SENATOR DOUGLAS. 25 percent? You would not be concerned with 25 percent?

MR. MARTIN. Senator, I am sorry but I just cannot say that I—

SENATOR DOUGLAS. You see, you are the doctor. You say, "Have faith in me."

MR. MARTIN. No; I—

SENATOR DOUGLAS. We want to find out what you are having faith in, what indexes you are watching.

MR. MARTIN. I am not saying, "Have faith in me."

SENATOR DOUGLAS. Let's turn to unemployment. The census says we have 4.5 million unemployed. If you add the part-time workers to this you get an equivalent of 1.2 million more or 5.7 million. The total working force is a little less than sixty-seven million. That is 8.5 percent. But this sixty-seven million includes the self-employed, nine million self-employed plus a million more wives and elder sons or elder daughters, self-employed. So you really have to deduct them in getting an index of unemployment. And when you come to the number of wage and salary workers in the country, a little less than fifty-seven million, then you have 5.7 million equivalent unemployed. That is a 10 percent unemployment ratio. Do you think that is significant?

MR. MARTIN. I certainly do. I think that—

SENATOR DOUGLAS. But you say it is not yet time for fiscal action. By how much would it have to increase before you think it would be time?

MR. MARTIN. Well, I cannot answer that categorically, but I want to say that these unemployment figures ought to be studied awfully carefully too. You have questioned the Consumer Price Index. I think all of these indexes have got to be put in the context of what is the truth about it.

SENATOR DOUGLAS. You see, here is the point. You will say, "I am moving because the Consumer Price Index is this way." Then you will shift. The pea will be under another thimble, and so on. You chase these around. What I am trying to do is assemble these various indexes and try to see when you would believe that fiscal policy should be carried out.

MR. MARTIN. Well, I cannot tell you precisely.

SENATOR DOUGLAS. You are not in control of fiscal policy. We are in control of fiscal policy. Presumably we have to make up our minds. We are coming to you for advice.

MR. MARTIN. Well, I am not trying to be presumptuous in what I am saying now, but I am saying that I think you, in studying your problem, just as we in studying our problem, should look at the whole picture and not just at one index or the trend in a few indexes.

The Tools
of Monetary Policy

The previous chapter discussed the goals of monetary policy. This chapter deals with the tools the Federal Reserve uses to reach these goals.[1] There are three major tools, open-market operations, the discount mechanism, and reserve-requirement changes. After discussing each of these major tools in the order given, the chapter takes up their interrelations and their relative advantages and disadvantages. This is followed by a discussion of the five minor tools: selective controls, moral suasion, direct action, publicity, and informal advice.

Mechanics of Open-Market Operations

Open-market operations are now the most important tool of monetary policy despite the fact that they were not even recognized as a monetary policy tool in the Federal Reserve's early history. The original Federal Reserve Act (1913) envisaged that the

[1] The Federal Reserve is not the only institution that possesses tools of monetary policy. The Treasury, too, has some monetary powers; for example, it can change bank reserves by shifting its cash holdings between the commercial banks and the Federal Reserve and has occasionally done so to give the Federal Reserve's policy a small assist. (See Irving Auerbach, "United States Treasury Cash Balances and the Control of Member Bank Reserves," in Commission on Money and Credit, *Fiscal and Debt Management Policies* [Englewood Cliffs, N.J.: Prentice-Hall, 1963], pp. 328–329.) Bank supervision powers provide both the Treasury and the Federal Deposit Insurance Corporation with some, though quite limited, potential for monetary policy. Government lending agencies, too, have some monetary powers. But, since the Federal Reserve is the only institution that systematically uses monetary policy on a continuous basis, this chapter discusses only the Federal Reserve's tools of monetary policy.

Federal Reserve Banks would hold government securities to obtain earnings and would, from time to time, buy and sell these securities to maximize their earnings. The Federal Reserve Banks soon realized, however, that by buying and selling securities they were changing bank reserves. Accordingly, starting in 1922, the Federal Reserve Banks decided to coordinate their purchases and sales. From this modest beginning evolved the modern, highly centralized, organization of open-market operations.

Decisions to undertake open-market operations are made by the Federal Open Market Committee (officially, the seven members of the Board of Governors and five presidents of the Federal Reserve Banks, though actually the presidents of other Federal Reserve Banks usually attend the sessions even though they do not vote). This committee usually meets every three weeks and its decisions are communicated for action to the "Trading Desk" of the Federal Reserve Bank of New York, which carries out the transactions. Its decisions are stated in fairly broad terms. For example, they might decide to allow only a small growth of the reserve base and to keep the money market under moderate pressure. Purchases and sales are undertaken in New York, the main money market of the country. All Federal Reserve Banks have a pro-rata share in the securities bought or sold.

The Federal Reserve Bank of New York deals with a handful of firms which make a market in government securities, the so-called primary dealers. The Trading Desk of the New York Bank is in constant touch with them, continually asking for bids and offers to sell, thus feeling out the money market. From these and other contacts in the market the New York Bank acquires a detailed knowledge of the market and prides itself on having the "feel of the market," to use a favorite Federal Reserve phrase. It is therefore able to adjust its purchases and sales to continually changing conditions. Note that nobody is forced to buy or sell to the Federal Reserve. Government securities are sold in an over-the-counter market, and the Federal Reserve buys or sells at the prices quoted by the dealers.

The securities in which the Federal Reserve deals are Federal government securities, primarily short-term securities.[2] Most transactions are in Treasury bills, the shortest-term securities issued. If the Federal Reserve undertakes open-market purchases which it intends to reverse later, it may let the market know this by using so-called "repurchase agreements." Under this arrangement, the Federal Reserve buys securities from dealers who commit themselves to repurchase these securities at a certain date, usually at a fixed price. It is an arrangement in-between a loan to the dealers and an outright open-market purchase. One of its uses is to provide dealers with temporary funds at a time of a Treasury financing or during some other temporary stringency in the money market. Sometimes the Federal Reserve undertakes reverse repurchase agreements selling securities to dealers with a commitment to repurchase them.

Effects of Open-Market Operations

Open-market operations are the principal method of changing bank reserves nowadays. If the Federal Reserve buys securities from a member bank (or a nonmember bank keeping an account with it) it credits the proceeds to the bank's reserve account, and bank reserves are increased directly. Conversely, if the Federal Reserve sells securities to a member bank it debits the bank's account.

The same effects occur if the Federal Reserve deals with a nonbank (that is, anyone except a bank). If the Federal Reserve buys securities, it issues a check to the seller and the seller deposits it in his bank. The bank then sends it to the Federal Reserve for clearance and the Federal Reserve credits the bank's account. Conversely, if the Federal Reserve sells securities to nonbanks, the seller draws a check on his bank, and the Federal Reserve debits the bank's account.[3]

---

[2] The Federal Reserve has the legal power to deal in a fairly wide variety of instruments, eligible bills of exchange, bankers acceptances, government securities, securities of certain government agencies, certain state and local securities, and foreign exchange.

[3] The only difference is that if the Federal Reserve deals with a nonbank, bank deposits are directly affected by the open-market operations, whereas if the Federal Reserve deals with a bank only bank reserves are directly affected. But unless banks decide to change their volume of excess reserves this makes no difference.

Expressed in the language of "T accounts," a $1,000 sale of securities by the Federal Reserve to a member bank has the following effects:

FEDERAL RESERVE SYSTEM		COMMERCIAL BANK	
Assets	*Liabilities*	*Assets*	*Liabilities*
Securities held − $1,000	Member bank reserves − $1,000	Deposits with Federal Reserve − $1,000	
		Securities held + $1,000	

If a nonbank had bought these securities from the Federal Reserve, the Federal Reserve account would look the same, but some commercial bank's account would change as follows:

Assets	*Liabilities*
Deposits with Federal Reserve − $1,000	Demand deposits − $1,000

In addition to this effect on the reserve base, open-market operations also have an impact on the economy through their effect on expectations. Money market analysts watch the weekly balance sheet of the New York Federal Reserve Bank and try to see if open-market operations indicate any changes in monetary policy. This "announcement effect" of Federal Reserve action is less for open-market operations than for discount rate changes, and will therefore not be discussed here, but in the following section.

Open-market operations are used by the Federal Reserve both for "defensive" and for "dynamic" operations. Numerous factors such as Treasury gold purchases, changes in float, and changes in currency in circulation continually impinge on the reserve base. The Federal Reserve Bank of New York goes to quite substantial trouble to forecast these "market factors" and then to offset them by open-market operations when they threaten to change the reserve base in an undesired direction or by an undesired amount. This is called "defensive operations" since the Federal Reserve is merely defending the reserve base against factors tending to change it.

On the other hand, Federal Reserve open-market operations to *change* the reserve base are called "dynamic operations." Unfortunately, it is not always easy to distinguish between the two. This is so for two reasons. First, assume, for example, that bank reserves have increased in a certain week and that the balance sheet of the New York Federal Reserve Bank shows security purchases. This does not necessarily mean that the Federal Reserve has adopted a dynamic policy to raise bank reserves. In undertaking defensive operations the Federal Reserve acts on the basis of *estimates* of the changes in reserves resulting from market factors. These estimates may be in error. Thus, in the particular week when reserves increased, the Federal Reserve may not have intended this to happen; it may have bought securities merely to offset an expected reserve drain which did not materialize.

The second difficulty is that changes in monetary policy are not usually abrupt. Often they occur in frequent, but almost imperceptibly small, steps. In the beginning, the Federal Reserve may merely tend in its forecast of market factors to lean more toward one side, say caution, than toward the other, expansion.[4] This sort of change is hard to notice in its early stages—defensive and dynamic policy are intertwined.[5]

Defensive operations account for a large part of total open-market operations. For example, in the six months from April to September, 1961, the Federal Reserve undertook total open-market operations (adding purchases and sales) of $10.5 billion. Purchases and sales, however, largely cancelled so that the re-

---

[4] Estimates of changes in reserves are necessarily within a range, and there is no reason why the Federal Reserve should use the mean of this range or even the most probable value as the "best" figure for action. After all, a driver who thinks that there is a 51 percent chance that he can pass a car without an accident, in other words, whose "best" estimate is that he *can* pass, will usually not try to do so.

[5] For a masterly example of the detective work necessary to separate intended from unintended reserve changes, see Hobart Carr, "Why and How to Read the Federal Reserve Statement," *Journal of Finance,* Vol. 14 (December, 1959), pp. 504–519.

sulting net addition to reserves was only $0.7 billion.[6] This great amount of market churning has been criticized as unnecessary. Critics argue that if the Federal Reserve would lengthen the reserve settlement period of member banks (that is, the period during which the reserves of banks are averaged and compared to required reserves) to one month, and, further, if it would stagger the reserve settlement dates so that they would occur on different days for different banks, market factors affecting reserves would, then, largely cancel out. Large scale defensive operations would, consequently, not be required.[7]

Advantages and Disadvantages of Open-Market Operations

Open-market operations are the best weapon of the Federal Reserve both for defensive and for dynamic operations for several reasons. First, the Federal Reserve can buy or sell enough government securities to determine the size of the reserve base as it pleases; there is more than enough ammunition. Second, open-market operations occur at the initiative of the Federal Reserve, unlike the case of discount-rate changes where the Federal Reserve can only encourage or discourage banks to borrow, but has no direct control of the volume involved. Third, open-market operations can be carried out in small steps, very small ones if need be. This allows the Federal Reserve to make quite precise adjustments in the reserve base. This ability to make small changes is, of course, most useful for defensive operations where the Federal Reserve may want to offset market factors causing minor changes in reserves.

Fourth, open-market operations can be used continually. This

---

[6] Albert Cox, Jr., and Ralph Leach, "Defensive Open-Market Operations and the Reserve Settlement Periods of Member Banks," *Journal of Finance*, Vol. 19 (March, 1964), p. 79.

[7] *Ibid.*, pp. 76–93. For a defense of the present arrangement, see Peter Sternlight, "Reserve Settlement Periods of Member Banks: Comment," *Journal of Finance*, Vol. 19 (March, 1964), pp. 94–98, and the debate between Cox, Leach, and Sternlight in *Journal of Finance*, Vol. 19 (September, 1964), pp. 534–543.

allows the Federal Reserve to adjust the reserve base on a continuous basis as it receives new information about the impact of market factors on reserves and as its "feel of the market" changes. Because of this ability to move rapidly and the ability to move in large or small steps the Federal Reserve really does have fingertip control over the reserve base.

Fifth and finally, the open-market operations can be reversed easily. The Federal Reserve can buy at 10 A.M. and sell at 11 A.M., and since the Trading Desk's assessment of money-market conditions is continually subject to revision, this ability to reverse the field is highly prized by the Federal Reserve. None of the other tools are so easily reversible. If the Federal Reserve were to change the discount rate continually, it might give the impression of not knowing what it wants to do. With open-market operations, however, actions which are reversed within the statement week do not come to the public's attention.

To be sure, open-market operations do suffer from one disadvantage. Their initial impact is concentrated in New York, and it takes some time until their impact spreads throughout the country. There is some evidence that it used to take a very long time. But now, as a result of the development of negotiable certificates of deposits and the growth of the Federal Fund market, monetary developments spread much faster throughout the country.[8]

The Discount Mechanism

Federal Reserve member banks can replenish their reserves by borrowing from the Federal Reserve Bank of their district if they meet certain not very restrictive conditions. (In principle, nonmember banks, as well as anyone else, can borrow from the Federal Reserve, but this provision of the law exists to take care of the special conditions of a financial panic, rather than for ordinary borrowing.)

[8] See Ira O. Scott, Jr., "The Regional Impact of Monetary Policy," *Quarterly Journal of Economics*, Vol. 19 (May, 1955), pp. 269–284. Roland Robinson, "Monetary Policy versus Credit Policy," George Horwich (ed.), *Monetary Prices and Policy: A Symposium* (Homewood, Ill.: Richard D. Irwin; 1967), p. 129.

Originally, member banks borrowed by *re*discounting the commercial paper (in other words, promissory notes) which they themselves had discounted for their customers. The Federal Reserve Banks imposed quite strict regulations on the type of paper they were willing to discount, or rediscount, as it is sometimes called. It had to be short-term paper arising from self-liquidating commercial operations.[9] Commercial paper which showed that the customer had used the proceeds for financial transactions, such as purchases of common stock, were not eligible for rediscounting. By limiting its discounting to a special type of paper called *eligible* paper, the Federal Reserve tried to control the *quality* of credit. This was in accordance with the real-bills doctrine (commercial credit theory) which had substantial support in the early years of the Federal Reserve's history.[10]

For many years now, however, banks have not actually discounted their customer's paper; instead they have usually borrowed on their own promissory notes secured by government securities.[11]

[9] Self-liquidating loans are loans used to finance transactions which *in themselves* generate the funds necessary to repay them. For example, a loan used by a merchant to acquire inventory is said to be self-liquidating since the sale of the inventory in the normal course of business provides the merchant with funds to repay the loan. Similarly, loans to merchants to pay wages are considered self-liquidating. By contrast, a consumer loan or a mortgage loan is not self-liquidating. Although the customer is able to repay the loan, he does not do so out of funds generated by the loan itself.

[10] The real-bills doctrine, or commercial loan theory, as it is sometimes called, is a theory which asserts that banks should make only short-term, self-liquidating loans. This view, now generally considered fallacious, had wide acceptance when the Federal Reserve was organized. Hence, to give banks an incentive to make short-term and self-liquidating loans, only commercial paper which met these criteria was "acceptable paper" for rediscounting.

[11] Banks can, and very occasionally do, use eligible paper to secure their borrowing, but for technical reasons it is more convenient for banks to use government securities (see George W. McKinney, Jr., *The Federal Reserve Discount Window* [New Brunswick, N.J.: Rutgers University Press, 1960], pp. 64–71). In a financial crisis the Federal Reserve has the power to suspend the regulations defining paper eligible for discount or eligible as collateral for bank borrowing. It may lend to banks on any security it pleases. This is known as the "doorknob clause," because the Federal Reserve could lend to banks on the security of their doorknobs.

Discounting or the use of eligible paper to secure borrowing may, however, be in for a modest revival. Since banks have to secure government deposits (Federal and state and local) by pledging government securities, a number of banks are running short of unpledged government securities needed as security when they borrow from the Federal Reserve on their own notes.

Another change has been the abandonment of the real-bills doctrine as a criterion for discounting. This does not mean that banks are allowed to borrow an unlimited amount—for any purpose. Banks are supposed to borrow only for short-term reserve adjustments. Borrowing should be for "need," and not for profit, that is, they are not supposed to borrow merely because the Treasury bill rate is above the discount rate so that they can make a profit by borrowing and buying Treasury bills with the proceeds.[12] Whether or not banks actually do borrow for "need" and not for profit is a controversial issue discussed in Chapter 3.

Quite recently the Federal Reserve has used the discount mechanism to influence the types of loans made by banks. A letter issued in December, 1966 announced that in granting discounts the Federal Reserve Banks would take into account whether the applying bank was cooperating with the Federal Reserve's attempt to curb the growth of business loans. The letter was withdrawn after a few months, and it is too early to tell whether the Federal Reserve has gone back to its earlier idea of using the discount mechanism for *qualitative* control. (In any case it is not the qualitative control envisaged by the real-bills doctrine.)

If it does invoke this power, it must charge the bank a discount rate one-half percent above the normal discount rate, a provision of the law the Federal Reserve would like to see repealed. This power was given to the Federal Reserve as a result of the experience in the 1930's.

[12] The distinction between borrowing for "need" and borrowing for profit is quite hazy at times. To be sure, if a bank borrows and then buys securities or makes loans it can be said to borrow for profit rather than for "need." But how about a bank which borrows to meet a deposit drain which it could also have met by selling securities? Is it borrowing for "need" or profit? Similarly, suppose that a bank operates on a very thin margin of excess reserves and therefore has to borrow frequently as unexpected deposit drains occur. Is it borrowing for "need" or profit? By and large, the term "need" has little place in economic analysis.

In principle, though perhaps somewhat less in practice, borrowing is considered by the Federal Reserve to be a privilege of membership and not a right.[13] The Federal Reserve feels that its funds belong to all the member banks and that it would be improper to allow any bank to make "undue" use of these collective funds to gain an unfair competitive advantage over other banks. To be sure, the Federal Reserve generally does not refuse a loan to a bank since a refusal might endanger the bank, but as a Federal Reserve official put it, "we help a bank decide not to borrow from us."[14]

Another limitation on borrowing from the Federal Reserve arises out of banking tradition and policy. American banks have a tradition against borrowing, a tradition at least in part explained by the disastrous effects of borrowing which showed up in nineteenth-century financial panics. Some banks are proud of the fact that they never borrow from the Federal Reserve. During a "fairly active year" about 20 percent of the member banks borrow at one time or another, and at any one time about 10 percent are currently indebted.[15] When a bank does borrow, it is under pressure to repay rapidly. The Federal Reserve therefore thinks that banks which borrow from it feel constrained in increasing their loans and security holdings, so that a dollar of borrowed reserves is less expansionary than a dollar of reserves owned by the banks.

Another limitation on borrowing relates to the use made of the borrowed funds. The Federal Reserve has a traditional distaste for speculation, and banks are not supposed to borrow if they are, at the same time, making an unduly large volume of loans to speculators. This regulation is limited in its effectiveness because a man may borrow from his bank for regular business purposes and then, consequently, be able to use his own funds for speculation.

[13] See John Kareken, "Federal Reserve System Discount Policy: An Appraisal," *Banca Nazionale del Lavoro, Quarterly Review,* No. 48 (March, 1959), p. 123.

[14] Robert Roosa, quoted in Charles Whittlesey, "Credit Policy at the Discount Window," *Quarterly Journal of Economics,* Vol. 73 (May, 1959), p. 211.

[15] *Ibid.,* p. 212.

The discount rate which the Federal Reserve charges is usually kept fairly close to the Treasury bill rate, though it often lags behind at turns.[16] Since the discount rate is changed fairly infrequently, the two rates do tend to get out of line.

Changes in the Discount Rate

Changes in the discount rate were originally the only major tool of monetary policy. This was copied by the framers of the Federal Reserve Act from the British system, where the Bank of England relied on changes in its "bank rate" to control the money market.

This did not last long. In the early 1920's the discount-rate mechanism was supplemented by the development of open-market operations as a credit control tool. For some years after 1933, bank reserves were greatly in excess of legal requirements and very little borrowing from the Federal Reserve took place. The discount mechanism seemed unimportant, and in the nineteen-year period 1934–1952 (inclusive) the New York Federal Reserve Bank changed its discount rate only eight times. Since then, money has become tighter, banks have had more incentive to borrow, and the Federal Reserve has put much more emphasis on the discount rate and has changed it much more frequently.

In the Federal Reserve's view, changes in the discount rate act to control the money stock and credit extension in two ways. First, there is the cost effect. Raising the discount rate makes borrowing more expensive and, hence, reduces the volume of borrowing, while conversely, lowering the rediscount rate encourages banks to borrow.[17]

Second, there is a more complex expectations effect, usually called the "announcement effect." Changes in the discount rate

[16] The Treasury bill rate is usually treated as the rate which is competitive with the discount rate because Treasury bills (the shortest-term government securities) have a highly organized market and are extremely liquid.

[17] The willingness of banks to adjust their borrowing to changes in the discount rate is clearly inconsistent with the notion that banks borrow *only* for "need," unless the term "need" is interpreted rather broadly. The Federal Reserve recognizes that there is a profit element in borrowing.

are dramatic—unlike open-market operations, they frequently make the front page of newspapers. Hence, even if it should turn out that the *cost* effect of the rate increase on bank borrowing is minor, the rise in the rate serves notice on the financial community that the Federal Reserve is likely to use its other, more powerful tools, soon. Thus, if the discount rate is raised, the public's expectations may be changed. Borrowers, the Federal Reserve asserts, will reevaluate their investment plans when they realize that interest rates are rising. At the same time, lenders will be less willing to lend because they expect interest rates to rise even further. Thus, a rise in the discount rate reduces *both* the supply and demand for loans and, hence, reduces investment.

Moreover, even firms not currently borrowing or lending are affected. When they see the discount rate rise, they interpret this as a signal that the Federal Reserve is concerned about the excesses of the boom, and consequently, they become more cautious in their investment. In addition, with the Federal Reserve fighting inflation there is less reason to expect price rises, and hence there is less of an incentive to undertake anticipatory buying. Conversely, during a recession, a reduction in the discount rate causes both the supply and the demand for funds to increase and makes the public less fearful of the recession because it feels that the Federal Reserve is taking counteractive measures. In the Federal Reserve's view the announcement effect of discount rate changes is, therefore, an important tool of countercyclical policy; it changes expectations in a direction that helps to counteract inflation or recession.

A number of economists have challenged the Federal Reserve's view that the announcement effect of the discount rate is likely to be favorable and have argued that the Federal Reserve could make its message clearer by issuing a forthright statement rather than by requiring the public to interpret the meaning of a change in the discount rate. The message the financial community reads in the change may be vague and even misleading. For example, if the Federal Reserve raises the discount rate merely to keep it in line with the Treasury bill rate, the market may interpret this increase not as the technical adjustment which it really is, but as an announcement by the Federal Reserve that it wants interest rates, in general, to rise.[18] As one critic, Professor Warren Smith, has put it:

> The truth is that changes in the discount rate constitute the crudest kind of sign language. Why this stone age form of communication should be regarded as superior to ordinary English is really quite difficult to understand. . . . While a long tradition has perhaps made discount rate increases a reasonably effective means of international communication in some situations of this kind, there are surely other equally satisfactory means available, e.g., English, French, Latin, or Zulu.[19]

Moreover, even if the public interprets the change in the discount rate correctly, the announcement effect may go in the opposite direction of the one intended by the Federal Reserve. It may be destabilizing.[20] The Federal Reserve view assumes that when the discount rate rises, lenders will expect interest rates to rise further, while borrowers will expect them to fall. There is little reason to expect such a convenient pattern of expectations. A rise in interest rates may cause lenders to expect further rate increases in the future as the Federal Reserve believes—or it may lead them to expect a subsequent fall. A priori, one cannot say which reaction is the more likely. In any case, it is highly improbable that borrowers and lenders would have different expectations as the Federal Reserve view discussed above assumes. The Federal Reserve's announcement effect argument can be revised to take care of this criticism, at least to some extent. But since this expectations argument is relevant for the evaluation of the strength of monetary policy in general, it is discussed in Chapter 4 and not here.

---

[18] As a rule, the Federal Reserve does not announce its reasons for changing the discount rate. And even if a Federal Reserve official does give reasons, they may not be accepted by the market, but may be treated merely as a smokescreen. Many observers of the money market are "inside dopesters."

[19] Warren L. Smith, "The Instruments of General Monetary Control," *National Banking Review*, Vol. 1 (September, 1963), pp. 60, 64.

[20] *Ibid.*, pp. 61–64.

Reform of the Discount Mechanism

Some economists have suggested that the discount rate should be handled in a way that avoids an announcement effect. This could be done by a technique tried by Canada at one time, as well as by some other countries, of linking the discount rate to the Treasury bill rate, setting it, say, at one quarter of 1 percent, above the bill rate. Changes in the discount rate, then, could not be misinterpreted—they would clearly *not* signal changes in monetary policy. Member banks could still borrow to replenish reserves, but they would have no incentive to borrow to buy bills. Admittedly, insofar as banks use borrowed funds to hold assets other than Treasury bills (commercial paper for example, or business loans), they may still have an incentive to borrow.

Moreover, this procedure would avoid a difficulty of the present system. As Professor Friedman has stressed, a stable discount rate does *not* mean a stable monetary policy.[21] As open-market rates change, the incentive for banks to borrow also changes, as does the volume of borrowing. For example, if the Treasury bill rate is 4 percent, a discount rate of 4.5 percent is associated with little borrowing and, hence, represents, *ceteris paribus*, a fairly tight monetary policy. But if the bill rate rises to 5 percent, the same 4.5 percent discount rate leads to more borrowing and, hence, is an easier money policy. Linking the discount rate to the bill rate would solve this problem of changing monetary policy unintentionally, by merely keeping the discount rate stable.

Not only do some economists (Professor Friedman, for example) challenge the utilty of the announcement effect, but they go further and advocate the complete abolition of discounting.[22] In their view the discount mechanism is unnecessary; open-market operations are quite sufficient to change bank reserves to any extent desired by the Federal Reserve. Using several tools of monetary policy, where one would do, is only likely to lead to con-

[21] Milton Friedman, *A Program for Monetary Stability* (New York: Fordham University Press, 1960), pp. 40–43.
[22] *Ibid.*, pp. 35–45.

fusion in policy making. Moreover, if one takes the view that open-market operations are *the* tool of monetary policy, the discount mechanism can be looked upon as a loophole in monetary policy. If the Federal Reserve adopts a tighter monetary policy, banks can escape this tightening, for some time at least, by borrowing from the Federal Reserve. Similarly, if the Federal Reserve adopts an easier monetary policy, this is offset in part by banks repaying loans as open-market interest rates fall. This view of rediscounting is sometimes called the "rathole" theory.

In addition, Professor Friedman has argued that allowing banks to borrow at a subsidized (that is, below-market) rate of interest is unjustified. This critical view of discounting is reinforced by the fact that discounting has lost most of its original functions. Originally, discounting had two main purposes. First, it provided a way in which banks could obtain funds to meet financial panics and runs on banks. Second, it provided a way in which banks would be able to obtain additional reserves as business "needs" for loans increased. The first of these functions is no longer relevant—deposit insurance is sufficient to prevent bank runs. The second function, taking care of business needs, has disappeared. The idea of an automatic link between business "needs" and reserve level is part and parcel of the outmoded real-bills doctrine.

There are, however, several points to be made in defense of the discount mechanism. The Federal Reserve has argued that the discount mechanism, far from weakening open-market operations, actually supports them. The Federal Reserve feels free to undertake strong restrictive open-market operations precisely because it knows that any member bank which is unduly hurt by these operations can replenish its reserves by borrowing.[23] An analogy may clarify this. Brakes slow down an automobile; but the fact that a car has brakes allows one to drive faster than would be possible without them. In addition, the discount mechanism provides funds for country banks *immediately*, some-

---

[23] It may be tempting to argue that any bank short of reserves would not buy securities and, hence, would not be affected by the Federal Reserve's sale of securities in any case. But this is wrong. A bank loses reserves if its depositors buy securities.

thing open-market operations often fail to do. Moreover, the Federal Reserve claims, although banks may borrow to offset the impact of open-market operations, such borrowing is only temporary. A borrowing bank is under pressure to repay. Hence if a bank loses a dollar of reserves through open-market operations and gains a dollar through borrowing, it will be less willing to make loans and buy securities than before.

To be sure, discounting allows member banks to borrow at a preferential rate, but this preferential treatment is justified since it offsets, or partly offsets, the burdens of Federal Reserve membership, such as a more onerous reserve requirement.

The Reserve Requirement

Nowadays, to economists, the primary function of reserve requirements is to limit multiple-deposit creation and, through variations of the reserve requirement, to provide the Federal Reserve with a tool of monetary management.

Reserve requirements have a long history in American banking. Their original purpose was to protect the depositor and only gradually did their primary purpose become the limitation of the quantity of money. As late as 1952, state bank supervisors generally regarded reserve requirements mainly as a device for protecting the bank's liquidity,[24] and for all one knows, they may still do so even now.

For member banks, reserve requirements are set by the Board of Governors within limits established by Congress while the states control the reserve requirements of nonmember banks. State requirements vary widely, ranging from no legal reserve requirement at all in Illinois, to 30 percent of demand deposit in Vermont.[25] State requirements tend to be less onerous than Fed-

---

[24] Warren Smith, "Reserve Requirements in the American Monetary System," in Commission on Money and Credit, *Monetary Management* (Englewood Cliffs, N.J.: Prentice-Hall, 1963), p. 178.

[25] However, none of this 30 percent need be kept in vault cash. See H. P. Gray, "Bank Regulation, Bank Profitability, and Federal Reserve Membership," *National Banking Review,* Vol. 1 (December, 1963), pp. 210–211. These figures relate to 1962.

eral Reserve requirements. This is so because they allow banks to count (up to a certain proportion) deposits in other commercial banks and sometimes United States government securities, and, occasionally, even state and local securities as part of their reserve requirement. Member banks, on the other hand, can count only vault cash and deposits with the Federal Reserve as reserves. The deposits they hold with other banks and the state securities they hold are in addition to, and not part of, their legal reserves. Hence even if the reserve requirement *ratio* is the same, member banks have a smaller proportion of funds available for loans and security holdings than do nonmember banks. However, quantitatively this differential burden does not seem to be as great as is sometimes supposed.[26]

Some Controversies about Reserve Requirements

The reserve-requirements arrangement has come in for considerable criticism. Limiting the quantity of money is a task which faces the whole banking system. Why should some banks be more limited in their deposit expansion than others? Why should banks be able to gain a competitive advantage by staying out of the Federal Reserve System? Defenders of the present arrangement have argued that since about 85 percent of deposits are held by member banks, little would be gained by imposing the Federal Reserve requirements on state banks. Moreover, the issues of states' rights and "checks and balances" have been raised.[27] Nonetheless, the Board of Governors, being concerned about

[26] See Clark Warburton, "Nonmember Banks and the Effectiveness of Monetary Policy," in Commission on Money and Credit, *Monetary Management, op. cit.,* pp. 346–350.

[27] Note, however, that there is no constitutional question involved. The federal government quite clearly has the power to set reserve requirements for state banks. Moreover, bankers and others who use the "checks and balances" argument do not indicate why "checks and balances" should be in equilibrium just at this particular point. One could, after all, argue that uniform reserve requirements provide the ground rules, and that the relative advantages and disadvantages of Federal Reserve membership other than differences in reserve requirements then provide the "checks and balances."

banks leaving the Federal Reserve System, has advocated extending Federal Reserve reserve requirements to all insured banks. In return, nonmember banks would be allowed to discount with the Federal Reserve on the same basis as member banks.

The Federal Reserve imposes different reserve requirements on member banks depending upon their location (see page 47 below). Banks located in so-called "reserve cities," some fifty major centers, face higher reserve requirements than do banks located elsewhere, the so-called "country banks." Actually, the situation is somewhat more complicated; the Federal Reserve can, and does, classify many small banks located in reserve cities as country banks. The main criterion for this decision is whether the bank holds substantial deposits of other banks (interbank deposits). This system of imposing higher reserve requirements on reserve city banks than on country banks was taken over by the Federal Reserve from the National Banking System, which had used a three-fold classification—as did the Federal Reserve until recently—country banks, reserve city banks, and central reserve city banks. Under the National Banking System, country banks could keep a part of their reserves in city banks, and reserve city banks could keep part of their own reserves in central reserve city banks. Differential reserve requirements, therefore, seemed to be a natural way of protecting depositors. Under present conditions where member bank reserves are not kept in other commercial banks, this system is less obviously desirable. Nowadays there is little reason why the holding of interbank deposits should lead to a higher reserve requirement.[28]

On the other hand, there are some things to be said in defense of the differential reserve requirement. First, since country banks tend to be smaller than reserve city banks one could argue that, to help small firms and limit the concentration of economic power, preferential treatment of country banks is justified. Note also that country banks tend to lend to smaller firms than do reserve city banks, so that favoring country banks tends to help small firms in general. Second, there is a traditional argument which says

[28] See Smith, "Reserve Requirements in the American Monetary System," *op. cit.*, pp. 182–183.

that an old tax is a good tax, since people who purchased an asset subject to tax did so at a price made lower by the old tax. Applying this argument here, purchasers of stock in reserve city banks would be given a windfall gain if the reserve requirements of reserve city banks were lowered to match those of country banks. Admittedly, this argument applies only to existing banks and not to banks started after the change in regulations. Third, since country banks are much less likely to join the Federal Reserve System than reserve city banks, a lower requirement for country banks can be defended as a way of making Federal Reserve membership more attractive to those banks less likely to join —a less polite way of putting this is to say that the higher reserve requirement for city banks means plucking the goose that squawks the least.

Apart from discriminating between deposits on a (partly) geographic basis, the present system also discriminates greatly between demand deposits and time deposits. This raises a much more complex issue. If the purpose of the reserve requirement is to control the quantity of money, then the same reserve requirement should be imposed on all types of deposit money. No reserve requirement at all is needed for any item which is *not* money. If time deposits *are* money they should be subject to the same reserve requirements as demand deposits, whereas if they are not money they should, in principle, not have a reserve requirement at all. Only if the effect on expenditures of a dollar of time deposits is one-third of the effect of a dollar of demand deposits, could one argue that the present system which requires approximately one-third as much reserves for a dollar of time deposits as for a dollar of demand deposits is justified.

But whether time deposits are money is a frequently debated issue. Economists who emphasize the "medium of exchange" function of money tend to exclude time deposits from the definition of money since they are not a medium of exchange, whereas economists who stress the "store of value" function of money tend to include time deposits since they are certainly a store of value. Looking at the "fundamental" nature of money is not the best way to decide the classification of time deposits. We are interested in the stock of money because it affects expenditures and, hence, income. The relevant question is therefore whether a dollar of time deposits has a similar effect on income as a dollar of demand deposits. This is a statistical issue on which, unfortunately, there is considerable disagreement. One difficulty is that our data do not give an accurate separation of time deposits from demand deposits until the mid-1930's. This data problem is one of the reasons why Professor Friedman includes time deposits in the money stock.

The issue is further complicated by another factor, the existence of nonbank depository institutions such as savings banks and savings and loan associations, which (as a general rule) have no cash minimum reserve requirement. If commercial banks are forced to keep minimum reserves against time deposits they are discriminated against vis-à-vis other depository institutions.

What we have in fact done is go part way with the proponents of both points of view; we impose reserve requirements on time deposits but much lower ones than on demand deposits. This is not necessarily the optimum policy; the prestigious Commission on Money and Credit and others as well have called for the outright abolition of the reserve requirement on time deposits,[29] while others have suggested solving the problem of competition among institutions by going in the other direction and imposing a reserve requirement on nonbank depository institutions.

Discrimination between various types of banks and deposits is not the only debatable aspect of reserve requirements. The very existence of a legal minimum reserve requirement has been challenged.[30] After all, even in the absence of any legal requirement, banks would want to keep a certain ratio of reserves to their deposits to meet deposit drains. As long as this reserve-deposit ratio is stable, its size is not so important—the Federal Reserve could simply reduce the reserve base to offset a decline in

[29] Commission on Money and Credit, *Money and Credit* (Englewood Cliffs, N.J.: Prentice-Hall, 1961), p. 69.

[30] See Deane Carson, "Is the Federal Reserve System Really Necessary?" *Journal of Finance,* Vol. 19 (December, 1964), pp. 652–661.

the reserve ratio. The critical question is whether a voluntary reserve ratio would not be more erratic than the legally imposed minimum reserve ratio and, hence, would lead to greater instability in the money supply. Even if one takes the view that a voluntary reserve ratio would *probably* be as stable as a legal one, does the removal of a legal reserve requirement have enough advantages to make it worth taking the *risk* of greater instability? Moreover, such a plan would operate like a reduction of reserve requirements in its effect on Federal Reserve and, hence, Treasury earnings—a point discussed below.

An alternative proposed would go to the other extreme and require banks to hold 100 percent reserves against deposits.[31] This 100 percent reserve plan would abolish commercial banks as we know them and replace them by two types of institutions; one would be a type of bank which would accept deposits and transfer them by check but would not make any loans—its income would come entirely from service charges. The second type of bank would be an institution accepting long-term savings and making loans. It would pay interest to its depositors, but its deposits would be illiquid instead of being available on demand. They would not be money. To prevent a radical reduction in the money stock at the time when the scheme would be inaugurated, additional reserves would have to be provided, perhaps by having the Federal Reserve buy securities and loans held by banks or by making an outright gift to banks.

The main advantage of the proposal is that it would abolish multiple-bank-credit expansion and, hence, give the Federal Reserve more precise control over the money stock. Each dollar

---

[31] For good discussions of this proposal, see George Tolley, "100 Percent Reserve Banking," Leland B. Yeager (ed.), *In Search of a Monetary Constitution* (Cambridge, Mass.: Harvard University Press, 1962), pp. 275–304; Albert G. Hart, "The 'Chicago Plan' of Banking Reform," reprinted in American Economic Association, *Readings in Monetary Theory* (Homewood, Ill.: Richard D. Irwin, 1951), pp. 437–456; Milton Friedman, *op. cit.*, pp. 65–71; Smith, "Reserve Requirements in the American Monetary System," *op. cit.*, pp. 286–296; and Clark Warburton, *Depression, Inflation and Monetary Policy, Selected Papers 1945–1953* (Baltimore: Johns Hopkins University Press, 1966), Chapter 18. The original idea is attributed to Henry Simons, Laughlin Currie, and Irving Fisher.

of reserves would result in one dollar, and in no more than one dollar, of money. There would not be the slippage existing under the present system where, on the one hand, banks can add to the money stock by utilizing excess reserves and, on the other hand, can prevent the money stock from rising as reserves increase simply by holding excess reserves. Another advantage is that changes in currency holdings of the public would no longer change the potential money stock. At present, if the public decides to hold more currency there is (in the absence of excess reserves) a *multiple* decline in bank deposits so that the total money stock (deposits plus currency) falls. Conversely, a decline in the public's currency holdings increases the potential money stock. With 100 percent reserves neither of these situations would arise—if the public deposits currency in the banks, required reserves would increase by exactly the same amount as bank reserves. Similarly, other factors such as shifts of deposits between member and nonmember banks could not change the money stock.

The most obvious disadvantage of the 100 percent reserve plan is the trouble and dislocation involved in setting it up. The banking system would have to be split into two parts (even though both parts could function under one roof), bank personnel and bank customers would have to be reeducated, and some uncertainty and confusion would result. Those who believe that small fluctuations in the money supply have strong effects on income may consider these once-and-for-all costs as unimportant when compared to the gains resulting from 100 percent banking, but those who believe that small fluctuations in the money stock have little effect on income are unlikely to consider the changeover worthwhile.

Moreover, there is a possibility that a 100 percent reserve plan would fail because high service charges on demand deposits would give the public an incentive to find some cheaper way of handling its money transfers. The historical records show at least one such episode. In 1863 a prohibitive tax was imposed on banknotes issued by state banks. These banknotes were driven out of circulation but deposits subject to check took their place.[32] There

32 Hart, *op. cit.*, p. 451.

is, however, a way of avoiding this difficulty; as Professor Friedman has suggested, interest could be paid to banks on their reserves so that they would not have to impose high service charges on their depositors.[33]

In spite of these disadvantages, the 100 percent reserve plan has considerable support among economists. This support comes in good part from conservative economists (such as Professor Friedman) for two reasons. First, they frequently place strong emphasis on the importance of fluctuations in the quantity of money; and, second, once a 100 percent reserve system is set up, it would require less government regulation of banking than we have at present.

There are also a number of other, less radical, proposals for reforming the reserve-requirement system. One is to impose reserve requirements, not on deposits, but on the bank's asset holdings. This would make it possible to influence the type of loans made and securities bought by a bank, by imposing different reserve ratios on the various types of loans and securities. Whether one wants the government to have this power depends to a large extent on one's political views.

A milder version of this proposal would merely impose lower reserve requirements on government securities than on other assets. During an expansion banks tend to shift out of government securities into business loans, a fact which (for reasons described in Chapter 4) has inflationary consequences. If such a shift by banks would raise the average reserve requirement, this would offset at least some of the inflationary effects of the shift.[34]

Still another plan, the velocity reserve plan, would base a bank's required reserve not on the volume of its deposits but on its total debits to accounts, that is, on the volume of deposits multiplied by their average (transactions) velocity. This proposal, which was advocated by a Federal Reserve System committee in 1931, would operate to stabilize total expenditures, MV, by reducing the volume of money as velocity increases.[35]

---

[33] Friedman, *op. cit.*, pp. 71–75.

[34] For criticisms of this proposal, see Smith, "Reserve Requirements in the American Monetary System," *op. cit.*, pp. 283–285.

[35] For a discussion of the difficulties of this plan, see *ibid.*, pp. 191–198.

Another proposal, which has the support of the Federal Reserve, is that lower reserve requirements be imposed on small banks than on large banks, a situation already existing in part, due to the fact that country banks, which tend to be small, have a lower reserve requirement than do city banks. Apart from the standard advantages and disadvantages of a discrimination in favor of small business, this plan also has a technical advantage. Small banks are not able to handle their reserve positions as accurately as large banks and, therefore, typically carry a higher ratio of excess reserves. Thus, the same stated reserve requirement for large and small banks actually imposes a greater de facto reserve requirement on small banks than on large ones.

Professor Tobin has proposed that the Federal Reserve should pay interest (at the discount rate) on *excess* reserves.[36] This would make for greater stability in excess reserves and, hence, give the Federal Reserve better control over the money supply. At present, banks have a stronger incentive to use their reserves more fully (that is, to carry less excess reserves) at a time when interest rates are high than when they are low. Since periods of high interest rates tend to be periods of excessive aggregate demand and periods of low interest rates tend to be periods of inadequate demand, the same volume of reserves leads to larger money supply in periods of inflation than in periods of serious unemployment. If banks were paid interest on their *excess* reserves, they would have no greater incentive to use these reserves (and expand the money supply) in a period of high demand than in a period of inadequate demand, and an "automatic de-stabilizer" would be removed. Professors Tolley and Friedman, on the other hand, have proposed paying interest on required, rather than excess, reserves.[37]

---

[36] "Towards Improving the Efficiency of the Monetary Mechanism," *Review of Economics and Statistics,* Vol. 42 (August, 1960), pp. 276–279.

[37] Tolley, *op. cit.,* pp. 289–295, and Friedman, *op. cit.,* pp. 71–75. The Tolley-Friedman argument is that (apart from service costs) the marginal social cost of allowing someone to hold a bank deposit is zero. If banks are required to hold interest-free reserves, that is, to forgo earnings on part of the deposit, they will pass this cost on to their customers so that the cost of holding a deposit for a customer exceeds the social cost of this deposit. Hence, unless interest is paid on reserves, a condition of optimal-resource allocation is not met, customers hold too few deposits,

Reserve Requirement Changes

Apart from acting as the fulcrum for open-market operations, the reserve requirement provides an independent tool of monetary policy because the Federal Reserve can change the required reserve ratio. This power was given to the Federal Reserve on a temporary basis by the Banking Act of 1933 and made permanent by the Banking Act of 1935. Under present legislation the Federal Reserve can change reserve requirements of member banks within the following limits:

TABLE   **2.1**   *Range of Reserve Requirements*

	LIMITS SET BY CONGRESS		*Present Reserve Requirements in Force (March 16, 1967)*
	Maximum	*Minimum*	
	(Percent)		
Demand deposits			
Reserve city banks	10	22	16.5
Country banks	7	14	12
Time deposits			
All member banks	3	10	3–6*

NOTES: Percentage of adjusted demand deposits. *Adjusted* demand deposits include, apart from demand deposits, certified checks and cashiers checks outstanding plus letters of credit and travelers' checks sold for cash. The following items are subtracted from this total: demand deposits in incorporated domestic commercial banks, cash items in the process of collection, and cash items on hand to be sent for collection within one day.

* Three percent on savings deposits as well as on the first $5 million of other time deposits; otherwise 6 percent.

---

and a net social loss results. (Professor Friedman also develops an equity argument along these lines.) But note that our tax system discriminates *in favor* of deposits. The holder of deposits receives a form of nonmoney income, the services of liquidity, from his deposit, and this nonmoney income is not taxed. This factor serves as an offset against the effects of requiring banks to hold reserves at no interest. It is, of course, not possible to say whether this tax discrimination more than offsets, or less than fully offsets, the above reserve-requirement discrimination. All that one can say is that, given our present reserve requirements *and* tax system, it is not clear whether deposit holders receive unduly favorable or unfavorable treatment.

When the Federal Reserve lowers reserve requirements, the potential money stock is increased in two ways. First, some reserves which were previously required reserves are now excess reserves and this allows banks to increase their deposits. Second, a lowering of the required-reserve ratio raises the deposit multiplier so that any increases in the reserve base allow a greater increase in the money stock than they did before. A raising of the required-reserve ratio works, of course, in the opposite direction.

Since the limits within which the Federal Reserve can change the reserve requirements are quite broad, this method of changing the *excess* reserves of banks is very powerful—as in the case of open-market operations, there is plenty of ammunition. But the Federal Reserve has used its powers to change the reserve requirement only infrequently. In ten years (1957–1966) the reserve requirement on demand deposits of reserve city banks and country banks has been changed only three times for each type of bank (though one should add to this the inclusion of vault cash in reserves as well as the abolition of the central reserve city classification). Thus, the Federal Reserve is using reserve-requirement changes as a method of bringing about broad secular changes in reserves rather than as a sensitive countercyclical device. For example, if a large-scale disarmament program were undertaken, a lowering of reserve requirements would be an obvious way of counteracting the decline in aggregate demand.

In the Federal Reserve's opinion, the power to change reserve requirements does not provide a flexible tool for three reasons. First, reserve-requirement changes cannot be used to bring about small changes in the reserve base since each change in the reserve ratio of half a percentage point involves a substantial dollar volume of reserves. Second, every time reserve requirements are raised, banks which do not hold sufficient excess reserves are forced to adjust their reserve positions either by liquidating other assets or by borrowing. Naturally, bankers dislike this pressure. Admittedly, this problem occurs only if reserve requirements are raised. If requirements are lowered, banks do not *have* to adjust their portfolios. (To be sure, their optimum portfolio balance changes if reserve requirements are cut, but this occurs also if the Federal Reserve increases reserves via open-market operations.) Third, not only is the process of raising their reserves troublesome for banks, but it also requires some time, and hence the Federal Reserve feels that it must give banks some notice before new, higher reserve requirements become effective. According to the Federal Reserve, raising reserve requirements is therefore a slower-acting tool than open-market operations.

It is by no means certain that this reasoning is correct. First, although each change in the reserve ratio by half a percentage point involves a large amount of reserves, why can't the reserve ratio be changed by, say, one-tenth of a percentage point?[38] Time after time, Federal Reserve statements about the inflexibility of reserve-requirement changes ignore this possibility. Second, if the reserve requirement were raised only by very small steps, then bankers would not find it so hard to meet the new requirement. After all, banks already have to adjust their reserve positions frequently as they experience deposit drains. Finally, if banks are given notice that the reserve requirement will be increased shortly, they will start to adjust their portfolios at once so that at least some of the effect will occur immediately. Moreover, if, as will be suggested below, the effect of monetary policy changes on income occurs only with a fairly substantial lag, the fact that one tool takes a week or two longer than another is not very significant. Reserve-requirement changes may not be as inflexible a tool as the Federal Reserve believes.

Interaction of Major Tools

Having discussed each of the major tools in isolation, the time has come to see how they interact. There are two aspects of this interaction. On the one hand, each of the tools has its own set of advantages and disadvantages and, hence, they can be used to com-

[38] See Joseph Aschheim, *Techniques of Monetary Control* (Baltimore: Johns Hopkins Press, 1961), p. 20; and Charles Whittlesey, "Reserve Requirements and the Integration of Credit Policies," *Quarterly Journal of Economics*, Vol. 57 (August, 1944), pp. 558–564.

plement each other. On the other hand, it can be said that, in a broad sense, all the tools do the same job since they all change excess reserves and that, therefore, a decision has to be made in each case as to which one should be used. In this way they are competitive. In its public statements, however, the Federal Reserve has emphasized their complementarity and has deemphasized their competitive nature.

In the Federal Reserve's view the tools should be used jointly. For example, as a business expansion proceeds, the Federal Reserve may decide to change its policy of "active ease" to a more cautious one.[39] This change will typically occur in small steps. At first, all that may happen is that in making its forecasts of the impact of market forces on bank reserves, the Federal Reserve may begin to resolve cases of doubt in the direction of restriction rather than in that of ease. Thus, the errors that inevitably occur tend to tighten money slightly rather than to ease it. As the expansion continues and the Federal Reserve begins to fear inflation, it purposefully reduces the growth rate of the reserve base by changing its open-market operations. With money tightened and the interest rate rising, the Treasury bill rate exceeds the discount rate. The discount rate is now increased. This is partly a defensive measure to curb bank borrowing and, in part, serves through the cost element as well as the announcement effect, to stimulate further increases in market interest rates.[40] If this action proves insufficient, the Federal Reserve may

---

[39] The Federal Reserve frequently uses terms like "active ease" and may announce, for example, that it is abandoning its policy of "active ease" in favor of a policy of "ease." While the direction of the movement is clear at least to the banking community, this type of terminology has no precise and quantitative meaning—at least to people outside the Federal Reserve.

[40] Here is a description of the process given in the 1957 *Annual Report* of the Board of Governors: "In summary, open-market policy and discount policy are complementary instruments of day-to-day monetary policy. In a period of monetary restriction, open-market policy limits the availability of bank reserves at the System's initiative. In effect this action places initiative in obtaining additional reserves with the member banks, many of which are reluctant to operate for extended periods on the basis of borrowed reserves. As restrictive monetary policy continues or becomes more intense, there are increases in the frequency, average duration, and

follow it up with greater open-market sales, or it may, though this is less likely, raise reserve requirements. If it does raise reserve requirements, it may well offset temporarily much of the resulting stringency in the money market by undertaking expansionary open-market operations. These expansionary open-market operations are then reversed over time. In this way excess reserves are reduced smoothly rather than abruptly, as they would have been had the Federal Reserve not used open-market purchases to cushion the sharp change in excess reserves resulting from the increase in the reserve ratio.

Once the Federal Reserve feels that the business outlook is changing, that the danger is now more likely to be a recession than an inflation, the Federal Reserve may undertake expansionary open-market operations which gather force as the recession becomes more and more obvious. (To be sure, if the Federal Reserve is too concerned about inflation, or if it uses the wrong money market indicators, this may take place only after the recession has gone quite far—this is a point made by many critics of the Federal Reserve.) As market rates of interest fall, the discount rate is again out of line with market rates, and the gap between it and the market rates discourages borrowing. This is deflationary and, hence, the Federal Reserve is likely to lower the discount rate. Moreover, since, in any case, it is necessary to increase the money supply due to the secular expansion of the economy, the Federal Reserve may lower the reserve-requirement ratio, cushioning the move by open-market sales at the same time.

But this picture of smooth orchestration of monetary instruments is only half the story; it omits the competitive element. At each step the Federal Reserve has to make a choice as to which of its tools to use. This choice frequently involves considerations other than those of monetary management, in the narrow sense.

---

volume of discounts, as well as in the number of member banks engaged in such borrowing. At such times, the cost of borrowing reserves—that is, the discount rate—may also be raised. Commercial bank lending and investing policies thus come under increasing restraint." Quoted in David Eastburn, *The Federal Reserve on Record* (Philadelphia: Federal Reserve Bank of Philadelphia, n.d.), p. 100.

Let us, therefore, look at the relative advantages and disadvantages of each of the major tools. To do this it is convenient to treat separately cyclical and secular policy actions. In addition to following a countercyclical policy the Federal Reserve also has the task of providing for a secular growth of the money stock. With potential output rising over time, price stability and full employment require a secular increase in the money stock unless velocity rises as much as potential output, which would be most unlikely. In practice, cyclical and secular elements tend to fuse —for example, the Federal Reserve may take care of the secular growth of the money stock, in part, by lowering reserve requirements during a recession and by not raising them during the subsequent expansion. But although cyclical and secular elements may be combined into one policy, one can analyze them separately.

Relative Advantages and Disadvantages of Major Tools for Countercyclical Policy

To start with the countercyclical problem, let us compare the relative advantages and disadvantages of discount-rate changes, open-market operations, and reserve-requirement changes. Comparing the first two of these, open-market operations have three clear-cut advantages over discount-rate changes. First, open-market operations are much stronger; they can bring about much bigger changes in the reserve base than can discount-rate changes. Second, they are more flexible; and third, they are much more precise. Unlike discount-rate changes, the Federal Reserve can undertake open-market operations to change the reserve base by the exact amount it wishes. Discount-rate changes, on the other hand, merely vary the incentives which banks have to borrow— the Federal Reserve has no way of knowing by exactly how much they will change their borrowing. In addition, open-market operations have less of an announcement effect than discount-rate changes. Some observers have stressed this point very strongly, believing that the announcement effect is *much* greater for discount-rate changes than for open-market operations. But note that the important financial decisions are made by sophisticated people who are quite aware of what the Federal Reserve is doing in the open market. Admittedly, discount-rate changes tend to make the observed changes in the money market "official," and in this way do have a greater announcement effect. In any case, as pointed out above, whether a strong announcement effect is an advantage or not is a debatable matter. But, on the other hand, discount-rate changes probably are superior to open-market operations in having a wider geographic impact immediately.

Comparing discount-rate changes with reserve-requirement changes, the latter have more strength. At least in the range within which the Federal Reserve has varied the discount rate, its effects on bank reserves are distinctly smaller than those which can be achieved with reserve-requirement changes. It is not easy to decide which one of these two tools is the more precise. Reserve-requirement changes are more precise in the sense that the Federal Reserve knows by how much it is changing required reserves. On the other hand, given the Federal Reserve's penchant for changing reserve requirements only by relatively large steps, discount rates can be used for smaller adjustments; that is, they are more precise in this way. (Note, however, that this precision is largely a reflection of the fact that discount-rate changes are not as powerful a tool as reserve-requirement changes.) Rightly or wrongly, the Federal Reserve seems to feel (or at least has felt in the past) that discount-rate changes are a more flexible weapon than reserve-requirement changes—at least the Federal Reserve has used them more flexibly. Thus, to summarize, discount-rate changes are weaker than the other two major tools, and while less flexible than open-market operations, they are, at least in the Federal Reserve's opinion, more flexible than reserve-requirement changes. This leaves open-market operations and reserve-requirement changes to be compared.

Reserve-requirement changes have two advantages over open-market operations as a countercyclical tool. First, reserve-requirement changes have a full geographic impact without a significant lag. As mentioned above, open-market operations may take a longer time to spread the effects to banks throughout the country.

A second advantage is that banks are more willing to expand their loans and deposits if they gain excess reserves through a cut in the reserve requirement rather than through open-market operations. Unless the bank itself sells securities, Federal Reserve open-market purchases show up for the individual bank as an increase in the deposits of customers. The bank has no way of knowing how long it will have these deposits; it has experienced an abnormal increase in deposits and may now expect to face an abnormal drain. When reserve requirements are lowered, however, the bank obtains excess reserves and has no reason to expect an abnormal deposit drain, hence it is more willing to use these reserves. To be sure, one could well argue that this difference is not very important—if banks are less willing to expand on the basis of a dollar of reserves generated by open-market operations than by reserve-requirement changes, the Federal Reserve could simply offset this by undertaking larger open-market operations. Thus this advantage seems rather minor.

Against these two advantages of reserve-requirement changes over open-market operations one has to balance disadvantages. First, reserve-requirement changes cannot be undertaken anywhere near as frequently as open-market operations can—continuous changes would make life too hard for banks and drive many out of the Federal Reserve System. Second, the Federal Reserve has argued that reserve requirements cannot be changed by small steps. But as pointed out above, this is a dubious point.

Third, and finally, according to the Federal Reserve, increases in reserve requirements, unlike open-market sales, create problems for banks. If reserve requirements are raised, all banks are affected regardless of whether they have excess reserves, and those banks without excess reserves must reduce loans, sell securities, or borrow. By contrast, if the Federal Reserve sells securities, banks without excess reserves need not buy any securities. But this is only partially correct. Open-market sales reduce the reserves of even those banks that do not participate themselves in the open-market transactions. If their depositors buy securities, their reserves are reduced. But the Federal Reserve *may* have something else in mind. If reserve requirements are raised, banks facing a shortage of reserves will know that the Federal Reserve is to blame for their trouble, but banks that lose reserves because their customers are buying securities will not know that the Federal Reserve's open-market operations are responsible.[41] Since the Federal Reserve likes to live at peace with its member banks, open-market operations make life easier for the Federal Reserve than do reserve-requirement increases.

To summarize this discussion, Table 2.2 illustrates the salient advantages of each of these tools.

Relative Advantages and Disadvantages of Various Tools for Secular Changes

Turning to the methods of increasing the money supply secularly, the problem is easier in one respect: discount-rate changes can be ignored: even a continually falling discount rate would not increase the money stock sufficiently, in the long run.

In deciding between open-market operations and reserve-requirement changes, the factors discussed above, in connection with countercyclical actions, are not relevant for secular increases in the money stock;[42] instead, what is significant is the distribution of gains between the Treasury and commercial banks. If the money supply is increased secularly by lowering reserve requirements banks are enabled to purchase additional earning assets without relinquishing any of the securities that they already hold. On the other hand, if the Federal Reserve increases bank reserves by open-market operations, banks obtain their additional reserves only by giving up some of their securities. Interest on

[41] For a statement by Chairman Martin which lends itself to this interpretation, see David Eastburn, *op. cit.*, p. 134.

[42] The fact that the impact of open-market operations is geographically concentrated is not relevant because in the long run the effects spread throughout the country. Similarly, the fact that changes in reserve requirements are more obvious to the banks is not important—eventually they will find out that the increase in their reserves is permanent. Lowering the reserve requirement continuously does not upset banks and, in any case, for secular changes, it is not necessary to proceed by continuous small steps; discontinuous large steps offset by temporary open-market operations can do the job.

TABLE 2.2 *Relative Advantages of Various Monetary Tools for Countercyclical Actions*

Comparing

	Discount-Rate Changes	Open-Market Operations	Discount-Rate Changes	Reserve-Requirement Changes	Reserve-Requirement Changes	Open-Market Operations
Strength	X	X	X	X	–[1]	–[1]
Flexibility	P[2]	X	P[2]	P[2]		X
Precision	P[3]	X	P[3]	P[3]		X
Faster geographic spread	X		–	–	X	
Willingness of banks to change assets	–	–	–	–	X	
Good relations with commercial banks	–	–	X[4]	–		X[4]
Relative strength of announcement effect	X[5]	–	–	–	X[5]	

X denotes superiority.   – denotes approximate equality.

NOTES:

1 Both have more than adequate strength.

2 The relative flexibility of these two tools is uncertain; the Federal Reserve appears to believe that discount-rate changes are the more flexible tool and, hence, uses this tool more flexibly.

3 The relative precision of these two tools is uncertain. Given present Federal Reserve practices, discount-rate changes are probably more precise. With a different Federal Reserve policy, reserve-requirement changes may be more precise.

4 Applies to increases on reserve requirements, not to decreases.

these securities is now paid by the Treasury, not to the commercial banks, but to the Federal Reserve which in turn hands it back to the Treasury.[43] As Professor Warren Smith has remarked, "To the extent that the central bank has power to change reserve requirements . . . it necessarily has a policy—whether explicitly or by default—with respect to the earnings of the banking system."[44]

Not surprisingly, this problem became a political issue and the Federal Reserve was criticized in the late 1950's for taking care of the secular increase in the money stock, at that time, by, primarily, lowering reserve requirements rather than by making open-market purchases.[45]

The critics argued that no reason existed to justify the Federal Reserve's increase of the money stock in a way which would give banks a capital gain at the Treasury's expense. Given the high social priority of public services and the difficulties in obtaining adequate tax revenue, the Federal Reserve, it was contended, should raise the income of the Treasury rather than of banks. To be sure, corporate and personal income taxes ensure that the Treasury recovers a good part of any gain accruing to banks and their stockholders, but critics asked, why should the Treasury get only a part of it?[46] Why should the Federal Reserve, in effect, subsidize banks?

[43] The same thing holds true if the Federal Reserve buys securities from nonbanks. The seller deposits the sales proceeds in his bank and bank reserves are increased. Both assets and liabilities of the bank rise. The bank is worse off than it would have been had reserve requirements been reduced instead, for a reduction in reserve requirements would have raised the bank's earning assets without raising its deposit liabilities.

[44] Smith, "Reserve Requirements in the American Monetary System," *op. cit.,* p. 227.

[45] In 1959, the Administration asked Congress to raise the interest ceiling on long-term government securities. Congress was willing to comply if the Administration would in turn accept a "Sense of Congress" resolution (which would not be legally binding, but would only be a Congressional recommendation) that the Federal Reserve, in raising the money stock, should use open-market operations more frequently. The Administration decided that this would constitute interference with the Federal Reserve's independence and did not accept it.

[46] Moreover, even the part which the Treasury receives through higher taxes is not costless. The collection of taxes imposes a social cost on the

Moreover, there is also a technical argument in favor of not lowering reserve requirements. If the Federal Reserve should make a mistake in forecasting the change in the reserve base resulting from market factors, this mistake in the Federal Reserve's defensive operations would have more serious effects if the reserve requirements are low than they would if these were high. This is so because a low reserve ratio ensures that each dollar of reserves supports a larger volume of deposits. Note, however, that the Federal Reserve can offset any mistakes in its forecasts quite rapidly.

The Federal Reserve replied that it is *not* the function of a central bank to earn income for the Treasury. It is a basic principle of central banking that the central bank should conduct its operations with complete disregard of profit and loss. However, the critics replied that while it is certainly true that a central bank should put the stabilization goal *ahead* of any desire to earn income, the central bank might still, legitimately, take its earnings into account by choosing between two methods of changing bank reserves when these two methods are known to be equally effective in doing the job.

This argument, however, is open to an objection. If the Federal Reserve acts to increase its earnings when it does not affect its stabilization function, there is a danger that, over time, it will gradually drift into a position of taking its earnings into account even in those cases when earnings should not be considered.

In addition, while it is possible to separate *analytically* secular and cyclical increases in the reserve base, *in day-to-day operations* they present a single unit of action. Thus, if the Federal Reserve wants to increase the reserve base during a cyclical downturn, it may want to do so by lowering reserve requirements, perhaps because reserve-requirement changes have a broader geographic impact. Then, during the subsequent expansion, when the Federal Reserve will want to restrict the growth of the re-

---

economy, largely by its interference with optimal-resource allocation. Some of this "excess burden" of taxation exists even when the increase in tax receipts is due to an increase of the tax base rather than the tax rate.

serve base, it may wish to use open-market operations, perhaps because these are more rapidly implemented than are reserve-requirement changes. If the Federal Reserve cuts reserve requirements during the recession, and does not raise them in the expansion, a secular downward drift in the reserve ratio develops, and, purely as a by-product of choosing the best countercyclical action, the Federal Reserve finds itself providing for the secular growth of the money stock by lowering reserve requirements. In other words, it is certainly *possible* that the Federal Reserve faces an asymmetry; cutting reserve requirements *may be* superior to open-market operations as an expansionary policy during a recession, but open-market operations *may be* preferable to raising reserve requirements as a countercyclical policy during the upswing. This is certainly a *possibility*. Whether it is more than a possibility is, of course, highly debatable. But it does suggest that it *may* be *incorrect* to argue that impact on government finance is the only relevant consideration, since changes in reserve requirements and open-market purchases are equally effective tools of secular expansion.

Another controversial aspect of the question is whether raising bank profits at the expense of the Treasury is necessarily a "bad" thing. Two replies can be given to the argument, stated above, that the Treasury should be allowed to capture the profit resulting from the secular increase in the money stock.

First, one could argue that bank profits, at present, are too low, that higher bank profits are needed to allow banks to raise more capital since the current capital-deposit ratio is too low. Note, however, that the microeconomic basis of this argument is unclear. Granted that higher earnings would *permit* banks to raise more capital, would a profit-maximizing bank actually do so? To some extent, raising profits would increase entry into banking, but given the severe limitations on free entry this factor may not be very important. Moreover, one might argue that the capital-deposit ratio is *not* too low, but merely reflects the fact that banks are now safer than they once were.

A second argument in favor of lowering reserve requirements is that reserve requirements were raised to too high a level in the period up to 1951, and the reductions in the reserve ratio since then merely represent a return to the proper ratio.[47] This argument is hard to evaluate since it is difficult to find criteria for determining the "proper" ratio.

Another argument takes a quite different line. If reserve requirements are lowered, it is pointed out, bank profits are raised only temporarily; in the long run, competition ensures that these higher profits are distributed in some fashion among bank customers. But this argument ignores the imperfections of banking competition, for example, the restriction on entry due to the bank chartering provisions.

Are All These Tools Necessary?

Having discussed which of the three major tools to use both for cyclical and for secular purposes, there remains one problem to be taken up. This is the basic issue of whether all three tools are really necessary. Professor Warren Smith has suggested that, once reserve requirements have been established at the optimal level, it may be desirable to eliminate, for normal times, the power to change reserve requirements.[48] Professor Milton Friedman would go even further and would abolish not only the power to change reserve requirements, but also the power to discount, leaving the Federal Reserve only one tool, open-market operations. In his view, open-market operations are perfectly adequate to change the reserve base. Giving the central bank more than a single tool merely confuses the issue.[49]

Although, in principle, it is certainly correct to say that open-market operations alone could be used to change the reserve base, the Federal Reserve feels that the use of all three tools in combination is much more effective. To a considerable extent, though not completely, this question is involved in a larger issue. As will be discussed below, Professor Friedman would have the

[47] Another aspect of this problem was discussed in footnote 37, p. 46–47.
[48] Smith, "Reserve Requirements in the American Monetary System," *op. cit.*, p. 216.
[49] Friedman, *op. cit.*, pp. 30–51.

central bank abandon countercyclical policy and would have it do only one thing—raise the money stock at a steady rate. For such a policy, little would be gained by having two tools in addition to open-market operations. But even given the present goals of monetary policy it is by no means clear that three tools do the job better than one would.[50]

Before leaving the comparison of major tools, it may be worth noting that the above analysis dealt only with the United States and does not necessarily apply to other countries. For example, in many countries the discount rate is more important than it is in the United States. In Japan it is the primary tool of monetary policy, and in Britain, too, the Bank Rate is more important than is the discount rate in the United States; not only business loans, but even interest rates on outstanding mortgages are linked to it. The Swiss central bank relies primarily on discount-rate changes; until a few years ago it did not even have the legal power to undertake open-market operations. Moreover, in many countries, developed as well as underdeveloped, open-market operations are not feasible because the government security market is too thin and inadequate. Open-market operations are a full-fledged tool of monetary policy in only a few countries, notably the United States, Britain, and Canada.[51]

[50] Professor Viner has argued that in a system such as ours which has a large number of small banks, the discount privilege is necessary since small banks may face substantial deposit drains and do not have easy access to the money market ("The Necessity and Desirable Range of Discretion to be Allowed to a Monetary Authority," Leland Yeager [ed.], *In Search of a Monetary Constitution* [Cambridge: Harvard University Press, 1962], p. 260). But the difference between Professors Friedman and Viner on this issue is not as great as it may seem. Under present regulations, banks not meeting their reserve requirements are subject to a fine. This fine could act like the discount mechanism if banks could somehow be induced to look upon the imposition of such a fine as a normal thing and not as a reflection on their virtue. A discount rate kept significantly higher than the bill rate would have a similar effect.

[51] Peter Fousek, *Foreign Central Banking: The Instruments of Monetary Policy* (New York: Federal Reserve Bank of New York, 1957), p. 31. See also Graeme Dorrance, "The Instruments of Monetary Policy in Countries without Highly Developed Capital Markets," *International Monetary Fund Staff Papers*, Vol. 12 (July, 1965), pp. 272–278.

Selective Controls

The major monetary tools discussed above are methods of changing bank reserves and, hence, aggregate demand, throughout the economy. Another set of tools focuses on specific areas of the economy. These "selective" controls have their initial impact on specific markets rather than on the whole economy. They do not possess one frequently claimed advantage of monetary policy, neutrality,[52] but instead affect particular markets which, it is claimed, are relatively insulated from the effects of overall monetary policy. They are designed to focus on trouble spots where demand may be excessive; their characteristics are those of a rifle, not of a shotgun.

At present there are only three selective controls, Regulations T, U, and G.[53] They limit stock market credit extended by security brokers and banks, and other lenders respectively. The method used is to set a minimum-margin requirement, that is, to set a minimum down payment for stocks registered on national security exchanges and for securities convertible into such stock. At present (1968) the margin requirement is 70 percent. This means that the purchaser must put up at least 70 percent of the value of the stock himself and may borrow only 30 percent from his bank or broker. For convertible securities it is 50 percent. The Federal Reserve has the power to vary the margin requirement and can raise it up to 100 percent.

The reason why the Federal Reserve was given this power by the Securities and Exchange Act in 1934 can be seen by look-

[52] The meaning of neutrality as well as its advantages and disadvantages are discussed in Chapter 5.
[53] Strictly speaking, Regulation A covering the types of paper the Federal Reserve is willing to discount is also a "selective control" but since Regulation A is fairly general, it is usually not included in the term "selective controls." The designations "Regulation T" and "Regulation U" come from the fact that when it commenced operations the Federal Reserve issued a series of regulations starting with "Regulation A" (discounting) and had reached the letters T and U by the time it issued the stock market margin regulations. The letter G, previously used to designate another regulation, was free at the time (1967) when the new regulation was imposed.

ing back at the situation in 1927–1929. In these y
Wholesale Price Index was stable but there was a spe
boom in the stock market. The Federal Reserve was in a
dary. It had no power to affect the stock market directly. By
raising the discount rate or by its conduct of open-market operations it could make credit generally less available and, hence, to
some extent limit the purchase of stocks on credit. But with stock
prices rising rapidly, it is unlikely that even a substantial boost
in interest rates would have had much effect on stock market
borrowing. And such a substantial rise in interest rates would
have been deflationary for the rest of the economy. At first,
the Federal Reserve relied on moral suasion to limit stock market
loans of banks; later, it raised the discount rate moderately. This
rise in the discount rate was too little and too late to curb the
stock market boom.[54] If the Federal Reserve had had Regulations
T, U, and G available to it at that time it could have limited
stock market credit without a deflationary effect on the rest of
the economy.

As so often happens, we locked the garage door after the
car was stolen. Since 1934 there has been no disastrous speculative boom in the stock market and, although the margin requirement was, on occasion, raised to 100 percent, it was probably
not a very important factor. An empirical study of Regulations
T and U suggests that they have not succeeded in reducing fluctuation and risk in the stock market or in limiting an "excessive" use of credit for security purchases.[55]

Potentially much more important are selective controls over
consumer credit. During World War II, as well as during the
Korean War and, briefly in 1948–1949, the Federal Reserve set
minimum down payments and maximum maturities for loans for

---

[54] For good discussions of this episode, see Milton Friedman and Anna
Schwartz, *A Monetary History of the United States, 1867–1960* (Princeton: Princeton University Press, 1963), pp. 254–266; and Emanuel Goldenweiser, *American Monetary Policy* (New York: McGraw-Hill, 1951), pp.
148–156.

[55] Hence, since they add to paper work and discriminate among buyers,
they are undesirable. See Thomas Moore, "Stock Market Margin Requirements," *Journal of Political Economy*, Vol. 14 (April, 1966), pp. 158–167.

consumer-durable purchases (Regulation W). At present, the Federal Reserve does not have the legal power to control consumer credit although in England and in some other countries consumer credit control is used as a countercyclical weapon.

From time to time a number of economists have proposed reinstituting consumer credit controls.[56] This idea gathered considerable support in 1955 when consumer credit rose rapidly in spite of a restrictive monetary policy. Since then, support for reinstituting Regulation W has waned. However, there has been some Congressional interest. The latest instance is a favorable report by the House Banking and Currency Committee of a bill which included standby authority for the President to regulate consumer credit.

The advocates of Regulation W point to several advantages of regulating consumer credit directly. First, consumer credit is a destabilizing factor since credit purchases conform positively to the business cycle. Given the size of credit sales in our economy, they are a significant destabilizer. Second, the argument runs, consumer credit extension is almost immune to monetary policy. An increase in interest rates has only a trivial effect on consumer borrowing. The demand for consumer credit is mainly a derived demand since the interest rate is only a relatively small part of the whole price of a durable bought on the installment plan. This tends to make the demand for consumer credit highly inelastic.[57] Moreover, it is said, credit rationing and

---

[56] See, for instance, James W. Angell, "Appropriate Monetary Policies and Operations in the United States Today," *Review of Economics and Statistics*, Vol. 42 (August, 1960), p. 251.

[57] The reason why derived demand tends to be less elastic than final demand is that a given percentage increase in the price of the particular input represents a smaller percentage increase in the final selling price. For example, if interest costs are 10 percent of the cost of an item, a doubling of interest costs raises the total cost by only 1 percent. (In principle, derived demand is not *necessarily* smaller than the final demand since there is the possibility of substituting one input for another but this is not relevant for consumer credit.) A somewhat related argument is that the demand for consumer credit is interest inelastic because consumers do not know how much interest they are paying for consumer loans. This argument is rather dubious. By analogy, one could argue that (apart from substitution in production) the demand for steel is completely inelastic since

the lack of availability of funds (factors to be discussed in Chapter 4) do not inhibit lenders in making consumer loans because the interest rate on such loans is very high and the repayment record is good.[58] Hence, conventional monetary policy puts a greatly disproportionate part of the burden of curbing aggregate demand on investment and too little on consumption. By discriminating against investment, the argument runs, a tight money policy reduces growth.

Another argument for using consumer credit controls is that they take less time to become effective than general controls since they affect consumption rather than investment. Since the purchase of a consumer durable does not involve a long planning period it responds to monetary policy faster than does business investment. (The importance of quick response is discussed in Chapter 7.)

One other point which seems to dispose some people favorably to Regulation W is a belief that some households are acting irrationally in taking consumer credit. They do not know the implicit interest rate they are paying on consumer credit and are taken advantage of by unscrupulous sellers.

Finally, in a defense emergency there is another reason for

---

the buyers of products made of steel do not know the cost of steel. Although households may not be aware of the true interest rate they pay on consumer credit, they do know the monthly payments—and these are affected by changes in interest rates. One can salvage a small part of the argument by saying that if households would know the true interest rate, and be aware of its fluctuations, they *might* defer demand to periods of low interest rates.

[58] Put in this, the usual way, the argument lacks rigor. In equilibrium, at the margin, profits are equal on all types of loans so that there is no difference between consumer loans and business loans on account of one being more profitable than the other. But it is possible to salvage the argument by restating it as follows: Consumer credit involves great clerical and administrative costs for the bank. In the short run these are fixed costs, since a bank would usually not want to dismantle its consumer loan division if consumer loans declined temporarily. For business loans, on the other hand, the fixed administrative costs are a smaller proportion of total costs. Hence, if the cost of money (pure interest rate) rises, banks will be more willing to cut back on business loans than on consumer loans. In this way they minimize the burden of excess capacity and set marginal revenue equal to marginal cost in each activity.

controlling installment credit. Many of the industries producing consumer durables can also produce military equipment; an automobile plant, for example, can shift from cars to tanks. In a partial mobilization period, the Korean War period, for example, we try to get these industries into defense production by offering them the carrot of government contracts. Regulation W, by cutting down on the civilian demand for their products, adds the stick to the carrot.

There is, however, a considerable amount to be said on the other side of this dispute.[59] First, one should control aggregate demand in a way that does not affect resource allocation. If demand is unstable in some industries, this should be offset by general stabilization policies and not by reducing the size of the destabilizing industry.

Second, one may question whether a reduction of consumer loans really reduces aggregate demand. From a strict quantity theory point of view, Regulation W does little to affect aggregate demand since it does little to reduce the money supply or its velocity. In a Keynesian model, Regulation W does reduce aggregate demand by excluding some borrowers from the market. This reduction in the number of borrowers lowers the interest rate, and the reduction in the interest rate, in turn, reduces velocity, that is, in strict Keynesian language it raises idle money holdings (M_2). Note, however, that even in a Keynesian model, the reduction of consumer credit would, in part, be matched by an increase in other borrowing and spending since a lower interest rate stimulates investment. The magnitude of this spillover depends upon the relative size of the slopes (with respect to the interest rate) of the demand for idle money and investment. These factors are discussed in Chapter 4.

[59] For excellent criticisms of consumer credit controls, see Milton Friedman, "Consumer Credit Control as an Instrument of Stabilization Policy," *Consumer Installment Credit* (Washington, D.C.: Board of Governors of the Federal Reserve System, 1957), Part 2, Vol. 2, pp. 73–103; Edward Simmons, "Consumer Credit Controls and Central Banking," in *ibid.*, pp. 112–138; and Elliot Zupnick, "Consumer Credit and Monetary Policy in the United States and the United Kingdom," *Journal of Finance,* Vol. 17 (May, 1962), pp. 342–354.

Third, there is the question of whether conventional monetary policy is really unable to affect consumer credit. The feeling that consumer credit is unaffected by monetary policy was stimulated in the year 1955 when consumer credit increased rapidly despite a tight money policy. One interpretation of these events is that monetary policy has no effect on consumer credit. But there is also another one. It can be argued that in these years there was a strong upsurge in the demand for consumer credit which, had it not been for the tight money policy, would have raised consumer credit even more than it actually did. The mere fact that consumer credit increased during a period of tight money does not mean that monetary policy had no effect on it.[60] Even if high interest rates have no effect on consumer credit, credit rationing and the general unavailability of funds may still reduce consumer credit extension.[61] There is evidence that sales finance companies, for example, may be hard pressed to obtain funds in a tight money market and, therefore, may have to limit their loan volume.[62]

Fourth, consumer-credit controls raise an equity problem; they discriminate against households who cannot meet the higher monthly payments set by Regulation W. In other words, households who have a low ratio of liquid assets to income are forced

---

[60] Thus, one study classified large- and medium-sized banks by the deposit change they experienced, which is a measure of the credit stringency felt by banks. It found that banks subject to credit stringency (as measured by deposit experience) increased their consumer loans substantially less than did other banks; in fact, they restricted the growth of their consumer loans to a greater extent than most other types of loans and security purchases. This suggests that credit stringency *does* affect consumer loans and that the rise of consumer loans in the mid-1950's would have been even greater had it not been for the restrictive monetary policy of the Federal Reserve. (See Paul Smith, "Response of Consumer Loans to General Credit Conditions," *American Economic Review*, Vol. 48 [September, 1958], pp. 649–655.)

[61] The meaning of credit availability and credit rationing is discussed in Chapter 4.

[62] See Donald P. Jacobs, "Sources and Costs of Funds of Large Sales Finance Companies," in *Consumer Installment Credit*, Board of Governors of the Federal Reserve System (Washington, D.C., 1957), Part 2, Vol. 1, pp. 324–413. In Britain in 1967 tight money appears to have had a powerful effect on automobile sales.

out of the market. These tend to be low-income households and young, newly-formed households. These young households, not yet equipped with the usual array of consumer durables, are particularly hard hit. Moreover, consumer-credit controls also discriminate against the factors of production employed in the consumer-durable industries as well as against consumer-lending institutions, particularly specialized institutions such as finance companies.

Fifth, consumer-credit controls have a political disadvantage: they limit economic freedom. The importance that one attaches to this limitation depends upon one's political outlook; to some people, this alone is enough to condemn consumer-credit controls. Sixth, and finally, consumer-credit control would create severe administrative problems for the Federal Reserve. All dealers who sell on the installment plan would have to be supervised, and supervising about 200,000 firms would create major problems of enforcement. Not only would this administrative problem create a great deal of work for the Federal Reserve but, in addition, it might simply not be possible to administer Regulation W efficiently in the long run. Dealers can profit by finding methods of evading the regulation, and, where there is a will, there is a way.[63] One possible solution to the administrative problem would be to control not the individual transaction, but, instead, to impose an overall limit on the amount of credit that a firm may extend.

During World War II and the Korean War, we imposed another selective control similar in many ways to Regulation W. This was Regulation X, control over mortgage credit. The purpose of this was to limit, during wartime, the use of scarce

[63] One method, among many, by which dealers were able to evade Regulation W was to give the purchaser an excessive price for his old car and to make it up by raising the price of the new car. In this way the old car might suffice as the down payment. For example, suppose a customer wants to buy a $3000 car, his old car is worth $500 and he has only $300 cash for a down payment. If Regulation W prescribes a one-third down payment, the dealer can offer the customer $1000 for his car and raise the price of the new car to $3500. The old car plus the $300 cash now meets the one-third required down payment. Obviously, this sort of operation is hard for the Federal Reserve to police.

resources in an industry in which demand was postponable. However, unlike Regulation W, there has been virtually no support for reinstituting Regulation X.

Moral Suasion and Direct Action

Another minor tool in the Federal Reserve's armory is moral suasion, sometimes called "open-mouth policy" or "jaw control." This simply means that the Federal Reserve uses its powers of persuasion to get banks, or the financial community in general, to change its behavior. Since the interests of the Federal Reserve frequently coincide with the long run self-interest of financial institutions, this form of control may *in certain cases* be more effective than it appears at first. For example, during an inflationary expansion, the Federal Reserve may urge lenders to be more cautious in their loan policies and lenders may treat this as sound business advice from an institution capable of forecasting business conditions better than they can. To be sure, banks and other institutions may sometimes feel that the stress is more on the "suasion" than on the "moral." For example, in 1965 when the President and the Federal Reserve laid down guidelines to limit foreign lending, some banks, at least according to some reports, were afraid that if they were to ignore the guidelines, they might find it more difficult to borrow from the Federal Reserve. Admittedly, these fears may have been groundless; for an outsider it is hard to say.

Direct Action means that the Federal Reserve can bring pressure to bear on particular member banks whose actions it considers undesirable. Clearly, it is a method of keeping a few black sheep in line rather than a method of controlling the great thundering herd of banks.

Publicity and Informal Advice

The Federal Reserve has many ways of making its opinions known to the general public. The Chairman of the Board of Governors is frequently invited to testify before Congressional

Committees, and journalists publicize Federal Reserve press releases. In addition, the Board of Governors publishes, each month, the *Federal Reserve Bulletin* and each of the twelve Federal Reserve Banks publishes a monthly review. Given the high regard in which the business community and its journalists hold the Federal Reserve, our central bank has no difficulty in getting its views and opinions across to the public.

This gives the Federal Reserve some influence over business expectations—exactly how much influence is hard to say. Some economists, though by no means all, attach a great deal of importance to expectations; they believe that, to a considerable extent, expectations tend to justify themselves. For example, if the Federal Reserve were to announce that it expects long-term interest rates to rise, lenders would refrain from buying long-term bonds, waiting for the rate to rise, while borrowers would try to float securities right away before the rate rise would take effect. Given such an increase in the demand for long-term funds and a decline in the supply, the interest rate would rise right away.

Finally, the Federal Reserve need not confine its publicity to the general public. The Chairman of the Board of Governors acts as one of the chief economic and financial advisors of the President. At present (1967) there is an informal economic "general staff" in Washington which meets with the President. It consists of the Secretary of the Treasury, the Chairman of the Council of Economic Advisers, the Director of the Budget Bureau —and the Chairman of the Board of Governors. A strong Chairman who has good relations with the President can exercise a great deal of influence here.

These, then, are the domestic tools of the Federal Reserve: open-market operations, discount-rate changes, and reserve-requirement changes. They carry the bulk of the burden, and they are reinforced by selective controls, moral suasion, direct action, publicity, and informal advice.[64]

[64] In addition, the Federal Reserve can at times use bank regulation powers as a tool of monetary policy. The Federal Reserve has control (Regulation Q) over time deposit interest rates. Hence, at a time when interest rates in general are rising, the Federal Reserve can reduce time deposits by not raising the interest ceiling.

International Tools

The Federal Reserve tries to meet its international responsibilities in several ways. One is to change interest rates and income by using the tools just discussed. Another way is to further international liquidity by collaborating with foreign central banks in so-called swap operations. In these operations a central bank, under temporary pressure, can swap its own currency against foreign currency and hence it can obtain funds to ride out a speculative attack or other temporary factors. In addition, the Federal Reserve collaborates with other leading central banks to try to stabilize the gold market, and deals in the forward exchange market to stabilize that market. Central banks also collaborate on a more general issue, that of interest rates. In setting their interest rates, central banks look not only at their own economy, but at times take at least some account of the effect of their actions on other countries.

Moreover, the Federal Reserve administers the current policy of trying to limit bank loans overseas. In addition, the Federal Reserve has a fairly large staff doing research on international financial problems and advises the President on international financial decisions.

The previous chapter discussed the goals that the Federal Reserve attempts to achieve, and now that we have seen what tools the Federal Reserve has for this purpose we are prepared to discuss, in the next chapter, how the Federal Reserve uses its tools in its day-to-day operations in the money market.

FURTHER READING

The references given throughout this chapter can really serve as suggestions for further reading; hence, the following list contains only a few selected items.

General Discussions

Ahearn, Daniel. *Federal Reserve Policy Reappraised, 1951–1959.* New York: Columbia University Press, 1963, Part II.

Aschheim, Joseph. *Techniques of Monetary Control.* Baltimore: Johns Hopkins Press, 1961.

Friedman, Milton. *A Program for Monetary Stability.* New York: Fordham University Press, 1960, Chapter 2.

Smith, Warren. "The Instruments of General Monetary Control." *National Banking Review,* Vol. 1 (September, 1963), pp. 47–76.

U.S. Board of Governors of the Federal Reserve System, *The Federal Reserve System, Purposes and Functions.* Washington, D.C., 1963, Chapter 3.

Open-Market Operations

Roosa, Robert. *Federal Reserve Operations in the Money and Government Securities Market.* New York: Federal Reserve Bank of New York, 1956.

Scott, Ira, Jr. "The Regional Impact of Monetary Policy," *Quarterly Journal of Economics,* Vol. 69 (May, 1955), pp. 269–284.

Discount Rates

Kareken, John. "Federal Reserve Discount Policy: An Appraisal," *Banca Nazionale del Lavoro Quarterly Review,* Vol. 12 (March, 1959), pp. 103–125.

McKinney, George. *The Federal Reserve Discount Window.* New Brunswick, N.J.: Rutgers University Press, 1960. (This is a detailed discussion of the institutional aspects of discount-window administration.)

Smith, Warren. "The Discount Rate as a Credit Control Weapon," *Journal of Political Economy,* Vol. 66 (April, 1958), pp. 171–177.

Reserve Requirements

Smith, Warren. "Reserve Requirements in the American Monetary System," in Commission on Money and Credit, *Monetary Management.* Englewood Cliffs, N.J.: Prentice Hall, 1963, pp. 175–315.

Selective Controls

Zupnick, Elliot. "Consumer Credit and Monetary Policy in the United States and the United Kingdom," *Journal of Finance,* Vol. 17 (May, 1962), pp. 342–354.

APPENDIX TO CHAPTER 2

Debt Management

In addition to the tools of monetary policy which the Federal Reserve possesses, the Treasury Department has one potentially major monetary stabilization tool which has received considerable attention in the postwar period. This is debt management. Our national debt is large and a significant part of it, close to half of the marketable debt, consists of short-term securities due within a year. Treasury sales and redemption of debt, therefore, amount to a substantial sum each year. As the Treasury borrows it has to decide whether to issue long-term or short-term securities. This is the essence of debt management. Note that debt management refers to changes in the *composition* of the debt, not to the total volume of debt outstanding. The volume of debt outstanding changes in accordance with deficit or surplus in the budget and, hence, is fiscal policy.

Shifting the debt between long-term and short-term securities can affect aggregate demand. There are several ways of approaching this problem. First, it can be said that if the public holds short-term securities, the greater liquidity of its portfolio makes it more willing to spend. Short-term government securities can serve as money substitutes. Put into Keynesian language, the public need not hold money to satisfy the precautionary and speculative demand for money, but can hold short-term securities instead. In some cases short-term securities serve as a money substitute even for transactions balances. Hence, if the Treasury issues short-term securities in place of long-term government securities, the demand for money drops, and the interest rate declines.

Another approach to the effects of changes in the maturity composition of the debt is to look at the term structure of interest rates. If the Treasury redeems long-term bonds and issues short-term securities in their place, this reduction in outstanding long-term securities tends, at least initially, to lower the long-term rate of interest. On the other hand, the greater supply of short-term securities, at least initially, raises the short-term rate of interest. Note, however, that this initial effect may not last. Chapter 3 discusses various theories of the term structure of interest rates. According to two of the theories discussed there, such a change in relative interest rates is only transitory and is eliminated by arbitrage. Another theory, the market segmentation theory, however, suggests that changes in the composition of the debt can have a lasting effect on relative interest rates. If this market segmentation theory is correct, changes in the composition of the outstanding debt can affect the volume of investment. Many, though not all, economists believe that the long-term interest rate has more effect on investment decisions than does the short-term rate. Hence, as the Treasury redeems long-term securities and issues short-term securities, the effect of the decline in the long-term rate is not fully offset by the effect of the rise in the short-term rate, and investment increases. Conversely, if the Treasury wants to restrain aggregate demand it should redeem short-term securities and issue long-term securities instead. Here, then, may be a method of influencing aggregate demand, a method which could supplement the tools used by the Federal Reserve. In the early postwar period when debt management was first brought to public attention, this new control mechanism aroused considerable enthusiasm, but this enthusiasm has cooled for several reasons in recent years.

One obvious problem is the behavior of the term structure

of interest rates—as mentioned below, whether changes in the composition of the debt can have any lasting effect on the term structure of interest rates is a matter of dispute. Empirical evidence can be cited for either view.[1] Similarly, while there is little dispute about the direction of the effect of issuing short-term securities in place of long-term securities on expenditures, there is still considerable dispute as to whether this effect is of significant size. Another problem is that selling long-term securities in the expansion, when interest rates are high, and selling short-term securities during the recession, when interest rates are low, serves to lock high-interest rate securities into the debt structure, and, thus, to raise interest costs to the Treasury. Secretaries of the Treasury tend to be unenthusiastic about a policy that raises their interest costs. Still another problem is created by the fact that if the Treasury sells short-term securities in the recession, these short-term security holdings of the public interfere with a subsequent tightening of monetary policy in the subsequent expansion. As is discussed further in Chapter 4, holders of these short-term securities can sell them to owners of idle balances and obtain the wherewithal for increasing their expenditures.[2] Moreover, having a substantial proportion of the

---

[1] See Arthur Okun, "Monetary Policy, Debt Management and Interest Rates: A Quantitative Appraisal," in Commission on Money and Credit, *Stabilization Policies* (Englewood Cliffs, N.J.: Prentice Hall, 1963), pp. 331–380; John Arena, "Monetary Policy and Debt Management Revisited," *National Banking Review*, Vol. 3 (September, 1965), pp. 65–87; Robert Scott, "Liquidity and the Term Structure of Interest Rates," *Quarterly Journal of Economics*, Vol. 79 (February, 1965), pp. 135–145, and "A Liquidity Factor Contributing to Those Downward Sloping Yield Curves, 1900–1916," *Review of Economics and Statistics*, Vol. 45 (August, 1963), pp. 328–329. For a critical discussion see Neil Wallace, "The Terms Structure of Interest Rates and the Maturity Composition of the Federal Debt," *Journal of Finance*, Vol. 22 (May, 1967), pp. 301–312. See also Franco Modigliani and Richard Sutch, "Debt Management and the Term Structure of Interest Rates: An Empirical Analysis of Recent Experience," *Journal of Political Economy*, Supplement, Vol. 75 (August, 1967), pp. 546–560.

[2] An additional disadvantage of countercyclical debt management is that it is very slow. Not only does it suffer from the usual lags in the effectiveness of monetary policy discussed in Chapter 6, but there is an additional lag. If long-term securities are issued during the expansion, these long-term

debt in short-term securities, as countercyclical policy would require at times, hinders monetary policy in another way. A short-term debt requires frequent Treasury refinancing, and such refinancing interferes with monetary policy. During a refinancing period the Federal Reserve is reluctant to tighten money, but tries to help Treasury financing by keeping the bond market on an "even keel." A large short-term debt severely restricts the times during which the Federal Reserve can feel free to move in a restrictive direction.

An alternative policy is, therefore, to try to limit the trouble that debt management may create for more conventional monetary policy. By placing the debt primarily into long-term (and hence relatively illiquid) securities, one can limit the shifting of the debt among various owners during the expansion phase of the cycle. In this way debt management does not support conventional monetary policy, but neither does it hinder it. But such a policy of lengthening the debt is also not popular with Secretaries of the Treasury because it raises, or seems to raise, the interest cost of the debt.[3] Moreover, if the market segmentation theory of relative interest rates discussed in Chapter 3 is correct, such a policy would lower the short-term interest rate relative to the long-term rate. Since foreign investment seems to depend more on the short-term interest rate than on the long-term rate, a policy of lowering the short-term rate would tend to reduce foreign investment in the United States and to increase United States investment abroad. This tends to increase the balance-of-payments deficit. Note, however, that this problem arises only if the market segmentation theory discussed in Chapter 3 is correct, a debatable matter.

---

securities stay in the debt structure during the next contraction and tend to reduce expenditures at that time too. A long time passes until these new long-term securities are redeemed so that a contractionary debt policy, unlike an expansionary debt policy, is *not* easily reversible.

[3] It is not certain that such a policy of lengthening the maturity of the debt would necessarily be costly. During the long-term security's lifetime, its interest rate may be the same as the average of short-term interest rates during the same period. However, there is some evidence—see Chapter 3 —that long-term securities do tend to involve greater interest costs, over the long run.

The third major alternative in public debt policy is to bypass the stabilization problem completely and to minimize the interest cost of the debt. It is usually assumed that this means putting a substantial part of the debt into short-term securities.[4] The rationale of this policy is that conventional monetary and fiscal policy can take care of the stabilization problem, and that debt management should deal only with the housekeeping task of keeping Treasury costs to a minimum. Since this policy is not directly relevant to stabilization policy, there is no need to discuss its pros and cons here.

FURTHER READING

Culbertson, John. "A Positive Debt Management Program," *Review of Economics and Statistics*, Vol. 41 (May, 1959), pp. 89–98.

Friedman, Milton. *A Program for Monetary Stability*. New York: Fordham University Press, 1960, Chapter 3.

Gaines, Tilford. *Techniques of Treasury Debt Management*. New York: Columbia University Press, 1962. This is a standard work stressing the institutional aspects of debt management.

Hollowell, Burton, and Kossuth Williamson. "Federal Debt Management, 1953–1958," *Review of Economics and Statistics*, Vol. 45 (February, 1963), pp. 47–54.

Rolph, Earl. "Debt Management: Some Theoretical Aspects," *Public Finance*, Vol. 16, No. 1 (1961), pp. 105–120. An interesting discussion of some aspects of debt management not taken up in this Appendix.

Smith, Warren. *Debt Management in the United States, Study Paper 19*, Study of Employment, Growth and Price Levels. Washington, D.C.: U.S. Congress Joint Economic Committee, 1960. An excellent short study.

---

[4] This is not necessarily the case. Although short-term securities have, for many years now, been usually below long-term interest rates this *average cost* of borrowing is not the relevant consideration. Like any other monopolist selling in differentiated markets, what the Treasury should look at is not the *average* costs in the two markets, but the *marginal* costs. See Warren Smith, *Debt Management in the United States, Study Paper 19*, U.S. Congress Joint Economic Committee, Study of Employment, Growth and Price Levels (Washington, D.C., 1960), p. 99.

Tobin, James. "An Essay on the Principles of Debt Management," in Commission on Money and Credit, *Fiscal and Debt Management Policies*. Englewood Cliffs, N.J.: Prentice-Hall, 1963, pp. 143–218. An unorthodox, but important, study.

Monetary Policy and the Money Market

The previous chapter dealt with the ways in which the Federal Reserve can change bank reserves. But, in and of themselves, changes in bank reserves have no further effect on the economy. What makes them important is that they lead to changes in the money stock and in interest rates. These effects are discussed in this chapter. The following chapter then starts with a change in the money stock and interest rates and shows how these changes affect money income.

A discussion of bank reserves and the money stock provides the tools for discussing an additional topic, money market indicators and the immediate goals of monetary policy. Chapter 1 talked about the Federal Reserve's goals in broad terms, such as full employment and price stability. But the Federal Reserve cannot aim at these goals directly since it has no *direct* impact on employment or prices. What the Federal Reserve has to do is to relate these broad, general goals to the tools which it wields. For example, the Federal Reserve may believe that to maintain price stability the money stock or perhaps the volume of bank credit must grow at a particular rate, and in order for the money stock, or else bank credit, to grow at this particular rate, the reserve base must grow at a given rate. Alternatively, the Federal Reserve may decide that to obtain the particular growth of the money stock, it must maintain excess reserves, or perhaps excess reserves minus bank borrowing, at a certain level. The choice of such intermediate goals raises difficult issues of monetary policy, issues which can be discussed in connection with the topics taken up in this chapter. Accordingly, this chapter deals first with the effect of changes in the reserve base on the money stock, then with the effect of changes in the money stock on interest rates, and finally with the monetary indicators and proximate goals used by the Federal Reserve. All of these topics are connected since they concern the way in which the financial sector responds to monetary policy.

The Reserve Base and the Money Supply

Until recent years the factors determining the money stock generally received rather skimpy treatment in discussions of monetary policy. Only in recent years has money supply theory been studied extensively.

Traditionally, there have been two approaches to this topic. One, a rather simple-minded approach, is the traditional textbook treatment of multiple deposit creation where the banking system expands deposits to a certain multiple of the reserve base. (This is not the place to discuss the mechanics of deposit creation, but since even advanced students are often unclear about this process, Appendix A provides a brief discussion of deposit expansion, a discussion stressing the principle involved rather than arithmetic examples.) This approach is quite mechanistic. Each bank as it receives a deposit finds that it now has excess reserves and gets rid of these excess reserves by making loans or buying securities.

The other traditional approach is to look upon the money stock as set not by supply conditions (that is, the reserve base), but as determined by demand conditions, that is by the demand for bank loans by sound customers. According to this view, banks usually have excess reserves and can make loans or buy corporate securities when business decides to borrow more. In the short run in this system the money supply is determined not so much by Federal Reserve policy as by the level of income. Here the money supply does not determine income, as it does in the quantity theory, but rather income determines the money stock.

In recent years a new view of money supply theory has emerged, a view which borrows something from both the traditional approaches. In this new view the commercial bank is treated neither as a mechanical expander of deposits, nor as a passive holder of excess reserves waiting for customers to come in. Instead, economists are more and more looking at banks as profit maximizers.[1] Banks do not necessarily create new deposits merely because they have excess reserves, nor are they necessarily satisfied to hold excess reserves if the demand for bank loans drops off. Instead, banks will create deposits if, and only if, the marginal revenue from doing so exceeds the marginal cost. Like any other industry, the banking industry has a supply curve showing the amount of products (deposits) it will supply at different prices (interest rates). Hence, it is possible to investigate the supply of money in the usual way we analyze supply. Let us now proceed to do so.

The marginal revenue which a bank obtains from making a loan or buying a security is the interest it receives on this loan or security.[2] The corresponding marginal cost consists of three elements, the cost of obtaining the loanable funds, that is, a deposit (the provision of free services to depositors and payment of interest to time depositors), the cost of the required reserves, and the administrative and advertising costs to the bank. Looked at from this point of view the legal minimum reserve requirement need *not* be the ruling consideration. On the one hand the

[1] This approach has been emphasized particularly by economists at Yale University under the leadership of Professor Tobin. For an excellent example, see his "Commercial Banks as Creators of 'Money'," Deane Carson (ed.), *Banking and Monetary Studies* (Homewood, Ill.: Richard D. Irwin, 1963), pp. 408–419. In this paper Professor Tobin deals mainly with the extent to which banks differ from other financial intermediaries, the question whether the ability to create money puts banks in a different category from other financial institutions all of which can create claims on themselves. This is an important issue which has been much discussed in recent years. For a discussion of this problem see Raymond Goldsmith, *Financial Institutions* (New York: Random House, in preparation), Chapter 3.

[2] Strictly speaking this is only true for a bank operating under perfect competition. But note that for security purchases perfect competition is a fair approximation. In making loans banks generally do not operate under perfect competition, but since they are able to indulge in a considerable amount of price discrimination they are often able to make additional loans without reducing their returns on other loans, so that here, too, price tends to equal marginal revenue.

profit maximizing bank may not expand deposits to the limit, but may keep some excess reserves. *Legally* excess reserves need not be *economically* excess, that is, redundant, reserves. Excess reserves safeguard the bank against a deposit drain and are useful in case profitable lending opportunities occur in the future. If interest rates are low banks may be reluctant to buy securities and may hold excess reserves instead. Just as an individual has a transaction, a precautionary and speculative demand for money, a bank has a transaction, precautionary and speculative demand for excess reserves. By and large, we find excess reserves concentrated in country banks. These banks, which tend to be smaller than city banks, have less access to the money market and possess only a relatively small dollar volume of excess reserves so that they do not find it profitable to manage their reserve position very tightly. But as interest rates rise they find it profitable to use their reserves more intensely.

On the other hand, if a bank finds it profitable to expand deposits but does not have sufficient reserves, it can undertake actions to acquire these reserves; it does not have to wait passively for an inflow of deposits and reserves. There are several ways it can obtain reserves. It can sell securities or run down its balances with correspondent banks. It can borrow from the Federal Reserve, or else it can borrow from its correspondent banks, or it can buy the excess reserves of other banks in the Federal Funds market. Alternatively, it can quickly attract deposits by raising the interest rate it pays on certificates of deposits, or, if it is a large bank, it can issue notes to the public.[3]

Note that the volume of reserves cannot be treated as something given to the banking system from the outside, but that by borrowing, or by repaying outstanding loans from the Federal Reserve, the banking system participates in determining the reserve base. This does *not* deny, however, that the Federal Reserve has ultimate control over the reserve base if it wants to

[3] In recent years there has been a substantial change in banking environment giving banks more freedom from reserve restraint on deposit creation. For an excellent discussion see Tilford Gaines, "Financial Innovations and Efficiency," George Horwich (ed.), *Monetary Process and Policy: A Symposium* (Homewood, Ill.: Richard D. Irwin, 1967), pp. 99–118.

exercise it. The Federal Reserve can be held responsible for the reserve base since it ultimately controls it. It has difficulty in controlling the volume of bank reserves only insofar as it makes errors in its forecasts of the behavior of banks and market forces, or if it allows its attention to be detracted by other factors (such as the behavior of interest rates).[4]

There have been several empirical investigations of the determinants of borrowing by member banks. The main question in this area is whether banks borrow for "need" or for "profit," that is, whether member bank borrowing depends significantly upon the gap between the discount rate at which the bank borrows and the rate at which it lends borrowed funds. Recent studies suggest that banks *do* borrow for profit as well as need; that borrowing increases as the gap between the discount rate and the Treasury bill rate rises.[5]

The money supply depends, of course, not only on the reserve base but also on the magnitude of the so-called money multiplier—the number of dollars of money (demand deposits plus currency) called into existence per dollar of reserves. In the simplest ex-

[4] If it wants, the Federal Reserve can offset member bank borrowing by selling securities. Moreover, although banks can offset, at least in part, contractionary open-market operations, the Federal Reserve believes that banks are reluctant to expand deposits on the basis of borrowed reserves since they know that they will shortly have to repay.

[5] See Stephan Goldfeld, *Commercial Bank Behavior and Economic Activity* (Amsterdam: North-Holland, 1966), p. 151; Frank de Leeuw, "A Model of Financial Behavior," James Duesenberry, Gary Fromm, Lawrence Klein and Edwin Kuh (eds.), *The Brookings Quarterly Econometric Model of the United States* (Chicago: Rand McNally, 1965), pp. 465–530; Karl Brunner and Allan Meltzer, "Some Further Investigations of Demand and Supply Functions for Money," *Journal of Finance,* Vol. 19 (May, 1964), pp. 240–283; Ronald Teigen, "A Structural Approach to the Impact of Monetary Policy," *Journal of Finance,* Vol. 19 (May, 1964), pp. 284–305; Stephen Goldfeld and Edward Kane, "The Determinants of Member Bank Borrowing: An Econometric Study," *Journal of Finance,* Vol. 21 (September, 1966), pp. 499–514; Murray Polakoff, "Federal Reserve Discount Policy and its Critics," Carson (ed.), *Banking and Monetary Studies, op. cit.,* pp. 190–212; A. J. Meigs, *Free Reserves and the Money Supply* (Chicago: University of Chicago Press, 1962). For a critical discussion of this book see Richard Davis, "Open-Market Operations, Interest Rates and Deposit Growth," *Quarterly Journal of Economics,* Vol. 79 (August, 1965), pp. 431–454.

ample of multiple bank-deposit expansion this money multiplier depends only on the required-reserve ratio. For example, if the required reserve ratio is 15 percent, the money multiplier is slightly less than seven. But in a more detailed analysis the legal minimum reserve requirement is not the only leakage in multiple-deposit creation. A second leakage is the drain of currency into circulation.[6] For each dollar of deposits the public may want to hold, say, 10 cents of currency. If so, an initial dollar increase in reserves allows the banking system to have $4 of deposits outstanding (the increase in reserves after the currency drain being $.60, that is, 15 percent of $4) and the money stock rises by $4 of deposits plus $.40 of currency, so that the money multiplier is only 4.4. A third leakage results from the public's desire to hold a certain ratio of time deposits to demand deposits. (A number of economists, among whom Professor Friedman is the most prominent, define money to include time deposits; in this case there is, of course, no time deposit leakage.) A fourth leakage results from the fact that banks want to keep deposits with correspondent banks, and these interbank deposits vary with the bank's deposit volume. Finally, an increase in deposits increases the excess reserves which banks find profitable to hold. In the contemporary American economy the sum of these leakages is about 30 to 40 percent so that this money multiplier has a value of about two to three and a half, not of six or seven as it

[6] The currency leakage can also be looked at in another, perhaps more fundamental way. The public wants to hold both currency and bank deposits. To provide the public with either currency or bank deposits (in the absence of market factors increasing reserves) the Federal Reserve has to acquire assets. (It provides currency or bank reserves in exchange against government securities if it undertakes open-market operations, or in exchange against a bank's IOU if its discounts increase.) For each dollar of demand deposits the public wants to hold, the Federal Reserve has to acquire only a fraction of a dollar of assets. But for each dollar of currency the public decides to hold the Federal Reserve has to acquire a whole dollar of assets. One can therefore think of a deposit multiplier which is, say, three, and a currency multiplier which is unity. The size of the money multiplier discussed above can then be looked upon as a weighted mean of the demand deposit multiplier and the currency multiplier. This way of putting things helps to bring out the fact that if the Federal Reserve does not offset a currency drain into circulation it is following a deflationary policy.

would have if the reserve requirement were the only leakage.[7]

Note that this lower value for the money multiplier does not hinder the Federal Reserve's control over the money market— all it means is that if the Federal Reserve wants to change the money stock by a given amount it must change the reserve base by much more than would be required if the legal reserve requirement were the only leakage. What is important is the stability, or more precisely, the predictability of the money multiplier. If the money multiplier were not predictable the Federal Reserve would not know by how much to change the reserve base to bring about a given change in the money stock. To be sure, by renewed open-market operations it could still offset errors in its initial predictions. But this would introduce a lag in approaching the desired money stock and would complicate the Federal Reserve's task.

In the traditional, mechanistic approach to bank deposit creation, it was assumed that the money multiplier was fairly easy to determine, though admittedly it might not be stable. All that was necessary to estimate the magnitude of the leakages was to take the ratio of currency, time deposit and so on, to total deposits. Excess reserves, to be sure, were often treated as much more volatile factors which introduced an erratic element into the deposit expansion process. (This is why many economists favor the 100 percent reserve proposal.)

Figure 3.1 shows the growth rates of the reserve base and of the money stock. It shows that there is a fair degree of cor-

[7] If time deposits are included in the definition of money the money multiplier is somewhat greater. In one model, for example, it changes from two and a half to approximately three. See Karl Brunner and Allan Meltzer, *An Alternative Approach to the Monetary Mechanism*, U.S. House Committee on Banking and Currency, Subcommittee on Domestic Finance, 88th Congress, Second Session (Washington, D.C.: 1964), p. 46. For a comparison of the money multipliers implied by various money supply functions, see David Fand, "Some Implications of Money Supply Analysis," American Economic Association, *Papers and Proceedings*, Vol. 62 (May, 1967), pp. 380–400. The above discussion has ignored shifts of deposits between member banks and nonmember banks as well as shifts between reserve city and country banks. Since reserve requirements differ among these types of banks, such shifts can affect the value of the money multiplier.

relation between the growth rates of the reserve base and the money stock, but that this correlation is by no means perfect.

In recent years a more complex approach has been developed, an approach which attempts to find not a single number which best represents the money multiplier, but which looks for a de-

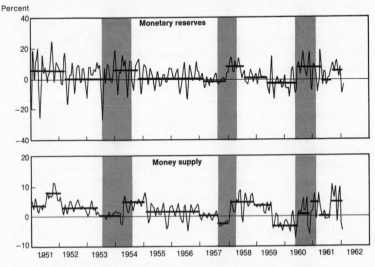

FIGURE 3.1   *Annual Percentage Rates of Increase in Monetary Reserves and the Money Supply*

NOTE: Semi-monthly data, seasonally adjusted three-period moving averages, weighted 1–2–1; shaded areas represent periods of business recession.

NOTE: Monetary reserves are total reserves less reserves required behind Treasury deposits. Adjusted for reserve requirement changes.

SOURCE: *Federal Reserve Bank of St. Louis Review,* Vol. 44 (March, 1962), p. 5.

posit supply *function.* Instead of assuming that the leakages are exogenous constants, they are explained by utility maximization and estimated by statistical techniques. For example, the time-deposit drain could be explained by making the demand for time deposits a function of the stock of wealth, interest rates paid on time deposits, open-market interest rates, and the imputed interest rate (consisting of free services paid on demand deposits).

Quite complex money supply functions have been developed in this manner. One such study, by Professors Brunner and Meltzer, found a quite stable money supply function which allowed them to forecast changes in the money stock with an average error of only 10 percent.[8] But another study of the money supply function, by Professor Teigen, found a supply function which was not stable.[9]

Another important problem relating to the supply function of money is its shape. Suppose that there *is* a stable money supply function, but that it is of such a nature that at very low rates of interest banks have an infinite demand for excess reserves, that is, there is a liquidity trap for banks.[10] If so, the Federal Reserve would be limited in counteracting a severe depression. Open-

---

[8] Brunner and Meltzer. *"An Alternative Approach to the Monetary Mechanism, op. cit.,* pp. 52–54. The predictions were for the period beginning with the first quarter of 1949 and ending with the last quarter of 1962. The estimates used for the prediction were drawn from the period first quarter 1949 to the fourth quarter 1958. If time deposits are included in the money supply the error of the prediction falls to 0.3 percent. But this good result may, at least in part, be due to a statistical bias. The high correlation between reserves and the money stock may be due not only to changes in reserves causing a change in the money stock, but also to changes in the money stock inducing changes in reserves. Under a policy of keeping free reserves (excess reserves minus borrowings) stable—a policy discussed below—the Federal Reserve would increase the reserve base whenever an increase in the money stock increases required reserves so that only part of the observed correlation between the reserve base and the money stock could be attributed to changes in the reserve base causing changes in the money stock. (See Jack Guttentag, "The Strategy of Open-Market Operations," *Quarterly Journal of Economics,* Vol. 80 [February, 1966], pp. 11–12.) In another study Professor Meltzer succeeded in explaining the level of the French money supply with an average error of only 1.5 percent. ("The Behavior of the French Money Supply 1938–1954," *Journal of Political Economy,* Vol. 47 [June, 1959], pp. 275–296.)

[9] Teigen, *op. cit.,* pp. 284–308. This study also found a much smaller value for the money multiplier, a value of unity or less. For a criticism of this low estimate see Donald Hester, "Discussion," *ibid.,* pp. 310–312.

[10] The liquidity trap is an idea mentioned by Keynes as a possible occurrence if interest rates fall very low. There may be a rate of interest so low that at this low rate the public prefers to hold money rather than to buy bonds. At this rate the demand for money is infinitely interest elastic and an increase in the money stock cannot lower the rate of interest. Applying this concept to banks, there *may* be a rate of return on securities and loans so low that banks prefer to hold excess reserves rather than buy earning assets at this low rate.

market security purchases from banks (or a lowering of reserve requirements) would not lead to an increase in the money supply, but would merely increase excess reserves. Only open-market purchases from nonbanks would increase the money stock, and they would do so only dollar for dollar rather than by a multiple of the securities bought. The postwar data give no evidence warranting such a pessimistic conclusion, but then there has been no severe depression during this period. Economists who believe that there is a liquidity trap for banks point to the experience of the 1930's when banks piled up a large volume of excess reserves, and the money supply seemed to be essentially divorced from the reserve base. In recent years this interpretation of the 1930's has been seriously challenged. Since this issue is so important it is discussed in some detail in Appendix B.

Before leaving this topic of money supply theory, it is only fair to warn the reader of two things. First, many different money supply functions can be constructed depending upon what factors one allows to vary. For example, the money supply function discussed above did take into account leakages into time deposits and currency, but did not allow for leakages into other liquid assets; nor did it take into account the repercussions through changes in income induced by changes in the money supply.[11] Second, the approach discussed above is not unanimously accepted. Some economists have argued that a meaningful supply function for money cannot be derived by looking at the reserve base and money multipliers because banks are nowadays able to adjust their reserve positions easily by issuing negotiable certificates of deposit and borrowing on their own notes.[12]

---

[11] For supply functions which do allow for these variables, see Fand, *op. cit.*

[12] See Lyle Gramley and Samuel Chase, Jr., "Time Deposits in Monetary Analysis," *Federal Reserve Bulletin*, Vol. 51 (October, 1965), pp. 1380–1406 and their "Money Supply versus Interest Rates: A Reply," *National Banking Review*, Vol. 4 (December, 1966), pp. 205–213; Gaines, "Financial Innovations and Efficiency," *op. cit.* For a criticism of the Gramley and Chase study see William Dewald, "Money Supply versus Interest Rates as Proximate Objectives of Monetary Policy," *National Banking Review*, Vol. 3 (June, 1966), pp. 509–522.

The Money Stock and Interest Rates

Having discussed the effect of changes in bank reserves on the money stock, it is time to take the next step and to see how changes in the money stock affect interest rates. In most, though not in all, Keynesian analyses, as well as in much of the older classical tradition, the stock of money does not affect income directly. Rather, it influences interest rates, and interest rates, in turn, affect investment and income. As will be discussed in the following chapter this view is by no means unanimous; some economists, such as Professor Friedman, relate money to income directly without focusing attention on interest rate changes. Nonetheless, discussions of monetary policy commonly do stress changes in interest rates, so let us look at interest rates, starting with the short-term rate.

Changes in the reserve base have a rapid impact on short-term interest rates. Indeed, if the reserve base is changed through Federal Reserve purchases of short-term securities, then the effect on short-term rates is instantaneous. In the process of buying securities the Federal Reserve bids the price of securities up so that the yield on securities changes automatically. Moreover, the additional reserves allow the banking system to expand deposits, and at least some of this deposit creation occurs through bank purchases of short-term securities which again lowers the short-term rate. If the reserve base is increased through a lowering of reserve requirements, banks find themselves with redundant reserves and, hence, buy short-term securities and this, too, lowers the short-term interest rate. Conversely, if the Federal Reserve reduces the reserve base banks attempt to restore their reserve position by selling short-term as well as other securities, and the short-term interest rate rises.

There is little doubt that if the Federal Reserve wants to, it can affect the short-term interest rate by changing the reserve base. This does not mean that the Federal Reserve has unqualified control over the short-term interest rate. First, there is a qualification applicable to the long run. If the Federal Reserve lowers the interest rate this tends to raise aggregate demand, and if the interest rate is maintained low enough it leads to inflation. Now as the price level rises, the demand for money rises along with it, and this increase in the demand for money, in turn, tends to raise interest rates. Most economists believe that this effect takes a long time to show up, but some economists, Professor Friedman for example, believe that it occurs fairly quickly so that an increase in the quantity of money depresses the interest rate only for a short time. If the Federal Reserve would try to keep the interest rate down, it would have to buy more and more securities on the open market (or lower reserve requirements) and eventually the Federal Reserve would run out of ammunition.

But it is highly improbable that this set of circumstances would actually arise. As inflation occurs the Federal Reserve is unlikely to try to keep the interest rate down; rather, it would encourage a rise to limit the inflation. In other words, the real limitation on the Federal Reserve's ability to maintain a low interest rate is danger of inflation.[13] This is a much more relevant and important qualification of the Federal Reserve's control over

[13] Federal Reserve spokesmen have frequently denied that the Federal Reserve has control over the short-term interest rate which, in their view, is determined in thousands of transactions by the grass roots of the country. But if the Federal Reserve wanted to, it could, in the short run, provide enough reserves to maintain a low interest rate. This is, after all, what it did in the pegging episode during World War II and the immediate following years. When the Federal Reserve says that it is incapable of setting an interest rate, it means that it is incapable of setting a low interest rate except at the cost of inflation, a cost it refuses to pay. Here, for instance, is some testimony about the money market by Chairman Martin before the Joint Economic Committee in 1956:

> I think it is a free market. I think one of the great blessings of our economy today is that neither the Federal Reserve nor the Treasury is strong enough to override the forces at the grass roots that are there in the economy. . . . Now you can vitiate the forces of supply and demand, but you pay a price for it, and when the Treasury does its financing, neither the Federal Reserve nor the Treasury can afford to ignore the forces of the market unless they want to have unbridled inflation.

(Quoted in Seymour Harris, *The Economics of Political Parties* [New York: The Macmillan Co., 1962], p. 101.)

the short-term rate than is the danger of running out of ammunition.

A third qualification, applicable to a period of less than adequate aggregate demand rather than to an inflationary period, is the possibility of Keynesian absolute liquidity preference. Keynes argued that at a very low rate of interest the public would prefer to absorb any quantity of money rather than buy securities so that the interest rate could not be forced down below this limit. But whether such an absolute liquidity trap exists is an empirical question, and the empirical evidence gathered in recent years has not supported the absolute liquidity preference idea.[14]

A fourth qualification arises from balance of payments considerations. If the interest rate is lower in the United States than in major foreign money markets, this leads to a gold outflow—hence the desire to defend the present exchange rate significantly limits the Federal Reserve's freedom to manipulate the domestic interest rate. Under current conditions this is perhaps the most

[14] See Karl Brunner and Allan Meltzer, "Predicting Velocity, Implications for Theory and Policy," *Journal of Finance,* Vol. 18 (May, 1963), pp. 319–355; Martin Bronfenbrenner and Thomas Mayer, "Liquidity Functions in the American Economy," *Econometrica,* Vol. 28 (October, 1960), pp. 810–834; and David Laidler, "The Rate of Interest and the Demand for Money—Some Empirical Evidence," *Journal of Political Economy,* Vol. 74 (December, 1966), pp. 543–555. The last of these studies found some evidence contradicting absolute liquidity preference for the broad definition of money, that is, currency, demand deposits plus time deposits in commercial banks. For the conventional definition of money its evidence is consistent with absolute liquidity preference but does not require it. For a theoretical criticism of the absolute liquidity preference theory, see Don Patinkin, *Money, Interest and Prices* (New York: Harper & Row, 1965), pp. 349–355. Although the *elasticity* of the liquidity preference curve does not appear to approach infinity as the interest rate falls, the liquidity preference curve does become flatter as the interest rate is reduced; and this means that as the interest rate falls it takes a greater and greater increase in the quantity of money to reduce the interest rate by a given amount. (See Robert Eisner, "Another Look at Liquidity Preference," *Econometrica,* Vol. 31 [July, 1963], pp. 531–538.) The above is subject to qualification. A new study (Ahmen Kooros, "The Demand for Cash Balances a la Latané, a Nonlinear Estimation," unpublished paper read at the December, 1967 Econometrics Society Meetings) does support the absolute liquidity trap hypothesis. (Last sentence added in proof.)

important of the several limitations on the Federal Reserve's ability to establish a low interest rate.

The belief is widespread among economists, though not unanimous, that changes in the long-term and intermediate-term interest rates have more effect on investment than do changes in the short-term rate. While the short-term rate has more effect on inventory investment, the long-term rate is more powerful in affecting construction and machinery investment. The extent to which monetary policy can affect the intermediate-term and long-term interest rates is, therefore, an important issue.

To consider the effect of changes in the reserve base on intermediate and long-term interest rates, it is worthwhile to look briefly at the reasons why securities with different maturities pay different rates of interest, the explanations of the so-called "term structure" of interest rates.

One theory of the term structure, the expectations theory, explains the difference in interest rates by expectations of future short rates.[15] This theory assumes that there is enough flexibility and arbitrage in the money market so that the expected yield to be obtained over a period of time must be the same for the buyer of a long-term security as for the buyer of successive short-term securities. Assume, for example, that a two year security yields 4 percent interest at a time when a one year security yields 3 percent. The public is then unwilling to buy the lower yielding short-term security unless it expects that in the next year (the second year in the life of the two year security) the interest rate which it could obtain on a new one year security will be higher. Ignoring compounding of interest, assume that the public expects the short-term rate in the second year to be 5 percent. If so, over the two year period, buyers could earn the same interest on both securities (4 percent for two years vs. 3 percent for one year and 5 percent for the other year) and

---

[15] For a classic exposition of this theory, see Friedrich Lutz, "The Structure of Interest Rates," reprinted in American Economic Association, *Readings in the Theory of Income Distribution* (Philadelphia: Blakiston Co., 1946), pp. 499–529. For a powerful empirical defense, see David Meiselman, *The Term Structure of Interest Rates* (Englewood Cliffs, N.J.: Prentice-Hall, 1962).

would therefore be indifferent whether they bought a two year security or two successive one year securities. Thus, for equilibrium to prevail, the long-term rate must equal the average of short-term rates expected over the life of the long-term security.

A somewhat similar theory, developed by Professor Hicks, adds another element to expectations.[16] This is liquidity preference. In the Keynesian system the public prefers to hold money rather than securities, because money is more liquid; hence, securities have to pay interest to induce the public to hold them. The same reasoning can be applied to the term structure. Short-term securities are more liquid than long-term securities and, hence, long-term securities must pay, on the average, a higher rate of interest than do short-term securities. This liquidity premium can be combined with the expectations effect so that the long-term rate is equal to the average of expected short-term rates plus a liquidity premium. This theory has obtained substantial support from recent statistical studies.[17]

Another explanation of the term structure takes a different view.[18] It assumes that there is considerable segmentation in the market. Although to some extent funds flow between the long- and the short-term markets in response to interest-rate differentials, this fluidity is fairly limited. Certain lenders, for example, banks, like to lend short term because their own liabilities are short term. Similarly, certain borrowers who need funds only temporarily, for example, buyers of inventories, like to borrow short term. At the same time, lenders with long-term commitments, such as insurance companies, prefer to lend long term while borrowers who hold mainly long-term assets, for example, owners of apartment houses, can minimize their risks by bor-

[16] *Value and Capital* (London: Oxford University Press, 1946), Chapter 11.

[17] See Reuben Kessel, *The Cyclical Behavior of the Term Structure of Interest Rates, Occasional Paper 91*, National Bureau of Economic Research (New York: Columbia University Press, 1965). However, one may well argue that the available evidence is not decisive. See Lester Telser, "A Critique of Some Recent Empirical Research on the Explanation of the Term Structure of Interest Rates," *Journal of Political Economy*, Supplement, Vol. 75 (August, 1967), pp. 546–560.

[18] See John Culbertson, "The Term Structure of Interest Rates," *Quarterly Journal of Economics*, Vol. 71 (November, 1957), pp. 485–517.

rowing long term instead of short term. Although some borrowers and lenders shift between the long-term and short-term markets in response to changing interest-rate differentials, not enough of them do this to keep the long- and short-term rates in a fixed relation to each other. To a considerable extent the two markets are independent.[19]

With this background let us see what happens to the long-term rate if the Federal Reserve buys short-term securities. According to the expectations theory (either with or without the liquidity premium) the resulting reduction in the short-term rate affects the intermediate- and long-term rates. But intermediate-term rates fall less than short-term rates and long-term rates fall by even less. The current short-term rate is only one component of all the consecutive short-term rates whose average must equal the intermediate-term rate (or the intermediate-term rate minus the liquidity premium). Hence, even if the new lower short-term rate is expected to prevail for *some* time (but for a lesser time than the life of the intermediate-term security) the interest rate on the intermediate-term security falls proportionately less than the current short-term rate.[20] For the twenty year bond the current short-term rate is of little importance—the market expects periods of easy money to alternate with periods of tight money. Hence, long-term rates are less responsive to countercyclical monetary policy than are intermediate-term rates.

The above discussion has been based on the expectations (or the expectations plus liquidity premium) theory of the term structure. The market segmentation theory implies that the reduction in the short-term rate has a small effect on the intermediate- and long-term rates. Since the money market is not perfectly segmented a decline in the short-term rate causes *some* lenders to shift their activities out of the short-term money market into the

---

[19] Actually, the situation is more complex. For example, short-term lenders may shift to intermediate-term securities which lowers the yield on these securities. This causes some lenders who were previously in the intermediate-term market to shift to the long-term market.

[20] Note, however, that a change in the current short-term rate may affect long-term rates indirectly by changing expected future short-term rates. See John Wood, "The Expectations Hypothesis, the Yield Curve and Monetary Policy," *Quarterly Journal of Economics*, Vol. 78 (August, 1964), pp. 457–470.

intermediate- or long-term markets, while at the same time, some borrowers shift out of the long-term and intermediate-term markets into the short-term market. Hence, to some limited extent in the intermediate- and long-term markets, supply is increased and demand decreased so that interest rates fall somewhat. The Federal Reserve could make its policy much more effective in the long-term market by buying, not short-term securities, but inter- mediate- or long-term securities. For a number of reasons the Federal Reserve prefers to deal in short-term securities, but even this obstacle could be avoided by having the Treasury support the Federal Reserve.[21] The Treasury could refrain from selling long-term securities and could sell short-term securities instead.[22]

[21] The Federal Reserve is reluctant, though not unwilling, to deal in inter- mediate- and long-term securities for several reasons. One is undoubtedly a revulsion against its earlier policy of bond pegging. Another reason is that the Federal Reserve does not enjoy being arbiter of the money market, determining interest rates. At least Chairman Martin feels that the Federal Reserve should concern itself with the quantity of money and bank credit, and should leave the structure of interest rates to be deter- mined by free-market processes—a point of view which has come in for considerable criticism by academic economists. Another reason is that Federal Reserve operations in intermediate- and long-term securities exposes government security dealers to losses and in this way hinders the smooth workings of the money market. Moreover, the Federal Reserve believes that because of multiple bank deposit expansion it makes little difference to the interest rate structure whether it buys long- or short-term securities. The main effect of open-market operations is to provide the banking system with reserves. The actual purchases of the Federal Reserve are only a small proportion of the total security purchases generated by open-market operations. (This argument is, however, an overstatement since, as pointed out above, the money multiplier is *not* six or seven, but is approximately three. These issues were involved in a major controversy about open operations in the 1950's and early 1960's, the dispute about the "bills only" policy. For a critical discussion see Deane Carson, "The Bills Only Doctrine in Retrospect," M. J. Brennan (ed.), *Patterns of Market Behavior: Essays in Honor of Phillip Taft* (Providence: Brown University Press, 1965), pp. 155–172. For a defense see Ralph Young and Charles Yager, "The Economics of 'Bills Preferably,' " *Quarterly Journal of Economics,* Vol. 74 (August, 1960), pp. 341–373.

[22] But the Treasury may be reluctant to do this. In a recession when the Federal Reserve is operating an easy money policy, interest rates are low, and, hence, the Treasury has an incentive to minimize its interest cost by selling long-term securities at that time. Conversely, in a boom when the Federal Reserve is undertaking a tight money policy, high interest rates make the Treasury reluctant to sell long-term securities which would lock the high interest rates into its debt structure for a long time.

Thus, all three term-structure theories suggest that inter-
mediate- and long-term rates are affected to some, though perhaps
only a quite limited, extent by open-market operations in short-
term securities.[23] Figure 3.2 illustrates how intermediate-term
interest rates fluctuate somewhat less than the short-term rate,
and also shows the stability of the long-term rate. To be sure,
this chart shows general movements of the interest rates rather
than only those induced by changes in monetary policy, but
there is little reason to think that a different conclusion would
emerge if it were possible to isolate the effects of monetary
policy changes.[24]

Money Market Guides

The preceding discussion of the money-supply function provides
the necessary basis for considering some problems connected
with Federal Reserve goals. The discussion of Federal Reserve
goals in Chapter 1 is incomplete because it dealt only with high
level goals. The Federal Reserve does not have any way of aim-

[23] The empirical evidence on the extent to which long-term and intermediate-
term rates are affected by changes in the short-term rate is mixed. One
study (Arthur Okun, "Monetary Policy, Debt Management and Interest
Rates: A Quantitative Appraisal," in Commission on Money and Credit,
Stabilization Policies [Englewood Cliffs, N.J.: Prentice-Hall, Inc., 1963], pp.
331–380) found that it makes little difference to the term structure whether
the Treasury sells long- or short-term securities. Presumably, this conclusion also applies to the Federal Reserve so that open-market operations in
short-term securities affect the whole spectrum of interest rates. (But for a
criticism of this study, see R. H. Scott, "Liquidity and the Term Structure
of Interest Rates," *Quarterly Journal of Economics,* Vol. 79 [February,
1965], pp. 135–145.) Another study (David Fand, "A Time Series Analysis of the 'Bills Only' Theory of Interest Rates," *Review of Economics and
Statistics,* Vol. 48 [November, 1966], pp. 361–371) found that "in a
cyclical context, the long rate is relatively independent of short-run movements in the short rates so that inducing changes in the short-term rate
is not a good way of bringing about quick countercyclical movements in
the long-term rate." See also Burton Malkiel, *The Term Structure of Interest Rates* (Princeton, N.J.: Princeton University Press, 1966).

[24] More direct evidence on the effect of changes in the money growth rate
on interest rates is given in Phillip Cagan, "Changes in the Cyclical Behavior of Interest Rates," *Review of Economics and Statistics,* Vol. 48
(August, 1966), pp. 219–250.

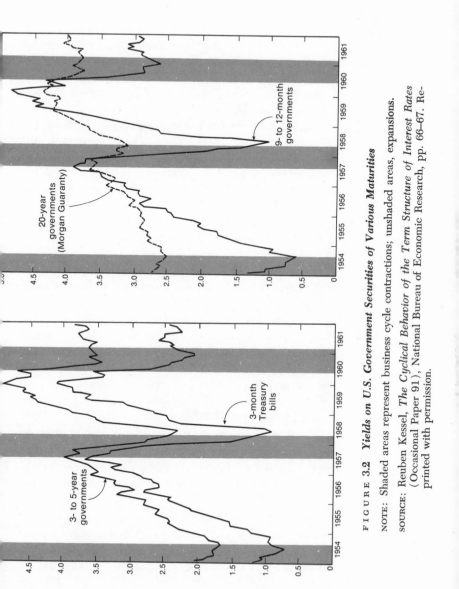

FIGURE 3.2 *Yields on U.S. Government Securities of Various Maturities*

NOTE: Shaded areas represent business cycle contractions; unshaded areas, expansions.

SOURCE: Reuben Kessel, *The Cyclical Behavior of the Term Structure of Interest Rates* (Occasional Paper 91), National Bureau of Economic Research, pp. 66–67. Reprinted with permission.

ing directly at high level goals such as full employment or price-level stability. Instead, the tools of monetary policy discussed in the previous chapter allow the Federal Reserve System to change bank reserves, and it then needs some intermediate goals and indicators to tell it how it should change bank reserves to achieve its high level goals.

There are a number of steps in the process linking changes in bank reserves to changes in money income and, in principle, the Federal Reserve could use each and every one of these steps as a target at which to aim. But it is convenient for the Federal Reserve to focus attention on the money market. Within the money market one can distinguish between intermediate goals of monetary policy and what are called money-market guides or goals.

To start with the intermediate goals, these are really the high level goals *within the money market*, the ultimate money-market variables the Federal Reserve wants to influence. They include such variables as the stock of money, the money stock plus time deposits, the long-term interest rate, the total supply of credit and the supply of bank credit. The first of these, the stock of money, is, of course, the strategic variable, and hence the obvious intermediate goal, to a believer in the quantity theory of money. The long-term rate of interest is the relevant variable for monetary policy in the Keynesian theory. The total supply of credit is the significant factor according to the liquid assets approach (discussed on pp. 142–143 below). The supply of bank credit, on the other hand, is a variable which is not at home in any widely accepted theory—presumably the Federal Reserve has adopted it in the (erroneous) belief that changes in the quantity of bank credit accurately mirror changes in the money stock.[25]

As can be seen from this multitude of intermediate goals the Federal Reserve takes an eclectic approach to monetary theory.

[25] Since bank credit comprises the bulk of bank assets and since demand deposits comprise a big part of bank liabilities (with demand plus time deposits comprising the bulk) one might expect a close relationship between bank credit and the money stock, or at least between bank credit

Such an attitude can be defended as the best alternative at a time when monetary theory is in an unsettled state—but it can also be criticized as demonstrating that the Federal Reserve has no well-explicated theory on which to base monetary policy.[26]

Turning to the money-market guides there are several alternatives open to the Federal Reserve. One obvious variable is the total reserve base. As the previous discussion of money supply theory indicated, there is probably a predictable relation between the growth of the reserve base and the growth of the

and the money stock plus time deposits. But for *short period changes* in these variables there is no such close relationship. This is illustrated by the following table showing seasonally adjusted annual rates of growth:

	Aug. 1964 through Nov. 1964	Dec. 1964 through Jan. 1965	Feb. 1965 through Mar. 1965	
Bank credit, all commercial banks	9.6%	12.2%	12.7%	
Money supply	4.9	3.4	1.1	
Money supply plus time deposits	9.2	10.1	7.7	

	Apr. 1965 through Aug. 1965	Sept. 1965 through Nov. 1965	Dec. 1965 through Jan. 1966	1959 to 1964
Bank credit, all commercial banks	9.0%	9.3%	11.5%	6.8%
Money supply	3.6	7.6	10.2	1.8
Money supply plus time deposits	8.8	11.6	10.5	5.6

SOURCE: Leonall Andersen and Elaine Goldstein, "Federal Reserve Open Market Operations in 1965," *Federal Reserve Bank of St. Louis Review*, Vol. 48 (June, 1966), p. 12.

See also Karl Brunner and Allan Meltzer, *Some General Features of the Federal Reserve's Approach to Policy* (Washington, D.C.: U.S. House Committee on Banking and Currency, Subcommittee on Domestic Finance, 88th Congress, Second Session, 1964), pp. 31–33.

[26] See Brunner and Meltzer, *Some General Features of the Federal Reserve's Approach to Policy, op. cit.*

money stock. Another variable is "free reserves" called net borrowed reserves, if negative. They are total reserves minus (1) required reserves and (2) borrowings from the Federal Reserve. The advantage claimed for free reserves is that they show more precisely than total reserves what is happening in the money market. By leaving out of account required reserves they omit reserves which are really not available to banks. Moreover, subtracting borrowing helps in gauging the state of the money market since banks are reluctant to expand credit on the basis of borrowed reserves. Hence, the argument asserts, free reserves can be used as a good indicator of money-market pressures.

In addition to free reserves, other money-market guides are the basic reserve position of money-market banks (free reserves minus purchases of Federal funds plus sales of Federal funds at eight New York money-market banks and at thirty-eight money-market banks outside New York), the Federal funds rate, member-bank borrowings, the inventories and outstanding borrowings of government security dealers, and the Treasury bill rate.[27] Due to the balance-of-payments problem, the Treasury bill rate is now more than a money-market guide, it is also a restraint on monetary policy and, as such, should also be classified with the intermediate goals. These variables, when combined with the Federal Reserve's evaluation of the attitudes and expectations of the various money-market participants, give the Federal Reserve an estimate of what it calls the "tone" of the market, or "the color, tone and feel." The tone of the market is not a measurable "scientific" variable but is imprecise and impressionistic.

For many years free reserves plus the "feel of the market" played a preponderate role in Federal Reserve policy making. However, the Federal Reserve has been severely criticized for

[27] Leonall Andersen and Jules Levine, "Implementation of Federal Reserve Open-Market Policy in 1964," *Federal Reserve Bank of St. Louis Review,* Vol. 47 (June, 1965), pp. 2–9; and Leonall Andersen and Jules Levine, "A Test of Money-Market Conditions as a Means of Short-Run Monetary Management," *National Banking Review,* Vol. 4 (September, 1966), p. 43. When a member bank is short of reserves it may borrow the excess reserves of another bank. This is known as buying "Federal funds," and the interest rate charged on this transaction is called the Federal funds rate.

relying on the feel of the market and on free reserves. The feel of the market is necessarily a vague, nonscientific affair as is illustrated by the following quotation from the minutes of the Federal Open Market Committee:

> Chairman Martin referred to Mr. Rouse's comment that the market had been "tight but not too tight," and he enquired whether it would also be correct to say that it had been "easy, but not too easy." Mr. Rouse responded that this statement would also apply.[28]

Since the feel of the market cannot be measured objectively, it does not provide any criterion which allows anyone, *including* the Federal Reserve, to see how successful monetary policy has been in establishing the correct tone of the market. For example, it is very hard to see how well the management of the Trading Desk is following the instructions of the Federal Open Market Committee.[29]

The free-reserve target has come in for even more severe criticism.[30] Free reserves, it is argued, are not a good target for monetary policy because they are a moving target. Free reserves are not simply reserves which banks hold because they don't know what to do with them; rather, they represent certain reserves which banks find profitable to keep at prevailing interest rates. Suppose that at current interest rates banks desire to hold $500 million of free reserves. If the Federal Reserve now attempts to raise free reserves to $600 million it will undertake $100 million of open-market purchases. But banks do not want to hold an additional $100 million of free reserves and will, therefore, get rid of these free reserves by making loans or buying securities, thus increasing deposits. If the Federal Reserve persists

---

[28] Quoted in Guttentag, *op. cit.*, p. 16.

[29] For details of these criticisms see Brunner and Meltzer, *Some General Features of the Federal Reserve's Approach to Policy, op. cit.*, pp. 13–16.

[30] See Milton Friedman, *A Program for Monetary Stability* (New York: Fordham University Press, 1960), pp. 41–42; Meigs, *op. cit.*; Karl Brunner and Allan Meltzer, *The Federal Reserve's Attachment to the Free Reserve Concept* (Washington, D.C.: U.S. House Committee on Banking and Currency, 88th Congress, Second Session, 1964); William Dewald, "Free Reserves, Total Reserves and Monetary Control," *Journal of Political Economy*, Vol. 71 (April, 1963), pp. 141–153.

in its attempt to raise free reserves the money stock continues to rise. Ultimately, a new equilibrium is reached as the rise in the money stock reduces interest rates and raises deposits enough so that at the lower interest rates and greater level of deposits banks *do* want to hold an additional $100 million of free reserves. But, at this equilibrium, the money stock is different from the one the Federal Reserve sought to establish. Thus, by aiming at a free-reserve target, the Federal Reserve relinquishes control over the stock of money.

Conversely, suppose that the Federal Reserve attempts to reduce free reserves to $400 million by open-market sales. Banks now find that their free reserves are below their desired level and, hence, they reduce outstanding deposits (or slow down the rate of deposit growth) until they have restored their free-reserve holdings. If the Federal Reserve counteracts this restoration of the free-reserve position of banks by selling more securities, banks again react by reducing the money supply (or its growth rate) still further. Hence, if the Federal Reserve attempts to obtain a certain money stock by aiming at a free-reserve target it will fail; the money supply will not respond in the desired way.

Moreover, looking at free reserves may mislead the Federal Reserve about its own policy. Suppose, for example, that it raises the discount rate. Banks now find it profitable to hold a greater volume of free reserves and, therefore, reduce their outstanding loans and security holdings. What looks like a situation of easy money when one uses free reserves as a criterion is actually an episode of tight money. Similarly, during a recession, as open-market rates fall, banks decide to hold more free reserves. The Federal Reserve sees an increase in free reserves and concludes that money is already easy, that, in fact, it may be too easy, and therefore decides to reduce the growth rate of the reserve base.[31]

---

[31] The Federal Reserve is concerned about the money becoming *too* easy in a recession for two reasons. First, if the reserve base is allowed to grow too much during a recession, it may take too long to mop up these excessive reserves during the ensuing expansion with inflationary results. A "sloppy" money market, as it is sometimes called, provides the Federal Reserve with too little control. Moreover, the Federal Reserve is concerned with another problem, the soundness of the banking system. It fears that if banks hold

Conversely, during an expansion, as interest rates rise and banks reduce their free reserves, the Federal Reserve may decide that money is too tight and, hence, may increase the growth rate of the reserve base. Thus, the use of a free-reserve target may trap the Federal Reserve into a policy of changing banks' reserves pro-cyclically rather than countercyclically. Not surprisingly, the opinion is very widely held that free reserves should be abandoned as a guide or target for monetary policy.[32] Fortunately,

---

a large volume of free reserves they will be tempted to make unsound loans and purchase unsound securities. This idea of protecting the banking system from its own alleged folly appears to have played a significant role in Federal Reserve thinking. To some outside observers this seems an utter misinterpretation of the uses of monetary policy. Bank examination plus the FDIC deposit insurance, the argument runs, are sufficient to protect the safety of deposits. Monetary policy should be concerned with the quantity of money and not with the *quality* of bank credit.

[32] This does not mean, of course, that nobody has a kind word to say about free reserves. Thus, Professor Guttentag (*op. cit.*, pp. 1–30) points out that free reserves can be used as a method of stabilizing the interest rate. A policy of keeping free reserves stable means that the Federal Reserve supplies additional reserves whenever the demand for free reserves increases and, conversely, that it reduces the supply of free reserves if the demand shrinks. Such an accommodation of supply to changes in demand reduces fluctuations of the interest rate. Stabilization of the interest rate has some advantages, particularly to the Federal government which is thereby enabled to sell large blocks of securities without experiencing a rise in interest rates. In addition he argues that there is no necessary inconsistency between using a free-reserve target for very short run policy decisions and a total reserve target for longer ones. He concludes (pp. 22–23) that:

> It is not clear that free reserves would be less effective than a reserve base measure in controlling money. . . . This is not to extol free reserves but simply to indicate that existing research provides little real basis for choosing between free reserves or some reserve base measure as the best intermediate target for controlling money. Additional research is needed . . .

See also the important paper by Richard Davis, "Open Market Operations, Interest Rates and Deposit Growth," *Quarterly Journal of Economics*, Vol. 79 (August, 1965), pp. 431–454. Professor Warren Smith believes that ". . . changes in the level of free reserves, if interpreted carefully, can be of some value as one indicator of changes in the state of the credit markets. . . ." Conference on Savings and Residential Financing, *1966 Proceedings* (Chicago: United States Savings and Loan League, 1966), p. 49.

there is some evidence that the Federal Reserve has moved away from its free-reserve notions.[33]

The use of free reserves has not been the only ground on which the Federal Reserve's approach to the money market has been criticized. Thus, a recent study found that the behavior of the intermediate goals (money, money plus time deposits, member bank total reserves, bank credit and long-term interest rates) did not respond at all closely to the behavior of the money-market guides.[34] Hence, the money-market guides the Federal Reserve's uses but does not give it adequate control over the variables it wants to control. In the same vein, another study concluded that:

> The analysis of the monetary mechanism contained in many of the Federal Reserve publications and statements reflects three basic features of the Reserve System: (1) they have an essentially short-run, day-to-day orientation; (2) their analysis of the monetary mechanism runs largely in terms of the operation of a single bank rather than in terms of the banking system as a whole; (3) their understanding of the monetary process consists of a series of unverified strands, often unconnected and obscure. These three factors are not unrelated. . . . Individual bankers and money deskmen must often take a day-to-day approach towards the management of their reserve positions. They often do not express great interest in analytical frameworks designed to separate the "systematic" from the "random." But the Federal Reserve has a very different role in the system and must be equipped with verified knowledge to effectively carry out the mandate of the Congress.

[33] For example, a Federal Reserve economist has stressed another money-market indicator, total reserves adjusted for seasonal changes and for the reserves required behind Federal government deposits. See Guy Noyes, "Short Run Objectives of Monetary Policy," *Supplement, Review of Economics and Statistics,* Vol. 45 (February, 1963), pp. 147–149.

[34] At most, indexes of money-market guides could explain about half the variation in the intermediate goals. See Andersen and Levine, "A Test of Money Market Conditions as a Means of Short-Run Monetary Management," *op. cit.* For a criticism of this study see Keith Carlson, "A Test of Money Market Conditions as a Means of Short-Run Monetary Management: A Comment," *National Banking Review,* Vol. 4 (March, 1967), pp. 347–349.

Knowledge that is adequate for the banker is often quite inadequate for the central banker.[35]

Professors Brunner and Meltzer buttress their criticisms by showing—see Table 3.1—that the money supply has behaved procyclically rather than countercyclically. At first glance this looks shocking; the Federal Reserve appears to have done exactly the wrong thing. But there are some qualifications to this conclusion.

TABLE 3.1 *Average Rates of Monthly Change in Money and "Credit" During Postwar Cycles, November, 1948 Through February, 1961*

Item	Peak to Trough	Trough to Peak
	(Millions of dollars)	
Change in money supply	120	229
Change in money supply plus time deposits	533	457
Change in bank credit	714	491

SOURCE: Karl Brunner and Allan Meltzer, *Some General Features of the Federal Reserve's Approach to Policy* (Washington, D.C.: U.S. House Committee on Banking and Currency, Subcommittee on Domestic Finance, 88th Congress, Second Session, 1964), p. 33.

First, the money supply plus time deposits (as well as bank credit) have behaved countercyclically and some economists such as Professor Friedman, define the money stock to include time deposits in commercial banks. Even those economists who prefer the conventional definition of money would agree that an increase in time deposits has *some* of the expansionary effect of an increase in demand deposits. Hence, whether one thinks that Table 3.1 shows bad behavior by the Federal Reserve de-

[35] Brunner and Meltzer, *Some General Features of the Federal Reserve's Approach to Policy, op. cit.,* pp. 40–41.

pends, in part, on one's view about the nature of time deposits.

Second, during part of the expansion period, though income is rising, it is still depressed, and a high rate of growth in the money stock *may* therefore be desirable, at least in the early stages of the expansion. The expansion phase of the cycle should not be confused with a period of excess demand. Third, if an increase in the money stock does take a long time to affect income (a matter discussed in Chapter 6) it *may* be good policy to increase the money stock at a relatively fast rate while still in the expansion phase of the cycle, and to slow down its rate of growth while still in the recession phase.

Fourth, Table 3.1 shows the money stock rather than the reserve base, the variable directly controlled by the Federal Reserve. If the Federal Reserve does not take strong enough defensive actions to offset the effects of changing interest rates on the money multiplier, the money stock may behave procyclically even if the reserve base behaved countercyclically.[36] But whether all of these qualifications are important enough to ameliorate the conclusions shown in Table 3.1 is a debatable matter.

In any case, perhaps as a result of these criticisms, the Federal Reserve appears to have modified its money-market behavior. In 1966 the Federal Open Market Committee started to use a so-called "proviso clause." While directives to the Trading Desk, according to this clause, are still issued in terms of the money-market guide, there is a proviso that the Trading Desk should aim at this guide only when a money-market goal, such as the money

[36] Whether or not reserves have behaved countercyclically is a controversial issue involving the definition of countercyclical and the relevant concept of reserves. See the testimony of Karl Brunner before the House Banking and Currency Committee's hearings (Committee on Banking and Currency, Subcommittee on Domestic Finance, *The Federal Reserve System after Fifty Years* [Washington, D.C.: 88th Congress, Second Session, 1964], pp. 1056–1058), William Dewald, "Money Supply versus Interest Rates: A Reply," *National Banking Review,* Vol. 4 (December, 1966), pp. 205–213. Another study found that the Federal Reserve had had the power to make the money supply move countercyclically had it only tried. See Robert Weintraub, "The Stock of Money, Interest Rates and the Business Cycle, 1952–1964," *Western Economic Journal,* Vol. 5 (June, 1967), pp. 257–270.

supply, behaves in a particular way. When the money supply does not behave in the desired way, the Trading Desk is required to try to get this market goal to behave in the desired way rather than to continue aiming at the money-market guide.[37]

The time has come to end this digression on the Federal Reserve's goals and guides and to return to the general line of discussion. Earlier sections of this chapter discussed the effects of changes in the reserve base on the stock of money and on interest rates. The following chapter takes the story from there and deals with the effect of changes in the money stock and interest rates on aggregate demand.

FURTHER READING

The Money Supply Function

There is really very little literature on this topic. Some of the earlier literature which includes important studies by Winfield Riefler, J. J. Polak and William White, and Robert Turner, is summarized in A. J. Meigs. *Free Reserves and the Money Supply.* Chicago: University of Chicago Press, 1962, a book which makes an important contribution to this topic. A powerful critique of this book is presented in Richard Davis. "Open Market Operations, Interest Rates and Deposit Growth," *Quarterly Journal of Economics,* Vol. 79 (August, 1965), pp. 431–454.

For recent statistical studies see David Fand. "Some Implications of Money Supply Analysis," American Economic Association *Papers and Proceedings,* Vol. 57 (May, 1967), pp. 380–400; Stephen Goldfeld and Edward Kane. "The Determinants of Member Bank Borrowing: An Econometric Study," *Journal of Finance,* Vol. 21 (September, 1966), pp. 499–514; Karl Brunner and Allan Meltzer. "Some Further Investigations of Demand and Supply Functions for Money," *Journal of Finance,* Vol. 19 (May, 1964), pp. 240–283, and their article prepared for U.S. House Committee on Banking and Currency, Subcommittee on

---

[37] See Elaine Goldstein and Leonall Andersen, "1966—A Year of Challenge for Monetary Management," *Federal Reserve Bank of St. Louis Review,* Vol. 49 (April, 1967), pp. 17–19.

Domestic Finance, *An Alternative Approach to the Monetary Mechanism*, 88th Congress, Second Session (Washington, D.C.: 1964); Ronald Teigen. "A Structural Approach to the Impact of Monetary Policy," *Journal of Finance*, Vol. 19 (May, 1964), pp. 284–305; Frank de Leeuw. "A Model of Financial Behavior," James Duesenberry, *et al.* (eds.), *The Brookings Quarterly Econometric Model of the United States*. Chicago: Rand McNally, 1965, pp. 465–532. For a critical view of this approach, see Lyle Gramley and Samuel Chase, Jr. "Time Deposits in Monetary Analysis," *Federal Reserve Bulletin*, Vol. 51 (October, 1965), pp. 1380–1406; and Tilford Gaines. "Financial Innovations and the Efficiency of Federal Reserve Policy," in *Monetary Process and Policies: A Symposium*. Homewood, Ill.: Richard D. Irwin, 1967, pp. 99–118. For a critique of the traditional approach, see the excellent paper by James Tobin. "Commercial Banks as Creators of 'Money,'" Deane Carson (ed.), *Banking and Monetary Studies*. Homewood, Ill.: Richard D. Irwin, 1963, pp. 408–419.

Major historical studies of the U.S. money supply are Milton Friedman and Anna Schwartz. *A Monetary History of the United States, 1867–1960*. Princeton: Princeton University Press, 1963; and Phillip Cagan. *Determinants and Effects of Changes in the Stock of Money 1875–1960*. New York: Columbia University Press, 1965. For an excellent study of the post World War I period see Patric Hendershott. *The Neutralized Money Stock: An Unbiased Measure of Federal Reserve Policy*. Homewood, Ill.: Richard D. Irwin, 1968.

Interest Rates

For the seminal discussions of the various term structural theories, see the following: Friedrich Lutz. "The Structure of Interest Rates," reprinted in American Economic Association *Readings in the Theory of Income Distribution*. Philadelphia: Blakiston Co., 1946; J. R. Hicks. *Value and Capital*. London: Oxford University Press, 1946, Chapter 11; John Culbertson. "The Term Structure of Interest Rates," *Quarterly Journal of Economics*, Vol. 71 (November, 1957), pp. 485–517. For empirical tests see David Meiselman. *The Term Structure of Interest Rates*, Englewood Cliffs, N.J.: Prentice-Hall, 1962 and Reuben Kessel. *The Cyclical Behavior of the Term Structure of Interest Rates, Occasional Paper 91*, National Bureau of Economic Research, New York: Columbia University Press, 1965. For an excellent detailed discussion of the controversy, see Joseph Conard. *An Introduction to the*

Theory of Interest. Berkeley: University of California Press, 1959, Part 3. A very good brief discussion is Frederick Struble. "Current Debate on the Term Structure of Interest Rates," in *Federal Reserve Bank of Kansas City Monthly Review* (January-February, 1966), pp. 10–16. Other aspects of interest rates and credit are discussed in *The Federal Reserve System: Purposes and Functions.* Washington, D.C.: Board of Governors of the Federal Reserve System, 1963, Chapters 5 and 6. For a major empirical study of the behavior of interest rates see Phillip Cagan. "Changes in the Cyclical Behavior of Interest Rates," *Review of Economics and Statistics,* Vol. 48 (August, 1966), pp. 219–251.

Money Market Guides and Targets

Andersen, Leonall, and Jules Levine. "A Test of Money Market Conditions as a Means of Short-Run Monetary Management," *National Banking Review,* Vol. 4 (September, 1966), pp. 41–51.

Brunner, Karl, and Allan Meltzer. *Some General Features of the Federal Reserve's Approach to Policy* and *The Federal Reserve's Attachment to the Free Reserve Concept.* Washington, D.C.: U.S. House Committee on Banking and Currency, Subcommittee on Domestic Finance, 88th Congress, Second Session, 1964.

Friedman, Milton. *A Program for Monetary Stability.* New York: Fordham University Press, 1960, pp. 41–42.

Guttentag, Jack. "The Strategy of Open Market Operations," *Quarterly Journal of Economics,* Vol. 80 (February, 1966), pp. 1–30.

Sternlight, Peter, and Robert Lindsey. "The Nature and Significance of Free Reserves," *Federal Reserve Bank of New York Monthly Review,* Vol. 40 (November, 1958), pp. 162–167.

Three other items cited in the first part of this bibliography, the studies by A. J. Meigs, Richard Davis, and the first-mentioned study by Karl Brunner and Allan Meltzer, are also relevant here. Important information (including brief summaries of the Brunner-Meltzer work) is also to be found in U.S. House Committee on Banking and Currency, Subcommittee on Domestic Finance, *The Federal Reserve System after Fifty Years, Hearings,* February 11–March 25, 1964, Vol. II. Washington, D.C.: 88th Congress, Second Session, 1964.

The Strength
of Monetary Policy

Contrary to the opinions of many contemporary economists (and to some of my own earlier views) I believe that monetary and credit policies have great potency to stimulate, stabilize or depress a modern economy. This belief is based on my evaluation of the tremendous amount of empirical data given by (1) history, (2) current statistics, and (3) case studies of business behavior. These data are diverse, conflicting, and often inconclusive, and therefore have to be interpreted with the help of all the tools of economic analysis inherited from the past and developed by the present generation of scholars.[1]

PAUL A. SAMUELSON

Introduction

The strength of monetary policy, that is, its ability to bring about changes in national income, is, of course, one of the most important questions, if not *the* most important question, that can be asked about monetary policy. To what extent does a change in the money stock really affect income? Is monetary policy strong enough to play a significant role or perhaps the predominant role in achieving the goals discussed in Chapter 1?

At one time the question of strength was just about the only major issue which divided the supporters and opponents of monetary policy. Recently, however, the issue of the strength of monetary policy has been supplemented by another issue, the question whether monetary policy is accurate or clumsy. (Clumsiness here means changing income in the *wrong* direction or having major undesirable side effects.) If monetary policy is strong but

[1] "Reflections on Central Banking," *National Banking Review,* Vol. 1 (September, 1963), p. 15.

clumsy, it may do damage rather than good. On the other hand, if monetary policy is weak but accurate, it will do some good, and while it may not be adequate as the major stabilization tool, it can be useful in supplementing other tools. These alternatives, as well as the other possibilities, are set out in the following matrix:

	Accurate	Clumsy
Strong	1	2
Weak	3	4

Only quadrant 1 yields a strong case for using monetary policy as a major stabilization tool. Quadrant 3 provides the case for using countercyclical monetary policy but relying primarily on other tools, and quadrants 2 and 4 describe the cases in which countercyclical monetary policy should not be used. The type of monetary policy to be used in these cases is discussed in Chapter 7.

In the early days of the Federal Reserve, up until the Great Depression, economists as well as other observers had great faith in monetary policy. They attached great importance to relatively small changes in interest rates. The justification for this was that interest is a cost of production which government policy can affect substantially. For example, consider a rise in the interest rate from 4 percent to 5 percent. This is not a 1 percent increase but a 25 *percent* increase in the cost of money. Admittedly, in most businesses interest costs are only a small proportion of total costs but, the reasoning ran, this does not prevent changes in interest rates from having a powerful effect on profitability because profits, too, are a small proportion of total costs. For example, assume that the selling price of an item is $1 and that the cost of production, apart from interest costs, is 96 cents and that interest costs are 2 cents. If the interest costs are doubled to 4 cents, the profit rate falls from 2 cents to zero. Although interest may be only a small proportion of total costs, it is a significant proportion of profits, the residual item.

Another way of treating the interest rate is to look upon it as the discount rate used to find the present value of a stream of income forthcoming from some investment project. For example, an asset producing $1000 per year in perpetuity is worth $20,000 if the income stream is capitalized at 5 percent, but only $16,667 if the interest rate used to capitalize it is 6 percent.

Moreover, the quantity theory, which had strong support among economists at that time, taught that the quantity of money dominates the behavior of prices so that from this point of view, too, monetary policy seemed very potent.

In the 1930's there was a sharp shift of opinion. Monetary policy was now believed to be weak. Fiscal policy rather than monetary policy was now thought to be the more promising stabilization tool. This change of opinion had several sources. First, there was the experience of the Great Depression. It was widely believed that easy money had been tried and found wanting; it seemed that despite low interest rates the economy refused to recover. This interpretation of the 1930's as illustrating the ineffectiveness of an easy money policy was widely accepted and has been challenged in a detailed fashion only in recent years. Since the correct interpretation of the monetary policy experience of the 1930's is so important, it is discussed in detail in Appendix B of this book.

The second reason for the decline of faith in monetary policy in the 1930's was the shift by so many economists from the quantity theory to Keynesian theory and the associated discovery of fiscal policy. In principle, in the Keynesian system the quantity of money *does* affect income and, depending upon what one assumes about the relevant interest elasticities, may do so powerfully. But in any theory which can properly be called a Keynesian theory (rather than a quantity theory expressed in Keynesian language), a change in the quantity of money has a less powerful impact on income than in the quantity theory. To be sure, this does not mean that a quantity theorist must necessarily place great faith in a countercyclical monetary policy. Far from it. If a quantity theorist believes as, for instance, Professor Milton Friedman does, that monetary policy is clumsy, he may still oppose countercyclical monetary policy. Similarly, a Keynesian may despair of the efficient and timely use of fiscal policy and may prefer countercyclical monetary policy. Nevertheless, the shift from Keynesian economics led to a de-emphasis of monetary policy.

Implications of the Quantity Theory and the Keynesian Theory for Monetary Policy

To explore this further, let us look in more detail at the implications which the quantity theory and the Keynesian theory have for monetary policy. In the simpler and older versions of the quantity theory the income velocity of money is taken as a constant so that aggregate demand depends upon the quantity of money. Put into the language of the equation of exchange, $MV = PT$ where M is the stock of money, V the number of times the average dollar becomes income during the year, T the volume of final output, and P the average price of output. Another way of putting it, the Cambridge or cash balance equation, is $M = KPT$ where K is the proportion of the year's income which is held in cash balances. The quantity theorist looks upon V or K as being very stable, and M as determined from the outside, so that income (which is, of course, PT) depends on the stock of money. Hence, monetary policy is able to change income.

In the more modern versions of the quantity theory V or K are no longer taken as constant numbers, but instead are treated as stable *functions* of other variables.[2] In Professor Friedman's version of the quantity theory velocity is a stable *function* of the level of "permanent income," that is, long-run income. In this system velocity decreases over time as permanent income rises (money being a luxury good) so that to maintain price stability and full employment the Federal Reserve must increase the

[2] For the modern versions discussed here, see Milton Friedman (ed.), *Studies in the Quantity Theory of Money* (Chicago: University of Chicago Press, 1956), particularly the essays by Professors Friedman and Selden. See also, Milton Friedman, "The Demand for Money: Some Theoretical and Empirical Results," *Journal of Political Economy*, Vol. 67 (August, 1959), pp. 327–351, and Karl Brunner and Allan Meltzer, "Predicting Velocity: Implications for Theory and Policy," *Journal of Finance*, Vol. 18 (May, 1963), pp. 319–354.

money stock sufficiently to offset both the secular increase in output and the secular decline in velocity. Consider the effect of an increase in the money stock in this system. Since permanent income is a weighted average of income over many years, it takes a substantial change in the income of any one year to change permanent income significantly. Hence, if permanent income is to rise enough within the year to make the public willing to hold the enlarged stock of money, income in that year must rise very much, though it will decline in subsequent years.

Another variant of the quantity theory developed by Professors Brunner and Meltzer makes the demand for money a function primarily of wealth and of the interest rate. Figure 4.1 shows how closely the Brunner-Meltzer model can predict income and the good fit suggests that changes in the quantity of money have a powerful effect on income.

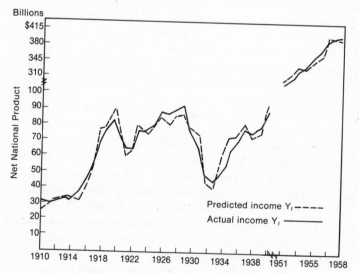

FIGURE 4.1 *Actual and Predicted Net National Product 1910–1940, 1951–1958*

SOURCE: Karl Brunner and Allan Meltzer, "Predicting Velocity: Implications for Theory and Policy," *Journal of Finance,* Vol. 18 (May, 1963), p. 341. Reprinted with permission.

In the Keynesian theory too, a change in the quantity of money affects income. If the money stock is increased, the rate of interest falls and the lower rate of interest stimulates investment which, together with the multiplier-induced increase in consumption, raises income. But note that in the Keynesian system the linkage between money and income changes is assumed to be such that the effect of a change in the quantity of money on income *may* (but need not be) minor. Consider first the case of complete price inflexibility so that income changes consist of changes in output rather than changes in prices. If the liquidity preference schedule is highly interest elastic, then an increase in the quantity of money has relatively little effect on the interest rate and, hence, on income. Alternatively, even if the liquidity preference schedule is relatively inelastic so that a sensible increase in the quantity of money *does* reduce the interest rate significantly, investment and consumption may be highly unresponsive to the rate of interest. If so, an increase in the quantity of money again has relatively little effect on income. In two extreme cases (cases A and B in Figure 4.2) the quantity of money has no effect *at all* on income. One is a situation where the liquidity preference schedule is completely interest elastic—the case of so-called "absolute liquidity preference." The second situation is one where investment and consumption schedules are completely interest inelastic. In either case a change in the quantity of money changes only velocity and not income.

The converse cases (C and D in Figure 4.2) are ones in which income changes in proportion to changes in the quantity of money, and velocity is constant. One of these cases occurs if the liquidity preference schedule is completely interest inelastic, the other if investment or consumption have an infinite interest elasticity. In between these extreme Keynesian and quantity theory cases are the empirically more likely ones (cases E and F in Figure 4.2) where the interest elasticity of these schedules is neither zero nor infinity. In these cases monetary policy has some effect, but not a completely dominating effect, on income. How much of an effect depends largely on the relative interest elasticities of the schedules.

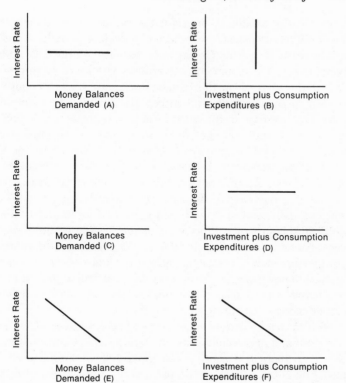

FIGURE 4.2   *The Interest Rate, Demand for Money, and Expenditures*

NOTE: A or B: Income completely unaffected by changes in the quantity of money. C or D: Income completely determined by the money stock. E and F: Changes in the money stock have some effect on income, but less than in C and D above.

So much for the price inflexibility case. Turning to the opposite case of completely flexible prices, where the change in income consists entirely of price changes, the situation is quite different. Unless the liquidity preference curve is infinitely elastic, or expenditure completely interest inelastic (cases A or B in Figure 4.2), a change in the stock of money causes a proportionate change in money income for the following reason. Suppose that the stock of money is increased. If so, the rate of interest falls initially. As a result the public moves down along the liquidity preference schedule and decides to hold a greater real quantity of money. Hence, as in the case of price inflexibility, expenditures and money income initially rise less than in proportion to the increase in the money stock. But since expenditures do rise to some extent, and prices are flexible, the price level rises. This increase in the price level lowers the real value of the money stock and continues to do so as long as the interest rate is below its (full employment-price stability) equilibrium, that is, until the money stock in real terms has declined back to its original level. At this new equilibrium point, the real money stock being unchanged, the rate of interest is back to where it was originally, and so is the public's demand for money balances. Thus, in this price flexibility case, as long as the liquidity preference curve is not infinitely elastic (or the expenditure curve completely interest inelastic) money income rises in proportion to the money stock regardless of the particular values of the elasticities. Conversely, if the nominal money stock is reduced, money income falls proportionately.[3]

But to a large extent monetary policy is concerned with the short run and most economists, though not all, believe that in the short run there is a considerable price inflexibility.[4] Hence, the next step is to go back to the price inflexibility case and to look at the interest elasticities of the liquidity preference and expenditure schedules. Unfortunately, relatively little is known about this and economists differ widely in their estimates. This is not surprising when one considers the great difficulties involved in estimating these elasticities by present-day statistical techniques.

To start with consumption, there is a widespread, though not unanimous, belief among economists that consumption is highly interest inelastic. The justifications for this view are, first, that adding an interest rate term to a consumption function does not improve the regression of the function on yearly data, and second,

[3] See Milton Friedman, "Interest Rates and the Demand for Money," *Journal of Law and Economics,* Vol. 9 (October, 1966), pp. 71–86. Moreover, insofar as price increases tend to make the public expect further price increases, the (money) rate of interest rises above its previous level.
[4] Professor Friedman believes that there is enough price flexibility so that an increase in the money supply soon raises interest rates.

that casual observation suggests that households disregard the interest rate in deciding how much to save.[5] (Note, however, that since consumption is a much larger dollar amount than is investment, even a small interest elasticity of consumption may be more significant than a fairly substantial interest elasticity of investment.[6]) Some responsiveness of consumption to interest rates may result from the effect of interest rates on consumer credit

[5] Regression analysis is a widely used statistical technique. It consists of relating the "dependent" variable, that is, the variable whose behavior we want to study, to one or more "independent" variables which serve to explain its behavior. For example, if we want to see if investment depends upon the interest rate, a simple (though bad) way of doing this would be to write an equation $I = a + bi$ where I is investment, i the rate of interest and a and b are constants. The regression technique can be used to fit this equation to the data. It chooses values of a and b so that it minimizes the square of the deviations between actual investment and the investment "predicted" by the equation. In other words, it picks the values of a and b which give the best fit.

Although this seems quite straightforward, there are a number of problems. First, suppose that the equation does yield a close relationship between investment and the interest rate. Does this mean that the interest rate determines investment, or that investment determines the interest rate, or some unholy mixture of the two? To use another example, suppose that we try to estimate a demand function for a commodity by regressing the quantity sold on price. Such a regression might yield a positive coefficient for price, suggesting that sales would increase if the price rises. If so, what the regression has produced is not a demand curve, but a supply curve, or perhaps a mixture of the two.

Another problem concerns the variables to be included. For example, a regression of investment on the interest rate might show that investment increases as interest rates go up. The reason for this peculiar finding is that during the upswing of the business cycle, both the interest rate and investment rise, while during the downswing both fall. Clearly, some variable measuring business activity should be included in the regression.

A third problem is the precise specification of the variables to be included. For example, a regression of consumption on income and on the interest rate paid on long-term government bonds might show that the interest rate has no significance whatsoever. But, if instead of using the currently prevailing interest rate on government bonds, the investigator had used a three year average of interest rates paid on savings deposits, the interest rate conceivably might have turned out to be significant.

[6] The elasticity measures the *percentage* change in one variable associated with the percentage change in the other. What is relevant for measuring the strength of monetary policy is the change in expenditures expressed in dollars. Hence, one has to multiply the elasticities of consumption and of investment by their respective dollar levels so that one can add them to find the total change in expenditures.

discussed in Chapter 2 as well as from the direct effects of the interest rate on consumer durable purchases. Moreover, the interest rate has some effect on corporate saving. In a period of tight money, corporations have an incentive to retain earnings.[7]

There is extensive literature on the interest elasticity of investment. As already mentioned, professional opinion on this topic changed radically in the 1930's. The view which became popular was supported both by theoretical analysis and by empirical studies showing that investment is quite insensitive to the interest rate.

On a theoretical level, the argument ran as follows: for short-term investment the interest rate is unimportant because for investment projects which last only for a few years interest is a quite unimportant element of costs. For long-run investment, on the other hand, interest costs are much more important; the present value of a future stream of income stretched over a long period of time is powerfully affected by the interest rate at which it is discounted to find its present value. But for such long-run investment projects, there is great uncertainty. Costs and prices may change radically over this long span of time, and compared to these uncertainties, changes in the interest rate are insignificant. Moreover, a great deal of investment is financed with internally generated funds (undistributed profits and depreciation reserves) and for such investment, the argument ran, the market rate of interest is irrelevant. In addition, many business firms use the "pay-out" method of evaluating investment projects; they ask how long it takes a piece of equipment to "pay for itself." In such calculations, the rate of interest does not seem to enter.[8]

[7] See John Brittain, *Corporation Dividend Policy* (Washington, D.C.: Brookings Institution, 1966), p. 199. Two recent statistical studies present evidence for a significant interest elasticity of consumption. See Colin Wright, "Some Evidence on the Interest Elasticity of Consumption," *American Economic Review*, Vol. 57 (September, 1967), pp. 850–854; and Michael Hamburger, "Interest Rates and the Demand for Consumer Durables," *American Economic Review*, Vol. 57 (December, 1967), pp. 1131–1153. (Last sentence added in proof.)

[8] M. Brockie and A. Grey, "The Marginal Efficiency of Capital and Investment Programming," *Economic Journal*, Vol. 66 (December, 1956), pp.

Empirically, this pessimistic view of the interest elasticity of investment found substantial support from two sources. First, a number of economists undertook surveys asking businessmen whether their investment plans were affected by the rate of interest. They concluded that there was little effect. Second, a large number of studies attempted to find the determinants of investment by using regression analysis. In these studies the rate of interest generally did not turn out to be an important variable. One survey of this literature lists fifteen such studies published in the period 1938–1951. In eight of these studies the interest rate variable was not significant. Even more damaging is the fact that many other studies got good statistical fits without using the interest rate.[9]

But this pessimism about the interest elasticity of investment can be challenged and, in fact, has been challenged in recent years. First, upon careful analysis it turns out that existence of considerable risk in long-term investment projects need *not* reduce their interest elasticity.[10] Moreover, one could make an a priori case for expecting the interest elasticity of investment to be high.[11]

662–675. Another argument used to show that the interest rate is unimportant is that with a corporate income tax the government "pays" part of any increase in the interest rate. But this argument is wrong because it leaves out of account that the government also obtains part of the profit from the investment project. One should look at both cost and return after tax.

[9] See John Meyer and Edwin Kuh, *The Investment Decision* (Cambridge, Mass.: Harvard University Press, 1957), pp. 23–35.

[10] See Lorie Tarshis, "The Elasticity of the Marginal Efficiency Function," *American Economic Review*, Vol. 51 (December, 1961), pp. 958–985; and Oliver Williamson, "The Elasticity of the Marginal Efficiency Function: Comment," *American Economic Review*, Vol. 52 (December, 1962), pp. 1099–1103.

[11] This case relies upon the fact that investment in any one year is only a small proportion of the total capital stock. Assume, for example, that the marginal efficiency of *capital* schedule is, as many critics of monetary policy assert, quite inelastic. Let us say it has an elasticity of 0.01. If the country's capital stock is equal to, say, 20 times its annual net investment, an increase of 0.01 percent in the capital stock induced by a 1 percent decline in the rate of interest is equal to a 0.2 percent of net investment. Even if one assumes that this investment is spread over two years, the 0.01 elasticity of the marginal efficiency of capital corresponds to a respect-

The empirical evidence on the inelasticity of the investment schedule has also been questioned. Dr. William White has pointed out several severe statistical biases in the interpretation of the surveys which asked businessmen about their reaction to interest rate changes and about their use of the "pay-out" method.[12]

The regression studies frequently contain several biases which tend to make them understate the importance of the interest rate as a determinant of investment.[13] Moreover, a number of—though, of course, by no means all—recent studies using sophisticated statistical techniques have concluded that investment *is* responsive to interest rate changes.[14] In addition, one should make

---

able 0.1 elasticity of net investment. As Professor Lerner has emphasized, one must sharply distinguish between the marginal efficiency of *investment* and the marginal efficiency of *capital*. (See his *The Economics of Control* [New York: Macmillan, 1944], Chapter 25.)

[12] "Interest Inelasticity of Investment Demand: The Case from Business Attitude Surveys Reexamined," *American Economic Review,* Vol. 46 (September, 1956), pp. 565–587; and "The Rate of Interest, The Marginal Efficiency of Capital and Investment Programming," *Economic Journal,* Vol. 68 (March, 1958), pp. 51–58.

[13] During a business expansion, as the marginal efficiency of investment increases, both investment and the interest rate rise. Unless the regression equation includes a variable which picks up *all* of this spurious positive correlation between investment and the interest rate, the true effect of the interest rate increases on investment will be, at least partially, hidden. Another bias is created by price expectations. If prices are expected to rise, the interest rate will rise, but since it is an increase only in the expected money rate of interest rather than in the real rate, investment is unaffected. Conversely, if prices are expected to fall, the decline in the money rate does not stimulate investment. In either case, a bias against the proposition that interest rates affect investment is introduced into a regression analysis. Still another bias may result from the fact that many empirical studies attempted to relate investment to the rate of interest instead of to the *change* in the interest rate. In equilibrium the stock of capital is already adjusted to the prevailing rate of interest. The *change* in the stock of capital, that is, investment, should therefore be related to the *change* in the interest rate, not to the *level* of the interest rate. For a discussion of these points, see Karl Brunner, "The Report of the Commission on Money and Credit," *Journal of Political Economy,* Vol. 69 (December, 1961), pp. 605–620, and Mayer, "Comments," in George Horwich (ed.), *Monetary Process and Policies: A Symposium, op. cit.,* pp. 316–321.

[14] A number of studies of plant and equipment investment published since 1960 have found the rate of interest to be significant. Professor Dale Jor-

allowance for the indirect effect of interest rate changes. Rising interest rates tend to reduce stock prices, because they raise the opportunity cost of buying stock and, hence, depress the stock market.[15] Stock prices, in turn, are likely to have some effect on investment.

---

genson found an interest elasticity of −0.15 for the very long run, and a substantially greater one for the short run ("Anticipations and Investment Behavior," James Duesenberry, Gary Fromm, Lawrence Klein and Edwin Kuh [eds.], *The Brookings Quarterly Econometric Model of the United States* [Chicago: Rand McNally, 1965], pp. 88–89). Yehuda Grunfeld, in his study of eight large firms, obtained an interest elasticity of −0.5 ("The Determinants of Corporate Investment," A. C. Harberger [ed.], *The Demand for Durable Goods* [Chicago: University of Chicago Press, 1960], p. 240) while Professors Edwin Kuh and John Meyer found an interest elasticity of −0.16 in the aggregate and one of −0.34 for the median industry ("Investment, Liquidity and Monetary Policy" in Commission on Money and Credit, *Impacts of Monetary Policy* [Englewood Cliffs, N.J.: Prentice-Hall, 1963], pp. 381–382). Another recent study found a short-run interest elasticity of −0.3 and a long-run one of −0.5 (Frederick Hammer, *The Demand for Physical Capital: An Application of a Wealth Model* [Englewood Cliffs, N.J.: Prentice-Hall, 1964], p. 112). Stephen Goldfeld, *Commercial Bank Behavior and Economic Activity* (Amsterdam: North-Holland, 1966), p. 166, found an interest elasticity of fixed investment of −0.5 or −0.6. Still another study (Robert Resek, "Investment by Manufacturing Firms: A Quarterly Time Series Analysis of Industry Data," *Review of Economics and Statistics*, Vol. 48 [August, 1966], pp. 322–333) found an interest elasticity for total manufacturing which varied from −1.0 to −1.4 in different models. See also Frank de Leeuw, "The Demand for Capital Goods by Manufacturers: A Study of Quarterly Time Series," *Econometrica*, Vol. 30 (July, 1962), pp. 407–423.

For residential construction there seems to be general agreement that credit conditions have a significant effect (see Leo Grebler and Sherman Maisel, "The Determinants of Residential Construction: A Review of Present Knowledge" in Commission on Money and Credit, *Impacts of Monetary Policy* [Englewood Cliffs, N.J.: Prentice-Hall, 1963], pp. 608–609). For inventory investment there is less evidence that interest rates have a significant effect on investment. On the other hand, for state and local government investment there is some evidence of responsiveness to interest rates. The results of recent studies on the interest elasticity of investment are surveyed in Michael Hamburger, *The Impact of Monetary Variables: A Selected Survey of the Recent Empirical Literature* (Washington, D.C.: Board of Governors of the Federal Reserve System, mimeographed edition, 1967).

[15] For a discussion of the effect of money supply changes on stock prices, see Beryl Sprinkel, *Money and Stock Prices* (Homewood, Ill.: Richard D. Irwin, 1964), Chapter 7.

This interest elasticity of investment has to be juxtaposed to the interest elasticity of the liquidity preference schedule discussed in the previous chapter. In recent years there have been numerous studies of the demand for money which have fitted regression equations to the data and estimated an interest elasticity. They have found little evidence that the liquidity preference schedule is either infinitely elastic or inelastic. Within the range of zero and infinity, many estimates of the elasticity of the liquidity preference schedule coexist; however, they are generally close to or less than unity.[16] When one compares the interest elasticities of investment and of liquidity preference, one can

[16] One's estimate of the interest elasticity depends in good part on whether one includes time deposits in the money stock and on whether one uses the short-term or long-term interest rate. For the short-term interest rate, and money defined to include time deposits, Dr. David Laidler found the "most likely range" for the income elasticity to be −0.16 to −0.19, with "absolute outside limits" of −0.01 and −0.59. See "The Rate of Interest and the Demand for Money—Some Empirical Evidence," *Journal of Political Economy*, Vol. 74 (December, 1966), p. 549. Henry Latané, using the long-term rate of interest, found an interest elasticity of −0.85 for the years 1909–1958 ("Income Velocity and Interest Rates—A Pragmatic Approach," *Review of Economics and Statistics*, Vol. 42 [November, 1960], p. 446). Professor Meltzer found an interest elasticity of −0.9 for money (as conventionally defined) for the period 1900–1958 (Allan Meltzer, "The Demand for Money: The Evidence from Time Series," *Journal of Political Economy*, Vol. 71 [June, 1963], pp. 219–246). A study by Gregory Chow found a similar elasticity ("On the Long-Run and Short-Run Demands for Money," *Journal of Political Economy*, Vol. 74 [April, 1966], pp. 111–131). In another set of studies, Brunner and Meltzer found various values for the interest elasticity ranging from −0.34 to −0.54 for the period 1930–1959 (Karl Brunner and Allan Meltzer, "Some Further Investigations of Demand and Supply Functions for Money," *Journal of Finance*, Vol. 19 [May, 1964], p. 266). Ronald Teigen estimated various interest elasticities ranging from −0.02 to −0.20 ("Demand and Supply Functions for Money in the United States: Some Structural Estimates," *Econometrica*, Vol. 32 [October, 1964], p. 505). Another study using the short-term interest rate estimated the short-run interest elasticity at −0.1 or −0.2 (Martin Bronfenbrenner and Thomas Mayer, "Liquidity Functions in the American Economy," *Econometrica*, Vol. 28 [October, 1960], pp. 817–820). Stephen Goldfeld obtained an interest elasticity for the short-term rate of −0.07 or −0.08, and a slightly higher interest elasticity using the rate paid on time deposits (*op. cit.*, p. 160). See also Milton Friedman, "Interest Rates and the Demand for Money," *Journal of Law and Economics*, Vol. 9 (October, 1966); and Michael Hamburger, "The Demand for Money by Households, Money Substitutes and Monetary Policy," *Journal of Political Economy*, Vol. 74 (December,

make a case that monetary policy is quite strong, though it does depend upon which estimate of these elasticities one prefers.

Institutional Factors Strengthening or Weakening Monetary Policy

All of the above has dealt with the problem as though the money market were a perfect market in which borrowers could borrow any amount they could repay at *the* interest rate while all lenders could lend at that rate. Moreover, it has been implicitly assumed that changes in this interest rate could be measured by looking at changes in the interest rate on government securities or the commercial paper rate which are the interest rates generally used by economists to estimate the interest elasticities of investment and of the liquidity preference schedule.

But we know that the real world money market does not look like this. Firms and households cannot borrow an unlimited amount at a fixed interest rate; banks ration credit. The amount they can borrow is affected by the sheer availability or unavailability of funds to the financial institutions. When money becomes tight, banks ration credit by turning down loan applications and by reducing the amounts and maturities of the loans they do make. Usually, there is a fringe of unsatisfied borrowers who would like to borrow at the prevailing interest rate but are unable to do so. When money becomes tight, some firms previously able to borrow become part of this unsatisfied fringe. Conversely, as money becomes easier, firms previously unable to borrow are now able to do so. Changes in the availability of funds *may* be as important, or even more important, than changes in the interest rate.

Looking only at the interest rate and the interest elasticity of

---

1966), pp. 600–623. In general, one would expect equations using the short rate to yield lower estimates of the elasticity than equations using the long rate. The elasticity is computed by dividing the percentage change in the money stock by the percentage change in the interest rate. The change in the money stock is the same regardless of what interest rate one uses, but since the short rate fluctuates more than the long rate, using the short rate means using a bigger denominator and, hence, one gets a lower value for the elasticity.

investment, therefore, involves abstracting from some of the observed behavior of the money market. Such an abstraction *may* be harmless. After all, we use many other heroic abstractions in economics. But there is a danger that such an abstraction may lead to wrong conclusions. Hence, the above analysis of interest elasticities should be supplemented, or perhaps even replaced, by an analysis which uses the availability of money rather than its costs.

Professor Friedman favors the latter, and has argued that we should look not at the rate of interest but at the quantity of money. *In principle*, it makes no difference whether we measure monetary conditions by looking at the real interest rate (that is, the interest rate adjusted for price changes) or at the real quantity of money. One can describe a demand curve either by taking a certain price and looking at the quantity demanded at that price, or else by taking a specific quantity demanded and looking at the price. Since price and quantity are uniquely related it does not matter whether one uses one or the other. Thus, *in principle*, it is irrelevant whether one talks about the real quantity of money or about the real interest rate. (Note, however, that what is relevant is *not* the *nominal* quantity of money as determined by the central bank, but the *real* quantity of money which is determined by the public.) But, in practice, we do not have an adequate measure of the rate of interest. The rate of interest which is relevant in determining expenditures is an average of the rates at which spenders can borrow and savers lend, that is, it is a weighted average of the rate at which households and firms borrow from or lend to a wide variety of sources. We do not have any statistical series which measures this rate—the interest rate on government securities, generally used to represent *the* interest rate, is a poor substitute. Hence, since we cannot measure the price of money, we should instead talk about a variable which we can measure—the real quantity of money.

Another approach is less radical. It argues that the interest rate approach is a useful way to look at the impact of monetary policy but that it must be supplemented by looking at the availability of money. This is essentially the position taken by the

Federal Reserve as well as by many monetary economists and must therefore be taken up in considerable detail.

To understand this "availability doctrine," as it is called, it is necessary to consider its historical background, that is, the conditions prevailing at the time when it was first formulated. During and after World War II, bond prices were "pegged," that is, the Federal Reserve had undertaken to support the price of government securities at par. Since interest rates had been kept very low during the war, this meant that during the postwar inflation the Federal Reserve was committed to an easy money policy.

This policy of supporting government securities at par was adopted in large part because policy makers faced an unfamiliar situation, a situation which they considered potentially dangerous. This new situation was the great increase in the public debt as a result of the war. This debt was widely held and dominated the portfolios of many financial institutions. The Treasury was afraid that if interest rates rose and government security prices declined, these financial institutions would be in serious trouble and might even fail. A condition which seemed to make the problem more severe was that the financial community had only a vague memory of life under a flexible monetary policy. Interest rates had been low since 1933 and the financial community was not familiar with rising interest rates. Another important background factor was the prevalence of the view that investment is highly interest inelastic so that even substantial increases in the interest rate would do little to curb inflation.

It was against this background that the Federal Reserve urged an abandonment of the pegging policy so that it would be able to use monetary policy as a curb on inflation. To do this, the Federal Reserve could not use the traditional argument that a substantial increase in interest rates would stop inflation by raising the cost of investing because there was the fear that such a *substantial* increase in interest rates would be damaging to the economy as well as be too costly for the country's chief debtor, the United States Treasury. The Federal Reserve therefore relied upon the availability thesis developed by Professor J. H. Williams and Dr. Robert Roosa of the New York Federal Reserve Bank.

This availability thesis argued that relatively small changes in the interest rate, changes too small to be dangerous, would suffice to limit inflation, and that the existence of a large and widely held public debt, managed by sophisticated money-market professionals, far from hindering monetary policy, actually aids it.

As the name implies, the availability doctrine does not stress the effect of interest rate changes on investment: instead, it talks about the *availability* of credit. In doing so it bases itself on the well-known fact that banks and other lenders ration credit, that in a period of tight money banks turn down loan applications of marginal customers even though the customers would be willing to pay a very high rate of interest. Interest rates are inflexible; to a considerable extent banks operate not by changing the price of credit, but by changing its quality. In a period of high demand for credit, they will turn down some less safe loan applications they would have granted at a time of easy money.

A second aspect of the availability thesis is that it puts a great deal of stress on expectations, particularly on the expectations of lenders. The theory has strong psychological overtones. Third, it emphasizes the effect of *rising* interest rates rather than of *high* rates. A fourth characteristic is its emphasis on institutional detail rather than on theoretical rigor. It presents the type of considerations which are likely to occur to men actually operating in the money market rather than to purely academic economists.

Finally, note that the availability doctrine does not consist of a single effect worked out in great detail, but rather it is a conglomeration of related points. These points are (1) the portfolio effect, (2) the locking-in effect, (3) the yield-differential effect, (4) the impact via investment banking, and (5) the expectations effect.

The portfolio effect works as follows. A rise in interest rates reduces the value of outstanding securities and, hence, lowers both the public's wealth and its liquidity.[17] And since the public is

[17] A rise in interest rates *reduces* the price of outstanding securities. The increase in interest rates does not apply to outstanding, that is, previously issued securities, and these old securities now have to compete with new securities paying a higher rate of interest, hence their price has to fall. To illustrate, consider the case of a "consol," that is, a security on which the

holding a very large volume of securities, even a small change in the rate of interest has a substantial effect. According to the proponents of the availability approach, this reduction in liquidity reduces investment in two ways. First, borrowers are less willing to invest as the value of their liquid assets declines. A simple equilibrium model suffices to show this. Assume that the firm or household possesses liquid assets and physical capital. Now, reduce its liquid assets; unless liquid assets are an inferior good it will react by partially restoring its stock of liquid assets at the expense of its stock of physical capital. (By analogy, consider a consumer who has apples and pears. If you take away some of his apples, he will reach an equilibrium only by swapping some pears against apples.)

The second way in which a reduction in wealth and liquidity reduces investment is through its impact on lenders. As the lender's liquidity is reduced by falling security prices, he becomes less willing to reduce it even further by exchanging liquid government securities for less liquid private securities or loans. The

---

issuer pays interest every year but which has no maturity date on which it has to be paid off. (At present, such securities do not exist in the United States, but in Britain the government has issued them.) Suppose that a consol pays an interest rate of 3 percent, and that the rate of interest now rises to 6 percent. The owner of the old consol still gets only $30 on each $1000 bond outstanding. If he sells his $1000 bond for $500 the buyer purchasing two of these bonds for his $1000 would get exactly the same return as he would by buying one new bond at $1000. Hence, to keep old securities competitive with new securities, the price of old securities has to fall by half as the interest rate doubles. This inversely *proportional* relationship applies only to consols, for with securities with a fixed maturity the price still moves inversely to the interest rate but no longer does so proportionately. If a bond is redeemable in, say, five years, the purchaser receives the old (lower) rate of interest only for five years, after that he gets his $1000 back and is able to invest that sum in the higher yielding bonds. Hence, although a doubling of the interest rate still reduces bond prices it does not cut them in half. The shorter the period until the maturity of the security, the less is the effect of a change in interest rates on its capital value.

In this way a rise in the interest rate reduces the public's liquidity, but it is not clear whether the public's wealth is necessarily reduced as the availability doctrine asserts. See R. C. O. Matthews, "Expenditure Plans and the Uncertainty Motive for Holding Money," *Journal of Political Economy,* Vol. 71 (June, 1963), pp. 201–218.

institutional framework of this argument is that in a period of tight money financial institutions can meet rising private demands for credit only by selling government securities. But banks, saving and loan associations, and other financial intermediaries hold government securities not only for earnings, but also to ensure their liquidity. Hence, a reduction in the value of their liquidity stock makes them less willing to reduce it even further by selling government securities. Conversely, during a period of falling interest rates and rising security prices, financial institutions find the liquidity of their portfolios increasing, and so they tend to restore these portfolios to equilibrium by selling government securities and making loans or purchasing private securities.

The second argument of the availability approach is the "locking-in" effect. This locking-in effect, too, relies on the fall in value of securities as interest rates rise, but unlike the portfolio effect just discussed it does not rely primarily on rational profit maximization, but on an irrationality. According to the availability doctrine, portfolio managers have an aversion to selling government securities at a loss, even if they could more than recoup these losses by using the proceeds of the security sales to make high yielding loans. If they sell government securities at a loss, this loss shows up on their balance sheets while the higher yield they obtain on private loans does not show up directly on their current balance sheets.[18] Hence, portfolio managers may be criticized by their superiors and by stockholders if they sell securities at a loss even if this action increases the long-run profits of the firm.[19] Conversely, during a recession when interest rates

---

[18] For accounting purposes banks may value their government security portfolios at cost; hence, if they hold on to their government securities as prices fall the price decline does not show up on their balance sheet.

[19] Note that this locking-in effect does not necessarily require irrationality on the part of the financial manager. He may maximize his salary by not selling securities even if this failure to sell securities reduces the income of the firm. The irrationality here is that the firm does not fire him.

Moreover, there is an aspect of the locking-in effect which is rational for the bank firm. Some regulations limit certain types of assets to a fixed proportion of the bank's capital. By not selling securities at a loss the bank maintains the book value of its capital and the amount of those assets it can hold.

have fallen and security prices have risen, portfolio managers can gain approval by selling securities and making lower-yielding private loans.

The third point of the availability thesis is the yield-differential effect. This argument relies upon the stickiness of interest rates on private loans and securities. It asserts that as interest rates rise on government securities, interest rates on private loans and securities increase too, but do so only with a substantial lag. Hence, for a significant period of time, government securities have a competitive advantage over private securities and loans, and banks and other lenders will tend to hold on to their government securities. Conversely, during a recession, a reduction in the interest rate on government securities makes lenders more willing to sell government securities and invest in private ventures, thus raising investment and income.

A fourth point raised by the proponents of the availability thesis deals with the reaction of investment bankers. The investment banker usually floats securities in the following manner. He obtains the securities from the original issuer, paying a fixed price for the issue, and then sells the securities for whatever he can get on the fluctuating market. If interest rates rise while he is holding them he may sustain a loss on the transaction, but if interest rates fall, and security prices rise, he will make a substantial profit. Hence, the argument runs, during a period of rising interest rates investment bankers tend to be unwilling to float securities and this retards investment spending. By contrast, in a period of falling interest rates, investment bankers are more willing to float securities and facilitate investment.

This leaves the expectations argument, one of the biggest and most controversial aspects of the availability doctrine. The argument has several facets. On the one hand, the argument states, if interest rates rise lenders expect them to rise even further. Hence, they reduce their lending and their security purchases while waiting for the rates to rise. It is not actually necessary that lenders have strong expectations that rates will rise; the mere creation of *uncertainty* about the possibility that rates may rise is sufficient. (This is an illustration of the workings of Keynes' speculative motive for liquidity preference.) On the other hand, borrowers have different expectations; as rates rise they expect rates to fall again and, therefore, they postpone borrowing and investing. Thus, both the supply curve and the demand curve for funds shift leftwards, and investment is reduced. Moreover, these effects on lenders and borrowers are supplemented by more general effects on investors, particularly investors in inventories. As investors see interest rates rise, they realize that the Federal Reserve is stepping in to control inflation and that there is now less need to buy ahead in order to protect against future price increases. Conversely, in a recession, as the Federal Reserve takes expansionary action businessmen feel more optimistic and, hence, are less prone to cut back on investment.

This availability doctrine has been criticized by a number of economists. Note that the whole approach is based on short-run market imperfections. Once the yield on private securities adjusts to compensate for the greater attractiveness of government securities, many of these imperfections vanish. Moreover, granted that the portfolio effect works in the direction indicated, how strong is it? Does a moderate reduction in the wealth and liquidity of financial institutions, and of borowers, really reduce investment substantially? To argue that monetary policy is strong, it is not sufficient to point out that it has an effect on investment. One must show that this effect is powerful. Unfortunately, both the proponents and the opponents of the availability doctrine have little hard empirical evidence to offer on the strength of the portfolio effect or, for that matter, on the other components of the availability doctrine.

The locking-in effect can be criticized on the grounds that, like other irrational behavior, it is not likely to be permanent. As one economist has remarked:

> The shortcoming of the theory of the locking-in effect is that it disregards other significant factors. . . . Old fashioned economic theory was by no means perfect. But surely a theory which starts from the assumption that the desire to maximize net [profits] is of primary importance in the actions of businessmen is more to be trusted than theory such as this that rests on far flimsier and more ephemeral assumptions. . . . At best the locking-in idea is a half-

truth which through continued repetition, has gained undue acceptance. It is as though it were assumed that a half-truth twice told becomes a whole truth.[20]

Admittedly, in the early postwar years when bond prices started to fall after many years of stability, portfolio managers and their superiors may have been unwilling to show losses on their books. But sooner or later they, as well as their stockholders, should learn that taking book losses may be a sign of efficient rather than inefficient portfolio management. To what extent is the availability doctrine guilty of taking the specific circumstances existing in the late 1940's and elevating them into a general theory?

There are two factors which tend to suggest that the locking-in effect is not very important. One is that banks and other financial institutions need not sell long-term government securities to obtain loanable funds; they can sell short-term government securities instead. And short-term securities can be sold with little capital loss. Second, the tax laws give banks a definite incentive at certain times to sell securities at a loss, which tends to make the locking-in effect work perversely by giving banks an incentive to sell securities during the expansion.[21] Some empirical tests of

[20] Charles Whittlesey, "Monetary Policy and Economic Change," *Review of Economics and Statistics,* Vol. 39 (February, 1957), pp. 36–37.

[21] Banks, unlike other security holders, do not have a maximum ceiling on the amount of security losses they can use as an offset against regular income in computing their taxable income. Since the corporate income tax rate exceeds the capital gains tax rate they have an incentive to offset capital losses against ordinary income rather than against capital gains. (Capital losses may be offset against ordinary income only to the extent that they exceed capital gains.) Hence, they have an incentive to take capital losses in a year in which they don't have capital gains to offset against them. They gain a tax advantage by massive selling of securities in the later stages of the expansion when security prices are low. See Robert H. Parks, "Income and Tax Aspects of Commercial Bank Portfolio Operations in Treasury Securities," *National Tax Journal,* Vol. 11 (March, 1958), pp. 21–34. For an analysis which points out some complicating factors which may delay the tax effect, see Burton Malkiel and Edward Kane, "U.S. Tax Law and the Locked-In Effect," *National Tax Journal,* Vol. 16 (December, 1963), pp. 389–396.

the locking-in effect have been undertaken with mixed results.[22]

In any case, at the present time an additional factor has entered the picture. Banks have to secure deposits of governments (federal, state, and local) by pledging government securities as collateral. As a result of this many banks currently have few government securities available they could sell, so that for banks the locking-in effect is both much less important and also much less necessary than in the past.

The yield-differential effect provides only a temporary aid to the availability doctrine. Granted that as interest rates rise on government securities, interest rates on private securities and loans do not follow right away. How long does it take until they catch up? Presumably, not very long. Hence, this component of the availability thesis is applicable only to a situation where interest rates keep on rising and not to one where they are allowed to stabilize at a higher level. This is not *quite* as serious a criticism as may appear at first because during an expansion when the Federal Reserve wants to limit investment, interest rates are generally rising. Usually the Federal Reserve puts bank reserves under continually growing pressure rather than reducing reserves in a once-for-all manner. Thus, interest rates not only are high, they are continually rising during a tight money period. But even then private yields may catch up.

The effect of tight money on the activities of investment bankers, too, is the result of *rising* interest rates rather than of *high* rates. Once interest rates have reached a new higher level and

[22] One study (Samuel B. Chase, Jr., "The Lock-In Effect: Bank Reactions to Security Losses," reprinted in Lawrence Ritter [ed.], *Money and Economic Activity* [Boston: Houghton Mifflin, 1961], pp. 171–177) found a strong locking-in effect for banks. However, this analysis is subject to criticism (see Malkiel and Kane, *op. cit.*, pp. 394–395). A second study covering both banks and other financial institutions (Daniel Ahearn, *Federal Reserve Policy Reappraised, 1951–1959* [New York: Columbia University Press, 1963], pp. 307–334) found that there is a locking-in effect, but that it is not as strong as Dr. Roosa's availability theory claimed. Still a third study, again covering other financial institutions as well as banks, found empirical evidence contradicting the locking-in effect. (See Michael Levy, *Cycles in Government Securities: Two Determinants of Changes in Ownership* [New York: National Industrial Conference Board, 1965], pp. 46 and 125.)

are stable at that level, investment bankers no longer face an extraordinary risk in floating securities. Hence, this component of the availability thesis is subject to the same criticism as the preceding one.

This leaves the expectations argument. Here the critics have challenged the assertion that if interest rates rise, lenders will hold off, waiting for the rate to rise even further. Why should lenders expect rates to rise? Would it not be more logical for them to think that if interest rates have risen they are likely to fall again? Why is one type of expectation more plausible than the other?[23] Moreover, even if, for the sake of the argument, we grant the assumption that if interest rates rise lenders expect them to rise still further, would not borrowers expect the same? Why should borrowers expect interest rates to fall as the availability thesis asserts? Borrowers and lenders are in constant contact with each other, and both read the same market forecasts, so why should their opinions differ?

The idea that lenders and borrowers have different market expectations appears to have been abandoned by one of the founders of the availability doctrine, Dr. Robert Roosa, who now argues that although borrowers and lenders have the same expectations, borrowers are often unable to act on them. If interest rates rise and are expected to rise further, borrowers are unable to rush in and borrow in anticipation.[24]

While this may be so, there is little reason to think that it will always, or even generally, be the case. But it is possible to develop a somewhat different defense of the expectations effect. Let us assume that many borrowers, like many lenders, expect

---

[23] To be sure, one could argue that expectations that a rise will be followed by a further rise are quite plausible. Interest rates generally rise or fall fairly continuously for substantial periods. Hence, if interest rates start to rise one could expect further increases in the future. But this reasoning is open to an objection. If the public believes that interest rates will rise and bond prices fall, they will sell bonds and, hence, bond prices fall and interest rates rise right away. Thus, expectations affect *current* bond prices and interest rates and once they have been adjusted to the new expectations there is little reason to expect future changes.

[24] Unpublished letter quoted in D. H. Robertson, *Economic Commentaries* (London: Staples Press, 1956), p. 70.

interest rates to rise in the future. (To be sure, not all lenders and borrowers can expect rates to rise in the future, otherwise interest rates would rise right away.) This gives borrowers an incentive to obtain financing, or a firm commitment for financing, right away. However, it does not give them much of an incentive to undertake the actual investment project at once. The rational borrower will secure his funds, but may hold them in short-term securities until the proper time for undertaking the investment project. Since it is spending rather than borrowing which is inflationary, the fact that borrowers expect interest rates to rise and therefore borrow does not add to inflationary pressure.[25] Thus, borrowers' expectations of rising interest rates are harmless and we are left with the deflationary effects of lenders expecting rates to rise, and hence, reducing lending. Admittedly, this argument assumes, somewhat arbitrarily, that many lenders expect interest rates to rise.

The final component of the expectations argument is that a move towards tighter money makes businessmen more cautious in their spending decisions even if they are not borrowers. This argument has met substantial criticism. While one can imagine expectations changing in this way, one can easily imagine the opposite, too. The adoption of a tighter money policy, that is, the cessation of an easy money policy, as the economy recovers from a recession, may be interpreted by businessmen as a signal that the recession is past and that this is a good time to expand capacity. Conversely, the adoption of an easy money policy when some economic indicators already suggest a downturn may be taken as a confirmation of the belief that a recession has started and that investment plans, therefore, should be cut back. In both cases expectations work against, rather than for, the Federal Reserve's policy.

Thus, each of the components of the availability doctrine is

[25] In fact, it may reduce them. If the prospective investor borrows long-term funds and lends them out temporarily on the short-term market, he is raising the cost of long-term funds and lowering the cost of short-term funds. Since investment is probably more responsive to conditions on the long-term money market than to conditions in the short-term market, this switch of funds may reduce investment.

open to a rejoinder by those who are skeptical of the strength of monetary policy. All in all, these criticisms suggest that the availability effect is not as strong as its originators took it to be. But, on the other hand, most economists would probably not be willing, by any means, to dismiss it completely; in spite of the above criticisms there does seem to be *something* to the availability thesis. Its exact strength, of course, still is an unresolved issue.

Economists who believe that monetary policy is weak have not merely attempted to refute each of the arguments of the availability thesis directly; in addition, they have pointed to a number of ways in which the existence of a large, widely held public debt has hindered monetary policy.[26] First, a large, widely distributed public debt facilitates the mobilization of idle funds throughout the economy. Turning idle balances into active balances raises velocity and, hence, allows the same quantity of money to finance a larger volume of expenditures. Federal Reserve attempts to control aggregate expenditures by controlling the quantity of money, therefore, are frustrated by offsetting changes in velocity.

The way in which a large, widely held public debt facilitates the activation of idle balances is by providing prospective spenders with liquid assets which they can easily sell to holders of idle money balances. For example, as customers request more loans, commercial banks can sell securities. As holders of idle balances purchase these securities from banks, their bank deposits are reduced. But since bank reserves have not fallen banks can create new deposits by making loans.

In this way deposits are transferred from one group of customers (who bought the securities) to another group (who obtained bank loans). As rising interest rates make it more profitable to hold securities, people buying securities from the banks are likely to be holders of relatively idle balances—if they had intended to spend these funds on goods and services they are unlikely to have bought securities instead. On the other hand, the

---

[26] For an outstanding exposition of this point of view, see Warren L. Smith, "On the Effectiveness of Monetary Policy," *American Economic Review,* Vol. 46 (September, 1956), pp. 588–606.

customers who borrow from banks probably spend these funds since people generally do not borrow in order to hold idle balances. Thus, velocity and expenditures are increased by this transfer of deposits. This process of activating idle balances is not confined to banks; other financial institutions such as savings and loan associations and life insurance companies may sell securities and lend the proceeds to prospective spenders.

Furthermore, given the widespread holding of the public debt, the process can operate directly without the help of financial intermediaries. Corporations or households wishing to spend can sell their government securities on the open market to holders of idle balances. In all of these ways velocity is increased and, therefore, expenditures can rise in spite of the Federal Reserve's tight money policy. Conversely, in a period of easy money, interest rates fall, and the public has less incentive to buy securities from banks and from potential spenders. Hence, there is a decline in velocity which tends to offset the increase in the money stock brought about by an easy money policy. In both cases (easy and tight money policies), changes in the interest rate induce changes in velocity which partially offset the effect of changes in the quantity of money. (Put into Keynesian language, the argument runs as follows: the liquidity preference schedule is interest elastic and the marginal efficiency of investment schedule is interest inelastic. Hence, changes in the quantity of money have but a limited effect on the interest rate, and the interest rate, in turn, has little effect on investment.)

Many economists who believe that monetary policy is powerful would agree that, in principle, the factors just described weaken monetary policy, but they would argue that the size of these effects is rather minor. In recent years the ratio of bank loans to deposits has risen very substantially. It is uncertain how much further banks would allow loans to rise in a period of tight money. In addition, as previously mentioned, banks have pledged a substantial proportion of their government securities as collateral for government deposits, and this limits their ability to increase velocity by selling securities. But note that these points apply only to banks and not to other financial institutions.

A second point raised by economists who are skeptical about a tight money policy is that tight money changes the structure of the money market; as interest rates rise, innovations occur in the money market which allow the participants to carry on their activities with a smaller ratio of money to sales or to income.[27] Not only do these innovations counteract the effects of a tight money policy, but later on when money is eased these innovations do not disappear; they become a permanent feature of the money market. As a result, periods of tight money induce a secular decline in the ratio of money to income and to debt. When this lower ratio of money to income and debt is combined with the effects of the banking systems' sales of government securities and their replacement by private securities, the money market becomes more and more vulnerable to shocks. As Professor Minsky, the leading proponent of this view, has put it:

> . . . every institutional innovation which results in both new ways to finance business and new substitutes for cash assets decreases the liquidity of the economy. That is, even though the amount of money does not change, the liquidity of the community decreases when government debt is replaced by private debt in the portfolios of commercial banks. Also when nonfinancial corporations replace cash with government bonds and then government debts with debts of bond houses, liquidity decreases. Such a pyramiding of liquid assets implies that the risks to the economy increase, for insolvency or even temporary illiquidity of a key nonbank organization can have a chain reaction, and affect the solvency or liquidity of many organizations. . . . the effort by the central bank to control inflation abets the development of unstable conditions in the money market . . .[28]

Again, defenders of monetary policy would raise the question of how strong these effects actually are. The fact that statistical

---

[27] See Hyman Minsky, "Central Banking and Money Market Changes," *Quarterly Journal of Economics*, Vol. 71 (May, 1957), pp. 171–187. For a description of some of the devices used, see also his "The Scramble for Money," Special Report, *Business Week* (November 17, 1956).

[28] Minsky, "Central Banking and Money Market Changes," *op. cit.*, pp. 184 and 187.

demand functions for money (which are based on the assumption that there are no such irreversibilities) get good fits suggests that these irreversibilities *may* not be very significant. Moreover, the argument runs, institutional changes since 1929 have made our financial system panic-proof.[29]

In addition to these changes, economists who believe that monetary policy is weak have often pointed to a third factor—the influence of nonbank financial intermediaries.[30] The operations of nonbank financial intermediaries may be destabilizing both in the short run and the long run. In the short run, during the expansion, as interest rates rise generally throughout the economy, the opportunity cost of holding demand deposits rises, and hence the public has an incentive to switch out of demand deposits and hold deposits of nonbank financial intermediaries instead. The financial intermediary holds its funds either as a deposit with a commerial bank, or else buys securities from, or makes loans to, someone who deposits the receipts in a commercial bank. In either case, commercial bank deposits are not reduced by this shift of bank customers to, say, a savings and loan association except to the trivial extent that the savings and loan association holds currency. All that happens is that instead of the original depositor holding a deposit in his bank the savings and loan association (or someone who received the funds from it) now holds the deposit. There has been pyramiding of financial assets; the total of bank deposits *plus* savings and loan deposits has increased. If expenditures depend in part upon the total stock of liquid assets rather than merely upon the quantity of money this development is inflationary.

[29] But this view, though widely held, is not beyond challenge. See Hyman Minsky, "Financial Crisis, Financial Systems and the Performance of the Economy," in Commission on Money and Credit, *Private Capital Markets* (Englewood Cliffs, N.J.: Prentice-Hall, 1964), pp. 173–380.

[30] The leading advocates of this approach are Professors Gurley and Shaw. For a brief statement, see their "Financial Aspects of Economic Development," *American Economic Review*, Vol. 45 (September, 1955), pp. 515–538; for a longer one, see their *Money in a Theory of Finance* (Washington, D.C.: Brookings Institution, 1960). In Britain this view has been strongly championed by the Committee on the Workings of the Monetary System, usually called the Radcliff Committee.

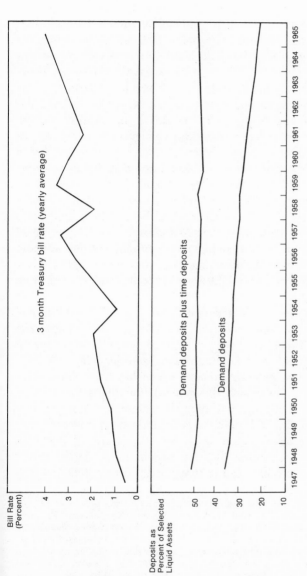

FIGURE 4.3 *Commercial Bank Deposits as Percent of Selected Liquid Assets and the Bill Rate 1947–1965*

NOTE: For liquid assets included see Table 4.1.

SOURCES: Table 4.1 and *1966 Economic Report of the President* (Washington, D. C.: Executive Office of the President, 1966), p. 266.

But Figure 4.3 shows little evidence of such a danger.[31] It is true that demand deposits as a percent of deposits in major depository intermediaries have declined since the end of the war while, at the same time, interest rates have been rising. However, this correlation has been one of secular movement only; cyclical changes in the bill rate have not been reflected in a decline of the demand-deposit ratio. This is not surprising. The rates paid by depository institutions change only with a lag as the money market changes. Moreover, there is probably a lag in the response of depositors to higher rates paid by these intermediaries. In addition, once a firm or household has decided to switch its deposit to a savings and loan association, it probably does not switch it back to a commercial bank if the interest rate paid by the savings and loan assocation declines. Hence, there is little danger of cyclical swings between demand deposits and other types of deposits offsetting Federal Reserve policy. Conceivably, such a danger might arise in the future but there is no indication of it in past data.

In addition to having a potential for cyclical destabilization, nonbank financial intermediaries may also create a longer run problem. As Table 4.1 shows, demand deposits as a percent of the public's liquid asset holdings have been declining secularly. According to one monetary theory which has been discussed a great deal in recent years, the general liquidity approach, aggregate demand depends not upon the quantity of money *per se* but upon the total of liquid assets or, indeed, of any debt. According to this view, liquid assets are readily turned into cash and provide the wherewithal for expenditures. Thus, during an expansion the public can raise expenditures by running down

[31] For support for this conclusion, see Ahearn, *op. cit.*, pp. 247–249, and Irwin Friend, "The Effects of Monetary Policies on Nonmonetary Financial Institutions and Capital Markets," in Commission on Money and Credit, *Private Capital Markets* (Englewood Cliffs, N.J.: Prentice-Hall, Inc., 1964), pp. 145–156. See also Patric Hendershott and James Murphy, "The Monetary Cycle and the Business Cycle: The Flow of Funds Reexamined," *National Banking Review*, Vol. 1 (June, 1964), pp. 531–550. This study shows that tight money slows the growth rate of nonbank financial intermediaries.

TABLE 4.1   *Commercial Bank Deposits as a Percent of Deposits in Private Depository Institutions and of Selected Liquid Assets Held by the Public, 1947–1966*

End of Year	Percent of Deposits in Private Depository Institutions*		Percent of Selected Liquid Assets**	
	DEMAND DEPOSITS	TOTAL DEPOSITS	DEMAND DEPOSITS	TOTAL DEPOSITS
1947	57.8	81.5	34.9	49.3
1948	56.5	80.4	33.3	47.5
1949	55.6	79.3	32.5	46.4
1950	56.1	78.8	33.3	46.8
1951	55.8	78.2	33.7	47.3
1952	54.2	76.9	33.2	47.1
1953	52.0	75.3	32.0	46.3
1954	50.3	73.8	32.1	47.1
1955	49.0	72.1	31.7	46.7
1956	47.2	70.3	31.0	46.2
1957	44.6	68.9	29.6	45.7
1958	42.8	68.3	29.5	47.1
1959	41.4	66.6	28.1	45.2
1960†	39.0	65.1	27.4	45.7
1961	37.1	64.2	26.6	46.0
1962	34.2	63.7	24.9	46.3
1963	32.0	62.9	23.6	46.4
1964	30.6	62.4	23.1	47.0
1965	29.2	62.9	22.3	48.0
1966	28.4	63.2	21.7	48.2
1967††	27.6	63.7	21.6	49.7

* Commercial banks, mutual savings banks, and savings and loan associations.
** Selected liquid assets include currency, demand and time deposits in commercial banks, mutual savings bank deposits, savings and loan association shares, postal savings deposits, U.S. Government savings bonds, and U.S. Government securities maturing within one year.
† Data for 1960 and subsequent years are not strictly comparable with data for earlier years. They exclude U.S. Government savings bonds and securities held by savings and loan associations.
†† Preliminary.

SOURCE: *1968 Economic Report of the President* (Washington, D.C.: Executive Office of the President, 1968), pp. 268–270.

its nonmoney liquid assets. Since there is no reason why prospective spenders have to hold money (except in the instant before expenditure) there is no reason why the quantity of money should govern aggregate demand—it is the total of all assets which can be turned into money that is relevant. (Put into Keynesian language, the public can hold its speculative and precautionary balances, as well as part of its transactions balances, in the form of nonmoney liquid assets.)

If this theory is valid the secular decline in the share of demand deposits as a proportion of total liquid assets may create a serious problem for monetary policy. If the Federal Reserve limits the growth of demand deposits in an economy in which other liquid assets are rising rapidly, the importance of demand deposits will decline further and further. According to Professor Gurley:

> Can the relationships among the sluggish growth of money, the relatively rapid expansion of other financial assets and the traditional base for monetary controls be purely accidental? No. The expansion of other highly liquid assets, at times so rapid as to threaten the stability of the economy, prompted the monetary authorities to clamp down on the one asset they could directly control—the money supply. The screws were tightened on commercial banks and the money supply to compensate for increasing liquidity elsewhere. Moreover, when borrowers were blocked at the doors of commercial banks, they turned to other financial institutions, and this added pressure stimulated the growth of these institutions. The result has been a diminishing role for money in the liquidity pool, and a relatively declining role for commercial banks within the family of private financial institutions . . .[32]

If the general liquidity approach is correct, and the quantity of money matters only insofar as it is part of total liquid assets, the decline in the share of demand deposits means that to get a given effect on expenditures the Federal Reserve will have to

[32] Testimony before the U.S. Joint Economic Committee, *Review of the Report of the Commission on Money and Credit, Hearings, August 14–18, 1961* (Washington, D.C.: 79th Congress, First Session, 1961), p. 285.

change the quantity of money by a greater and greater proportion all the time.[33] Since very large changes in the volume of demand deposits may prove disruptive to the economy, the Federal
Reserve is, in this way, losing control over the economy. Therefore, it may be necessary either to impose controls over nonbank
financial intermediaries, or else to reduce controls over commercial banks so that they are able to compete better with their
more freewheeling competitors.

But there are qualifications to this view. First and most fundamentally, there is the question of whether the liquidity approach
is correct. If, as the quantity theory asserts, it is the quantity
of money that matters rather than the stock of liquid assets,
then the growth of nonmoney liquid assets is irrelevant. The fact
that a number of empirical studies have found stable demand
functions for money for the postwar period when nonmoney
liquid assets were growing rapidly suggests that the growth of
these assets may not have made the relation between money and
income more unstable.

The second qualification is created by the difficulty in deciding on the proper definitions of money and liquid assets. If one
uses a broad definition of money and therefore looks at time deposits in commercial banks as well as at demand deposits, and
if one defines liquid assets as the "selected liquid assets" used in
Table 4.1, then commercial bank deposits, as a share of liquid
assets, have *not* declined, and the problem discussed above does
not exist. But if one defines liquid assets as deposits in private
depository institutions, or if one uses the narrower, conventional
definition of money, and therefore looks only at demand deposits,
then, as Table 4.1 shows, there has been a decline. It is by no
means certain which is the proper set of definitions.

A third qualification is that although total commercial bank
deposits as a proportion of total deposits in all depository insti-

[33] This reasoning assumes that the changes in the money stock do not lead
to corresponding, roughly proportional or more than proportional changes
in the stock of nonmoney liquid assets. This is a debatable issue. For a
good discussion of this type of problem, see Donald Shelby, "Some Implications of the Growth of Financial Intermediaries," *Journal of Finance,*
Vol. 13 (December, 1958), pp. 527–541.

tutions have declined substantially, the data for the last few years suggest that this trend may have come to an end. It is too early to tell. (The demand deposit percentage, however, is still declining.) In any case, we have already started to impose controls over nonbank intermediaries to some extent. Under temporary legislation passed in 1966, the Federal government can impose—and currently has in force—a ceiling on interest rates paid by saving and loan associations and savings banks. In addition, a quite simple change in regulations, a change advocated in any case by many economists for other reasons, may put a limit to the decline in the role of demand deposits. This is to permit banks to pay interest on demand deposits so that the public has less of an incentive to economize on the use of demand deposits.[34]

Before leaving the subject of financial intermediaries it is worth noting that in addition to the professional financial intermediaries, monetary policy also has to contend with what might be called amateur financial intermediaries. In a tight money period firms, particularly large firms, extend trade credit to their customers. This may allow the economy to carry out a larger volume of transactions with a given money stock and, thus, by raising the income velocity of money it has an inflationary potential.[35]

[34] As interest rates on time deposits have risen in recent years the volume of commercial bank time deposits has grown substantially, thus suggesting that, in the long run, the form in which the public chooses to hold its liquid assets is responsive to interest rates. For a defense of interest payments on demand deposits see Albert Cox, Jr., *Regulation of Interest Rates on Bank Deposits* (Ann Arbor, Mich.: University of Michigan, 1966). For criticisms of interest payments on demand deposits, see Clark Warburton, "Prohibition of Interest on Demand Deposits," *The Federal Reserve System After Fifty Years*, Vol. III (Washington, D.C.: U.S. House Banking and Currency Committee, 88th Congress, Second Session, 1964), pp. 2080–2092.

[35] See R. G. Lipsey and F. P. R. Brechling, "Trade Credit and Monetary Policy," *Economic Journal*, Vol. 73 (December, 1963), pp. 618–641. But in reply see William H. White, "Trade Credit and Monetary Policy: A Reconciliation," *Economic Journal*, Vol. 74 (December, 1964), pp. 935–945. See also R. G. Lipsey and F. P. R. Brechling, "Trade Credit and Monetary Policy: A Rejoinder," *Economic Journal*, Vol. 76 (March, 1966), pp. 165–167.

Overview

The above discussion has dealt with many arguments pro and con about the strength of monetary policy. Since the large number of points to be considered is confusing, it may be useful to pull them together. Unfortunately, it is not possible to do so in a manner which would be acceptable to all economists—there is just too much disagreement. But in broad outline, the following picture may be acceptable to a considerable number of economists.

Starting with the findings of the elasticity studies, it appears that the demand for money is neither highly interest elastic nor highly inelastic, but is in between. Hence, monetary policy, by changing the quantity of money does have a significant effect on interest rates. Other evidence suggests that residential construction and, more controversially, plant and equipment investment, does respond to changes in the interest rate. If one combines what appear to be fairly reasonable estimates of the interest elasticity of demand for money and the interest elasticity of investment, it seems that changes in the quantity of money have a significant effect on income.[36]

These effects which operate through the interest rate are reinforced by other effects which work through changes in the availability of money—exactly by how much is hard to say.[37] Admittedly, there are a number of institutional factors, such as the ability of banks to sell securities to holders of idle balances, that tend to counteract the effect of changes in the quantity of money. But the very fact that empirical studies of the demand for money

[36] See Thomas Mayer, "Multiplier and Velocity Analysis: An Evaluation," *Journal of Political Economy*, Vol. 72 (December, 1964), pp. 563–574; and Donald Tucker, "Mayer's Test of Keynesianism: A Correction," *Journal of Political Economy*, Vol. 73 (August, 1965), pp. 394–395.

[37] Since changes in the availability of money and interest rates are by no means perfectly correlated, studies of the interest elasticity of investment do not capture all of the effects of changes in availability. Hence, to some extent, the availability effects have to be added to the effects of interest rate changes found in studies using the interest rate.

that do not have very large interest elasticity coefficients have frequently obtained good results suggests that these factors, while not necessarily negligible, do not predominate. This conclusion is reinforced by the upshot of some statistical studies that attempted to discover if there is in the United States a better correlation between money and consumption than between autonomous expenditures (the Keynesian "investment") and consumption.[38] Although these studies yielded sharply different results, depending upon the definition of "investment" used, in most of them the stock of money turned out to be important. All in all, much recent evidence supports the view that the stock of money and, therefore, monetary policy, has a substantial effect. Note, however, that this reading of the evidence is by no means acceptable to all economists. Some, Professor Friedman and Dr.

[38] These studies computed the correlation between autonomous expenditures and consumption rather than between autonomous expenditures and income. Since autonomous expenditures are part of income, correlating autonomous expenditures with income would mean correlating income with a part of itself and this would introduce a bias. One of these studies is by Professors Friedman and Meiselman, "The Relative Stability of Monetary Velocity and the Investment Multiplier in the United States, 1897–1958," in Commission on Money and Credit, *Stabilization Policies* (Englewood Cliffs, N.J.: Prentice-Hall, 1963), pp. 165–268. It found that the money stock could explain consumption very successfully, while autonomous expenditures had no explanatory power. But if one uses a different definition of autonomous expenditures than that used by Professors Friedman and Meiselman, this conclusion is changed and both autonomous expenditures and money turn out to be important, thus suggesting that monetary policy, while not dominating, is by no means powerless. (See Albert Ando and Franco Modigliani, "The Relative Stability of Velocity and the Investment Multiplier," *American Economic Review*, Vol. 55 [September, 1966], pp. 693–728; Michael DePrano and Thomas Mayer, "Tests of the Relative Importance of Autonomous Expenditures and Money," *ibid.*, pp. 729–752.) This source also carries replies by all the participants to the debate. See also Donald Hester, "Keynes and the Quantity Theory: A Comment on the Friedman-Meiselman CMC Paper," *Review of Economics and Statistics*, Vol. 46 (November, 1964), pp. 364–368. Another study (Gregory Chow, "Multiplier, Accelerator and Liquidity Preference in the Determination of National Income in the United States," *Review of Economics and Statistics*, Vol. 49 [February, 1967], pp. 1–15), found some role—albeit a relatively small one—for money. One warning is in order, however. All of these tests compared very simple models of the Keynesian and quantity theories, and what is true for very simple models need not necessarily be true for more complex models.

Warburton for example, argue that changes in the stock of money do have a *dominant* effect on income, at least in the long run, while others such as Professor Hansen believe that changes in the stock of money are largely offset by opposite changes in velocity.

The Relationship of Strength and Magnitude

There is one line of thought which suggests that regardless of any of the qualifications discussed above, monetary policy is always strong enough to do the job. If a given change in the reserve base does not suffice to change income enough, all the monetary authorities would have to do is to change the reserve base by greater and greater amounts, and eventually income would change to the desired extent. If variations in velocity offset much of the effect of changes in the quantity of money, this merely means that a substantial change in the money stock is required to do what a small change would do if velocity were stable. Since the Federal Reserve *can* change the money stock very substantially, it can be argued that the offsetting changes in velocity do not really matter. In fact, Professor Ritter has argued that changes in velocity facilitate monetary policy by providing a safety valve. If the Federal Reserve tightens money too abruptly, velocity increases and the Federal Reserve can modify its policy before it causes significant damage.[39] The same argument applied to the case of rediscounting applies here: The existence of brakes allows cars to be driven faster.

The view that a tight money policy, if carried far enough, could choke off a boom has been accepted for many years, but for a long time it was argued that the power of monetary policy is asymmetrical. If money is made tight enough it can end the boom, but however far an easy money policy is carried, it cannot stop a depression. As two popular clichés have it, "You can't push on a piece of string" and "You can lead a horse to water, but you can't make it drink." This viewpoint (based in good part on the standard Keynesian interpretation of the Great Depression discussed in Appendix B) has been severely chal-

[39] "Income-Velocity and Anti-Inflationary Monetary Policy," *American Economic Review*, Vol. 49 (March, 1959), pp. 120–129.

lenged in recent years, and the belief in the asymmetry of monetary policy has lost much of its support.[40]

This approach to monetary policy is extremely important; if it is correct, the whole problem of the strength of monetary policy is irrelevant. All that is required is that the Federal Reserve have the courage of its convictions and initiate very substantial changes in the money stock. It is therefore worth seeing if there are any qualifications to this view.

One qualification is that the change in velocity may not be predictable accurately. If so, the monetary policy adopted may turn out to be either too strong or too weak. To be sure, in either case follow-up action could be used to correct the error, but such delayed adaption would lengthen the lags of monetary policy and, as will be shown in Chapter 6, may create instability. Given the Federal Reserve's great uncertainty both about underlying conditions and about the impact of its own policies, it is very hard for the Federal Reserve to proceed in any but small steps. As a Staff Report of the Congressional Joint Economic Committee put it:

> . . . until we are unable to forecast near-stern economic developments with more confidence than is presently possible, monetary policy will necessarily contain an element of hesitancy and caution which is natural in the case of officials charged with important responsibilities, uncertainty as to exactly what kind of action the situation calls for, and concerned lest a mistake in policy might do serious harm to the economy.[41]

A second difficulty with the idea of simply reducing bank reserves until the desired change in aggregate demand occurs is that a sharp rise in interest rates might disrupt financial markets. For example, the 1967 Report of the Council of Economic Ad-

---

[40] According to Professor Harry Johnson ("Monetary Theory and Policy," *American Economic Review*, Vol. 52 [June, 1962], p. 366), ". . . in the United States . . . the wheel has come full circle, and prevailing opinion has returned to the characteristic 1920's view that monetary policy is probably more effective in checking deflation than in checking inflation."

[41] U.S. Joint Economic Committee, *Staff Report on Employment, Growth and Price Level* (Washington, D.C.: 86th Congress, First Session, 1960), p. 361. This report is often called the "Eckstein Report."

visers expressed the belief that in August, 1966 "monetary policy was probably as tight as it could get without risking financial disorder."[42] At first glance this reasoning seems fallacious. The very purpose of a tight money policy is to cut back investment. To say that a very large increase in interest rates reduces investment too much is to leave oneself open to rejoinder that if a small increase in interest rates does not do enough, and a very large increase is much too powerful, there must be some intermediate increase which is just right. The only answer to this argument is that this optimal intermediate increase is too hard to determine and that the penalty for overshooting the mark is too great to take the risk. But this argument is really nothing but a special case of the previous point about uncertainty.

A third objection to the view that a tight money policy can be pressed as far as needs be, is its interference with public debt management. Given the large proportion of the public debt that is in the form of short-term securities, the Treasury is undertaking substantial refinancing operations very frequently. To help the Treasury in placing this debt, the Federal Reserve refrains from tightening money when the Treasury is refinancing, and tries to keep security markets "on an even keel." This need to help the Treasury hinders the maintenance of a powerful, tight money policy. Note, however, that this problem would not arise if the Treasury would keep a much smaller proportion of the debt in short-term form, or if it would be less worried about an unsuccessful refinancing operation. But even then a substantial rise in interest rates would be expensive for the Treasury, the country's biggest debtor.

Fourth, a very sharp, tight money policy would cause some reallocation of resources and some redistribution of income (matters discussed in Chapter 5) which many people would consider undesirable.

Fifth, there is the danger that sharp increases in the interest rate would cause the financial community to innovate new methods of economizing on cash balances, so that, over time,

[42] *Economic Report of the President* (Washington, D.C.: Executive Office of the President, 1967), p. 60.

velocity would tend to rise substantially. As Professor Minsky has emphasized, a high ratio of credit to final means of payment and to income flows creates danger of a financial collapse during a cyclical downturn.[43]

All of these arguments refer to pushing a tight money policy very far and, with the exception of the first one dealing with uncertainty, are not really objections to a very strong easy money policy. There are, however, in the Federal Reserve's view, two objections to a very aggressive easy money policy. As Chairman Martin has frequently said, a powerful easy money policy creates a large amount of liquidity for banks and for the economy in general. When economic conditions change and warrant a tight money policy it takes a long time until the Federal Reserve can mop up this excess liquidity. This delays the "bite" of a tight money policy too long. Moreover, the Federal Reserve is afraid that very low interest rates and a too great supply of bank credit would tempt banks into making loans they would otherwise realize are too risky.

How important are these qualifications? Again, there is no unanimity on this question. The majority of economists would probably agree that there is enough substance to these qualifications so that one cannot simply settle the question of the strength of monetary policy by saying that the Federal Reserve should adopt so radical a policy that it can get any effect it wants. On the other hand, the possibility of inducing greater changes in the reserve base than have been usual in the past does reinforce the conclusion suggested in the previous section that monetary policy can have a substantial effect on income. One factor supporting this conclusion is that in recent years there has been a very great improvement in the Federal Reserve's research on monetary policy. As we obtain more knowledge of how monetary policy operates we will be able to use stronger policies with less fear of making a mistake.

[43] See, for instance, "Can 'It' Happen Again?" Carson, (ed.), *Banking and Monetary Studies* (Homewood, Ill.: Richard D. Irwin, 1963), pp. 101–111.

International Aspects

So far this chapter has dealt only with the power of monetary policy to achieve its domestic goals. But in addition to this task, monetary policy also plays a role in obtaining balance-of-payments equilibrium. It does so in two ways. First, an increase in money income, whether due to price rises or output increases, raises the demand for imports and tends to move the balance of payments in a deficit direction. Hence, by limiting the level of money income the Federal Reserve is able to help achieve balance-of-payments equilibrium. Second, monetary policy affects the balance of payments by changing interest rates.

If foreigners invest in United States securities or deposits, this generates a demand for dollars and is a positive item on the United States balance of payments.[44] Conversely, if United States residents purchase foreign securities, or undertake direct investment in a foreign country, this enters the balance of payments as a negative item. Now, the decision to invest in one country rather than in another is made, in part, on the basis of the relative interest rates ruling in different countries. Hence, by changing interest rates, the central bank can affect the balance of payments.

The size of the effect which can be obtained by relatively small changes in the interest rate on foreign investment is still undetermined.[45] Again, one could argue that since a *substantial* rise in interest rates would attract large foreign funds (as well as limit capital outflows), monetary policy is powerful enough. But there are qualifications to this optimistic view.

[44] This statement needs qualification. The Department of Commerce computes the U.S. balance of payments in two different ways. One way does not count short-term foreign investment in the United States as a positive item; the other way does.

[45] For one estimate as well as for criticisms of some other estimates, see Jerome Stein, "International Short-Term Capital Movements," *American Economic Review*, Vol. 55 (March, 1965), pp. 40–66; H. P. Gray, D. G. Heckerman, A. B. Laffer, P. H. Hendershott, and T. D. Willett, "International Short-Term Capital Movements: Comments," *American Economic Review*, Vol. 57 (June, 1967), pp. 548–565; and Jerome Stein, "Reply," *ibid.*, pp. 565–570.

First, as pointed out in Chapter 1, there is a potential conflict among goals. Balance-of-payments equilibrium may be incompatible with full employment, and even with price stability. Although a higher interest rate may ameliorate the balance-of-payments problem, it may make other problems worse. Second, other countries may retaliate by raising their interest rates.[46]

One method which has been used to reduce this conflict is to play on the structure of interest rates. The foreign investment which is most easily influenced by central bank manipulation of the interest rate is short-term investment. Thus, if the central bank can raise the short-term rate without raising the long- and intermediate-term rates, it *may* succeed in helping the balance-of-payments goal without seriously hindering the achievement of full employment. This policy of twisting the yield curve (called "operation twist") has been tried by the United States in recent years. Note that the feasibility of this operation depends upon the interrelation of long- and short-term rates discussed in Chapter 3. According to some views of the interest rate structure described there, it is simply impossible to twist the yield curve. In addition, the success of this policy depends upon investment being substantially more sensitive to the long- and intermediate-term interest rates than to the short-term rate. While there is a widespread belief that this is the case there is little firm evidence on this subject.[47]

Another difficulty with raising interest rates to cure a balance-of-payments deficit is that high interest rates, by reducing domestic income, may make long-term domestic investment less profitable, and in this way may stimulate foreign investment. If income is depressed in the United States, corporations may prefer

---

[46] One outstanding international trade authority, Professor Charles Kindleberger has gone so far as to state: "If foreign central banks raise interest rates, it affects the spread between New York and their market; if New York changes its rate, it alters the whole level." U.S. Joint Economic Committee, *The 1967 Economic Report of the President, Hearings, February 20–23, 1967* (Washington, D.C.: 90th Congress, First Session, 1967), p. 836.

[47] For a criticism of effectiveness of operation twist, see Myron Ross, " 'Operation Twist': A Mistaken Policy?" *Journal of Political Economy*, Vol. 74 (April, 1966), pp. 195–199.

to use their limited funds to build plants in more buoyant markets abroad rather than in the United States. Moreover, United States commodity exports are influenced by the degree of technological innovation in our economy. By retarding domestic investment, tight money may conceivably make the balance-of-payments problem worse in the long run. In any case, high interest rates are no cure for a long-run balance-of-payments problem. Although an inflow of foreign funds helps the balance of payments while it occurs, the subsequent interest payments on these funds make the balance-of-payments deficit worse. And the same thing applies to a reduction in United States foreign investment which reduces future inflows of interest and dividends. It is hard to know how important these offsetting factors are—but it is doubtful that they should be dismissed out of hand.

FURTHER READING

Ahearn, Daniel. *Federal Reserve Policy Reappraised, 1951–1959*. New York: Columbia University Press, 1963, Part 3.

Alhadeff, David. "Credit Controls and Financial Intermediaries," *American Economic Review,* Vol. 50 (September, 1960), pp. 655–671.

Aschheim, Joseph. *Techniques of Monetary Control*. Baltimore: Johns Hopkins University Press, 1961, Chapters 6 and 7.

Benavie, Arthur. "Intermediaries in a Macroeconomic Model," *Journal of Finance,* Vol. 22 (September, 1967), pp. 441–454.

Crockett, Jean, Irwin Friend, and Henry Shavell. "The Impact of Monetary Stringency on Business Investment," *Survey of Current Business,* Vol. 47 (August, 1967), pp. 10–27.

Gurley, John. "The Radcliff Report and Evidence," *American Economic Review,* Vol. 50 (September, 1960), pp. 672–700.

Gurley, John, and Edward Shaw. "Financial Aspects of Economic Development," *American Economic Review,* Vol. 45 (September, 1955), pp. 515–538.

————. *Money in a Theory of Finance*. Washington, D.C.: Brookings Institution, 1960.

Lindbeck, Assar, *The "New" Theory of Credit Control in the United States*. Uppsala, Sweden: Almquist and Wikesell, 1962.

Mayer, Thomas. "Multiplier and Velocity Analysis: An Evaluation," *Journal of Political Economy*, Vol. 72 (December, 1964), pp. 563–574. But see also Donald Tucker. "Mayer's Test of Keynesianism: A Correction," *Journal of Political Economy*, Vol. 73 (August, 1965), pp. 394–395.

Minsky, Hyman. "Central Banking and Money Market Changes," *Quarterly Journal of Economics*, Vol. 71 (May, 1957), pp. 171–187.

―――. "Money, Other Financial Variables, and Aggregate Demand in the Short Run," George Horwich (ed.), *Monetary Process and Policy: A Symposium*. Homewood, Ill.: Richard D. Irwin, 1967, pp. 265–294.

―――. "Can 'It' Happen Again?" D. Carson (ed.), *Banking and Monetary Studies*. Homewood, Ill.: Richard D. Irwin, 1963, pp. 101–111.

Meiselman, David. "Strotz and Minsky on Monetary Variables and Aggregate Demand," George Horwich (ed.), *Monetary Process and Policy: A Symposium*. Homewood, Ill.: Richard D. Irwin, 1967, pp. 322–329.

Ritter, Lawrence. "Income Velocity and Anti-Inflationary Monetary Policy," *American Economic Review*, Vol. 49 (March, 1959), pp. 120–129.

Rousseas, Stephen. "Velocity Changes and the Effectiveness of Monetary Policy, 1951–1957," *Review of Economics and Statistics*, Vol. 42 (February, 1960), pp. 27–36.

Scott, Ira O. "The Availability Doctrine: Development and Implication," *Canadian Journal of Economics and Political Science*, Vol. 23 (November, 1957), pp. 532–539.

Shelby, Donald. "Some Implications of the Growth of Financial Intermediaries," *Journal of Finance*, Vol. 13 (December, 1958), pp. 527–541.

Smith, Warren. "On the Effectiveness of Monetary Policy," *American Economic Review*, Vol. 46 (September, 1956), pp. 588–606.

―――. "Financial Intermediaries and Monetary Controls," *Quarterly Journal of Economics*, Vol. 73 (November, 1959), pp. 533–553.

Strotz, Robert. "Empirical Evidence on the Impact of Monetary Variables on Aggregate Expenditure," George Horwich (ed.), *Monetary Process and Policy: A Symposium*. Homewood, Ill.: Richard D. Irwin, 1967, pp. 295–316.

Thorn, Richard. "Nonbank Financial Intermediaries, Credit Expansion and Monetary Policy," *International Monetary Fund, Staff Papers,* Vol. 6 (November, 1958), pp. 369–383.

Tobin, James. "Monetary Policy and the Public Debt: The Patman Inquiry," *Review of Economics and Statistics,* Vol. 35 (May, 1953), pp. 118–127.

Tobin, James, and W. Brainard. "Financial Intermediaries and the Effectiveness of Monetary Controls," *American Economic Association Papers and Proceedings,* Vol. 53 (May, 1963), pp. 383–400. (See also A. P. Lerner. "Discussion," *ibid.,* pp. 401–407.)

Tussing, Dale. "Can Monetary Policy Influence the Availability of Credit?" *Journal of Finance,* Vol. 21 (March, 1966), pp. 1–14.

U.S. Joint Economic Committee, *Staff Report on Employment, Growth and Price Levels.* Washington, D.C.: 86th Congress, First Session, December, 1959, pp. 344–394.

White, William. "Interest Inelasticity of Investment Demand: The Case from Business Attitude Surveys Reexamined," *American Economic Review,* Vol. 46 (September, 1956), pp. 565–587.

Whittlesey, Charles. "Monetary Policy and Economic Change," *Review of Economics and Statistics,* Vol. 39 (February, 1957), pp. 31–39.

Monetary Policy
and Resource Allocation

The previous chapter started out with a matrix for the evaluation of monetary policy, a matrix that covers the issues of strength versus weakness and efficiency versus clumsiness. Having discussed the first of these issues, the question of whether monetary policy is clumsy or efficient remains. Efficiency here means having few major unfavorable side effects and having the main effects occur at the right time. The latter issue is discussed in the following chapter; this chapter investigates whether or not a countercyclical monetary policy has unfavorable effects on resource allocation. If monetary policy does seriously distort resource allocation, then the case for using countercyclical monetary policy is substantially weakened even if monetary policy is strong. After all, monetary policy is not our only stabilization tool; fiscal policy, too, affects aggregate demand. The choice between the two hinges, in good part, on two issues, speed and resource-allocation effects.

One of the main claims made in favor of monetary policy is that it does not interfere with resource allocation, that it changes aggregate demand in a neutral manner so that there are no unfavorable side effects. By contrast, the argument runs, fiscal policy impinges on specific sectors of the economy (for example, a public works program) or on specific income groups (for example, tax reductions). In doing so it interferes with the resource allocation and income distribution patterns resulting from the interplay of free market factors.

Economists who are critical of this line of argument have taken either one of two stands. They have either argued that monetary policy is in fact *not* neutral, or else they have argued that neutrality is not "a good thing."

To evaluate both of these arguments it is necessary to clarify the meaning of neutrality. One possible interpretation is that a neutral policy is one that has a proportional effect on all sectors of the economy. For example, if a tight money policy cuts aggregate demand by, say, 3 percent, all types of investment as well as consumption are reduced by 3 percent. If one uses this definition of neutrality, the problem is very simple, monetary policy is far from neutral—different types of investment are affected differently. But this interpretation of neutrality involving proportionality misses the point completely. Proportional change in all sectors of the economy is *not* an adequate welfare criterion. Proportionality would generally be inconsistent with optimal-resource allocation.

An adequate definition of neutrality requires a more sophisticated treatment. Neutrality must be interpreted as letting the free market decide where to increase or reduce demand. And generally it is *not* decided to increase or reduce demand proportionately in all sectors, any more than a household experiencing a doubling of income would decide to double its expenditures on each and every commodity. Consider, for example, a tight money policy instituted in an inflationary environment. Aggregate demand is too high and the Federal Reserve now brings about an increase in the interest rate. The increase in the interest rate means that the cost of using resources for either current consumption or investment has increased. This operates as a signal to the economy to reduce its demand. Households cut back on consumption until the marginal loss from postponing consumption from this year to the next is equal to the interest rate, and similarly, firms reduce investment until the rate of return on investment, once again, equals the interest rate. If one can take the distribution of income as optimal (or as exogenously given) and if the other welfare conditions are met, the reduction in aggregate demand occurs where the least loss of utility to the economy is involved.[1]

[1] As usual in applied economics, the difficulties of constructing a social

Contrast this with fiscal policy. Suppose that government expenditures are cut to curb inflation. If one assumes for illustration that the equilibrium value of the multiplier is two, half the reduction in aggregate demand occurs within the governmental sector. If the public were allowed to choose where its expenditures would be cut, it is unlikely that it would decide to concentrate half the cut in one category, government services. A somewhat similar situation applies to the other side of fiscal policy, changes in tax rates. Here, a tax cut gives the public more disposable income which it can allocate in an optimizing manner, but there is still an interference with income distribution since the tax cut usually affects different income groups differently. Unlike monetary policy, fiscal policy is not neutral—it substitutes the decisions of government officials for the decisions of the free market.

Note that a neutral policy does not cure existing maladjustments and distortions in the economy—it leaves them unaffected. In principle, it is possible to analyze the effect of monetary policy on resource allocation without worrying about misallocations which exist independently of monetary policy. In many discussions, however, this line of distinction becomes blurred. People who are very concerned about a particular type of resource-allocation problem want a stabilization policy to help solve this problem too. A stabilization policy which is merely neutral vis-à-vis this problem seems inferior to one which ameliorates this particular resource-allocation problem. Hence, in popular arguments both lines of criticism tend to merge. But for analysis it is necessary to separate them, so let us start with the argument that neutrality, as defined above, is not desirable.[2]

---

welfare function are handled in the most convenient way—by simply ignoring them.

[2] However, before getting into this discussion, it is necessary to discuss whether a tight money policy really raises interest rates in the long run. One could argue that if the Federal Reserve did not adopt a tight money policy in an inflationary situation, the resulting inflation would raise the interest rate and, by reducing the real quantity of money, would tend to perpetuate high interest rates for a long time. But note that it is not the real rate of interest that rises in an inflation, but only the money rate, and criticisms of tight money should actually relate to the real rate.

The preceding argument that neutrality is desirable is valid only if all the conditions for welfare maximization in a free enterprise system are met. These conditions are an optimal distribution of income, full employment, perfect competition in all markets, and an absence of uncompensated external economies or diseconomies. If they are not met, fiscal policy (or any other policy) which is *not* neutral *may* increase welfare. The fact that monetary policy does not interfere with a nonoptimal situation is not necessarily a point in its favor. For example, a number of economists believe, rightly or wrongly, that a free market system saves too small a proportion of its income. Let us assume, for the sake of the argument, that this is correct. If so, the fact that a tight money policy brings about a proportionately greater reduction in investment than in consumption is a drawback of a tight money policy, even if such an allocation of resources corresponds to the free choice of the participants in the marketplace. Similarly, if the distribution of income is not optimal, changes in tax rates, though they interfere with the free market system, *may* raise economic welfare.

Now clearly, the conditions necessary for optimal-resource allocation in a free market are not fully met in practice, and it may therefore be tempting to argue that the neutrality of monetary policy is a "bad thing." But this does not necessarily follow. Although resource allocation and income distribution are not optimal, a policy which is not neutral *could* make resource allocation and income distribution worse than they otherwise would be, and *not* better. Some of the provisions of our tax laws surely distort, rather than improve, resource allocation. The best case for a free market is not that, in the absence of government interference we would live in a perfect world, but rather that government interference often makes an already poor situation still worse. From this it follows that one's reaction to the neutrality of monetary policy really involves one's political views. Liberals, who take the shortcomings of a free market system seriously but have faith in governmental policy, tend to favor fiscal policy because they believe that the government is efficient enough to ameliorate the shortcomings of a free market. Conservatives hold the opposite view. The issue of the relative efficiency of governmental policies and the workings of the free market clearly transcends the topic of monetary policy and, hence, will not be discussed here.

Now let us look at the other line of criticism which asserts that monetary policy is *not* neutral. This criticism relies upon the fact that there are many imperfections in the capital market and that, therefore, the interest rate does not serve as an efficient signal. In a way this second line of criticism is merely a special case of the first type of criticism since it relies on the fact that one of the welfare conditions, perfect competition in the capital market, is not met.

One important imperfection of the money market is the existence of credit rationing already discussed in the previous chapter. To a considerable extent banks do not allocate their funds to the highest bidder, but instead they ration credit among their customers. This means that the interest rate does not serve as the allocating device. While a rise in the rate of interest serves to cut back investment where its yield is lowest, credit rationing does not necessarily do this. Hence, the argument runs, monetary policy does not further the optimal allocation of resources. The decision as to where to cut investment is made, not by an impersonal market, but by bankers. Like fiscal policy, the argument goes, monetary policy involves "the rule of men" rather than the rule of impersonal economic forces. To be sure, one could counter this argument by saying that the rule of men involved in monetary policy is that of a large number of widely dispersed individuals, whereas in the case of fiscal policy the men who do the ruling are a small number of politicians and bureaucrats. But, one could turn this argument around and say that it is better to have decisions made by democratically elected officials than by an oligarchy of bankers. Evidently this discussion is about to intrude on political issues and will therefore have to stop.

It is worth noting, however, that capital rationing by banks is not the capital market's only imperfection. Small business has only limited access to the capital market, so that capital is not perfectly allocated between large and small business. Moreover, many interest rates are inflexible and do not reflect the movements of the more sensitive rates. For example, in the early stages of a tight money policy, when interest rates paid by depository institutions have not yet risen, the signal to reduce aggregate demand has not yet reached households. The locking-in effect is another imperfection.

The frequent claims made that monetary policy distorts resource allocations are generally concerned with tight money rather than easy money.[3] At first glance this looks invalid, since countercyclical monetary policy serves to raise interest rates at one time and to lower them at other times. The average interest rate ruling over the cycle is left essentially unaffected. If this is so, how can it be claimed that monetary policy discriminates against certain sectors of the economy because these sectors are more sensitive to interest rates and credit availability? Presumably, countercyclical monetary policy reduces investment in these sectors at one time, but raises it at other times. There are two answers to this argument. First, monetary policy, by causing countercyclical fluctuations in a sector, may increase instability for that particular sector. This hurts the factors of production employed in this sector and, perhaps, also hurts potential customers. Another answer takes a different approach. As will be discussed in Chapter 7, one of the alternatives to countercyclical monetary policy is a policy of maintaining low interest rates throughout the cycle. And some economists who are unwilling to go quite this far, believe that the Federal Reserve has in recent years generally been too restrictive. In this way, for some observers, countercyclical monetary policy has become almost identified with tight money policy.

Specific Sectors

With this background let us look at those sectors of the economy where, it is claimed, monetary policy has distorted resource allocation, starting with those sectors where this claim does not

[3] Criticisms of the allocative effects of easy money are scarce. Occasionally Federal Reserve spokesmen claim that if money is too easy banks are induced to make too many marginal loans and, hence, the safety of the banking system is reduced and unsound investment occurs.

deny that monetary policy is neutral but, instead, asserts that neutrality is undesirable.

One of these is the saving-income ratio of the economy. Although there is no unanimity among economists that we should raise our rate of capital accumulation to spur economic growth, a number of economists do advocate such a policy. One way to raise capital accumulation is to make investment more profitable by lowering the interest rate. The inflationary impact of this increase in investment can then be offset by raising income taxes; this will lower consumption. By using monetary and fiscal policy in this combination, investment can be raised.[4] If this policy is accepted, it then follows that the rate of interest should be kept low and that a tight money policy (which reduces investment proportionately more than consumption) is undesirable even in an inflationary period. If monetary policy is to be used to curb inflation, it should not be a neutral monetary policy, but one that curbs consumption rather than investment. To put it another way, it should consist of controls over consumer credit.

But there are three qualifications to this conclusion. First, the notion that we should raise the rate of capital accumulation is open to debate.[5] Second, if we do decide to increase the rate of capital accumulation, a low interest rate is not the only way to accomplish this. Tax incentives for investment could accomplish the same purpose. Third, there is a more fundamental issue. A firm quantity theorist would argue that, if the Federal Reserve increases the quantity of money in order to lower interest rates, prices will then rise proportionately in spite of the tax increase, and, as pointed out in Chapter 4, this raises the real interest rate again. Fourth, the argument refers, basically, to the *average* level of interest rates over the cycle. A low average interest rate is compatible with raising the interest rate during an expansion and lowering it during a contraction.

---

[4] For a discussion of the use of monetary and fiscal policy in this combination, see Abba Lerner, *The Economics of Control* (New York: Macmillan, 1964), Chapter 24.

[5] For an excellent discussion of this issue, see James Tobin, "Economic Growth as an Objective of Government Policy," American Economic Association *Papers and Proceedings*, Vol. 64 (May, 1964), pp. 1–20; and Harry Johnson and Herbert Stein, "Discussion," *ibid.*, pp. 21–27.

There is a closely related argument which involves the contrasting of industrial plant and equipment investment with consumer credit. The argument asserts that industrial investment should be fostered because it contributes to economic growth; by contrast, consumer credit finances less socially desirable items. It is then pointed out that plant and equipment investment is more responsive to conventional monetary policy than is consumer credit. Hence, the argument claims, conventional monetary policy has an unfavorable resource-allocation effect and should be replaced, or at least supplemented, by a different type of monetary policy, namely a revival of consumer credit controls. Whether one accepts this view depends, in good part, on one's attitude toward a free market system. In addition, as pointed out in Chapter 4, it is by no means certain that consumer credit is really so insensitive to a restrictive monetary policy.

A second area where monetary policy is said to hurt resource allocation is Federal government finance. The Treasury is the biggest debtor in the country. Interest charges in the Federal budget (excluding payments to trust funds) are now running at a rate of over $10 billion a year.[6] If interest charges on the debt increase the government may raise taxes. Taxes impose a deadweight burden on the economy because the transfer of a dollar from the taxpayer to the Treasury involves a certain cost. (Probably the most important component of this cost is the distortion in resource allocation resulting from the taxpayer arranging his affairs to minimize his tax burden.) Insofar as higher interest rates add to taxes, they add to the deadweight burden borne by the economy. Another alternative is to have the government finance the higher interest payments by cutting government expenditures. To those who believe that government expenditure is wasteful this may seem desirable, but those who believe that

[6] To be sure, the higher interest cost applies only to that proportion of the public debt which is financed, or refinanced during the period of high interest rates—interest payments on other securities remain unaffected. But this is offset by the fact that the securities floated at the higher interest rate stay in the public debt structure when interest rates decline. See Ervin Miller, "Monetary Policy in a Changing World," *Quarterly Journal of Economics,* Vol. 70 (February, 1956), p. 26.

we are already starving the public sector find it undesirable. Finally, the government may finance the higher interest payments by running a deficit, but such an expansionary fiscal policy works counter to the tight money policy.

Note that this argument, too, relates to the average level of interest rates and not to countercyclical monetary policy per se. Moreover, most economists would probably agree that the deadweight burden of taxation is not so great that we should abandon a major stabilization tool merely to reduce the interest burden of the Treasury

Third, there is the distribution of income. This provides the basis for one of the most popular criticisms of tight money. A high rate of interest, it is said, helps lenders at the expense of borrowers. Since lenders tend to be the "rich," the argument continues, and borrowers tend to be the "poor," tight money makes the distribution of income more unequal than it is. Monetary policy should, therefore, be employed to keep interest rates low rather than be used as a countercyclical tool. Actually, the situation is complicated by the fact that much of the interest payments are received not by households, but by financial institutions such as banks and life insurance companies. When these institutions receive an increase in interest income it is hard to say how this receipt is distributed among customers and stockholders. A recent statistical study found that low income groups *gain,* relative to high income groups, when interest rates rise.[7] Note also that if countercyclical monetary policy causes interest rates to rise at one time, it causes them to fall at others. In any case, if we want to make the distribution of income more equal, we do not have to use monetary policy for that purpose. Even if tight money were to make the distribution of income more unequal we could offset this by making the tax system more progressive.

Let us now turn to those sectors of the economy where monetary policy is said to cause a distortion of resource allocation

[7] See Oswald Brownlee and Alfred Conrad, "Effects upon the Distribution of Income of a Tight Money Policy," *American Economic Association Papers and Proceedings,* Vol. 51 (May, 1961), pp. 74–85. This paper is a summary of a study done for the Commission on Money and Credit.

because its impact is *not* neutral but is unduly great. One sector which is said to be hurt excessively by tight money—and, indeed, to bear the brunt of it—is residential construction. For example, the Council of Economic Advisers stated its belief that the effects of tight money on aggregate demand in 1966 operated primarily through the mortgage market.[8] Residential construction is powerfully affected by changing conditions in the money market, and even observers who are generally not "cheap money men" have at times felt that monetary policy was hurting residential construction too much.[9]

But the mere fact that a sector is sensitive to monetary policy does not prevent monetary policy from being neutral. As explained above, neutrality does not mean proportionality. Since residential construction is long-term investment one would expect it to be relatively responsive to monetary policy. In many cases, the homeowner can maximize his utility by postponing the purchase of the house until the interest rate falls. Hence, the countercyclical pattern shown by residential construction should not be too surprising and is not inconsistent with the view that monetary policy is neutral. There are, however, two ways in which monetary policy may fail to be neutral in its impact on residential construction. Since banks and other financial institutions ration credit, even borrowers who are willing to pay more than the prevailing interest rate may be unable to obtain mortgage financing. In addition, though this is a much debated issue, interest ceilings on FHA and VA supported morgages may be responsible for a part of the countercyclical behavior of residential construction.[10]

---

[8] *Economic Report of the President* (Washington, D.C.: Executive Office of the President, 1967), p. 60.

[9] For example, on July 14, 1966, all the Republican members of the House Banking and Currency Committee called upon the President to appoint a committee to investigate the decline in residential construction resulting from tight money. ("U.S. Stands Pat on Discount Rate," *The New York Times,* July 15, 1966, p. 39.)

[10] Mortgages supported by FHA or VA underwriting have legal ceilings on the interest rate. Hence as interest rates rise it may become unprofitable to make mortgage loans. However, this factor is counteracted by the discounting of such mortgage loans (the payment of "points"). The empirical

Before leaving the topic of residential construction it is worth noting that even if the sharp cutback in residential construction during periods of tight money is the result of a neutral monetary policy, it is still open to criticism. Since perfect competition does not prevail, a cutback in construction tends to lead to unemployment of construction labor rather than to a shift of this labor into other, lower-paying, occupations. Some of the complaint about the impact of tight money of residential construction may therefore be justified as a criticism of a neutral monetary policy.

Another area in which tight money is said to have an undue effect is investment by state and local governments. A number of observers, led by Professor Galbraith, believe that we are seriously slighting investment in schools and other government facilities. If this is correct then any cutback in such investment caused by monetary policy is a serious matter. Again, since state and local government investment is long-term investment, a substantial response to monetary policy is consistent with monetary policy being neutral. But there is one institutional factor that causes tight money to have a more than neutral effect on state and local government investment. This is that many state and local government projects have a restriction on the interest rate they may pay; bond elections or state law give the maximum rate of interest on the bonds. Hence, as interest rates rise, a number of state and local projects find themselves priced out of the money market. (Moreover, people who are concerned about the inadequate level of state and local investment would in many cases be concerned about a cutback in state and local investment even if it were a response to a neutral monetary policy. If the level of

---

evidence on the importance of these interest ceilings suggests that while they may be of some importance, they are not important enough to account for the whole countercyclical pattern of residential construction. One recent study found that they did have some influence (Eugene Brady, "A Sectorial Econometric Study of the Postwar Residential Housing Market," *Journal of Political Economy*, Vol. 77 [April, 1967], pp. 147–158). On the other hand, they are unlikely to account for the whole countercyclical pattern since another study found that mortgages not covered by the FHA or VA ceilings also show countercyclical behavior. See Jack Guttentag, "The Short Cycle in Residential Construction," *American Economic Review*, Vol. 51 (June, 1961), pp. 275–298.

such investment is below its optimal, then a *neutral* policy would not maximize welfare. The criticism that tight money reduces state and local government investment unduly really applies to both lines of criticism outlined above.)

Three replies can be made to the argument that counter-cyclical monetary policy hurts state and local investment too much. First, note that this argument relates to high interest rates over the long run rather than to a countercyclical monetary policy. Second, if state and local government investment is too low, it can be increased without making money easy for the whole economy by having the Federal government subsidize it to a still greater extent than it does at present. Third, there is an empirical question. Does a tight money policy really cut back state and local investment substantially? One study concluded that:

> . . . the impact of monetary controls on state and local governments since 1952 constitutes a model of what monetary policy should be expected to accomplish. At no time during the period studied did a restrictive monetary policy "throttle" or severely curtail state and local capital projects. Its impact appears to have been limited to roughly the marginal 5 percent of capital projects, those having a more postponable nature. Projects having high social priorities, such as schools and water and sewer projects, appear to have gone ahead largely independently of the state of the money market. The contracyclical fluctuations of state and local government bond sales, contract awards, and construction work, although relatively small in amplitude, have made a substantial contribution to the stabilization of the economy since 1952. The most ardent advocate of a compensatory monetary policy could hardly have hoped for a better performance.[11]

[11] Frank Morris, "Impact of Monetary Policy on State and Local Governments: An Empirical Study," *Journal of Finance*, Vol. 15 (May, 1960), p. 249. Another study found that in 1955–1957 tighter money caused a postponement or cutback of municipal capital expenditures by 4 to 7 percent. (See Charlotte Phelps, "The Impact of Monetary Policy on State and Local Government Expenditures in the United States," in Commission on Money and Credit, *Impacts of Monetary Policy* [Englewood Cliffs, N.J.: Prentice-Hall, 1963], p. 647.) See also William Shropshire, "Interest Rates and Local Government Spending: The North Carolina Experience, 1955–1958," *Southern Economic Journal*, Vol. 32 (April, 1966), pp. 440–450.

Another area where tight money is said to have an unduly harsh effect is the financial market. There are two separate problems here. First, there is the effect on the money market as a whole. Clearly, monetary policy impinges on the money market more directly than on other markets and this may raise the cost curves of the financial industry. But most economists would probably agree that this is a cost worth paying.

Another argument relates to the impact of monetary policy on commercial banks. A restrictive monetary policy, the argument goes, limits the loans and security purchases of banks. Bank profits are therefore reduced and, in addition, banks lose a part of their market to nonbank financial intermediaries. But this argument is open to serious question. Whether a tight money policy reduces bank profits depends on the elasticities of demand and supply for bank funds. The fact that banks are generally advocates of tight money suggests that they do not lose excessively by a restrictive monetary policy. Moreover, nonbank financial intermediaries, too, feel some effects of tight money. As Figure 4.3 indicates, the market share of banks, while declining secularly, does not show any cycles corresponding to periods of tight and easy money.

The impact of tight money on small business, one of the biggest, if not *the* biggest, issues in the debate on the allocational effect of monetary policy still remains to be discussed. As background to this debate remember that regardless of monetary policy there is considerable concern about the difficulties that small business faces in obtaining adequate financing.

There are several reasons why tight money may impose a greater burden on small business than large ones. First, small business is more dependent on bank financing than is large business because small firms find it very costly to float securities. Since much of the initial impact of monetary policy centers on banks, small firms who are dependent on banks may find that a restrictive monetary policy cuts their access to capital substantially. Second, it is argued that in rationing credit banks discriminate against small firms. When credit is rationed banks are more concerned with meeting the demands of their good customers than of their weaker customers, and large firms generally meet the usual criteria of credit worthiness better than small firms do. Not only does credit rationing lead to discrimination against small firms, but it also causes discrimination against new firms since banks try to take care of the needs of their old customers before taking on new customers.

Moreover, if a large firm is denied credit by one bank it can turn to another bank, but small firms find it much more difficult to do this. Small firms have to borrow from banks in their own area since they are not known outside of it. Large firms, on the other hand, have access to banks throughout the country. In addition, if interest rates rise banks may find it unprofitable to lend to small firms. Interest rates on loans to small firms are higher than rates on loans to large firms, and as interest rates rise generally, the interest rate paid by small firms may be limited by the ceiling imposed by state usury laws, thus making it relatively unprofitable to lend to small firms.[12]

But there is another side to this debate, too. There is one way in which a rise in the interest rate may favor small firms over large ones. The interest rate charged on a loan consists of three components. First, there is the so-called "pure" rate of interest, which is what we mean when we use the term "rate of interest" in economic theory. Then there is a risk premium component of the lending rate which offsets the risk involved in any private loan. Third, there is a service charge component which compensates the bank for the administrative expenses involved in making the loan. Now, in a period of tight money the increase in the interest rate which occurs reflects an increase only in the pure rate. The pure rate of interest is a smaller proportion of the total interest rate for small firms than it is for large ones. Hence, the same increase in the pure rate raises the total interest rate *proportionately* less for small firms than for large firms. If the effect of a

[12] Another point, raised by Professor Galbraith, is that competitive firms are unable to pass the higher cost of funds on to their customers by raising their prices. Large oligopolistic firms, on the other hand, usually have an unexploited margin of potential profit and, hence, can raise their prices and pass the higher interest costs on. (See Kenneth Galbraith, "Market Structure and Stabilization Policy," *Review of Economics and Statistics,* Vol. 39 [May, 1957], pp. 124–133.)

rise in the interest rate depends upon the percentage increase rather than absolute size of the increase, then, *ceteris paribus,* we would expect a restrictive monetary policy to reduce investment more for the large firm than for the small firm. Unfortunately, too little is known about the determinants of investment to be able to say whether it is the absolute increase in the interest rate or the proportional increase that is relevant.

Moreover, in a period of tight money large firms lend to their smaller customers by extending trade credit. According to Professor Meltzer:

> Given the magnitude and direction of the redistribution of the money stock which takes place through net receivables alone, there is little evidence of the often cited "discrimination" against small firms.[13]

But there are two qualifications to this optimistic conclusion. First, trade credit is often very expensive for firms, and hence, while the extension of trade credit itself ameliorates the impact of tight money for small firms, the very fact that so many small firms are willing to take trade credit suggests that they experience great difficulty in obtaining financing in a period of tight money. The second qualification is that trade credit is a competitive weapon. If small firms have difficulty in obtaining financing and are therefore inhibited in *extending* trade credit, they are at a competitive disadvantage vis-à-vis their larger competitors.[14]

[13] Allan Meltzer, "Monetary Policy and the Trade Credit Practices of Business Firms," in Commission on Money and Credit, *Stabilization Policies* (Englewood Cliffs, N.J.: Prentice-Hall, 1963), p. 494.

[14] There is still another way in which a restrictive money policy could favor investment by small firms over investment by large firms. Large firms are, at least in many cases, sophisticated enough to know that a tight money policy is likely to reduce demand for their output and, hence, they may reduce investment even if they have no difficulty in financing it. Small firms are less likely to take into account the repercussion of monetary policy on their market. One study for Britain, dealing with the reaction of small- and medium-sized firms to a restrictive monetary policy, found that tight money had had a similar effect on investment of small firms and medium-sized firms. But the reasons for the response to tight money differed. Among small firms financing difficulties were more important and among medium-sized firms expectations about the effect on customers were more important. (See H. F. Lydall, "The Impact of the Credit

One study tried to test the proposition that banks discriminate against small firms empirically and concluded that they do not. This study divided banks into three groups, those which experienced a severe reserve stringency (tight banks), those whose reserve position remained fairly easy (loose banks), and an intermediate group (medium banks).[15] If banks discriminate against small business as their reserve position tightens we would expect to find the tight banks making proportionately fewer loans to small business than do the medium banks, and the medium banks, in turn, making proportionately fewer small business loans than the easy banks. The data do not show this pattern, and hence, they reject the hypothesis that a restrictive monetary policy causes banks to discriminate against small firms.[16]

Thus, to summarize this discussion, monetary policy does seem to create some distortion in resource allocation in the sense of changing resource allocation from what it otherwise would be, but does so to a much smaller extent than many of its critics allege. Three questions emerge in this connection: first, are the distorting effects so serious that a restrictive monetary policy should be avoided; second, are the distortions so small that it

---

Squeeze on Small- and Medium-Sized Manufacturing Firms," *Economic Journal*, Vol. 67 [September, 1957], pp. 415–431.) The particular tight money episode covered by this study was a well advertised, rather unorthodox measure; a more pedestrian and familiar monetary policy might have had less effect on the expectations of medium-sized firms. Note, too, that the effects on the investment programs of large and small firms is not the only relevant criterion. The profitability of small firms is important, too. Insofar as small firms undertake too much investment because they are unable to see that demand for their product will drop, a restrictive money policy hurts small business.

[15] See G. L. Bach and C. J. Huizenga, "The Differential Effects of Tight Money," *American Economic Review*, Vol. 51 (March, 1961), pp. 52–80.

[16] This conclusion has not gone unchallenged. See Deane Carson, "The Differential Effects of Tight Money: Comment," *American Economic Review*, Vol. 51 (December, 1961), pp. 1039–1042; G. L. Bach and C. J. Huizenga, "Reply," *ibid.*, pp. 1042–1044; Dale Tussing, "The Differential Effects of Tight Money: Comment," *American Economic Review*, Vol. 53 (September, 1963), pp. 740–743; and G. L. Bach and C. J. Huizenga, "Reply," *ibid.*, pp. 743–745. See also Donald Hodgman, *Commercial Bank Loan and Investment Policy* (Champaign, Ill.: Bureau of Economic and Business Research, 1963), pp. 156–157.

would be feasible to use monetary policy much more vigorously than we have in the past; and third, does monetary policy create fewer distortions than fiscal policy? Different people will read the evidence presented above differently. Probably the majority of economists would answer the first question in the negative. Whether the majority would answer the second question in the affirmative and would favor a much stronger monetary policy, is hard to say, since this depends, also, on the timing of monetary policy, the problem discussed in the next chapter. The third question, the relative distortions of monetary and fiscal policy, is an extremely difficult question since its answer depends upon the type of fiscal policy being considered as well as on one's own value judgments.

FURTHER READING

Bach, G. L., and C. J. Huizenga: "The Differential Effects of Tight Money," *American Economic Review*, Vol. 51 (March, 1961), pp. 52–80. See also the critical comments by Deane Carson. "The Differential Effects of Tight Money: Comment," *American Economic Review*, Vol. 51 (December, 1961), pp. 1039–1042; and by Dale Tussing. "The Differential Effects of Tight Money: Comment," *American Economic Review*, Vol. 53 (September, 1963), pp. 740–743; and the replies by G. L. Bach and C. J. Huizenga which follow these papers.

Fand, David, and Ira Scott, Jr. "The Recent Questioning of Monetary Policy," *Current Economic Comment*, Vol. 21 (August, 1959), pp. 17–28.

Miller, Ervin. "Monetary Policy in a Changing World," *Quarterly Journal of Economics*, Vol. 70 (February, 1956), pp. 23–43.

Morris, Frank. "Impact of Monetary Policy on State and Local Governments: An Empirical Study," *Journal of Finance*, Vol. 15 (May, 1960), pp. 232–249.

Schlesinger, James. "Monetary Policy and Its Critics," *Journal of Political Economy*, Vol. 68 (December, 1960), pp. 601–616.

U.S. Joint Economic Committee. *Staff Report on Employment, Growth and Price Levels*. Washington, D.C.: 86th Congress, First Session, 1959, pp. 363–393.

Chapter 6

The Problem of Lags

Let us suppose that the strength of monetary policy could be demonstrated beyond doubt. Let us further suppose that we could prove that it has no unfavorable resource allocation effects. These conditions alone would not suffice to make monetary policy a useful stabilization tool. If monetary policy is badly timed it may *de*stabilize rather than stabilize the economy. Like fiscal policy, countercyclical monetary policy may create a stabilizer's nightmare. Suppose that as inflationary tendencies develop the central bank reduces bank reserves. If this action cuts aggregate demand right away, well and good. But suppose that, for reasons discussed below, it takes a long time until a change in bank reserves affects income. If so, the reduction in aggregate demand may take place, not during the inflation, but only after the economy has passed the turning point in the business cycle and is in a recession. During this recession the central bank may reverse itself and adopt an expansionary policy. But if this policy, too, takes a long time to affect income, then it may serve not to ameliorate the recession but may reinforce an inflation during the subsequent expansion. Thus, as is shown in Figure 6.1, a countercyclical *policy* may have procyclical effects. Good intentions are not enough.

This danger is serious enough to warrant considering it in greater detail. In an ingenious paper, Professor Friedman formalized this problem by treating it as a problem in statistics and, hence, was able to bring mathematical analysis to bear on it.[1]

---

[1] See Milton Friedman, "The Effects of a Full Employment Policy on Economic Stability: A Formal Analysis," *Essays in Positive Economics* (Chicago: University of Chicago Press, 1953), pp. 117–132.

In statistics the fluctuation of a series can be measured by its variance, and we can therefore measure fluctuations in income which would occur in the absence of a countercyclical monetary policy by the variance of this income series.[2] Similarly, we can

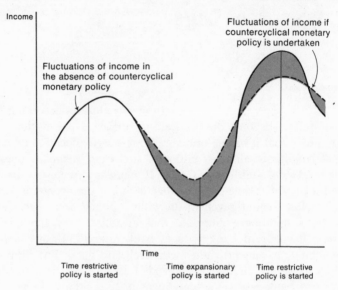

Figure 6.1

NOTE: Shaded areas denote changes in income induced by monetary policy.

[2] The variance (which is the square of the standard deviation) is obtained by taking the deviation of each observation from the mean of the series and squaring it. These squared deviations are then added and divided by the number of cases to find their mean which is the variance. As an illustration, consider the following example:

	Series	Deviation	Deviation Squared
	2	-1	1
	4	1	1
Mean $= 3$	5	2	4
	1	-2	4
			Sum: 10

$$\text{Variance} = \frac{10}{4} = 2.5$$

consider the changes in income brought about by a countercyclical monetary policy as another series with its own variance. To find the total variance in income which exists if countercyclical monetary policy is used we merely have to add these two variances. The sum of the two variances is given by the following formula

$$\sigma_z^2 = \sigma_x^2 + \sigma_y^2 + 2R\sigma_x\sigma_y$$

where σ_z^2 is the variance of income existing if a countercyclical monetary policy is used, σ_x^2 is the variance of income in the absence of monetary policy, σ_y^2 measures the variance in income brought about by a countercyclical monetary policy, and R is the coefficient of correlation between the original fluctuations in income and the fluctuations induced by monetary policy.[3] If monetary policy is perfectly timed, then it expands income at a time when income would otherwise be low, and reduces income at a time when it would otherwise be high. If there is a perfect negative correlation between the original fluctuations in income and the offsetting fluctuations induced by monetary policy, then by adoption of a policy strong enough to set $\sigma_x = \sigma_y$, monetary policy would eliminate all fluctuation in income. Conversely, if R is positive, monetary policy is very badly timed, and we have the case of the stabilizer's nightmare described above.

The above formula brings out two important points. First, it suggests that there is a real possibility that monetary policy may be destabilizing.[4] To have a substantial stabilizing effect the coefficient of correlation must be negative and fairly large. If the policy is timed randomly with respect to the original fluctuations in income so that the coefficient of correlation is zero, then the above equation shows that *monetary policy is increasing the fluctuations experienced by the economy*. It can be shown that

[3] The coefficient of correlation is a measure of how well two series are correlated. If both series show exactly parallel movements, the coefficient of correlation is unity; if they show exactly inversely parallel movements it is minus one; if there is no relation at all between the two series the coefficient of correlation is zero.

[4] Note that it is the timing of *effects* of monetary policy on income which is relevant, *not* the timing of the *taking of action* by the central bank.

a monetary policy strong enough to offset the whole of the original fluctuations in income (that is, a policy which sets σ_y equal to σ_x) will be stabilizing only if the coefficient of correlation lies between -0.5 and -1.0, and destabilizing if it lies between -0.5 and 1.0.[5]

Second, monetary policy can be too strong as well as too weak. For each value of the coefficient of correlation there is an optimal size for the monetary policy—a policy greater than that would do less to stabilize income, and may even destabilize it.[6] For example, assume that the coefficient of correlation is -0.5. If so, the optimal policy would be one which would reduce the fluctuation in income by 25 percent; a policy of trying to offset the original fluctuation in income fully would, in fact, not reduce the fluctuation at all.[7] This is certainly a far cry from the traditional criticism of monetary policy that monetary policy is too weak.

Professor Friedman's approach of looking at monetary policy in terms of the sum of two variances is extremely interesting, but since it deals only with the *fluctuation* of income, it has to be supplemented by considering the effect of policy on the *level* of income. Stabilizing income is not the only, and often not even the predominant, goal of monetary policy.[8] What we want to achieve is full employment, price stability, etc. These goals are only imperfectly related to the elimination of *fluctuations* in income. The problem may be to raise aggregate demand in most periods, rather than to keep it stable at its average level. For example, suppose someone had told President Roosevelt in 1933 that he had an infallible method of stabilizing employment. To be sure, it would involve continuous unemployment for one-third of the labor force, but it would be a *stable* level of unemployment. Presumably, President Roosevelt would have preferred a

[5] Friedman, *op. cit.*, p. 125.
[6] The optimal size of the policy, $\hat{\sigma}_{-y}^2$, is given by the equation $\hat{\sigma}_{-y}^2 = -R\sigma_x$; *ibid.*, p. 125.
[7] *Ibid.*, p. 126. If $R = -0.5$, then the optimal size of σ_y is $\frac{1}{2}\sigma_x$.
[8] See Lloyd Orr, "A Note on the Inflexibility of Monetary Policy," *Review of Economics and Statistics*, Vol. 42 (August, 1960), pp. 329–331.

policy which lowered unemployment substantially on the average, even if it meant some fluctuation in unemployment.

Moreover, note that any attempt to relate fluctuations in income to welfare gains and losses necessarily involves a value judgment. The formula for the variance counts a deviation of one unit above the mean in the same way as a deviation of one unit below the mean. But, taking the mean level of income to denote price stability and full employment, a deviation below the mean involves unemployment and a deviation above the mean involves price increases. Depending on one's value judgment one may consider the unemployment resulting from a $1 billion deficiency of demand to be better or worse than the inflation resulting from $1 billion excessive demand. Most economists would probably consider the unemployment to be the greater of the two evils. In any case, this issue should be treated explicitly as a choice between goals and should not be tucked away as an arbitrary assumption made in the process of calculating the variances.[9] But, in spite of these problems the author feels that Professor Friedman's analysis of the timing problem in terms of the variances has added greatly to our insight into it.

The Length of the Lag

Having seen how important a lag in policy can be, let us now look at the probable magnitude of the lag. The total lag involved in the operation of countercyclical monetary policy is usually divided into three components. First, there is a lag between the time the need for the action arises and the time this need is recognized. Statistical data become available only with a lag, and moreover, cyclical turning points are not clear-cut, certainly not at the time they occur. At what we afterwards consider to be the

---

[9] In addition, there is a more technical point. In computing the variance the deviations from the mean are squared. This means that a single deviation of $4 billion is given more weight than two deviations of $2 billion each. Hence, in considering the minimization of the variance of income to be our goal, we are using a quadratic utility function. This type of utility function is certainly used in economics, but it does restrict the generality of the result and, again, involves an implicit value judgment.

upper turning point some series are still turning up while some are turning down. Even by hindsight it is hard to decide in what month to place the turning point.

The second lag is the time elapsing between the recognition of the need for action and the taking of that action. For monetary policy, unlike fiscal policy, this second lag would normally be quite short. These two lags are often combined into one concept and called the "inside lag."

The third lag, the so-called outside lag, is the time between the taking of action and its consequent effects. Suppose that the Federal Reserve increases bank reserves. Banks then make credit available more readily and lower interest rates. This could have a quick effect on consumer loans and, hence, consumer purchases, but, at least according to most expositions of monetary policy, the main effect is on investment. Now, investment projects usually take a substantial time to get going. Plans may have to be drawn up, and the construction process itself is often long.

As Table 6.1 indicates, in recent years the inside lag has been short. But the outside lag appears to be considerably longer, a fact which is not surprising since we know that investment takes time. It is only in the postwar period, and particularly in recent

TABLE **6.1**   *Lag Between Cyclical Turning Point and First Indication of Major Change in Federal Reserve Policy[a]*

Peaks		Troughs	
July, 1953	− 1 month	August, 1954	4 months
July, 1957	3 months	April, 1958	4 months
May, 1960	− 2 months	February, 1961	10 months
MEAN	0 month	MEAN	6 months

[a] Turning points are National Bureau of Economic Research turning points.

SOURCE: Based on Karl Brunner and Allan Meltzer, *The Federal Reserve's Attachment to the Free Reserve Concept* (Washington, D.C.: U.S. House Committee on Banking and Currency, Subcommittee on Domestic Finance, 88th Congress, Second Session, 1964), p. 42.

years, that economists have studied the outside lag in detail. A number of estimates of this outside lag are available. They are summarized in the appendix to this chapter.

This appendix shows that there is much disagreement between the various studies which suggests that there is still a great deal to be learned about the lag of monetary policy. Yet in spite of this disagreement, all but one show an average lag of two quarters or more.[10] The fact that the studies found a lag of two quarters or more provides strong evidence that the lag is actually at least two quarters. This is so because these studies used a wide variety of different approaches so that even if *some* of the studies contain errors, the overall result would still hold. This is important because a number of the studies listed in the appendix have been subjected to strong criticism.[11]

[10] One study (for Chile) shows a two-quarter lag if quarterly data are used and a one-quarter lag if yearly data are used. For determining the lag, the former are clearly more reliable.

[11] For a discussion of the Friedman-Schwartz study, see John Culbertson, "Friedman on the Lag in the Effect of Monetary Policy," *Journal of Political Economy*, Vol. 68 (December, 1960), pp. 617–621; John Culbertson, "The Lag in Effect of Monetary Policy: A Reply," *Journal of Political Economy*, Vol. 69 (October, 1961), pp. 467–477. See also John Kareken and Robert Solow, "Lags in Fiscal and Monetary Policy," in Commission on Money and Credit, *Stabilization Policies* (Englewood Cliffs, N.J.: Prentice-Hall, 1963), pp. 14–25. For a reply see Milton Friedman, "The Lag in Effect of Monetary Policy," *Journal of·Political Economy*, Vol. 69 (October, 1961), pp. 447–466. For an excellent justification of Professor Friedman's technique see Arthur Okun, "Comment," *Review of Economics and Statistics, Supplement*, Vol. 45 (February, 1963), pp. 72–77. For criticisms of the Kareken and Solow study, see Milton Friedman, "Note on the Lag in Effect of Monetary Policy," *American Economic Review*, Vol. 54 (September, 1964), pp. 759–761; Thomas Mayer, "The Lag in the Effect of Monetary Policy: Some Criticisms," *Western Economic Journal*, Vol. 7 (September, 1965), pp. 324–342. Rhomberg's study is criticized in Harry Johnson and John Winder, *Lags in the Effects of Monetary Policy in Canada* (Ottawa: Queen's Printer, 1964). A critical discussion of the author's study can be found in William White, "The Flexibility of Anticyclical Monetary Policy," *Review of Economics and Statistics*, Vol. 43 (May, 1961), pp. 142–147, and William White, "The Inflexibility of Monetary Policy: Reply," *Review of Economics and Statistics*, Vol. 46 (August, 1964), pp. 322–324. For replies, see Thomas Mayer, "Dr. White on the Inflexibility of Monetary Policy," *Review of Economics and Statistics*, Vol. 45 (May, 1963), pp. 209–211, and "Rejoinder," *Review of Economics and Statistics*, Vol. 46 (August, 1964), pp. 322–325. For a

If the outside lag is two quarters or more, perhaps very substantially more, does this create a danger that countercyclical monetary policy may be destabilizing rather than stabilizing? Very little work has been done on this topic. In a study listed in the appendix, the author attempted to answer this question by using Professor Friedman's sum-of-variances approach. The results showed monetary policy as having some effectiveness in stabilizing prices, but little effectiveness in stabilizing industrial production.[12] However, these conclusions are extremely tentative, and deal only with a monetary policy which is of optimal strength. Any actual policy is likely to be either stronger or weaker than that and, hence, a less effective stabilizer. These results, therefore, cannot be used to contradict Professor Friedman's view that monetary policy is likely to be destabilizing. Moreover, as shown in the appendix, the lags found in this study are shorter than the ones found by Professor Friedman and Mrs. Schwartz. If their estimate of the outside lag *is* correct, countercyclical monetary policy probably *is* destabilizing.

Variability of the Outside Lag

Its *average* length is not the only important characteristic of the outside lag. Variability is important, too. Suppose that the outside lag is long but quite stable. If so, it may be possible to operate an effective countercyclical monetary policy by basing action, not on current business conditions, but on a forecast. Even if, at present, forecasts are not accurate enough to serve as a guide to monetary policy (a subject still open to debate) they may become accurate enough in the future. But if the outside lag is highly (and unpredictably) variable, then even an accurate business cycle forecast would not suffice. Suppose the forecast predicts that income will be too high for the next nine months, after which there will be a downturn. If the outside lag

---

criticism applicable to a number, but by no means all, of these studies, see Donald Tucker, "Income Adjustment to Money-Supply Changes," *American Economic Review,* Vol. 56 (June, 1966), pp. 433–450.

[12] This is due to the fact that during the period covered the Wholesale Price Index lagged behind the Industrial Production Index.

varies greatly from case to case, then even a knowledge that its *average* is, say, six months or a year does not provide the central bank with an adequate guide to action in a specific situation.

Unfortunately, little work has been done as yet on the variability of the lag. In their study Professor Friedman and Mrs. Schwartz concluded that the lag is highly variable. Table 6.2 shows the extent of the variability they found.[13] However, their estimate of the variability is subject to debate since they measure the lag as the difference between the turning points of the rate of money growth series and the business cycle turning points instead of the length of time it takes a given dollar change in bank reserves to affect income. At a time when investment incen-

T A B L E **6.2**   *Array of Lags, 1908–1961*

Measured from:			
Step Dates[a]		*Money Cycle Turning Points*[a]	
Peaks	*Troughs*	*Peaks*	*Troughs*
− 8	− 3	13	4
− 2	− 1	13	5
0	0	13	6
7	0	15	8
7	1	15	9
7	3	20	10
10	4	20	11
12	4	20	11
13	4	21	13
13	8	23	14
16	10	27	17
22	11	29	18
—	17	—	21

[a] For a definition see the Appendix to this Chapter.

SOURCE: Friedman and Schwartz, "Money and Business Cycles," *Review of Economics and Statistics, Supplement,* Vol. 45 (February, 1963), p. 37.

[13] Dr. Warburton's study, cited in the appendix, also shows substantial variability of the lags, but he was not dealing with this topic and, hence, did not emphasize this finding.

tives are strong it may take longer for a given decline in the rate of money growth to terminate the expansion than at a time when investment incentives are weak, even though in both cases a dollar change in bank reserves may require as much time to have its particular effect on income.[14]

To summarize this discussion, it has been shown that a badly timed monetary policy may be destabilizing rather than stabilizing. And the various empirical estimates of the lag of monetary policy which have been undertaken suggest that the lag is long enough for this possibility to be one which must be taken seriously. There is some empirical evidence that the lag is highly variable, but it is subject to some objections. All in all, a great deal of additional work will have to be done before we have an adequate knowledge about the lags of monetary policy.

FURTHER READING

Obvious sources for further reading are the various studies of the outside lag listed in the appendix, together with the criticisms listed in footnote 11 on page 183. Several of these studies are summarized in V. Argy, "The Lags in Monetary Policy: An Assessment of Alternative Approaches," in Banca Nazionale del Lavoro, *Quarterly Review*, No. 73 (June, 1965), pp. 3–13. This list, together with the Friedman paper discussed in the beginning of the chapter, comprise close to all of the literature available on this topic. But for a general mathematical discussion of the timing of stabilization policy see also A. W. Phillips, "Stabilization Policy and the Time-Forms of Lagged Responses," *Economic Journal*, Vol. 68 (June, 1957), pp. 265–277; and William Baumol, "Pitfalls in Contracyclical Policies: Some Tools and Results," *Review of Economics and Statistics*, Vol. 43 (February, 1961), pp. 21–26. For studies of the outside lag see also Patric Hendershott, "The Inside Lag in Monetary Policy: A Comment," *Journal of Political Economy*, Vol. 74 (October, 1966), pp. 519–523; and Mark Willes, "The Inside Lags of Monetary Policy: 1952–1960," *Journal of Finance*, Vol. 22 (December, 1967), pp. 591–594.

[14] For a critique of the Friedman-Schwartz estimate of variability, see Mayer, "The Lag in the Effect of Monetary Policy: Some Criticisms," *op. cit.*

APPENDIX TO CHAPTER 6

Brief Description of Studies of the Outside Lag

AUTHORS.

WARBURTON: A comparison of turning points in the trend-adjusted series of GNP and the trend-adjusted money stock.

FRIEDMAN *and* SCHWARTZ: Specific money cycle turning points—a comparison of turning points in the series measuring the rate of growth of the money stock with the National Bureau of Economic Research turning points.

Step dates—essentially a similar procedure. The difference is that instead of using the peaks and troughs in the money growth series, Friedman and Schwartz use the date at which the money growth series moved up or down by a step. The series does exhibit steplike movements.

KAREKEN *and* SOLOW: Estimation of lags in several sectors of the economy by the use of lagged regression. The study does not provide an average lag for the whole economy, but states that the lag is shorter than that found by Friedman. But the lags estimated for the various sectors suggest a long average lag for the whole economy.

LIU: The lag in the effect of changes in the money stock on income is estimated as part of a quarterly econometric model.

MAYER: Lags are estimated for various sectors of the economy in various ways, such as the use of questionnaires to obtain information on the lag between the decision to build an industrial plant and the start of construction as well as the completion of construction.

DE LEEUW *and* GRAMLICH: The lag in the effect of changes in free reserves is estimated using an econometric model.

EVANS *and* KLEIN: The lag in the effect of changes in the discount rate and in free reserves is estimated using an econometric model.

RHOMBERG: The lag in the effect of changes in the money supply is obtained as part of an econometric model.

JOHNSON *and* WINDER: Lagged regression between the money stock and income.

MACESICH: Similar to the Friedman and Schwartz study using money cycle turning points.

WALTERS: Correlation of the money supply and income.

HARBERGER: A correlation of the percentage increase in the money stock with the inflation.

COLACO: Similar to the Harberger study.

UCHIHASHI, MACHINAGA, *and* KODERA: Comparison of discount-rate changes with turning points in industrial production and GNP growth rate.

T A B L E **6.3** *Mean Lags of Monetary Policy*

	Peaks[a]				Troughs[b]	
	Number of Quarters					
United States:						
Warburton[c]	4^d	5^e			3^d	2^e
Friedman and Schwartz[f]						
Specific money cycle						
turning points	6^g				4^g	
Step dates	2^g				2^g	
Kareken and Solow			Long Lags[h]			
Liu			6^i			
Mayer	2^j	3^j			2^j	3^j
de Leeuw and Gramlich			7^k	8^k		
Evans and Klein			4^l	5^l		
Canada:						
Rhomberg			5^m			
Johnson and Winder			$2\text{–}4^n$			
Macesich[o]	4				2	
Great Britain:						
Walters			2			
Chile:						
Harberger			2^p	1^p		
Brazil:						
Colaco			4^q			
Japan:						
Uchihashi, Machinaga,			Very short or Non-			
and Kodera			existent Lags			

NOTES:

[a] Lag at peaks, or lag of restrictive policy, depending upon the study.

[b] Lag at troughs, or lag of expansionary policy, depending upon the study.

c From turning points in bank reserves to National Bureau turning points. Using the turning points in GNP instead of the National Bureau turning points does not change the result.

d Using turning points in total reserves.

e Using turning points in reserves applicable to demand deposits.

f Beryl Sprinkel, "Monetary Growth as a Cyclical Predictor," *Journal of Finance*, Vol. 14 (September, 1959), pp. 333–346) found results similar to the Friedman-Schwartz specific money cycle estimates. Since his methods are quite similar to those of the Friedman-Schwartz study, his study is not listed in this table.

g Monthly data only.

h Insufficient information to specify the average lag.

i Time required for a once-for-all increase in the interest rate to reach its maximum effect on GNP. For a maintained increase in the interest rate the lag is still longer.

j Half the effect is reached within second quarter, three-quarters of the effect is reached within third quarter. These lags do not include the lags of the multiplier effects.

k Half the twelfth quarter effect is reached in the seventh quarter; three-quarters is reached in the eighth quarter.

l Half of the maximum effect on disposable income is reached in the fourth quarter; three-quarters of the effect is reached in the fifth quarter. For GNP, the lag is longer.

m Both half and three-quarters of the full effect are reached in the fifth quarter. The model shows oscillations with the peak effect of monetary policy subsequent to the fifth quarter exceeding the equilibrium effect. The figure shown refers to Rhomberg's fixed exchange rate model. With flexible exchange rates half the effect is reached in the second quarter and nearly the full effect in the third.

n Johnson and Winder have "relatively greater confidence" in their model showing a six months to a year lag, but admit that the lag may be as long as two and a half years.

o Keith Hay ("Money and Cycles in Post-Confederation Canada," *Journal of Political Economy*, Vol. 75 [June, 1967], pp. 263–273) found a five quarter lag for peaks. I have not included it in the table since his method is similar to Macesich's.

p This study, like the following one, does not deal directly with the lag problem but with the rate of change of prices. The equation shows an approximate two-quarter lag of price changes behind changes in the money stock when quarterly data are used and a one-quarter lag when yearly figures are used.

q Based on yearly data using the money stock of the current and previous two years.

SOURCES: Based on Clark Warburton, unpublished study, "Central Bank Operations and Business Fluctuations in the United States, 1919–1964," prepared for the House Banking and Currency Committee; Milton Friedman and Anna Schwartz, "Money and Business Cycles," *Review of Economics and Statistics, Supplement*, Vol. 45 (February, 1963), pp. 32–64; Albert Ando, E. C. Brown, Robert Solow, and John Kareken, "Lags in Fiscal and Monetary Policy," in Commission on Money and Credit, *Stabilization Policies* (Englewood Cliffs, N.J.: Prentice-Hall, 1963), pp. 1–163; Ta-Chung Liu, "An Exploratory Quarterly Econometric Model of Effective Demand in the Postwar United States," *Econometrica*, Vol. 31 (July, 1963), pp. 301–348; Thomas Mayer, "The Inflexibility of Monetary Policy," *Review of Economics and Statistics*, Vol. 40 (November, 1958), pp. 358–374; Rudolph Rhomberg, "A Model of the Canadian Economy under Fixed and Fluctuating Exchange Rates," *Journal of Political Economy*, Vol. 72 (February, 1964), pp. 1–31; George Macesich, "The Rate of Change of the Money Stock as a Leading Canadian Indicator," *Canadian Journal of Economics and Political Science*, Vol. 28 (August, 1962), pp. 424–430; Harry Johnson and John Winder, *Lags in the Effects of Monetary Policy in Canada* (Ottawa: Queen's Printer, 1964); A. A. Walters, "Monetary Multipliers in the United Kingdom 1880–1962," *Oxford Economic Papers*, Vol. 18 (November, 1966), pp. 270–283; Arnold Harberger, "The Dynamics of Inflation in Chile," Carl Christ (ed.), *Measurement in Economics* (Stanford: Stanford University Press, 1963), pp. 219–250; Francis Colaco, private communication; Frank de Leeuw and Edward Gramlich, "The Federal-Reserve–MIT Econometric Model," *Federal Reserve Bulletin*, Vol. 54 (January, 1968), pp. 11–40; Michael Evans and Lawrence Klein, *The Wharton Econometric Forecasting Model* (Philadelphia: Wharton School of Finance and Commerce, University of Pennsylvania, 1967), pp. 64–65; Yoshiro Uchihashi, Sogo Machinaga, and Takeshiro Kodera, "Lags in Monetary Policy: Cases in Japan," Kwansei Gakun University *Annual Studies*, Vol. 16 (1967), pp. 107–113.

Alternative Monetary Policies

The previous chapters have discussed the goals and methods of monetary policy as well as its strength, its resource-allocation effects and its timing. This material can now be combined by considering alternative monetary policies which have been proposed, or more specifically, alternative evaluations of the desirability of countercyclical monetary policy. Obviously, it is not possible to consider all alternative policy views here; instead this chapter deals with four policy positions. One is the position currently taken by the Federal Reserve, another is that of the advocates of easy money, a third is that of the monetarists, and fourth is the proposal to replace countercyclical monetary policy with a policy of increasing the money supply at a constant rate regardless of the business cycle. These four alternatives compose the position of the great majority of economists, though there are substantial points of disagreement even between supporters of the same general position and many economists take an in-between position. The policy positions described below are, in most cases, not those of any single individual or institution but an amalgam of fairly similar views.

Before coming to the disagreements, it is worth noting that there is substantial agreement on one important issue, namely that financial panics should be prevented. Traditionally, this has been an important task of monetary policy, though nowadays deposit insurance has taken over much of this task. There is little discussion on the issue, in part because there is widespread agreement on it, and in part because most economists feel that financial panics are a thing of the past.

The Dominant View

The label "dominant view" is not really an ideal description; the term "establishment view" would be better if it were not for the fact that the term "establishment" is so often used in a derogatory sense. In any case, the policy to be described in this section is the one favored by the Federal Reserve as well as by what the newspapers call "the financial community" as well as by very many economists.

In this view, the average level of interest rates over the business cycle is not very important—what is important is that interest rates and credit availability should behave countercyclically. By using monetary policy in a countercyclical fashion the Federal Reserve can, through the processes described in Chapters 3 and 4, moderate the business cycle. To be sure, interest rates and credit availability may not be the most important factor impinging on the businessman's decision to invest, but they do have a significant effect. Monetary policy may not be strong enough to do the whole stabilizing task by itself—particularly if fluctuations are severe—and may have to be supplemented by countercyclical fiscal policy. But all the same, monetary policy should be operated in a countercyclical manner so that it contributes as much as possible to stabilization and balance-of-payments equilibrium. Granted that monetary policy does not have its main impact on income immediately, and that its effectiveness may be reduced to some extent by lags, yet monetary policy is still fast enough to be stabilizing rather than destabilizing.

On the whole, the resource-allocation effects of a countercyclical monetary policy are not very unfavorable. When advocates of easy money disparage the resource-allocation effects of tight money, they really complain about the way in which a free market allocates a scarce resource and they attempt to impose their own social priorities on the economy. As a nation we have, by and large, chosen to let resource allocation and income distribution be guided by free market processes. Monetary policy should not be used to upset this decision.

Moreover, the argument runs, since tax increases are polit-

ically unpopular, the alternative to tight money is usually inflation, and inflation distorts resource allocation much more than
tight money does. Not only is inflation an evil in and of itself,
but an inflation makes the subsequent recession more severe
and, hence, increases the overall level of unemployment over the
cycle as well as making the balance-of-payments problem worse.[1]
This fear of inflation, it should be noted, is widespread in the
financial community, and is an important component of the dominant view, at least in its Federal Reserve variant. Professional
economists who accept the dominant view in other ways often do
not share the Federal Reserve's great fear of inflation, and are
more concerned than is the Federal Reserve with unemployment.

In the dominant view monetary policy should be the main
stabilization tool, at least in the case of relatively moderate cycles,
because it is much more efficient than fiscal policy. Admittedly,
fiscal policy can have a powerful effect on income but, the argument runs, it is clumsy compared to monetary policy. Both
changes in government expenditures and tax-rate changes usually distort resource allocation; they are often centered on very
narrow segments of the economy and lack the generality and
market guidance of monetary policy. Moreover, fiscal policy is
very slow. It takes a long time to get a public works program
into motion, and Congress may be slow to institute tax cuts. In
an expansion, fiscal policy is even less reliable. While tax cuts
are politically popular, tax increases are shunned as long as
possible. Congress may not be willing to raise taxes in an election
year, and even if it does raise them it may do so only after a
long delay.

Whether all of this is correct is hard to say. Certainly many
public works programs are slow, and some tax bills have spent
a very long time in Congress. But some public works programs
can come into operation rapidly,[2] and Congress has passed some

---

[1] As Chairman Martin said: "I think one of the reasons we have had so
much unemployment as we have had, and you may think this is silly, is
because we have had too easy money." Cited in John Culbertson, *Full
Employment or Stagnation?* (New York: McGraw-Hill, 1964), p. 156.

[2] See E. J. Howenstine, "The Alleged Inflexibility of Compensatory Public
Works Policy," *Journal of Political Economy,* Vol. 59 (June, 1951), pp.
233–241.

tax bills speedily. Moreover, it is simply incorrect to say that Congress is reluctant to raise taxes in an election year.[3] On the whole, though, fiscal policy probably is slower than monetary policy.

In the dominant view monetary policy should "lean against the wind." In doing so, it should concern itself with many variables, such as the stock of money, interest rates, credit conditions, and the volume and quality of bank credit. All of these variables are important and policy has to be based on a mature judgment regarding the overall pattern they indicate. In arriving at such a judgment, the level of interest rates can be used as a good indicator of the current posture of monetary policy.

The Monetarist Countercyclical Policy

Many economists accept the above point of view in one respect; they believe that countercyclical monetary policy is desirable. However, they differ sharply from the Federal Reserve in the type of countercyclical policy they advocate.

To the countercyclical "monetarists" the stock of money is the critical variable the Federal Reserve should look at. Instead of concerning itself with interest rates, credit conditions, and so on, the Federal Reserve should ensure that the stock of money grows at the proper rate—that is, slower in the expansion than during the recession. This might seem an innocuous statement. After all, is this not what "leaning against the wind" implies? But as pointed out in Chapter 3, using the conventional definition of money, this is not what the Federal Reserve has done. In recent cycles, the stock of money has increased faster in the expansion than in the recession, suggesting that the Federal Reserve was leaning *with* the wind. The monetarist explains this by the fact

---

[3] As Professor Shoup has pointed out, ". . . if we go back over the history of the past 40 or 50 years, and make a tabulation of the years in which the heaviest tax increases occurred, we find that most of them were election years." (Testimony before the hearing of the Joint Economic Committee. See U.S. Joint Economic Committee, *Review of the Report of the Commission on Money and Credit* [Washington, D.C.: 87th Congress, First Session, 1961], p. 190.)

that the Federal Reserve has been paying too much attention to the absolute level of interest rates and to free reserves, and so on. A policy which tends to stabilize the interest rate causes destabilizing changes in the growth rate of the money stock. During the expansion, as the marginal efficiency of investment and economic activity in general rise, interest rates tend to rise, too. This rise in the interest rate reduces expenditures and, hence, tends to limit the expansion. Conversely, during a recession, as activity falls the interest rate declines, which tends to limit the recession. But if the Federal Reserve is concerned with interest rate stability, it will attempt to limit interest rate changes by allowing the money stock to grow at a more rapid rate in the expansion, when interest rates are rising, than in the contraction, when they are falling. This means that it introduces a *procyclical* element into the growth of the money stock. To the monetarist, what is important is not the rate of interest *per se*, but only the rate of interest *relative to the marginal efficiency of investment*. For example, during a recession a discount rate of 4 percent may represent a restrictive monetary policy. If the Treasury bill rate is, say, 3 percent, banks would tend to repay borrowing, and keep a relatively large volume of excess reserves. Conversely, during an expansion a 5 percent discount rate may be an easy money policy. If the Treasury bill rate is, say 6 percent, a 5 percent discount rate would give banks an incentive to borrow and to keep only a low level of excess reserves, both factors tending to raise the money stock.

Now the Federal Reserve no longer explicitly considers interest stabilization to be one of its major goals, but according to the monetarists, its policies work in the direction of interest stabilization for three reasons. First, one of the criteria used by the Federal Reserve in deciding whether its current monetary policy is expansionary is the ease with which borrowers can obtain bank loans at the prevailing rate of interest. If the rate of interest is high, the fact that banks are ready to make loans at this high rate does not show that money is easy, but indicates instead that money is tight.[4] Moreover, the heights of the interest

[4] See Culbertson, *Full Employment or Stagnation?, op. cit.,* Chapter 12.

rate must be related not to previous levels of the interest rate, but to the marginal efficiency of investment and to expected price level changes.

Second, in a recession the Federal Reserve is sometimes reluctant to let the interest rate fall very much because it thinks that very low interest rates and "excessive" availability of credit, a so-called sloppy money-market, would tempt banks into making "unsound" loans.[5] To the monetarist this concern with the quality of credit is unwarranted. Bank examination can ensure the safety of the banking system, and the Federal Reserve should concern itself with the quantity of money.

Third, there is the fact that the Federal Reserve has frequently used a free-reserve goal. As pointed out in Chapter 3, aiming at a fixed free-reserve target tends to stabilize interest rates at the cost of destabilizing movements in the quantity of money. In this way the Federal Reserve has indirectly used an interest stabilization goal.

To the Federal Reserve the monetarist case is oversimplified. It ignores the complexity of the money market and also misinterprets Federal Reserve policy.[6]

[5] All of this has a long history. In its early days the Federal Reserve was bound to the real-bills doctrine that stabilization depends not on the quantity of money, but on the *quality* of bank loans. Interest rates should be kept fairly stable and the money stock should be allowed to increase during the expansion when the demand for short-term self-liquidating business loans increases. The Federal Reserve says that it has abandoned these ideas; its critics claim to find their residue affecting current policies.

Apart from concern about a sloppy money market the Federal Reserve believes that if the reserve base is expanded too much in the recession, it will be difficult to mop up these reserves in the upswing. Moreover, the Federal Reserve has asserted that at low interest rates investment is quite interest inelastic.

[6] For a good example of this type of reply see the statement of Governor Mitchell before hearings of the U.S. House Committee on Banking and Currency, Subcommittee on Domestic Finance, *The Federal Reserve System after Fifty Years*, Vol. III (Washington, D.C.: 88th Congress, Second Session, 1964) pp. 1955–1958.

The Easy Money Position

A third position on monetary policy is that of the advocates of
easy money. This view has significant support in Congress and
among borrowers. It also represents the position of quite a number of economists. According to this view countercyclical monetary policy is desirable with one important limitation: Interest
rates should not be allowed to rise to high levels at any time.
The Federal Reserve should keep interest rates low and credit
readily available throughout the cycle, with interest rates being
pushed below their average during the expansion. In other words,
it is a position favoring countercyclical monetary policy with one
important restraint, namely, really tight money must be avoided.
The degree of emphasis placed on this restraint and the willingness to abandon it in special circumstances varies among advocates of the easy money view, but they are united in their dislike
of tight money.

The easy money case consists of three components. First, there
is the argument that inflation is often the result not of excess
demand, but of excessive income claims by the factors of production—labor being the villain to conservatives, and business
oligopolists being the culprit for liberals. If inflation is the result
of "cost-push" rather than "demand-pull," the argument claims,
monetary policy is unable to prevent it. If money is tightened and
aggregate demand falls, it is employment rather than the price
level which is affected. A tight money policy creates unemployment, not price stability. To be sure, if aggregate demand is
reduced sufficiently, the rise in unemployment and in excess
capacity will *eventually* put a stop to wage and price increases,
but since it will do so at a level of unemployment which is
socially unacceptable, tight money is not a useful weapon against
inflation.

Some easy money advocates would go even further than this
and argue that an increase in interest rates raises prices by increasing the cost of production so that tight money is really
inflationary. Although this argument is sometimes heard in Con-

gress, it has but little support among economists.[7]

The second component of the easy money argument is that tight money has many serious disadvantages. By reducing investment rather than consumption it reduces the rate of growth. Moreover, it discriminates against particular industries and makes the distribution of income more unequal. These are points discussed in some detail in Chapter 5 and will not be discussed here. Suffice it to say that advocates of easy money, unlike the supporters of the dominant view, consider the discriminatory effects of tight money to be substantial and attach a great deal of importance to them.

Some proponents of the easy money view argue that though tight money, if carried far enough, would be able to stop inflation, even a quite substantial increase in interest rates may have little effect on aggregate spending. The marginal efficiency of investment is interest inelastic and velocity can easily increase as interest rates rise. Moreover, lags inhibit the efficient operation of a countercyclical monetary policy. Hence, unfavorable income-distribution effects of tight money are not balanced by a favorable performance as an economic stabilizer. Tight money is not the answer even to a demand-induced inflation.

Some other supporters of the easy money position take a different view and believe that tight money has a powerful—and unfortunate—effect on output. If the Federal Reserve adopts a strong tight money policy in the expansion it is likely to carry this policy too far and to maintain it too long. The effect of this is to bring on a recession. Monetary policy is a very dangerous tool. A number of observers feel that the Federal Reserve has a deflationary bias, that it attaches much too much importance to price stability, and much too little importance to full employment. According to this view, an unwarranted fear of inflation has led the Federal Reserve into adopting policies which have sharply reduced the growth rate and has therefore imposed a substantial cost on the economy.

[7] For a refutation see George Horwich, "Tight Money, Monetary Restraint and the Price Level," *Journal of Finance,* Vol. 21 (March, 1966), pp. 15–33.

To many adherents of the easy money position, the Federal Reserve's deflationary bias is no accident; they look upon the Federal Reserve as being the representative of the financial interests. Five of the voting members of the Federal Open Market Committee come from the twelve Federal Reserve Banks and two-thirds of the directors of these Federal Reserve Banks are elected by commercial bankers. Moreover, until recently, the members of the Board of Governors tended to come from the financial community. However, in recent years there has been quite a radical change: In 1967 four of the seven members of the Board of Governors were professional economists and only one of the other members a former banker. Moreover, the Federal Reserve has frequently said that when a commercial banker takes office at a Federal Reserve bank he looks upon himself as representing the public interest rather than the interest of the banking community. But the problem of excessive banker influence at the Federal Reserve goes deeper than that. It has frequently been observed that a government agency set up to regulate an industry tends to become too sympathetic to the industry and frequently protects the industry against the consumer and other government agencies. This is not the result of any ill will or malfeasance. It is not surprising that officials who deal primarily with the problems of an industry and talk, to a large extent, to members of that industry, will sooner or later tend to have the point of view of that industry. Many critics of the Federal Reserve feel that this is what has happened to it.

The main line of criticism which can be directed at the easy money approach is to challenge its empirical suppositions. There is considerable question whether inflation is cost induced rather than demand induced, but this topic cannot be discussed here. Moreover, as was pointed out in Chapter 4, one can make a case that monetary policy is powerful. The argument that monetary policy has unfavorable effects on resource allocation was discussed in Chapter 5.

Rules versus Authorities

The fourth and last major position on monetary policy is one developed many years ago at the University of Chicago by the late Henry Simons; its leading present day exponent is Professor Friedman.[8] But, in addition to many members of the so-called Chicago School, a number of other economists, such as Professors Angell and Shaw, and Dr. Warburton, though they differ from Professor Friedman on a number of important points have accepted this position in broad outline.[9] And a very moderate variant of this proposal has received strong support in Congress.[10]

[8] See the basic paper of Henry Simons, "Rules versus Authorities in Monetary Policy," *Journal of Political Economy*, Vol. 44 (February, 1936), pp. 1–30; Milton Friedman, *A Program for Monetary Stability* (New York: Fordham University Press, 1960), Chapters 1 and 4; and his testimony before the U.S. Joint Economic Committee, *Employment, Growth and Price Levels Hearings, May 25–28, 1959* (Washington, D.C.: 86th Congress, First Session, 1959), pp. 605–637.

For a discussion of the Chicago School which provides an excellent background to the "rules versus authorities" debate, see the following three short papers: Henry Miller, Jr., "On the 'Chicago School of Economics,'" *Journal of Political Economy*, Vol. 70 (February, 1962), pp. 64–69; George Stigler, "On the 'Chicago School of Economics': Comment," *ibid.*, pp. 70–71; and Martin Bronfenbrenner, "Observations on the 'Chicago School(s),'" *ibid.*, pp. 72–75.

[9] Professor Angell's proposal would apply to bank reserves rather than the money stock. He allows for exceptions to the rule and, moreover, he advocates a wide range of selective controls. His version, therefore, differs substantially from the "orthodox" Chicago version. See James W. Angell, "Appropriate Monetary Policies and Operations in the United States Today," *Review of Economics and Statistics*, Vol. 42 (August, 1960), pp. 247–252. Professor Shaw states that he is arguing "partly out of conviction and partly to incite controversy" ("Money Supply and Stable Economic Growth," Neil Jacoby (ed.), *United States Monetary Policy* [New York: Praeger, 1964], p. 77) and, hence, it is not clear to what extent he is really supporting the proposal. Dr. Warburton's plan also differs widely from the Chicago plan. For an analysis of the differences see Richard Selden, "Stable Monetary Growth," Leland Yeager (ed.), *In Search of a Monetary Constitution* (Cambridge, Mass.: Harvard University Press, 1962), pp. 326–331. This paper, incidentally, provides an excellent discussion of the rules versus authorities issue.

[10] In its *Report on the 1967 Economic Report of the President*, the Majority of the Joint Economic Committee urged "that the monetary authorities

Since the Friedman version of this proposal has received most attention, this section deals primarily with his variant of the plan.

In brief, the proposal is to abandon discretionary monetary policy and instead to follow a policy of increasing the money stock at a constant rate each month regardless of the stage of the business cycle. The money stock is defined by Professor Friedman to include time deposits in commercial banks, but this is not basic; the same rule could be applied to the money stock as conventionally defined (currency plus demand deposits). If the money stock is to be increased at a steady rate, monetary policy cannot be used to counter balance-of-payments disequilibrium. Professor Friedman advocates that the balance of payments be kept in equilibrium in another way, namely by a system of flexible exchange rates.[11] Professor Friedman advocates adoption of 100 percent reserve banking, but while this would facilitate the operation of the rule, it is not necessary for it.

Professor Friedman's case for increasing the money stock at a constant rate runs as follows. As a quantity theorist, he believes that after making allowance for the secular trend in velocity (induced by the rise of real income), changes in money income mirror changes in the money stock. Hence, if the money stock is increased at a constant rate, there will be relatively few fluctuations in income. To be sure, not all fluctuations in income are due to fluctuations in money growth, so that adoption of the rule

---

adopt the policy of moderate and relatively steady increases in the money supply, avoiding the disruptive effects of wide swings in the rate of increase or decrease . . . Such rate of increase should be more or less consistent with the projected rate of growth—generally within a range of 3–5 percent per year." The Minority stated: "We therefore recommend that the Federal Reserve increase the money supply in 1967 at an annual rate of 2 to 4 percent. Monetary growth should vary between the upper and the lower end of this range, as economic conditions indicate, but we urge the Federal Reserve to avoid the extremes of 1965 and 1966." U.S. Joint Economic Committee, *Report on the January, 1967 Economic Report of the President* (Washington, D.C.: 90th Congress, First Session, 1967), pp. 14 and 60.

[11] Professor Friedman advocated flexible exchange rates quite apart from their relationship to the monetary rule. See his "The Case for Flexible Exchange Rates," in his *Essays in Positive Economics* (Chicago: University of Chicago Press, 1953), pp. 157–203.

would not eliminate *all* fluctuations. But since much of the instability of income and, particularly, the more severe fluctuations are due to instability in the money growth rate, the rule would give greater stability than we experience now.

But can we not do better than the rule? Granted that the abolition of discretionary policy would prevent monetary management from adding to the instability of the economy, can we not use discretionary monetary policy to reduce the instability introduced by other factors? Professor Friedman's answer is "No," for two reasons. First, there is the problem of lags. If monetary policy takes a long, and unknown, time to have its main effect on income, a countercyclical monetary policy may be destabilizing. "Leaning today against next year's wind is hardly an easy task in the present stage of meteorology."[12] Second, there is the problem of divergent goals. Since discretionary monetary policy has several potentially conflicting goals, such as full employment and balance-of-payments equilibrium, there is always the danger that the Federal Reserve will be diverted from its domestic stabilization goal. One classical example of this type of thing occurred in the postwar period when the Federal Reserve followed an easy money policy at a time of inflation in order to maintain the price of government securities at par.

Given both the less than perfect devotion of the Federal Reserve to its domestic stabilization goal and the difficulties of determining the correct policy in the face of long and variable lags, it would not be surprising to find that, in the past, the Federal Reserve has been destabilizing rather than stabilizing. And, the argument runs, when we look at the history of the Federal Reserve we do find that it has been perverse more frequently than not. The money stock has been more unstable in the years following the establishment of the Federal Reserve System than in the prior years for which we have adequate data, 1867 to 1914. According to Professor Friedman, a monetary rule would therefore have been preferable.

The simple rule would have avoided the excessive expansion of the stock of money from 1919 to 1920 and the very sharp con-

[12] Friedman, *A Program for Monetary Stability, op. cit.,* p. 93.

traction thereafter, the fairly mild but steady deflationary pressure of the late 1920's, the collapse of the stock of money from 1929 to 1933, the rather rapid rise thereafter, and the sharp decline in the course of the 1937–38 recession. In the period since World War II, the simple rule would have produced a lower rate of growth in the stock of money until the end of 1946 than was in fact realized, almost the same rate of growth during 1947, a faster rate of growth from sometime in 1947 to the end of 1949, which is to say, throughout the closing phases of the 1946–48 expansion and the whole of the 1948–49 contraction.[13]

Given this inferior record of discretionary policy, Professor Friedman concludes that:

> In light of experience, the most urgent need is not to have some everpresent back-seat driver who is going to be continually correcting the driver's steering, but to get off the road the man who has been giving the car a shove from one side to the other all the time and making it difficult for the actual driver to keep it on the straight and narrow path. . . . I am tempted to paraphrase what Colin Clark once wrote about the case for free trade. Like other academicians, I am accustomed to being met with the refrain, "It's all right in theory but it won't work in practice." Aside from the questionable logic of the remark in general, in this instance almost the reverse of what is intended is true. There is little to be said in theory for the rule that the money supply should grow at a constant rate. The case for it is entirely that it would work in practice. . . .[14]

In addition to this argument that the Federal Reserve's record is worse than that which would have resulted from the rule, there are two other arguments for the rule. One is that a rule involves less government interference with the economy than does discretionary policy. Professor Friedman attaches a great deal of importance to limiting government controls. The other is that a monetary rule would create confidence. If businessmen know that the money stock will be increased at a steady rate they will expect

[13] *Ibid.,* pp. 93–94.
[14] The first part of this quotation is from Professor Friedman's testimony before the U.S. Joint Economic Committee, *Employment, Growth, and Price Levels, Hearings, op. cit.,* p. 615. The second part is from his *A Program for Monetary Stability, op. cit.,* p. 98.

stability, and this facilitates the maintenance of stability. For example, during a recession, businessmen would know that demand is depressed only for a short time and would not cut back so much on investment.

The rate at which the money stock should be increased each year is given by Professor Friedman as somewhere in the 3 to 5 percent range, if money is defined to include time deposits in commercial banks. A 4 percent increase in the money stock would offset the projected 3 percent rate of increase in physical output and the 1 percent secular decline in velocity. But Professor Friedman is not very much concerned with the precise rate of increase which is selected as long as this rate of increase is maintained steadily. If the rate of increase of the money stock exceeds the rate at which output is growing and velocity is declining there will be secular inflation. But as long as prices rise steadily the inflation is predictable and, hence, does little harm. All wages, debts, and other contracts could be adjusted for this expected increase in prices so that inflation would not redistribute income. Conversely, if output is growing at a faster rate than 3 percent or if velocity is declining at a rate greater than 1 percent, the rule would result in a falling price level. Professor Friedman feels that this, too, would be acceptable; contracts could be written to make allowance for this and, hence, it would not create a serious problem. While Professor Friedman believes that, on the whole, price stability is preferable to a secular trend in prices, his main concern is to avoid *fluctuations* in the price level, not a steady trend. The monetary rule is not necessarily a rule of price level stability.

Another variant of the rules position which antedates the Friedman variant is that of Dr. Warburton.[15] He concluded from his empirical studies of previous business fluctuations that they are due to unsteadiness in the rate of money growth, and there-

15 See his statement before the U.S. House Committee on Banking and Currency, Subcommittee on Domestic Finance, *Hearings, The Federal Reserve System after 50 Years,* Vol. 2 (Washington, D.C.: 88th Congress, Second Session, 1964), p. 1317; and *Depression, Inflation, and Monetary Policy, Selected Papers* (Baltimore: Johns Hopkins University Press, 1966), Chapters 17–18. See also Selden, *op. cit.,* pp. 326–331.

fore advocates letting the money stock grow at a 3 percent rate until the Federal Reserve has completed studies which allow it to do better. In his view, exchange-rate flexibility is not required by the rule and, unlike Professor Friedman, he would allow the monetary authorities, *on occasion*, to offset changes in velocity and output by departing from the rule.

But these arguments favoring a rule are accepted only by a minority of economists. A number of points have been raised by the supporters of discretionary policy.[16] One point is political. Quite apart from the technical reasons of lags, and so forth, proponents of the rule frequently claim that a monetary rule would limit government interference. To some of the opponents of the rule this great antipathy towards government regulation seems unwarranted.[17] A second point is that past experience with an automatic rule has not been very encouraging. As Professor Viner has put it:

> In the economic field important rules affecting important social issues have in fact been extremely scarce, and to the extent that they have had a substantial degree of durability this has been largely explicable either by the fact that they evolved into taboos, or ends in themselves, and were thus removed from the area of open discussion and rational appraisal, or by the tolerance of widespread evasion. The most conspicuous instances of economic rules with a substantial degree of durability were the prohibition of lending at interest and the maintenance of fixed monetary standards in terms of precious metals. The most enthusiastic advocate of rules can derive little comfort from the availability of these historical precedents.[18]

[16] The leading publications criticizing the rule are: Abba Lerner, "Review of Milton Friedman, *A Program for Monetary Stability*," *Journal of the American Statistical Association*, Vol. 57 (March, 1962), pp. 211–220; Jacob Viner, "The Necessity and Desirable Range of Discretion to be Allowed to a Monetary Authority," Yeager (ed.), *op. cit.*, pp. 244–274; and Daniel Ahearn, *Federal Reserve Policy Reappraised, 1951–1959* (New York: Columbia University Press, 1963), pp. 225–233.

[17] Professor Viner has argued along a different line, namely, that government control is control regardless of whether it takes the form of a rule or of discretion, *op. cit.*, pp. 244–245.

[18] *Ibid.*, p. 248.

Moreover, there is the problem that monetary policy has a plurality of goals. To Professor Friedman this plurality is unwelcome, and one of the reasons for his advocacy of the rule is precisely the fact that he thinks it is better to give monetary policy a single task rather than to let various goals pull it in various directions. But to other economists, the existence of multiple goals provides a reason for opposing a rule. If one considers the various goals to be desirable and achievable preferably by monetary policy, then the adoption of a rule may involve a social loss. To illustrate by just one example: To advocates of fixed exchange rates, a monetary rule would have a great disadvantage—it would prevent the use of monetary policy to adjust the balance of payments.

On a more technical level, economists have questioned Professor Friedman's belief in long and variable lags in the effect of monetary policy and his view that discretionary monetary policy is destabilizing. Moreover, there is a problem about the definition of money. If liquid assets, such as savings and loan shares, are important in determining expenditures, or may become so in the future, a monetary rule may do little good. As one critic has put it, "If a fixed rule had in the early 1800's fixed a regular percentage increase in the supply of banknotes—the major component of the money supply at the time—the rule would have become largely irrelevant with the emergence of demand deposits as the major type of money."[19]

A number of criticisms have focused on the compatibility of the rule with future requirements. For example, suppose that velocity should decrease at a faster rate in the future or that productivity should increase at a faster rate. Given the rule, full employment would then require falling prices—but are prices flexible enough to allow a declining price level to coexist with full employment? Professor Friedman believes that the answer is yes and points to the rapid increase in output during the decade of the 1870's when the price level fell substantially. But probably the majority of economists would feel that whatever

---

[19] Ahearn, *op. cit.*, p. 226. For a similar criticism based on the general liquidity approach, see Richard Sayers, *Central Banking after Bagehot* (Oxford: Oxford University Press, 1957), pp. 55–56.

may have been true in the 1870's, at present there is so much price rigidity that inadequate aggregate demand is more likely to result in a fall in output than in a fall in prices.[20]

A related point is that velocity may change at an irregular rate. If so, given full employment, a constant rate of growth of the money stock would result in an irregular movement of prices. (And the same is true if velocity declines at a regular rate but potential output increases at an irregular rate.) With irregular price movements some of the benefits of the rule would be lost since businessmen's price expectations could be destabilizing. This consideration suggests the use of something in-between a rigid rule and discretion. This is to adjust the money stock for changes in potential output and in velocity during the previous period.[21] Moreover, if, as some economists believe, we face a situation of secular cost-push inflation, then the monetary rule would require substantial unemployment.

A central issue in the whole dispute is the efficiency of the Federal Reserve. Opponents of the rule, while conceding past errors by the Federal Reserve, have argued that the Federal Reserve is unlikely to repeat such errors in the future. The fact that a child cannot be trusted to drive a car does not mean that an adult should not be allowed to drive. Thus, what is relevant is not the successes or failures of the Federal Reserve since 1914, but its successes or failures in recent years.

For the postwar period several studies have attempted to evaluate discretionary monetary policy and to compare it to the monetary rule.[22] They have computed the stock of money required to maintain price stability and full employment and have compared this to both the actual increase in the money stock and to

---

[20] On the other side of stability line, there is probably more support for the proposition that a predictable inflation would do no harm.

[21] See Martin Bronfenbrenner, "Monetary Rules: A New Look," *Journal of Law and Economics*, Vol. 8 (October, 1965), pp. 173–194.

[22] See Martin Bronfenbrenner, "Statistical Tests of Rival Monetary Rules," *Journal of Political Economy*, Vol. 69 (February, 1961), pp. 1–14, and "Statistical Tests of Rival Monetary Rules: Quarterly Data Supplement," *Journal of Political Economy*, Vol. 69 (December, 1961), pp. 621–625; Franco Modigliani, "Some Empirical Tests of Monetary Management and of Rules versus Discretion," *Journal of Political Economy*, Vol. 72 (June, 1964), pp. 211–245. A study for Canada found little difference

the increase which would have resulted under the monetary rule. One study, by Professor Bronfenbrenner, ended by advocating a modified rule in which the money stock is increased at a rate depending on the previous year's increase in potential output and decrease in velocity; another study, by Professor Modigliani, found discretion superior to a rule. But both of these studies are subject to the criticism that they make inadequate allowance for the lag of monetary policy so that they are testing Professor Friedman's proposal by neglecting an important part, perhaps the most important part, of his case.[23]

Note that most of these criticisms merely point out why a rule would not work well. Most of them do not focus on the basic case for the rule, namely that long and unpredictable lags may make countercyclical monetary policy destabilizing. As was pointed out in Chapter 6, we know relatively little about the length and variability of the lag, and we *may* not, at the present time, really be in a position to decide the rules versus authorities issue. Moreover, there is another difficult problem. In recent years our knowledge of monetary policy has grown significantly. There has been a substantial upsurge in work on monetary economics, both within the Federal Reserve and in universities. Even if long and unpredictable lags make it impossible to operate an effective countercyclical policy now, in time we may learn to predict the lag for individual cases and, hence, to base monetary policy on a forecast. Whether we will reach this stage in the foreseeable future is difficult, if not impossible, to say.[24]

---

in the success of the rule and discretion, though the latter was perhaps slightly superior. See Charles Schotta, Jr., "The Performance of Alternative Monetary Rules in Canada 1927–1961," *National Banking Review*, Vol. 1 (December, 1963), pp. 221–227.

[23] For criticisms of these studies see Donald Tucker, "Bronfenbrenner on Monetary Rules: A Comment," *Journal of Political Economy*, Vol. 71 (April, 1963), pp. 173–179; Richard Attiyeh, "Rules vs. Discretion: A Comment," *Journal of Political Economy*, Vol. 73 (April, 1965), pp. 170–172; and Thomas Mayer, "The Lag in the Effect of Monetary Policy: Some Criticisms," *Western Economic Journal*, Vol. 5 (September, 1967), pp. 324–342.

[24] Professor Friedman has suggested that we should now adopt a monetary rule which we could abandon once we learn enough about monetary policy. But a danger of this proposal is that if we abandon discretionary monetary policy we may not get back to it readily later on.

FURTHER READING

Obviously, many of the issues discussed in this chapter have political implications. For a discussion of these aspects see Seymour Harris, *The Economics of Political Parties.* New York: Macmillan, 1962, Chapters 11–14.

For the dominant position see *The Federal Reserve System, Purposes and Functions.* Washington, D.C.: Board of Governors of the Federal Reserve System, 1963, Chapters 7 and 8; and Lawrence Ritter. "Official Central Banking Theory in the United States, 1939–1961," *Journal of Political Economy,* Vol. 70 (February, 1962), pp. 14–29.

Among monetarist criticisms of the dominant position see John Culbertson. *Full Employment or Stagnation?* New York: McGraw-Hill, 1964; and his "The Use of Monetary Policy," *Southern Economic Journal,* Vol. 28 (October, 1961), pp. 130–137, as well as the various studies of Professors Brunner and Meltzer published by the House Banking and Currency Committee and referred to in the "Further Reading" for Chapter 3.

A very moderate exposition of the easy money position can be found in U.S. Joint Economic Committee. *Employment, Growth, and Price Levels, Staff Report,* Washington, D.C.: 86th Congress, First Session, 1960, Chapter 9. (This chapter is largely the work of Professor Warren Smith.) For an extreme version of this position see Conference on Economic Progress. *Tight Money and Rising Interest Rates.* Washington, D.C.: Conference on Economic Progress, 1966. Culbertson, in his *Full Employment or Stagnation?, op. cit.,* does not deal with the overall easy money case, but sharply criticizes recent Federal Reserve policy as being much too tight.

The main expositions of the rules versus authorities view are Simon's. "Rules versus Authorities in Monetary Policy," reprinted in American Economic Association, *Readings in Monetary Theory,* New York: Blakistone, 1951, pp. 337–368; Milton Friedman. *A Program for Monetary Stability.* New York: Fordham University Press, 1960, Chapters 1 and 4, and his testimony before the May 25–28, 1959 hearings of the U.S. Joint Economic Committee, *Employment, Growth, and Price Levels,* Washington, D.C.: 86th Congress, First Session, 1959. An interesting variant of the Friedman rule is advocated by

Martin Bronfenbrenner in "Monetary Rules: A New Look," *Journal of Law and Economics*, Vol. 8 (October, 1965), pp. 173–194. A very good survey of the argument is given in Richard Selden. "Stable Money Growth," Leland Yeager (ed.), *In Search of a Monetary Constitution*. Cambridge, Mass.: Harvard University Press, 1962, pp. 322–355. For criticisms see Jacob Viner. "The Necessity and Desirable Range of Discretion to Be Allowed to a Monetary Authority," *ibid.*, pp. 244–275; Abba Lerner. "Review of Milton Friedman, *A Program for Monetary Stability*," *Journal of the American Statistical Association*, Vol. 57 (March, 1962), pp. 211–220; and Ahearn. *Federal Reserve Policy Reappraised, 1951–1959, op. cit.*, pp. 223–233. An excellent discussion of various other monetary rules can be found in Clark Warburton. "Rules and Implements for Monetary Policy," *Journal of Finance*, Vol. 8 (March, 1953), pp. 1–21.

For a fascinating discussion of less orthodox views not discussed in this chapter, see Albert Hart. *Money, Debt and Economic Activity*. Englewood Cliffs, N.J.: Prentice-Hall, 1953, Chapter 26, entitled "Monetary Panaceas." For considerably more orthodox proposals, as well as for a discussion of many of the problems taken up in this book, see the report of the prestigious Commission on Money and Credit. *Money and Credit*. Englewood Cliffs, N.J.: Prentice-Hall, 1961, Chapters 1, 3, and 9.

To conclude, the following are three excellent surveys of monetary policy: Phillip Cagan. "A Commentary on Some Current Issues in the Theory of Monetary Policy," Michael Brennan (ed.), *Patterns of Market Behavior*. Providence: Brown University Press, 1965, pp. 135–154; Howard Ellis. "Limitations of Monetary Policy," Neil Jacoby (ed.), *United States Monetary Policy*. New York: Praeger, 1964, pp. 195–214; and Harry Johnson. "Monetary Theory and Policy," *American Economic Review*, Vol. 52 (June, 1962), pp. 335–384.

Appendixes

Multiple Bank
Credit Expansion

The key to understanding multiple deposit expansion is to remember that what is being expanded is an abstraction—entries on the books of banks—rather than physical objects such as currency. Students often have difficulty grasping the process because it seems to have a magical quality: something is being created out of nothing. In actuality, bank deposits are not being created out of nothing, but out of something, namely paper and ink.

One way of showing the process of multiple bank credit expansion is to start with a very simple and unrealistic model and then to add realistic detail. So let us consider a country which (1) does not use currency, all money being bank deposits, (2) does not have a legal reserve requirement, (3) has only a single bank, and (4) has no other financial institutions. This monopoly bank finds it profitable to issue deposits, that is, to sell the public claims on itself which the public then uses as money—an occurrence which has inflationary consequences. This simple monopoly bank creates deposits the same way in which an individual can create claims on himself by signing IOUs. There is nothing magical about this.

Now let us complicate matters by removing one assumption and introducing currency. For each dollar of deposits outstanding the public wants to hold, say, 10 cents of currency. The monopoly bank can now no longer create as many deposits as before. If it starts out with $100 of currency it can create deposits, by making loans and buying securities, only up to $1000. Once $1000 of deposits are outstanding all of the $100 will be withdrawn from the bank, and if it were to try to issue an additional dollar it would not be able to meet the depositor's claim for 10 cents of currency.

One can complicate the model slightly by removing another assumption and adding a legal reserve requirement. Suppose the law forces the bank to keep 10 cents with the central bank for each dollar of deposits outstanding. Now the $100 of currency allows the bank to have only $500 of deposits on its books. With $500 of deposits outstanding, the public has withdrawn $50 of currency from the bank and the bank has to keep the remaining $50 of currency as a reserve with the central bank.

Now comes the big complication. Instead of assuming that there is only one bank, assume that there exist a great multitude of banks. This puts each bank in a quite different position. Suppose that a bank having a $100 of currency (or other reserves) makes a loan giving the borrower a $500 deposit in exchange for his IOU. The borrower, of course, proceeds to use these funds by writing a check on his deposit, giving the check to somebody who deposits it in another bank. When this bank presents the check to the first bank for payment, the first bank has only $100 of currency (or other reserve) to meet this $500 and is in trouble. Hence, any single bank cannot indulge in multiple deposit creation. For each $100 of excess reserves it has, a bank can create $100 of new deposits, but no more than that because once it creates a deposit it will lose it.[1] But the essence of the process is that it loses this deposit *to another bank,* the bank into which the check is deposited. This second bank can now use the reserves it thus received to expand its deposits. Since the checks stay within the banking system (there being no other place for them to go) the banking *system* as a whole is in the same position as the previously discussed monopoly bank. Hence, the whole banking system can expand outstanding deposits to a multiple of the original deposit, a multiple determined by the legal-reserve ratio and the public's desired ratio of currency to deposits. Note again, however, that no single bank possesses the power of multiple deposit creation, only the system as a whole does.

---

[1] When a bank creates a deposit it must assume that it will lose it because a person generally does not borrow from a bank to keep an idle deposit. On the other hand, when a bank passively receives a deposit, it can assume that this deposit will stay in the bank since a customer will maintain his balance at the bank.

To see why banks jointly are able to do what each individual bank on its own is unable to do, let us take an example where a bank sells a security to the Federal Reserve for A. This bank can then create deposits of A.[2] As this deposit is drawn upon, the bank loses both the deposit and the A of reserves it started with, to another bank. This second bank now obtains a deposit as well as reserves of A. If the required reserve ratio plus the currency drain are q, the bank can lend out $A(1-q)$. As it lends out $A(1-q)$ this amount is deposited in another bank which can again lend out the proportion $(1-q)$, that is, it lends $A(1-q)^2$. As this process continues, we get the following sequence: $A(1-q) + A(1-q)^2 + A(1-q)^3 \ldots \ldots A(1-q)^n$. The sum of this geometric progression is $A(1/q)$ so that the sum of the deposits in all banks together is the same as the amount of deposits which could be created by a single monopoly bank.

[2] Had the bank obtained the deposit by a customer bringing in currency, rather than by selling a security, the bank would not be able to lend out A because it would have to keep a reserve against the customer's deposit. It would be in the position of the second bank in the sequence described in this paragraph.

The Role of Money in the Great Depression

The monetary experience of the United States economy in the 1930's furnishes an extremely interesting case study of the operation of monetary policy and the monetary variables. To a considerable extent, the view that monetary policy is weak and ineffective originated in the experience of this period. Let us, therefore, look at it to see whether it really supports this point of view. More specifically, we can ask the historical record the following questions. First, can the experience of the 1930's be cited in support of the proposition that in a severe depression the Federal Reserve is incapable of increasing the money stock sufficiently because banks will pile up excess reserves? Second, in those years in which the money stock did increase during the 1930's, did a liquidity-preference trap prevent interest rates from falling? Third, insofar as interest rates *did* fall, was the marginal efficiency of investment so interest inelastic that easy money failed to bring about recovery? In other words, we can take the three factors which can prevent changes in bank reserves from affecting income and see to what extent they were operating in the 1930's.

Before doing this, here are some general facts about the depression. The upper turning point was reached in August, 1929, that is, a few months prior to the stock market crash. The recession continued until March, 1933 when an upswing started. This upswing reached a submerged peak, a peak which still had very substantial unemployment in May, 1937. The following recession reached its trough in June, 1938. The ensuing expansion carried us into and through World War II. In the period 1929–1933, Net National Product fell by more than one-half when measured in current prices; real Net National Product fell by more than one-third as did the Wholesale Price Index. In 1930, 13 percent of non-farm employees were unemployed; in the next year this percentage reached 23.3 percent to rise to a peak in 1933 of 35.3 percent. Not once in the ten years 1931–1940 did the unemployment rate fall below 20 percent.[1] Clearly, it was the most serious depression on record.

Turning to the monetary data, from August, 1929 to March, 1933 the stock of money fell by one-quarter and the stock of money plus time deposits in commercial banks fell by more than one-third. This decline in the stock of money was the accompaniment of widespread bank failures, failures which occurred in three waves, one in 1930, one in 1931, and the final one which led to the bank holiday when all banks were closed for a time, in 1933. Figure A.1 shows the behavior of interest rates. The discount rate fell radically in this period. It was reduced from a level of 5 to 6 percent in various Federal Reserve Banks in the fall of 1929 to a level of 1½ to 3 percent in September, 1931. Other short-term rates declined sharply, too. However, in this period the rate on long-term government securities did not decline as much and the rate on *Baa* corporate bonds, that is, bonds of "lower medium grade" quality, actually rose substantially in the early part of the period, then fell, and in 1939 was not far from its 1928 level. Moreover, note that the price declines which occurred in the early 1930's meant that for these years the real rate of interest was substantially greater than the money rate of interest shown in Figure A.1. For subsequent years the real rate of interest was less than the money rate. Since the price level was lower in 1939 than in 1929, for the decade as a whole, the real rate exceeded the money rate of interest.

These are the facts; now to the interpretation. The view which had by far the widest acceptance among economists for many years—the Keynesian view—is that the Great Depression

---

[1] Stanley Lebergott, "Annual Estimates of Unemployment in the United States," in Universities-National Bureau on Economic Research, *Measurement and Behavior of Unemployment 1900–1950* (Princeton: Princeton University Press, 1957), pp. 215–216.

was a period in which an easy money policy was tried and found wanting.[2] According to this view there was a massive drop of the marginal efficiency of investment, which was reinforced by banking failures and the collapse of the international financial system. Essentially, many of the weaknesses built into our economy during the 1920's now took their toll.

In this situation the Federal Reserve adopted an easy money policy very promptly. The discount rate was reduced quickly, short-term rates fell and, with two brief exceptions, stayed very low throughout the 1930's. Long- and intermediate-term rates

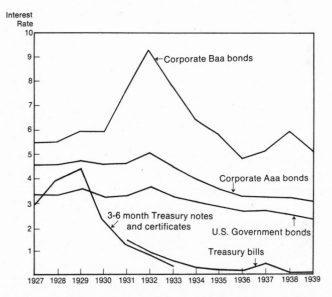

FIGURE **A.1** *Selected Interest Rates, 1927–1939 (Annual Averages)*

SOURCE: *Banking and Monetary Statistics* (Washington, D.C.: Board of Governors of the Federal Reserve System, 1943), pp. 460, 468.

[2] For expositions of this view see Alvin H. Hansen, *Fiscal Policy and Business Cycles* (New York: W. W. Norton, 1941), Chapter 3; and an empirical study by George Horwich, "Effective Reserves, Credit, and Causality in the Banking System of the Thirties," D. Carson, *Banking and Monetary Studies* (Homewood, Ill.: Richard D. Irwin, 1963), pp. 80–100.

declined, though they did so to a much lesser extent. Excess bank reserves rose to a very high level as shown in Figure A.2. The Federal Reserve was pumping reserves into the banking system but it was to no avail. Given the amount of excess capacity as well as the general pessimism generated by the depression, business did not want to borrow and banks were faced with little demand for loans. Since interest rates were too low to induce them to buy many securities, banks simply reacted by holding excess reserves. The easy money policy, while it was a move in

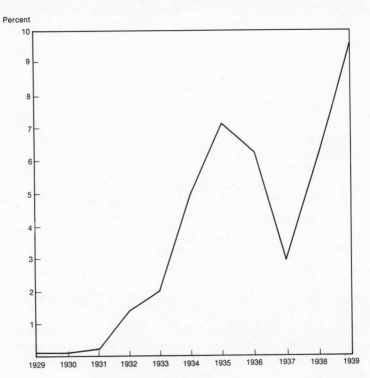

FIGURE A.2   *Member Bank Excess Reserves as a Percent of Total Member Bank Deposits, 1929–1939*

SOURCE: *Banking and Monetary Statistics* (Washington, D.C.: Board of Governors of the Federal Reserve System, 1941), pp. 73–75 and 368.

the right direction, was ineffective. Although monetary policy can choke off a boom, it cannot start a recovery because if business-men have no incentive to invest, the availability of funds does little to stimulate investment.

In this interpretation, the evidence for the 1930's shows mone-tary policy failing on all counts. The great increase in excess re-serves of banks demonstrates that—at least in severe depressions—an expansion of the reserve base does not lead to an adequate increase in the money stock. The stock of money depends more on the availability of customers for loans than on the volume of reserves. Moreover, velocity fell during the 1930's as interest rates declined, thus suggesting that at low rates of interest, the demand for money becomes quite interest elastic. Even if the stock of money is somehow increased it has little effect on expen-ditures; the public is simply willing to hold most of the additional money as idle balances. Moreover, the failure of long-term interest rates to decline to any great degree also showed a weakness of monetary policy. Finally, although interest rates did fall, the interest elasticity of investment was so low that investment did not increase much. Thus, the argument asserts, in every respect monetary policy was ineffective.

The above view has been challenged very seriously in a series of articles by Dr. Warburton and in a voluminous study by Pro-fessor Friedman and Mrs. Schwartz, which appeared in 1962.[3] According to these authors, the Great Depression, far from show-ing the weakness of monetary policy, was a major example of the importance of monetary factors. In this interpretation the depres-

[3] Friedman and Schwartz, *A Monetary History of the United States, 1867–1960* (Princeton: Princeton University Press, 1963), Chapters 7–9. Dr. Warburton's articles which appeared in the early 1950's are reprinted in his *Depression, Inflation and Monetary Policy, Selected Papers, 1945–1953* (Baltimore: Johns Hopkins University Press, 1966), Chapters 3, 15 and 16. For supporting evidence see also Phillip Cagan, *Determinants and Effects of Changes in the Stock of Money, 1875–1960* (New York: Columbia University Press, 1965), Chapters 6–7; George Morrison, *Liquidity Preference of Commercial Banks* (Chicago: University of Chicago Press, 1966); and John Culbertson, "United States Monetary History: Its Implications for Monetary Theory," *National Banking Review,* Vol. 1 (March, 1964), pp. 359–380.

sion started out as a routine one and was turned into a major disaster by the great decline in the stock of money that resulted from bank failures. Since changes in the money supply have a powerful effect on income, it is not at all surprising that a great decline in the stock of money brought about a great depression. Warburton, Friedman, and Schwartz dispute the view that monetary policy was easy during the 1930's. They argue that the interest rate was not really low. To be sure, the discount rate was cut substantially, but according to Dr. Warburton this was offset by another policy.

> Prior to 1929 the Federal Reserve authorities had made strenuous efforts to establish a tradition against continuous member-bank borrowing. . . . By 1930 . . . it became apparent that these efforts to reduce rediscounting had become effective. . . . In addition, as bank failures became frequent, the Federal Reserve banks developed an extremely hard-boiled attitude towards member banks which needed to borrow to meet deposit withdrawals. In combination these policies made it impractical for the member banks in the early 1930's to prevent their reserves from contracting by taking advantage of the low discount rates. . . . The Federal Reserve authorities had discouraged rediscounting almost to the point of prohibition. . . .[4]

Moreover, it is not the level of the discount rate or any other interest rate which is relevant, but the relation between the discount rate and open-market interest rates. If interest rates on the open market fall more than the discount rate, the discount rate will be restrictive even if it is low by historical standards. Warburton, Friedman, and Schwartz are monetarists. As pointed out in Chapter 7, monetarists believe that the rate of interest is but a poor guide, that one should look at the quantity of money instead. They argue that the Federal Reserve was following a *tight* money policy because it did not undertake anywhere sufficient open-market operations to provide adequate reserves to a banking system faced by runs from depositors. Federal Reserve policy was restrictive, as becomes clear when one looks not at the largely

[4] Warburton, *Depression, Inflation and Monetary Policy, Selected Papers, 1945–1953, op. cit.,* pp. 320 and 340.

irrelevant discount rate but at the relevant variable, open-market operations.

> In the context of the changes then occurring in the economy and in the money markets, the policy followed should be regarded as one of monetary "tightness" not "ease." During a period of severe economic contraction extending over more than a year, the System was content to let its discounts decline by nearly twice its net purchases of government securities, and to let its total credit outstanding decline by almost three times the increase in the gold stock. Through early 1932, the most striking feature of the System's portfolio of government securities and bills bought is the usual seasonal pattern of contraction during the first half of the year and expansion during the second. From August 1929 to October 1930, the whole increase in government securities plus bills bought came in the second half of 1929. The System's holdings of government securities plus bills bought was nearly $200 million lower at the end of July 1930 than they were at the end of December 1929.[5]

The failure of business investment to expand should therefore be blamed on the utter ineptitude of the Federal Reserve which failed to adopt an expansionary policy, rather than on the weakness of monetary policy. Monetary expansion did not fail; it simply was not tried.

But how can this interpretation explain the great increase in excess reserves shown in Figure A.2? According to Friedman and Schwartz, when banks found out through bitter experience that the Federal Reserve would not provide them with adequate reserves during a panic they decided that they would have to hold a greater volume of excess reserves to guard against future runs.[6] In the Friedman-Schwartz view, what we call "excess" reserves are only legally excess reserves, they are not economically excess. This fact is illustrated by what happened in 1936–1937 when the Federal Reserve doubled reserve requirements, raising them to a level which still left the banks with excess reserves. If these re-

[5] Friedman and Schwartz, *op. cit.*, p. 375.
[6] Another hypothesis, favored by Morrison, *op. cit.*, is that banks treated the increase in their reserve base as temporary.

serves were really excess in the economic sense, the banks would not have reacted to this in any way but would have been willing to give up the excess reserves readily. But we find the banks did not behave in this way; instead, they sold securities to protect their excess reserves. In other words, say Friedman and Schwartz, the demand schedule of banks for excess reserves shifted outward because of the great uncertainty that banks faced.[7]

While the behavior of banks in 1936–1937 creates a problem for the previously discussed view that excess reserves were due merely to a lack of borrowers, the Friedman-Schwartz view also faces one difficulty.[8] This is that excess reserves did not really start to pile up to a great extent until 1934. If banks were shocked by bank failures into wanting more reserves why did they not increase their reserves right after the bank failures? Why did they wait so long?[9]

This leaves the decline in velocity. The previously discussed view attributed this decline to the low level of interest rates which made us approach the Keynesian liquidity trap. But studies of the demand for money cited in Chapter 3 find little evidence for a liquidity trap in the 1930's.

---

[7] Their interpretation, however, does not completely ignore interest rates; they point out that at the lower level of short-term interest rates prevailing in the mid- and later parts of the decade, banks had little incentive to use their excess reserves to buy Treasury bills (Friedman and Schwartz, *op. cit.*, p. 538).

[8] An alternative interpretation of the 1936–1937 episode is that prior to the increase in reserve requirements banks did have *economically* excess reserves, but that the increase in required reserves was large enough to take away not only their economically excess reserves, but also some of the reserves they wanted to hold. See John Kareken, "Our Knowledge of Monetary Policy," *American Economic Association Papers and Proceedings*, Vol. 51 (May, 1961), pp. 41–42.

[9] Karl Brunner ("Institutions, Policy and Monetary Analysis," *Journal Political Economy*, Vol. 73 [April, 1965], pp. 205) argues that the great increases in excess reserves resulted from banks chasing a moving target. Banks would raise their deposits when they found they had excess reserves, but reserves simply grew at a faster rate. This explanation raises the question of why banks consistently underestimated the growth of their reserve base. For a sharp criticism of the Friedman-Schwartz explanation of excess reserves, see James Tobin, "The Monetary Interpretation of History," *American Economic Review*, Vol. 55 (June, 1965), p. 472.

Thus, at present we have two explanations of the 1930's—one interpreting events of this period as showing the weakness of monetary factors, and the other showing their strength. In the author's view, much more research is needed before we can decide definitely between these two competing explanations. Both now contain some part of the truth.[10] But he believes that Warburton and Friedman and Schwartz have established enough of a case for their side so that the burden of the proof now lies with those who claim that the experience of the Great Depression demonstrates the unimportance of money.

[10] For example, one possible explanation of the increase in excess reserves which combines elements of both interpretations is that as a result of bank failures, the portfolio preferences of banks shifted in favor of both short-term securities and cash, and away from long-term securities and loans. The low level of the short-term interest rate then caused banks to favor excess reserves over short-term securities. Hence, both a movement *of* the liquidity-preference schedule and a movement *along* the schedule may have been involved. Friedman and Schwartz do state that the low level of interest rates was a factor in the increase in excess reserves (*op. cit.*, p. 538) but do not stress this point. The more one stresses the movement along the liquidity-preference schedule relative to the shift of the schedule, the closer one comes to a Keynesian position.

Another possible compromise position would be to argue that the early stages of the downturn monetary restriction caused a collapse of confidence so that what would otherwise have been a normal recession turned into a great depression.

INDEX

Index